THE CULTURAL DIMENSION OF DEVELOPMENT

THE CULTURAL DIMENSION OF DEVELOPMENT

Indigenous Knowledge Systems

Edited by
D. MICHAEL WARREN, L. JAN SLIKKERVEER,
DAVID BROKENSHA

Technical Editor: Wim H.J.C. Dechering

INTERMEDIATE TECHNOLOGY PUBLICATIONS 1995

Intermediate Technology Publications Ltd,
103–105 Southampton Row, London WC1B 4HH, UK

A CIP catalogue record for this book is available from the British Library

ISBN 1 85339 264 2 *(Hardback)*
1 85339 251 0 *(Paperback)*

Typeset by the LEAD Programme of Leiden University in The Netherlands
Printed in Great Britain by SRP, Exeter

Contents

Abbreviations

AAACU	Association of Asian Agricultural Colleges and Universities
ACFOD	Asian Cultural Forum on Development
ANGOC	Asian Non-Governmental Organizations Coalition
ARCIK	African Resource-Centre for Indigenous Knowledge
CAAP	Centro Andino de Acción Popular
CENDHRRA	Centre for the Development of Human Resources in Rural Areas
CET	Centro de Educación y Technología
CETEC	Centro de Technología Campesina
CIED	Centro de Investigación, Educación y Desarrollo
CIKARD	Centre for Indigenous Knowledge for Agriculture and Rural Development
CIRAN	Centre for International Research and Advisory Networks
CLADES	Consorcio Latino Americano sobre Agroecología y Desarrollo
CPCC	Centro de Promoción Campesina de la Coordillera
CTTA	Communications for Technology Transfer In Agriculture Programme
ERASMUS	Programme of the European Commission
FAO	Food and Agriculture Organization of the United Nations
FES	Field of Ethnological Study
GTZ	Deutsche Gesellschaft fur Technische Zusammenarbeit
HD	Historical Dimension
IIED	International Institute for Environment and Development
IIRR	International Institute of Rural Reconstruction
IK	Indigenous Knowledge
ILEIA	Information Centre for Low External Input Agriculture
INIREB	Institute for the Study of Biological Resources
INRIK	Indonesian Resource-Centre for Indigenous Knowledge
IRRI	International Rice Research Institute
IUCN	International Union for Conservation of Nature
KENRIK	Kenya Resource-Centre for Indigenous Knowledge
LEAD	Leiden Ethnosystems and Development Programme
LEISA	Low External Input and Sustainable Agriculture
MAB	Man and the Biosphere Programme
NIRCIK	Nigerian Resource Centre for Indigenous Knowledge
NISER	Nigerian Institute of Social and Economic Research
ORT	Oral Rehydration Therapy
OXFAM	Oxford Committee for Famine Relief
PTD	Participatory Technology Development
PRATEC	Proyecto Andino de Technologias Campesinas
PV	Participants' view
RRA	Rapid Rural Appraisal
REPPIKA	Regional Programme for the Promotion of Indigenous Knowledge in Asia

RDP	Rural Development Programmess
RRAFA	Rural Reconstruction Alumni and Friends Association
SARRA	South Asia Rural Reconstruction Association
SDN	Sustainable Development Network
SEMTA	Servicios Multiples de Technologías Apropiadas
SUAN	South East Asian Agricultural University
TEK	Traditional Ecological Knowledge
TFAP	Tropical Forest Action Plan
UNESCO	United Nations Educational, Scientific and Cultural Organization
UNCED	United Nations Conference on Environment and Development
UNDP	United Nations Development Programme
UNICEF	United Nations International Children Education Fund
WHO	World Health Organization
WDCD	World Decade for Culture and Development (UNESCO)
WWF	World Wildlife Fund

Dedication

This book is dedicated to Oswald Werner, Professor of Anthropology, Northwestern University, Evanston, Illinois, for his selfless dedication to the development of methodologies for recording Indigenous Knowledge Systems and for stimulating and supporting so many of us who followed in his footsteps.

Acknowledgements

We would like to acknowledge the extraordinary efforts of the individuals who worked with us to format the contents of this book into a camera-ready copy: Ank Amesz, Martin van Bakel, Kristine Burrows and John Burrows, Deborah Calhoun, Roddie Grant, Yolanda Martin, Mady Slikkerveer, Margot Starkenburg, and Gill Steenvoorde.

Preface

ROBERT CHAMBERS AND PAUL RICHARDS

IN THE PAST, indigenous knowledge was widely regarded among development professionals as an academic, if not dilettantish, concern limited largely to social anthropologists. Much of it was seen as superstition. In the dominant model of development, useful knowledge was only generated in central places – in universities, on research stations, in laboratories, then to be transferred to ignorant peasants and other poor people.

In the past two decades, these views have been changing. Social anthropologists have come out of their cloistered villages and contributed more and more, as development anthropologists, to the understanding and processes of development. A substantial and growing minority of agricultural scientists have recognised the value of working closely with farmers. In university curricula, in programs for rural research and development, in project identification, design and implementation, in agricultural research and extension, and in discussion of paradigms for development, the balance of rhetoric has shifted, with less stress on the transfer of technology and more on learning from and with rural people.

The reality, though, has changed less than the rhetoric. The awareness, attitudes and behaviour of many development practitioners have changed less than the language they have learnt to use. Many have acquired the easy skill of using words like 'participation' and even 'empowerment' but without changing the way they see poor people or the way they feel development should be undertaken. The language has become bottom-up but the inclination remains top-down. If we include all those who work in international agencies, national governments and their field agencies, and NGOs, then, even now in the early 1990s, the great majority of development professionals undervalue indigenous knowledge and the capacities of local, especially rural, people. For this majority of professionals, 'they' and 'what they do not know' are still the problem; and 'we' and 'what we know' are still the solution.

This book is therefore timely, for it presents overwhelming evidence, carefully researched and from many countries and sources, of the great range, validity and usefulness of indigenous knowledge. It does not argue for the untenable fundamentalist view that poor and rural people always know best. The authors would surely agree that there are spheres in which modern scientific knowledge has a comparative advantage. Yet in the past, the advantage has been assumed to be almost universal. What this book shows is that in many fields, indigenous knowledge is far more relevant, valid, and useful than had been supposed. The power and prestige of modern science have been so heavily weighted against the indigenous knowledge that the counterweight of evidence, such as that presented in this book, is vital for a balanced view.

We hope therefore that *Indigenous Knowledge Systems: The Cultural Dimension of Development* will be widely available to development practitioners and academics throughout the world. It should be read not just by those who, though still a minority, are convinced of its evidence and point of view.

It should be read, even more, by those many sincere professionals who are sceptical and who believe that poor people are largely ignorant and incompetent. The evidence it presents shows how radically our knowledge of their knowledge has changed and needs further to change. It shows the need for humility, the need to learn from people before trying to teach them. To our discomfort, it shows that 'we' are much of the problem and 'they' are much of the solution.

Introduction

D. MICHAEL WARREN, L. JAN SLIKKERVEER
AND DAVID BROKENSHA

INDIGENOUS KNOWLEDGE – the local knowledge that is unique to a given culture or society – contrasts with the international knowledge system which is generated through the global network of universities and research institutes. Indigenous knowledge is important as it forms the information base for a society which facilitates communication and decision-making. By taking the time and effort to document these systems, they become accessible to change agents and client groups.

A relationship based on understanding and respect helps to establish an environment conducive to participatory approaches to decision-making in development. During the past decade or so, when ignorance of local knowledge often resulted in failure of development projects, more professionals have begun to see the value of documenting the existing systems and of working with and through the local systems to improve upon them.

Meanwhile, on a global scale, indigenous knowledge systems as a prime part of culture have come to play an important role in the international debate on cultural policy and development planning. UNESCO, as the supranational advocate of humanising the economic development process, has recently provided a central platform for discussion. Introduced in the 1970s by the Regional UNESCO/OAU Conference in Accra (AFRICULT), the key concept of cultural identity gradually evolved, marking a striking feature of contemporary history in Africa and elsewhere in the developing world. This concept helped encourage endogenous development through the introduction of programmes for alphabetisation, and the study and documentation of the cultural heritage.

The international discussion on the relationships between economic, social and cultural development has gradually emphasised the re-discovery of the concept of culture. A broader, anthropological conception of culture was introduced, which goes beyond arts and literature to encompass a whole complex of distinctive material, non-material, and emotional characteristics of a society or group, based on systems of knowledge, technology, values, traditions, and beliefs. This widened concept of culture has brought a whole range of cultural aspects within the scope of international development activities during the last decade, stressing the concept of the cultural dimension of development.

As a result of the increasing awareness of the international community and of the re-orientation in scientific thinking, UNESCO proclaimed in the mid-80s the World Decade for Cultural Development (WDCD), parallel to the Third Development Decade of the United Nations. The cultural dimension of development has now become a key concept for the international development strategy for the concluding part of the twentieth century. Subsequently, the other organisations of the United Nations, such as the United Nations Development Programme, the Food and Agriculture Organisation, the World Health Organisation, the United Nations Children's' Fund (formerly the United Nations International Children's' Emergency Fund), the Economic Commission for Africa, the Economic Commission for Latin America and the Caribbean, and the International Monetary Fund, have acknowledged the cultural dimension of development strategy, and new ways are presently being sought to effectuate incorporation of cultural components in development plans and programmes. In this context, the current efforts to record, document, and make accessible the contextual information on indigenous knowledge systems, as presented in this volume, seek to shape further the cultural dimension of development from the points of view of different disciplines. Thus, they bring to the forefront the eminent role of ethno- and area-specific knowledge systems of distinct cultures in the determination of their own course of development for the years to come.

In 1980, *Indigenous Knowledge Systems and Development* by Brokensha, Warren and Werner (ed) was published, with most of the contributions coming from anthropologists and geographers. The book was widely used in both academic and development circles. It had, and still has today, a considerable influence on a variety of academic disciplines and development agencies.

The contributors to this present volume represent not only anthropology and geography, but also agronomy, plant pathology, soil science, entomology, rural sociology, agricultural extension, agricultural physics, library science, agricultural education, agricultural economics, forestry, agroforestry, agroecology, linguistics, botany, veterinary medicine, fisheries science, range management, and natural resources management science. Several chapters are co-authored by social and biological scientists. This interdisciplinary approach is a very important and a very welcome circumstance.

Contributors to this volume come from the United States of America, the United Kingdom, The Netherlands, Burkina Faso, Norway, The Philippines, India, Chile, Germany, Nigeria, and Zimbabwe. They represent a wide range of academic institutions, such as Iowa State University, the University of California at Berkeley, Cambridge University, the University of Sussex, Michigan State University, the University of Missouri, Tuskegee University, the Indian Institute of Management, the University of Minnesota, the University of Wisconsin, the University of Florida, Cornell University, Leiden University, and the University of Southern California.

Unlike the contributors to the 1980 volume, the contributors to this volume also represent a variety of international development agencies and agricultural research institutes. These include the United States Agency for International Development, the International Potato Centre, the International Rice Research Institute, the Food and Agriculture Organisation, the United Nations Educational, Scientific and Cultural Organisation, the United Nations Children's' Fund, the International Centre for Living Aquatic Resources Management, the International Union for the Conservation of Nature and Natural Resources, the Intermediate Technology Development Group, the Information Centre for Low External Input Agriculture, the International Institute for Environment and Development, the International Institute of Rural Reconstruction, the Transformation Resource Centre, the Indian Institute of Management, the International Centre for Living Aquatic Resources Management, the Academy for Educational Development, the International Resources Group, the Agency to Facilitate the Growth of Rural Organisation and ActionAid. This is very encouraging. What was once regarded as the academic domain of anthropology has now generally been recognised as a much broader, interdisciplinary field of study which can facilitate development activities in cost effective ways.

This volume is far broader in scope than that of the 1980 volume. In the latter, most of the chapters were limited to a description of indigenous knowledge systems, although several discussed their role in the decision-making process.

Today, we visualise indigenous knowledge systems as a more dynamic conception of culture and as the ultimate foundation upon which decision-making takes place.

Part I consists of chapters with a focus on indigenous knowledge. Part II is devoted to studies showing how the knowledge is used in decision-making. Part III goes a step further, with contributions focused on the role that indigenous organisations play in the decision-making process. These studies demonstrate that by working with and through existing organisations, the development process can be greatly facilitated. Part IV is on indigenous experimentation and innovations. In 1980, little attention was devoted to the dynamic nature of the indigenous knowledge systems or about the variability one could find within them, depending on such variables as gender and occupational role.

These new studies, however, indicate clearly the dynamic nature of indigenous systems. People are constantly creating and experimenting in response to a constantly changing set of circumstances. This innovation process provides an internal dynamic to the existing systems. People are also evaluating, adopting, and adapting new technologies presented through a variety of channels external to the local system.

Several contributions indicate how appropriate, skillful, and cost-effective many of the indigenous contributions can be. There are examples of indigenous research, development and extension systems which operate parallel to the national systems without the development professionals recognising their existence. It is quite apparent that indigenous innovations, which are found to be effective in one part of the globe, can be equally effective when made available to populations in similar ecological conditions in other parts of the world. The documentation of the vast amount of unrecorded, often rapidly disappearing, indigenous knowledge could provide the basis for many effective development interventions, if this knowledge could be shared.

Contributions in Part V describe how different development institutes are using indigenous knowledge to facilitate the development process. Part VI consists of bibliographical essays, which explore the attention provided to indigenous knowledge in the literature of the past decade in the areas of agriculture and rural development and natural resource management.

We now have a far clearer understanding of the role that nineteenth century social science and colonialism played in popularising the belief that non-European knowledge systems are primitive and had little to offer to the world. Today, a growing number of scholars from both the developing nations and the West realise that the indigenous knowledge systems, which have accumulated in many parts of the world over generations and, in some places, millennia, are important national and international resources. There is now a move to establish a global network of regional and national resource centres for indigenous knowledge. Following the establishment of the Center for Agriculture and Rural Development (CIKARD) at Iowa State University, Ames (USA) in 1988, global (LEAD and CIRAN), regional (REPPIKA) and national (ARCIK, KENRIK and INRIK) centres have joined the global network, focusing its activities to study, document, analyse and provide a data base for indigenous knowledge, technology and decision-making systems in the context of development.

Once the methodologies for documenting these systems are introduced into training institutes in a given country, the recorded systems can be systematically deposited and stored for use by development practitioners. The global network of indigenous knowledge resource centres will facilitate the exchange of indigenous knowledge as currently occurs through the international knowledge systems. As the worlds' population becomes more concerned with environmental issues, sensitivity to the value of indigenous knowledge grows. Considerable effort has been made to preserve the germplasm of plants as biodiversity declines. It is anticipated that the decade of the 1990s will include considerable effort to document the human knowledge accumulated about this plant material, particularly that which is at high risk.

It is hoped that this volume will further facilitate cross-cultural understanding, participatory and sustainable approaches to development, and the realisation that existing indigenous knowledge systems represent a critical resource base for the process of development.

1. Ethnobotanical Knowledge Systems – A resource for meeting rural development goals

JANIS B. ALCORN

Introduction

THIS CHAPTER WILL summarise some of the contributions that ethnobotanical knowledge can make to development. I will focus on ethnobotanical knowledge as a system of knowledge in use in real situations. I will not focus on plant classification systems (sometimes called ethnobotanical-botanical knowledge systems), as elicited by cognitive anthropologists.

Ethnobotanical knowledge can be acquired by studying agricultural landscapes and agricultural systems, as well as by talking with individual rural residents. I will discuss seven kinds of resources that can be mined from ethnobotanical knowledge:

- principles;
- facts;
- technologies;
- crops;
- farming systems;
- strategies, and
- information about local constraints and opportunities.

The current practice of extracting and transferring isolated bits of information from a few ethnobotanical knowledge systems makes limited use of a widespread resource that has tremendous potential for application in designing locally adapted, sustainable agricultural systems.

Resources derived from ethnobotanical knowledge can contribute to the attainment of rural development goals including:

- improved rural livelihoods;
- sustainable use of the natural resource base;
- improved well-being, health, and nutrition;
- strengthened institutional capacity to meet the needs of rural people;
- generation of capital surplus for financing industrialisation.

Contributions are especially valuable in regions of 'marginal' farmland or pasture where high-input, capital-intensive systems are unprofitable or unsustainable.

For ethnobotanical knowledge to be mobilised as a resource to meet development goals, greater interaction is needed between the users of ethnobotanical knowledge – rural residents – and specialists contracted to design, carry out, and evaluate development projects. Two barriers have limited this interaction: the status difference between ethnobotanical knowledge bearers and development specialists, and botanical illiteracy of development specialists. Ethnobotanical knowledge systems are currently associated with the lowest socioeconomic classes – tribal peoples and peasant farmers. That status association has led the élites who design development interventions to think of the knowledge base of these lower classes as the cause of their low socioeconomic status.

Elites have not recognised that the knowledge of the lower classes might be valuable in improving socioeconomic conditions if coupled with modern insights and other development intervention activities. Secondly, rural sociologists or agronomists who access and transfer knowledge are generally not educated to pay attention to natural vegetation or to recognise techniques in indigenous resource management that manipulate non-crop vegetation as a resource. Instead, outsiders tend to see non-crop vegetation as 'weeds', 'brush', 'useless forest', or 'wasteland'. On the other hand, local people often manage that same vegetation as a multiple-use resource to ensure future productivity of their farmlands, and to meet their needs for food, fuel, construction materials, micro-enterprise inputs, and medicine.

Increasing interest in Indigenous Knowledge Systems (IKS) and sustainable agriculture is making outsiders appreciate the ways in which wild plants and minor crops are integrated spatially and temporally into dynamic agricultural systems that exploit and conserve biodiversity as a natural resource. Efforts to enable farmers to direct agronomic research on crops (Chambers and Jiggins 1987) should be extended to enabling farmers to teach agronomists how to manage native plants as an element of agriculture. By bringing rural people with ethnobotanical knowledge of plants, plant ecology, crops and farming systems into a dialogue with scientists, agronomists, development planners, and extension agents, rural development can proceed at a steady pace, instead of lurching through expensive ventures piloted by outside experts that often leave no lasting impact (see Richards 1985, and Lambert 1985, for a few examples from Africa and Asia).

Resource 1: principles

Principles that guide successful adaptation to the advantages and disadvantages of tropical ecosystems can be gleaned from ethnobotanical knowledge used in agriculture and medicine. Study of traditional land-use systems reveals the principles upon which tropical farmers base their agriculture. Temperate-zone agricultural practices are based on principles derived from farming relatively simple ecological systems in a region where capital-intensive inputs are readily available. Such practices, however, are generally not well-adapted to the more complex conditions offered by tropical soils, vegetation, and climate where capital-intensive inputs are less available to farmers.

Traditional farming systems are designed to use the resources available to them. Natural processes and elements are manipulated so they can be used as inputs and energy harnessed to a farmer's advantage. These principles affirm B. L. Gordon's (1982) assertion that indigenous farmers make a living as applied ecologists. Some of the principles that relate to agricultural management include the following:

Wild plants are not necessarily weeds. Whether they are viewed as weeds or not depends on where they grow and what benefits they can offer (*cf.* Gliessman 1987). Farmers manipulate wild plants as resources for the value of their products, the ecological services they mediate, or for the ecological services they provide directly.

The preferred landscape holds a mosaic of wild and crop biodiversity. Diversity is desirable at all levels. A diversity of native vegetation provides resources to meet the needs for food, medicine, shelter, and ecological services, yet requires minimal energy inputs. In some cases, the diversity of the native ecosystem is enhanced to support a greater concentration of native species than would occur naturally. For example, Kayapó farmers of Brazil build artificial forest in the savanna (Posey 1985) as part of the complex mosaic landscape they maintain. Likewise, crop diversity is appreciated. It spreads risks, maintains crop evolutionary processes, and provides variety in the diet. Diversity is maintained in the landscape at two levels: within units containing different types of crops and wild vegetation, and in the form of mosaics made up of these units at the level of the farmer's or community's holdings, so that the farmer and the community have access to multiple units.

Wild plants can be managed to sustain agricultural systems. Cropping systems make trade-offs to balance advantages for current and future crops and wild non-crops. Soil conservation on slopes can be achieved by short fallow swidden systems that use native secondary vegetation to hold the soil (Alcorn 1990a). Wild plants are used to regulate soil fertility. Farmers use weeds to make water and nutrients available to crops at appropriate times and over time. They use native vegetation to shade the soil between crop plants from the sun's heat and rays, thereby maintaining conditions necessary for positive microbial processes in the soil. They allow wild plants to continue to trap nutrients from air and subsoil and hold them for future crops so the nutrients are not leached and lost.

Topographically related variation in wild plant communities is valuable. Farmers appreciate the diversity created by topographic variation. For example, seasonally flooded riversides and raised fields in marshes use water-borne organic matter (largely derived from wild plants) to fertilise crops, and they include useful wild plants adapted to annual flooding. In Mexico, raised fields relying on natural processes in Tabascan marshes achieve higher yields than drained areas under capital-intensive agriculture in the same area (Gliessman 1990).

Seed selection is a joint venture between the farmer and the environment. Farmers use natural selection to shape crop evolution in their fields (*cf.* Oldfield and Alcorn 1987). They select their next season's crop seeds and the wild individuals to be spared from genotypes that have thrived under pressure from local pests and other local environmental constraints. They do not rely on seeds with narrow genetic base adapted to the conditions in the trial fields of seed companies.

Experimentation with biological elements (wild plants, new crops, or traditional varieties of current crops from other regions) can improve local systems. Such experiments are usually done on a small scale, often in plots near the home where they can be monitored easily. For example, the Tiv of Nigeria evaluate new plants for ecological requirements, as well as suitability of food for local processing and diet. Most communities include at least a few people who are particularly interested in experimentation with new crops or new ways of mixing crops (*e.g.* McCorkle, Brandstetter and McClure 1988; Alcorn 1984a).

Experimentation with new ways of integrating crops and wild plants can improve local systems. This includes dedicating effort to integrate cropping systems with weed communities that are hard to eliminate under standard agricultural regimes. For example, Indonesian farmers have developed successful ways to farm Imperata grasslands that agricultural extension agents claim can only be managed by removing the Imperata through the use of expensive inputs (Dove 1987).

Optimal use of space can be achieved by copying blueprints from the local community structure of wild vegetation. For example, many traditional systems in moist tropical areas, like native wild plant communities, make use of vertical space to increase productivity per unit area. Researchers are now creating modern agroforestry systems based on this principle (*e.g.* Ewel 1986).

Conservation of useful, rare plants is a priority goal that can be achieved locally. This may be achieved through local sacred groves or sacred gardens, or by individual farmers who take pride in having certain rare wild plants on their farms or in maintaining certain rare crop varieties (*e.g.* Nabhan *et al.* 1990; Gadgil and Vartak 1981; Alcorn 1989a, 1990b).

Ethnobotanical knowledge found in traditional medical systems likewise demonstrates some principles different from our own. The healing principles of sweat therapy, sub-lethal poison shock therapy, tactile stimulation with fragrant herbs, and other non-conventional therapeutic techniques are of interest to biomedical researchers.

Resource 2: plant uses and other facts

Facts extracted from ethnobotanical knowledge systems include information about:

o the uses of material from particular local plants;
o the ecological requirements and characteristics of particular species, and
o agriculturally useful information that can be 'read' from understanding the ecological reasons for the occurrence of particular natural plant associations.

Local uses of plant materials have long been recognised as good 'leads' for developing modern applications for plant materials. These facts can lead to the development of new industries or commercial products. There are numerous examples of this happening in the past. Many common modern medicines and new 'wonder' drugs are derived from herbal medicines. Plant extracts are useful in demonstrating novel activities to pharmacologists as well as providing chemical blueprints which can be improved. Rotenone is a major natural pesticide derived from a plant traditionally used as a fish poison. Rubber, coffee, and fruit industries are but a few of many based on traditionally valuable trees. (For other examples, *see* Oldfield 1989). Many regionally important industries, such as the bidi industry in India, the rattan furniture industry of The Philippines and Indonesia, and the candelilla wax industry of Mexico, to name only a few, are built upon wild plant products. Alternative fodder for livestock is an increasingly important goal of rural development initiatives. In the future, as we look for multi-purpose tree species to meet rural needs, more attention will be paid to local knowledge of trees with leaves that make good or unsuitable feed for livestock. For example, following up on local use of ramón (*Brosimum alicastrum*), researchers in Mexico found that this tree has a remarkable potential as a high-yielding producer of highly nutritious livestock feed (Peters and Pardo-Tejedo 1982).

Commercially under-used timber species are wasted when tropical forests are harvested, because these species are unknown to commerce and science. Local knowledge of wood qualities, such as rot resistance, wood strength, suitability for particular uses, and uses for non-wood forest products can provide the basis for planning better use of tropical forests (Nor 1989).

Facts related to the ecological requirements of particular species or crop varieties, speed of growth of particular species, relative values of local plants for firewood, site renewal, or plant indicators of soil quality are less commonly tapped by outsiders. These are used by farmers engaged in traditional agriculture systems and could be used by those who would improve farming in a region as a key to local soil and water resources.

Resource 3: technologies

Agricultural, medical, and industrial technologies based on plant materials or plant communities can be modernised to improve efficiency, or provide the basis for adapting modern methods to local circumstances. There is a tremendous variety of agricultural technologies involving the use of plants that can be incorporated into modern systems. For example, traditional plant protection methods include soaking seeds, before they are planted, in an extract from poisonous wild plants. Certain plants are used for soil improvement. Such practices range from swidden agriculturalists' selective protection of native leguminous trees in natural secondary regrowth to renew a site, to mulching with leaves from particular local species.

Aumeeruddy and Pinglo (1989) have recently compiled a survey of traditional crop culturing techniques that includes ways to control the flowering time of fruit trees, ways to train tree growth to influence fruit production, vegetative propagation methods, mechanical stresses that improve production, and others. Other indigenous technologies include seed storage methods, assisted natural reforestation, weed suppression, and vegetation management techniques to achieve soil conservation. Pharmaceutical companies are investigating unconventional methods of drug delivery used in traditional societies, such as transdermal delivery of certain compounds through herbal baths, herbal steam baths, and oily herbal salves.

Another use of ethnobotanical knowledge is to build upon local, plant-based industries by starting with local methods and to offer minor improvements that will increase efficiency and thereby contribute to better incomes.

Resource 4: locally adapted crops

Locally adapted crops that are part of local knowledge systems include varieties of major and minor crops, multi-purpose trees, and pasture. Such crops are often ignored by outsiders who introduce new crops and exotic multi-purpose trees without considering the value of the resources being replaced. Local varieties of major crops have value to local people and to outsiders.

Plant breeders build modern varieties by breeding in disease resistance, drought hardiness, and similar qualities from traditional varieties and their wild and weedy relatives. The Consultative Group on International Agricultural Research (CGIAR) network has emphasised collection, storage, and use of local varieties of major crops, but they have not incorporated conservation of traditional varieties for the benefit of local farmers and breeders (Oldfield and Alcorn 1987). Traditional varieties have value to local farmers because they are well adapted to local, rough farm conditions, unlike high-yielding varieties created for growing under optimal conditions with inputs of fertiliser, pesticides, and herbicides. Improving the yield of locally adapted, traditional varieties or integrating the management of local and high-yielding varieties are seldom taken as goals by outsiders. For example, in Malawi, yields of local varieties of maize equalled or bettered yields of introduced high-yielding varieties when fertilisers were applied (Hansen 1986). Yet, extension agents and researchers resisted testing the effects of fertiliser on local varieties because they had been instructed that applying fertiliser to local varieties was useless. Local minor crops fulfil local food needs and offer critically important nutritional variety to diets (Dewalt 1983; Dewey 1981; Fleuret and Fleuret 1980). Their cultivation also complements the time demands of local major crops or other labour-demanding activities. Minor crops often are displaced as modern agricultural systems are adopted. This process happens almost unconsciously. The target of modernisation is not to reduce crop diversity, yet, this is a common side effect. As they modernise their farms, families find themselves with less and less diversity available to them. Many of these minor crops are adapted to marginal lands and are drought tolerant, water-logging tolerant, and salt tolerant. They have great potential for development into major crops for marginal lands.

Local trees with multiple uses are well known to local people. Firewood, fruits, construction materials, and thatching are among the needs met by such trees. Farmers know which wild trees can be incorporated into their farmsteads, and often transplant or protect them where they grow. For example, in Nepal, a significant amount of the reforestation observed on farms is produced by farmers using native species in this way (Gilmour 1988). In other cases, communities set aside woodland groves of native and exotic trees to meet community needs (*cf.* Alcorn 1990a; Olofson 1983). Outsiders, nonetheless, almost invariably promote plantations of a handful of exotic species that have proven themselves in trial plots on research stations. The risks of this practice are clear in the failed eucalyptus plantations, which were established in areas ill-suited for eucalyptus but where native species would have succeeded. Another example of a failure is in the poor performance of Leucaena following psyllid insect attack on ipil-ipil plantations promoted over wide areas in Southeast Asia. These practices were advocated instead of the promotion of the genetic diversity of local native species that would not risk large losses from a single pest to which large populations of introduced exotics with a narrow genetic base are susceptible.

The values, seasonal availability, and ecological niches of local pasture grasses are well known to pastoralists. Improved management of these grasslands based on scientific and ethnobotanical knowledge could significantly increase their productivity. By understanding current grazing practices and the reasons behind them, outsiders could devise better management schemes that use existing grasses, or enrich existing grasslands by mixing native grasses with a few modern exotics, rather than replacing existing diversity of grasslands with pastures of a few exotic grasses with a narrow genetic base.

Resource 5: agricultural systems

Ethnobotanical knowledge is not only held by individual farmers, it is also held in the customary 'scripts', or ways of farming that farmers learn from their parents and pass on to their children (Alcorn 1989a). These are methods of farming that have been fine-tuned to local conditions by farmers experimenting with basic plans over generations. Farmers often do not know the reasons for following these scripts, it is simply 'just the way it is done'. Farmers do not describe the details of their traditional farming activities well. It is necessary to try to learn to farm as they do, learn the decisions that are made, to learn exactly what they are doing and, thereby, discover the wisdom held in their methods.

Traditional agricultural systems often take advantage of 'subsidies' from nature – the natural processes of biologically mediated decomposition and site-renewal that follow the planting of a field. They also use natural vegetation for the ecological services it provides (*e.g.* watershed management, erosion control). Below, I focus on four areas of particular interest to development planners:

o packages of practices for major crops;
o integrated pest management;
o agroforestry and reforestation; and
o home gardens / homestead forests.

Packages of practices for major crops

Traditional farmers have developed packages of practices for tropical forested lands, arid lands, steep lands, swamp lands and other marginal lands where standard, temperate-zone agricultural packages do poorly. Most of these systems renew fertility, control erosion, and maintain biodiversity through fallowing. A number of these systems are types of swidden (slash-and-burn) agriculture. Long cast as ignorant misuse of forests, swidden is now recognised as a complex system based on ecological principles, some of which may provide the basis for better modern, permanent field systems for moist tropical areas. (Traditional swidden should not be confused with slash-and-burn used by colonists to convert forest into 'permanent' pasture or cropland, which often fail to become permanent, but are rather abandoned because they are degraded through inappropriate management.)

Traditional systems that can be viewed as packages of practices for major crops include:

o the milpa system of corn cultivation with versions adapted to Mexican and Central American wetlands, tropical forests, and arid highlands;
o the chacra system of manioc cultivation in the moist tropical forests of South America;
o the lowland and upland systems of rice cultivation in Southeast Asian forests; and
o the highland Andean potato systems.

(Documentation of these elaborate systems can be found in Alcorn 1990a; Lambert 1985; Marten 1986; Mayer 1980; Olofson 1983; Wilken 1987, and others.)
In addition, there are also many complex, locally adapted systems for crops minor on the global scale but locally or regionally important (Klee 1980). Examples include:

o the eleusine systems in Africa;
o the sago palm systems in Polynesia;
o the peach palm systems in northern South and Central America; and the
o the acai palm system in the Amazonian estuary (Anderson 1990).

These systems integrate useful wild plants into their management regime.

Integrated pest management

Integrated Pest Management (IPM) makes use of natural predators and crops' spatial and temporal distribution patterns to control crop pests (Risch *et al.*

1983). At present, IPM is enjoying much interest in international development circles. However, IPM, by its nature, requires research into local plant, pest, and predator communities and their effective management. Investigation of how traditional farming patterns are affecting pest population size and distribution can provide information to scientists working to develop site-specific guidelines for IPM.

Traditional farmers often manage weeds and other wild vegetation to create a 'vegetational architecture' that controls insect population sizes in fields of crops (Altieri and Letourneau 1982) through providing habitats for pest predators, and preventing pest population build-ups because of the size and distribution of host patches. Yet, when interviewed, farmers are often unaware of why pests are not a problem in their traditional systems.

Agroforestry and reforestation

During the past decade, development experts have begun to appreciate the values of agroforestry systems. For hundreds of years, traditional farmers have developed an incredible array of complex agroforestry systems adapted to local conditions and designed to meet local needs. In one geographical area, it is often possible to document many agroforestry combinations. For example, 72 different agroforestry combinations have been observed among Panamanian Kuna farmers (Castillo and Beer 1983). Traditional agroforestry systems differ from the simple modern forms in a number of ways (Alcorn 1990a).

- o they integrate native species;
- o they make use of natural environmental variation;
- o natural forest regeneration processes are used as management tools;
- o a large number of species are included in each system;
- o agroforestry plots are integrated into a diversified farmstead;
- o there is variation among farms using the same basic system; and
- o they are designed to meet the needs of farm families in the context of uncultivated wildlands available for community exploitation.

Additionally, native and introduced trees are integrated into agricultural systems in a tremendous variety of ways:

- o trees border agricultural fields (*e.g.* living fences of multiple species);
- o they are part of the field as living supports (*e.g.* for vanilla or betel leaves);
- o they are intercropped with annuals by alley cropping, contour plantings, or as scattered small patches in a field;
- o they are used to create a field (*e.g.* honey production groves); and
- o they are the final orchard stage of a plot sequentially harvested of annuals, short-lived perennials, and eventually long-lived trees.

Artificial forests or woodland groves, that complement the production of agricultural plots, are created by allowing selected natural seedlings to become established, enriching the plot with introduced species, and sometimes by manipulating the soil and sunlight conditions. This technique is now being given the scientific name of 'assisted natural regeneration' as restoration ecologists use it to attempt to restore degraded lands and reforest denuded hills where single species plantations have failed. These ecologists need to seek out the knowledge of indigenous people who have managed local species using this technique for centuries.

Home gardens and homestead forests

Indigenous knowledge includes knowledge of how to create complex gardens incorporating native plants. Generally a riot of useful native species and minor crops, these gardens provide families with access to nutritious fruits and vegetables, medicinal plants, firewood, poultry feed, and high-value tree crops for income. It is not uncommon for such gardens to contain 80 to 100 species. Home gardens can be found in dooryards of the homestead, in the corners of agricultural fields, at the edges of coffee plantations, in pits dug along dry river beds, along pathways, and like places; they are not restricted to dooryards. They take a variety of forms and often do not resemble the typical temperate-zone garden (Alcorn 1989a). In some regions, such as Bangladesh, dooryard gardens are better described as homestead forests or orchards because trees are dominant. A given family may have several different types of gardens in different spots on their land.

Resource 6: mixed farming values and strategies

Knowledge of facts, principles, technologies, and scripts are applied in mixed farming strategies. Mixed farming here refers to farming strategies that manipulate a mixture of four elements: livestock, annual crops, perennial crops, and wild resources. These strategies are reflected in the regional, mosaic-like landscapes they create. Such landscapes are constituted in one of two ways. They may consist of repeated units of farmsteads that include sub-units emphasising each of the four elements listed above. Alternatively, the wild resource element may be emphasised in nearby areas that are not farmed, such as common pasture lands, forest greenbelts along ridges and creeks, or in narrow belts along common path/road right-of-ways, for example.

In the first type (strategy A), the native plant element depends on individual farmer or community decisions, depending on land tenure rights. Farms build in all four elements to provide multiple options to spread risk (different cash crops; drought tolerant, wild famine foods for people and livestock; subsistence foods) and provide social security (*e.g.* subsistence food for times when jobs are not available or when a worker is disabled). Native plants are integrated with cash crops in unique ways in different regions (see Alcorn 1990a for examples).

In the second type (strategy B), native plants may either simply be harvested from free access areas or they may be managed by the community as common property resources. In strategy B, the community relies on harvesting wild plants, from some place other than individuals' farmlands. Development projects often ignore the value of wild plants on 'wastelands' that are not being farmed, and unwittingly destroy community resources – as in the case of 'wasteland' social forestry in India (*e.g.* Jodha 1986).

Traditional common property systems have been undercut by pressures of privatisation, technological advances in harvesting, and commercialisation (NAS 1986). Jodha (1985), for example, has analysed the degradation of Rajastani grassland and forest common property resources. These lands were traditionally classified as marginal and restricted from agricultural use by local rulers who taxed users of the common property to pay the costs of managing them. Jodha determined that privatisation and conversion of common property resources into free access resources led to inappropriate land use practices and subsequent degradation of the resource base (reduced production from overexploited wild plants, soil erosion).

Re-empowerment of traditional common property systems based on ethnobotanical knowledge combined with modern insights may restore marginal lands to their earlier productivity (*cf.* Messerschmidt 1987). Biodiversity is consistently under-valued in economic analyses, and this has contributed to policies that have resulted in its degradation. Development planners need to realise real costs of eliminating biodiversity from the landscape if a sustainable path for development is to be pursued.

Accurate quantification of the economic benefits of traditional, diversified farming requires the inclusion of the economic values of goods and services derived from wild plants. One effort to do this (Alcorn 1989b) demonstrates that a system that mixes strategy A (farmers build their farms on four subunits that include native plants: maize swidden fields, sugar-cane, livestock, and forest groves) and strategy B (the community also manages common forested lands) provides farmers with an average net benefit higher than the benefits earned from employment in towns of the same region.

Resource 7: information about constraints, opportunities, and needs

The constraints that limit the options, the opportunities available to rural communities, and the needs felt by local communities are revealed in indigenous knowledge systems. Rural residents manipulate their social and natural environment in attempts to achieve a successful livelihood. Plant use and management are shaped by:

○ the strategies for success chosen by farmers and farm communities;
○ history;
○ the social and natural environmental constraints and opportunities perceived by local people; and
○ by the real structures and functioning of the social and natural environments.

Careful study of the ways in which indigenous knowledge is being applied will reveal the windows of opportunity available to local people. Constraints revealed by analysing local ethnobotanical knowledge include evidence of lack of access to reasonably priced capital, the lack of local species to provide biologically mediated services, and the progressive loss of useful species so that the species of choice is not easily available (*cf.* Alcorn 1981).

Opportunities revealed by the analysis include natural processes that can be used as subsidies from nature as well as the availability of species that have particular uses. Analysis will also identify local specialists with green thumbs who experiment with plant breeding or seed traders with well-developed networks of clients who can collaborate in trying out and spreading new techniques/seeds. Another opportunity is identification of local groups that have organised to meet a need, *e.g.* communal labour groups that maintain common property resources. These groups can be strengthened and encouraged to expand as necessary.

Local needs are also revealed. For example, analysis of knowledge of famine foods may indicate that famines are a problem in some segment of the society. The presence of many herbal treatments for diarrhoeal diseases may indicate that water pollution is a major problem. Marketability of current crops and wild plants can also be learned by investigating ethnobotanical knowledge systems.

Conclusion: ways to facilitate the use of ethnobotanical knowledge to meet development goals

Farmers have ethnobotanical knowledge of value to those interested in meeting development goals. Ethnobotanical knowledge can be used to improve rural livelihoods, especially in marginal areas, by providing the basis for integrating useful native plants and low-input technologies into modernisation packages that meet rural needs. Knowledge of biologically-mediated processes that improve and maintain soil resources can contribute to sustaining the resource base. Rural health and nutrition can be improved by encouraging the maintenance of gardens and orchards that produce a wide variety of foods and medicinal plants. Encouraging the use of proven herbal medicines among people who do not have access to pharmaceuticals can also improve rural health care in many areas (*cf.* Bastien 1987).

Investigation of the distribution of ethnobotanical knowledge and management regimes of plant resources will reveal local institutions that regulate resource use. Among these are common property institutions, which should be supported by development efforts (NAS 1986). Such studies also reveal the needs around which local people will organise themselves. Knowledge of perceived needs is a valuable foundation upon which to build development.

Finally it can be argued that the social security provided by subsistence production elements of a farmstead frees up a nation's capital for investment in industrialisation instead of subsidising social services.

To achieve development goals through the use of ethnobotanical knowledge, two actions must be taken. First, policy reform must be undertaken to ensure that biodiversity is assigned a more realistic value in economic cost-benefit analyses; forest-based systems are recognised and encouraged as viable land uses; and decentralised control of common property resources is strengthened. Secondly, farmers must be encouraged to participate in development as informed actors and as teachers.

These actions would have to be complemented by a broadening in the orientation of development specialists. Development planners should look at the landscape with a botanical eye. They should assume that any patch of wild vegetation (wasteland, forest, grassland, or pathside swath) is providing something of use to someone. They need to find out what this something is and who that someone is before they replace that patch with some other land use system. They should make every effort to design new land uses in ways that include native vegetation to meet the needs in the existing land use system.

Planners need to understand the current system of managing common property resources, as well as the system for managing wild plants on farmstead. They should determine how wild vegetation is being used as a subsidy to maintain cropped fields, and as a subsidy to maintain families. They should understand how the existing structure was created and how it has changed in the recent past if it appears that the resource base is being degraded. Labour allocations for maintaining the native plant resources must be considered in relation to labour allocations envisioned for the new systems being considered for development-introduction. Those interested in pursuing this strategy for development will find no written documentation of the ethnobotanical knowledge of most regions. They must interact with local residents. One method might be to use a form of Rapid Rural Appraisal (RRA) that incorporates a focus on native plants. Richards (1985) has included some of the critical questions about productive activities, local skills, facilities, equipment and raw materials, and social and political organisation, although he does not address the specifics of ethnobotanical knowledge.

Questions would range from specifics like: Where did construction materials used in your house come from? What minor crops are being cultivated? How many local varieties of rice are being grown? Where does livestock fodder come from in all seasons? to conversations designed to determine what products and services are currently being provided by the specific wild plants and plant communities seen by the observer in a given village/region's landscape. A simple, computerised program could be designed to enable planners to elicit ethnobotanical information, then analyse and apply it.

Ultimately, use of ethnobotanical knowledge systems depends on an attitude change by extension workers, by development specialists, and by rural people (Alcorn 1988; Compton 1989). Extension agents must change their attitudes that the only good knowledge originates in universities and experiment stations. The onus for making that change lies with those institutions. More social scientists and agronomists need to recognise nature as a resource, instead of equating all native plants as background generic forest, weeds, or brush, and internalise the principles noted above. This is not an easy transformation to catalyse, because an unfortunate side effect of modernisation and urbanisation has been the loss of common appreciation for the critical roles played by plants in our ecosystem. Perhaps, a national effort to educate professionals and the general public about the importance of plant life would be useful (Wilkes 1990).

Finally, rural residents have often come to accept outside attitudes that what they know is of no value to others. 'Foxfire' projects that encourage young people to document and appreciate 'old ways' (as suggested by Compton 1989) and participatory research projects may enable greater interaction between development specialists and local people by helping to erase distrust of outsiders and by giving pride in a local resource of global value: ethnobotanical knowledge systems.

2. *Taman Obat Keluarga (TOGA)*: Indigenous Indonesian medicine for self-reliance

L. JAN SLIKKERVEER AND MADY K.L. SLIKKERVEER

Introduction

OVER THE AGES, indigenous Indonesian medicine has evolved as a distinct body of knowledge of health and healing, relying upon the balanced interaction of the community with the rich domains of the natural environment of the Southeast Asian Archipelago. Despite ignorance and supersession of the traditional medical system by the former Dutch colonial power and the post-war influx of Western pharmaceuticals, and more recently, the imminent depletion of natural resources under the pressure of commercial production and increasing population, Indonesian medical plants and herbs have continued to provide the majority of the rural people with the appropriate ingredients for traditional medicaments. In addition to the common knowledge of certain natural produce beneficial for health maintenance, healing and the preparation of home remedies constituting a basic, pan-Indonesian culture trait, the retention over generations of intimate, often secret recipes of particular herbal mixtures among virtually each of the more than 300 ethnic groups of present-day Indonesia indicates the complex ethnospecific character of the indigenous medical knowledge system in this part of the world. Apart from the linguistic differentiation in the term 'medicine' along ethno-cultural lines, the classificatory names used for different categories of medicaments of the wide variety of specific names referring to distinct remedies for particular ailments or complaints, the approved knowledge of a whole range of herbal, animal and mineral *materia medica* used in the preparation and application of traditional Indonesian medicine reflect the intricate structure of this system in a rapidly modernising society.

While the term *obat*[1] in *Bahasa Indonesia* (the official language since Independence) encompasses the collective term for 'medicine', *obat asli Indonesia*[2] refers exclusively to 'indigenous Indonesian medicine'. In this context the term *jamu*[3] is generally used to define ready-made 'indigenous herbal medicine' prepared from plant materials, *ramuan*,[4] such as leaves, flowers, fruits, bark, roots, etc. Beside the lay-person's knowledge and practice of these indigenous remedies within the family, several categories of traditional healers, *dukun*[5] master their wisdom in a more professional mode of availing their clients and patients with traditional care (Suparlan 1991). However, since the beginning of this century, the preparation and use of certain *jamu* proved to be so successful, that part of it became commercialised into a small-scale home-industry of fully-prepared, indigenous medical products. Later on, it developed into the establishment of manufacturers of 'modern' *jamu* providing the market with local 'ready-to-use' medicines in an effort to compete with imported *obat paten*.[6] In contrast with these 'modern' *jamu* still prepared out of natural ingredients, the latter encompassed innovative, patented medicines, largely composed of compounds which were introduced from Europe during the colonial era.

During the Japanese occupation of Indonesia (1942–5) and subsequently, in the course of the Indonesian Revolution (1945–59) prior to Independence, a revaluation of herbal medicine by medical doctors and public health services

13

initiated such massive resort to the indigenous medical system that a first wave of medical revivalism was induced throughout the country. Initially triggered off by the discontinuation in the supply of imported pharmaceuticals as a result of the crisis of war, the cosmological re-appreciation of the 'good' of 'mother earth', *ibu pertiwi*,[7] and the popular response to the nationalist appeal for the common heritage of the new nation provided the wider historical and cultural context of this movement (*cf.* Crozier 1977; Afdhal and Welsh 1988).

Although shortly after the recovery from the Second World War the medical interest and use of *jamu* declined in favour of the prescription of newly imported medicines, both the traditional medical belief system, and the success of increased manufacture and sale of *jamu* had firmly secured the place of herbal medicine within the pluralistic medical configuration of the new nation. Later on, the early eighties even witnessed a second, more institutionalised wave of revivalism of the indigenous medical system, when increased commercial production of 'modern' *jamu* was reinforced by government legislation and subsequent promotion.

BERDIKARI: the concept of self-reliance

In line with these fluctuations in revivalist movements in Indonesia, the changing values and attitudes towards traditional pharmaceuticals after independence had fostered a re-orientation and trust among different groups of the population towards their own culture. In the wake of expensive, modern medicines, rural people relied increasingly on the easily accessible, relatively cheap herbal medicines from their own familiar 'environment' largely used for health maintenance and the preparation of home remedies. Whereas previously, most ingredients for herbal medicines had been collected from the forest by professional traditional healers, it was no exception for them to cultivate certain medicinal plants in their botanical gardens, *kebun obat*.[8] With the popularisation of both the 'secret' herbal recipes of ancient *jamu* of particular families – usually from the *keraton*[9] – and the professional wisdom of *dukun*, exchange and spread of indigenous medical knowledge soon evolved into a common effort at village level to put such knowledge into practice and have some families planting and harvesting their own selection of medicinal plants.

Easily incorporated into the social system of *gotong royong*[10] reintroduced by the former President Sukarno and widely adopted as a renewed cooperative movement of cultivating medicinal herbs and plants for largely private use soon became a community activity at grassroots level. Given the substantial involvement of women in this active form of self-reliance in family health, initially referred to as '*Apotik Hidup*', a 'living pharmacy',[11] it is not surprising that already in the course of the seventies, *Apotik Hidup* readily was adopted in the early development stages of the Village Family Welfare Movement, *Pembinaan Kesejahteraan Keluarga* (PKK 1984). This cooperative movement had originated in the late sixties out of local self-help activity among village women of Java and subsequently spread into other villages and urban neighbourhoods throughout the country. Later on, when the World Health Organisation (WHO) in its *Global Strategy for Health for All by the Year 2000* (1981) at the beginning of the eighties recommended each member state to explore and utilise its natural medicinal resources, the Government of Indonesia decided to comply and formally promote the cultivation and use of indigenous medicinal herbs and plants in its efforts to enhance the self-reliance of communities, particularly in the rural areas. To this end, the practice of *Apotik Hidup* of PKK was further institutionalised in all villages and named *Taman Obat Keluarga* (TOGA) or *Family Medicinal Gardens* (FAME Gardens) supporting the national policy of self-reliance in health and related areas of food, nutrition and environmental conservation (TOGA 1983; Sutrisno 1984; Esche 1987).

This policy of self-reliance in health was based on the general concept of *berdiri atas kaki sendiri* (BERDIKARI), the motto of 'standing on one's own feet' that had characterised the development philosophy of the country since Independence.

As the Declaration of Alma Ata of WHO/UNICEF (1978: 79) specifically refers to the *self-reliance* of communities and national authorities in Primary Health Care, initiatives are implied to assume the population's own responsibility for health development. It refers to the extent to which individuals are able to maintain their health and solve their medical problems within the context of available resources.

The age-old indigenous knowledge and practice of herbal medicine – revived since the end of the seventies – provided an appropriate 'vehicle' for the implementation of the concept of self-reliance in health promotion and care throughout Indonesia, supported by non-governmental organisations and community-based voluntary groups, associations and cooperatives. The underlying interest of the government in the promotion of herbal medicine has generally been focused on future self-reliance with regard to the production of medicines, as part of the Primary Health Care delivery system.

Although pharmacological and phytochemical research on medicinal plants in Indonesia has been initiated under the impetus of WHO's research policy on traditional medicine in Primary Health Care (1978, 1983), the study of the cultivation, preparation and use of medicinal plants in this part of Asia is still in its infancy.

As Leslie (1988) notes, it is at least remarkable that in the numerous studies on the sociocultural context of the production and utilisation of different kinds of Western and indigenous medicines in the Third World which started to emerge about two decades ago in medical and pharmaceutical anthropology literature, the substantial role of indigenous herbal medicines in Indonesian society so far has only been addressed to in a handful. Whereas a few recent studies have concentrated on the impressive transnational marketing of modern *jamu* pharmaceuticals, the underlying principles and premises as well as the practical utilisation of indigenous resources at community level have hardly experienced any scientific investigation. Equally, interest in phytopharmacology and phytotherapy under the impetus of the current recommendations of WHO (Bannerman, Burton and Ch'en Wen-Chieh 1983) to enter into preliminary research on the efficacy and safety of herbal medicine has only very recently evolved within a number of university schools of pharmacy in Indonesia.[12] This is not only in sharp contrast with the numerous studies on comparable systems of herbal medicine elsewhere in Asia such as China, India, Sri Lanka, Thailand, Malaysia and The Philippines, but also with the increased interest among different individuals and groups of Indonesia itself. Apart form the popularity through public promotion and advertising of *jamu*, local 'do-it-yourself' publications on *Obat Asli Indonesia, Apotik Hidup, Apotik Hijau, Obat Tradisional* and *Jamu* containing specific lists of plant names, disease classifications and instructions for cultivation and use of local medical plants reflect an ongoing process of the renaissance of indigenous Indonesian medicine. It underlines the readiness 'from below' to bring in local medical knowledge and resources into the all-embracing effort of primary health care development which certainly deserves further investigation, in particular from the applied-oriented, medical social sciences.

Although indigenous medical knowledge and practices in Indonesia have aroused the interest of many scholars including botanists, geographers and ethnologists, even from pre-colonial times onwards, the comparative study of the relationship between medicine, culture and society in its particular geo-historical context of Southeast Asia has been hampered by both theoretical and methodological problems. Theoretical in the sense of a protracted absence of a holistic approach to the different bio- and ethnomedical systems operating in the region and the neglect of the behavioural dimension of medical ideas and practices, and more generally, the over-emphasis on the rather 'exotic' magico-religious and ritual aspects of health, illness and healing. Methodologically, an arbitrary delimitation of the concept of a medical system, the lack of systematically collected data and wavering in the application of advanced analysis, conventional methodology has equally hampered a better understanding of the public health situation in present-day Indonesia. However, these shortcomings have for a long time been overshadowed by more detrimental views of nineteenth-century social and natural scientists whose writings, as Warren (1989: 177) accurately notes: '...generated the belief in Westerners that there was little of value in non-Western cultures, that progress for non-Westerners was a function of acquiring Western knowledge, building upon an indigenous knowledge base which was presumed to be both elementary and filled with error.' Although during the last decades, a more realistic study of ethnomedical systems in non-Western societies has developed in the medical social sciences, a truly comparative study of indigenous Indonesian medicine in terms of its multiple functions, its different socio-cultural contexts and, last but not least, its behavioural nature is still in its infancy.

In this light, it is the objective of this chapter to assess the historical setting and renewed significance of indigenous Indonesian medicine in the context of rapidly modernising society. In particular, it seeks to highlight an intriguing phenomenon of the traditional systems: adaptation and development of a unique, grassroot-movement of self-reliance of local groups in a new concept of Primary Health Care, unparalleled in this region of Asia.

The evolution of Indonesian herbal medicine

Presently, as in most societies, the daily life of health and healing in Indonesia is comprised of a wide range of medical beliefs, knowledge and practices, and of distinct categories of functionaries including 'Western' medical doctors, nurses and specialists, folk healers, herbal doctors, traditional birth attendants, drug vendors and pedlars, dispensing chemists and pharmacists. In the application of their medical knowledge, these doctors and healers use different forms of diagnosis, therapy and medicines. In the analytical study of such complex medical configurations which are also found elsewhere in Asia, it was especially Leslie (1977: 9) who developed a very useful, non-normative concept of 'medical pluralism', based on historical analysis, in which medical systems can be regarded as: '...pluralistic structures in different kinds of practitioners and institutional norms'. The theoretical implications of this pluralist perspective on medicine have clearly been perceptible in the emergence of new orientations in the medical social sciences: it introduced a more realistic approach to the study of 'non-formal', 'irregular' or even 'illegal' medical traditions as part of pluralistic structures: '...in which cosmopolitan medicine is one component in competitive and complementary relationship to numerous "alternative therapies."' (cf. Leslie 190: 191). As a result, an expanding research interest in medical anthropology has recently focused on medical pluralism in various settings, laying the foundation for the further development of a 'new' ethnomedical approach to medicine with a special interest in indigenous medical knowledge (*cf.* Leslie 1977, 1978, 1980; Janzen 1978; Rubel *et al.* 1986; Weidman 1979; Kleinman 1980; Warren 1974, 1982; Warren *et al.* 1982; Slikkerveer 1982, 1983, 1990).

The employment of such new approach to the study of the Indonesian situation, in which different ethnic groups in this region over the centuries have developed and adapted their medical knowledge systems for health maintenance and healing practices requires a rather specific geo-historical classification, as introduced by Dunn (1977). In this way, the prevailing different perceptions and practices in Indonesia can usefully be classified as the *local medical systems*, accommodating the indigenous folk medicine of *i.a.* the Javanese, Sundanese, Madurese, Balinese and Buginese, the *regional medical systems* such as the traditional Chinese and Indian humoral traditions and the *cosmopolitan medical system* of 'modern' or 'scientific' medicine, introduced from the West. As these systems in the course of historical processes of acculturation all had interacted and differentiated into hierarchic and lay traditions of learned, scholarly systems of the 'Great Tradition' and popular, lay systems of the 'Little Tradition', it seems appropriate, first to access the evolution process of these traditional medical knowledge systems in the area, before focusing on the diffusion of indigenous herbal medicine, which undoubtedly has been at the 'roots' of the present pluralistic medical configuration (*cf.* Redfield 1956).

Historically, as Foster (1976, 1983, 1987), Leslie (1977), Bürgel (1977), Kleinman (1978) and Udupa (1975) among others have well documented, the three major 'Great Tradition' humoral systems are: the Hippocratic-Galenic of ancient Greece, the Ayurvedic of India and the Chinese systems. All three systems, as opposed to ethnomedical systems of Africa, Oceania, Australia and the Americas, share certain common characteristics such as a 'naturalistic' cosmological view of the universe encompassing an equilibrium model to explain health and disease and to indicate proper cure, a conception of elements with ascribed values, the significance of bodily fluids or humours and the belief in a metaphorical 'breath of life'. Most intriguing, as Foster (1987: 359) indicates, is the similar, ancient notion that: '...foods, medicinal remedies, and other substances are characterised by pairs of metaphoric values of qualities: Hot or Cold, paired with Wet or Dry'. Consequently, therapy is practiced according to the 'principle of opposites' whereby Hot remedies cure Cold diseases and *vice versa*. Here, the pre-eminence of the knowledge of the *materia medica* in terms of the right classification of Hot and Cold medicinal plants and herbs, and the associated method of mixing is widely reflected in the major role, pharmacies have played in these traditional medical systems. Medical historians have retraced the diffusion of these 'Great Traditions' from around the Mediterranean to have followed different routes: Ayurveda penetrated India, Nepal, Sri Lanka, and partly eastward into Burma and Malaysia, while Chinese medicine proliferated into Korea, Japan, Thailand and southward into the islands of Southeast Asia. Greek humoral medicine spread substantially with the expansion of Islam. Eastward, it has diffused through Iran, Afghanistan, Pakistan,

India, Bangladesh, Malaysia and, according to Foster (1987), into parts of Indonesia. In view of the rather scattered information on the historical interaction among and between 'Great' and 'Little Traditions' in Indonesia, and sometimes conflicting interpretations of traces of humoral systems in different contexts, a more systematical, 'new' ethnomedical approach towards the complex situation in Indonesia is needed.[13]

Since early times, one of the outstanding elements in traditional Indonesian medicine, herbal medicine, has attracted particular attention from foreign, mostly Dutch, travellers and scientists. Although early accounts of Bontekoe (1689), Rumphius (1741) and Van Bloemen-Waanders (1859), generally remained limited to the collection, description and taxonomy of indigenous medical plants and herbs, occasionally additional information was provided on local practices of preparation, use and efficacy of remedies. At the turn of the century, however, Vorderman (1894, 1900) widened his research interest in herbal medicine in Java and Madura to include the attributed magico-religious significance and the underlying belief system of the local population. His treatise on the two main doctrines of 'transmigration' and 'signature' of Javanese medicine dominated the structural-functionalist orientation towards 'primitive medicine' in Indonesia during the first half of this century. Following Elshout (1923), Drewes (1929), Hidding (1935), Kleiweg de Zwaan (1914, 1931, 1933) and Van Ossenbruggen (1911), it was above all Weck (1937, 1938) who elaborated on the historical context of the mystical and ritual nature of medical beliefs and practices in Indonesia. He based his study on healing and tradition in Bali on ancient medical manuscripts on palmleaves, *lontar*, illustrating that the traditional medical systems on the island had evolved from historical contacts between, on the one side, indigenous Balinese notions largely corresponding with Old Javanese and Lesser Sundanese views, and on the other side, imported Hinduistic and Hindu-Javanese perceptions into a blended form of 'medical dualism'.

Weck (1937) contrasted the philosophical-mystical perceptions of learned Hinduistic tradition with the magical beliefs and practices of folk medicine, a significant dualism which he also observed in the wider context of both the Balinese caste system, as well as in its segregated religion. Similarly, the traditional healers in Bali were classified as *balian*, different categories of learned priests, and as *dukun*, the pragmatic healers. His analysis of the traditional medical literature in *usada* or *usana*[14] and *tutor* or *tutur*[15] on the *lontar*[16] clearly indicates the strong influence of learned medical tradition of the Hindus of India on Balinese medicine, which goes back to the fifth professional knowledge of *ruwa binedia*, based on the healing fluid of the body, *idhep*, as opposite to bodily fire, *bayu*. Also, the concept of elements, abundantly recorded in several local monographs, is expressed in the five elements, *mahabhuta*, adopted from the Indian *Mahabharata* which refers to both the macrocosm of the universe and its image of the microcosm of the human body. The five elements include space, air, fire, water and soil. In addition to the magical remedies such as charms and amulets, the traditional medicaments include herbal, mineral and animal ingredients, which are mostly applied in combination with water and according to qualities such as temperature and colour. The importance of such qualities in Balinese remedies have also been described by Covarrubias (1986: 353) who notes: 'The keystone of Balinese medicine is the principle of 'hot' and 'cold', irritating and refreshing, also applied to foods.' Similar classifications, in which the proper balance of 'fire' and 'water' confers 'health', while imbalance results in 'disease', has recently been documented by Howe (1984).

The view of the universe

Interest in the relationship between ritual behaviour, symbols and the sociocultural system has long been the domain of the anthropological study of symbolism. The specific methodology of semantic analysis and the introduction of binary models have retrieved complex symbolic systems, ethno-specific cosmologies and the significance of ritual language (*cf.* Fox 1975; Jackson 1975). A useful, extended perspective on the interaction between symbols and changes in the environment has widened recent anthropological studies of symbolism to encompass the influence of fluctuations in daily life – such as health and disease – on the prevailing cosmology. In this way, Karim (1981) documents the classificatory, opposed sets of rules and practices in the context of illness and injury among the *Mak Betisek* of the Malay Peninsula. The description of the defining elements of the *abangan* world-view by Mulder (1983: 262) stresses the basic model for the 'order of life' among the Javanese, in which rituals are: '…important devices for maintaining or restoring equilibrium and ensuring social harmony.' The location of such a view as much in human society as in a wider cosmic context is sustained by the elaborate mythology of Indian inspiration, *Mahabharata*, as reflected in the popularity of the shadow theatre *wayang* among the Javanese (*cf.* Geertz 1976: 262-278). More recently, Schefold (1990) documents the conception of a symbolic, common order among the *Sakuddei* of the Island of Siberut, west of Sumatra, encompassing similar religious principles which dominate the entire environment, both natural and cultural. In his analysis of the culinary code of the *Puliaijat* ritual, the author notes that a disturbance of the ideal of balance and harmony in life may even lead to illness and death, illustrating the important role of rituals, often performed by medicine-men in restoring the cosmological order (*cf.* Schefold 1982).

Recent medical-anthropological studies on the harmonious interconnection between the physical world and the spiritual world, between the microcosms and the macrocosm, and between culture and nature refer to an *all-embracing equilibrium model of the universe*, in which the indigenous medical knowledge system in Indonesia – as elsewhere in the Southeast Asian region – is embedded (Durrenberger 1977; Geertz 1977; Leslie 1977; Foster 1983; Jordaan 1985). With specific reference to health and disease in Indonesia, several components of this model have been sparsely documented including the concept of basic elements, each with certain metaphorical qualities: water (moist), air (cold), soil (dry), and fire (hot). Additionally, bodily fluids or humours have been recorded to the categories *blood*, *phlegm* and *wind* (Hart 1969; Gould-Martin 1978; Manderson 1981). The explanation of illness and the selection of appropriate treatment are equally found to be conceived of as disturbance of the hot–cold balance and the subsequent restoration of the equilibrium through the application of medicines with opposite humoral values (Foster 1987).

Finally, the adherence to a conception of a mystical 'life-breath', a secret manifest of God in one's breath is shown among several groups to be associated with the essence of life, which is located within the body (*cf.* Needham and Lu 1969).

Such traces of a humoral pathology in the context of a 'naturalistic' paradigm of an all-enfolding cosmology have been reported by Jaspan (1969, 1977) in Southwest Sumatra. Here, among the *Rejang*, traditional pathology and therapy related to a conception of balance and imbalance are associated with four main categories: the action of natural elements such as water and wind; deistic or ancestral retribution; sorcery, and witchcraft and poisoning. Geertz (1976) high-lights three cultural types reflecting Javanese cosmology: *abangan*,[17] *santri*[18] and *prijaji*,[19] associated with a balanced, historical integration of respectively Animistic, Hinduistic and Islamic elements which evolved into a basic form of Javanese syncretism. Whereas *abangan* religious tradition encompasses a complex set of theories and practices of curing, sorcery and magic of the 'Little Tradition' of the peasantry, *santri* and *prijaji* undoubtedly refer to 'Great Traditions' of the Islamic and Hinduistic systems. The *prijaji* worldview's binary structure is built upon different pairs of concepts such as *alus* (pure)[20] versus *kasar*[21] (rough), *lair*[22] (external human behaviour) versus *batin*[23] (inner human experience). These recurrent elements are – broadly speaking – generally categorised in four main categories: the action of natural elements, generally fire (hot), wind (cold), earth (dry) and water (moist); deistic or ancestral retribution; sorcery and witchcraft; and poisoning (*cf.* Burkhill and Haniff 1930; Jaspan 1969, 1976, 1977; Kimball 1979; Laderman 1984; Foster 1987). As far as the first category of the concept of elements is concerned, several studies have documented the widespread adherence to a matrix of health–illness dichotomy, expressed in pairs of metaphorical qualities such as 'hot' or 'cold' versus 'wet' or 'dry' and attributed to foods, plants and medicines. Such classifications have direct bearing on the different types of remedies and treatment, which are equally classified in qualities of 'hot' and 'cold'. The elements operate in a certain mode of equilibrium to be kept in harmony in order to prevent illness.

In Madura, the maintenance of correct relationships among the natural and supernatural forces, mainly through the performance of certain rituals has early been documented by Vorderman (1900) and later by Jordaan (1982, 1985). Here again, the manifold classifications of metaphoric 'hot' and 'cold' values or qualities to diseases and remedies such as foods and plants and their 'opposite' use to restore the balance, equally conform to an equilibrium model.

Similarly, Adimihardja (1990) underscores the basic adherence to the equilibrium model in the worldview of the Sundanese in West Java, the largest ethnic group in Indonesia. In their cosmology, the Sundanese conceptualise four basic elements in the macrocosm: *api* (fire), *tanah* (soil), *air* (water) and *flesh*, to which equally the 'hot' and 'cold' qualities are attributed. While disturbances in the equilibrium in either the macrocosm or microcosm will influence human life, the attempts to restore the balance include ritual service (*sesajen*) and the application of opposite 'hot' or 'cold' medicine by the traditional healer (*dukun*). The Sundanese system, according to Adimihardja (1990) also resembles the Javanese concept of 'life-breath' (*urip*)[24] in the similar concept of *hurip* which distinctly refers to 'being alive' or 'having the soul'.

In the light of such abundant historical and anthropological evidence of traces of classical Graeco-Arabic humoral medicine in the culture area of Indonesia, supported by previous studies in the region of Hart (1969), Hiroko (1980) and Manderson (1981) supplemented with richly documented ethnographic-historical studies of Leslie (1977) and Foster (1987), presuppositions on traces of an older 'Austronesian medical tradition' of *e.g.* Jordaan (1985) can hardly be maintained. By consequence, the homogeneity of humoral medicine is accentuated, as it is found in Latin American, in the Caribbean and in Southeast Asia in terms of the same equilibrium model of health and disease and similar hot–cold classificatory systems (*cf.* Foster 1987). The less apparent occurrence of a wet–dry dimension among certain ethnic groups in Indonesia refers to a process of 'degeneration' commonly found in interactive 'Great' and 'Little' medical traditions in Afghanistan (Penkala 1980; Centlivres 1985), North Iran (Bromberger 1985), Hong Kong (Lee 1989) and the Horn of Africa (Slikkerveer 1990).

The ascriptions of classificatory properties of 'hot' and 'cold' to foods and medicines, and in particular to the essential 'popular' remedies such as medical plants and herbs and their widespread utilisation underscores the preeminence of indigenous herbal medicine in the plural medical system of Indonesia.

Over the centuries, herbal medicine has been the major medical resource in the indigenous medical system of Indonesia, providing medicinal plants and herbs for a wide variety of applications in health maintenance, disease prevention and healing. Although nowadays a special interest has evolved into the practical utilisation of local plant resources in Primary Health Care, for most Indonesians the underlying principles of herbal medicine encompass a much wider area of human life being an intrinsic part of the whole universe.

As mentioned before, the special properties of many Indonesian medicinal plants attracted the attention of foreign scientists as early as in the sixteenth century, when Dutch botanists started to collect, describe and classify medical herbs and plants all over the archipelago (*cf.* Lehner and Lehner 1973). Later on, some researchers widened their attention to include in their accounts the 'mystical' and 'magico-religious' principles governing the use of specific plants by the local people. In this way, during the colonial era, Vorderman (1894), interpreted Javanese traditional pharmacology to comprise of supernatural doctrines of 'transmigration' and 'signatures' (*cf.* Van der Pijl 1990). Although traces of these doctrines are also found in medieval European theories of pharmacology and alchemy, the exotic character of both 'primitive' assumptions on the transition of the powers of the consumed into the consumer and on the indication in the exterior appearance of the plant to its use dominated his otherwise meritorious work. Later on, nineteenth century scientists such as Van Bloemen-Waanders (1859), De Kat Angelino (1909), and Van Eck (1878) all in their rather ethnocentrist descriptions of traditional healers in Bali, *balyan* or *balian*[25], and their practices and medicaments elaborate on the extensive use of incantations, amulets and charms, not seldom referring to these functionaries as '"quacks" with minimal knowledge, who virtually had no part in the healing of their patients.' However, with the later development of anthropological and ethnomedical, applied-oriented studies of traditional medicine on the one hand, and the persistent use of predominant plant remedies in Indonesian society – despite an influx of foreign medicine – on the other, a renewed interest in indigenous herbal medicine has evolved over the past two decades. Interest in the spread of such indigenous medical knowledge over the 'Anthropological Field of Study' of Indonesia has shown that several species of medical plants, described in the *Taru premana lontar*, an ancient indigenous pharmacopoeia from Bali and still vividly in use on the island, have also been recorded under their local name, in *i.a.* Java (Geertz 1976; Soeparto 1986; Van der Pijl 1900; Kloppenburg-Versteegh 1934; Adimihardja 1990), Kalimantan (Kimball 1979), Madura (Vorderman 1900; Jordaan 1985) and Sulawesi (Slikkerveer 1987).

Linguistic evidence of the spread of knowledge of certain medicinal plants over the Archipelago is found in some of the modern pharmacopoeia. Soeparto (1986: 162) in the classification of names of medicinal plants, indicates the regional differentiation in the nomenclature. So, for instance, the herb *ketumbar* (*Coriandrum sativum L.*) from the Balinese *Taru premana* is found in Sumatra under the name *keutumba* (Aceh), *ketumeur, ketumber* (Gayo), *hatumbar*

(Batak), *katombhar* (Madura); in Sulawesi *katumbali* (*gorontalo*), *katumbara* (Makassar) and in Bali *katumbah*. Similar regional variation in names of plants and herbs, currently used in the Indonesian home gardens have been recorded by Soeparto (1986) for over sixty species.

Home gardens and the concept of *TOGA*

Home gardens have been a widely used practice of near-the-homestead use of small plots of land throughout Indonesia for generations. As these gardens have particularly been used for specific needs of rural families, they have been providing a whole range of traditional food and medicinal plants and crops. The practice of home gardens links up with other forms of indigenous agroforestry systems of local farmers forest garden systems elsewhere in Asia, such as the Kandyan spice gardens in Sri Lanka (Everett 1987, this volume; McConnell and Dharmapala 1973; Bavappa and Jacob 1981; Jacob and Alles 1987).

With regard to Indonesia, a number of studies have focused the attention on traditional agroforestry systems in Indonesia. Christianity, Abdullah, Marten and Iskandar (1986) have documented two types of traditional agroforestry systems in West Java: the *pekarangan* (home garden) and *kebun-talun* (annual-perennial rotation). Soermarwoto and Soemarwoto (1984) describe the Javanese rural ecosystem, while Hardjono (1991) provides an environmental context for several traditional and modern food production systems in Indonesia.

As noted before, traditional medicine, particularly indigenous herbal medicines have recently undergone revived interest, both among government circles as well as among local population groups. Supported by international programmes of WHO (1978, 1985, 1987) both small-scale and large-scale production of *jamu* boomed in view of a possibly cheaper and safer alternative to imported, expensive drugs from Western countries (Haryadi 1986).

Based on the general form of self-help and mutual cooperation *gotong-roy-ong*[26] the initial community involvement in self-reliance in family health, activated by the Village Family Welfare Movement (PKK) in the early seventies has resulted in the practice of establishing a small garden for the cultivation of medicinal plants and herbs, called *Apotik Hijau*, the 'Green Pharmacy', or more widely known as the *Apotik Hidup*, the 'Living Pharmacy'. In principle, *Apotik Hidup* refers to a garden around the house, planted with trees, shrubs and grasses needed for home-preparation of indigenous remedies and medicines (*jamu*).

Traditionally, the local classification of the flora in Indonesia encompasses five categories:

- ○ trees (*Jenis phon*);
- ○ shrubs (*Jenis perdu*);
- ○ vegetables and herbs (*Jenis bumbu dan sayur*);
- ○ grasses (*Jenis rumput*), and
- ○ creepers (*Jenis tumbuhan merambat*).

In contrast with the collective term *obat* for 'medicine', prepared from chemical or natural ingredients, *obat asli* is exclusively used for indigenous medicine for combating disease or healing wounds, based on *natural materials*. The term *jamu*, however, refers to ready-made indigenous herbal medicine, prepared from mixtures (*ramuan*) of plant and, to a lesser extent, animal materials. The local taxonomy of such raw materials, used for the preparation of *jamu*, and which possess beneficial properties, includes:

- o 'Pure' materials (*bahan baku*), comprising of (a) plant materials, such as sugar cane, mahogany seeds and carambola leaves, and (b) animal materials, such as honey and eggs;
- o 'Additional' materials (*bahan pelengkap*), which in combination with the 'pure' materials complete the mixture by increasing its efficacy. These 'additional' materials can also be of plant or animal origin.

As mentioned before, several types of *jamu* are found in Indonesia. Departing from the assumption that all types of *jamu* share a common feature of *natural* ingredients, three broad categories are distinguished:

- o 'indigenous' *jamu*, individually prepared for household-use. The materials are fresh or dried, and subsequently pounded, boiled and poured over with fresh or boiled water;
- o 'manufactured' *jamu*, prepared by hand on a limited scale from pure materials, dried, boiled and poured over with boiled water, and
- o 'industrial' or 'modern' *jamu*, factory-prepared from dried materials which are pounded into power by machines. This type of *jamu* is processed in a laboratory and machine-packed in sachets or capsules.

The original term of *Apotik Hidup* ('Living Pharmacy') has initially been used to refer to a garden near the house, in which medicinal plants are cultivated to supply the household with locally available, herbal medicines (*cf.* Esche 1987). However, since the term *Apotik* has been legally protected by the Article of Law no. 25/1980 to strictly indicate a place in which the pharmacist practices his profession and provides the population with medicines after he has taken his oath, a new, better suited term has recently been introduced officially to describe a garden for medicinal plants.[27] Therefore, the term 'TOGA' as an acronym for *Taman Obat Keluarga* has recently been chosen by the government, literally referring to a 'Garden for Medicine for the Family' (TOGA 1983). It links up with the term *Taman Gizi Keluarga* which indicates a 'Garden for Food for the Family'.[28] Moreover, the term *taman* linguistically refers correctly to the empirical situation, which Poerwadarminta (1976: 1000) describes as a 'Garden for Flowers and Plants'. It is noteworthy, that the medicinal plants are also sometimes cultivated in red earthenware pots – particularly in urban areas – on the verandah or near the house.

In general, the practical use of plant material, and in particular that of medical plants, has been widely conceived among the population as of yielding several advantages over the use of chemical components.

First of all, the effects of medicines, based on 'pure' plant ingredients, are less drastic than of chemical medicaments. Secondly, the effect of herbal medicine is regarded to be better mainly because of its combination with other plant components *vis-à-vis* strictly 'isolated', chemical elements form industrial processes. Thirdly, the use of herbal medicines generally hardly causes any side-effects as 'modern' medicines tend to do. This notion is based on the belief, that *jamu* in fact are composed of elements, which are basically regarded as 'food', be it for specific internal treatment of ailment or disease, free from any poisonous or toxic materials: roots from a young coconut tree, root from the avocado tree, eggs and honey, etc. This belief in the beneficial efficacy of *jamu* has been strengthened by the confidence in its use, as transmitted over generations as part of the local culture and cosmology.

Following the Recommendation of the International Conference on Primary Health Care of the WHO/UNICEF (Alma Ata 1978, No 14: 29): ...*that proved traditional remedies be incorporated* in national health care services, and the subsequent *Global Strategy for Health for All by the Year 2000* (1981), the Government of Indonesia recently has officially incorporated the use of herbal medicine in its policy aimed at the improvement of the health care system. The legal basis of the use of traditional medicine has been provided in three legal positions: (a) Paragraph No 4, Article of Law No 9/1960 on the guidelines for national health care; (b) Paragraph No 7, Article of Law No 7/1963 on pharmacy, and (c) the National Health Care System and its policy on the use of traditional medicines. In short, traditional medicines have not only proved their usefulness for the population, but are also officially recognised as such by the Government, which eventually has started to promote and stimulate the utilisation of indigenous medicine as a means to achieve better health for the entire nation. The access to local plant materials has further been increased by the legitimation and spread of *TOGA*, and related efforts in education at regional and local level.

As *TOGA* (1983) indicates, the further spread of the concept and practice of *TOGA* on account of the Government is promoted by a number of activities which are presently being conducted, such as:

o the extension of information on *TOGA* and its significance for health improvement to the entire population (*Sarana untuk memperbaiki status gizi masyarakat*);
o the supply of the community with seeds and seedlings of medical plants, of which the beneficial properties have empirically and scientifically been confirmed (*Sarana untuk pelestarian alam*);
o the provision of education on the cultivation of certain species of medicinal plants and herbs, with special attention to the preconditions for growth, such as irrigation, type of soil and fertilisation (*Sarana penyebaran gerakan penghijauan*);
o the extension of information on the use of specific parts of plants such as seeds, flowers, roots, leaves, barks, juices, etc. (*Sarana pemerataan pendapatan masyarakat*);
o the extension of knowledge on the use of '*simplisia*', the parts of medicinal plants which have undergone a particular treatment. This includes the way of harvesting, the preparation of '*simplisia*' and the storage in order to guarantee the quality (*Sarana memotivasi gerakan koperasi masyarakat*);
o the provision of education on the preparation of the mixtures, such as drinks, powders and pills, whereby the quantities used are important elements (*Sarana keindahan*).

At community level, such extension activities are now performed by functionaries of the health centres (*puskesmas*) or health stations (*puskesmas pembantu*)[29] as part of the national health care delivery system. Following the above mentioned support by the social system of *gotong royong* and the actual promotion of *TOGA*, the use of herbal medicine has recently been extended under the guidance of the present Family Planning Movement (*Kegiatan Terpadu Keluarga Berencana*). The interconnected activities of the spread of the concept and practice of *TOGA* is schematically represented in Figure 2.1.

It is interesting to note, that in all official documents and pamphlets, it is stressed that the recognition of the efficacy of indigenous herbal medicine and the promotion of *TOGA* should not prevent the population from visiting the *puskesmas* for Primary Health Care in case of illness or disease. Indeed, the potential of this type of traditional medicine is specifically indicated in the *prevention of illness* and in the *promotion of the health status* of the population.

These latter two objectives of *TOGA* are embedded in the interconnection of two local terms: *upaya-upaya kuratif* (the cure of illness or disease) and *upaya-upaya promotif* (improvement of health status).

Further to these two principal objectives, *TOGA* (1981) has several additional functions :

- the improvement of daily intake of nutritious substances from fruits and roots of medicinal plants, such as *pare* (bitter cucumber), *lobak* (black radish), *tomat* (tomato), *bortol* (carrot), *sledri* (celery), *pisang* (banana), *papaya* (papaya), *sawo* (very tasty fruit). etc.;
- the conservation and protection of particular species of medicinal plants;
- he promotion of a 'green movement' throughout Indonesia, including the cultivation of trees such as the *pulai* tree (*Alstonia scholaris*), the *asam* tree (*Tamarinde*), the *kedawung* tree (*Parkia biglobosa*), the *jati* tree (*Tectona grandis*), etc.;
- the provision of additional income for rural families;
- the stimulus for an extra motivation for extension of a cooperative movement, such as the *Koperasi Unit Desa (KUD),* which embodies a sales cooperation of traditional medicines and *'simplisia'* at the village level; and
- a revaluation of the aesthetics of family gardens.

It is evident, that in line with the adopted Alma Ata Declaration of Primary Health Care of WHO/UNICEF (1978), integration is sought between traditional and modern medicine, and in this context in particular between indigenous herbal medicines and imported pharmaceutical medicines. Figure 2.2 refers to such an integration model of indigenous and modern medicines in Indonesia.

Medicinal plants and their use

Traditionally, the use of Indonesia's richness of medicinal plants has been facilitated over many generations because of fostered wisdom within the community as part of the local culture, the easy access to wild plants and crops in the forests, the uncomplicated cultivation in home gardens, and their relatively cheap and local availability.

Beside the secret recipes of herbal medicines in the hands of particular families, herbalists have preserved the knowledge and practice of traditional medicines, often in combination with the use of spiritual powers. The role of the underlying cosmology of an integrated concept of nature and culture, recently revitalised through a revaluation of Indonesia's indigenous knowledge and wisdom in the context of development, has strengthened national and international efforts to study, document and integrate traditional medicine in Primary Health Care programmes.

A computerised data system such as the one used by the Special Programme on Research, Development and Research Training in Human Reproduction of the WHO – located within the University of Illinois – has been operational in

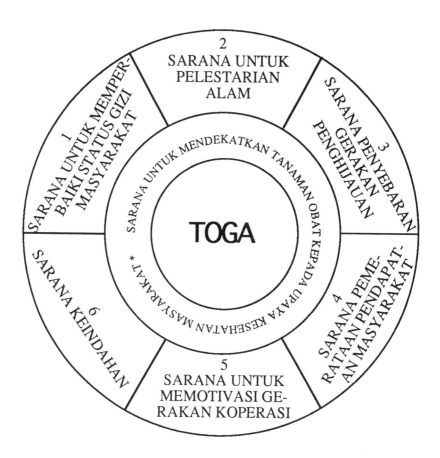

Figure 2.1: *Scheme of the 6 activities of* TOGA
          Source: *TOGA* Report 1981

chemistry and pharmacology since 1975 under the acronym NAPRALERT (*cf.*
Farnsworth 1983). In addition to the review of several *Abstracts*, more than 200
current scientific periodicals are regularly reviewed, while also reports on folklore and ethnomedical use of medicinal plants are computerised. As far as
Indonesia is concerned, Soejarto (1978) has collaborated with NAPRALERT in
the field of fertility-regulating plants. Although initially, the knowledge and
practice of indigenous herbal medicine has been transferred orally – enhancing
its persistent dynamic and adaptive character – the recent emerging interest has
also resulted in a whole range of locally available publications on the subject. In
the mainstream of a wide variety of local books and manuals on the preparation
and use of *jamu,* a few of these publications deal specifically with the concept
and practice of *Apotik Hidup, Apotik Hijau, Taman Obat Keluarga* and *Taman
Gizi Keluarga.*

     While local, popular publications on *jamu,* such as Endra (1980), Daryanto
(1981), Abadi (1983a), Lingga (1983), Sahly (1983), Lubis (1984), Pringgohusodo (1986), Sartono (1986) Soeparto (1986), Ibrahim (1986), Jarvis (n.d.) and

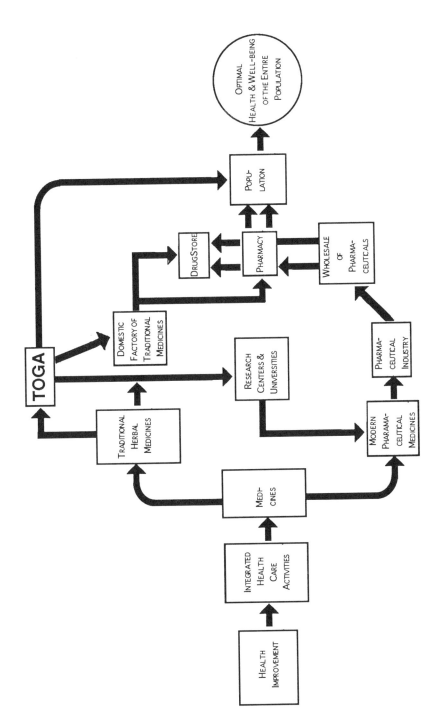

Figure 2.2: *Integration model of indigenous and modern medicines in Indonesia*
Source: *TOGA* Report 1983

Hayuningrat (n.d.), generally include elaborate descriptions of symptoms, their remedies and the necessary components of specific, often well-illustrated medicinal plants for the preparation of herbal recipes from Java, and sometimes from China, only a few books have been pubiished in Indonesia on the actual practice of do-it-yourself cultivation and use of medicinal plants. The latter include the practical manual of Natawidjaja (1982), and the richly illustrated publications on *Apotik Hidup* of Abadi (1983b, 1983c), Sayahbuddin (1984, *cf.* figure 2.3), strengthened by the *TOGA* Report (1983), the Journal of the *Association for Traditional Indonesian Medicine YAPTRI* (1989), and the well-documented and instructive manual of Esche (1987) on *Apotik Hidup* (*cf.* figure 2.4)

In view of such an abundance of lists of medicinal plants transpiring from these popular publications, of which designated parts are described to be used in elaborate recipes for traditional remedies, the *TOGA* Report (1983) has compiled a list of 89 medicinal plant species in Indonesia, which have been recognised in the *Tanaman Obat Editsi II* of 1981 (*cf.* Appendix). This list is completed with specific instructions and requirements for the cultivation of these plants in family gardens, followed by a detailed botanical description of each of the plant species mentioned. The instructions encompass the preparation of the soil and the design of the seedbed in the garden, the use of direct planting or transplanting, the rearing, protection and watering of the actual plants, the application of humus and the different harvesting methods.

In addition to these publications on *jamu* and *TOGA*, some local books are also dealing with religious healing perceptions and practices of the Koran through the use of recently translated reprints of classical 'medical books' of famous Arabic healers such as Jalaluddien As-Suyuthy. This phenomenon has also been documented for other culture areas under influence of Islam, such as the Horn of Africa, where similar contemporary reprints of medical textbooks of Jalal-ad-Din as Syuti (1505) and Dawud al-Antaki (1579) are used (*cf.* Slikkerveer 1990). Equally, local publications on traditional medicines include the standard book of Sastroamidjojo (1965) on the history, cultivation, and application of indigenous herbal medicines, and the book of Sartono (1986) on ancient *jamu* recipes from Javanese scripts. *LESTARI*, the Journal of the *Association for the Promotion of Traditional Indonesian Medicine* has recently come out with a Special Issue on 'Original *Jamu* from Java' under the editorship of Soeparto (n.d.).

Conclusion

Following the converging social and scientific forces and interests that recently have renewed the attention on approaches of self-reliance as crucial components in health maintenance and Primary Health Care delivery in Indonesia, the official recognition and support of the government has recently enhanced the long-standing practice of use of indigenous herbal medicine, enabling the concept of *TOGA* to emerge 'from below' as a social movement throughout the dom of health and healing, the community has been able – despite ignorance and supersession in the past – to maintain and revitalise its local and regional indigenous medical systems centred around the preparation and use of herbal medicine as a pan-Indonesian culture trait.

While the preparation and use of certain mixtures of herbal medicines, *jamu*, proved to be so successful, that part of it became commercialised into modern factories and subsequently legalised by the Government, the local cultivation of

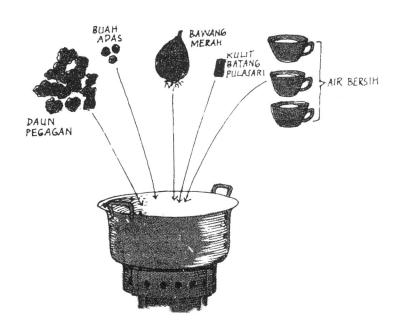

Figure 2.3: *The Practice of* TOGA: *Instructions for the cultivation and preparation of indigenous herbal medicine*
Source: Syahbuddin 1984

KENCUR

Bahasa Daerah

Sumatra	: Ceuko, tekur, kaciwer; cakue, cokur
Jawa	: Kencur, cikur, kencur, kencor, cekor
Sulawesi	: Batako, waian, sukhur, humpoto, cakuru, ceku
Nusatenggara	: cekuh, cekur
Maluku	: asauli

Nama Tanaman (Latin)

Kaempheria galanga

Syarat Tumbuh

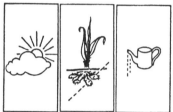

Guna	**Bagian & Khasiat**
Obat batuk	rimpang
	→ melancarkan dahak
Obat kurang gizi	rimpang
	→ penambah nafsu makan
Obat sakit perut	rimpang
	→ anti racun
	→ menetralisir dalam saluran pencernaan
	→ menghilangkan kembung
	→ menghilangkan mual
Obat bengkak	daun
	→ menghilangkan bengkak (obat kompres)
Obat bisul	rimpang
Obat penghilang rasa capai	→ mempercepat pemasakan
	rimpang
	→ penghilang rasa nyeri

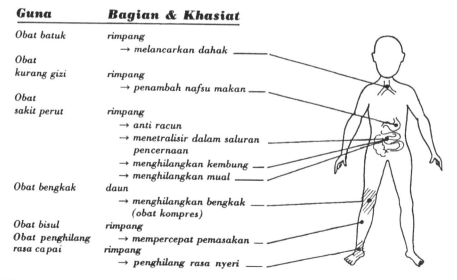

Figure 2.4: *A Reference for Apotik Hidup: Identification, Latin and local nomenclature, cultivation and symptoms to be treated*
Source: Esche 1987

medical plants and daily use of the prepared remedies at the family level recently witnessed a revaluation and re-introduction through the Village Family Welfare Movement (PKK). Initially launched as *Apotik Hidup*, and later on further institutionalised by the Government as *TOGA* or 'Family Medicinal Gardens', a movement has developed supporting the national policy of self-reliance in health and related areas such as food, nutrition and environmental conservation. Evidently, such movement has only been able to emerge from a deeply-rooted adherence to prevailing cosmologies among different ethnic groups in which the conception of an equilibrium between the natural and supernatural forces is reflected in the balanced interrelationship between health and disease. Traces of classical Graeco-Arabic humoral medicine, introduced during past centuries into the culture area of Indonesia in the form of basic elements in the macrocosm and their corresponding 'hot' and 'cold' qualities have been found in the ascriptions of classificatory properties to popular remedies such as medicinal herbs and plants, and their widespread utilisation – recently enhanced through the nationwide introduction of the concept of *TOGA* – throughout the archipelago.

Facilitated by a whole range of popular books and manuals on medicinal plants and recipes, complemented with several manuals on the practice of cultivation of herbs, the concept of *TOGA* not only links up with national and international efforts to promote such use of indigenous herbal medicine for future self-reliance in pharmaceuticals, but it equally reinforces the scientific interest, not only in commercially viable components of medicinal plants, but even more so in the local perceptions and practices of individuals and groups in this part of Southeast Asia.

In addition to international efforts of pharmaceutical research in medicinal plants of agencies such as NAPRALERT, there is now an urgent need to study, analyse and document for development the actual *knowledge and practice* of the local cultivation and use of home gardens for health and disease purposes among different ethnic groups, as presently is undertaken by institutions such as CIKARD and LEAD at the international level, as well as national centres such as the newly-established Indonesian Resource-centre for Indigenous Knowledge (INRIK) at Padjadjaran University in Bandung.

Acknowledgments

The authors wish to thank Dr. Kusnaka Adimihardja from Universitas Padjadjaran in Bandung and Dr. Hans Siwon from Universitas Airlangga in Surabaya for kindly providing particular data on respectively the perception and the use of medicinal plants in Indonesia.

Also, we are grateful for the information on the role of the Women's Village Family Welfare Movement in promoting indigenous herbal medicine for self-reliance at village level, given by Mrs. Atik Adimihardja and the Members of PKK of North Bandung.

Notes

1. For the term *obat*, see Echols and Shadily (1975: 259); Poerwadarminta (1984: 682).
2. For the term *obat alsi Indonesia* , *see* Echols and Shadily (1983: 22), and for *asli, see* Poerwadarminta (1984: 62); Echols and Shadily (1975: 22).
3. For the term *jamu, see* Sastroamidjojo (1965: 19); Poerwadarminta (1984: 400).

4. For the term *ramuan*, *see* Echols and Shadily (1975: 290); Poerwadarminta (1984: 796).
5. The term *dukun* generally refers to sorcerer as well as to healer. *See* Echols and Shadily (1975: 104), and Poerwadarminta (1984: 261). Geertz (1976: 86) classifies *dukun* into a whole range of functionaries: *dukun baji*, midwives; *dukun pidjet*, masseurs; *dukun prewangan*, mediums; *dukun tjalak*, circumcisors; *dukun wiwit*, harvest ritual specialists; *dukun temanten*, wedding specialists; *dukun petungan*, experts in numerical divination; *dukun sihir*, sorcerers; *dukun susuk*, specialists who cure by inserting needles under the skin; *dukun djapa*, curers who rely on spells; *dukun siwer*, specialists in preventing natural misfortune (keeping the rain away when one is having a big feast, preventing plates from being broken at the feast, and so on); *dukun tiban*, curers whose powers are temporary and the result of their having been entered by a spirit. Poerwadarminta (1986: 261) also mentions *dukun beranak*, traditional midwife, which is also known as *bidan*.
6. For the term *obat paten*, *see* Poerwadarminta (1984: 682, 717).
7. For the term *ibu pertiwi*, *see* Echols and Shadily (1975: 150); Poerwadarminta (1984: 368).
8. For the term *kebun obat*, *see* Echols and Shadily (1975: 171); Poerwadarminta (1984: 455).
9. For the term *keraton*, *see* Echols and Shadily (1975: 183); Poerwadarminta (1984: 489).
10. For the term *gotong rojong*, *see* Echols and Shadily (1975: 132); Poerwadarminta (1984: 328).
11. *Pembinaan Kesejahteraan Keluarga* (PKK) refers to the Indonesian organisation which provides guidelines for women to secure the well-being of the family throughout the nation.
12. Major institutes in Indonesia, involved in research in herbal medicine include Universitas Indonesia, Jakarta; Universitas Padjadjaran, Bandung; Institute Teknologi, Bandung, Universitas Airlangga, Surabaya, and Universitas Gajah Mada, Yogyakarta.
13. Such 'new' ethnomedical approach encompasses the study of indigenous medical knowledge in conjunction with practice over longer periods of time, and in particular, socio-cultural settings. This is in line with the etic perspective in the work of authors such as Fabrega (1977), Good *et al.* (1979), Leslie (1977, 1980), Young (1982), Warren (1974, 1979) and Slikkerveer (1982, 1983, 1990).
14. For the term *usada* or *usana*, *see* the description of Covarrubias (1986: 37).
15. For the term *tutor* or *tutur*, *see* the description of Covarrubias (1986: 296).
16. For the term *lontar*, *see* Poerwadarminta (1984: 607, 608).
17 For a description of the term *abangan*, *see* Geertz (1976: 5).
18. For a description of the term *santri*, *see* Geertz (1976: 5).
19. For a description of the term *prijaji*, *see* Geertz (1976: 6).
20. For a description of the term *alus* or *halus*, *see* Poerwadarminta (1984: 341).
21. For a description of the term *kasar*, *see* Poerwadarminta (1984: 448).
22. For a description of the term *lair*, *see* Geertz (1976: 232).
23. For a description of the term *batin*, *see* Geertz (1976: 232).
24. For a description of the term *urip*, *see* Poerwadarminta (1984: 1134).
25. For a description of the term *balyan* or *balian*, *see* Poerwadarminta (1984: 81).
26. For a description of the term *gotong-royong*, *see* Poerwadarminta (1984: 328).
27. The literal meaning of the term *apotik* is established in the *Peraturan Pemerintah* (Article of Law) No. 25/1989, which replaces No. 26/1965, restricting it to a special locality for the pharmacological preparation and distribution of medicines. Moreover, 'pharmacological preparation' has been established in Article of Law No. 7/1963, Par. 2e as:' *production, elaboration, preparation, changing of the form, mixing, storage and distribution of medicines and raw materials*', while 'production of pharmacological supply' according to Article of Law No. 7/1963 refers to: '*the*

cultivation of medicinal plants and the support and care of animals needed for the pharmaceutical industry etc.

28 As the concepts of *Taman Obat Keluarga (TOGA)* and *Taman Gizi Keluarga* both refer to a garden to cultivate respectively. medicinal and health food plants, they do not have any legal consequences.

29 The term *PUSKESMAS* refers to *Pusat Kesehatan Masyarakat* (health centre), while the term *PUSKESMAS pembantu* refers to *Pusat Kesehatan Masyarakat pembantu* (health station).

Appendix: List of traditional medicinal plants for use in Indonesian home gardens (Edition II, 1981) Source: *TOGA* 1982.

1.	Adas	*Foeniculum vulgare* Mill
2.	Angsana	*Pterocarpus indica* Willd
3.	Anyang-Anyang	*Elaeocarpus grandiflora* J. Sm.
4.	Asam	*Tamarindus indica* L.
5.	Bawang merah	*Allium cepa* L.
6.	Bawang putih	*Allium sativum* L.
7.	Belimbing wuluh	*Averrhoa bilimbi* L.
8.	Beluntas	*Pluchea indica* (L.) Less
9.	Besaran	*Morus alba* L.
10.	Brotowali	*Tinospora crispa* (L.) Aliers. Hookb & Them
11.	Ceguk	*Quisqualis indica* L.
12.	Cengkeh	*Eugenia aromatica* O.K.
13.	Dadap serep	*Erythrina subumbrans* Merr
14.	Daun dewa	*Gynura procumbens* Backer
15.	Daun encok	*Plumbago zeylanica* L.
16.	Daun sendok	*Plantago major* L.
17.	Daun wungu	*Graptophyllum pictum* (L.) Griff
18.	Delima putih	*Punica granatum* L.
19.	Dempul lelet	*Glochidion molle* Bl.
20.	Gambir	*Uncaria gambir* Roxb
21.	Gandarusa	*Justicia gendarussa* (L.) Burm.f.
22.	Garut	*Marantha arundinacea* L.
23.	Iler	*Coleus atropurpureus* Benth.
24.	Jagung	*Zea mays* L.
25.	Jambu biji	*Psidium guajava* L.
26.	arak	*Ricinus communis* L.
27.	Jarak pagar	*Jatropha curcas* L.
28.	Jeruk nipis	*Citrus aurantifolia* Swingle.
29.	Jinten hitam	*Nigella sativa* L.
30.	Kacapiring	*Gardenia augusta* Merr
31.	Katuk	*Sauropus androgynus* Merr
32.	Kayuangin	*Usnea misaminesis* Not.
33.	Kayuputih	*Melaleuca leucadendra* L.
34.	Kayu ules	*Helicteres isara* L.
35.	Kecombrang	*Nicolaia speciosa* Horan.
36.	Kecubung	*Datura metel* L.
37.	Kedawung	*Parkia roxburghii* G. Don.
38.	Kelapa	*Cocos nucifera* L.
39.	Kelembak	*Rheum officinale* Baill.

40. Kembang sepatu	*Hibiscus rosa-sinensis* L.
41. Kemiri	*Aleuritis moluccana* (L.) Willd.
42. Kencur	*Kaempferia galanga* L.
43. Urang-aring	*Eclipta alba* (L.) Hassk.
44. Kendal	*Cordia dichotoma* Farst.
45. Ketepeng cina	*Cassia alata* L.
46. Ketumbar	*Coriandrum sativum* L.
47. Kumis kucing	*Orthosiphon stamineus* Benth.
48. Kunyit	*Curcuma domestica* Val.
49. Labu	*Lagenaria leucantha* Rusby.
50. Labu merah	*Cucurbita moschata* Duchesne
51. Lada	*Piper nigrum*
52. Landep	*Barleria prionitis* L.
53. Langkuas	*Languas galanga* (L.) Merr.
54. Lempuyang emprit	*Zingiber amaricans* Bl.
55. Lempuyang gajah	*Zingiber zerumbet* J. Sm.
56. Lempuyang wangi	*Zingiber aromaticum* Val.
57. Lidah buaya	*Aloe vera* L.
58. Lobak	*Raphanus sativus* L.
59. Manis jangan	*Cinnamomum* Spec.
60. Meniran	*Phyllanthus niruri* L.
61. Mentimu	*Cucumis sativus* L.
62. Merica bolong	*Melaleuca leucadendra* L.
63. Padi	*Oryza sativa* L.
64. Pare	*Momordica charantia* L.
65. Patikan cina	*Euphorbia prostrata* Ait
66. Pegagan	*Centella asiatica* (L.) Urban
67. Pepaya	*Carica papaya* L.
68. Pinang	*Areca catechu* L.
69. Pisang	*Musa paradisiaca* L.
70. Ploso	*Butea monosperma Lamk.* O.K.
71. Pohon merah	*Euphorbia pulcherrima* Willd
72. Poko	*Mentha arvensis* L. var Javanica (Bl.) Backer
73. Pulasari	*Alyxia Spec.*
74. Saga	*Abrus precatorius* L.
75. Salada air	*Nasturtium officinale* (L.) R. Br.
76. Sambiloto	*Andrographis paniculata* Nec
77. Sembukan	*Paederia foetida* L.
78. Sembung	*Blumea baisamifera* (L.) DC.
79. Sidaguri	*Sida rhombifolia* L.
80. Sirih	*Piper betle* L.
81. Sosor bebek	*Kalanchoe pinnata* Pers.
82. Teh	*Thea sinensis* L.
83. Tembakau	*Nicotiana tabacum* L.
84. Tembelekan	*Lantana camara* L.
85. Temugiring	*Curcuma heyneana* Val & V. Zip
86. Temukunci	*Boesenbergia pandurata* (Roxb.) Schlet
87. Temulawak	*Curcuma xanthorrhiza* Roxb.
88. Trenguli	*Cassia fistula* L.
89. Ubi jalar	*Ipomoea batatas* Poiret

3. Neem in Niger: A new context for a system of indigenous knowledge

EDWARD B. RADCLIFFE, GREGOIRE OUEDRAOGO,
SONIA E. PATTEN, DAVID W. RAGSDALE AND PETER P. STRZOK

Introduction

THE CONUNDRUM OF integrating local knowledge systems with externally
designed and managed projects is an abiding problem. In the Sahelian zone,
this problem is exacerbated by the institutional arrangements which evolved in
the training and education of local administrators, first during the colonisation
of the region and later during the early years of the independent Sahelian
states. From the beginning of formal colonial education, traditional methods
were identified as native, simple, and primitive; colonial methods were European, modernising, and civilised. These two systems became hostile to and
uncommunicative with each other. The educational system served as a vehicle
of divisiveness, wherein the best rural students, brought into the colonial value
system, were educated and then employed in bureaucratic or related functions
in jobs in the metropolis or major towns of a country.

A 1954 study of rural Senegalese students, who had successfully completed
12 years of formal education, showed that only two per cent remained farmers
five years after completion of their education. This continuing exodus of the
brightest of rural youth was seen as Africa's greatest social problem. This pool
of graduates produced the technical agents who were sent back to rural areas,
if only on short visits, as extension agents, to infuse the traditional farmers
with external, so-called improved, practices for enhanced agriculture production. This arrangement was found to have no economic impact and a negative
social impact to rural communities and constituted a significant barrier to rural
development well into the first decade of governance of the newly independent Sahelian countries (David Hapgood in Lewis 1965).

Concurrently, colonial rule provided commercial outlets for primary products through construction of rail and road networks to coastal ports. The integrated economies of the savanna and the desert, which had operated for 2000
years, became moribund. Significant surplus production was moved through
the new network to feed production facilities in Europe. Large-scale monocultures were developed as cash crops for export; food production by traditional
practices languished because of reduced radii of comparative advantage, which
reduced incentives to production, and dampened innovative practices and
marginalised the interior Sahelian communities (Baier 1976).

The large number of failures of development projects in the Sahel in the
1960s and 1970s caused donor agencies and national development planners
alike to re-examine the assumptions and conditions for project success. Concurrently, three large economic shocks battered these countries at that time:
one external – the oil crisis and high energy costs of the late '70s – and two
internal – the droughts of 1974–78 and 1983–85. These events strengthened
joint planning, and regional agencies evolved to manage problems of large-
scale environmental degradation which transcended national borders. Methods of survivability were re-examined, including traditional rural production

practices. The realisation spread that these systems contained important elements to combat or ameliorate natural disasters and provided for an efficient use of endowments under a wide range of conditions in a fragile physical setting (De Lattre and Fell 1984). This was the general socioeconomic setting for a University of Minnesota / AFGRO project relating to the utility of a locally available natural insecticide against the ravages of grasshoppers and locusts.

The project was developed in early 1987, as part of a response by the United States Agency for International Development (USAID) to assist Sahelian countries against the grasshopper/locust threat. The project was designed by the Agency to Facilitate the Growth of Rural Organisations (AFGRO), a small non-government organisation (NGO). AFGRO's principal objective is to contribute to the endogenous growth and development of agricultural and educational activities and crafts among the rural peoples of West Africa, with only a minimum of input from an external organisation. In considering various Sahelian countries, Niger was seen as the first choice, largely because of recent intensive efforts by the national administration to revive the esprit of rural communities and fully integrate traditional food production practices into the national socioeconomic framework.

The project provided for an evaluation of the efficacy of neem seed extract as a pesticide against locusts and grasshoppers in an agricultural setting in the Sahel. The process involved crushing neem seeds, soaking the mixture in water and using the liquid residue as a spray to protect millet and sorghum plants. The neem tree is found everywhere in the Sahel and local communities use it in a variety of ways: firewood, lumber, wind erosion control, medicinal uses ranging from potions for malaria, diarrhoea, and rheumatism to soap from the seed oil for dermatological problems. Concurrent with the entomological studies, a socioeconomic study was done on selected rural villages relating to land-use issues, ownership of neem trees and their products, availability of labour to employ the technology proposed and competing uses of labour. The project was to determine major constraints which would impinge on the adoption of the technology proposed. Technical supervision for the two components was to be provided by scientists from the University of Minnesota. AFGRO would act as a facilitator knowledgeable about conditions and to identify bridging mechanisms to bring the research into the repertoire of local technologies of the Sahel as rapidly as possible. The constraints to technology transfer in this environment have been the object of intense concern by developers for a long time. In this case, the technology proposed appeared to have immediate and important benefits to the Sahelian farmer, could be implemented with local tools and skills with a minimum of external training and assistance, and appeared relatively cheap and without harmful side-effects.

In the following two parts, the scientists involved in this project elaborate on the execution of the project, the results and findings. As a general finding, we believe that the operational techniques employed here provide an important framework for mounting an on-site field research and bridging this research into local communities for inclusion in their agricultural practices. There are also important cautions. Each community studied demonstrated significant differences in land tenure, division of labour (both by age and gender), and in ethnic practices and associations. Nomadic/sedentary arrangements, which evolved over time into symbiotic relationships among common ethnic groups, are variable from local village to local village because of variations of factors such as soil differences and pastures, degree of access to water and differences in other endowments. These result in significant variations in the way an individual community plans and executes its annual agriculture production strategy. Accordingly, we believe that on-farm trials and implementation of research efforts such as undertaken in our project require micro-knowledge and micro-management. Integration of these local micro units at an early planning stage are essential for a meaningful bridging of exogenous science and technology to local practices.

We are not prepared to say that our model is complete and mature, but we do believe it provides a means by which expatriate scientists can leave behind appreciable institutional memory of their accomplishments, accelerating the test of acceptability by local agriculture producers and, at the same time, providing these visitors with a better understanding of the paradigms which local small-scale agriculture producers use in managing their agriculture production decisions.

Socioeconomic feasibility of producing and using neem extract as a crop protectant

Low-resource farming practices dominate the Sahelian agricultural landscape. Family incomes in rural areas average $150 or less per annum. Production activities are focused on meeting household subsistence needs first, and then moving any surplus into the market. Under such circumstances, any new agricultural technology which requires more than the most modest cash outlay, or which modifies any of the basic agricultural inputs of land, water, seed and labour, may be rejected by the members of peasant families because it represents a level of risk that is too high relative to the potential for enhanced production.

The calculus of maximising production while minimising risk in the peasant farming enterprise must include considerations of subsistence requirements, the farming cycle, rents owed, markets for subsistence and cash crops, and various domestic group and community obligations. The family must maintain sufficient land, labour, and capital to carry out the production process to meet its fixed needs and obligations. Under such conditions, conservative decision-making is probably a most rational strategy (Greenwood 1973: 51).

The production and use of neem solution as a crop protectant would seem to be compatible with peasant farming in the Sahel. The neem is a common tree throughout the area, and the production of neem solution can be accomplished with equipment already in use for carrying out farm tasks. But the crucial question of compatibility cannot be second-guessed, or argued from a distance. It must be examined at the micro level, particularly in an ecological situation as fragile as that of the Sahel.

Socioeconomic research, Niger

It has been demonstrated that African farmers regularly expand their indigenous knowledge base by experimenting with new techniques, testing and selecting for new seeds and cultigens, and adapting new technologies to specific physical and socioeconomic environments (Richards 1983). Given this, and having established that Niger neem powder in solution is an efficacious crop protectant for grasshoppers (see section on Entomology), how feasible is it for Sahelian peasant farmers to adopt and adapt this new use for a material that has been part of their social and ecological environment for fifty years? Is it likely to be adapted for use on the basic grain crops of millet and sorghum or the various vegetable crops grown during the counter season?

The socioeconomic component of this project was designed to assess these feasibilities. It was clear that land and tree accessibility and management, water availability, and organisation of agricultural work (deployment of family and other labour) were potential limiting factors in the production and use of neem solution as a crop protectant. We anticipated that other limiting factors might emerge during the field research.

The project was initiated in late 1987 by choosing a purely Sahelian zone in Niger as the research site. The Tera *arrondissement* in the far south-western part of the nation was selected. It shares problems and potentials in physical and human resources with neighbouring Burkina Faso and Mali: low and irregular rainfall, delicate ecology, enclosed areas with relatively high population density, lack of mechanised agricultural equipment, low level of essential infrastructures for support, hard-working people, periodic episodes of grasshopper plagues, and the presence of neem trees in most places.

With the help of the local government administrators and the Agriculture Extension Service, four villages were selected which were representative of the area in both agroclimatic and human terms:[1]

- Dargol, a Songhay village with more than 7500 inhabitants, about 60 km south-east of Tera. It is an administrative centre of an agricultural district and has an agricultural extension agent posted in the village;
- Bellekoira, a Songhay village in Bella territory, inhabited by more than 1000 people, around 100 km north-west of Tera;
- Mehanna, a cosmopolitan village on the Niger River with a population of more than 3500 Songhay-Zarmas, Hausa, Bella and Kado, located about 80 km south of Tera. It is an administrative centre of an agricultural district, and thus has an agricultural agent posted in the village; and
- Diagourou, a Fulani village of approximately 1000 people, located about a dozen km south of Tera.

After a general study of the environment, we carried out two group interviews in each village, interviewing men and women separately. Approximately one hundred individual representatives of the four villages were also interviewed; these individuals were selected to include a range of ages and size of landholding. It was more difficult to secure adequate representation of women amongst the individual interviewees.[2] Only older women with the status of widow could speak for themselves in this context. Therefore, the group discussions with women became especially important.

The group interviews consisted of approximately twenty questions concerning land management and agricultural production systems, organisation of agricultural work, and other elements relating to the possible use of neem as a crop protectant. The individual interview schedule also contained approximately twenty questions. These questions concentrated on the following elements: family composition and occupations, land holdings in the form of fields and gardens, number and age of neem trees on family property, tools and equipment used, availability of year-round or seasonal water sources and their relative proximity to property, presence of crop pests and damage caused, knowledge of or familiarity with approximately ten species of grasshoppers,

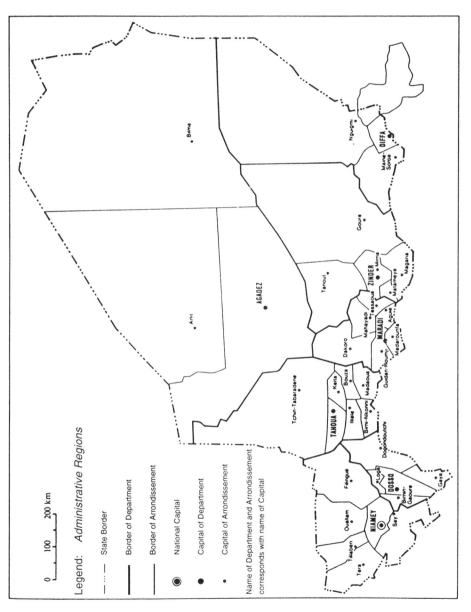

Map 3.1: *Niger Administrative Regions*

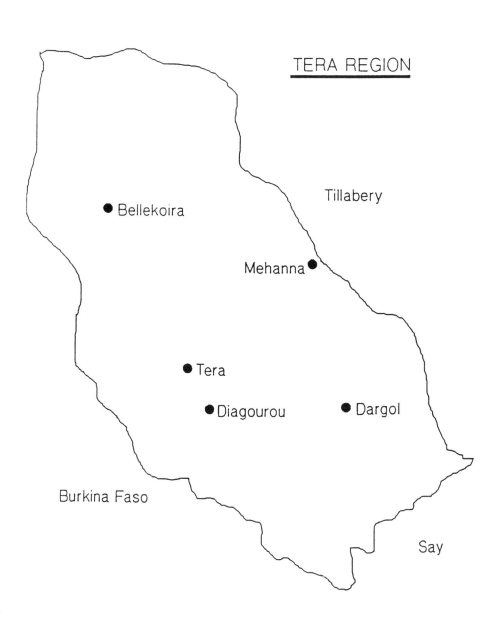

Map 3.2: *Tera Region*

and opinions about which members of the family would carry out the various tasks necessary to use neem as a crop protectant.

Characteristics of the study zone

The *arrondissement* of Tera, in which the four villages are found, is located in the far west of the Republic of Niger, in the department of Tillabery. It is between latitude 13° 30′ and 14° 58′ north and longitude 0° 20′ and 2° east. It is bordered on the south by the Sirba River, on the east by the Niger River, on the north by the border with Mali, and on the west by the border with Burkina Faso. The area of the *arrondissement* is 20,200 km², representing about 22.5 per cent of the department in which it is found, or 1.6 per cent of the total area of the country. Its population, as established in a national census carried out in May and June of 1988, is 293,869, representing 22 per cent of the department or 4 per cent of the country. The population density of the *arrondissement* is about 15 inhabitants per km².

The climate of the *arrondissement* corresponds closely to that of the south Sahelian region of the country. It is of the classic Sahelian type, with an annual rainfall ranging from 350 mm at Dolbel in the north to 500 mm at Gotheye in the south. Rainfed farming of millet and sorghum is practiced, with recession agriculture and gardening carried out during the counter or dry season. Rain falls between May and October. The principal water collectors are three tributaries coming into the right bank of the Niger: the Goroul, about 100 km. long, the Dorgol (130 km), and the Sirba (80 km). The Niger flows year-round in its 150 km course through the *arrondissement* of Tera. The water table is often near the surface in valleys, and people dig shallow wells for their water supply. About 20 permanent and semi-permanent water impoundments are found in the *arrondissement.* A number of wells have been dug to supplement available water supplies. From these wells, water is drawn up by means of manual or foot-powered pumps. However, a large proportion of these wells has become unusable, due to either pump break-down or the lowering of the water table.

Plants and animals found in the *arrondissement* of Tera are characteristic of the Sahel climate. Species must survive a temperature range of 30° Celsius, between 10° and 40°, coupled with slight and irregular rainfall. Recent droughts, rapid increases in numbers of fields due to population pressures and soil degradation, and deforestation have all compounded to modify profoundly the classification of plant varieties. Fifty-year-old farmers talk about the forests and forest animals of their youth which are no longer seen today. The bushes, which were found in the savannas of the north on the Dargol–Diagourou line and the shrubs on the steppes in the south on the Kokoro–Mehanna–Goroul line, are now dying out.

The countryside is currently characterised by large bare spots, trees and spiny shrubs between 5 and 15 m tall, tufts of bushes, grass, and trees about 10 to 20 m tall planted along roads and near houses. The trees and spiny shrubs are representatives of the Balanitaceae (wild date tree or *Balanites aegyptiaca*), the Mimosaceae, (*Acacia albida, Acacia nilotica, Acacia senegal, Prosopis africana*), and the Rhamnaceae (*Ziziphus mauritania*). The others are species of Meliaceae (*Azadirachta indica, Khaya senegalensis*), Combretaceae (*Combretum glutinosum*), Palmae (*Hyphaene thebaica*), Ebenaceae (*Diospyros mespili-formis*), and leguminous Caesalpiniaceae (*Piliostigma reticulatum*).

Climatic conditions are such that only a sparse and spotty plant cover has survived, composed of trees and spiny shrubs interspersed with grasses that wilt and disappear around January under the effects of over-grazing.

Sand, clay and silt, or their combinations make up visible soils in the *arrondissement*. They can be grouped into three major types whose distribution and characteristics are linked to geology and topography: dune soils, soils on glacis and pediment, and hydromorphic soils. Traditionally, dune soils have been used for rainfed farming of millet with cowpeas and sorrel. Soils on glacis and pediment have been used as pasture for animals, but today's population pressures are causing them to be used for food crops. Hydromorphic soils are used for rainfed farming of sorghum, vegetables and legumes. These latter soils are also the ones used for gardens and vegetable farming, or counter-season crops, grown after the end of the rainy season, but before water sources dry up completely.

Types of soil and crops

Millet and sorghum are intercropped with legumes on the three major types of soil encountered: dunes, flat soils, and sandy, clay, silty bottom-lands. Sandy soils are found in all four villages where millet, cowpeas and sorrel are grown together. Farmers in Diagourou add peanuts to these three crops. Songhay-Zarma farmers call sandy soil *hondu*, whereas Fulani call it *seno*. Silty soils exist in all four villages, where everyone intercrops millet, cowpeas and sorrel. In Dargol, corn and peanuts are added to these. In the Songhay-Zarma language, *goru* and *tansamia* are used to designate silty soil, whereas the Fulani use the term *tohelol* in Fulfulde.

Clay soils (*botogo*) are found in Mehanna and used to grow sorghum. Sandy clay soils exist too, as well as silty clay soils. The former, called *gangani* in Songhay-Zarma or *kolagal* in Fulfulde, are used to grow sorghum in Bellekoira and Diagourou. Dargol, Bellekoira and Diagourou farmers use sandy clay (*goru* or *bolare*) to intercrop sorghum, cowpeas and sorrel. Dargol often adds millet, corn and peanuts to these three crops. Diagourou has bottomland soils called *tasheko* in Fulfulde, which are used for growing sorghum. Some farmers in Mehanna grow rice, thanks to the waters of the Niger River.

Organisation of agricultural tasks

The rhythm of everyday rural life and the agricultural calendar in the four villages is determined by the alternation of a rainy season of three to four months, with a dry season of eight to nine months. The intensity of village activity is also dictated largely by the amount of rain that falls in the country side. Abundant and well-distributed rainfall promotes abundant crops, and perhaps an appreciable surplus of produce. By selling a portion of the extra produce, if there are surpluses, a family may be able to buy some favourite food items, or better clothes, a better dwelling, or better farming implements.

Lack of rain, on the other hand, is an indication of subsequent food shortages, famine, and possible epidemics. If a family's granary does not contain supplies from the previous season, or if a family has not been able to rent out land to someone else to get back a part of the leasee's harvest as a rental fee, the chances of holding out until the next growing season can become doubtful. In the same way, a major grasshopper invasion threatens a family's ability to survive from one growing season to the next.

Table 3.1: Agricultural calendar for rainfed crops in the arrondissement of Tera

Period	Procedure	Duration	Tools
March – May	*Field preparation* Clear underbrush. Pull up dry stems from preceding season and burn dried vegetable matter. Spread manure, sometimes.	7-15 days	Short hoe Long hoe Rake
June – August	*Sowing of crops* Make small holes in wet soil and sow seeds in pockets. Protect young sprouts, if necessary. One or two re-plantings may be necessary	3-7 days	Short hoe Long hoe Containers
	Weeding – hoeing Eliminate weeds before and after emergence of food plants. Protect young plants, if necessary.	0-50 days	Long hoe Short hoe Pick
	Crop protection Prop up fallen plants. Chase pests away.	Constant after flowering	Appropriate implements such as long sticks
September – November	*Harvest* Cut off the heads of cereal grains and tie them in bundles Pick vegetables. Dig up peanuts.	7-25 days	Knife Scythe Hands Short hoe Long hoe Containers
	Seed selection Pick out and put aside the best grain heads	2-5 days	Hands Containers
	Crop storage Place bundles in grain storage houses. Protect seeds.	3 days, at most	Hands Containers
	Harvesting wild crops	Intermittent	Short hoe Long hoe Containers
December – February	*Counter season* Counter season farming or vegetable gardening, or both Departure to seek paid employment for many people 15-40 years of age	45-90 days	Short hoe Long hoe Containers

The agricultural calendar

The majority of crops grown by rainfed agriculture in the Sahel have a vegetative cycle of 90 to 110 days, but they require, from the farm family, sustained work effort spread out over 270 days. This calendar is summarised in Table 3.1.

Family members in the sample are all involved in agricultural work. Both the collective and the individual surveys of village men and women confirm that men, women, and children all participate, directly or indirectly, in all the farming operations in the agricultural calendar.

Between March and May, the men and children arm themselves with the long-handled and the short-handled hoes to clear away the brush from the fields. They sometimes fertilise the fields with animal manure. Women are often involved in the one- or two-week period of hard work, which is necessary to prepare the fields for planting.

In June, if the rainy season begins, all members of the family sow millet and sorghum for a period of no more than a week. As soon as the emerging shoots are about two weeks old, the tasks of weeding and, shortly thereafter, hoeing are carried out primarily by the men and children, while the women tend their small plots not far from home. Weeding and hoeing are carried out over a period ranging from 30 to 50 days. During this same period, the men and children prop up stands of grain which have been knocked down by the wind or rain and make sure that their fields are not invaded by predators.

The crops bloom and are already beginning to head in August and September. As soon as the grain is ripe, all the members of the family in most locations participate in the harvest, using knives and baskets. Men and children select seeds and put them into storage. By October or November at the latest, the traditional agricultural calendar has come to an end and counter season activities begin: recession agriculture, which permits the growing of grains in low, moist areas, and vegetable gardening. The procedures necessary for using neem would begin with the gathering of the seeds in May-June. Grain crops would be treated between June and September, and vegetable crops, including seedlings, from November through February.

In addition to direct involvement in many phases of agricultural labour for producing grain, women are responsible for other important tasks. It is their job to get water that may be more than 5 km from the living quarters. It is their job, too, to gather firewood, which is harder and harder to find and further and further from home. It is they who are responsible for the regular rise and fall of the pestle in the mortar when grain must be ground. They have full responsibility for all food preparation in the household. Most women are actively engaged in gardening during the counter season. This provides important supplements to the family diet and usually results in a surplus that women can sell in local markets to generate cash for their own use. In three of the four villages, women were engaged in rearing animals as a source of wealth to give to their children.

Farming techniques

Sahelian soils are delicate because they are exposed to very trying conditions caused by the sun, rain, and wind. In the past, a good farmer regenerated farmland by changing or rotating crops, intercropping or multiple cropping, and letting fields lie fallow. Fertilising with manure was not unknown. Pest control and crop protection were carried out prophylactically, using traps or various other tactics to scare away or kill the pests. The farmers of the Sahel know that a given crop always removes the same nutrients from the earth. In the long run, growing the same crop exhausted the soil, so in the past, they changed crops annually in a given field. Crop rotation was usually carried out with legumes and cereal grains. Thus peanuts or cowpeas, which provide abundant nitrogen to the soil, were grown before a cereal grain, which needed lots of nitrogen.

The farmers of both today and yesterday are aware of intercropping, a technique that resembles crop rotation. Intercropping constitutes a better use of the land and available rainfall, when the plants complement one another. If the plants do not have the same water and nutrient needs, certain of them give back to the soil nutrients that are needed by others. In Sahelian areas, where rainfall is undependable and often insufficient, intercropping diminishes the risk of having nothing to harvest by increasing the survival chances of whichever plant needs the least water. It produces essentially the same results as crop rotation, but in less time. Growing complementary crops amongst one another can constitute an improvement over mere intercropping. In mixed cropping, short plants may be set in among taller ones in order to protect them from the wind. The practice of letting land lie fallow is observed very rarely today. Population pressures are no doubt the principal cause of this failure to practice what was once an important technique for sustaining soil fertility.

Land access and distribution – gifts, leasing, lending

The founder, first occupant, or conqueror of a given site is the master of that land. The village chief, his descendant, has the right to distribute land. He charges a rental fee. Heads of the extended Songhay family gave him this *fukurmey* in form of bundles of millet after each harvest. This rental fee amounts to one bundle per field, or 14 kg , in Mehanna, and ranges from two to ten bundles of millet in Dargol. Although the *fukurmey* still exists in Dargol and Mehanna, the fee is not obligatory. In contrast, the *fukurmey* fee is no longer practiced in Bellekoira. The Fulani village chief in Diagourou receives a fee, called *zakka*, equivalent to one tenth of the family harvest.

A villager who holds lands has always been able to make a gift of land to a relative or friend, or lease land, and may still do so. Gifts are not subject to any fees in the Songhay and Fulani families in all four villages. Any ethnic minority in any of the villages respects the practices of the ethnic majority. Leasing, or *ngudja*, is the most commonly practiced mode of land access in the Fulani village of Diagourou. The lease becomes effective once it is witnessed, and its duration is fixed in advance, but may be prolonged beyond the expiration of the original term. In the case of the Songhay, lending or leasing used to be carried out in mutual confidence by the two parties. But the presence of witnesses has become more and more necessary in order to resolve conflicts and disputes over land rights. Leasing or lending did not traditionally involve obligatory fees, but the lessee generally expressed gratitude to the land owner by giving a certain amount of the produce. The nature and quantity of this expression of gratitude, *labu albarka*, as well as its frequency, depended on the lessee in the case of the Songhay. Whereas the *labu albarka* was once discretionary and a matter of choice, it is now required of the lessee by the landowner. In one of the Songhay villages, if the lessee dies, the family is more and more frequently called upon to renew the verbal lease in the presence of witnesses if they want to continue to farm the tract of land in question.

The practice of pawning or pledging land does not exist among the Songhay of Bellekoira and Dargol, nor among the Fulani of Diagourou. In Mehanna, which is a river village on the banks of a branch of the Niger, the practice seems to have existed but only in reference to rice paddies. The notion of pawning or pledging is called *tolme*. Traditionally, the practice of selling tracts of land did not exist, and it is not a current practice even now in the country-side of Niger. Even today, the sale of land is almost inconceivable in village society. It appears that someone who might attempt to sell land would be banished from the area.

Land access and distribution – inheritance and partition

In the Songhay village of the past, the basic economic and agricultural social unit was the extended family, composed of married households within a lineage whose rules of succession were continuously observed. The family land-holdings constituted a collective heritage, called *tubuyan*. The collective and individual management of these family landholdings was incumbent upon the head of the extended family. The colonial period had the effect of weakening the extended family. Its continued atrophy ended up by transforming the core household into the basic economic and social unit in a Songhay village. The idea of partitioning the land, called fayan, was born with the weakening of the extended family and the progressive pre-eminence of the core household, autonomous and increasingly isolated. In the current era, partitioning of extended family landholdings among core families is a powerful trend. Today, among the Fulani of Diagourou, partitioning of the landholdings of a deceased father comes into play when there are dissident children involved, in most cases, born of different mothers. An unmarried daughter and a widow may inherit land from their father. But Songhay and Fulani societies seem to expect them not to claim their shares, because in these societies brothers keep or care for their sisters, whether they are unmarried, married or widows. Minor children of widows are also cared for by their uncles.

Land litigations

Litigations involving landholdings appear to be numerous throughout the *arrondissement* of Tera. Litigations are entered into most often by the parties to a lease or a loan. The tendency to lease land seems to result from the increasing scarcity of good farmlands. Good land is more and more difficult to find because of the frequent droughts of the last ten years, the sand storms that degrade the soils, and the tendency of the farmers to devote more and more field area to crops to compensate for decreasing crop yields. Many people who lease land argue today that the land belongs to the person who farms it. Other cases of litigation over leasing are born of the refusal of the lessee to pay a fee to the landowner. Wandering livestock and brush fires can also be causes for law suits in rural environments.

The use of neem as a natural crop protectant

Different species of grasshoppers pose different degrees of danger, depending on their preferred feeding habits and environments. Detailed line drawings of ten of the most abundant species found in the zone were presented to individual interviewees in each of the four villages to see if the species were recognised and identified as pests. Of the ten species in the questionnaire, the best known in the villages is, without any doubt, the Senegalese grasshopper or

Oedaleus senegalensis. Two (Dargol and Mehanna) of the four villages knew it very well, whereas the other two knew it well. The second best known species is *Kraussaria angulifera.* It is well known in Dargol and Mehanna, but only fairly well known in Bellekoira and Diagourou. Third best known is the African migratory locust which has breeding grounds in the interior delta of the Niger River. This species, *Locusta migratoria*, is known for the damage it does in three out of the four villages (Dargol, Bellekoira and Mehanna).

Finally, there are three species that are known in two of the villages and two species that are known in only one. These are *Anacridium melanorhodon* (Dargol and Mehanna), *Hieroglyphus daganensis* (Bellekoira and Mehanna), *Aiolopus simulatrix* (Dargol and Bellekoira), *Schistocerca gregaria* (Bellekoira), and *Cataloipus fuscocoerulipes* (Bellekoira). At the micro level, then, different species of grasshoppers present different magnitudes of problems to farmers. It would only be appropriate to introduce neem as a crop protectant against grasshoppers, if it had been established that it is effective against the particular species which are most problematic and generally recognised in a particular micro setting.

The following activities would need to be carried out in the villages, if neem were to be used as a crop protectant.

Picking, gathering, harvesting:
- o Climb tree and shake it to make ripe fruit fall to the ground.
- o Gather up fallen fruit.
- o Gather fruit that has been picked or seeds that fall from tree after fruit is eaten by birds.
- o Operation requires some form of container to hold the fruits or seeds.
- o Timing of operation: May-June

Peeling, depulping, cleaning:
- o Using picked or harvested fruit, remove skin and pulp by pressing with hands or feet.
- o Clean gathered fallen seeds by removing pulp from them, if needed.
- o This operation requires sand or water and sometimes a container.
- o Timing of operation: Immediately after picking or gathering.

Drying:
- o Spread out seeds, from which pulp has been removed, on a stand or in acontainer to evaporate water and make seed dry.
- o This traditional solar drying presupposes regular, sustained human intervention to protect the product or gather it up in the event of wind or rain storms and to stir the spread-out seeds to keep the drying even and prevent mould. Usually some portion of the product is lost due to the simple drying procedure.
- o Operation can be carried out right on the ground with a mat, a piece of cloth, or a tray.
- o Timing of operation: Immediately after peeling, depulping and cleaning.

Pounding, grinding, milling:
- o Powder the dried seeds with the following equipment: stones for pounding, mortar and pestle for grinding, millstone or flour mill for milling.
- o Crushing, pounding and grinding are operations which are slower and which incur greater losses than milling. Moreover, the millstone, mortar and pestle, and flour mill need to be cleaned well if these implements are to be used with other products.
- o Timing of operation: Dependent on user's needs.

Preservation and storage:
- Keep seeds or powder in container and in dry, well-ventilated area to protect them from the sun, wind and rain (or humidity).
- Powder can be kept with clay, sand or sawdust in appropriate place.
- Seeds can be stored in burlap bags, and others.
- Timing of operation: User can decide to keep dried seeds until he or she needs to grind them into powder for use in fields or else make them into powder first prior to storage.

Mixing:
- Neem powder is mixed with water to obtain an aqueous solution or aqueous extract of neem.
- Dosage for aqueous solution is 1 kg neem powder to 20 l water. About 20 to 30 kg of powder and 400 to 600 l of water are needed to treat one hectare of adult plants. This is approximately the productive capability of one mature neem tree in a year.
- Powder-water mixture should stabilise for at least several hours and be stirred well before filtering.

Filtering:
- Separate particles or residue in aqueous solution by using appropriate filter, such as cloth, sieve, and others.
- Timing of operation: Filtering operation immediately follows mixing and stabilisation. Treatment is carried out after filtering.

Transporting:
- Take the treatment product to place where it is to be used.
- Product prepared at treatment site does not need to be transported, but it is necessary to transport ingredients of the mixture in advance.
- If treatment of grain fields (millet, sorghum) that are located far from a permanent water source is to be attempted, it is perhaps advisable to transport water and powder to fields separately before mixing them together.
- The transportation operation needs only strong arms in cases where 20 l of water and 1 kg of powder are needed to treat a 25 m x 20 m garden with an area of 500 m², but to treat a 5-hectare field, 100 to 150 kg of powder and 2000 to 3000 l of water must be moved. In the lattercase, a cart and a draft animal that would make at least three trips would be needed in addition to 1 or 2 sacks of powder and 10 to 15 barrels of water.

Spraying operation:
- The principal operation to be carried out is spraying neem, in aqueous solution, to treat food crops for protection against harmful insects. Perhaps it would be more appropriate to talk about sprinkling rather than spraying, for one finds far fewer sprayers than buckets and sprinkling cans among farmers. Tools available to the farmer for spreading liquid products are, ranging from the home-made to the manufactured, clay water jars, water-skins, buckets, metal containers and sprinkling cans. The latter three may be made from plastic or metal.
- Grain-producing plants are very vulnerable to insect attack when they are still young shoots and again when their fruits are in the milky stage. These two periods correspond to approximately the beginning of the rainy season and the most regular rainfall in the Sahel regions. Vegetable crops are very vulnerable as seedlings, and remain susceptible to grasshopper damage throughout their growth cycle. This corresponds to the counter, or dry season, from December to March.

○ Spraying or sprinkling has to be carried out in calm weather conditions without wind or rain. The frequency of crop treatment with aqueous extract depends mainly on the availability of neem powder, water to put it into solution, and adequate equipment for transportation and application, as well as the labour force available to village farmers. A rainfall occurring just after an application could necessitate a repetition of the operation.

Social organisation

Aspects of social organisation which could influence the use of neem by farmers in the study zone were investigated. Of primary importance are size of family and normal work carried out by family members.

There are two types of families present in each of the four villages surveyed. The smaller of these, which we will designate as *core family* is composed of a man, his wife or wives, and the dependent children born to these wives. At any given time, one or more of these members may be temporarily absent. Core families may live separately from other kin. The term *household* is used to denote such dwellings and those who occupy them. The second type of family incorporates several patrilineally related core families; we refer to it as an *extended family*. The term *compound* is used for the physical dwelling and the extended family which occupies it.

These are the most important social units of co-operation in relations of production and consumption. When labour supplies in the household prove inadequate, the kin ties within an extended family facilitate mutual assistance. Other researchers have indicated that breakdown of the extended family is occurring rapidly among Zarmaphone people of Niger, more rapidly than among the Hausa to the east (Painter 1986: 201). However, we found that in the Tera region, the extended family, with patrilineally related males heading the member core families, is still a dominant and very important kin unit.

In each of the four villages in the study, the nature of the research project was explained to the chief of the village and his council of male elders. Permission was sought and given to interview individual representatives of households and compounds as well as a group of men and a group of women. For the individual interviews in each village the elders were asked to identify about 25 people representing a range of ages and size of landholdings, and including both men and women, who were heavily involved in farming and would thus be knowledgeable about the details of farm operations. A total of 103 such respondents were named across the four villages.

We are well aware that this in no way constitutes a random sample. We do believe that it is a representative sample. Furthermore, it was the only way for a group of strangers and bureaucrats to rapidly accomplish the tasks at hand in a conservative Muslim village setting. Of the 103 individuals identified and interviewed, 15 were women, all widows.

Sixty-one interviewees represented core family households and 42 represented extended family compounds. A total of 255 core families resided in the context of these 42 extended families. Thus, 316 core families were represented, with 255 (81 per cent) existing as units within extended families and 61 (19 per cent) existing as independent households. The 61 core family households represented in the sample contain a total of 564 members; the 42 extended family compounds contain 1104 members. Clearly, the extended family constitutes the primary social and economic unit within the study zone, in spite of a trend toward individualisation which began during the colonial period. It should also be noted that 97 per cent of all married men in the households and compounds represented in the sample were polygynous. 'Other' members of the households and compounds surveyed, *i.e.* those who were neither married into nor born into the core families represented, totalled only 87 people out of the overall sample population of 1668. They would not constitute significant additions to family labour for most family units.

Compounds and core families

Table 3.2 displays information on core and extended families which was gathered from interviewees in each of the four villages. It is quickly apparent that the people of Diagourou, the Fulani village, are organised quite differently from members of the other three villages. All 25 of the interviewees are part of core families which are in separate households; none are in extended family compounds. This does not necessarily imply that farmers in Diagourou can rely only on the labour of core family members, but it is an indication that decision-making processes about production and consumption may be different for the Fulani than for the Songhay. What is clear is that large extended family compounds are not a significant social unit for the Fulani.

Table 3.2 also reveals different levels of absenteeism among the four villages. The data were collected during February, a part of the counter season. It is very common for villagers to migrate into cities, and south toward the coast, during this period. They seek paid employment to send remittances home, accrue a capital fund for themselves, and relieve pressure on family food stores. Older male children and husbands are most likely to leave the village temporarily. Table 3.2 illustrates that families across the four villages seem to have different experiences with migration. It was not a major demographic factor in Diagourou, the Fulani village, when these data were collected in 1988; Fulani core families were not losing family agricultural labour to migration. In Dargol, Bellekoire, and Mehanna, however, the impact was more substantial.

Extended family compounds very commonly had some of the husbands and children absent at the time of the study. In the case of the largest compound, in Dargol, fully 40 per cent of the compound husbands were absent. This would indicate that, if a labour-intensive innovation such as the production and use of neem solution as an anti-feedant were to be accepted and used and if the family has lost key labourers to migration, labour from outside the core family would have to be accessible. This could come from voluntary (communal) labour, or from paid labour. Recourse to paid labour seems to be more and more common in all four villages. The Bella appear to make up the primary agricultural labour pool, but some Fulani and Kado are also available. Everywhere, the daily wage for agricultural work is 500 francs CFA. Farmers in Dargol added that, during the hoeing and weeding period, farm labourers prefer to receive their pay in the form of a bundle of millet rather than 500 francs.

Voluntary (communal) aid takes two forms, depending on the nature of the participants: either the general populace contributes, or young people stratified by age form work groups. Both forms are still practiced, but the form carried out by young people tends to come more and more through the para-gov-

Table 3.2: Compounds and core families

Village	Extended family compounds	Core families	Core families per extended family	Present				Absent			Total individuals
				Hu[b]	Wi[c]	Ch[d]	Other	Hu	Wi	Ch	
Dargol	In HHs[a]	2		2	2	7	0	0	0	1	12
	1	2	2	1	3	5	0	1	0	0	10
	4	12	3	7	8	18	5	5	4	12	59
	5	20	4	13	25	34	0	7	2	4	85
	4	20	5	14	20	42	3	6	3	1	89
	1	6	6	4	4	4	0	2	1	0	15
	2	14	7	10	22	18	6	4	0	4	64
	1	8	8	7	7	9	0	1	2	1	27
	1	12	12	11	9	6	0	1	0	2	29
	1	14	13	8	8	10	0	6	0	4	36
	1	58	58	34	56	80	0	24	7	0	201
Total	21	168		111	164	233	14	57	19	29	627
Diagourou	In HHs	24		24	35	121	28	0	1	5	214
	In HH of Widows	1		0	1	5	0	0	0	0	6
Total		25		24	36	126	28	0	1	5	220
Bellekoira	In HHs	10		10	14	37	2	0	0	8	71
	In HH of Widows	3		0	8	6	0	0	0	2	17
	5	10	2	10	14	30	16	0	0	0	70
	3	9	3	8	15	31	9	1	0	10	74
	2	8	4	7	6	22	0	1	0	0	36
	1	9	9	6	8	31	2	3	0	0	50
	1	16	16	13	10	21	0	3	0	0	47
	1	17	17	11	16	29	2	6	1	1	65
Total	13	82		65	91	207	31	14	1	21	430
Mehanna	In HHs	16		16	25	131	8	0	0	48	228
	In HH of Widows	5		0	5	4	2	0	0	5	16
	2	10	5	9	12	49	2	1	1	0	74
	2	6	3	5	8	31	0	1	1	2	48
	1	4	4	4	5	14	2	0	0	0	25
Total	5	41		34	55	229	14	2	2	55	391

a = household
b = husband
c = wife
d = child

ernment youth movement known as *Samariya*. In the past, young unmarried men were obligated to contribute communal labour to their prospective in-laws. Voluntary aid offered by the populace at large, called *boogu* in the Zarma language and *baala* in Fulfulde, is requested by a farmer who wishes to carry out a one-day farming operation. The farmer who organises the *boogu* or *baala* invites the village community, and sometimes other communities, to come and help carry out the project.

The farmer's obligation is to furnish participants with food, drink, cola nuts, and tobacco or cigarettes. Sometimes people must also be put up for the night, if they come from far away. If the job is that of putting grain up for storage, the obligation may entail giving people bundles of millet. Painter (1986: 207) has pointed out that such communal labour in South-western Niger is most frequently available to those who occupy a high status in the village.

It is not easy to estimate the cost of voluntary aid, which is underwritten by the organiser. From information supplied by two farmers in Dargol, it may be estimated that an organiser of voluntary aid in the Tera Arrondissement spends between 300 and 500 francs CFA to give each participant cola nuts, chewing tobacco or cigarettes, goat meat, food and drink.

An invitation to participate in voluntary aid may attract anywhere from a dozen to a hundred participants.

Table 3.3: Division of labour in grain-farming operations

Farming operations	Village			
	Dargol	Bellekoire	Mehanna	Diagourou
Field preparations	M, Ch	M, Wo, Ch	M, Ch	M, Ch
Sowing	M, Wo, Ch	M, Wo, Ch	M, Wo, Ch	M, Wo, Ch
Hoeing and weeding	M, Ch	M, Wo, Ch	M, Ch	M, Ch
Early millet harvest	M, Wo, Ch			
Regular harvest	M, Wo, Ch	M, Wo, Ch	M, Wo, Ch	M, Wo, Ch
Storage	M, Ch, Comm	M, Ch, Comm	M, Ch, Comm	M, Ch, Comm

M=men, W=women, Ch=children, Comm=communal

Table 3.3 delineates the division of labour in grain farming operations by village. These data were collected from the 103 individual interviewees. They were asked to indicate who in the family participated in particular categories of farming tasks – adult men, adult women, or children. They were also asked if communal labour was requested.

It must be noted that information collected during the group interviews with women both supplement Table 3.3 and raise some questions. Women indicated that bird scaring is a significant farming activity to which they and their children are major contributors; it was not a category on the interview schedule for individuals. Women in all four villages also indicated that they helped to carry the harvest in from the fields, and assisted with the winnowing.

During the rainy season each woman also works on a small number of plots of land close to the village; these are her husband's plots, and she has the use of them. Usually crops such as okra, cowpeas, or peanuts are grown on these plots, although sometimes the women will also plant millet. Women perform all farming tasks on these plots, including field preparation and weeding. Men who were interviewed may have tended to under-report women's involvement in farming operations.

Tools and equipment

Existing tools which could be used in employing neem as a natural crop protectant would be primarily the mortar and pestle, the water jug, and the water-skin. The mortar and pestle would be used to pound the neem seeds and reduce them to a powder.

The water jug or water-skin could be used to carry water. These two latter implements, however, could only hold 10 to 15 l, so they would only be practical for use in small gardens. Nevertheless, they could be used to carry hundreds of l of water, if the voluntary aid system were practiced.

During the counter season, women in all four villages are involved in gardening. The tasks in gardening are the same in all the villages:

o Just after the grain harvest is in from the fields, the gardens are cleaned.
o Gardens are tilled.
o Gardens are divided into beds and planted with seedlings.
o Watering is done as needed. Water is hauled or lifted from ponds or wells. Children provide assistance.
o Gardens are manured. Children help with this.
o Gardens are cultivated twice for weed control.
o Bird scaring is done as needed.
o Crops are harvested as they ripen and are either used in the household or sold in local markets. Sometimes vegetables are harvested semi-ripe and then held for awhile before they are used or sold.
o Seeds are saved for the following year.
o After the harvest, animals are allowed to graze in the gardens to leave their
excrement and break up the soil with their hooves.

The women rotate crops from year to year in their gardens; they do not practice intercropping, which is a significant practice in grain farming. They reported major problems with insect pests, rats, and birds. Seedling beds and new growth are especially vulnerable. In all four villages, women have individual gardens, but may likewise participate in collective gardens as members of local chapters of the *Association des Femmes du Niger*, the national organisation for women which was part of the Niger's response to the UN Decade for Women. The land for collective gardens is usually designated by the village chief. The women must also ask the chief for the use of individual garden plots. In Bellekoire and Dargol, women inherited use rights in garden plots from their mothers and fathers.

One of the interesting aspects of the gardening is that women conduct their seedling operations quite differently across the four villages. In Mehanna, each woman makes seedling beds for just one crop, and then the women exchange seedlings until all have what they need. In Bellekoire, the women use a communal fund to buy seeds. They make one collective seedling bed for all gardens, individual and collective; each woman can then take what she needs from these beds. In Diagourou, each woman saves or buys seeds and makes her own seedling beds. In Dargol, each woman also makes her own seedling beds. If her nursery plants do not grow, then she will buy them from another woman.

Sizes and types of fields and gardens

The size of a farmer's fields depends today on a combination of how many mouths there are to feed and the number of hands available to wield a pick or a hoe. This is one reason why the farmer needs many children and also why a male farmer is often polygynous in the Sahel. But the poverty in rural environments and the hard work in the fields are causing the youngest and the strongest to flee the countryside. When a farmer acquires a field, its size is measured by the number of paces between natural landmarks, and it is referred to as the big or little field between such and such a tree and the termite mound, the water hole, and other landmarks.

Analysis of the results of the individual survey allows us to confirm or infer information gathered through environmental observation and the collective surveys on holdings of compounds and married households. During the individual survey, each representative of either gender was asked to give the number of large fields, small fields and gardens possessed by the compound or nuclear family. These landholdings are classified according to their proximity to (under 5 km) or distance from (more than 5 km) the living quarters according to the type of crops raised.

In all 349 fields, with an estimated area of 2,030 ha, were tallied for the 103 compounds and households in the overall sample. Fields which are termed large, number 225; those that are called small total 124. The respective areas of these are 1,475 ha and 555 ha. Thus, large fields average 6.6 ha and small fields average 4.4 ha. The overall total is 2,030 ha. Table 3.4 displays the distribution of cultivated fields. It is apparent that average land holdings display a wide range when compared by village, by core family, and by individual. Bellekoira, with the largest average landholding per individual, is also the village under the greatest ecological stress.

Table 3.4: Distribution of cultivated fields

Village	Fields			Ha	Com- pounds	House- holds	Core families	Indi- vid- uals	Ha per core family	Ha per individ- ual
	Large	Small	Total							
Dargol	69	31	100	638	21	2	168	627	3.80	1.02
Bellekoira	82	51	133	747	13	13	82	430	9.11	1.74
Mehanna	56	19	75	468	8	21	41	391	11.41	1.20
Diagouru	18	23	41	177	-	25	25	220	7.08	0.80

The majority of fields are located less than 5 km from the living quarters. These nearby fields (273 totalling 1,528 ha) represent 75.27 per cent of the total area. Both absolute and relative disparities exist between villages and within the same village. Fields located more than 5 km from the residence (76 totalling 502 ha) constitute 24.7 per cent of the total area. Here again, both absolute and relative disparities exist between villages and among the compounds and households of a single village. Travel time, by foot or wagon, would appear to be, on the average, at least 60 minutes between living quarters and fields located less than 5 km away. A one-way trip between the living quarters and fields located more than 5 km away would appear to average between 75 and 90 minutes. A total of 152 gardens were reported in the sample: 45 in Dargol, 65 in Mehanna, 19 in Bellekoira, and 23 in Diagourou. Their absolute or relative areas were not calculated. However, these gardens are rarely larger than 500 m² Finally, it should be noted that nearly all these gardens are located very near the living compounds, generally within a 15-minute walk.

In most cases, mortars and water-skins seem to be in sufficient supply in each extended family compound to handle normal present needs. The same equipment would not necessarily be in sufficient supply for all the core family households contacted. Equipment of a more intermediate sort is in short supply. A good example of this lack of available equipment may be seen in the area of carts, wheelbarrows, and similar conveyances. Intermediate level tools, such as barrels, buckets and sprinkling cans, are also deficient in number.

The following is an inventory of tools and equipment which would be used in production and application of neem solution across the four villages:

Mortars	193
Barrel	37
Buckets	375
Sprinkling cans	3
Carts	40
Wheelbarrows	3
Draft animals	160

With the exception of buckets, which appear to exist in sufficient numbers for all core and extended families, ratios of other tools and equipment range from 1 for every 2 to 1 for every 105 core families:

Mortars	2 per compound; 2 for each of 3 core families
Barrels	1 for each of 3 compounds; 1 for each of 9 core families
Buckets	4 per compound; 1 per core family
Sprinklers	1 for each of 34 compounds; 1 for each of 105 core families
Carts	1 for each of 3 compounds; 1 for each of 8 core families
Wheelbarrows	1 for each of 34 compounds; 1 for each of 105 core families
Draft animals	Perhaps 2 animals available per compound; only 1 for each of 2 core families

Water

Each interviewee was asked to identify the number of water sources (water-holes, wells, lakes, ponds, dams, rivers) located in or near the compound or property. These water sources were classified by the proximity (0–1 km) or distance (1–5 km) from the living quarters, gardens, and fields of each individual surveyed.

A distinction was finally made between permanent water sources, which were not subject to drying up, and semi-permanent water sources, which were subject to drying up seasonally. In reality, the essential information needed was proximity of a permanent water source to compound, gardens and fields. Analysis of responses to the water question allowed us to pinpoint the compounds and other village property with access to a permanent water source located less than a kilometre away. Table 3. 5 shows a summary of our results.

Table 3.5: Water accessibility

Location	Permanent water less than one kilometre away		
	Compound or household	Gardens	Large and small fields
Dargol	3	3	1
Bellekoira	5	9	0
Mehanna	25	5	11
Diagourou	25	4	0

A total of 58 compounds or households out of 103 have access for the entire year to a permanent water source located less than 1 km. away. This total amounts to 56 per cent of the compounds and households in the overall sample. However, absolute and relative disparities between villages are very great. In Mehanna, 25 of the 29 compounds or households in the local sample have practically no water problems all year round, unless the deep well pumps break down. Furthermore, in this village, there is also the river which hardly ever dries up. At Diagourou, all 25 households surveyed have well water nearby all year.

On the other hand, at Dargol, 87 per cent of the 23 compounds or households do not have access to a nearby permanent water source. In Bellekoira, only 5 out of the 26 compounds or households have access to a nearby permanent water source. However, it should be pointed out that UNICEF was drilling several deep wells at Bellekoira that had not yet been finished at the time of our survey.

With regard to gardens, 21 out of 152, or only 14 per cent, had a permanent water source located no more than 1 km away. Only 12 fields out of 349 are located less than 1 km from a water source which is reliable all year round, including 1 field out of 100 at Dargol and 11 fields out of 75 at Mehanna. Of the 2030 ha of total area comprised by the 349 fields, 1528 ha (75.27 per cent) are located between 1 and 5 km from the compound, and 502 ha are more than 5 km away.

It quickly becomes apparent that water, equipment, and human labour are all limiting conditions in the local production and application of neem solution to large and small fields during the major growing season. A few mathematical calculations establish that, with the human and water resources presently available in the study zone, it is not socioeconomically feasible to use neem solution as a crop protectant on field crops. Minimal amounts of water needed for the preparation of neem solution would be in the order of 611,200 l to be transported a distance of at least 5 km for 1528 ha, and 200,800 l to be transported more than 5 km for 502 ha.

Containers needed to transport the necessary 812,000 l of water could be either water-skins with a capacity of 10 to 15 l carried on the head, or 200 l barrels transported in carts pulled by animals or humans. Around 54,134 trips would be needed using 15 litre water-skins, at one skin per person, or more than 13,350 trips with one of the locally used conveyances called a *pousse-pousse* loaded with four water-skins at a time. This little home-made cart which is frequently seen in certain parts of Burkina Faso, is made out of wood or metal and has a bicycle or motorcycle wheel and room for two, three, or four water-skins. If water is transported in ox or donkey carts, which are common in the rural areas of Niger, a maximum of four or five 200 litre barrels can be carried at a time, in which case it would take about a thousand trips.

Neem within the study zone

Another crucial variable and possible limiting factor in using neem solution as a crop protectant is, of course, the neem itself. Treatment of one hectare of crop area requires 20 kg of neem seed powder, approximately the productive capability of one mature neem tree in a year. When mixed with 400 l of water, the effective ratio is one hectare:one tree, as revealed in the entomological trials reported under the section on 'Entomology' in this chapter. Interviewees were asked to indicate the number of neem trees present in their compound or household. Table 3.6 indicates, by village, the number of compounds and households represented in the study, and the number of neem trees available to their members.

Table 3.6: Availability of neem trees

Village	Neem trees			Number of compounds and households	Number of core families
	Total	Immature	Mature		
Dargol	137	44	93	23	168
Diagourou	22	10	12	5	25
Bellekoira	235	63	172	26	82
Mehanna	216	96	120	26	42

Clearly, the number of neem trees is not sufficient to permit households and compounds to protect field crops during the growing season. The average land holding for a compound or household, across the four villages, is 19.71 ha. A household or compound would need 20 mature trees and 8000 l of water to prepare an aqueous solution sufficient for a single application. To treat this average land holding in three hours time, the labour of approximately 100 people would be needed to transport the solution and spray or sprinkle the crop, in the event of a grasshopper attack.

Constraints and possibilities

The socioeconomic component of this research project was conducted to ascertain if neem, which is already present and used for a multitude of purposes in the Sahel, could feasibly also provide an accessible, non-monetised, albeit labour-intensive way to produce a crop protectant which would be effective against grasshoppers. The following realities have emerged from the study:

○ neem trees planted in the compounds and in other family property do not, at this time, exist in sufficient numbers to allow treatment of the areas planted to grain crops during the regular agricultural year. They would be sufficient to treat gardens and recession agricultural plots, which are worked during the counter season;

○ sufficient permanent water sources for preparing crop protectant are not available within 5 km. of households and compounds such that large-scale application could be done. The water resources are sufficient for the small areas such as gardens and recession plot, and.

○ tools and implements required for the production of the neem solution are available in all the villages. Equipment and containers for transport and application are available for use on small areas such as gardens and recession plots, but not for use on the fields normally planted to grains.

Table 3.7: Division of labour in production of neem solution

	Dargol	Diagourou	Bellekoire	Mehanna
Women	Grinding seed Carrying water Filtering	Grinding seed Carrying water	Grinding seed Carrying water	Depulping fruit Drying seed Grinding seed Carrying seed Filtering Transporting solution
Men	Drying seed Filtering Transporting solution	Depulping fruit Filtering	Drying seed Filtering Transporting solution	Depulping fruit Drying seed Transporting solution
Children	Gathering neem Depulping fruit Carrying water Transporting solution	Gathering neem Transporting solution	Gathering neem Depulping fruit Carrying water Transporting solution	Gathering neem Depulping fruit Drying seed Carrying water Transporting solution

Individual interviewees were asked who would perform the labour steps in producing and applying neem solution. Table 3.7 shows the projected division of labour in the production and transport processes. The interviewees indicated that application would be done by men, women, and children, if buckets or sprinkling cans were used. However, when asked who would do the application if a new item of technology, the hand-held sprayer, was introduced into the villages, the response was unanimous: men.

Because the major opportunities for use of neem as a crop protectant are clearly for use on gardens and recession plots, and gardening is an important counter season activity for women, it is clear that women will be key in the decision-making process to adopt a new use for a familiar material. When farmer trials are mounted as the next logical step in the introduction of neem solution as a crop protectant, men and women will be crucial actors. Research and extension activities will be most productive if both men and women are encouraged and assisted to experiment and innovate with materials already present in their environment (McCorkle, Brandstetter and McClure 1988).

Entomology

Seeds and leaves of the neem tree, *Azadirachta indica* A. Juss (=*Melia azadirachta* L.), have been used for their insecticidal properties for hundreds, possibly thousands, of years on the Indo-Pakistan subcontinent. Traditional uses of neem included protection of clothing, books, and stored grain by layering with leaves and incorporation of the leaves in making earthen storages (Ahmed and Grainge 1986). The earliest scientific research on neem was almost entirely on stored-product insects (Jotwani and Srivastava 1981a). The use of neem to protect standing crops is a very recent development (Jotwani and Srivastava 1981b).

It has been observed that neem trees are essentially immune to attack by the desert locust, *Schistocerca gregaria* Forsk. (Mann and Burns 1927, cited in

Jotwani and Srivastava 1981, Schmutterer 1981). Locusts confined on neem trees die of starvation without feeding (Jotwani and Srivastava 1984). However, attempts to protect crop plants with sprays made from neem leaves met little success (Pradhan *et al.* 1962). In the 1950s, it was discovered that highest concentrations of biologically active constituents in neem occur in the seed kernel. Using this information, Indian scientists successfully protected standing crops against invading locusts in 1962 by spraying with a 0.1 per cent neem kernel suspension (Pradhan *et al.* 1962, 1963).

Subsequent research has demonstrated the efficacy of neem extracts against more than 120 species of insects (Jacobson 1986) and that list is being extended rapidly. Neem extracts are now known to have activity against many insect taxa including Orthoptera, Hemiptera, Homoptera, Thysanoptera, Lepidoptera, Coleoptera, and Diptera, as well as ticks, mites, nematodes, and certain bacteria and fungi.

Neem-based insecticides appear to be exceptionally safe in terms of human exposure or environmental effects. Indeed, medicinal properties were attributed to neem from the earliest of Sanskrit medical writings (Waring 1868). Amazingly, most of the remarkable medicinal benefits claimed appear to have basis in fact (Jacobson 1988). Beneficial insects are generally little affected because the contact toxicity of neem is typically one to two orders of magnitude less than levels which deter feeding by phytophagous insects and two to four orders of magnitude less than the dietary levels disruptive to growth and metamorphosis (Steets 1976; Rembold 1988).

Biological activity and the chemical nature of neem

Butterworth and Morgan (1968) isolated a phytochemical anti-feedant common to neem and chinaberry, *Melia azedarach L.* Applied to plants at concentrations as low as 5 ppm, this chemical, which they named azadirachtin, completely inhibited feeding by the desert locust. The chemical structure of azadirachtin was first elucidated by Zanno *et al.* (1975). Azadirachtin is a highly oxidised triterpenoid in which carbon atoms 24-27 have been lost and the remaining carbon atoms cyclised into a furan ring (Jones *et al.* 1988). In 1979, it was discovered that some neem constituents did not deter insect feeding, but were nevertheless potent disruptants of growth and metamorphosis (Schmutterer and Rembold 1980). Exposure to minute quantities of these substances caused suspension of metamorphosis or resulted in larval-pupal intermediates (Rembold *et al.* 1984). This indicated interference with the neuroendocrine system. Titers of ecdysone and juvenile hormone are affected.

It was subsequently learned that azadirachtin itself is a disruptant of insect growth and, indeed, the most important such constituent in neem (Schmutterer and Rembold 1980). Other of the insect growth inhibiting constituents were found to be stereo isomers of azadirachtin (Rembold *et al.* 1983; Rembold 1988). To date, more than 50 biologically active constituents have been identified (Jones *et al.* 1988) all tetranortriterpenoids (C_{26} triterpenoids= liminoids).

Potential application of neem in Third World agriculture

In many developing countries, ever expanding human populations and limited resources for agricultural production have made conditions of rural subsistence increasingly intolerable. A common consequence has been massive migration of the rural poor to urban centres. In cities, these migrants often encounter an inadequacy of employment opportunities and experience even greater poverty. Such dislocations can also endanger the traditions and culture of the people. Rural development strategies are typically intended to keep rural populations on the land (Ahmed and Grainge 1986). To accomplish that, ways must be found that enable resource-limited agriculturalists to increase production. Improved insect control is one of the most obvious possibilities since in developing countries, insects commonly destroy 40 per cent or more of potential crop production (Cramer 1967; McEwen 1978).

For subsistence farmers, available insect control measures are often limited or ineffective. Synthetic chemical insecticides may be unavailable or prohibitively expensive. Lack of suitable application equipment and inadequate information as to proper use and handling can result in inefficient use or other problems, some potentially serious. Alternative pest control methods that are effective, safe and require minimal capital inputs are desperately needed. Ideally, farmers should be able to control pests by means available in their own villages. Botanical insecticides, such as neem, that can be grown on-site could provide that alternative (Radwanski 1982). Ahmed and Grainge (1986) listed attributes desirable in plants and their extracts when used for pest control by limited-resource farmers. The plant should be:

○ perennial;
○ require little growing space, labour, water or fertiliser;
○ not be destroyed when harvested for its pesticidal components;
○ not become a pest itself or host pests; and
○ possess complementary uses.

The crude extracts should:

○ provide effective pest control with minimal disruption of non-target organisms;
○ be easy to process/formulate with village-level technology;
○ be easy to use with skills and resources available; and
○ be environmentally safe.

Of the more than 2400 plants now known to possess insecticidal properties (Ahmed and Grainge 1986), no plant better satisfies these criteria than does neem.

As mentioned previously, scientists with the Indian Agricultural Research Institute New Delhi were the first to demonstrate the practical use of neem in crop protection. Despite the success of Indian scientists, the insecticidal properties of neem attracted little attention in other countries before 1970. That year, Justus-Liebig University in Giessen, Federal Republic of Germany, initiated research on neem (Schmutterer 1981). Since 1978, that research, now involving cooperators around the world, has been financed by the German Agency for Technical Assistance (Deutsche Gesellschaft für Technische Zusammenarbeit (GTZ)).

Application of neem technology at the village level received scant attention until just the past decade. Now classic is the 1982–85 work of Adhikary (1981, 1985) and Dreyer (1984, 1987) in Togo to determine if simple neem insecticides, as prepared with only indigenous resources, could be used by subsistence farmers to protect vegetable and field crops in the field. Fortunately, the active constituents of neem are water soluble (Feurerhake 1985). Possibly, the saponins and saccharides in the seed serve as natural emulsifiers (Ascher 1981).

Effective spray suspensions could be prepared by simply grinding dried, decorticated seed to a fine powder and allowing it to stand in water for some hours. The suspension was then filtered through fine gauze and applied by knapsack sprayer. Sprays prepared with 25-50 g of neem kernel per litre gave control of various insect pests of crucifers, cucurbits, and eggplant that was generally comparable to that obtained with conventional insecticides. Other useful preparations were made by expressing neem oil (by hand or mechanical press) or by powdering the neem kernel and diluting it with sawdust.

Since the First International Neem Conference was held in 1980 (Schmutterer, Ascher and Rembold 1981), interest in neem has greatly increased worldwide. At the Second and Third International Neem Conferences (Schmutterer and Ascher 1987), many of the presented papers concerned implementation research in developing countries. At the conclusion of the Third conference, participants adopted seven resolutions supporting the concept that use of aqueous neem extracts and other simple neem products should be promoted in developing countries for purposes of pest control and that the growing of neem should be encouraged (Schmutterer and Ascher 1987). Neem is now recognised as the world's pre-eminent botanical insecticide (Schmutterer 1985; Jacobson 1986).

University of Minnesota/AFGRO Neem Project, Niger

The University of Minnesota/AFGRO Neem Project in Niger was initiated in 1986, with funding provided by USAID/AFR/OEO (USAID Project DAN-4141-C-00-5122-00). Our objectives were to conduct entomological and socioeconomic studies relating to the utility of neem kernel extract to protect pearl millet, Pennisetum americanum (L.) Leeke, and sorghum, Sorghum bicolor (L.) Moench, against grasshoppers and locusts. The project was undertaken as a co-operative venture between the University of Minnesota and AFGRO. For the University, this arrangement was an experiment with a model we may wish to use in future international activities. AFGRO provided project scientists with on-site expertise and a network of contacts we would not otherwise have. The University provided AFGRO with technical expertise to advance its objectives of developing and promoting indigenous technologies that may facilitate the survival and growth of rural organisations in West Africa.

Entomology experiments, Niger

The entomological component of this project was designed to test the efficacy of locally produced neem kernel extract as a grasshopper and locust antifeedant on millet and sorghum seedlings in Niger. Our first two series of experiments were done at the International Crops Research Institute for the Semi-Arid Tropics (ICRISAT), Sahelian Centre, Sadore, 28 August to 3 September 1987 (Radcliffe *et al.* 1990) and 16 July to 10 September 1988, respectively. The next series of experiments were done on farmer-owned fields near the village of Mozague, 17 to 27 November 1988. The July-September experiments were done during the season when production of rain-fed crops is possible. Pearl millet is the principal cereal of Niger with some sorghum production in areas where rainfall is highest. The November experiments were done during the 'counter season', when there is essentially no rainfall. Counter season production of field crops is limited to the recession plains with planting proceeding as the water recedes (recession agriculture). Sorghum is the principal counter season cereal with most production from transplants.

Experiments were done in screen cages (1 m³) using both millet and sorghum seedlings (3–5 leaf stage). Trials used either nursery-grown plants transplanted into the field or field-grown millet. Cages were placed over 4 'hills' of transplants (4–7 plants per hill) or a single row of field-grown seedlings (about 25–35 seedlings). Plants in each cage were randomly assigned to treatment groups and either sprayed with neem or left untreated (choice experiments). In a few cages, all plants received the same treatment (no-choice experiments). Neem seed collected from the streets of Niamey or the villages of Diagourou, Gotheye, Tsernawa, and Mozague, and two methanolic neem extracts, 'Beltsville neem' (provided by J. D. Warthen Jr., USDA) or the commercial product, Margosan-O (W. R. Grace & Co.) were used in these trials.

In the 1987 experiments, defoliation was visually estimated and scored (1–5 scale) as follows: 1= < 5 per cent defoliation, 2=5–25 per cent, 3=26–74 per cent, 4=75–95 per cent, and 5 > 95 per cent. In the 1988 experiments, defoliation was less extensive with most grasshopper species tested so damage on each leaf was visually scored (0–3 scale) as follows: 0=no feeding, 1=one or two feeding scars, 2=three to six feeding scars and no more than the terminal third of the leaf eaten, and 3=more than six feeding scars or more than 50 per cent of the leaf eaten. Plant damage was scored 1 to 8 days after introduction of the insects. Usually, the same plants were scored several times over successive days. Neem kernel extract spray suspensions were prepared from decorticated and dried seed, ground to a fine powder, water extracted for 2 to 4 hours before use, filtered through cheesecloth and sprayed with a low pressure hand-pumped sprayer. Strength of the neem kernel extract spray solutions of all local neem sources was standardised by extracting 50 g neem powder per litre. Beltsville neem was used at 10, 20 and 40 ppm, Margosan-O was used at 20 ppm (the recommended 1:150 dilution rate). Plants were sprayed until run off (25–50 ml. spray suspension per cage) with the selected treatment.

Because some grasshopper species were relatively scarce, a priority ranking of treatments was designed. Local neem sources were tested before the methanolic extracts (standards) and the priority for rates were 1x > 0.5x > 0.5x + PBO (the synergist piperonyl butoxide) > 1x + PBO. Niamey neem and Beltsville neem were used only in the 1987 experiments; neem seed from Tsernawa and Mozague were used only in the November 1988 experiments. In some of the November 1988 experiments, neem kernel extract was used as soil-applied root drenches to newly transplanted seedlings to determine systemic activity.

Grasshoppers were introduced after treated plants had dried, usually within one hour of application, but in some experiments residual activity of neem-based sprays were tested by introducing grasshoppers at 0, 2, 4, or 6 days after treatments were applied. In the July–August 1987 experiments, a single grasshopper species was used, *Kraussaria angulifera*. In 1988, 11 grasshopper and locust species were used: *Acrotylus blondeli, Cryptocatanops haemorrhoidalis, Diabolocatantops axillaris, K. angulifera, Oedaleus nigeriensis, O. senegalensis, Pseudosphingonotus canariensis, Pyrgomorpha cognata, Ornithacris turbida cavoisi, Chrotogonus senegalensis,* and *Schistocerca gregaria*.

Treatments in the 1987 experiments included: source of neem, concentration of neem, pH of the water used to prepare spray suspension, addition of a synergist (PBO), days since application, and Kraussaria life stage (nymphs or adults). Data were analysed with Student's-t (one-tailed) or Student's paired comparison t tests (one-tailed).

Treatments in the July–September 1988 experiments were: source of neem, concentration of neem, addition of synergists, days since application, seedling species (millet or sorghum), and grasshopper or locust species. Effects of treatments were analysed using the ANOVA procedure (Statistical Analysis System) as a completely randomised design. Where effects of neem treatment differences were not statistically significant, cages were considered as replicates and mean plant rating per cage of treated and untreated plants was used for the analysis (rather than individual plant data) for each grasshopper/locust species using Student's-t test.

Treatments in the November 1988 experiments were source of neem, concentration of neem, days since application, method of application (foliar spray or root drench), seedling species, and grasshopper species. All treatments had 8 replications, and were analysed using the ANOVA procedure with separation of means of significant interactions by Duncan's Multiple Range Option (Statistical Analysis System).

Results and discussion

In the 1987 choice experiments, neem-protected sorghum seedlings had significantly less ($P < 0.05$, 9-26 d.f.) Kraussaria feeding damage than the untreated controls in evaluations 1–3 and 5–6 days post-treatment (Table 3.8).

Niamey neem-treated plants had mean damage scores of 1.56 (n=10) at 48 h post-treatment and 2.06 (n=14) at 72 h post-treatment. Corresponding scores

Table 3.8: Feeding responses of *Kraussaria angulifera* (nymphs or adults) on caged sorghum seedlings with neem (aqueous or methanolic extracts), or a conventional insecticide. ICRISAT, July 1987

Days post-treatment	Choice experiments[a]			No-choice experiments[a]		
	Neem	UTC[b]	Significant paired-t test	Neem	Cygon/ cymbush	UTC
1	1.65 (10)	2.20 (10)	0.05	–	1.00 (1)	2.75 (1)
2	1.83 (24)	2.92 (24)	0.005	1.50 (5)	1.50 (5)	2.67 (3)
3	2.41 (27)	3.13 (27)	0.005	2.85 (5)	1.50 (5)	3.75 (1)
4	3.83 (3)	4.33 (3)	n.s.	–	–	–
5	2.86 (18)	3.19 (18)	0.005	2.75 (4)	1.25 (2)	3.50 (1)
6	3.22 (18)	3.47 (18)	0.05	3.38 (4)	1.00 (2)	4.00 (1)

a Plants scored on a 1–5 scale:
  1 = <5 per cent defoliation
  2 = 5–25 per cent
  3 = 25–75 per cent
  4 = 75–95 per cent
  5 = >95 per cent
b UTC = untreated control

Table 3.9: Response of various grasshopper and locust species to foliar application of aqueous and methanolic extracts of neem to millet. ICRISAT, July–September 1988

Species[b]	Stage of development	Average plant damage rating[a]		Probability t[d]	No.of cages
		UTC[c]	Neem		
ABL	Adult	2.07	1.20	0.0003	27
CHA	Adult	1.76	1.19	0.17	8
DAX	Adult	1.74	0.97	0.05	3
KAN	Nymph	2.69	1.67	0.029	6
ONI	Adult	1.40	1.40	0.99	21
OSE	Adult	1.85	1.30	0.0007	40
PCA	Adult	1.29	0.46	0.019	9
PCO	Adult	1.78	1.00	0.0001	27
SGR	Adult	0.99	0.13	0.0001	43
SGR	Nymph	1.60	0.25	0.0001	22

a Plant damage scored:
  0 = no feeding;
  1 = one or two feeding scars
  2 = three to six feeding scars and no more than the terminal third of the leaf eaten
  3 = more than six feeding scars or more than 50 per cent of the leaf eaten
b Grasshopper/locust species identified by the following acronyms:
  CHA = *Cryptocatanops haemorrhoides*
  DAX = *Diabolocatantops axillaris*
  KAN = *Kraussaria angulifera*
  ONI = *Oedaleus nigeriensis*
  OSE = *O. senegalensis*
  PCA = *Pseudosphingonotus canariensis*
  PCO = *Pyrgomorpha cognata*
  SGR = *Schistocerca gregaria*
c UTC = untreated control
d Significance based on Student's paired comparison *t* test (one-tailed)

for Beltsville neem-treated seedlings were 2.05 (n=10) and 2.62 (n=17). Spray suspensions prepared in pH 4.5 water were slightly more efficacious than sprays prepared in pH 7.0 water (mean score 1.33 (n=6) compared to 2.00 (n=18) and 1.83 (n=6) compared to 2.57 (n=21) at 48 h and 72 h post-treatment, respectively). Effects of neem concentration or addition of PBO were not evident. In these same experiments, nymphs were more deterred from feeding than were adults, mean score 1.56 (n=17) compared to 2.5 (n=7) and 2.06 (n=18) and 3.11 (n=9). For the first 72 h post-treatment, neem-sprayed plants were not significantly more damaged than were Cymbush/Cygon-sprayed plants.

In the July–September 1988 experiments, we had highly significant treatment effects for grasshopper/locust species (F=4.95, 7 and 253 df, p=0.0001) and post-treatment evaluation date (F=6.90, 6 and 253 df, p=0.0001) effects. However, effects of neem source, rate, or additives (PBO) were not significant (F=0.84, 14 and 253 df, p=0.63) (Table 3.9).

Neem-based sprays significantly reduced feeding on millet for seven of the nine grasshopper/locust species tested. Of the two species where neem did not

Table 3.10: Response of various grasshopper and locust species to foliar application of neem (aqueous and methanolic extracts) to sorghum. ICRISAT, July–September 1988

Species[b]	Stage of development	Average plant damage rating[a]		Probability t[d]	No.of cages
		UTC[c]	Neem		
ABL	Adult	1.78	1.32	0.25	2
CHA	Adult	1.40	1.16	0.55	8
DAX	Nymph	1.24	0.4	0.14	3
KAN	Adult	1.88	0.72	0.02	6
ONI	Adult	2.28	1.34	0.35	2
OSE	Adult	1.79	1.14	0.05	10
PCA	Adult	1.29	0.46	0.019	9
PCO	Adult	1.45	1.57	0.19	2

a Plant damage scored:
 0 = no feeding
 1 = one or two feeding scars
 2 = three to six feeding scars and no more than the terminal third of the leaf eaten
 3 = more than six feeding scars or more than 50 per cent of the leaf eaten
b Grasshopper/locust species identified by the following acronyms:
 ABL = *Acrotylus blondei*
 CHA = *Cryptocatanops haemorrhoides*
 DAX = *Diabolocatantops axillaris*
 KAN = *Kraussaria angulifera*
 ONI = *Oedaleus nigeriensis*
 OSE = *O. senegalensis*
 PCA = *Pseudosphingonotus canariensis*
 PCO = *Pyrgomorpha cognata*
c UTC = untreated control
d Significance based on Student's paired comparison t test (one-tailed)

significantly reduce feeding damage, one, *Oedaleus nigeriensis*, suffered heavy daily mortality in the cages from a tachinid parasitoid which may have impaired the insects' feeding responses.

The other, C. haemorrhoidalis is primarily a forb feeder. In experiments with those species that are important pests of millet, K. angulifera; desert locust, S. gregaria; and Sengalese grasshopper, O. senegalensis; plants protected with neem-based sprays sustained significantly less feeding damage. With the exception of K. angulifera and S. gregaria, all species were evaluated only as adults.

Most of the grasshopper species tested on millet in the experiments of July–November 1988 were, at the same time, subjected to limited testing on sorghum (Table 3.10). Neem was generally less efficacious on sorghum. Sorghum is usually not planted during this time of year so this is not a commonly encountered host plant for these grasshoppers. We suspect this is the reason for the poor response to neem-based sprays.

Neem kernel extract residues significantly reduced feeding damage to millet by *K. angulifera* nymphs when the grasshoppers were introduced 0 or 2 days after spray application, but not when they were introduced 4 or 6 days after treatment. On days 4 and 6, treated plants were less damaged than the untreated control, but differences were not significant (Table 3.11). We cannot

Table 3.11: Analysis of residual activity of foliar sprays of neem (aqueous and methanolic extracts) on defoliation caused by Kraussaria angulifera on day 0, 2, 4, or 6 after treatment (cages evaluated 2 days after introduction of grasshoppers). ICRISAT, July–September 1988

Treatment	Average plant damage rating[a] when introduced on day[b]			
	0	2	4	6
UTC[c]	2.13	1.74	1.49	1.34
Neem	0.66[d]	1.01	1.18	1.09
Probability t	0.0001	0.0003	0.17	0.11
N	12	12	12	12

Legend: see Table 3.12

conclude from this that residual effects of neem kernel extract is less than 4 days. It is important to note that since our experimental design confined the insects, repellent effects could not be adequately tested. We speculate that in an open field, grasshoppers encountering neem-treated foliage would probably disperse without feeding. In experiments with the desert locust, all neem treatments significantly reduced feeding on treated plants ($P < 0.001$) for the entire 6-day duration of the test (Table 3.12). However, it is important to remember that all post-treatment defoliation indices are cumulative from day 0.

In the November 1988 experiments, neem kernel extract from various

Table 3.12: Feeding injury caused by the Desert Locust, Schistocerca gregaria, to millet seedlings treated with neem (aqueous and methanolic extracts), on days 2, 4, and 6 after treatment. ICRISAT, July–September 1988

Stage of insect development	Days post-treatment	Average plant damage rating[a]		Probability t
		Control	Neem	
Adult female	2	1.04	0.22[b]	0.0001
	4	1.22	0.14	0.0001
	6	1.28	0.36	0.0001
Adult male	2	0.76	0.18	0.0001
	4	1.06	0.19	0.0001
	6	1.40	0.39	0.0001
Nymph	2	1.52	0.21	0.0001
	4	1.85	0.38	0.0001
	6	1.68	0.53	0.0007

a Plant damage scored:
   0 = no feeding
   1 = one or two feeding scars
   2 = three to six feeding scars and no more than the terminal third of the leaf eaten
   3 = more than six feeding scars or more than 50 per cent of the leaf eaten
b All cages were evaluated two days after introduction of grasshoppers.
c UTC = untreated control
d Significance based on Student's t test

Table 3.13: **Average plant damage[a] caused by two grasshopper species to millet seedlings treated with neem (aqueous and methanolic extracts). Mozague, Niger, November 1988**

Treatment	Days post-treatment							
	1		2	3	4		6	
	OTU[b]	CSE	OTU	CSE	OTU	CSE	OTU	CSE
Diagourou	0.3a[c]	–	0.9a	–	1.3a	–	1.5a	–
Gotheye	0.5a	0.0a	0.6a	0.9a	0.9a	1.4a	1.0a	1.4a
Tsernawa	0.3a	–	0.8a	–	1.0a	–	1.0a	–
Mozague	–	0.3a	–	0.6a	–	1.4a	–	1.5a
Margosan-O	–	0.1a	–	0.6a	–	1.0a	–	1.9a
UTC[d]	1.8b	1.1b	2.4b	2.4a	2.8b	2.3a	3.0b	2.1a

a   Plant damage scored:
   0 = no feeding
   1 = one or two feeding scars
   2 = three to six feeding scars and no more than the terminal third of the leaf eaten
   3 = more than six feeding scars or more than 50 per cent of the leaf eaten
b   Species of grasshopper
   CSE = *Chrotogonus senegalensis*
   OTU = *Ornithacris turbida cavoisi*
c   Columns with the same letter are not significantly different (a=0.05), using Duncan's New Multiple Range Test
d   UTC = untreated control

sources significantly reduced feeding by both *C. senegalensis* and *O. t. cavoisi* for as long as 6 days on both millet and sorghum (Tables 3.13 and 3.14). In further experiments with neem drenches, significant reduction in defoliation by *O. t. cavoisi* was observed on days 4 and 7 (Table 3.15) after application indicating systemic activity. However, when neem kernel extract was applied as drenches to transplanted sorghum and millet seedlings, phytotoxicity was noted within 24 h, but plants began to recover by day 6. This application method needs further work to determine how long the systemic activity will continue and at what rate neem kernel extract can be applied without phytotoxicity.

Table 3.14: **Average plant damage[a] caused by *Chrotogonus senegalensis* to sorghum seedlings treated with aqueous extracts of neem kernel. Mozague, November 1988**

Neem source	Days post-treatment[b]			
	1	2	4	6
Diagourou	0.03a[b]	0.4a	1.4ab	1.9bc
Gotheye	0.0a	0.0a	0.5a	0.8a
Tsernawa	0.0a	0.3a	0.8a	1.3ab
UTC[c]	1.8b	2.3b	2.4b	2.5c

Legend: see Table 3.15.

Table 3.15: Defoliation of millet and sorghum seedlings by *Ornithacris turbida cavoisi*, when aqueous extracts of neem kernel are supplied as a soil drench. Average plant damage rating[a]

Neem source	Days post-treatment[b]					
	2		4		7	
	Millet	Sorghum	Millet	Sorghum	Millet	Sorghum
Diagourou	0.8a[b]	0.2a	1.0a	0.6a	1.4	1.2a
Gotheye	0.8a	0.0a	1.6a	0.0a	1.6a	1.2a
Tsernawa	1.4a	0.0a	1.2a	0.2a	1.4a	2.6b
Margosan-O	0.6a	0.2a	1.4a	0.8a	1.6a	2.2ab
UTC[c]	0.4a	0.8a	2.4a	2.0b	3.0b	2.8b

a Plant damage scored:
  0 = no feeding
  1 = one or two feeding scars
  2 = three to six feeding scars and no more than the terminal third of the leaf eaten
  3 = more than six feeding scars or more than 50 per cent of the leaf eaten
b Means within each column followed by the same letter are not significantly different
  (a=0.05), using Duncan's New Multiple Range Test
c UTC = untreated control

Phytotoxicity of neem sprays to millet and sorghum seedlings was determined in the 1987 and 1988 summer experiments, by spraying foliage with 4x and 2x concentrations of three local neem sources. No phytotoxicity was observed 24–48 h post-treatment. We also sprayed a cowpea, Vigna ungulicula (L.) Walp., field at the 3–4 leaf stage with two of the same local neem sources (1x) and no phytotoxicity was observed on this crop after 7 days.

Neem kernel extract from all local sources provided excellent protection of millet seedlings from grasshopper and locust feeding. Control on sorghum was not as consistent, but some of the grasshopper species tested are not usually sorghum feeders. Protection was not perfect, as some feeding did occur on treated plants, especially as the new growth appeared.

However, had the insects been free to disperse, the neem treatments might have provided adequate protection. In some experiments, it appeared that after some days of confinement the grasshoppers became sluggish and feeding diminished even on unprotected plants.

We have demonstrated that a wide variety of grasshoppers and locusts are easily controlled using simple, readily available technology. Neem kernel extract as a locally available crop protectant has great potential. Large-scale field experiments were beyond our capability in short term visits, but this probably needs to be done, if we are to move this technology from research to implementation. If neem kernel extract could be shown to be effective on high value vegetable crops and against a wider variety of pests, extension of this technology should be pursued vigorously. Implementation might be best promoted by establishing a series of grower-managed demonstration trials (AFGRO 1989).

Counter-season crops such as vegetables and transplanted-sorghum would seem ideal candidates for the application of this technology (Schmutterer and Hellpap 1988).

Notes

1. Field trials using neem solution on recession crops were conducted in late 1988 in the Hausa village of of Mozaque near the border with Nigeria. The entomological results supported the conclusions reached in the highly-controlled station research reported in this chapter. No socioeconomic data were systematically collected in Mozague. What is clear is that this is a rather isolated and very conservative village, which not only practices subsistence agriculture, but also conducts a lucrative trade in food crops, especially cowpeas and peanuts, with the Hausa who live across the border.
2. The spatial and social ambiguity of Songhay women is described by Jeanne Basilliat (1983). Although their labour complements, the cultural elaboration of gender differences does not define a corresponding significant political role for them. Thus, their interaction with visitors is rather tightly controlled.
3. The principal food crops grown in the Tera arrondissement are millet, sorghum, haricot or cowpea, corn, and sorrel. Peanuts and sesame are minor crops, which are intercropped with cereal grains. Two cucurbits, squash and calabash, are also intercropped with cereals. The calabash is not a source of food – it is used as a container or a musical instrument. Some rice is grown near the river in Mehanna. The major fruit-bearing trees are lemon, guava, mango, and papaya. Counter season gardens contain a mix of the following: peanuts, calabash, carrots, cabbage, squash, okra, lettuce, corn, manioc, cowpea, onion, sweet potato, peas, white, potato, tomato, eggplant, and pepper.

Acknowledgments

The research reported here was the result of the efforts of many professionally qualified individuals, in addition to the present authors. Those who participated in the socioeconomic studies included:

o Kimba Idrissa, historian, University of Niamey, Niger
o Aïssatou Souley, educator with Institut National de Documentation, Recherche et Animation Pédagogique, Niamey.

Those who contributed to the entomological studies included:

o Sani Adam, entomologist, Direction de la Protection des Végétaux du Ministère de l'Agriculture, Niamey
o Florence V. Dunkel, entomologist, Montana State University (formerly with the University of Minnesota)
o Habib Khoury, consulting entomologist, Montréal, Québéc
o David M. Noetzel, entomologist, University of Minnesota

Many others provided important and much appreciated assistance with various aspects of this project. We thank:

o Morris D. Lukefahr, cereal entomologist, ICRISAT, Sadore (for permitting us to share his field research facilities and equipment.)
o Phil Serafini, farm manager, ICRISAT, was also very gracious in providing resources and assistance.

In 1987, pulverised kernels of Niamey neem were provided by:

o Peter Reckhaus   (Deutsche Gesellschaft für Technische
o Christian Pantenius   Zusammenarbeit, Niamey)
o Peter Engels

Neem kernel extract was also provided by:

o Martin Jacobson   (USDA Agricultural Research Service
o Hiram Larew   Beltsvile, Maryland)

- J. D. Wharten Jr.   (USDA-ARS, Eastern Regional Research
- M. F. Kozempel   Centre Philadelphia, Pennsylvania)

In 1988, Margosan-O was provided, courtesy of:
- R. O. Larson,   Vikwood Botanicals, Inc., Sheboygan,
           Wisconsin

We also wish to thank the men and women of Mehanna, Dargol, Bellekoire, Diagourou, Mozague, and Tera for their hospitality and their contributions of time and information to this project.

4. The Lari Soils Project in Peru – A methodology for combining cognitive and behavioural research

*DAVID W. GUILLET, LOUANNA FURBEE,
JON SANDOR AND ROBERT BENFER[1]*

Introduction

ADVANCES IN CULTURAL anthropology generally come from one of three directions. First, anthropologists attempt to uncover cognitive aspects of an unfamiliar culture through the analysis of rules, plans, schemes, symbols and categories. Mental patterns may be unconscious and unformulated but capable of being discovered by posing the right questions, or conscious and explicit and the subject of ordinary conversation. Second, actual events and activities are observed and analysed in order to discover patterns of behaviour. Lastly, mental rules, plans, and values are compared with actual cultural behaviour to determine congruences, exceptions, and the rules for breaking the rules for behaviour.

Of the three, the relationship between cognitive and behavioural aspects of culture is the most problematic. While one expects some link between what people think they should do and what they actually do, the degree and character of the correspondence between cognitive rules and behaviour is the subject of much controversy and may vary depending on cultural sphere or context. Partly for these reasons, attempts at synthesis have been few and problem ridden (Chibnik 1980: 88). The debates, often vociferous, over the importance of mental versus material factors remain inconclusive.[2]

The aspect of the difficulty in assessing the correspondence which we wish to address in this paper is methodological. Cognitive and behavioural aspects of culture are approached through quite different lines of inquiry: the former through sophisticated and complex cognitive and linguistic procedures requiring considerable training; the latter through observation and often the mastery of specialised data-gathering techniques (Whiting and Whiting 1970).[3] Control of the subject matter and methodological procedures of fields such as psychology, agronomy, or astronomy may be essential to behavioural analysis. Combining mental and behavioural approaches to culture may, thus, place excessive demands on an individual researcher.

Pooling the specialised skills of several researchers offers a potentially constructive solution to the dilemma. While teamwork in sociocultural anthropology dates to at least the collaboration of Walter Baldwin Spencer and Frank Gillin in Southwestern Australia in 1896 (Stocking 1981: 78–79), its use today as a method is rare, particularly in comparison with archaeology. Part of the reason stems from difficulties intrinsic to teamwork in sociocultural anthropology. Training in data-gathering techniques and methods usually includes explicit or implicit exposure and socialisation into narrow theoretical orientations. Thus, training in cognitive and linguistic methods may be biased toward explications of culture which stress the role of mental over material factors. Training in the use of specialised observational techniques may pay only tip service to language and cognition. Incorporating investigators from each methodological tradition into a team may entail different interpretations attached to seemingly identical concepts, such as mind and culture, and quite distinct epistemological assumptions.

Different epistemological assumptions are a particularly intractable dimension of the problem since observational and interview data are usually considered to represent divergent ways of human knowing. It is well known that interview material, the product of linguistic discourse, is subject to the need of exegesis. It is less recognised that while actions can be observed through sensory perception, they are filtered through the conceptual and theoretical lenses of consultant and anthropological field worker producing the need for a different sort of exegesis. Another consideration is the need for cognitive and behavioural models to be constructed separately, lest an uncritical mixing makes it impossible to discern whether a given piece of information is the product of interview or of observation (Werner and Schoepfle 1987: 272–3). Lastly, when brought together, cognitive and behavioural models often lapse into poorly formulated, weak comparisons. Too often there is a failure to devise formal tests of the correspondence between cognitive and behavioural models.

In this chapter, we present a methodology for combining cognitive and behavioural research developed during the course of an interdisciplinary investigation of native Andean soil management. It involves teamwork, the construction of rule-based decision models using expert-system computer programs, and formal tests to assess the correspondence between the cognitive and behavioural models.

Cultural ecology and soil management

Cultural ecology is particularly appropriate for exploring the relation between cognition and behaviour, at issue in the recent emergence of ethnoecology, a reaction against the earlier relegation of cultural knowledge to a 'black box' (Ellen 1982: 204–235; Hardesty 1977: 215–243). Yet, ethnoecological studies rarely move beyond the description of folk categories. Studies that compare semantic organisation and rule sets with behaviour in the explanation of material provisioning are uncommon (Johnson 1974). These failings have led to criticisms that ethnoecological studies are unable thereby to capture the dynamics of traditional production systems (Brush, Carney and Huamán 1981).

This criticism applies with equal force to soil ethnoscience (Ellen 1982). While ecologically oriented studies have occasionally touched on native knowledge of soils (Rappaport 1984), research that focuses on the correspondences between folk knowledge of soils, soil management behaviour, and the prescriptions of western soil science is rare (see Ollier, Drover and Godelier 1971 and Williams and Ortiz Solorio 1981 for exceptions). Nonetheless, it is precisely in the domain of land use where it has been suggested that cognitive rules may most closely correspond to behaviour (Harris 1979: 271; Johnson 1974; Jochim 1981: 9).

The Colca Valley and the village of Lari

In order to address these and other questions, a multidisciplinary study focused on native Andean soil management was designed and carried out in Lari, a village of Quechua-speaking farmers in the Colca Valley in the highlands of the Peruvian Department of Arequipa. The Colca Valley is a region noted for extensive prehistoric agricultural terracing and has been the site of recent research on long term agrarian change (Denevan 1986). This research had found evidence of good soil management and agriculturally excellent soils since the prehistoric periods (Sandor 1987). Ethnographic fieldwork also suggested an unusually rich set of terms for classifying soils and a wide range of measures for soil management used by farmers in the region (McCamant 1986).

Fieldwork and the division of labour

Given the multidisciplinary nature of the problem and the need to combine cognitive and behavioural perspectives, field research was designed to be carried out simultaneously by a team, which included an ecological anthropologist, cognitive anthropologist, and soil scientist. Each investigator was familiar with the region having carried out research in or around it. This allowed several potential problems to be averted. Entry had been established, consultants identified, and logistical problems, such as housing and food, resolved. We turn now to a description of the division of labour in the fieldwork.

Folk models of soils and soils management

Standard ethnosemantic methods of anthropological linguistics and cognitive anthropology were employed in determining two folk models, the folk classification of soils (Furbee 1989a), and the cognitive rules of crop rotation (Furbee 1989b). Classical methods for the acquisition of knowledge are formal, well-documented, and well-tested (Frake 1961; Goodenough 1970; Young 1981). To help understand the underlying cognitive structure and the contribution of individuals to group knowledge, we used individual multidimensional scaling.

The classical methods of ethnosemantic study involve eliciting in the native language the names of a semantic domain (terms, in this case names of kinds of soil) and appropriate questions (frames, also in the native language) with which to learn culturally relevant information about organisation of the terms and questions. Terms are collected by asking a question in the native language such as 'What kinds of soils are there?' until no more terms are forthcoming. Additionally, elicited terms may be compared by the consultant using dyadic, triadic, or general sorting tasks to create comparative similarities among the terms. One proceeds from a minimum of external assumptions, and consultants largely determine relevant materials and comparisons for study.

Two kinds of consultants, primary and secondary, were used in this study. Ten primary consultants were consulted. They were bilingual (Quechua/Spanish) residents of Lari who helped with the design of survey protocols in Quechua and completed a variety of tasks for the study of semantic structures (for example, sorting). The ten primary consultants aided in the construction of the folk model of soil management, as well as in giving consultant exegesis of the results. The secondary consultants were also Lari residents and native speakers of Quechua; 21 were selected from the universe (n=237) of households in the community, a sampling frame of 8.8 per cent. Secondary consultants completed some, but not all of the tasks designed in consultation with primary consultants, and they did not all complete the same tasks. When the domain of soil names was exhausted, sorting tasks carried out by primary consultants were used to investigate the semantic organisation of the terms and the distinctive properties recognised for each.

To determine the soil taxonomy and variations in patterns of cognition of soils for inhabitants of the village of Lari, beliefs about the various types of soils were elicited from the primary consultants. What are the properties of the soil? What are appropriate uses for a soil type? If there are implicational conditions for certain soil use (or soil modification) decisions, what are they? Answers to inquiries such as these formed the bases of the questions used in a general, formal survey completed by all primary and five secondary consultants. Once relevant information about soil types was collected, these beliefs about soils, their uses, and their improvement, were cast as questions in Quechua about each of the named soil types. Those questions (frames) were formulated as yes/no questions in Quechua (e.g. Does ... need a lot of water?), back translated into Spanish to test whether they were indeed asking what the investigator wished, and tested to be certain that they were appropriate. A selection from them became the survey administered in Quechua (see Furbee 1989a for a copy of the survey questionnaire).

Three tasks were designed to help relate the folk classification of soils to the western scientific one. For the first, 13 samples of top soils were selected and identified by the soil scientist. These samples were then presented to 6 secondary consultants for identification in the folk classification. The second task involved having one primary consultant draw a map of the land holdings of the community and identify particular kinds of soils in each zone. This folk soils map (Furbee 1989a) was designed to be compared with the 'scientific' soils map prepared by the soil scientist (Sandor 1989). The third task involved a triadic sorting of a possible triples from 12 soil terms. That task was completed by the soil scientist, representing the Western classification system, and two of the primary informants, representing the folk classification system. Formal comparison of the two systems, using the results of the three tasks has been reported by Furbee and Sandor (1990).

Toward the end of the work on the classification of soils, the focus shifted to the elicitation of two rule-based folk decision models: one of folk soil classification as an aspect of soil management, the other of cognitive rules of crop rotation. These models were constructed in the fields using an expert system computer program (*see* below). For soil classification, rules were extracted by induction from a series of hypothetical cases elicited from consultants. For crop rotation, consultants were presented with hypothetical fields and asked to plan a soil management strategy for the following year. The rules we deduced were modelled as a backward-chaining expert system and then tested interactively with consultants.

Soil management and land-use

To the ecological anthropologist fell the task of constructing a rule-based behavioural model of soil management using standard observational techniques from ecological and economic anthropology (Guillet 1989a). To approach this task he obtained cases of soil management behaviour and farmer's exegesis of their behaviour in these cases. Farmers in this community own small fields scattered throughout the cultivated areas of flats and terraced slopes. These fields constituted the unit of analysis for the collection of cases of soil management. A survey instrument was constructed with the assistance of the primary consultants, pretested, and administered to the owners of a range of fields deemed representative of the major soil types encountered in the village. It contained questions on soil type, soil management practices for the current agricultural season and cropping practices for each of the five previous growing seasons for each field. To the extent that memory is imperfect, one would expect recent seasons to reflect actual behaviour, decisions as to cropping practices to grade into an ideal or modal pattern for the earlier seasons (D'Andrade 1974). Questions concerning soil management practices included, for example, the addition of dung, ash and chemical fertiliser, fallowing, and the cultivation of alfalfa. We collected information for each field on altitude, field type, area, distance from the village, the availability of water and yields, based on the ratio of harvest to seed, for the current (May–June 1987) harvest. The survey instrument was administered to 13 landowners and covered 22 fields.

We used open-ended questions to elicit farmer's logic for soil management procedures followed in their fields. These questions were triggered by the responses to the questions in the survey and by non-directed interviewing techniques. This approach allowed us to direct our inquiries to a specific field. The management of the soils in a field probably cannot be decomposed into sums of attributes each of which, taken independently, produced an element of the decision. Each field is a small ecological system in which a soil management decision is an attempt to maintain a key element of the system and to produce sustainable yields of a crop. Soils interact with other edaphic variables in systemic ways, and farmers often possess a tacit understanding of these interactions which can be drawn out through the interviewing process.

A rule-based behavioural model of soil management was built with data from the field survey and farmer's interviews (Guillet 1989a). This process began early in the fieldwork with a graphic prototype subsequently expanded and refined. After the fieldwork, data from the field survey were entered into an expert-system computer program and rules induced from it, producing a second prototype. Ensuing development of the expert system involved reconciling and combining the two prototypes, making it conform to the cultural logic of Lari farmers.[4]

Soil science

The soil scientist was charged with evaluating agricultural soils and their productivity from the perspective of 'Western' soil science. A related objective was to determine the characteristics and distribution of natural soils in the area and to study soil-geomorphic relationships in the Colca Valley. This objective is tied to the first in two ways. First, potentials and limitations of soils for agriculture are dependent on natural soil properties to varying degrees. Second, the natural soils provide a reference against which the major changes resulting from long-term agriculture and soil management in the region can be measured.

The methodology adopted to meet these two objectives included a dual sampling strategy based on the need to sample broadly enough to describe the total range of soils, but also to sample intensively in some representative sites to adequately characterise the composition and variability of important soils and the distribution of soils within farmer's fields.[5] To describe the range of soils, an 'extensive' survey was conducted which included all 22 of the fields visited with the ecological anthropologist and his 13 consultants. Most of the consultants took us to two different fields containing different soils. While the ecological anthropologist was interviewing the farmers, the soil scientist excavated the soil by auger near the middle of the field. A short description of each soil was made using standard soil survey methods (USDA-Soil Conservation Service 1981). A small sample (about 200–300 grams) from the agriculturally important 0–15 cm. depth was also collected from each site for laboratory analysis.

After completing 'extensive' samples from 10 widely distributed fields, conducting a reconnaissance survey around Lari during the first week of field work, and getting a sense for the types of soil recognised by Lari farmers, we designed an 'intensive' sampling phase to characterise major soil types more closely. One of the primary means by which Lari farmers distinguish soils is by texture – the relative amounts of sand, silt, and clay in the soil. Lari farmers also note rock fragment content as part of their textual classification. Because most of the soils were identified by Lari farmers as being either sandy *(acco),* clayey *(llink'i),* or intermediate *(allin hallpa,* which also implied the most productive, desirable type of soil), we decided to intensively sample soils in each of these three classes. Two 'intensive' samplings of each of the three soil types were conducted in widely distributed fields.

Laboratory analyses of soil samples, after the field period, evaluated soil properties relevant to present and potential productivity of currently farmed, fallowed, and abandoned land. Properties measured to assess tilth, water retention, water movement, and aeration included texture, bulk density, and available water capacity. Soil fertility includes organic carbon, total nitrogen, nitrates, total phosphorus, available phosphorus, carbonate, and pH (Sandor 1989).

Data on soil distribution in Lari were used in conjunction with an aerial photo series to prepare a detailed 1:17,000 soil map. This map is designed, in part, to be compared with the folk soil map described earlier.

Expert system implementation of rule-based models

Cognitive and behavioural aspects of soil management were formulated as rule-based decision models. Current formulations of rule-based models, based on natural decision-making, do not contain the implied tests of rationality that hindered earlier cross-cultural work. Lastly, rule-based models can be supplied with data from real or hypothetical cases of decisions which allows a more formal test of correspondence than other formulations such as interpretive models.

The rule-based cognitive and behavioural models in this project were represented as expert systems, formal, computer-based, models of decision-making in a well-defined bounded domain.[6] Expert systems have several advantages over other rule-based representations, such as matrices, flow-charts, and decision trees.

First, expert system programs are able to separate procedure from facts, which can be manipulated by a separate inference engine, based on first-order predicate calculus. The conceptual separation of procedural knowledge (propositions, functions, rules for combination of degrees of confidence, etc.) from factual knowledge gives expert systems the ability to closely mimic human reasoning in narrow domains. Rules-of-thumb, or heuristics, are the ways people use to simplify complex decisions; they can be incorporated into the expert system as procedural knowledge (Gladwin 1980; Quinn 1978; Tversky 1972).

Second, expert systems accommodate varying levels of certainty that accompany outcomes by attaching confidence factors, quantitative measures indicating the degree of confidence that a conclusion is valid, to conclusions in rules. For example, one expert system software program used in the project indicates confidence factors by an integer between 0 and 100. A confidence factor of 75 assigned to the conclusion of a rule signifies that the conclusion is drawn with 75 per cent confidence.[7] Consultants can assign this subjective weighting. Confidence factors are then combined and computed during the course of the running of the program. While a single incorrect or sub-optimal choice in decision tree representations will lead the user inexorably down a path farther and farther from where they should be going, this is not the case with even simple expert systems.

Third, expert systems satisfy criticisms of ethnocentric observations deriving from semantic interference, by using actual cases of decision-making supplied by consultants to induce prototypes, and then submitting the refined and expanded model to consultants for their approval. For example, one of the elements of the construction of the expert system model of soil management behaviour is the assignment of confidence factors for rules. One can check to see if the confidence factor given in the final conclusion, under various combinations of circumstances, agrees with the intuition of a consultant. The ability to construct an expert system with a laptop computer in the field and teach a consultant to run it and supply a running commentary, as occurred in the construction and evaluation of one of the expert systems in Lari, enhances considerably the validity of the model, meeting suggestions of submitting all observations to review by consultants (Whiting and Whiting 1970; Werner and Schoepfle 1987: 260).

Fourth, many expert system programs have the capability to backward chain – to reason from a possible outcome to the factors necessary and sufficient to produce the outcome. This is a reverse procedure from reasoning characteristic of other decision representations, such as a flow chart or decision tree, but it probably corresponds more closely to actual goal-directed human reasoning.

Lastly, expert systems can now be constructed with software 'shells' running on microcomputers rather than programmed with a complex, declarative, language such as LISP or PROLOG on a powerful mainframe computer. Translating 'common sense' reasoning, often extracted from anecdotes and case material, into modular decision rules involves long and painstaking trial-and-error. Expert system software shells reduce this effort considerably with troubleshooting capabilities to check for missing, logically inconsistent, and redundant rules. Expert systems models can be immediately tested and debugged by the field worker, in the field, interactively with a consultant. The increase in validity, reliability, and speed in construction of a rule-based model is significant.

In our implementation of expert systems, we have attempted to account for individual differences. Some domains of folk knowledge inhere not in one or a few specialists, the usual case for application of expert systems until now, but rather in the individual. It is the individual who must manage his or her specific plots using his or her personal knowledge. Adding the individuals as a feature permits evaluation of the characteristics of individual differences. While some differences are obviously due to errors, others are explicable given knowledge of holdings, length of time in Lari, and other idiosyncratic factors.

Comparison of models

The last step is to test correspondences between the cognitive and behavioural models. Competing rule-based models of the same cultural domain help to isolate congruences and divergences allowing a high degree of comparability. The research produced three rule-based models represented as expert systems: a cognitive model of soil classification (Furbee 1989a), a cognitive model of the crop-rotation component of soil management (Furbee 1989b), and a behavioural model of soil management (Guillet 1989a). In addition, one can test correspondences between folk soil classification and Western soil classification and between cognitive mapping of soil spatial relationships and Western geomorphological and soil distribution mapping (Furbee and Sandor 1990).

Tests of these correspondences indicate a considerable degree of fit between certain of the models. Two examples exemplify this. In the domain of folk soil classification, many characteristics with which Lari residents classify soils tend to reduce the meaning dimensions to texture and productivity, and in fact, the textural quality of a soil probably implies production properties. Certainly, texture pertains to water-holding properties. It is also involved with the ease of working soils, since soil hardness is an important negative characteristic which consultants often mentioned treating by adding ashes to make the soil more soft *(blanda)* (Furbee 1989a). The emphasis on texture in folk soil classification fits closely with its role in Western soil classification (Sandor 1989).

Comparisons of the cognitive model of the crop-rotation component of soil management and the crop choice subset of the behavioural model of soil management indicate a high degree of commonality in that soil management emerges as a pragmatic consequent to crop choice, rather than an independent decision process with soil states as abstract goals. Where differences occur in the structure of the models, they involve the priority placed in the role of soil class: the cognitive model places soil class as an antecedent to crop choice while the behavioural model gives predominance to rules-of-thumb involving field type with soil class being rather unimportant in crop choice (Guillet 1989a, 1989b; Furbee 1989a). Research into possible correspondences between the cognitive map of soil spatial relationships and the geomorphological and soil distribution maps is currently being conducted and will provide additional tests of correspondences between and among the cognitive, behavioural, and Western soil science models.

Discussion

The methodology presented in this paper can be applied to the comparison of cognitive and behavioural cultural domains that involve rule-based decision processes. Rule-based decision processes are characterised by many independent, nontrivial, states relative to the number of actions. These would include, for example, dynamic adaptations to environmental settings (Orlove 1980), medical treatment decisions (Young 1981) and the class of problems covered by formal economic anthropology (Barlett 1980). Decisions in which a few tenets serve to embody much of the required knowledge are less appropriate to this methodology. Examples of inappropriate problems would be those solved through intuition, metaphor, and analogy.

Teamwork and the separation of cognitive and behavioural culture

The research design used a distinction between cognitive and behavioural culture as the organising vehicle for the division of labour. Indiscriminate mixing makes it impossible to discern whether a given piece of information is the product of interview or of observation (Werner and Schoepfle 1987: 272–3). During the research, the tightly drawn boundaries between cognitive and behavioural models proved difficult to maintain. First, eliciting native categories of soils and soil management rules and plans was demanding without reference to specific illustrative cases. In abstract discussions of soil management, farmers preferred to use a specific field to illustrate a principle and a visit to the field often helped to clarify the discussion. This was expected; when confronted with a new situation, one often will recall a similar situation experienced in the past and reason by analogy to apply that experience to the present. Similarly, understanding farmer's classification of the soils in their fields and explanation of their management practices was difficult without some knowledge of their linguistic and cognitive patterns.

The maintenance of a strict division between cognitive and behavioural culture, while laudable from the perspectives of an efficient division of fieldwork labour and a safeguard of the 'purity' of the resulting models, thus proved difficult. We resolved the problem as follows. Whenever it came up, we decided to go back to our basic starting points: fields for the cultural ecologist and soils scientist and language for the cognitive anthropologist. Fields were illustrative cases for the cognitive anthropologist and were used to elicit cognitive distinctions among soil categories and soil management rules. For the ecologist anthropologist and soil scientist, however, fields were the units of analysis from which were induced soil management behavioural rules and practices. Contradictions and confusion over soil terms which emerged at the level of field observations were cleared up by a dialogue among the members of the team.

Teamwork and the translation problem

One of the most intractable difficulties in fieldwork is the 'translation' problem: lack of full competency in the language of the 'other.' To be competent in this sense, a field worker must be able to discriminate among phonemic and phonetic linguistic differences and to decenter, achieve the closest equivalence between the native language and the language of the field worker . Research of the kind described here compounds the problem. Beyond the cultural differences between the field workers and Quechua-speaking consultants, there are significant disciplinary and sub-disciplinary differences of a sub-cultural nature among the members of the fieldwork team.

The skills required for achieving translating competence are well-known and explicit (Werner and Schoepfle 1987), yet team members may vary widely in the degree to which they command them. Linguists and cognitive anthropologists receive the specialised training to make these distinctions and to be able translators. Ecological anthropologists rarely receive more· than minimal language training. There are no provisions in the usual professional training of an agronomist for acquiring linguistic skills beyond a reading knowledge of a European language.

The inclusion of a cognitive anthropologist in the team provided a solid control over the translation problem. Other team members have access to linguistic analysis of the difficult phonetic issues that arise in local language use. The translation process can be expedited and the quality enhanced. The soil scientist can interact through the ecological anthropologist with the consultant and the ethnoscientist can monitor the translation process. Certainly, the difficulties of translating between anthropological perspectives of team members in the field invite speculation that one might achieve equivalent advantage if each party were to act independently. Results of the two (or more) studies could be compared later as a separate exercise. There are several reasons to reject such a suggestion.

First, as previously mentioned, the very independence of such studies leads to results that are difficult to relate because the units of analysis may be incomparable. That non-comparability lies at the heart of the translation problem and is best confronted early. More positively, the exercise of seeking accommodation early in the study, both in the design phase and in the execution of the project in the field, rewards participants by permitting them to share insights from the different approaches. Research within a single tradition is constrained by the tenets of that framework. There are cognitive constraints on the investigator comparable to the familiar cultural ones attributed to Whorfian effects. Investigators representing cognitive and materialist traditions will tend to seek different sorts of data and relate those findings to models derived from different assumptions about the character of cause and explanation. In effect, they will be treating of slightly different realities – for us, the realities were psychological and behavioural, respectively.

For other anthropologists, 'reality' might lie in the social world, or material artifacts, or some other area. Certainly, no anthropologist would claim that only one such realm is sufficient, but the claims of theoretical approaches assure that one will predominate in our models. We tend to begin from that one, and consider data relevant to it as primary. Beginning with the one, we then extend to other realms of inquiry, for example from cognition to behaviour, or the reverse. A good ethnographer of one sort probably obtains information similar to that acquired by a good ethnographer who adheres to a different canon. The two may start at different points, but they eventually discover the same kinds of information. In a team such as we suggest here, members approach the same problem from different points of view, depending on their theoretical biases, but they tend to converge rapidly in data gathering as they proceed. As they work, their task is aided by input from colleagues who have begun at different points. Those colleagues will have collected data early in the study as primary data that team members will see as important to them as secondary information. Since translation has been maintained throughout the study, data will be in a form that all can readily use, thus accelerating the investigative process. In addition, persons working from different points of view of course tend to find slightly different kinds of information relevant, and their sharing of these observations then greatly enriches each others work.

Finally, and perhaps most important, the inherent advantage of convergence of results from different approaches is the cross validity check the effort provides. In problem-oriented research such as our soils study, a result arrived at independently from two or more perspectives convinces more readily. The methodology proposed here incorporates such a test of cross validity.

Notes

1. The research reported here was supported by the National Science Foundation BNS-8615807 (David Guillet, principal investigator; Louanna Furbee, co-principal investigator).
2. Attempts to use formal, theoretically-generated models to predict observed behaviour have similarly failed to meet earlier promises. When this occurs, anthropologists usually fall back on qualitative, post-hoc explanations (see Johnson 1980).

3. Participant-observation and, in general, ethnographic method have come under attack from a number of directions in recent years. From the interpretive and reflexive camps comes criticism of the naive assumption that a short 1–2 year field period is sufficient to acquire cultural knowledge in depth, the assertion that a minimal language competency is sufficient to solve complex 'translation' problems, and the adequacy of visual interpretation of behaviour, all leading to an assault on the mantle of 'authority' worn by the ethnographer (Watson 1987; Clifford 1983). From cognitive anthropology and related endeavours comes a startling disclosure that about half of what informants report concerning past events and behaviour is probably incorrect in some way (Bernard, Killworth, Kronenfiel and Sailer 1984). Criticisms, such as these, suggest two responses: outright rejection of ethnographic method and, in particular, participant-observation, a retreat from the rich traditions of field work, the hallmark of sociocultural anthropology, on the one hand, and attempts, on the other, to improve the enterprise by focusing on the construction of reliable, valid, and accurate primary data (Bernard *et al.* 1986). The methodology espoused in this paper was devised in the spirit of the latter.

4. Procedures used for the development of the expert system are discussed in Guillet (1989).

5. See Sandor (1989) for a description of the evolution of the methodology that was eventually adopted for the field work.

6. See Guillet (1989a) and Furbee (1989a).

7. This is not the same as a 75 per cent statistical probability; rather, it represents the relative degree of confidence that a conclusion is valid.

5. Indigenous Soil Classification Systems in Northern Zambia

CAROL KERVEN, HILDE DOLVA AND RAGNHILD RENNA

Introduction

AGRICULTURAL ON-FARM and extension must be based on a knowledge of local soils to be useful to the farming clientele. In Zambia, as elsewhere in the Third World, highly technical methods for describing and classifying soils have been developed, which, however, often have little practical value and are therefore rarely used for research and extension aimed at small-scale peasant farmers. There are several reasons why this is the case. First, the criteria used by technical scientists for classifying the soil may not match the criteria considered by farmers – the latter being concerned with the soil's usefulness for cropping. Second, sampling and analysis required to classify a soil using conventional technical methods are often too laborious, time-consuming, and costly for applied ('on-farm') researchers and extensionists to carry out. Third, researchers and extensionists may lack the skills and training required to identify and analyse a soil in the field. Fourth, interpretation of conventional soil classification manuals may be beyond the technical ability of some researchers and extensionists.

It was recently noted in Zambia's Northern Province that for all these reasons, very little, if any, attempt to relate different soils and their characteristics to local farming practices was made by applied researchers and extensionists in their work with peasant farmers. At the same time it was noted that considerable soils field research had been undertaken and was still being undertaken by technical scientists attached to the Soil Survey Unit of the Ministry of Agriculture and Water Development (now Ministry of Agriculture and Cooperatives). This data source was simply not being used by those concerned with the subsistence and semi-commercial peasant farming population. Finally, it was noted, in the course of anthropological field research being conducted as part of an applied on-farm agricultural research project (Adaptive Research Planning Team [ARPT], Misamfu Regional Research Station, Kasama, Northern Province, Zambia), that members of the peasant farming communities had a breadth of knowledge and opinions about the local soils they used for farming. This was not a new finding – in the 1930s vernacular soil terms and indigenous knowledge on soils had been recorded both by an anthropologist (Richards 1939) and an ecologist (Trapnell 1953).

A curious situation has occurred in which two quite distinct and unrelated systems for describing soils coexist but are unknown to each other, and neither is being used by the agents for agricultural development. Clearly, farmers, soil scientists and agriculturalists have information on soils of value to each other; the problem is to transfer the information from each group to the others. It was therefore proposed to carry out a joint study involving farmers, social scientists, soil scientists and agriculturalists to collect information on indigenous terms, descriptions and uses of local soils, and to compare this information to that available from technical soils research in Zambia.

This research program has evolved into several phases, the first two of which are reported here. As may be expected with any unconventional, multidisciplinary research, the program has met with opposition and criticism in some quarters, and has also changed its focus since beginning in 1987. A major challenge has been to gain acceptance by some local Zambian scientists of the validity of an indigenous knowledge system regarding soils. Perhaps this notion was resisted because the existence of an indigenous classification system was perceived as inimical to the adoption of the technical classification system by agricultural researchers.

More fundamentally, acceptance of an indigenous system, as articulated by uneducated peasant farmers, seemed to question the scientific credentials of formally educated local scientists. Furthermore, the indigenous system is still very imperfectly recorded and understood, and much more research is required. Questions about the validity of data on the indigenous system were therefore raised and hotly debated. However, these challenges have highlighted the need for soil scientists, social scientists, farmers, extensionists and agriculturalists to create a bridge between the discrete systems of soil classification in Zambia. Until the different knowledge about soils can be transmitted between farmers and technical scientists, (and this can only happen when more conclusive data are available) members of these groups will not be able to communicate effectively about the soil upon which agriculture is based.

Research on indigenous soil classification in Northern Province, Zambia

A multidisciplinary field program was essential to the research objectives, which were initially to:

o collect vernacular terms, descriptions and uses of soils used by farmers;
o determine the criteria used by farmers to identify a soil;
o compare the technical and indigenous soil classification systems;
o test the hypothesis that farmers' indigenous classification systems were non-hierarchical, based on contextual and definitive features of soil and landscape, and that this system could be correlated to the technical Zambian soil classification system.

The first phase of field research consisted of several case studies in communities located within different agro-ecological zones of Zambia's Northern Province. These case studies used anthropological interviewing techniques to elicit local knowledge about soils and micro land systems exploited by farmers in each community (Kerven and Sikana 1988). These studies were part of a diagnostic study of farming systems and production constraints undertaken for a farming systems research project (ARPT), and revealed an extensive local knowledge of soil variation and of the responses of the various local crops to different soils. As a result, it was felt by the ARPT social scientists that interpretation of data from on-farm agronomic trials and extension demonstrations being implemented by other ARPT professionals could benefit by using farmers' local knowledge on soils.

Crop performance was clearly site-sensitive. Farmers selected field sites according to soil characteristics which, in their experience, were particularly suited to individual crops. Moreover, on-station soil productivity research in Zambia's northern region (a high rainfall area) , which had been carried out for the past decade, could become more relevant to the client group by replicating on-station trials on similar soils to those selected by farmers. In this event, research on soil productivity could investigate more closely the soil–crop interactions already noted by the farmers, rather than siting trials on 'bench-mark' soils as classified under the technical system.

The second phase of the field research was broader in scope. It consisted of detailed data collection at five sample sites representing different major soil and land regions within the Northern Province of Zambia. The study was conducted by a team of agriculturalists, soil surveyors and social scientists drawn from the Soil Productivity Research Project (SPRP), the Soil Survey Unit and the Adaptive Research Planning Team (ARPT), all under the Research Branch of the Ministry of Agriculture and Water Development, in collaboration with the Agricultural University of Norway (Dolva, Mwale, Renna and Simute 1988).

Briefly, the research at this phase involved comparing technical analysis of indigenously named soils with the farmers' own evaluations of these soils. This was done by digging auger pits to a depth of 1.5 m, followed by chemical and physical laboratory analysis to correlate these data with farmers' statements about the soils. The results of this research phase are discussed later, but overall it revealed little correlation between soils as classified by the Zambian soil series technical method and those as defined by farmers in the indigenous classification (Dolva and Renna 1989).

Both the researchers and government soil and agricultural scientists concurred, after the second phase, that the research objectives and scope should be expanded in a third phase of field work. It was agreed to increase the number of sample soil observations and the number of farmers interviewed per site in order to validate the findings and to be able to generalise the use of an indigenous classification system to the northern region as a whole. In particular, any practical application of indigenous soil terms by researchers and extensionists in carrying out work with local farmers needed to have an adequate data base.

The new objective of the third research phase was to produce a Field Guide Handbook, listing all vernacular soil terms (including the different language groups occurring in the region), the chemical and physical properties of these locally named soils, and finally, the soil-crop interactions both from farmers' and technical scientists' perspectives. This third phase is currently being implemented by the Soil Surveyor for Northern Province and several social scientists from the Adaptive Research Planning Team. The Field Guide Handbook will provide a reference for applied on-farm agricultural work, which combines for the first time the indigenous and technical knowledge systems regarding soils in Northern Zambia.

The third phase began with a sample survey of farmers participating in ARPT on-farm agronomic trials, located in six distinct agro-ecological zones. The farmers were asked to describe the soils they had selected for different crops, then to comment on the suitability of the soil for each crop on fertility indicators before and after fallowing, and lastly to describe vegetation associated with each locally distinguished soil type. The main purpose of this survey was to link ARPT agronomic trial results with soil conditions as viewed by farmers on specific sites, without having to use technical soil analysis methods. A second purpose was to examine the pattern of fallowing in relation to particular soil types, cropping histories and vegetation species, as part of a longer-term joint study on soil fertility monitoring and management being carried out by the Soil Productivity Research Project (SPRP).

The nature of the indigenous classification system

Farmers identify soils in Zambia's northern region along several axes of a classification system, the primary axis being that of land systems comprising microecological zones, typically on a slope. Since settlements are usually within walking distance of a stream or river, cultivation occurs along valley bottoms, slopes, and on uplands or crests associated with river valleys. Cropping systems depend on the specialised use of different parts of the terrain, in relation to drainage patterns and soil changes along the slope.

An illustration of this system of land and soil classification in relation to agriculture is from one of the case studies (Kerven and Sikana 1988). Farmers in one community use two dimensions, slope and predominant vegetation, to describe the their land systems. From these two dimensions, two main land systems are identified, namely an upland forest zone *(mulundu/mpanga)* and an open-wooded valley zone *(chipiya/mumana)*. The soils of the upland area are described as sandy, light soils which are 'hungry' (requiring fertilisers), with other soils described as red and clayey or again, other soils which are gravelly and heavy, dry up quickly but are more fertile than the sandy light soils. The soils of the slopes and plains, in contrast, are designated by farmers as clayish, dark in colour and more fertile than the upland soils. Small pockets of an especially fertile dark soil occur within the plains area.

Present-day cropping patterns within these two land systems reflect the limitations and advantages offered by each type of soil, as well as reflecting recent technological and economic changes at the national level in Zambia. The settlements within this community lie along the valley crest, at the junction of the two land systems. The hinterland, in the more thickly forested upland, is reserved for the slash-and-burn system for cultivation of finger millet and beans.

Farmers prefer not to use the heavier soils for the finger millet subsistence crop, but instead, since the introduction of a 'technical package' involving cultivation of hybrid maize with fertiliser as a cash crop, have begun growing maize on the heavier, more fertile valley soils. These richer soils were avoided before the introduction of the hybrid maize cash crop package. They are harder to cultivate and their greater fertility leads to thick growth of grass and weeds, which farmers view as the major limiting factor due to the labour required for weeding. The lighter, less fertile sandy soils of the forest, on the other hand, while not fertile enough for maize, are suitable for finger millet and beans, with the enhanced fertility and need for weeding eliminated through the effect of burning in the densely wooded upland area.

The indigenous classification system briefly outlined here is typical of the northern region of Zambia, in that a matrix of factors is considered by the farmers in identifying and selecting different soils for particular crops. Soils are viewed in relation to drainage, associated vegetation, crop suitability, labour constraints, available technology, and proximity to settlements.

A second aspect of the indigenous soil classification system is the farmers' method of naming and describing individual soils. Here one must distinguish analytically between the names versus descriptors used by farmers to refer to soils. Names are terms used to identify or label a particular soil type, whereas descriptors may either be used in place of a specific name, or as qualifiers to a name. Thus, farmers call a certain soil *nkanka*, by which they refer to an upland red clayey fertile soil, defined by its red colour. *Nkanka* is preferred for cereals and some legumes and, indeed, for most of the crops, due to its fertility. Technical observations on this named soil were largely uniform and thus corroborated farmers' descriptions (Dolva and Renna 1989). The term *nkanka* is also used in association with descriptive terms translating as sandy, really red, big, small, and moldable (in the hands), to refer to what farmers may view as subsets or variations of *nkanka* soil.

Some descriptive terms, however, such as red and sandy, are also used as the sole referents for other non-*nkanka* soils. Thus, in the farmers' terminology *nkanka* soils are also sometimes sandy but not all sandy soils are necessarily *nkanka*. In contrast, an important widely-occurring group of soils are termed as sandy *(muchanga)*, with various qualifiers added by the farmers such as fine, mixed with black or hard soil, dusty and small. Variation of properties within the sandy-named *muchanga* group is wide on *some* technical criteria (such as colour and chemical properties) but uniform on texture (sandy loam) and drainage (well drained) (Dolva and Renna 1989).

From this evidence we can conclude that farmers primarily consider the definitive features, *from their perspective*, in naming or describing a soil. Some soils in the farmers' experience are sufficiently discrete in their visible proper-ties to warrant an exclusive name, such as *nkanka*. Other soils merge under a general characteristic such as sandy *(muchanga),* but with significant visible variations which constitute subsets of all sandy soils – such as particle size (hence, 'dusty', 'coarse', 'small', 'fine' used as qualifiers to separate the classes of *muchanga*). These qualifiers are important as a means of identifying poorer quality from better quality sandy soils, from the farmer's viewpoint.

The lack of a comprehensive taxonomic hierarchy in the indigenous system is clear. Farmers do not necessarily group soils according to logical subsets but according to the soil's most significant and empirical features from a farming perspective. In particular, many farmers were able to provide detailed informa-tion on how a specific soil performed according to the various crops planted on that soil, and during, as well as, after fallowing. In the example just given, many of the soils named as *muchanga* (with qualifiers) would, technically, be differen-tiated on the basis of colour and chemical properties into sub-groups, but in this class farmers have 'lumped' categories together which share the overriding char-acteristic of having a sandy texture. Texture alone would not be a sufficient cri-terion for distinguishing a separate soil type in the technical classification sys-tem.

Conclusions

An outline has been presented of how a research program on indigenous soil classification systems in Northern Zambia has developed as part of a larger set of research programs on soil and agriculture aimed at small-scale peasant farm-ers. To date, some 73 different types of soil named in the vernacular languages have been recorded and analysed. These 73 terms could probably be combined into about 27 major soil groups, not all of which are used for cultivation (Dolva and Renna 1989). Samples of each named soil type have been tested using stan-dard laboratory techniques. A low degree of correlation with the official Zam-bian Soil Series classification on most indices was obtained. This indicates that the indigenous criteria for classifying a soil type differ radically from the techni-cal criteria.

Reasons for this divergence in criteria can be summarised as follows. First, farmers mainly consider topsoil in describing a soil, while soil scientists use sub-soil and parent material as one criterion for classification. Second, farmers judge their soils empirically, while soil surveyors identify soils deductively based on predetermined indices. Third, farmers consider limiting factors such as hard-ness, stoniness, and presence of weeds in assessing soils; these factors are not included in conventional soil classification, but are considered in land evaluation studies. Soil classification is a contentious subject, but as one soil surveyor has remarked, 'There is no point in...defining classes [of soils] that do not correspond to the differences which the farmer or other users perceive to be important.' (Butler 1980: 9).

It is to discover what these differences are that led to research on indigenous soil classification systems in northern Zambia. Agricultural researchers and extensionists were not only unable to communicate with farmers about their soils, lacking a common terminology, but were unaware of what farmers viewed as important differences in the properties of the soils they selected for particular crops. The ultimate objective of the research outlined here is to facilitate communication between farmers and scientists by interposing the indigenous and technical bodies of knowledge, following the advice of the ecologist Trapnell who first recorded indigenous terms for land and soil in Zambia during the 1930s: '...it may be held that improvements in African agriculture are likely to have their best prospect of general adoption where it is possible to build on the foundations of the existing system or on what is best in their practice.'

6. Indigenous Knowledge Systems and Agro-forestry Projects in the Central Hills of Nepal[1]

ERIC P. RUSTEN AND MICHAEL A. GOLD

Introduction

PLANNING FOR AGROFORESTRY projects, as for all development efforts, generally involves several basic activities, including:

- identification and definition of the problem(s);
- collection, organisation, and interpretation of information on project population, their biophysical, agricultural, and socio-political environments, their problem(s), and possible solutions;
- decisions about what actions should be taken to address the problem, and what goals need to be achieved;
- design of a project to achieve the desired goals;
- identification of strategies and methods for mid-course project modification; and
- establishment of monitoring and evaluation procedures.

Of these activities, the information component, specifically the importance of incorporating an understanding of indigenous knowledge systems[2] into project plans will be the focus of this paper. With reliable and appropriate information, there exists the potential to develop an accurate understanding of the problems, needs, and socioeconomic characteristics of a target population. In addition, research on the indigenous knowledge systems of a rural society can help project planners learn about indigenous technologies involved in the management of natural resources, and understand how people perceive and conceptualise their biophysical and socio-political environments. Information concerning different development options can then be integrated with extent knowledge systems to better address the identified needs and problems of the developing community.

The high value that planners place on reliable and appropriate information in the planning process is partially attributable to its relative scarcity, and the high cost and difficulty of acquiring, analysing, and applying it. An examination of the chronology of the diagnosis and design activities for the Kathama agroforestry project in Kenya, as presented by Duchhart, Steiner and Bassman (1989), is further testament to the value of information in agroforestry planning. The process of generating this information addresses several interrelated issues:

- What information is needed and obtainable?
- How should this information be collected?
- How should raw data be analysed and presented?
- How will the final information product be used?
- What financial and time constraints impinge on this phase of the planning process?

The decisions about what information is needed and how it should be collected are often overly predefined and limiting, and not based on the information needs of the project or on the character of the population and area under investigation. This may immediately result in a loss of reliability and completeness of collected data and, in turn, lead to a reduction in learning and understanding about the project population and environment.

This may also result in lost opportunities for involving members of local populations in the planning process. We are not suggesting that structured parameters for research and data collection should not be used. We are suggesting that flexible approaches to research and data collection be used; flexibility that reflects the general lack of understanding of the societies and environments in which an intervention is planned.

One major problem with formal surveys is that the meanings ascribed to terms and concepts in survey questions often differ widely between the researcher and the respondents. The following question regarding trees, drawn from a forestry survey used in Nepal, will help illustrate this concern:

It is common for formal household-level surveys to be used as a preferred means of collecting information and data on the character and attitudes of project populations. Problems associated with cross-cultural surveys are well-documented, and when surveys are improperly used, the accuracy and validity of data collected using this method with rural populations in low income countries are open to debate (Whyte 1977; Hill 1984; Fisher 1987). Additionally, the disadvantages associated with formal surveys are often compounded by using survey instruments that have been 'borrowed' from other projects, regions, or countries, in place of carefully constructing a customised instrument designed to meet specific needs of the research at hand .

Trees owned by the household (HH)

Types of trees	Number of trees	Number of trees planted by HH members
Fruit		
Fodder		
Fuelwood		
Construction timber		
Bamboo		
Other (specify)		

This question assumes that the different terms and concepts present, when properly translated into the local language, would mean the same thing to researcher and respondents. However, can it be assumed that all concepts present in this questionnaire have equivalent meanings to everyone? For example, what defines a 'tree'? Does this definition include seedlings, shrubs, vines, or bushes? Would both dead and living trees be counted? Is ownership of trees a straightforward universal concept for all societies? How is a household defined? What makes a tree a fodder or a fuelwood tree? Is bamboo a tree, or a grass? Can trees that are used to build tools, beehives, or seasonal sheds be classified as construction timber trees?

Beside careful consideration of what needs to be learned and what techniques and methods should be used for the data collection, the issue of local participation in this process must also be considered. It is inappropriate to limit participation of indigenous populations in the planning process to that of 'respondents.' A sincere effort should be made to cultivate more meaningful participatory roles for residents. However, this is much easier said than done. One possible reason for this difficulty is, as an official in the Nepalese Department of Forestry put it: 'They [local people] are so difficult to work with.

This comment reveals two important concepts. First, development workers often feel that the responsibility for the difficulty of improving local participation in planning and development lies with the local population. Second, planners and development workers do not often understand indigenous populations and their sociophysical environment well enough to communicate with them on their own terms. It seems far easier to expect peasants to learn to operate in our world – to leave the problems and difficulties of cross-cultural understanding and communication to rural farmers.

The attitudes and orientation of people involved in the decision making and planning process towards these issues will influence significantly the character of an agroforesty intervention, and its potential for success. As many planners have received most of their training from formal 'Western' educational systems,[3] it is logical to assume that their information and planning approach will be biased by a Western orientation. In fact, the basic concept of development, or directed change, on which the development planning process is based, has emerged from and is based on Western knowledge systems.

Despite the rhetoric and sincere attempts to include 'grassroots' participation in planning of development projects, planned and directed change efforts are consistently dominated by Western systems of categorisation, definitions, and classifications. It is not uncommon for planners to assume that indigenous non-Western knowledge systems are either non-existent or very simplistic in nature and scope. Consequently, these biases may contribute to the formulation of an inappropriate and ineffective project (Dove 1984).

For agroforestry development activities to be more successful, it is essential that planners respect and cultivate an understanding of indigenous knowledge systems. They should also test their own assumptions, definitions, and understandings about problems and solutions against the local systems of knowledge and understanding. Planners should likewise foster the attitude that the difficulties of working with indigenous people be viewed as opportunities for project success rather than as constraints and impediments that need to be overcome. Furthermore, it is unrealistic to expect entire project populations to understand the Western knowledge systems and models on which development efforts are based, and to understand all the cultural characteristics and assumptions of the outsiders involved in a project. This burden rests with the outsiders, who must accept the responsibility for developing an understanding of the local system from an insider's (emic) point of view.

Indigenous knowledge systems and agroforestry

As noted in the literature, traditional agroforestry historically precedes experimental agroforestry and agroforestry development projects. As such, it is a strategy and principle already well-accepted by many agricultural groups around the world. Many rural societies have been experimentally developing different forms of agroforestry for centuries (Conklin 1957; Salisbury 1962; Radwanski and Wickens 1967; Rappaport 1971; Johnson 1972; Wilken 1977; Rambo 1981; Rice 1981; Advisory Committee on the Sahel 1983; Nations and Kromer 1983; Olofson 1983; Clay 1988). These indigenous agroforestry systems are thus potentially rich sources of knowledge about the cultivation of woody perennials in different time and space arrangements with annual crops. For this reason alone, research on indigenous knowledge systems is warranted. However, in addition to knowledge about such ecological relationships, research on indigenous knowledge systems is also important because it can help us develop an understanding of indigenous perception and cognition of the environment.[4] The critical need to incorporate an understanding of indigenous agroforesty into the planning process is clearly summarised by Olofson (1983: 150): 'Quite a literature [exists on how] so-called Western Scientific agriculture has been applied in the tropics without full understanding of the ecological context, leading to disastrous consequences. To divorce the concept of agroforestry from its indigenous roots is to unfairly underplay (1) its historical significance as the precursor to modern agroforestry, (2) the goodness of fit which often obtains between indigenous agroforestries and their environments, and (3) the potential contribution of indigenous agroforestry to modern agroforestry in terms of part or even whole models of agroforestry systems.'

Indigenous knowledge systems research has the potential of providing a variety of benefits to the planning process, resulting in opportunities for enhancing project success. One commonly cited benefit involves the 'discovery' of factual information to further our understanding of the ecology of an area and the way that people interface with their environment. Studies in ethnobotany, ethnomedicine and ethnoecology have led to the 'discovery' of economically important plants and new understandings of ecological relationships. For example, an ethnomedical study contributed to the discovery of a traditional Chinese herbal treatment for malaria using an extract from the herb *Artemisia annua*. This led to the development of a drug that has been shown to restore the consciousness of comatose patients with cerebral malaria more rapidly and, at times, more effectively, than commercial drugs (Klayman 1985).

In another example that is relevant to agroforestry, a very effective indigenous technique for propagating *Ficus nemoralis*, an important tree fodder species in the middle hills of Nepal was 'discovered' through research on indigenous knowledge systems (Rusten 1989). *Ficus nemoralis* is a major source of tree fodder for many hill communities in Nepal, but because of its palatability, grazing animals make it very difficult to propagate, especially on public lands. This difficulty has been overcome by farmers in one community who use *Neolitsea umbrosa*, a small bushy tree that grazing animals ignore, as a nurse plant for *F. nemoralis*. From field observations and according to farmers who use this technique, companion planted *F. nemoralis* grows more quickly than trees grown without *N. umbrosa*. This technique has obvious application to forestation projects in Nepal and possibly elsewhere.

Potential benefits also result from learning about the ways that different segments of local populations use and manage their environment and associated resources. Scott and Gormley (1980) describe pastoral development projects in the Sahel that had often contributed to further resource degradation because the traditional mechanisms of resource management practiced by pastoral people in this region were not studied and understood. In contrast, the authors describe an Oxfam project that was based on an understanding of pastoralists' survival strategies, and on the custom of the 'animal of friendship' relations. As a result of this improved and expanded understanding, the project helped to improve herd productivity without creating a loss of adaptive abilities of the people.

Cashman (1988) describes another situation where knowledge of indigenous methods of communication and perception of the local environment facilitated successful extension of alley cropping technology to a Nigerian village. Constraints to the extension of this technology were transformed into opportunities for success by using the 'tradition of sharing information through stories and songs' characteristic of Nigerian villages. In addition, the names of *Leucaena spp.* and *Cassia spp.* were changed to 'the fertiliser bush,' a phrase that embodied a more acceptable and appropriate concept for the village farmers.

A final important element of indigenous knowledge research involves understanding how members of the local population categorise, classify, and label perceptions of their social and biological environments, and how different forms of indigenous knowledge flow through a social system. A classic example is provided by Berlin, Breedlove, and Raven's (1974) research on the botanical ethnography of an indigenous population in Mexico. They brought a new understanding of the ways that indigenous people organise and classify elements of their natural world. Similarly, the research described in the second half of this paper falls within this category of indigenous knowledge research.

To fulfil the need for investigating indigenous knowledge systems, planning efforts commonly call on the skills of sociologists and anthropologists. If time and money were not constraints, this would be an appropriate strategy. For all projects, time or money or both are scarce resources, and the need to investigate local knowledge and cognitive systems may not be met because specialists cannot be employed. However, a lack of time and money should not be sufficient cause to neglect such investigations. Techniques and approaches exist, and they could be learned and applied by foresters, agronomists, other natural science specialists, economists, and administrators who wish to investigate local knowledge and cognitive systems.

The remainder of this paper will present elements from one case study to illustrate the potential of using a positive attitude in development-oriented research. It will also show how practical, low cost, multidisciplinary research techniques were used to investigate the indigenous knowledge on tree fodder resources in one rural community in Nepal. The lessons learned from this case study are important because of their wide utility in learning about and understanding complex traditional agroforestry systems. We demonstrate how this approach may assist planners and researchers in developing an understanding of indigenous knowledge systems, and the people with whom they wish to work, in the formulation of agroforestry activities.

Case study from the middle hills of Nepal

Description of research site This research was carried out in one *panchayat*[5] of Parbat District in Central Nepal from November 1987 to June 1988. The primary purpose of this research was to investigate attributes of indigenous systems of management,[6] cultivation, perception, and use of private tree fodder resources in one community in the middle hills of Central Nepal. In addition, this research investigated the existence of an indigenous system of classification and evaluation for animal fodder. To achieve these goals, an multi-method research approach was used.

Although this research was not part of an agroforestry planning initiative, the impetus for the research was to contribute to a national emphasis on incorporation of fodder trees in Nepali farming systems. The approach taken could be adapted to the information gathering needs of other agroforestry planning efforts. Also, the results from this study could contribute to the design of either an agroforestry project or the development of an agroforestry extension system for this and other middle hill areas of Nepal.

This research was conducted in three of the nine wards of Dhali Gaun Panchayat (2, 6 and 7). These three wards comprised the village area of Upper Dhali Gaun.[7] (For the remainder of this paper, Dhali Gaun will be substituted for Upper Dhali Gaun.) These three wards lie east to west across a steep south-facing ridge and range between 1,800 to 2,300 meters in altitude. Differences in altitude, aspect, and exposure to warm air from the valleys below, create daily and seasonal climatic differences between the three wards.

Unlike many areas of Nepal, the households in the study area are not organised in nuclear villages. Instead, they are dispersed across the southern face of the sloping ridge that forms this *panchayat*. For this reason, the term village area is used to refer to the inhabited portions of the research area. The total area of the Dhali Gaun Panchayat is 800 ha. According to a 1976 survey (Wormald and Russell 1976), the composition of land in this *panchayat* is: 234 ha forest land, 520 ha grass and scrub land, and 46 ha cultivated land. In the 12 years since this survey, the amount of land under forest cover has decreased (Lumle 1987), and the area of grass/scrub and cultivated land has increased. This change is primarily the result of agricultural expansion and degradation of forest areas.

General methodology and sampling procedure

The goal of developing an understanding of indigenous knowledge systems surrounding tree fodder required the use of an integrated research approach based on five distinct methods. This integrated approach facilitated the collection of different types of data and information essential to achieving this goal, and it helped to overcome many of the problems endemic to cross-cultural research. Even though each of these methods was applied individually, they were developed and used in an integrated fashion, and the data were analysed both individually and collectively.

It needs to be emphasised that the conclusions from this research were made possible because of this 'multi-method' approach. If only a subset of methods had been used, the results and conclusions would have been quite different and less valid. To test this contention, analyses were performed on and conclusions drawn from individual data sets. In all cases, these conclusions, although related in some ways, exhibited important differences from the conclusions developed through comprehensive integrated analysis of data collected from all methods. Throughout the study observations of community life, informal discussions with residents of Dhali Gaun, and participation in household activities took place.

To complement participant observation, a formal survey questionnaire was used to measure socio-economic variables at the household level. This was closely associated with a comprehensive inventory of all trees grown on land owned by the households which participated in the survey (Appendix A). Knowledgeable farmers were interviewed using a Fodder Knowledge Interview/Discussion Guide (Appendix B) that was developed with the help of community members. This fourth method provided some structure to informal interviews. The final method, based on the personal construct theory (Kelly 1955), made use of triad tests and the repertory grid. This technique provided data used to formulate a description of a system of classification used by residents of Dhali Gaun to evaluate and classify different types of tree fodder.

Local women and men of the Dhali Gaun village area who participated in this research are referred to here as consultants.[8] All research assistants[9] were native residents of Dhali Gaun. Beside being the primary source of data and information used to derive conclusions from this research, consultants assisted in its development and implementation. For example, the fodder resource discussion guide was gradually developed throughout the course of the research to incorporate suggestions and thoughts from several consultants. Also, both the formal survey and inventory forms were extensively edited and improved through consultations with different men and women of Dhali Gaun.

The decision to hire community members as research assistants was not based on the need to conserve money, because sufficient funds were available to hire highly educated and experienced people from Kathmandu and bring them to Dhali Gaun. This decision was based on a belief in the value of participatory research, and the recognition that people generally accept new and unfamiliar experiences more quickly if they are involved in them in a meaningful way. Using educated outsiders might have made much of the research easier to accomplish since communication with these professionals would have been less difficult. However, we contend that research assistants hired from outside the community would have been unable to work and communicate with research consultants as successfully as resident assistants.

There are obvious logistic advantages of hiring local women and men as research assistants. More important, it is highly probable that this local participation and cooperation contributed greatly to the fidelity of this research and is significantly responsible for the character and validity of the results. By sharing in this research effort, villagers not only learned about their own village area, but their natural distrust of the research and the researcher was quickly dispelled. The research did not just happen *to* them, but it happened *with* them, and it was successful *because of them*. These people were not 'simply' nameless and faceless respondents, disconnected from the research purpose and process – they were *participants*.

The three wards in the study area were purposively selected for this study based on the expert judgment of Mr. Judhbir Pun, the resident forester of Dhali Gaun for the last 12 years. Mr. Pun's decision was based on the need to select three areas of this panchayat: one was judged as the 'richest' in terms of private fodder tree planting; a second judged to be the 'poorest' in private tree fodder planting; and a third area judged as being midway between these two extremes. The accuracy of this subjective judgement was validated by a reconnaissance of the *panchayat* by the principal researcher, and results from the private tree inventory.

Panchayat officials prepared the lists of all households present in each of the three wards, consisting of the names of each head of household, the household head's gender, an estimate of the amount of land owned by each household, and the household's caste composition. Approximately 25 per cent of the households from each ward list was selected randomly to form a representative sample population of potential consultants for the household survey and private tree inventory. This resulted in a final sample of 28 women and 26 men from 54 different households in the three wards (8 women and 7 men came from Ward 2, 6 women and 6 men from Ward 7, and 14 women and 13 men from Ward 6).

Major research methods

Survey procedure Three male teachers from Dhali Gaun middle school, and three women, who were the most educated women in Dhali Gaun, were hired to carry out the survey. Before any consultant was interviewed, the principal researcher and his assistants visited each sample household and spoke with the selected consultants about the purpose of the research, about who would be visiting them, and about the sort of questions they would be asked.

This introductory process not only fitted well within the cultural norms of this village area, and contributed to a reduction in respondent fear of the survey and interview, but it also allowed the researcher to observe the household, the surrounding land, the type of trees growing around each house, and the intensity of tree cultivation. This process may have contributed to some survey leakage and stimulated some thought and conversation about the survey before the interview. Any possible loss in survey quality was, however, likely offset by gains brought about by respondents being more relaxed and less fearful during the interview. The introduction process, coupled with the knowledge that the community leaders supported the research project, contributed to the fidelity of research results.[10]

Introduction of the researcher and the project was specifically important because half of the informants were women. Women in many villages of Nepal are often very shy, and they are rarely given the opportunity to engage in activities such as surveys or discussions with foreign visitors. In fact, none of the women respondents in this survey had ever been interviewed before, while some of the men had taken part in earlier surveys. Thus, great pains were taken to explain what the survey procedure entailed, to make them as relaxed as possible about this very foreign experience.

Discussions with different villagers after the survey had been completed leads to the conclusion that the introduction process was very successful, and it is recommended that other field researchers consider using this technique. This recommendation holds true for both expatriate and Nepalese researchers, as both groups can be considered outsiders in rural villages.

By design, each assistant conducted one survey a day. After each interview, the principal researcher met with each interviewer to go over the survey and discuss the questions and responses. This not only allowed for the immediate translation of the survey answers and interviewer's comments, but it also permitted the extraction of additional information about survey conditions and problems, about written comments, correction of mistakes, and interpretation of local word usage.[11]

Inventory procedure Eight young men from the three wards were hired to carry out an inventory of all trees growing on each sample household's property. (See Appendix A for a copy of the inventory sheet.) As with the survey, only one inventory was done per day, since some landholdings took between six to nine hours to inventory, and when each person finished with that day's inventory he or she met with the principal investigator to discuss the results. These discussions provided opportunities to learn more about each household's land use and tree cultivation practices, and to examine and press leaf and twig samples collected by these men from uncommon trees they encountered during the inventory.

While inventories were being carried out, spot checks were made by the principal investigator and two research assistants to ensure that the inventory was being carried out properly. In all cases it was learned that the workers in the inventory and the survey took great care and pride in all aspects of this work. The quality of their work was to a great extent the result of their being residents of Dhali Gaun. It is strongly believed that an equivalent degree of quality could not have been achieved by using people brought into Dhali Gaun from Pokhara or Kathmandu.

Tree fodder knowledge discussion guide

The fodder knowledge discussion guide (Appendix C) was used to collect detailed information on specific fodder species via informal interviews with purposively selected consultants. This guide was not used to structure a formal interview. It was only used to make recording information easier and less intrusive, so that the flow of conversation was not disrupted by such recording. It helped to ensure that important questions were not overlooked during a discussion, and to maintain some consistency in data that were collected from each consultant. Most of the questions in this guide originated from discussions with farmers in Dhali Gaun.

Because of the great variety of trees, vines,[12] grasses, and agricultural by-products that are used for animal fodder, it was decided to focus these detailed discussions on a limited number of trees identified as major sources of fodder in Dhali Gaun. This permitted the collection of data from several consultants on a select group of species that were identified as important fodder trees by knowledgeable men and women consultants. This also provided a means of identifying contradictions in information and of following up on interesting statements. Most of the consultants who participated in these interviews were purposively selected.

However, some discussion occurred in an opportunistic manner. For example, during the project introduction process, some farmers would spontaneously start to talk about one or more specific fodder species, and these natural openings often developed into informal interviews.

This method illustrates one way that residents can productively participate in research activities. It is important to realise that the absence of formalised Western research approaches from non-Western societies does not mean that local people are not curious, do not have questions, do not formulate hypotheses, and are not keen observers of their environment. Their survival depends in part on their ability to observe, understand, and explain phenomena around them, and they use such understanding and explanations to formulate predictions and experiment with modifications in their farming systems.

The triad tests and repertory grid

One of the goals of the grid technique was to extract an array of categories used by consultants to order, classify and evaluate attributes of tree fodder. Another goal was to arrange the resulting categories into a structured classification scheme that is used by villagers in their evaluation and management of different types of tree fodder.[13] By using this method, it was possible to develop a more accurate image of the internal local or emic view of tree fodder, and to avoid imposing the researcher's outside or etic view on the research.

Consultants for this activity were selected purposively from the original sample population, based on two primary criteria:

o the judgement that the person was knowledgeable about tree and vine fodder, and
o that the person would be able to participate effectively in this activity.

Table 6.1: Latin names of leaf samples used in triad tests

Nepali names	Latin names	Tree/vine
Phultiso	Colquhounia cocciea[a]	tree
Maya	Eriobotrya elliptica	tree
Bhokre	Ilex doniana	tree
Halaure	Hedera nepalensis	vine
Bhango	Quercus incana	tree
Seto Chuletro	Brassaiopsis hainla	tree
Paiyu	Prunus cerasoides	tree
Shirmoo	Michelia spp.	tree
Jhyanu	Eurya acuminata	tree
Kharsu	Quercus semecarpifolia	tree
Bhains	Salix babylonica	tree
Dudhilo	Ficus nemoralis	tree
Rajeli[a]		vine
Pain lahara	Vitis repanda	vine
Dhurse	Buddleja asiatica	tree

a The Latin name could not be determined or the accuracy is in question.

Not surprisingly, older consultants were found to be much more knowledge-able about tree and vine fodder and less shy in dealing with an outsider. The original goal of involving 15 male and 15 female consultants in this activity had to be reduced to 7 men and 6 women. This was done because of complications regarding the interaction between consultants and both the researcher, on one hand, and consultants and this technique, on the other. Therefore, finding 30 suitable consultants was not possible. Due to this low number of consultants, the level of statistical analysis of the resultant data was limited to content analysis.

To perform triad tests, each consultant was provided with fresh leaf samples in groups of three, a triad leaf sort, from a collection of the 15 different fodder samples listed in Table 6.1. To avoid consultant fatigue, only nine different triad leaf sorts were used. Each triad leaf sort was determined randomly with repeat groups being excluded. After consultants were presented with a leaf sort, they were asked to name the leaves and then arrange them into two groups: one group consisting of the two leaves they felt to be most similar to each other, and the second consisting of the remaining dissimilar leaf. After this grouping activity, the consultant was asked to explain her or his reasons for the groupings. These responses were recorded on the Triad Test Record Form (Appendix C), and used to formulate composite verbal labels thought to be important in the evaluation of tree and vine fodder.

Once this first grouping and associated verbal label were established, the consultant was presented with another leaf sort and asked again to group them and to give her or his reasons for the grouping. When all nine leaf sorts had been presented, the consultant was reminded, one at a time, of each of his or her verbal labels and leaf groups, and was then asked to place the remaining 12 leaves in one of the two groups of each leaf sort. The record form was marked to indicate whether a specific leaf sample agreed or disagreed with a specific verbal label.

This procedure, repeated for all verbal classification labels mentioned by the consultant, made it possible to test each leaf sample against a verbal classification label. In some situations, it also led to new classification labels when the consultant felt that a new leaf did not fit well in either group, but required a new group, or fit equally well in both original groups. This in turn made it possible to construct a repertory grid composed of all fodder types involved in this test and the various verbal classification labels that were elicited.

Standard research procedure for the repertory grid technique requires that consultants be asked to use only one bipolar verbal classification label[14] to explain their grouping of each triad leaf sort (Kelly 1955; Fransella and Bannister 1977). Also, once a verbal label is used, consultants are generally not allowed to use the same label again for other sort groupings. However, because one of the primary goals of this research was the development of an understanding of what factors villagers in Dhali Gaun use to discriminate between fodder types and to identify attributes of the indigenous knowledge system surrounding fodder, this research did not force consultants to restrict the verbalisation of their grouping rationale to single elements. Furthermore, consultants were permitted to repeat verbal labels for other sort groupings.

This deviation from standard research method was also based on pre-test results. During the pre-test, an attempt was made to restrict consultants to the strict procedural requirements of this research technique. However, this rigid application of research procedure had a negative effect on the performance of consultants. Pre-test consultants exhibited great reluctance to verbalise their rationale for their arrangements of leaves within a triad leaf sort when restricted to only one exclusive statement. These consultants also appeared to be uncomfortable and tense under these conditions, and this caused some to stop participating in the activity. Additionally, the information gathered through the strict application of this technique lacked the richness of detail that was common during more open discussions. These and other difficulties lead to the use of a more flexible procedure, which resulted in a more relaxed and open interchange between the consultants and researcher. However, in exchange for effective consultant participation and the collection of data rich in detail, the level of analysis that is possible with the resultant data is essentially limited to qualitative content analysis of the verbal labels through inspection.

Results and discussion

For this chapter, two condensed examples of preliminary research findings are presented. These examples focus on results that came primarily from the repertory grid and triad test procedures, but were interpreted by using information from the other methods. The first example demonstrates how an understanding of indigenous knowledge can help identify differences in the way that men and women perceive their environment. Identification of such gender-related differences in perception can be used in project design not only to take advantage of differences in resources used, but also to meet the needs of different segments of a community.

The second example demonstrates how indigenous knowledge research could contribute to an understanding of indigenous schemes of classification and evaluation of natural resources, and how this could be used to improve an agroforestry intervention. Knowing how people perceive, conceptualise, and speak about elements of their environment is essential for effective cross-cultural communication and diffusion of innovations.

Gender-related differences in fodder perception

All verbal labels provided by consultants were grouped into 16 categories based on similarities among labels (Table 6.2). Table 6.3 shows the differences in the frequencies of responses for each category between women and men. It can be seen that there is a noticeable difference in the number of women and men who used the five categories (in bold letters) to distinguish between fodder types. For the remaining categories, there were negligible or no differences at all between the responses of men and women.

Table 6.2: Frequency of construct labels by gender[a]

Category	Total Labels	% of Total	Male	Female
Winter fodder	28	18.3	22	6
Good for milk production	24	15.7	13	11
Nutritious, healthy	19	12.4	10	9
Eaten well	12	7.8	8	4
Health problems	11	7.2	9	2
Good for milk and *ghui*[b]	9	5.9	7	2
Available all seasons	9	5.9	5	4
Source of fodder and fuel	7	4.6	1	6
Obano fodder[c]	7	4.6	4	3
Chiso fodder[d]	7	4.6	7	0
Easily obtainable	6	3.9	2	4
Generally good	5	3.3	2	3
Manure production	5	3.3	2	3
Available in same season	2	1.3	2	0
Satisfying fodder	1	0.6	1	0
Hot season fodder	1	0.6	0	1
Total	153	100.0	95	58

a   Seven men and six women provide the data.
b   *Ghui* is the Nepalese word for clarified butter. This product is made from buffalo milk and serves as an important cooking oil, seasoning, and source of cash in Dhali Gaun household.
c   *Obana* is the Nepalese word for dry.
d   *Chiso* is the Nepalese word for cold and wet. See footnote 10 and Figure 6.1 for more information on this term relative to fodder.

It was hypothesised that men and women would share common domains of knowledge about tree fodder use, cultivation and management, as well as have unique gender-related domains of knowledge. This hypothesis was based on the realisation that divisions of labour based on gender are common in rural Nepalese households (Bennett 1983; Molnar 1981).

Even though the sample was small, a Chi-square statistics was calculated for the data presented in Table 6.2 to determine if the differences in the exhibited frequencies was significant to the 0.01 confidence level. The resulting Chi-square proved significant only to the 0.25 confidence level. Therefore, we cannot definitively conclude, based on the analysis of repertory grid alone, that for all the categories taken together, there is a significant difference between perception and evaluation of different fodder types between men and women.

However, if individual categories are given closer examination within the context of village life and in relation to data collected from the survey and inventory, an argument can be made to support the hypothesis that gender-related differences in fodder perception and evaluation exist. Data on fodder tree preference by gender, presented in Table 6.4, support this conclusion. A clear majority of women consultants (85.6 per cent) selected *Ficus nemoralis (Dudhilo)* as their first choice for the best fodder tree. In contrast, only 27 per cent of the men consultants selected this species, with 35.7 per cent of them selecting *Quercus semecarpifolia (Kharsu)*.

Table 6.3: High and low frequencies of responses for label categories by men and women[a]

Labels	Men		Women	
	High	Low	High	Low
Winter fodder	X			X
Good for milk production	N[b]		N	
Nutritious, healthy	N		N	
Eaten well	N		N	
Health problems	X			X
Good for milk and *ghui*	X			X
Available all seasons	N		N	
Source of fodder and fuel		X	X	
Obano fodder	N		N	
Chiso fodder	X			X
Easily obtainable	O[c]		O	
Generally good	O		O	
Manure production	O		O	
Available in same season	O		O	
Satisfying fodder	O		O	
Hot season fodder	O		O	

a   The determination of high and low depends on whether or not the frequency of responses from male or female consultant groups for a category if 50 per cent higher or lower than the frequency of responses from the other group for that category.

b   'N' indicates that the differences were not greater or lesser than 50 per cent in that category.

c   'O' indicates that there were too few comments to make this computation meaningful.

Table 6.4: Frequency of first choices in fodder tree preference by gender

Species	Where common	All wards		% of total	
	Women and men	Women	Men	Women	Men
Ficus nemoralis	farm	24	7	85.6	27.0
Quercus semecarpifolia	forest	1	9	3.6	34.7
Ilex doniana	forest	0	2	0.0	7.7
Colquhounia coccinea	farm	1	0	3.6	0.0
Brassaiopsis hainla	farm	0	1	0.0	3.6
Salix babylonica	farm	1	0	3.6	0.0
No answer		1	7	3.6	27.0
Total		28	26	100.0	100.0

Interpretation of the differences in species preference between men and women is possible when two contrasting attributes of these two species are compared:

Ficus nemoralis
  o This species is almost exclusively cultivated on private land and 2167 trees of this species were counted during the inventory.
  o A majority of consultants reported that this is the best species for milk production. Milk is not commonly sold in Dhali Gaun.
Quercus semecarpifolia
  o This species is almost exclusively found in the forest and is not commonly cultivated on private land. Only 408 trees of this species were recorded during the inventory.
  o A majority of consultants reported that this is the best species for the production of *ghui* (clarified butter). *Ghui* is an important cash commodity in Dhali Gaun. About 50 per cent of those households who make *ghui* also sell it.

Also, most women consultants reported that they preferred *Ficus nemoralis* over *Quercus semecarpifolia* for three reasons:
  o *Ficus nemoralis* was readily available near their homes.
  o *Ficus nemoralis* was an easier tree to climb. One woman said, 'Kharsu in the forest are very big trees and I am a small woman, climbing them is difficult and dangerous for women; only men collect fodder from this tree.'
  o *Ficus nemoralis* does not have thorns on its leaves.
In contrast, many men consultants reported that they preferred *Quercus semecarpifolia* over *Ficus nemoralis* for the following reasons:
  o *Quercus semecarpifolia* is available during the winter season when other animal fodder is scarce.
  o *Quercus semecarpifolia* is good for the health of livestock.
  o Feeding *Quercus semecarpifolia* produces more *ghui* than other fodder.

When these three sets of data are considered together, it could reasonably be concluded that differences exist in the way men and women evaluate fodder. These differences could have important implications for an agroforestry project. This conclusion would not have been possible if only one or two of the five research methods had been used.

Classification categories for fodder evaluation

As stated previously, one of the goals of the grid technique is to extract an array of categories that can be used to order, classify, and evaluate fodder from comments of consultants. Another goal is to arrange the resulting categories into a structured classification scheme. The analysis of the repertory grid data alone, however, did not reveal an ordered classification system into which the different categories could be arranged. Nevertheless, by integrating these results with those from other research methods, a plausible classification scheme was formulated. Based on this integrated analysis, and the assumption that major categories of classification are general and broad in character, with subcategories being more specific, it is proposed that the primary scheme for the evaluation and classification of tree and vine fodder, used by residents of Dhali Gaun, consists of a bipolar scale, with the two poles defined as *chiso* and *obano* (Table

6.5). It appears that tree and vine fodder, and possibly grass fodder and agricultural residues, are identified as being either more-or-less *chiso* or *obano*. Tree and vine fodder can be arranged along this sliding scale according to an evaluation of their *chiso* and *obano* character.

Table 6.5 Bipolar scale of evaluation for tree fodder

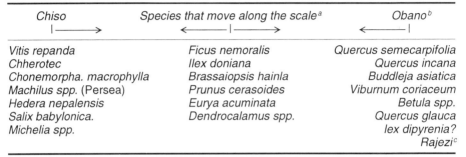

Chiso ⟶	Species that move along the scale[a] ⟵—⟶	Obano[b] ⟵—
Vitis repanda	Ficus nemoralis	Quercus semecarpifolia
Chherotec	Ilex doniana	Quercus incana
Chonemorpha. macrophylla	Brassaiopsis hainla	Buddleja asiatica
Machilus spp. (Persea)	Prunus cerasoides	Viburnum coriaceum
Hedera nepalensis	Eurya acuminata	Betula spp.
Salix babylonica.	Dendrocalamus spp.	Quercus glauca
Michelia spp.		lex dipyrenia?
		Rajezi[c]

a Species are arranged for the Nepali month of *Magh* (January-February).
b *Obano* is the most common term used by villagers, but another term *garimi*, which means warm or hot, is occasionally used along with or in place of *obano*.
c Vernacular

The Nepalese word *chiso* is used to describe something that is cold and damp, and *obano* is used to describe something that is dry and possibly warm. However, when used to describe the character of a fodder, the meanings of these words are expanded to describe several attributes of fodder quality, and what may result from feeding too much of a *chiso* or *obano* fodder to livestock. As reported by the consultants, the best quality fodder usually have obano attributes, which not only describe the physical character of leaves, *i.e.* being relatively dry, stiff, and leathery, but it also infers that this fodder will generally:

○ lead to the production of good firm relatively dry dung without causing constipation;
○ improve the general health of livestock;[15]
○ cause the livestock to gain weight;
○ be eaten well and satisfy the animal's appetite, and
○ contribute to the improved production of milk and *ghui.*

Conversely, fodder referred to as *chiso* are often poorer quality fodder which usually need to be mixed with other more obano fodder before being fed to livestock. As with the term obano, the term *chiso* describes both physical attributes of the fodder, i.e., being relatively succulent, supple, and smooth, and more importantly, it describe the physiological effects of this fodder on livestock. According to consultants, if *chiso* fodder is fed to livestock as the sole feed, it will generally:

○ cause the animal to produce watery dung;
○ in some cases, cause livestock to loose weight;
○ weaken the animal and cause it to lose its appetite, and possibly cause a blockage in the stomachs or throat of the livestock;
○ not satisfy the animal's appetite; and
○ not increase the production of *ghui*, but may improve the productivity of milk.

It should be emphasised that *chiso* fodder is not necessarily thought of as 'bad' fodder. For example, *Vitis repanda* (*Pani Lahara*) is considered to be one of the most used *chiso* fodder in the Dhali Gaun area, and one of the best for milk and *ghiu* production. However, because of its *chiso* quality, this fodder needs to be fed in limited quantities and mixed with fodder which have a relatively high *obano* state. Similarly, all *obano* fodder cannot be considered free from problems. For example, one consultant explained that during the Nepali month of *Asar* (June-July) fodder from *Prunus cerasoides* (*Painyu*), which is relatively *obano*, can be fed because there is sufficient water around for animals to drink. According to this woman, since this 'is a *garimi* (*obano*) fodder, it will cause the udder to dry up and the teats will develop pimples' if this is the sole fodder fed to cows and buffaloes.

It appears that only a few fodder species are classified as purely *obano* or *chiso*, a majority fall between these two extremes of classification, forming two major groups. Both groups of fodder move along this scale, becoming more *chiso* or more *obano* during different times of the year. Many species like *Ficus nemoralis* (*Dudhilo*), one of the most popular fodder in Dhali Gaun, could be classified as very *chiso* in the spring, when there is a new flush of leaves. As the leaves mature they become progressively more *obano* and the fodder quality of this species improves. A few species which make up the second group may slowly approach less *chiso* or less *obano* states as seasons change. It appears, however, that they never really achieve the character of fodder defined by the opposite pole.

Because not all leaves on a tree mature at the same time, most trees will generally have leaves that are both *obano* and *chiso*. Therefore, fodder collection often requires the selective lopping of *obano* leaves from trees, leaving more *chiso* leaves to mature for later use.[16] It appears that farmers in Dhali Gaun use two basic techniques to determine the relative *chiso* or *obano* condition of fodder. In one technique, the species and the season of the year are used. This method seems to be most commonly used for fodder that are more or less fixed at either pole. For a majority of fodder species that lie between the two extremes, farmers need to apply the second technique, consisting of qualitative analysis of the leaves of a tree or vine using their senses. Table 6.5 presents techniques that many of the consultants in Dhali Gaun used in the evaluation of the different fodder that were discussed.

An understanding of this indigenous system of tree fodder evaluation could be valuable to planners in designing an agroforestry project or an extension effort. For example, if there was a desire to introduce an exotic fodder species to this community, knowledge on how this tree would be evaluated in terms of its *chiso* or *obano* character would aid in the introduction effort.

Also, if extension agents were aware of this evaluation, they would be better able to communicate with farmers about fodder and fodder trees in ways that would be meaningful to villagers. This would improve the effectiveness of an extension effort.

Conclusions

This research has demonstrated that there is much more to the collection, management, and use of tree fodder than meets the eyes of outsiders. By using their knowledge of individual fodder species, their indigenous classification scheme (Table 6.5), and their skillful qualitative analysis of available fodder (Table 6.6), knowledgeable villagers could efficiently evaluate the relative quality of different fodder and provide good feed to their livestock.

Table 6.6: General methods of sensory analysis of leaf samples of tree fodder.

Sense	Analytic technique
Sight	Both surfaces of the leaves were closely inspected by holding the leaves so as to take the best advantage of natural lighting.
Touch	Both surfaces of the leaves were gently felt between the thumb and the fingers. The leaves were tugged, bent, and crumpled. The leaf margins were caressed and thorns teased. The leaf petioles were also rolled between the thumb and forefinger.
Smell	Leaves were smelled in both crumpled and uncrumpled states.
Taste	Some consultants chewed some leaves or parts of leaves.

As mentioned earlier, this research 'discovered' that woody vines are considered tree fodder, and that *Neolitsea umbrosa* is used as a nurse tree for the propagation of highly valued fodder trees. These 'discoveries' are very important in that they provide insights that may lead to opportunities for further research into intensification of agroforestry systems, and to more general applications well beyond the scope of this research project.

We have demonstrated that conducting this type of research is viable and feasible within a reasonable time frame and when financial resources are limited. Extensive participation of villagers as research consultants and assistants was also shown to be highly effective because they:

○ lessened the cost of obtaining reliable and appropriate information;
○ reduced the time required to carry out this research;
○ helped to dispel the fear villagers had of the research and the researcher;
○ refined research methods to reflect more appropriately the needs and character of this community, and
○ provided very important insights to the indigenous knowledge systems and environmental cognition in this village.

One of the major results of this research was the formulation of the integrated research strategy described in the preceding sections. The value of this strategy for this type of research became apparent both during field work and data analysis. The major goal of developing a more complete understanding of the use, cultivation, and knowledge about fodder trees in a Nepalese village could probably not have been accomplished, if only one or two of the preceding methods were used.

One of the key advantages of this approach was that, when data obtained from each method was inspected and analysed, anomalies and problems that came to light could be cross-checked with information provided from other methods. In many cases, what were problems of understanding at first became insights into the workings of this complex rural system.

Notes

1. This research was carried out from November 1987 to June 1988, and was supported

by a research grant from the Nepal Mission of the United States Agency for International Development, grant number 367-0132-G-SS-8001-01. Logistic assistance was provided by the Institute of Forestry, Pokhara Campus, Nepal.
2. Indigenous knowledge systems, as used in this paper, includes two major concepts: (1) the concept of indigenous technical knowledge (IDS Bulletin 1979), *i.e.* factual knowledge about local environments, and technologies used by indigenous people to survive; and (2) the concept of environmental perception and cognition (Moore and Gooledge 1976), *i.e.* how indigenous people perceive and conceptualise their environments and express this in language, symbolism, and behaviour.
3. This includes both those from Western nations and those from non-Western countries who have been trained in Western-oriented formal educational systems.
4. Defined as the mechanisms people use to comprehend and conceptualise their environment, the labels they use to define, classify, and communicate about their environment, and how this knowledge and associated perceptions are passed on from one generation to the next.
5. A *panchayat* is the primary political and geographic unit in Nepal, and each one is divided into nine wards *(wadda)*.
6. It is interesting to note that the term management was initially used in describing the focus of this research. However, from the perspective of the Nepalese farmers in the research area, this term was found to be inappropriate because there is not single, commonly used and understood Nepalese word for 'management' of fodder trees or other natural resources. Discussions with farmers about their 'management' of fodder trees in their farming systems, lead to the use of a more appropriate term, the Nepalese equivalent of 'to cultivate' – *umaru* or *launu* – in place of the relatively modern and uncommon term *byawasthaa garnu* (to manage). This is an excellent example of how difficult it is to carry out cross-cultural research and why it is so difficult to do so.
7. Dhali Gaun is not the real name for this village area. It is a oponym used to protect the people of this study area and their management of the community forest.
8. The term consultant is used in place of the more common, and somewhat pejorative, term respondent to reflect more accurately the role that village members played in this research. Additionally, this term was used to grant these participants the respect they deserve as advisers, teachers, and people who possess unique and useful knowledge.
9. These included: two village men who helped in the general logistics of the research and in the improvement of the research tools, three men and three women who carried out the survey, and eight men who carried out the private tree inventory.
10. It is common for local leaders of rural communities to be distrusted by residents, but Dhali Gaun appears to be an exception. The leaders of this community were active in bettering their community and caring for the less fortunate community members.
11. This proved to be very important. For example, the Nepalese word *chiso* generally means damp or cold. However, when used in reference to fodder, it describes the quality of fodder, not its temperature. One attribute of *chiso* fodder is that it can cause livestock to have diarrhoea. In describing a fodder as *chiso*, villagers infer that it will cause livestock to produce watery dung, which is more difficult to collect by hand, and less useful as a fertiliser, than the preferred drier dung.
12. Before the field research, there was no indication of the important role that vines and climbers play as a source of fodder, nor of how it was viewed as a tree fodder by village farmers. Nowhere in the literature review or during discussions with knowledgeable people in Kathmandu and Pokhara was the value of fodder vines and climbers mentioned.
13. Farmers of this area make a major distinction between tree fodder, grass fodder, and agricultural residue. However, included with tree fodder is fodder collected from shrubs and vines. For this reason, the term fodder type is used. Vines and shrubs are included with trees when the term tree fodder is used.
14. Bipolar verbal labels refers to the way consultants explained their grouping of each

triad leaf sort. For example, the group with two of the three leaves may have been grouped together because they were considered as winter fodder, while the remaining leaf was excluded because it was considered a summer fodder. This dichotomous label, winter fodder/non-winter fodder, is thus bipolar.

15. There are a variety of terms used to describe a fodder that contributes to an animal's health, including *pashilo* (nutritious) and *nirogi* (healthful).

16. This lopping behaviour was commonly observed for the collection of fodder from *Ficus nemoralis (Dudhilo)*.

Appendix A: Fodder tree inventory sheet

Household No. _____ Name _____ Date _____ Inventory No. _____

Use	Tree Name	Age estimate		Place of planting						
		<10Yrs	>10 Yrs	Khar Barri	Barri	Khet	Stream	Marginal	House-hold	Trail
A B	Dudhilo	|||| |||	|||	||||			||||		||||	
Code										

This total = the rest of the row

Translation Key:
Barri   – Non-irrigated agricultural land
Khet   – Irrigated agricultural land
Khar barri   – Land where thatch grass is grown (marginal land)

Inventory Form Key:
Codes   – Use or utility codes (A, B, C, etc) were written in the order of importance based on comments by farmers
Age Estimates – These were made by the farmers

Appendix B: Fodder knowledge data sheet

1. Species: (Nepali) _____ 2. (Latin) _____

3. Site/Location: _____ Sample No. _____

4. Elevation: _____ 5. Aspect _____ 6. Date: _____

7. Consultant(s): [F], [M] _____ 8. Age: _____

9. BIO-DATA: _____

10. Plant is a: Tree ☐ Shrub ☐ Vine ☐ Grass ☐ Other _____

11. Fodder Quality: E ☐ G ☐ F ☐ P ☐ Not fodder ☐
    11.1. Comments:
    _____

12. Are there months when this fodder cannot be used? [Y] [N].
    12.1. Explain/Comments:
    _____

13. Fodder for: Buffalo ☐☐ Cow ☐☐ Goats ☐☐ Sheep ☐☐ All ☐☐

14. Fodder for: Older animals ☐ Younger animals ☐ Both ☐
    Pregnant animals: [Y] [N].   Milking animals: [Y] [N].

15. Other uses with rating   [E, G, F, P]:
    Fuel ☐ Timber ☐ Tools ☐ Medical ☐ Fiber ☐ Fruit ☐ Bed/fertiliser ☐
    Other: _____

16. Does fodder cause health problems? [Y] [N].
    Details:
    _____

17. Can both old and young (new) leaves be fed to animals? [Y] [N].
    Explain:
    _____

18. How are other parts of the tree used?
Sap	Leaves	Flowers	Seeds	Roots	Bark	Fruit
☐☐	☐☐	☐☐	☐☐	☐☐	☐☐	☐☐

    If human food or other (medicine/religious), explain:
    _____

19. How often should fodder be harvested? Why?
    _____

20. How heavily should this tree be lopped?
    All leaves   ☐
    Only a fraction of the leaves   ☐ _____%
    Only new leaves   ☐
    Only old leaves   ☐
    Explain reasons for this lopping intensity:
    _____

Appendix B: Fodder knowledge data sheet (continued)

21. How old should tree be before it is first lopped? _____

22. Can lopping be used to control the shape of the adult tree? [Y] [N].
    22.1. How is this lopping done?
    _____

23 Can this tree be coppiced (*tusaaunu*)? [Y] [N] [DK]

24. How often do you harvest this fodder? Why?
    _____

25. Primary months for lopping and collection of fodder:

Baisakh	Jeth	Asad	Saun	Bhadau	Asoj	Kattik	Mangsir	Pus	Magh	Phagun	Chait
1	2	3	4	5	6	7	8	9	10	11	12

26. Which month(s) is fodder quality best? (Use nos.) _____

27. Which month(s) is fodder most available? (Use nos.) _____

28. Tree grows: mainly in farm ☐ mainly in forest ☐ both ☐
    28.1. If grown in farm area, grown in khet? ☐ and/or barri? ☐

29. Best site/location for growth:
    _____

30. How fast does this tree grow? Fast ☐ Moderate ☐ Slow ☐
    30.1. Explain:
    _____

31. Is it grown near crops? [Y] [N]. Which crops? _____
    _____
    31.1. If not, why not? _____
    _____

32 What effect does this tree have on crops?
    _____

33. How is this tree generally propagated (grown)?
    Seed Cutting ☐ Transplanting ☐ Nursery ☐ Seeding ☐ Other: ☐
    33.1 Description of procedure:
    _____

34. Does this tree harbor pests? [Y] [N].
    Explain:
    _____

35. Do epiphytes grow on this tree? [Y] [N].
    Explain:
    _____

36. Is there anything else that you can tell me about this tree?
    _____

Appendix C: Triad test record form

Triad Test Record Form

Consultant:_____   Date:_____   Time:_____

Constructs labels	Name of leaf samples															Notes
	PHULTISO	MAYA	BHOKRE	HALAUE	BANJO	CHULERO	PAIYU	SHIRMOO	JHYANU	KHASRU	BAINS	DUDHILO	RAJELI	PAINLAHARA	DHURSE	
			X			X						X				
			X	X								X				
	X					X						X				
										X	X				X	
	X								X	X						
				X									X	X		
						X	X		X							
							X					X			X	
New construct																
New construct																
Problems with crops																

X = Triad member
[X] = Triad pair
+ = Construct agreement
− = No agreement

Appendix D: Illustrative Repertory Grid

Illustrative Repertory Grid

(Adapted from one consultant's form.)

Consultant: __Narmati Pun__   Date: _3-88_   Time: _8:35 a.m._

Name of leaf samples															ELICITED VERBAL LABELS
PHULTISO	MAYA	BHOKRE	HALAURE	BANJO	CHULERO	PAIYU	SHIRMOO	JHYANU	KHASRU	BAINS	DUDHILO	RAJELI	PANILAHARA	DHURSE	
+	−	X +	−	+	−	X −	+	+	+	+	X +	+	−	+	Available during the same season + / Not available during the same season −
−	−	X +	−	X +	−	+	+	+	+	−	X −	+	−	+	Winter fodder + / Not a winter fodder −
X −	+	+	+	+	X +	−	+	−	+	−	+	X +	−	+	*Pashilo* (nutritious) fodder + / Not *pashilo* −
−	−	+	−	−	−	−	+	−	X +	X −	−	+	−	X +	Winter and *pashilo* + / Not winter and *pashilo* −
X −	−	+	−	+	−	+	+	X +	X +	−	−	+	−	+	Winter fodder + / Not winter fodder −
−	−	+	X +	+	−	−	+	−	+	−	−	X +	X −	+	Available all year long + / Not available −
−	−	+	−	+	−	X +	X −	−	X +	−	−	−	.	+	Fodder and fuelwood + / Fodder only −
−	−	+	−	−	−	−	−	+	+	−	X +	−	+	X +	Good for hot season + / Not good for hot season −

KEY:

X = Triad member

X̲ = Triad pair

+ = Construct agreement

− = No agreement

7. Indigenous Communication and Indigenous Knowledge

PAUL A. MUNDY AND J. LIN COMPTON

Introduction

MOST DEFINITIONS OF indigenous knowledge refer to the accumulation of experience and the passing down of information from one generation to the next within a society (Wang 1982, CIKARD 1988). Yet, despite frequent expressions of concern for enculturation, little attention has been given to how knowledge is accumulated and shared within local societies. Communication is one of several processes essential for the continuity and spread of knowledge and the culture in which it is embedded.

Every society seemingly has evolved elaborate ways for transmitting information from person to person. Such indigenous communication includes the transmission of not only technical information, but also all other messages: entertainment, news, persuasion, announcements and social exchanges of every type within the expansive sweep defined by Doob (1960). This chapter deals primarily with the communication of technical information, though it will be necessary to mention other types of content also. We choose to concentrate on technical communication because this has been relatively ignored in the literature. The neglect by outsiders of the interface between indigenous knowledge and indigenous communication is despite its central place in the perpetuation of culture. This chapter describes indigenous communication and proposes a heuristic framework for studying this interface.

In the following discussion we must keep in mind the distinction between knowledge and information. Knowledge is the process of knowing, of individual cognition (Freire 1971, 1973). It resides in people. It cannot be communicated but is created in the minds of individuals as a result of each person's perceptions of the environment or through communication with others. An information sender must first encode knowledge into a form of information and transmit this. The receiver then decodes and analyses the information, forming connotations with schemata and memorised experiences and relating it to knowledge he or she already has. The receiver's verbal or other reactions form feedback, which in turn may create new knowledge in the mind of the sender. The communication process thereby enables both partners to create new knowledge in their minds.

Communication may occur without any conscious or deliberate attempt by an information sender. Observers may infer much from others' actions, dress and body language. Much childhood learning consists of imitation. Animals, plants, and inanimate objects such as stars and clouds convey much information to those able to interpret it. The receiver must similarly decode the incoming information and match it with existing knowledge.

This encoding, decoding and matching process produces 'noise' in the communication channel and results in no two people having exactly the same knowledge about anything. It also means that rural people and scientists see the same item of 'indigenous knowledge' in completely different ways. For this reason, in this chapter we are careful not to talk of the 'communication of indigenous knowledge'; rather, we talk of the 'communication of indigenous information' to refer to the process of encoding and decoding and the associated generation of new knowledge in the sender's and receiver's minds.

What is indigenous communication?

The problems of defining indigenous communication are very similar to those facing a formal definition of indigenous knowledge (*see*, for example, Swift 1979 and Howes and Chambers 1979). Gradations, overlaps and exceptions abound. Wang's (1982: 3) definition of the indigenous communication system implies that changes in technology and organisation make it difficult to draw a firm line separating indigenous from non-indigenous, or exogenous, communication: 'the communication system which existed before the arrival of mass media and formally organised bureaucratic system, and is still existing today despite changes.'

This historical perspective fits the developing world – where mass media and bureaucracies are relatively new – better than the developed world. One might argue, however, that small-circulation newsletters, telephones, personal correspondence and electronic mail in the West perform the same functions as more traditional channels in developing countries. Wang (1982: 3) goes on to list examples of indigenous communication: 'folk media such as puppet shows; folk drama; storytelling; interpersonal communication channels, including the Korean village meetings, the Chinese loaning club; or even local meeting places (community teahouse and open market). Although the primary function of these media and channels may not be communicative, together they interact with one another to form a network which constitutes the information environment of people in most of the rural areas in the Third World.' We will mention many other instances of indigenous channels in this chapter.

We can see indigenous communication as operating at different levels in society. Interpersonal communication operates primarily at the individual and small group levels. Grassroots organisations such as irrigation associations and housing cooperatives allow structured discussions involving organisation leaders and larger audiences than is possible in unstructured situations. The audiences of folk media are larger still and may involve virtually everyone in a community as well as people from outside.

Why study indigenous communication?

Indigenous communication has value in its own right It is an important aspect of culture and is the means by which a culture is preserved, handed down, responds to new situations and adapts. The erosion of indigenous communication systems by exogenous education and media endangers the survival of much indigenous knowledge.

Exogenous channels have limited range Television and newspapers are largely confined to urban areas in the Third World. Even the most widespread of exogenous channels, extension personnel and radio, fail to reach many rural people. Indigenous channels, by contrast, are ubiquitous. They are needed to convey messages to people out of the reach of exogenous channels.

Indigenous channels have high credibility Because they are familiar and are controlled locally, indigenous channels are highly credible. Audiences throughout the world often greet with scepticism or hostility messages transmitted through the externally controlled mass media.

Indigenous channels are important conduits of change Because of the above factors. Research on the diffusion of innovations has shown the importance of informal, interpersonal contacts in persuading people to adopt, or reject, innovations (Rogers 1983). Such contacts are often made through indigenous channels.

Development programmes can use indigenous communication For both information collection and dissemination. Outsiders can tap indigenous channels for information about the local situation and responses to outside initiatives. Much can be learned by attending village or organisation meetings and interviewing local individuals who have accumulated knowledge through direct experience and communication. Integrating indigenous and exogenous communication systems can strengthen both (Howes 1979): for instance, Schwabe and Kuojok (1981) propose an animal disease surveillance system using indigenous veterinarians in southern Sudan. Collaboration between the local hospital and indigenous healers in central Ghana has allowed the healers to refer patients to the hospital and vice-versa (D. M. Warren 1989).

Many projects rely on information diffusion processes to carry innovations and development messages to their intended beneficiaries. Some projects target opinion leaders and people likely to be innovators in the expectation that indigenous channels will spread the message. Others have made explicit use of indigenous channels such as folk media and village organisations.

Indigenous channels offer opportunities for participation by local people in development efforts. They allow local people to communicate among themselves and with development professionals and decision makers. Local people can retain control over more indigenous more easily than over technologically intensive media.

If ignored, indigenous communication can result in inappropriate development efforts For instance, failure to recognise the role of a network of 'water temples' in controlling irrigation in Bali, Indonesia, led to the introduction of cropping technologies and the construction of canals and dams that were not appropriate to local conditions (Cowley 1989; Lansing 1987).

Indigenous and exogenous communication compared

We may conveniently contrast indigenous communication channels with exogenous channels: mass media (radio, television, newspapers, magazines, and the like) and such bureaucratically organised networks as firms, schools, banks, postal and telephone services, agricultural extension and other government agencies.

In general, indigenous communication systems have three features: they have developed locally, are under local control, and use low levels of technology. Many indigenous communication systems share a fourth characteristic: a lack of bureaucratic organisation. However, some systems we might regard as indigenous (mosques, churches) are organised bureaucratically, while some exogenous forms (computer bulletin boards, small-circulation newsletters) are not. Despite these exceptions, we might describe exogenous systems as 'institutionally organised communication,' a phrase parallel to Compton's (1984a) term for science and technology 'institutionally organised knowledge systems'.

As with exogenous and indigenous knowledge, there is sometimes no sharp line between exogenous and indigenous communication. The two systems overlap in all four elements of the SMCR model of communication: source, message, channel, and receiver.

- While the two systems are distinguishable primarily by the *channels* used (radio, TV and the printed word vs. informal face-to-face communication and folk media), exogenous communication also makes ample use of interpersonal communication, as in extension activities and telephones.
- The *sources* often are different. Exogenous communication is originated by an outside institution such as a television or radio station, while indigenous communication derives from local people. But here too there is overlap. A television program may show a local source such as a village farmer who has adopted and benefited from a new technology, while folk media such as puppets have been widely used to convey family planning and other developmental messages designed by national governments.
- *Messages* conveyed by the two systems are sometimes similar. News and entertainment may travel through either network, for instance. However, most indigenous information flows through indigenous channels, while exogenous information typically is carried by exogenous channels. Later in this chapter we discuss exceptions to this. The smaller, more intimate audiences typical of indigenous channels mean that messages are more easily tailored to local conditions than is possible in mass exogenous channels (Wang and Dissanayake 1984: 22). Some forms are unique to exogenous communication systems (television soap operas and satellite weather forecasting, for instance) while others are found almost exclusively in indigenous systems (such as indigenous healing methods). Even here there may be mutual borrowing, though, as in a TV documentary about traditional acupuncture methods or the puppet shows about family planning mentioned above.
- The *receivers* of both types of communication also coincide, though the mass media forms of exogenous communication typically reach a much larger audience than do indigenous channels (Wang and Dissanayake 1984: 22). While television and newspapers have limited ranges, radios are common even in remote areas. And even the most highly educated urbanite still relies on indigenous communication for much information.

We discuss each of these aspects of indigenous communication in more detail below.

Indigenous communication channels

We divide indigenous communication channels into six types: folk media, indigenous organisations, deliberate instruction, records, unorganised channels, and direct observation.

Folk media Folk media are the indigenous equivalents of exogenous mass media. This broad range of art forms is used primarily for entertainment, but also is used to promote education, values and cultural continuity. They are distinguishable from indigenous organisations, the following category, because they entail a performance by an actor or actors before an audience.

Types of folk media include festivals, plays and puppet shows, dance, song, storytelling, poetry, debates such as the Filipino *balagtasan*, parades and carnivals (Valbuena 1986). These traditional forms of entertainment were thought to be in danger of being superseded by radio and television, but fears of cultural imperialism and realisation of the limitations of the mass media have sometimes led to their revival (Wang and Dissanayake 1982). This sometimes has occurred with the aid of modern broadcast media, with traditional performances, albeit somewhat changed in form, being broadcast over television and radio (Lent 1982).

Indigenous organisations and forms of social gatherings Indigenous organisations include religious groups, village meetings, irrigation associations such as Balinese *subak* (Lansing 1987), mothers' clubs and loan associations. These organisations orchestrate much communication through formal meetings of members, by messages sent about activities and obligations, and through work activities. There is inevitably overlap between this and other categories. For instance, indigenous organisations often arrange folk media performances, though performance is not usually their major aim. They provide many opportunities for unorganised communication among organisation members.

Deliberate instruction A large part of the enculturation process occurs through what C. P. Warren (1964: 10) terms 'deliberate instruction': 'an institutionalised act or set of acts performed by an individual to modify the behaviour of another individual and induce habit formation'.

Thus defined, deliberate instruction includes both 'directed learning' ('...informal acts of teaching...') and 'schooling' ('...formalised institutional activity...found only in literate societies with a few exceptions') (C. P. Warren 1964: 3-4). It includes child-rearing practices such as feeding, sphincter control and weaning, training during childhood and adolescence, as well as traditional (often religious) schools, and the instructions given by parents and other older people as a child works and plays in the fields or at home (Mosende 1981). It continues during adolescence and adulthood through initiation rites and other rites of passage, apprenticeship arrangements and the instructions given by indigenous authorities.

C. P. Warren (1964: 22) points out that the number of *agents of deliberate instruction* (those giving the training) increases as an infant grows into an adult. An infant typically receives training only from immediate kin (parents and older siblings); as the child matures, he or she interacts with larger and more diverse groups of kin and non-kin as a result of greater awareness and mobility, increasing reciprocal obligations and numbers of siblings. The relative influence of the immediate kin consequently decreases. Deliberate instruction continues after adolescence, however (C.P. Warren 1964: 6): 'any individual can learn and habituate something – an act or an idea – throughout the entire life cycle; the ability to learn is a matter of degree and is not confined to any particular phase of the life cycle.'

Despite the importance of deliberate instruction in enculturation and innovation diffusion, this topic has received little attention from development specialists. It seems that deliberate instruction is far more important in the communication of information than are occasional Indonesian *wayang kulit* puppet performances or village festivals, or even than the more ubiquitous exogenous channels of radio, television and schools.

Records Formal records – written, carved, painted or memorised – are another way of communicating indigenous information. Examples of this are the South Asian treatises on animal management written on palm leaves (FAO 1980), ancient scripts on *bai lan* leaves preserved in Thai Buddhist temples, and similar leaves containing records of land ownership and tax obligations in Bali (Geertz 1980: 179; Rupa 1985). Perhaps a study of 'indigenous librarianship' would turn up many examples of knowledge thus recorded. Such records do not have to be written. African storytellers narrate memorised historical epics and genealogies at length. Proverbs and folklore are other vehicles for transmitting cultural information.

Unstructured channels Indigenous communication occurs in many other settings: talk at home and at the well, in the fields and on the road, in the teahouse and coffee shop, in the chief's house and at the market, and wherever else people meet and talk. This communication is not organised or orchestrated but is spontaneous and informal. Communication among peer groups forms a major part of it. Folk media and indigenous organisations provide many opportunities for such unstructured communication before, during and after meetings and other activities. The importance of such channels is illustrated by the role of informal networks in Iranian bazaars in the overthrow of the Shah (Mowlana 1979).

Direct observation Doob (1960) points out that communication does not have to be intentional to take place. A farmer may see another's bumper crop and infer that the variety or technique used is good. An example of this process is given by Johnson (1983), who describes how a group of Machiguenga Indians in Peru began planting coffee after seeing others experiment with the crop. Nor does the source have to be another person. A dark cloud alerts us to a coming thunderstorm just as clearly as a verbal warning from another person could.

Indigenous communication sources

Not everyone in a society has the same indigenous technical knowledge (Swift 1979). Differences among individuals occur because of age, gender, experience, profession and personality. A person may be a highly skilled smith but know little of farming; another may be held in high esteem for her midwifery or gardening skills. In general, we can differentiate five different types of sources of information:

Indigenous experts are referred to as 'farmer paragons' by McCorkle *et al.* (1988: 71), are generally recognised as being skilled in areas such as crop or livestock raising. Everyone engaged in these activities has these skills to some degree; but the indigenous experts are sought out for advice on farming and other problems. These experts are probably opinion leaders in their specialties. Because men and women often perform different tasks, knowledge may be gender-specific or held in common by people of both sexes (Norem *et al.* 1989).

Indigenous professionals are a special type of indigenous expert with knowledge and skills not widely distributed among others in the society. This category includes healers, sorcerers, shamans, scribes, midwives, blacksmiths, irrigation-tunnel builders (in Bali) and water-temple priests who oversee irrigation systems in whole watersheds (also in Bali) (Lansing 1987). They may belong to certain clans or guilds and derive status or income from their skills, which they learn through long apprenticeships or on-the-job training. The 14 categories of indigenous veterinarians in Nepal, for instance, receive various types of training, ranging from formal government-sponsored instruction to experience and observation on the job (FAO 1984: 4-8). Non-indigenous counterparts of this group also are seen as professionals: doctors, lawyers, car mechanics and accountants; however, their knowledge and skills are based on exogenous knowledge and are acquired through formal education as well as apprenticeships.

Innovators are often considered deviants in their societies; they deliberately experiment and try out new ideas. Examples in the literature are 'Mr. Radio' and 'Mr. Researcher,' Nigerian farmers who experimented with new millet varieties (McCorkle 1988); 'El Loco,' a Peruvian farmer who successfully planted potatoes 1000 m. below the lowest elevation at which the crop normally grows (Rhoades and Bebbington 1988); and Mukibat, an East Javanese who developed and gave his name to a method of grafting hardy cassava tops onto high-yielding roots (Aumeeruddy and Pinglo 1989: 26). These innovators may develop new knowledge themselves, or they may introduce ideas they have obtained elsewhere through their frequent travels. They are a major source of the indigenous innovations that enter the society.

*Intermediaries1*who are formally designated as such. One example is the *juru arah* or herald in Balinese irrigation associations, who is responsible for informing association members about meetings and maintenance duties (Rupa 1985). Other examples are the linguists attached to West African rulers' courts (Doob 1960), town criers in West Africa, *akyeame* in Ghana and griots in francophone West Africa (McCorkle 1989a, personal communication). Non-indigenous equivalents of this group are the extension agent, interpreter and journalist – who do not originate but merely report, information.

Recipient-disseminators (Doob 1960) are informal intermediaries in the information chain. Unlike the previous category, the recipient-disseminator may receive an item of information and react to it (for instance by testing a new crop variety) before passing it on. Everyone in a communication system acts as a recipient-disseminator at some time. Recipient-disseminators who have links outside the local society are important conduits for the lateral exchange of both indigenous and exogenous innovations.

Table 7.1: Typology of the interface between knowledge and communication types

Communication systems	Knowledge systems	
	Exogenous	Indigenous
Exogenous	A. Technology transfer	C. Indigenous knowledge-based development
Indigenous	B. Diffusion; co-opting of traditional media	D. Cultural continuity and change

Information diffusion theory and network analysis provide a useful approach to studying the roles of these sources. Much indigenous communication occurs within highly homophilous groups or cliques. Such cliques facilitate efficient communication among their members but act as a barrier preventing new information from entering the clique. Boundary spanners such as bridges, liaisons and cosmopolites have links with people outside their own cliques; together with innovators, they introduce information to the network (Rogers and Agarwala-Rogers 1976).

A typology of the knowledge and communication interface

Despite the overlaps between types of communication, and corresponding problems in distinguishing indigenous from exogenous knowledge, it is helpful to think of a matrix that opposes both exogenous and indigenous types of each system (Table 7.1). The four quadrants represent the communication of each type of information through each type of channel. For ease of explanation, we deal first with the two quadrants on the diagonal (A and D) and then briefly discuss quadrants B and C.

Quadrant A: exogenous communication of exogenous information

Exogenous communication systems are used for many functions: to entertain, inform, educate, persuade and advertise. Perhaps the main channel for exogenous *technical* information in many countries is the school system. Technical information is a small part of most mass media fare; entertainment has the lion's share of most television and radio programming, while newspapers contain mainly news and advertising. The transmission of technical knowledge typically is relegated to unused time slots at inconvenient hours on the broadcast media and to the inside pages of newspapers. Books, pamphlets, newsletters and – in the developed world – magazines, are the main printed channels for technical information. The extension service is charged with delivering exogenous information to farmers through interpersonal contacts and the mass media.

This quadrant is the focus of most research in advertising and development communication. Much of the literature on agricultural technology transfer (for example, see Hornik 1988; World Bank 1985) is devoted to discovering how best to disseminate researcher-developed crop varieties and agricultural practices through the mass media and extension system. The idea behind the technology transfer strategy is to develop technologies that are clearly superior to current practices and to disseminate them through channels over which the disseminating agency has some control. Indigenous channels are seen as multipliers that will take over the dissemination process once the innovation has proven superior.

Quadrant D: indigenous communication of indigenous information

Just as exogenous information is communicated mainly by exogenous channels, indigenous information is transmitted almost exclusively through indigenous channels. But there seems to be very little in the communication literature about this topic. Most studies have concentrated on the spread of exogenous innovations rather than of locally generated information. Study of traditional communication systems has fallen largely into the realm of cultural anthropology rather than communication. But many anthropologists have not regarded the communication of technical knowledge as worthy of study, and what information there is on this topic likely is buried within ethnographies and studies devoted to other topics. There is a need to search for clues on how these communication systems work and to incorporate this knowledge into communication studies and development projects.

Information about technical knowledge forms only a small percentage of the total volume of messages in indigenous (or exogenous) communication. Other information in the realm of indigenous knowledge pertains to social organisation, actions and decision processes, values and beliefs, while entertainment, news, instructions and everyday social discourse account for the greater part of messages. Each of the six indigenous channels described earlier can carry technical messages, though some are more suited to this task than others. It seems that deliberate instruction is likely to be more important than folk media, for instance, despite the disproportionate attention the latter have received from anthropologists and communication scientists.

Technical messages may contain information, take the form of an object, or both. *Information* may be about an indigenous innovation or an item of traditional knowledge. It may relate to knowledge (cognitive domain), skills (psychomotor) or attitudes (affective). It may encapsulate the indigenous knowledge in verbal form ('plant maize on this type of soil') or may be in the form of news ('the store has some new seed' or 'the healer in the neighbouring village cured my daughter'). The distance travelled by such messages is shown by the far-flung reputations of traditional healers in Central Ghana, who attract apprentices from as far afield as Mali, Burkina Faso, Togo and Ivory Coast (D. M. Warren, personal communication).

The message also may take the form of an *object:* tools, for example, or germplasm such as seeds or cuttings. McCorkle *et al.* (1988: 38) describe how a man collected millet grains that had fallen to the ground after hearing a neighbour describe the benefits of the seed. Markets enable the exchange or purchase of such items as the orange cuttings that farmers in Central Java planted in their rice fields after the price of rice plummeted and that of oranges soared in the mid 1980s.

As Richards (1989) points out, indigenous knowledge is not static; it is constantly changing, adapting to new conditions and technologies. We can thus view indigenous knowledge, and hence messages about it, as having stable and dynamic components. The *dynamic* component arises through the introduction of innovations from outside (such as from neighbouring villages) and through the generation of innovations locally. These innovations are generated by farmers and other local people through a variety of means: deliberate experimentation, chance discoveries, or adapting practices introduced from outside. Rogers (1983) calls the last process 'reinvention'.

Intergenerational communication The *stable* component is derived from the stock of existing knowledge held in the society. This is re-created through communication from one generation to the next – the process of accumulation and passing down referred to by Wang (1982) and CIKARD (1988) and alluded to earlier in this chapter. This component has a stabilising function because it perpetuates the knowledge base of the society and serves to maintain the culture.

Much indigenous knowledge is not written but is preserved in peoples' minds, often with remarkable accuracy. Because of the failings of memory, however, it must be repeated to ensure it is not forgotten. Such repetition can take two forms: *use*, as when an indigenous professional practices his or her skills, and *communication* to others. The process of communication can thus be seen as a method of preserving the body of indigenous knowledge within a culture.

Breakdowns in intergenerational communication can have disastrous effects on culture. For instance, the Kayapó Indians in the Amazon are thought to have changed from a peaceful tribe to a number of warlike, mutually hostile groups because introduced diseases wiped out the tribe's older people, destroying the seat of culture (Posey 1987). Barth (1975) mentions a tribe in Papua New Guinea that lost most of its traditional initiation rites because all the older men died. Similar cultural destruction is occurring today in refugee camps in many parts of Africa.

Lateral communication Lateral communication is the diffusion of information, including indigenous innovations, from one area to another or among peer groups. These lateral networks bring new ideas into the culture; they are thus a *dynamic* aspect of indigenous communication. McCorkle *et al.*'s (1988) case study of the spread of indigenous innovations in Niger is one of the few studies of such mechanisms. It is possible that the same networks are active for indigenous as for comparable exogenous innovations. Techniques used in diffusion research (Rogers 1983) could be applied to the study of these networks.

Through the process of development, acceptance, adaptation, use and communication to others, both indigenous and exogenous innovations may enter the corpus of knowledge that is replicated in successive generations. The acceptance and communication of such information to the next generation within the culture are features that distinguish indigenous from exogenous knowledge.

Quadrant B: indigenous communication of exogenous information

As with indigenous technical information, any of the six indigenous communication channels may transmit exogenous messages, though some are more likely to than others. For instance, news about a successful new crop variety will spread quickly through direct observation and unorganised channels. Lent (1982) gives several examples of successful uses of indigenous opinion leaders in spreading family planning and other innovations. The spread of exogenous information and technologies through such interpersonal networks has been the focus of much of the vast literature on innovation diffusion. While most of this research has been conducted in the United States, numerous studies of innovation diffusion also have been made in Third World societies, identifying such features as opinion leadership, the importance of homophily, socioeconomic status, interpersonal networks, and so forth. Much effort has been put into identifying characteristics of key actors (innovators and opinion leaders) in order to target them for development messages (Rogers 1983).

Organised channels and folk media are also frequently coopted to spread exogenous information. Many extensionists try to use traditional organisations to spread family planning and agricultural messages. In the last two decades much attention has been given to the folk media. Kidd (1982) lists 1779 references on their conscious use to promote social change. Successful examples include Cashman's (1987) use of plays to advertise the 'fertiliser bush' (alley cropping using leguminous trees) in Nigeria and the Indonesian government's use of *wayang* puppet plays to spread family planning messages (Surdjodiningrat 1982). Kidd (1982), Lent (1982), Parmar (1975), Rangagath (1980), Valbuena (1986), and Wang and Dissanayake (1982, 1984) discuss such uses of folk media. The advantages of using these media as an element in a communication campaign include their familiarity and credibility to local people and the potential for the involvement of the audience in performances.

Two problems are evident in using folk media to spread development messages produced by others. The first is that even though in their original forms they may contain morals or substantive messages, these media carry primarily entertainment in the same way as Western mass media do. Audiences may therefore not perceive or understand the development messages included in the script (Lent 1982).

The second problem is that audiences may resent the use of traditional forms to convey development messages (Lent 1982; Diaz Bordenave 1975; Compton 1980). Because message production is outside local control, such adaptation may lead to 'domestication' ('the process whereby groups in power seek to channel and neutralise...oppressed peoples' (Freire 1973)) rather than 'liberation.' One way to avoid this is to enable local people to develop their own messages and performances, as described by Compton (1980) in the Philippines.

There is also a need to follow up the folk media campaign with practical support, as with the use of literacy workers to organise reading groups following performances by Filipino *barrio* cultural groups.

Quadrant C: exogenous communication of indigenous information

Few examples exist of indigenous information being transmitted via exogenous channels, though this has great growth potential. One example if the Foxfire Project in Georgia, in which school children collect information on traditional skills from older people in the area and public it in the form of magazines and books. Another example is the growing scientific literature on indigenous knowledge (for example, Brokensha *et al.* 1980) and the documentation efforts of Iowa State University's Centre for Indigenous Knowledge for Agriculture and Rural Development (CIKARD) and other institutions described elsewhere in this volume. A third example is the emphasis given to farming systems research in many countries, and within this, the movement toward farmer-managed research. Technology emerging from field surveys and on-farm trials is inserted into the scientific information system, and from there may filter through to the extension services or is disseminated directly to neighbouring farmers (*e.g.* McCorkle 1989b).

A major area of potential growth is in the use of exogenous communication techniques to enable farmers to learn directly about indigenous knowledge. Among the few examples of this in the developing world is *Minka*, a low-cost magazine devoted to recording and disseminating the knowledge of local farmers to other farmers in the Peruvian Andes (Altieri 1984). The 'farm tips' pages of US farm magazines and the growing number of sustainable agriculture newsletters are First World equivalents. The potential for developing research and extension systems that draw on indigenous knowledge and farmers' proclivity to experiment is enormous.

Indigenous communication: where do we go from here?

Indigenous communication has been touched on by specialists in various disciplines, including development communication, extension, sociology, cultural anthropology, education, folklore and theatre, as well as by scientists in several agricultural and health-related disciplines. Much of this work has, however, concentrated on using indigenous channels to promote exogenous innovations (quadrant B in Table 7.1). While more work is clearly needed in this area, development efforts are likely to be less effective if we continue to ignore the communication of information on indigenous knowledge (quadrants C and D). It is necessary to study communication patterns to design interventions that benefit from this knowledge. While each of the disciplines mentioned has a role to play, we believe that ethnographic methods will prove particularly useful in discovering how indigenous communication operates.

Any development strategy based on indigenous knowledge must consider the repositories of that knowledge. The benefits of integrating indigenous and exogenous specialists into a single system are illustrated by a benefit-cost analysis (Zessin and Carpenter 1985) that showed that Schwabe and Kuojok's (1981) proposal to use indigenous veterinarians as a disease surveillance system in southern Sudan was cheaper than a conventional mass-vaccination programme.

We echo Compton's (1973) plea that indigenous specialists not be regarded as paraprofessional aides to exogenous professionals. Rather, they must be seen and treated as experts in their own right, for that is what they are. Training activities for such specialists should seek to build on their existing knowledge rather than replace it with alien practices. And these specialists should be used as expert consultants to advise in the planning and implementation of development efforts.

We are deceiving ourselves if we think we can manoeuvre local people into doing what we think is best for them. Local initiative has often been neglected in the design of development efforts. Tapping indigenous communication channels can help ensure that this initiative is incorporated. An understanding of indigenous communication improves the chances of true collegial participation by local people and outsiders in such efforts.

8. Incorporating Farmers' Knowledge in International Rice Research[1]

SAM FUJISAKA

Introduction

ALTHOUGH STUDIED BY social scientists for the last 30 years, the technical knowledge of farmers has only recently been incorporated into agricultural research leading to the generation of new technologies. Ethnoscientific techniques developed by ethnobotanists as early as the 1950s revealed how swidden agriculturalists applied detailed botanical knowledge (Conklin 1957, Johnson 1974). The 'Green Revolution' later stimulated research on farmers' decision making relative to technology adoption (Gladwin 1983), risk and uncertainty (Cancian 1972, Ortiz 1980), crop protection (Norton 1976) and external factors (Barlett 1976). By the early 1980s, agricultural researchers not only worked to understand indigenous or farmers' technical knowledge, but also began to explore ways to enlarge its practical role in development (Brokensha, Warren, and Werner 1980).

The incorporation of farmer's knowledge and practice in technology generation gained momentum when anthropologists and post-harvest technologists from the International Potato Centre (CIP) worked with farmers to develop diffused light post-harvest storage technologies for seed potatoes. One result is that such storage technologies are now used by farmers in more than 50 countries (Rhoades 1984, Horton 1984). The work also resulted in a much needed farmer-back-to-farmer model of technology generation (Rhoades and Booth 1982).

Others have shown cogently how development specialists or 'outsiders' need to really understand the knowledge and practices of the rural poor (Chambers 1983), and to build upon adaptation by and inventiveness of farmers (Richards 1985). More recently, a Centre for Indigenous Knowledge for Agriculture and Rural Development was created (Warren and Cashman 1988).

Awareness of the need to incorporate farmers' perspectives in research at the International Rice Research Institute (IRRI) has increased, as the institute's emphasis has shifted from the irrigated lowlands to rainfed lowland and upland rice ecosystems, and as the sustainability and stability of these systems have started to be addressed as research problems. Rice provides 35–60 per cent of the caloric intake of 2.7 billion people in Asia where 90 per cent of the world's rice is grown and eaten. Criteria such as area, production, dependent consumers, and efficiency argue for research in irrigated areas: 49 per cent of the world's 138 million ha of rice is irrigated; and this area accounts for 72 per cent of world production. On the other hand, large numbers of poor producers, a predominance of the less favourable rice ecosystems in poorer rice producing countries, and worsening environmental degradation underscore the need for rice research in non-irrigated areas.

The rainfed lowlands account for 29 per cent of the world's rice area and 19 per cent of production; uplands account for 13 per cent of rice area and five per cent of production; and deepwater accounts for nine per cent of area and four per cent of production (IRRI 1989). Fifty per cent of world rice production is

124

consumed by the producers, mostly resource-poor farm households; and numbers of marginal farmers and rural landless are increasing, possibly to more than one billion by 2020. Many of these people are moving into the uplands and, where still possible, into less favourable rainfed lowland areas (IRRI 1989).

In response to these needs – which heightened in the 1980s – interdisciplinary teams of agronomists, plant protection specialists, plant breeders, agricultural economists, and agricultural anthropologists at IRRI are seeking to incorporate farmer perspectives into the development of appropriate rice technologies and have provided farmer-oriented assessments of rice research priorities for collaborative country programs. The purpose of this paper is to discuss methods and to describe an example of each of these research activities from the rainfed lowland and upland rice environments.

Methods

Methods needed to discover farmer knowledge are well known to social anthropologists and ethnobotanists, but these have rarely been applied to agricultural research and the technology generation process. Probably the most useful are ethnographic field methods in which samples of farmers are interviewed using open-ended guide questions.

Responses are evaluated and directions of inquiry followed or abandoned as interactive discussions, which are conducted on farmers' fields, unfold. Categories used by farmers, classification systems, and technical knowledge are elicited. Relevant questions for subsequent interviews are identified or refined in initial interviews. On-farm work also includes monitoring of farmers' crop management practices and of weeds, fallow succession, soils, insect pests, and sampling of crop cuts. Analysis includes simple descriptive statistics, partial budgets, and descriptive accounts of whole farm systems.

Claveria: a Philippines test site

IRRI's key site for on-farm research for improving upland rice-based systems is at Claveria in the southern Philippines (Figure 8.1). The majority of Claveria farmers are migrants from the Visayas who have arrived since the 1940s seeking a broader land base. The municipal population has doubled since the 1960s, reaching almost 30,000 by the early 1980s (NCSO 1980). The settlers' semi-shifting cultivation and logging resulted in conversion of more and more of the forest to crop and grassland. Although pasture leases of up to 1000 ha are found, the farm sizes of most owners, tenants, and land reform beneficiaries are less than three ha. The small-scale farmers are faced with making a living in a difficult but typical upland area of Asia. Acid, infertile soils, characterised by moderately well-drained clays of pH 3.9-5.2, predominate. More than half the land is above 15 per cent slope and severely eroded. Although mean annual rainfall is 2200 mm, most of this falls during July–December leaving a dry season of uncertain rains from October to March. Weeds and diseases, especially blast, are also major problems in rice production.

Cropping pattern trials were a main part of the initial work to develop improved upland technologies at the site. Trials were located on the more favourable but limited flatter lands. This section describes how a better understanding of the problems facing most farmers in the area led to new approaches to the development of technologies for managing sloping lands.

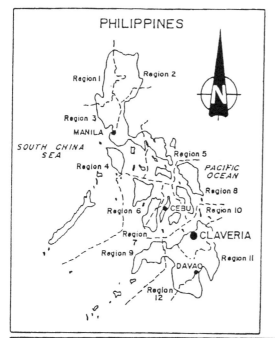

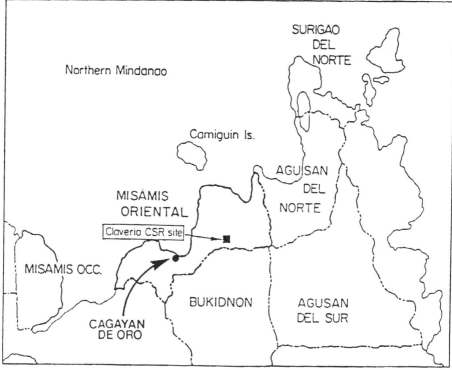

Figure 8.1: *Claveria, Misamis Oriental, Philippines. Key IRRI on-farm research
site for acid upland rice ecosystems*

Farmers' practice and knowledge

In a set of initial interviews, 55 farmers readily shared their knowledge concerning the local environment, identified crop production problems, discussed related changes in land and soil, and described what they had tried to do about the problems. Although from different areas of the country, farmers had acquired a shared knowledge base pertaining to local conditions. They tested land, soil, crop, cultivar and input combinations. Land was classified by slope and elevation, and soil by fertility, colour, texture, acidity and friability. For example, red *(puwa puwa)* soils were poor *(niwang,* 'thin') and acidic *(aslom,* 'sour'), and poor soils were red (Table 8.1).

Table 8.1: Claveria farmers' land and soil categories

Soil		Land	
Undesirable characteristics			
puwa puwa	red	bakilid	sloping
niwang, umau	poor, thin	buntod buntod	hilly
walay sustancia	nothing left	batohon	rocky
aslom	'sour' or acidic	nagasgasan	washed out, lit,
pundok pundok	spotty fertility		'scratched'
pagkumot magbuwag/	disintegrates when		
magkabuwag	held		
Desirable characteristics			
tambok tambok	fertile, rich	patag patag	flat
itom itom	black, dark	bunkag	newly opened
bukakhaon	absorbs/holds water	kabugon	low-lying area
madali madayao	not easily dried	basak	
waterway/lowland			
pughay na, humok	friable		
balason	sandy		
medyo mopilit	quite sticky		
bonbon	silt (rich)		
More neutral characteristics			
mogahi, mobagtik	crusty	nahanay hay,	
tibuok	coarse	nahandig	gently sloping
**	sakom	kaingin	

Soil erosion was considered a major problem: 90 per cent of the respondents reported yield declines due to soil erosion. They discussed erosion due to rainfall run-off, called attention to parts of fields and crops damaged, and identified different types of erosion in local terms. About 15 per cent said non-contour plowing contributed to problems. Respondents welcomed nutrients eroded from neighbors' slopes, especially pastures, but they described how heavy rains led to destructive flooding in lower areas. Farmers observed changes in their soils. Many said soils initially had been dark on top and reddish underneath but, over time, the top layer had eroded away. Poorer red sub-soils were exposed and increased while more fertile dark soils were lost. Farmers gave estimates of losses of darker soils, *e.g.*, from 50 cm depth in 1976 to 10 cm in 1986. Farmers described ways to conserve soils. Planting perennials in upper slopes, diversion canals, and bananas planted in gullies to trap soil and utilise eroded nutrients were each cited by 50 per cent. Some 20 per cent named grassy strips across slopes or along field borders, *Leucaena leucocephala* strips, weed or crop residue piled across gullies, contour plowing and cover crops. Practices adopted, however, fell short of knowledge: 20 per cent of the farmers interviewed constructed diversion canals. Others left weedy strips between plots, piled weeds and crop residues across, or planted banana in channels. Only a few land owners planted perennials on slopes. No one planted trees in strips or on upper slopes. Some left trees on fallowed areas; but most reported that they lacked enough land to plant trees. Farmers also discussed perceptions and practices pertaining to soil nutrients. Of the 55 informants, 96 per cent claimed that inorganic fertilisers, lime, and chicken manure are needed to boost production and to maintain or improve soils; but that these were wasted on slopes because of erosion.

In practice, few purchased inputs are used for the main crops. Plot selection, however, is carefully considered. Traditional maize is planted on better soil, rice or cassava on poorer type. Highest levels of inputs are applied to tomatoes given potential high returns, residual P benefits from chicken manure, and risks usually shared with a financier. Lower levels of inputs are applied to hybrid maize and an improved upland rice, UPLRi5.

No one used green manures, and no farmer who had grown legumes saw soil nutrient benefits from crop or biomass. Eight switched from burning to crop residue incorporation. Some 70 per cent mentioned compost benefits; but only six farmers had pits. Labour (including hauling water) and lack of raw materials limit compost production. Although farmers thought dung increased soil fertility, they generally grazed draft animals and did not husband manure. Farmers knew that field fallows were supposed to lead to nutrient regeneration, but had observed few positive effects of fallows in Claveria. The researchers analysed fallow weeds and soils, and the farmers' perceptions were discovered to be essentially correct. Vegetative succession no longer proceeds past grasses *(Imperata cylindrica, Saccharum spontaneum, Paspalum spp.).* Organic matter increased, but levels of nitrogen and phosphorus remained low.

Technology identification and transfer

The initial studies indicated several things about Claveria farmers. Although mostly migrants from other areas, they had learned about and had adapted their farming practices to local conditions. Farmers with sloping lands were very concerned about soil erosion. They knew of several ways to conserve soils and had tried a few of the measures on their farms. Farmers were knowledgeable about various alternatives for soil nutrient management, but faced cash and labour constraints. Based on such findings and on discussions between farmers and researchers (Fujisaka and Garrity 1988), an agroforestry-based technology of contour ditches and bunds established by A-frame (Figure 8.2) and planted to hedgerows seemed potentially appropriate for soil erosion control. The technology harnesses erosive forces to form terraces between planted strips and is appropriate for areas with sloping land, permanent plow agriculture, intense rainfall, and land scarcity. Contour hedgerows have been tried in various countries (Young 1986) including the Philippines (World Neighbors n.d.). It also seemed appropriate and cost effective to link farmers from different areas in a system of 'farmer-to-farmer' communication rather than follow traditional procedures in technology transfer.

World Neighbors, a non-governmental organisation working with upland

Table 8.2: Examples of Claveria farmers' concepts/statements concerning sustainable crop production

Crops and soil nutrients

Cassava adds soil acidity
Cassava gobbles up soil nutrients
Rice is more tolerant of acidic soils than is maize
Rice is more vigorous on an area previously planted to tomato
The effect of decomposed rice straw is like that of lime
Intercropping is good only if there are complete chemicals

Nutrient depletion

Soil fertility has been used up
The soil is weak
Fertility is spotty
Soils are over-trained
The soils are getting older
Poor, but not used up in the sense of hardest part within a log

Fallows

The decomposing leaves of the weeds help to enrich the soil
The land is resting so the soil can store some nutrients
Rich because it is rested
Fertility is added and the soil is made cool
The soil is slightly enriched if left a short time

Weeds

Rice was harmed by *cogon (I. cylindrica)* roots
Poor soil if *cogon* dominates
D. longiflora and *cogon* consume soil nutrients and destroy soil quality
Acidity increases where *cogon* dominates
Weeds are thin on infertile soils
R. cochinchinensis rapidly produces seed, thus easily soars in population
If not weeded, it exceeds the height of rice or corn
Fertility is added and the soil is made cool *(Calapogonium spp.)*
Soil is good where there are weeds/grasses with nodules

Soil erosion

Soil slides down and floats away
Nutrients are drawn down
Plants are eroded along with soil
Soil was drawn down and fertility was washed out
The land was shaven and eroded after trees were removed
Fertiliser is collected (on lower plots) due to rain

Erosion control

Banana and coconut are better because they hold the soil
Contour plowing reduces downslope erosion losses
Weedy strips can decrease erosion effects
Trees planted above and below fields can decrease erosion effects
Banana planted above and below fields can decrease erosion effects

Figure 8.2:   *The A-frame. The A-frame transit is shaped like the capital letter 'A'.*
              It is made of three pieces of wood or bamboo, twine or nails and a
              rock or other weight
              Source: World Neighbors Brochure for farmers

farmers in Cebu (an island with high population and very eroded uplands), successfully employed a 'menu' of contour technologies by facilitating farmer participation, group cooperation and minimal farmer subsidies. In response to a
request by the team from IRRI, farmers from Cebu agreed to teach contour
farming to a group from Claveria. The Claveria participants chosen were those
who had described soil erosion and nutrient depletion, had tried to address the
problems, and did not want degraded land to force them to migrate again to a

new arca. With fares paid by IRRI, they went to Cebu for 'hands-on' training in establishment of contour bunds, ditches, and hedgerows of fodder grasses (napier, *Pennisetum purpureum*) and legume trees *(Gliricidia sepium)*. Upon return from Cebu, the farmers worked as a cooperative group, and other farmers joined the group, as work got underway. Local *G. sepium* and *P. purpureum* were located and planted. Heavy storms damaged the work, causing a new member to drop out.

Most of the farmers who had been trained in Cebu recalled the warning that substantial maintenance was needed for about three years. The first group established almost 7000 m of hedgerows on 10 parcels, with a mean size of 0.8 ha. Labour per ha varied, but averaged 29 days/ ha (with 55 per cent spent for shoveling). The 673 to 1555 m per ha reflect variation in slope and distances between strips. Differences in soil compaction and ground cover meant that 17 to 57 m/person-day of planted strip were established.

Farmer and researcher adaptive research

Farmers immediately started to experiment with the technology. They tested combinations of hedgerow species, including grasses (*e.g.*, *Panicum maximum*), trees (local *Cassia spectabilis*), cash perennials (coffee, cacao, fruit), wild sunflower *(Helianthus annus)*, and weeds that are otherwise pests *(D. longiflora, Paspalum conjugatum)*. Compared to trees, grasses appeared to provide more effective, faster terracing. Grasses, however, may exacerbate problems of root aphids *(Tetraneura nigriabdominalis* or *Rhophalosiphum rufiabdominalis)*, and white grubs *(Holotrichia spp. or Leucopholis irrorata)*, a problem being examined at various upland rice areas (Litsinger *et al.* 1987).

Some farmers added hedgerows between initial strips. One researcher assumed the reason was to increase biomass production, but the farmers named terracing and erosion control as their goals. As a result, emphasis of the formal research conducted at the site shifted from nutrient cycling alone to more work on soil erosion control. Farmers noticed *G. sepium* on the down-slope of the bund suffered from competition from napier grass above. A farmer's experiment of tree above and grass below provided a superior alternative. Researchers thought *P. purpureum* grown for goat fodder in Cebu was inappropriate for Claveria because local forage appeared to be adequate and because legumes are more desirable for potential nutrient cycling benefits. Large pastures, however, are not accessible to small farmers, and fodder for draft animals is often scarce, and is therefore valued.

Farmers tried different ways of planting *G. sepium* cuttings once problems of termites and poor rooting became apparent. Because seedlings are not affected, farmers and researchers built a small nursery to supply and test *G. sepium* and *C. spectabilis* seedlings. Seed germination of *C. spectabilis* was low. One farmer had no trouble, but no 'secret' was discerned from his methods. Timing of seed gathering and sowing is being tested.

Although some researchers were impatient for farmers to 'do it right' (*e.g.*, modify bunding methods to save labour, grow legume trees for biomass, cut weeds and grass to reduce competition with *G. sepium*), farmers accepted technology adaptation as a step-by-step process. As their lands were terraced, the Cebu farmers switched crops from cereals to flowers or vegetables, and started to use manure and fertiliser for these cash crops. Claveria farmers expect to be able to make similar changes.

The farmers' willingness to solve problems over time was well matched to the evolutionary nature of the hedgerow system. A field with broken bunds was temporarily abandoned, but then terraced well as weeds and napier grass took over the bunds. Napier grass on the bunds was too competitive with crops planted in the alleys. Farmers then wanted to try other grasses or legumes, as well as penned goats to convert fodder to manure. Hedgerow-crop competition was investigated. Forage varieties are being screened and goats are being tested as parts of an improved nutrient cycling system.

An additional 25 farmers have since adopted contour hedgerows. In addition to contour bunds and ditches planted to trees and grasses, some of the more experimental forms include grassy hedgerows formed by laying down crop and weed residues along the contour, stone-walled bench terraces, and even contours planted to cassava with rice in the alleys.

Participation of farmers in technology dissemination

The Department of Agriculture (DA) of the Philippines and IRRI are working to develop methods that can be used by national agricultural programs that facilitate technology adoption. A past approach targeted farmers with sloping lands next to the road and featured lectures by 'experts' and fixed technology packages. The IRRI team, however, opted for the participation of farmers concerned about their soil losses, farmer-to-farmer training, and farmer participation in technology generation.

Other on-farm research

On-farm team research is also conducted at an infertile, flood and drought-prone rainfed lowland rice area in NE Thailand. Farmers' lands, soils, and cultivar combinations and management were studied. Understanding manure management led to experiments combining manure and pre-rice green manures such as *Sesbania rostrata*. On-farm research in the Philippines also examined a seeding/modern variety/weed control technology for upland rice in South Cotabato as well as the use of green manures in rainfed lowland rice in Northern Luzon. These farmer's practices are being compared to experimental data and possibilities for diffusion of such farmer-developed innovations are being examined.

Kampuchea: an example of research priority identification

Kampuchea's rice yields (1.2 t/ha) are the lowest in Asia, and rice is regularly imported. Constraints to increased production include few human resources for rice research and extension, a poor production and marketing infrastructure, and a lack of improved technologies appropriate to farmers.

In 1987, the Australian International Development Assistance Bureau (AIDAB) funded IRRI for ten months to plan collaborative rice research in Kampuchea. A draft proposal was prepared, but AIDAB responded that it did not demonstrate a sufficient understanding of Khmer farmers and their circumstances. The work described below followed. Based on a better understanding of farmer perspectives (Pingali 1988, Fujisaka 1988a), IRRI was funded for an initial three years of work in Kampuchea. This section discusses the rainfed lowlands, farmers' knowledge and practice, *krom samakki* ('solidarity group') organisation, and research recommendations.

The rainfed lowland rice environment

Only 17 per cent (3.1 million ha) of Kampuchea's 18.1 million ha is cropped. Rice is grown on 1.8 million ha, 80 per cent of which is rainfed lowland. Lands range from level to gently undulating. Problems include poor soils and drought in upper terraces and flooding in lower. The mostly sandy topsoils are infertile, with pH ranging from 4.5 to 6.0 (excluding alkaline soils near Takeo, Prey Veng). Rains (averaging 1400–1800 mm.) start in April–May, and large areas flood from July–August to October–November. The dry season starts December–January.

Farmers' perception and practice

Farmers were interviewed in Takeo, Kandal and Kampong Speu. These provinces represent eight per cent of the nation's land area, 24 per cent of the population, 20 per cent of the rice area, and 22 per cent of rice production. Farmers described the systems in which rice cultivars and management practices are carefully matched to different landscape and hydrologies.

Farmers described most of their land as upper paddy *(dey kpous)* with 0–15 cm water and sandy *(ksach)* or silt with sand *(dey lbay ksach)* soils. Middle or 'normal' *(dey tommada)* paddy had 15 cm water and sands to sandy clays *(dey kanding lea ksach)*. If not waterlogged or if crops are not flooded out, lower paddies *(dey trapaing, dey thip, dey chumrau)* are the most productive. These paddies have earlier and longer lasting water of 30–80 cm and from sandy to silty *(dey lbop)* or sand mixed with clay soil *(dey ath leay ksach)* (Table 8.3).

Table 8.3. Kampuchean farmers' land and soil classifications

Khmer	Translation	Equivalent
Landscape position/relative water depth		
kpous	high/shallow; normal for MVs	0-15 cm water
tommada	middle fields; normal for TVs	10-30 cm
chumrau, thip, trapaing	lower/deep	30-80 cm
Soil texture		
dey ksach	sand	sand
dey lbop	silt	silt
dey ath	clay	clay
Textural classes		
dey ksach	sandy soil	all of the sand group
dey ath	(infertile) clay soil	clay
dey ath leah ksach	sandy clay	sandy clay
dey kanding leah, kasch	sandy-silt clay	silty clay/silty; clay loam
dey lbay ksach	silt and sand	silt loam
Soil tilth/bulk density		
reng	hard/compacted	
tun	soft/friable	

Traditional cultivars (TVs), which are photoperiod-sensitive, and of long duration, flower in December and are adapted to medium-long flooding of various depths up to 50 cm. They accounted for about one million ha in 1986-7.

Both modern varieties (MVs, especially IR36 and IR42), which are non-photoperiod-sensitive and of short duration, and the weakly-sensitive short-medium duration TVs, are now planted on shallow rainfed or partially irrigated areas in the wet season. Reported MV yields were about 2.0 t/ha in the wet season and 2.5 t/ha in the dry. TV yields were 0.6–3.0 t/ha. Table 8.4 lists some respondents' cultivars, respective micro-environments, and yields.

Table 8.4. Cultivars, rice environment, reported yield, and other comments of rainfed-rice farmers in Kampuchea.

Variety	Land, soil	Yields tons/ha	Comments
Pram Bae Kourt	hip-kpous, ksach, dey ath leah ksach	1.5–2.0	shallow–medium depth 165 days, PP sens
Lum Ong Ksak	tommada, ksach	1.9	medium (15–25 cm) water depth, 180 day
Chmar Chang Kom	thip, ksach	2.8	50+ cm water, 190–95 days, tall PP sens
Sambok Angkong	kpous, dey lbay ksach	1.2	
Phkar Kgney	kpous, dey lbay ksach, dey ath	0.6–2.0	0.6 empty grains drought at flowering 2.0 manage like IR36
Srov Sor	tommada, dey kanding leah ksach	0.7	late transp, drought at flowering
Pkasla	chumrau, dey lbop	1.2	
Kong Plouk	trapaing, lbay ksach or dey ath	3.0	40+ cm water depth, 180 days, 0.6 tons/ha farmyard manure
IR36	kpous, dey ksach	2.0–3.0	inorganic fertiliser 30–45 kg N/ha
IR42	kpous-tommada, ksach	2.0–3.0	30–45 kg N/ha
Phkar Phneou	kpous, dey ath leah	2.0	weak/non-sensitive,
Sor Kroop	ksach, dey kanding		medium duration TVs
Pkar Dong	leah ksach, dey lbay ksach		no inorg. fert. used
IR36	same as above	1.5–4.8	usual yield 2.5 tons/ha; 70 kg. N/ha and pump gave 4.8t; prob. seed dormancy
IR42	kpous-tommada	1.5–3.0	shatters

The traditional rice crop management practices rely on human labour. Problems faced by farmers include labour scarcity, lack of inputs such as inorganic fertiliser, and drought and flooding. On the positive side, the TVs suffer from relatively few pests and diseases, and farmers have developed various means to cope with their resource poor circumstances. The main wet season crop is transplanted June–September and harvested late September to early February. Land is plowed twice and harrowed once or twice in mid-May to mid-September using simple breaking plows (with or without steel shares) and crude wooden comb harrows drawn by ox pairs. About 15 person-days/ha are spent per plowing. TV seedbeds are sown early June to late July. Pulling and transplanting requires about 14 person days/ha and is done mid-July to as late as early October if delayed by drought. Late rains result not only in poor land levelling, late transplanting, and reduced yield, but in late paddy fish and frogs, smaller fish, and a smaller catch as well. Most TVs are harvested December to January, although short- and medium-duration varieties are harvested as early as October. Stalks are cut with sickles, sheaved, and threshed by beating against slanted boards. Paddy is air dried on mats. Winnowing is by hand using flat baskets. Paddy is stored in large baskets, wattle-and-daub huts on stilts, or fertiliser sacks, and is generally milled by hand or in small local mills.

Women do most of the pulling, transplanting, weeding, harvesting, threshing, winnowing, drying, hand milling and seed management. Men do much of the plowing, harrowing, and some threshing. Males made up only 28 per cent of working-age adults in the villages visited. The low proportion of adult males throughout Kampuchea was due to deaths during the Pol Pot period and because of their service in the army.

Weeds were not a major problem, except for the drought-prone upper paddies that need three to four hand weedings. 'Rice-like' weeds *(smao srov* and *sro ngair,* probably *Leptochloa chinensis* and *Echinchloa crus-galli)* were reported as problems. A few broadleaves and sedges *(Monochoria hastata, Ludwigia adscendens, Sphenoclea zeylanica, Fimbristylis miliacea, Cyperus ferax, C. iria)* appeared to be the worst weeds. Lower paddies are not weeded.

Insects were not considered a serious problem. Stemborer, *Chilo spp.* or *Scirpophaga spp. (dong khao),* is a pest of MVs and is sprayed up to three times with monocrotophos or unnamed Soviet pesticides. Some medium deep water cultivars *(e.g., Kong Pluok)* reportedly had no insect problems. Leaffolder, *Cnaphalocrocis medinalis (dangkov mou slek),* was present but not a problem. Rat losses were considered serious, but no means of control were reported.

As is typical of rainfed lowland rice areas, upper paddies suffer from drought and lower paddies from submergence and flooding. Some farmers with land next to water sources use manual water lifting devices *(e.g.,* pedal *rohat* or tripod mounted water shovel *snach).* Several areas visited were awash, overtaxing irrigation, drainage, and water control systems. Of the canals, reservoirs, dikes, and drainage systems built during the Pol Pot period, some were poorly designed; others are inoperable due to lack of maintenance or the disappearance or breakdown of pumps.

Little inorganic fertiliser is used for rice. Amounts depended on what the government could allocate to cooperatives. The co-ops visited received at most 43 kg N/ha of MV planted at costs of 3 kg paddy/kg of 16-20-0 and 2 kg/kg urea. Farmyard manure (FYM) management varied, but was more intensive where animals and manure have been privatised. FYM was applied to shallower, middle paddies at the rate of up to 3 t/ha. Farmers appeared to be familiar with green manures. They incorporated or added to FYM *Chromalaena odorata (tontrean khet),* a common dryland weed. Earlier studies had found that 20 t/haof fresh biomass provided 112 kg N, 12 kg P, and 87 kg K per ha, and that rice yields were higher with the green manure than with inorganic fertiliser plus FYM (Litzenberger and Ho Tong Lip 1968). Some farmers incorporated rice straw, a practice that can be beneficial if the flooded period before transplanting is adequate. Farmers trade paddy to the state for consumer goods. The low state paddy price (US$ 0.02/kg) is offset by exchange goods being 3–4 times cheaper than open-market. Farmers sell milled rice on the private market for US$ 0.08/kg. Other income sources include vegetables, fruit, cottage industries *(e.g.,* silk weaving), pedicab *(cyclo)* driving in Phnom Penh, palm sugar, and, importantly, fishing in paddies and watercourses.

Krom Samakki Any farmer-participatory work conducted in Kampuchea would have to consider changing structure of farmer cooperatives. In 1979 farmers were organised into *krom samakki*, groups of 10–15 families, which were supposed to share resources, jointly farm up to 25 ha, and follow official rules, record keeping and crop management. Cooperatives ideally provided for widows, orphans, and the old or disabled.

There were 3 *krom* levels. At level 1, productive resources were pooled, produce was divided among working members , and inputs and taxes were paid collectively. At level 2, land (still state-owned) was distributed to families according to number of members. Implements, animals and labour were private, and traditional exchange labour *(provas dai knia)* was allowed. At level 3, all means of production were privately managed. Level 3 groups were common where land and draft animals were plentiful, such as in Prey Veng, Kampong Thom, Kampong Cham, and Battambang provinces.

The government is allowing changes in the *krom* structure. From 1979 to 1987, level 1 *krom* increased from 3 per cent to 19 per cent, level 2 from 27 per cent to 73 per cent, but level 3 decreased from 70 per cent to 7 per cent. Although members experienced the problem of 'waiting for each other to work', level 1 *krom* are now either those most in need of state welfare or are really irrigation pump coops that the government provided with pump and fuel. Transition from level 1 to 2 was accompanied by private income diversification. Level 3 groups declined because they were given the least access to fertilisers, pesticides, MV seed, credit, international aid, and pumps.

Recommendations for research

The goal of the study was to identify priorities for a collaborative IRRI-Kampuchea project in rice research. These priorities had to consider constraints at the national level and had to reflect the needs and potentials of the country's poor rice farmers and consumers. Some of the recommendations – which are now being implemented – are described as a further example of building farmers' perspectives into proposed research.

1. Additional research on farmers' circumstances was suggested. A better understanding is needed of how farmers manage and make decisions regarding diverse yet limited resources, implications of a farm population dominated by women and children, and potentials for farmer's participation and technology transfer, given a changing krom samakki structure.
2. Given the diversity of local rice cultivars adapted to equally varied environmental conditions, it was suggested that research on varietal improvement should first consider farmers' TVs and corresponding management practices. An ideal variety for much of the rainfed lowland areas would (Mackill 1987: 4):

   ○ be photoperiod-sensitive;
   ○ flower in late November or early December;
   ○ have intermediate plant height; and
   ○ be submergence-tolerant.

   Observation and replicated yield trials using local and introduced entries have already started, and multi-location testing throughout the country was recommended.

3. Given farmers' knowledge and adaptation to their rainfed lowland rice ecosystems, monitoring of existing crop management practices and resulting productivity in specific micro-environments was recommended. Such work would further identify TVs adapted to local conditions. Evaluation of best local cultivars, pure line selections, introduced traditionals, and modern varieties could then be integrated with farmer-managed on-farm research based in part on existing practices and knowledge. Future interdisciplinary on-station and on-farm research was recommended. Training of national scientists in working on-farm and with farmers was suggested.

4. Because of limited cash, credit, and available agricultural inputs, research on low-input soil nutrient management was recommended, including:

   ○ use of grain or forage legume green manures within improved cropping systems;
   ○ use of local resources such as *C. odorata*;
   ○ farmyard manure management;
   ○ incorporation of rice straw; and
   ○ more efficient use of N fertilisers (*e.g.*, urea incorporation before flooding, slow release fertilisers, and deep placement).

   It was assumed that research using low input levels could address current circumstances, and that research using higher levels can anticipate improved national conditions.

5. To address widespread problems related to water management, it was recommended that the systems be assessed and that farmers' knowledge of local hydrologies be considered as a planning resource.

6. Given few reported insect or weed problems and limited use of pesticides, there was little awareness of a future need for integrated pest management (IPM). Knowledge of economic thresholds or natural enemies was limited. A group of farmers identified a lady beetle (Harmonia octomaculata) as a harmful insect. Farmers were, however, concerned about potential pesticide poisoning of wild paddy fish. Furthering an awareness of IPM technologies, at the national, provincial, district, krom, and farmer levels as new varieties and management practices are adopted, was recommended.

7. Because women and children provide most of the labour for rice farming, work to develop appropriate improved plows (e.g., sole ard to moldboard plow), harrows (comb to box), water lifting devices, and harvest and post-harvest technologies was recommended.

8. Characterisation of the country's agroecosystems was recommended. Knowledge of actual land areas and uses would help establish national research priorities and locate key field sites. The government agreed to allow work with satellite imagery and ground surveys.

Overall, the work in Kampuchea resulted in an understanding of farmers' practices and underlying agricultural knowledge within different rice micro-environments, an identification of research issues based in part on such understanding, and a program design and proposal.

Research priorities in other countries

Lowland rice environments, farmer crop-soil nutrient management, and changing social organisation were examined in Madagascar's Central Highland

(Fujisaka 1988b) to assist the national agricultural research program in making its work more farmer-responsive and appropriate. Rice environments and farmer practices were examined in the southern rainfed lowlands, the irrigated Vientiane Plain, and the northern slash-and-burn areas of Laos. As in Kampuchea, results (Fujisaka 1988c) were used to develop collaborative research.

Farmers' knowledge and rice research

Rice research in rainfed lowland and upland agroecosystems seeks to generate technologies that improve productivity and sustainability. Given many techni-cally-sound adaptations by farmers to these diverse, complex, and more difficult agroecosystems, such research has attempted to learn about and then build upon farmers' practice and knowledge. Ethnographic techniques have been employed to examine farmers' management strategies and to elicit and make sense of their technical knowledge underlying practices. That is, researchers – to learn from farmers – need not only a technical understanding of agriculture, but also an understanding of ethnoscientific techniques, methods to unravel kinship and local social organisation, field monitoring of farmers' crop management, soils and vegetative analysis, and crop cut sampling. Acceptance of such meth-ods by members of the interdisciplinary team clearly facilitated the research described.

Biological scientists from IRRI have been willing adaptors of approaches that make research more farmer-appropriate or more farmer-participatory. Most have had enough experience in investigating farmers' practices to appreciate being able to entrust the job to disciplines specialising in studying human behav-iour. For on-farm research at Claveria, efforts to improve cropping systems were redirected to address also the main farmer problem of soil erosion. In the process, farmers learned about contour hedgerows from other farmers, and the farmers' experimental adaptation of the hedgerow system became closely tied to the formal work. Rather than trying to fully, finally, and separately develop technologies for eventual 'release' to farmers, potential innovations introduced by the researchers were farmer-tested and evaluated as a first step in the local adaptation of the technology.

Methods are now being developed by which such farmers' knowledge and related technology adaptation and dissemination can be factored into work con-ducted by national agricultural programs. The same approach was applied to establishing priorities for collaborative rice research in Kampuchea, and will continue to be applied to the research activities that were proposed.

The cases presented suggest that on-farm research can coordinate the contri-butions of farmers and scientists in the development, adaptation and dissemina-tion of appropriate innovations, and, to do so, needs to include:

- understanding existing farmer practices in terms of underlying technical knowledge and as adaptations to local agroecosystems;
- problem identification based in part on such understanding;
- learning from farmers and their problem-solving adaptive experimentation as a starting-point for technology generation;
- substantial participation by farmers having a demonstrated interest in solving the identified problems;
- technology transfer from adapter-adopters to farmers wanting solutions to the problems addressed by the technologies; and

○ development of methods by which national programs can implement the same type of technology generation and transfer.

Overall, this paper has maintained that the knowledge of farmers can be used first to identify and prioritise research issues. Such knowledge can then be applied via farmers' participation in the design, testing, and adaptation of appropriate technologies. Finally, such knowledge can be efficiently shared via farmer-to-farmer technology transfer. At the same time, it appears that some of the scientists involved in the cases described have learned from farmers to the point that they have started to reexamine their assumptions about the technology generation and transfer process.

Note

1. Paper presented at the CIP-Rockefeller Foundation Conference on Farmers and Food Systems, Lima, Peru, September 26–30, 1988.

9. Raised Beds and Plant Disease Management

H. DAVID THURSTON AND JOANNE M. PARKER

Introduction

THE MANAGEMENT OF wetlands for agriculture by using raised beds or fields has been practiced extensively by indigenous peoples of the Americas for at least 2000 years. Denevan (1970) and Parsons and Denevan (1967) describe the approximately 170,000 ha of raised field remnants found in South America. Extensive systems of intensive raised field management known as *chinampas* were found in Mexico and were also common in Central America (Adams *et al.* 1981; Barrera, Gomez-Pompa and Vasquez-Yanes 1977; Gomez-Pompa 1978; Siemens 1980; Siemens and Puleston 1972; Turner 1974; Turner and Harrison 1981). North American Indians used raised-bed agriculture before European arrival in several states of the USA (Fowler 1969). Raised-bed management was also common in Africa (Jurion and Henry 1969, IITA 1988) and Asia (King 1926; Harwood and Plucknett 1981; Williams 1981). The practice seems to be quite ancient as raised-bed farming was developed in China in the 5th Century B.C. (Wittwer *et al.* 1987). Raised beds in the Wahgi Valley of New Guinea have been dated as older than 350 BC (Lampert 1967).

Denevan and Turner (1974) define a raised field as 'an agricultural feature created by transferring earth to raise an area above the natural terrain.' Denevan (1970) differentiates the following types of wetland cultivation that indigenous American peoples have used:

- soil platforms built up in permanent water bodies;
- ridged, platformed, or mounded fields on seasonally flooded or waterlogged terrain;
- lazybeds or low, narrow ridges on slopes and flats subject to waterlogging;
- ditched fields, mainly for subsoil drainage;
- fields on naturally drained land, including sandbars, river banks, and lake margins;
- fields diked or embanked to keep water out.

Hills or mounds, a type of broken raised field, are routinely used for many root and tuber crops. Raised beds, ridged fields, drained fields, and cambered beds are also terms found in the literature used to describe raised fields (Webster and Wilson 1980).

Raised field systems

Chinampas Probably the best known raised field system is the *chinampas* or 'floating gardens' of the Valley of Mexico which the Spanish conquistadors erroneously thought floated. When the Spanish arrived in Mexico in 1521 and entered the capitol of the Aztec civilization located on an island in Lake Texcoco, they were amazed by the immense areas in *chinampas*. *Chinampas* apparently interfered with the Spanish conquest. As Squire (1858: 556) noted: 'The lands around the Lake were highly cultivated, as appears from the references which are made by Villagutierre to "great fields of maize", surrounded by fences and deep ditches which the Spanish horsemen found it impossible to leap'.

Despite clumsy attempts by the Spanish at draining Lake Texcoco for flood control purposes which diminished greatly the area in *chinampas*, they are still farmed near Mexico City at Xochimilco (Armillas 1971; Gomez-Pompa 1978; Jimenez-Osornia and Del Amo 1988) and Tlaxcala (Wilken 1969). Only 1000 ha of *chinampas* remain, one-tenth of the area the Aztecs possibly had under cultivation 2000 years ago (Salas 1988). The high productivity of *chinampas* has been cited as a major factor that allowed the Aztecs to grow from a small tribe to a powerful group that essentially dominated most of Mexico when the Spanish arrived. Armillas (1971) has estimated that the Aztec *chinampas* may have fed 100,000 people.

Chinampas were probably first developed by the Maya and then subsequently used by other Indian cultures in Mexico and Central America (Adams *et al.* 1981; Siemens 1980; Siemens and Puleston 1972; Redclift 1987; Turner and Harrison 1981; Chen 1987). Adams *et al.* (1981) state: 'New data suggest that Late Classic period Maya civilization was firmly grounded in large-scale intensive cultivation of swampy zones.' Many investigators do not believe that slash and burn agriculture could have provided sufficient food for the large Maya populations that constructed Tikal, Palenque, and other similar Mayan centres. Only a more intensive food production system such as raised field agriculture could have produced the food necessary to support the large populations that existed then. Pollen data indicate the possibility of raised fields on the Hondo River (between Mexico and Belize) going back to 1800 BC Radiocarbon dating of worked timbers in the area dates them at 1110 + or - 230 BC (Puleston 1978). A system similar to *chinampas* was being used by Venezuelan Indians on the swampy shores of Lake Maracaibo when the Spanish arrived (Simon 1923).

The *chinampas* constructed in the shallow Lake Texcoco in Xochimilco are generally rectangular in shape (90 m by 4.6 to 9 m) and separated by canals (Coe 1964). The surface of the *chinampas* is usually several feet above the water level in the canals. Two operations build up the *chinampas*. First, mud rich in nutrients from the bottom of the canals is dredged up using a hand tool and spread on the *chinampa* surface. This maintains the canals and enriches the *chinampas*. In addition, aquatic weeds and animal manure, (and in the time of the Aztecs, human waste) are also spread on top.

A wide variety of crops were grown by the Aztecs on the *chinampas* and many diverse crops are still seen today (Muñoz 1986). Maize is planted directly in the *chinampas*, but other crops are first planted in seedbeds prepared by spreading a layer of mud over vegetation, cutting it into small rectangular blocks called *chapines*, and planting a seed in each *chapin*. The *chapines* are subsequently transplanted to the soil of the *chinampas*, thus giving the crops a good start. The *chinampas* are perpetually moist, and cropping can continue year round, even through the dry season. Yields of the system are very high (Armillas 1971). In 1978, Venegas (cited by Redclift 1987) calculated maize yields of 4–6 tons/ha while Gomez-Pompa (cited by Chen 1987) reported yields of 6–7 tons/ha in Tabasco on *chinampas*.

Chapin (1988) describes the unsuccessful attempts to reintroduce *chinampa* technology into the lowland tropics of Mexico. He is highly critical of these attempts and identifies many of the technical, social, and political reasons for the failure. Nevertheless, his strong implication that *chinampas* are not a valid model for increasing food production in tropical areas seems superficial and premature. *Chinampa* construction and maintenance require considerable labour. This meant that the discovery of immense oil reserves in Tabasco which increased greatly the cost of scarce labour, poor planning and coordination of government projects, and lack of marketing opportunities and planning contributed more to failure than a faulty conceptual model.

The *chinampa* system, in sum, allows continuous cropping made possible by sophisticated water control, multiple cropping, high levels of organic material and nutrients periodically added to the system, and transplanting of healthy, selected seedlings (*chapines*) with strong root systems (Gómez-Pompa 1978; Jiménez-Osornio and Del Amo R. 1988). The diversity of crops grown on traditional *chinampas* also may have contributed to the success of the system by inhibiting the spread of disease. In actuality, little is reported on the utility of raised fields in general for plant disease control; but there is little doubt that, in addition to their obvious irrigation, drainage, and agronomic value, disease management is often an additional benefit.

Lumsden *et al.* (1987) studied *chinampa* soils relative to disease. They compared relative levels of damping-off disease caused by *Pythium* spp on seedlings grown in soils from the *chinampas* versus those grown in soils from modern systems of cultivation near Chapingo, Mexico. They found that disease levels were lower in the *chinampa* soils. When they introduced inoculum of *Pythium aphanidermatum* the fungus was suppressed by *chinampa* soils. From their studies they concluded: In the chinampa agroecosystem, apparently a dynamic biological equilibrium exists in which intense management, especially of copious quantities of organic matter, maintains an elevated supply of organic nutrients and calcium, potassium and other mineral nutrients which stimulate biological activity in the soil. The elevated biological activity, especially of known antagonists such as *Trichoderma spp.*, *Pseudomonas spp.*, and *Fusarium spp.*, can suppress the activity of *P. aphanidermatum*, other *Pythium spp.*, and perhaps other soilborne plant pathogens.

More recently Zuckerman *et al.* (1989), in a cooperative study between scientists from Mexico and the USA, also studied suppression in *chinampa* soils, but of plant parasitic nematodes rather than fungi. The authors point out that the high organic content of the soil is probably responsible in part for the relatively few nematodes in *chinampa* soils, but they also found nine organisms which had antinematodal activity. Their results were summarized as follows: Soil from the *Chinampa* agricultural system in the Valley of Mexico suppressed damage by plant parasitic nematodes in greenhouse and growth chamber trials. Sterilization of the chinampa soils resulted in a loss of the suppressive effect, thereby indicating that one or more biotic factors were responsible for the low incidence of nematode damage. Nine organisms were isolated from chinampa soil which showed antinematodal properties in culture. Naturally occurring populations of plant-parasitic nematodes were of lower incidence in chinampa soils than in Chapingo soil.

Waru Waru Erickson (1985), Garaycochea (1985), Lennon (1982), and Sattaur (1988) have described over 80,000 ha of raised fields called *waru waru* or *camellones* at 3660 m elevation near Lake Titicaca bordering Peru and Bolivia. Denevan (1985) suggests some may be 2000 years old. When some of the raised fields were rebuilt according to specifications obtained from archaeological studies, potato yields of 8 t/ha were obtained on them compared to the 2-3 t/ha average in the surrounding Puno district. In addition to better water management, the raised beds contribute to flood and frost control. The Peruvian government now gives farmers credit to reconstruct the raised fields and some 1500 ha have been reconstructed. Thus, farmers in the Andes are learning from their traditional ancestors.

Tablones The use of systems such as ridge terraces, erosion dikes, and bench terraces in modern tropical agriculture, as described by Ochse *et al.* (1961), attests to their value today. Besides the *chinampas*, many other examples of raised fields can be found today. The Maya in the Panajachel River delta of the highland Lake Atitlan basin grow a large number of crops, especially vegetables, on raised beds called *tablones* (Mathewson 1984; Wilken 1987). Both authors suggested that the *tablones* are probably pre-Colombian. Separated by irrigation trenches, they vary in height from 20–65 cm. During construction, a trench is made in the centre of the *tablón* and weeds, ground litter from nearby coffee plantations, and animal manure is placed in the trench, covered and allowed to decompose. Later, muck from the irrigation ditches may be added to the *tablón*. No mention was made of the possible presence or absence of root pathogens in this system, but it is worth investigating.

Flooding and raised beds

In Southern China, two or three crops of paddy rice are often grown after which the land is ridged for growing various vegetables and ginger (King 1926; Williams 1981). A similar system is described in Taiwan (Su 1979). Flooding for rice culture destroys many soilborne pests and pathogens (Cook and Baker 1983). A similar system is used in West and Central Africa. According to IITA (1976), there are 85 million ha of inland valleys in Sub-Saharan Africa, and 80 per cent of the inland valley fields found in this region practice an annual cycle of mounding for vegetables, cassava, or sweet potatoes during the dry season and flat tillage for rice in the wet season. In the construction and destruction of mounds, organic matter and soil nutrients are recycled through incorporation of crop residues and weeds and, in flooding, many pests and pathogens in the soil are destroyed.

Raised beds in Asia

Raised beds, ridges, and mounds are commonly used in Asia for agriculture, especially in high rainfall and swampy areas (Chandler 1981; Harwood and Plucknett 1981; King 1926; Marten and Vityakon 1986; Herklots 1972; Villareal 1980). Their importance is described by Herklots (1972) as follows: 'Throughout the monsoon countries of Southeast Asia this is the almost universal technique adopted where water is abundant or too abundant. In the vast silted plains of the river valleys of Thailand, of the Mekong delta of Cambodia and of the Pearl River of South China and even of the smaller rivers of Taiwan raised vegetable beds are a feature of the countryside especially near the large cities.'

Extensive vegetable and flower growing on large raised beds is common in swampy areas near Bangkok, Thailand. In many areas of China the use of raised beds is still common. As in *chinampas*, large quantities of organic material consisting of manure, aquatic plants, mud from canals, and crop and plant debris are incorporated into the soil in many of these systems (McCalla and Plucknett 1981; King 1926). Kelman and Cook (1977) suggest that: 'the practice of flooding fields for paddy rice and the use of organic material as fertilizers are apparently key factors in the general absence of soilborne diseases in China.'

Crops grown in raised field systems

Root and tuber crops Many investigators report that root and tuber crops such as cassava, yams, and sweet potatoes are usually grown by traditional farmers in Asia, Africa, and Latin America in raised beds, mounds, and ridges (Nyoka 1983; Miracle 1967; Okafor and Fernandez 1987; Okigbo and Greenland 1976; Waddell 1972; Denevan and Treacy 1987; IITA 1988). According to Curwen and Hatt (1953), when Captain James Cook discovered New Caledonia in 1774, he found taro planted in ridges. Jones (1959) states that as early as 1854 the missionary David Livingstone saw cassava planted in raised oblong beds near the Belgian Congo.

At that time Europeans thought cassava indigenous to Africa, whereas, in reality, it had been introduced into Africa with the slave trade by the Portuguese. Prinz and Rauch (1987) describe raised beds used in West Cameroon which were adapted from a form of traditional mounds. Reichel-Dolmatoff (1965) and Parsons and Denevan (1967) note that many of the ancient South American raised fields probably were used for producing cassava although positive evidence is lacking. Furthermore, Denevan and Turner (1974) suggested that root crops probably dominated raised-bed agriculture in South America.

Sweet Potatoes The 'mound builders' of New Guinea (Brass 1941; Lampert 1967) provide another fascinating example of traditional farmers who have worked out a sustainable system of agriculture by cultivating sweet potatoes on mounds, producing high yields for long periods of time, with no apparent disease problems. Waddell (1972) describes the system in detail. Although the sweet potato gardens in his study area covered almost two-thirds of the cultivated area, other types of farming were practiced such as mixed gardens, kitchen gardens, and cash-crop gardens.

Sweet potato culture is primarily on large mounds called *modó*. The mounds average 3.8 m in diameter and 0.6 m high. Smaller mounds are also made. The modó mounds permit continuous cultivation without fallow. Sites in the study area are known to have been in continuous cultivation since 1938 (when Europeans first found these people). When a new mound is prepared, approximately 20 kg of old sweet potato vines, sugar cane leaves, and other sources of vegetation are placed in the centre of the mounds. When this material begins to decompose, the mound is closed with soil and subsequently planted with sweet potato cuttings. Two to three harvests are obtained a year, totaling 19 tons/ha of sweet potato roots (Waddell 1972: 120). The only reference to disease in this excellent, detailed study is the following : 'It [sweet potato] is also less susceptible to disease than taro (*Colocasia esculenta*), which has suffered greatly in recent years from the depredation of the taro beetle (*Papuana spp.*) and the virus *Phytophthora colocasiae* in various parts of the Pacific.'

The error regarding the nature of *Phytophthora colocasiae* (an oömycete fungus, not a virus) is perhaps illustrative of the level of knowledge and interest that ethnobotanists, anthropologists, archaeologists, economists, and rural sociologists have achieved regarding disease problems. Rarely are diseases even

mentioned in their published studies. On the other hand, plant pathological literature seldom references work in the above disciplines.

In their recently published compendium on sweet potato diseases, Clark and
Moyer (1988) state: The rows may be prepared as level beds or raised beds,
depending on local requirements. Raised beds are generally preferable to flat
beds when it is necessary to improve drainage. Although almost all of the sweet
potatoes in the USA are grown on raised beds (C.A. Clark, personal communication) nothing further was found in the compendium on the effect of raised
beds on plant disease.

Maize The use of mounds or ridges in maize culture appears to be a very old
practice in the Americas (Weatherwax 1954). When plants have reached a
height of about 60 cm, a considerable amount of soil is mounded up around the
plant. In Guatemala, the practice is called *calzando*, putting boots on the corn.
This practice is still common in higher elevations of Mexico, Central America,
and parts of the Andes.

According to Carrier (1923), North American Indians also planted maize in
mounds which were 30-50 cm in diameter. Only the soil in the mounds was loos-
ened and, as the maize grew, soil was scraped around them and the mounds
were carefully weeded. These mounds were apparently used repeatedly and
thus became rather large. Remnants of such large mounds in abandoned fields
were frequently found by early colonists in North America. In Mississippi,
Georgia, Texas, Illinois, Michigan, and Wisconsin ridged fields were found
which had probably been used by Indians for maize culture (Fowler 1969).
Whether these practices of growing maize in hills and ridges had any effect on
plant disease is unknown, but the better physical conditions for roots and better
drainage probably reduced soil-borne diseases.

Raised beds for plant disease management

In addition to the obvious benefits of better water management, ridges, mounds,
and hills are undoubtedly also used because of their value in reducing a high
incidence of various root rots in poorly drained soils. Barta and Schmitthenner
(1986), Matheron and Mircetich (1985), Mueller and Fick (1987), Wicks and
Lee (1985) and Wilcox and Mircetich (1985) indicate that flooding increases
host susceptibility to the various *Phytophthora spp.* they studied. Raised beds
would often prevent or reduce such predisposition from flooding.

Several species of *Phytophthora* cause serious root rots of cassava in tropical
areas (Booth 1977; Oliveros *et al.* 1974). Planting in well drained raised beds or
ridges was found to be an effective control against cassava root rots caused by
Phytophthora spp. (Booth 1977; Lozano and Terry 1976). According to Lal
(1987), shifting cultivators in Africa construct yam mounds around termite
mounds, recognizing the importance of termite mounds in the ecology of the
area. For potato production, exceptionally large hills (0.7–0.9 m high) are commonly made by traditional farmers in some parts of the Andes Mountains.
Tuber infection caused by the fungus *Phytophthora infestans* (causal agent of
late blight of potatoes) is rare in the Andes. The soil in the very high hills probably filters out the spores before they can reach the tubers (Thurston and Schultz
1981). Thus, planting root and tuber crops in mounds and ridges appears to be,
in part, a disease management practice.

The losses caused by *Rhizoctonia spp*, causal agent of bottom rot of lettuce
(Pieczarka and Lorbeer 1974) and *Erwinia caratovora*, causal agent of bacterial

softrot of Chinese cabbage in the USA (Fritz and Honma 1987) and China (Williams 1981), is reduced by the use of raised beds or ridges. Raised beds are used extensively in California and help to control red stele disease of strawberry *(Phytophthora fragariae)* and root rots of lettuce. Knowles and Miller (1965) recommend that safflower be planted in raised beds in California for control of *Phytophthora drechsleri.*

Planting in ridges in New Jersey contributed to the control of *P. capsici* (Phytophthora blight of pepper) (Johnston and Springer 1977). Arneson (1971) found that the use of raised beds helped control white rot of peanut (caused by *Sclerotium rolfsii*) in Nicaragua. Abawi, Crosier and Cobb (1985) recommend raised beds for control of *Pythium* root rot of snap beans in New York. Despite many such reports, raised field technologies receive surprisingly little if any attention in most plant pathology texts, and the terms 'raised bed' and 'ridges' are rarely found in the index of plant pathology texts.

Conclusion

In areas as widely separated as tropical America, Asia, and Africa, traditional farmers evolved raised bed systems of agriculture with striking similarities. Drainage, fertilization, frost control, and irrigation were among important considerations in these systems. How much the control of plant diseases or other pests entered into the evolution of these systems is unknown. Nevertheless, there is no doubt that planting in raised fields, raised beds, mounds, and ridges are, in part, practices in disease management.

Most knowledge regarding raised beds in agriculture comes from anthropologists, archaeologists, ecologists and ethnobotanists, rather than from plant pathologists or other agricultural scientists. Cooperation and communication among disciplines to make the principles and knowledge regarding the merits of raised beds available to farmers worldwide would be highly desirable. Determining the value of these practices should become part of the research agenda of governments and international agencies in developing countries.

10. Indigenous Knowledge and Famine Relief in the Horn of Africa

PETER J.C. WALKER

Introduction

FAMINES ARE NEITHER a new nor an abnormal state. In communities where famine is still present, a person may expect to live through three or more periods of what they define as famine. As a consequence of the repetitive nature of this threat, most communities have evolved ways of coping with or at least mitigating famine's worst effects. Today, alongside this indigenous system of coping is the externally derived and much publicised relief aid. Both systems are presumably aiming to do the same things: to mitigate the effects of this famine and to prevent future ones.

Famine relief, from the point of view of aid agencies, is a messy process. It always seems to end up being a last ditch attempt to save lives, usually by pumping food into the affected area. An analysis of the way aid agencies respond draws one to the inevitable conclusion that famine is seen as a nutritional crisis brought about by a general scarcity of food and alleviated by an injection of food. But does this diagnosis and remedy square up with the victims' perception of what is happening to them? Do the victims and aid agency share a common analysis of famine causes and the purpose of famine relief? As a practitioner of relief aid, I would have to answer no to both these questions.

For the relief agency, famine is typified as a crisis, one which requires a 'fire fighting approach'. Like most definitions in development, this is the view of the rich man who assumes he knows what the poor require. But for most at-risk communities, famine is seen as a process which *may* end in crisis and which can be tackled by a series of strategies, usually aimed at safeguarding the long term rather than short term future. This is well exemplified by the way famines are defined by those who suffer them.

The victim's view of famine

Almost by definition, victims' descriptions of famine are few and far between. It is the most vulnerable and least powerful who suffer during a famine: a group which has little access to the written word and its dissemination.

The great Irish famine of the 1840s is thought to have killed around one and a half million people and caused another million to emigrate (Woodham-Smith 1962). In a collection of oral histories, Charles McGlinchey (1986: 119) recalls his father talking about *the great hunger*: 'The women pulled Charlock round the fields and made it into a kind of broth...There were a lot of travelling people on the roads coming from the place where the famine was worst.'

He recalls children being found dead beside the road, farm land being sold for £17 when it would normally have fetched £500, and the price of grain rocketing. To those familiar with the recent crisis in the Horn of Africa, there is something sickeningly familiar about this description. The use of 'famine foods', 'out-migration', 'reduced value for assets' and 'increases in basic food prices' seem to be common features.

147

In countries where famine is endemic, multiple terminologies for naming and describing it have developed. In Bangladesh, the culture defines three types of famine: scarcity is *akal* (when times are bad); famine is *durvickha* (when alms are scarce) and nationwide famine is *mananthor* (when the epoch changes) (Currey 1978: 90). As Currey points out, these subtle terms contrast starkly with the West's commonly accepted monolithic picture of famine. The people of Darfur in West Sudan recognise two types of famine. *Maja'a al katala* (periods of dearth when people are forced to do unpleasant things to survive) and *maja'a* (Famine that Kills) (de Waal 1987).

Not only do victims tend to perceive famine in a qualitatively different fashion than do outsiders; they also react to it in a qualitatively different way. A number of studies have shown that victims respond to the attack on the *sustainability of their livelihoods*, not to the threat to their personal food supplies as such. Most communities suffering famine have responded to the crisis a number of times in their history. Famine victims do not respond to stress from a position of ignorance, but from a position of knowledge. They have knowledge of both the stress processes their community suffers and the long term consequences of their individual actions.

This traditional knowledge is neither fossilised nor stagnant. It is a means of survival. Traditional wisdom, like any system of knowledge, is constantly evolving, as are the factors causing famine and the political and economic context within which it is set. Today, famine victims have recourse to sources of casual employment or state benefits denied to their grandfathers. On the other hand, today's victims have to cope with stresses unknown to their forefathers. Civil wars fought with submachine guns and aircraft put a stress unknown 50 years ago on a peasant society.

The logical and sequential nature of coping strategies provides, for the outsider, an insight into the manner in which famine develops and an indication of possible appropriate forms of relief and warning. However, caution should be exercised when creating generalisations from the literature. Its breadth and depth are in fact pitifully limited. There is no mass of data upon which to build theories, only a few isolated case studies. Most of these examine coping strategies in Africa during the famines of the 1970s and 1980s.

Ethiopia

In Wollo province, Rahmato (1987) identifies three stages that famine victims experience: *crisis anticipation, crisis management* and *exhaustion and dispersal*. He maintains that the peasants of Wollo have developed an 'early warning' technique, which in many ways, is analogous to that being used by the national government. 'Indigenous peasant warning techniques concern themselves also with crop conditions, weather and environmental change, and rural market behaviour' (Rahmato 1987: 140). This technique is exercised by individual farmers and in the past, by traditional mystics or 'spirit men'. Rahmato points out that the predictive value of these techniques is often just as good, and usually more locally relevant, than present day national warning systems.

Crisis anticipation allows the peasants to start mapping out the coping strategies open to them. These strategies form the basis of the crisis management stage. Cutler (1984), using a different terminology, divides crisis management into two stages. In the first stage, crop failure forces households to seek alternative sources of income which do not involve selling off those assets which are needed to ensure the long-term viability of the household, such as oxen, farm tools, and seeds. Throughout this stage farmers may react by (1) migrating in search of work to crop surplus areas outside the famine zone, (2) by going into debt, and (3) by selling off less important assets (Cutler and Stephenson 1984: 6). If these strategies prove insufficient, then a second stage may be entered when households must choose between the sale of these key assets, or male heads of household migrate in search of food.

Rahmato is highly critical of this analysis on the grounds that it is incomplete. He lays much greater stress on the kinship support strategies that are adopted and maintains that during the period of stress poorer families will exchange food with, or borrow food from, wealthier relations. 'One of the tasks of the male household head is to make arrangements with other families to acquire assistance or to set up mutually beneficial deals. Assistance often involves borrowing grain or other food stuff, while deals may take the form of barter exchange, mortgaging assets in exchange for food, setting up credit arrangements and the like' (Rahmato 1987: 203). He makes the crucially important point that 'These exchanges or deals are inter-family affairs and not open and routine business transactions. A stranger cannot walk into a prosperous peasant household and ask for food on credit or on barter.' Thus, while Cutler's 'external' analysis of coping strategies may be correct, it may well be that as a visiting outsider he has failed to detect a whole sub-culture of family support mechanisms.

During the crisis management stage, all observers agree that the role of the market becomes critical in determining the peasant's ability to survive. For now, if kinship credit and barter fail, the peasant's survival depends on the acquisition of cash to buy food. As Seaman and Holt (1980) point out, only about 5 per cent of the population are dependent upon the market for food in normal times in Wollo, yet when famine strikes the market may be the only source of food. A study of how the Mursi of Southern Ethiopia dealt with the threat of famine, asserts that: 'the single most important factor which enabled them, as a group, to survive this crisis, was undoubtedly access to grain through market exchange in the highlands' (Turton 1985).

One consequence of this shift is that the value of an asset is now determined by how saleable it is. In normal times, on the other hand, its value is determined by its contribution to a more long-term strategy and to other social and cultural practices. Famine victims enter the market at a distinct disadvantage. The mass sale of assets tends to push their market value down and the mass demand for food pushes their value up. Assets are sold by many and bought by a few. Food, on the contrary, is sought by many and sold by a few. Whether as seller or as purchaser, the market is largely outside the victims' control.

Both Cutler and Rahmato agree that the final stage of the famine process in Wollo was wholesale mass migration in search of relief and that this was distinctly different from the migration of individual members of a household in search of work or 'take home' relief. Cutler portrays mass migration out of a famine area as a final act of desperation, when all else has failed. While not disagreeing with its definition as a final act, Rahmato holds that it is a much more positive and deliberate undertaking. As he puts it: 'peasants understand the impact of numbers.' In his view mass migration should be viewed as a cooperative act of silent protest and a: 'collective articulation of the demand for the consecration of the right to life' (Rahmato 1987: 188).

Sudan

In a study of survival strategies in West Sudan, de Waal (1987) asserts that the overall objective of households is to maintain the subsistence basis of their livelihoods. He identifies three sequential stages of destitution in which this subsistence base is progressively eroded. The first involves the use of unusual sources of income which do not eat into the subsistence base of the household. In the second stage, activities are undertaken which do cut into the subsistence base, and in the third stage, it is assumed that the subsistence base has collapsed and that households are reliant upon charity.

Corbett (1988), quoting de Waal and El Amin (1986), lists the responses made during each of these three stages:

First stage of destitution

- gathering of wild foods;
- selling animals which are surplus to requirements;
- borrowing money or food from relatives;
- other forms of inter-household assistance;
- work as day labourers;
- sale of non-essential possessions;
- migration with herd to distant pastures.

Second stage of destitution

- sale of animals which are required for subsistence;
- borrowing food or money from merchants;
- sale of required possessions;
- paid work which interferes with the running of the household farm;
- clientage;
- out-migration to seek work or charity in towns.

Third stage of destitution

- starvation;
- dependence on charity.

Many of the first-stage strategies are the ones employed in times of 'normal' stress and are used routinely by very poor families. When households first seek to protect their subsistence base during famine times, they do so using *normal* strategies. In its early stages, famine is no different from the seasonal poverty routinely experienced by African peasantry. On the eastern side of Sudan, in Red Sea Province, Cutler (1986) shows a similar succession of coping strategies.

Adaptive strategies

- sale of excess livestock;
- labour migration;
- diversification of income through petty commodity production and trade;
- use of credit from merchants.

Sale of key productive assets

- sale of land;
- sale of tools;

o sale of breeding animals;
o sale of household belongings;
o mass migration;
o households to towns and road sides in search of charity.

In Cutler's Red Sea Hills study, most interviewees put the start of the drought, which they saw as the cause of the famine, at around 1979–80 and the suggestion is that adaptive strategies would have been practiced at this time. By the end of 1984, it is estimated that 90 per cent of the herds of these pastoral people had been destroyed. It was then that mass migration in search of charity began (Walker 1988). At this point, many coping strategies used previously were no longer available to the pastoralists. Once assets were sold, there was no getting them back. Once herds were destroyed, reliance upon the normal livestock/grain trading to provide food was no longer possible. A survey conducted in early 1987 showed that animal sales, the 'normal' source of income, still only accounted for a tiny fraction of household income. Food aid followed by wage labour were now the biggest sources of income (Walker 1988).

Taking an overview of the three examples given above, the support structures, both kinship and non-kinship related, which are used to mitigate the effects of famine seem to fall into four classes.

Those strategies which people would employ to overcome normally experienced seasonal stresses

o cropping and pasturing practices are altered;
o food is rationed;
o use of kinship transfers and loans is increased;
o income sources are diversified;
o temporary migration in search of work during slack periods in the farming calendar take place;
o non-essential possessions are sold;
o excess animals are sold.

None of these strategies affects the underlying basis of the potential victim's economy. Thus, for the subsistence farmers, their land, tools, seeds, and labour potential remain intact. For the pastoralists, their breeding herd is intact. For the landless labourers their ability to work at peak employment periods is preserved. All these strategies are reversible. They do not force the practitioners down a path which limits their options for the future.

If stress is prolonged, then strategies are employed which trade off short-term gain for long-term problems

o essential livestock are sold;
o agricultural tools are sold;
o money is borrowed from outside kinship relations;
o land is mortgaged;
o land is sold;
o children are taken into bondage.

The essential difference between stage one and stage two strategies is that those in the second stage directly undermine the basis of the victim's normal means of survival. The sale of essential livestock or land means that the victim sees the household's position as being so desperate that they are willing to sacrifice future security for present survival. If one wished to mark the true beginnings of famine, as opposed to seasonal food shortage, this might well be the appropriate place.

If all these fail, then the victim can only resort to outside charity

○ distress migration;
○ reliance upon food aid.

If coping mechanisms fail, then the final stage may be reached

○ starvation;
○ death.

As the famine victim moves along this sequence, the household's options for future survival are progressively curtailed. Distress migration, particularly if it is across an international boundary may have so curtailed a victim's options, that they have no way of re-entering their old mode of survival.

The above sequence of strategies is of course a generalisation. Not every famine-prone community will have access to all these strategies or be able to use them all. Not every household in a 'famine' area starts off from the same level of vulnerability. The larger farmer, the more prosperous pastoralist and the well-connected merchant may never have to move past stage one in the coping sequence. Those households, which in normal times only just survive, will find themselves very quickly at the bottom of the coping sequence.

Lessons for famine warning

The first and most obvious lesson is that the above analysis points very clearly to that phenomenon which a famine warning system should be trying to predict. Famine warning should not be about predicting mass starvation. It must be geared to warning of the erosion of the subsistence base of the victim's society. The real crisis emerges when famine victims shift from using reversible, non-asset stripping strategies, to non-reversible ones which cut into their long-term options. This is the point at which the warning needs to be sounded.

Secondly, the socioeconomic responses to stress, which we call the famine process, are extremely complex, typically localised, and often producing contradictory signals. To understand and use such signals as a warning, one needs to understand the motivations and constraints upon individual households. Warning systems which use that data must themselves be localised in nature.

Lessons for famine relief

Traditional responses to famine have implications also for the way in which outside agencies should conduct their relief programs. At present, the standard practice of relief agencies is to intervene at the junction of stages three and four. To delay the input of emergency aid to this point is to totally misunderstand the nature of the real needs of the victims.

From the point of view of preserving livelihoods, not just lives, there is a growing case for emergency intervention between stages one and two. This, after all, seems to be the point at which the victim sees famine beginning. Clearly, the actions to be taken to stave off famine will be highly location-specific. They must have regard for the manner in which the local economy functions and should be based upon the same rationale as lies behind the traditional coping mechanisms.

Thus, they should aim at safe-guarding people's capital and assets. In a recent analysis of famine vulnerability, Jeremy Swift (1989) argues for a much broader definition of the term assets. He sees three different categories: *investments*, *stores* and *claims*. Investment could be in education, farm tools, animals, collective investment in irrigation systems or soil conservation schemes. Stores can be interpreted as food stores, or money in the bank, or goods which can be sold such as jewelry. Finally, claims may be those by households upon kinship groups or upon local patrons. Claims can be made upon governments and international relief agencies.

Aid, which enables people to keep their livestock, tools and seeds, will build for the future as well as helping for today. Of equal importance will be maintaining social structures. A recent FAO report highlighted village level associations as being one of the key components in overcoming famine in a number of African countries. The possession of structures to organise locally on both a kinship and peer-group basis seems to be of paramount importance in facing adversity. Famine aid should encourage the formation of such self-help groups and, where possible, work through those that already exist.

By taking this approach, there is the potential not just to avert famine but also to actually reduce people's vulnerability. Indeed, this should be a prerequisite of any relief plan. If the landless labourers are vulnerable to famine because they depend upon a single volatile source of income, then their vulnerability can be reduced by helping them diversify. If the peasant farmers are vulnerable because their crop varieties are susceptible to drought, then the introduction of improved seed varieties and help with seed replication at the village level will reduce future vulnerability.

Finally, we have to ask who should control the relief program. If the program is to build upon the aspirations and knowledge of the victims, then clearly they have to be involved in the formulation and execution of the aid package. They must, therefore, have a degree of control over its implementation. While it is naive to suggest that the victims should have total control over the program, there clearly must be a true partnership between the aid agency and the victims if implementation is to be successful.

Unfortunately, such long-term and well-integrated approaches to famine mitigation are not always successful. Often stresses may be too great to counter and a state of starvation may ensue. For the foreseeable future, the key tool in mass starvation relief will remain food aid. It is not just a source of calories; it can likewise be viewed as an income transfer to the vulnerable. In the Red Sea Province of Sudan in 1985–6, the relief agency Oxfam based its assessment of the food aid needs of the province not on the nutritional status of the people but on the 'income gap' between what they actually earned and what they needed to purchase sufficient food to survive.

Food aid can be used to safeguard assets directly. In many pastoral societies, mass starvation is preceded by the selling off of animals at ridiculously low prices to purchase grain at ever increasing prices. Food aid can intervene in this process to protect the pastoralist from the harshness of the market. This has been tried successfully in both Mali and Kenya in the recent past.

Conclusion

In conclusion, we have to acknowledge that those of us involved in relief and development aid are essentially outsiders to the process we wish to affect. We must recognise that the vulnerable and the victims know far more about the localised processes that are affecting them than we do. Therefore, we must approach our work with a sense of humility and an openness to learn from those with whom we are trying to work.

For the future, it seems clear that the effectiveness of the indigenous responses to famine are in danger of being eroded rapidly through urbanisation, the increased role of the national state, and the rapidity of environmental and climatic change. The challenge for the state and international agencies is to find a humanitarian and effective way of building upon these previously localised and self-controlled systems of survival.

11. Indigenous Decision-making in Agriculture – A reflection of gender and socioeconomic status in the Philippines

VIRGINIA D. NAZAREA-SANDOVAL

Introduction

IN AGRICULTURE, WELL-MEANING development efforts are sometimes met with passive indifference or outright resistance by their intended beneficiaries. Between the cost-benefit analysis of planners and the cost-benefit analysis of farmers is a dark middle phase. This middle phase, often neatly labelled and then dismissed as a 'black box', consists of opportunities and constraints as experienced and perceived by the farmers themselves.

An in-depth study of farmers' perception and evaluation of alternatives, access price, and limiting factors can contribute basic information towards the elucidation of agricultural decision-making (Quinn 1978; Ortiz 1979; Gladwin 1980). Such knowledge will be helpful in evolving and communicating development strategies that are scientifically sound, technologically feasible, and economically viable and, at the same time, culturally and cognitively acceptable. If the last criterion is met along with the others, promising options may have a better chance of being seriously considered for their possible merits instead of being haphazardly dismissed by local farmers who find them too complicated, threatening, and incompatible with their agricultural regime.

One important but often neglected dimension in the search for cognitively and culturally acceptable strategies is that even within one community, different categories of farmers operate under various decision-making environments due to systematic differences in access to knowledge, resources, and rewards (Cancian 1972; Roumasset 1976; deWalt and deWalt 1980). This is true not only with respect to socioeconomic standing but with respect to gender as well (Abbott 1976; Heyzer 1986). These decision-making 'environments' consist of different sets of opportunities and constraints which define and delimit their decision-making framework and give rise to distinctive decision-making criteria.

An example, too glaring to qualify as hindsight, of what happens when this caveat is overlooked is the effect of the Green Revolution on different categories of farming households (Burke 1979; Ledesma 1982; Ardnt 1983; Heyzer 1986). The assumption of scale-neutrality and trickle-down effect justified the introduction of capital-intensive agricultural technology which led to greater polarisation between rich farmers who could afford to adopt and poor farmers who could not, between males who could dominate the technology and females whose labour became redundant in the process. This illustrates how critical the decision-maker's position in the internal differentiation of society is in agricultural development and underdevelopment.

It is critical in another sense. In the process of socialisation, different categories of individuals acquire familiarisation with his or her social and material world – an orientation about its potentials and limitations – that endows

155

the individual with a vantage point that is characteristic of the niche in which that socialisation took place. As a consequence, what alternatives are feasible and what are not is determined not just by the actual means to pursue such alternatives but by the cognitive 'filters' which block out certain options as not even worth considering because of the decision-maker's station in life. Ultimately, according to Keesing (1987: 387): 'What actors know, what perspectives they take, depend, even in the least complex classless societies on who they are, whether they are male or female, young or old, leader or led.'

This study analyses the response of different categories of farmers in a Philippine rural community to changing social, economic, and ecological conditions. It focuses on the decision-making criteria of households and individuals who are currently developing new adaptive strategies. The variability in choice among various alternatives is analysed in relation to the social distribution of indigenous knowledge pertaining to agriculture and nutrition as well as the decision-maker's position in the internal differentiation of society.

Adaptive strategies of a rural population

The study area, Sitio Kabaritan of Barrio Sto. Domingo in Bay, Laguna was traditionally devoted to wet-rice cultivation, its inhabitants either full-time farmers or full-time fishermen of the nearby Laguna de Bay. They farmed on rich alluvial soil, and irrigation was never too much of a problem since the sitio is bounded on its two sides by bodies of water. On the west is the Maitim River and on the north is Laguna de Bay into which the Maitim River drains (Figures 11.1 and 11.2). Due to the location of their community, Kabaritan people always appeared to have one foot in water and one foot on land in securing their livelihood. The amphibious adaptations have recently culminated in the culture of tilapia *(Tilapia nilotica)* in aquatic nurseries which have been dug in former rice fields, along the lake shore area, and in vacant residential lots. A few are experimenting with other aquaculture options such as raising carp or edible 'golden' snails instead of tilapia.

It was largely through the farmers' own initiative that some rice paddy fields have been converted to aquatic hatcheries and nurseries for fingerlings. These are subsequently sold to operators of fishpens in neighbouring provinces. Thus, where there used to be a distinct dichotomy between farmers and fishermen in the area, interests are now converging to rice-aquaculture combination as a means of livelihood. This is supplemented by backyard vegetable gardening. For women, there is a growing interest in the cultivation of ornamental plants, which are purchased by middlemen from urban areas. In addition, the women buy and sell farm inputs and produce, thereby acting as middlepersons themselves. The new opportunities have also attracted migrants who considerably expanded the landless sector of the population. These transitions have ushered in novel choices, altered constraints, and restructured relationships, thus providing a good opportunity to study agricultural decision-making of rural cultivators under conditions of on-going development change.

Elicitation of indigenous decision-making criteria

One important physical manifestation of agricultural decision-making is land use. Patterns of land utilisation reflect not only immediate concerns but also

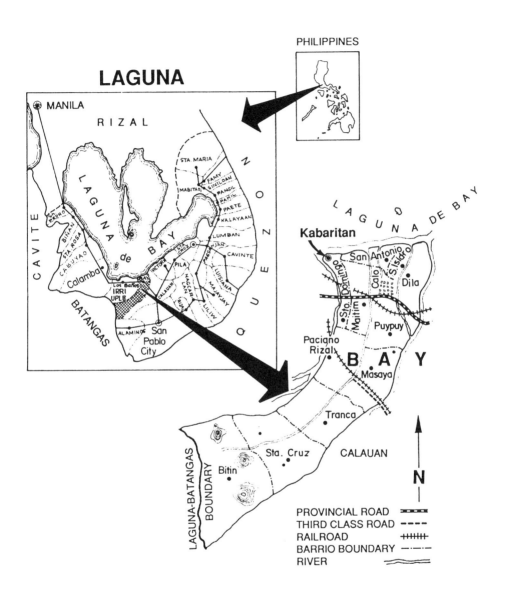

Figures 11.1: *Location map of study area*

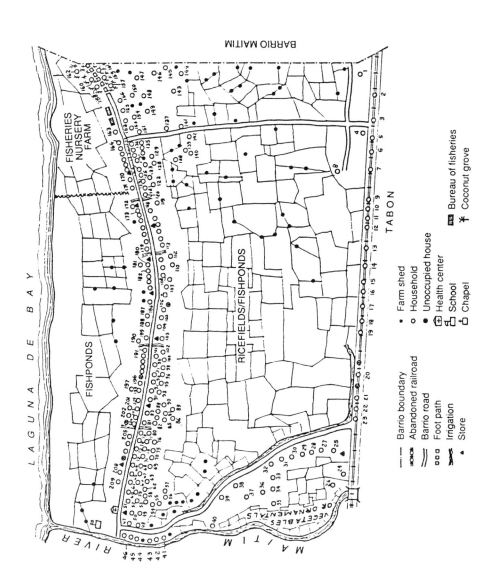

Figure 11.2: *Land use map of Kabaritan*

past failures and successes as well as future plans. In Kabaritan, the land use options commonly engaged in are of four general types – wet-land rice culture, aquaculture, vegetable gardening, and cultivation of ornamental plants. A stratified sample of twelve male and twelve female informants (husbands and wives representing different socioeconomic groups) were asked to evaluate each of the options currently used in Kabaritan, though not necessarily by them. All the informants have direct experience with at least one option in the capacity of owner-operator, contract-worker, care-taker, or hired labourer and were familiar enough with all the others to be conversant about their advantages and disadvantages. The 24 informants were interviewed separately to minimise the effect of inter-informant influence.

Local perceptions and evaluations of each of the land use options were investigated by using an adaptation of contrastive elicitation technique (Gladwin 1980; Young 1981). This method consisted of a series of questions, usually in the form of 'Why this and not that?', which were designed to make the decision-makers verbalise the reasons for their choice by consciously going over the range of possibilities. This range was established before hand by compiling a list of predominant crop and livelihood options in Kabaritan. Hence, the aspects which are considered important were identified and the process of elimination of inappropriate alternatives was illuminated.

Folk evaluation of major options of land-use

When the 24 informants were asked to evaluate the major land use options in Kabaritan, some responses were common to all informants while others were given by some but not by others. The former are considered here as basic and prototypical evaluations[1] which are known to, and used by, all members of the culture (Table 11.1). The latter, herein referred to as marginal comments, are apparently neither completely shared nor totally idiosyncratic but, rather, are characteristic of informants who share a common niche in society (Table 11.2).

With respect to rice, for example, modern varieties such as IR 36, IR 42, and *Malagkit* IRRI were characterised by every informant, regardless of socioeconomic status or gender as early-maturing but 'sickly' ('sickly' or *sakitin* being a gloss for low resistance to many 'enemies' of rice, including insects and fungi, but excluding birds and rats), and high-yielding but producing grains of less desirable cooking and eating quality, which consequently command a lower price in the market. On the other hand, C4, *Sinandomeng*, and the traditional *Malagkit sungsong* were viewed as delicious and aromatic rices that command a higher price in the market. However, the plants were evaluated as prone to lodging because of their tall soft stalks and highly inviting to birds and rats because their panicle is tall and open, thus wafting the aroma of the grains in the air (Table 11.1).

On the other hand, if Table 11.2 is examined, it will be seen that evaluations like 'good to plant so we won't buy any more', 'relatively new in Kabaritan', 'not as familiar as other IR's', and 'not tried yet', 'no problem is anticipated but we would rather stick with IR 42 which has been tried and tested' are more characteristic of middle class informants. By comparison, disjointed, experiential, and closer to the ground comments like 'difficult to thresh because the grains are more difficult to detach from the panicle', 'sends out a lot of shoots (*masuwi*)', and 'rice plants have excessively sharp

Table 11.1: 'Prototypical' comments regarding major land-use options

Land-use option		Local evaluation	
General category	*Specific category*	*Perceived advantages*	*Disadvantages*
Glutinous rice	*Malagkit sungsong*	• delicious and fragrant when cooked • commands a good price in the market	• low yielding • prone to rat and bird infestation
	Malagkit, IRRI	• high yielding	• does not command a good price in the market • firm and sticky when cooked • not as delicious and fragrant as *Malagkit sungsong* when cooked
Non-glutinous rice	IR 36	• high yielding • short maturation period	• 'sickly,' not resistant to pests • not very good eating quality, grains are hard when cooked
	IR 42	• grains expand a great deal when cooked • high yielding, especially during the dry season	• hard and not fragrant when cooked • 'sickly,' especially during the wet season
	Super 42	• better tasting than other IR's • commands a better price in the market • yields well	• longer maturation period • 'sickly,' especially during the wet season • grains are not firm when cooked
	IR 62	• high yielding • resistant to pests and floods • good eating quality • easy to sell because it is relatively cheap	• not as well-known and well-tested as IR 36 and IR 42 • somewhat hard when cooked • does not command a good price in the market
	C4	• good eating quality; smells and tastes good when cooked • high yielding • commands a good price in the market	• 'sickly,' and prone to rat and bird in-festation • tall, soft stems tend to lodge during rainy season
	Sinandomeng	• very delicious, soft and aromatic, when cooked • high yielding • commands a high price in the market	• attractive to birds and rats because of its aroma • prone to lodging • relatively new to Kabaritan, therefore not yet tested

▶

Table 11.1: 'Prototypical' comments regarding major land-use options (continued)

Land-use option		Local evaluation	
General category	*Specific category*	*Perceived advantages*	*Disadvantages*
Vegetables	Taro	• good vegetable, delicious and versatile, all parts are edible • easy to cultivate, not much care required	• some varieties are itchy • exacerbates coughing and rheumatisms
	Sweet potato	• delicious and nutritious, can be used as vegetable dish, or as dessert, many edible parts • does not require a lot of care	• can cause gas if eaten in excessive amounts • usually eaten by goats if not fenced or watched
	Eggplant	• good source of income • long life span, continues to yield for one year • delicious and versatile vegetable, fruits and young shoots can be eaten	• highly susceptible to pests • difficult to cultivate, requires a lot of care and attention • can be easily destroyed by floods • not very nutritious
	Bell pepper	• commands a good price in the market • requires only moderate care, not difficult to cultivate • provides delicious flavouring for viands	• very few people buy this except during special occasions • eaten by goats unless fenced • can cause hemorrhoids and indigestion if eaten in excessive amounts
	Tomato	• good source of income, can be easily sold in the market • prolific, bears a lot of fruit especially during the dry season • delicious and nutritious ingredient in cooking	• demands a lot of care, susceptible to pests • soft stem easily rots during the rainy season • seeds can cause appendicitis
Ornamental plants	*Pisaray*	• additional source of income • can also be used as house decoration • requires moderate amount of care	• does not thrive on ordinary soil, needs good potting. Medium rich in humus • needs to be carefully tended so its foliage will be beautiful • needs to be separated and propagated regularly to prevent overcrowding

▶

Table 11.1: 'Prototypical' comments regarding major land-use options (continued)

| Land-use option | | Local evaluation | |
General category	Specific category	Perceived advantages	Disadvantages
Ornamental plants (continued)	Aster	• very good source of income because it commands a high price in the market	• requires too much care • needs a big piece of land • demand is seasonal (only during special occasions), so timing is critical
Aquaculture	Tilapia	• adults can be eaten, fingerlings can be sold • good source of income • does not require too much care	• reeders and fingerlings can escape when the water floods over, and fishponds overflow • there are times when there are no buyers
	Carp	• commands high price (carp fingerlings cost more than tilapia fingerlings)	• requires too much work • very few buyers are interested because of the high cost and care requirements
	Golden snail	• can be eaten by some • can be sold, even exported	• voracious rice pests, no benefit to farmers • imported variety is too flabby and slimy, unlike native variety

leaf blades and spikelets (*masungot*) and a lot of powdery materials which are 'itchy' (*mabulo*)' are more characteristic of low socio-economic informants who toil in the fields as transplanters, weeders, or harvesters.

Also notable is their frequent use of the evaluation 'nice to watch' or 'good to look at' versus 'not nice to watch' or 'not good to look at.'Being landless and at the same time living very close to the rice fields, they can only view the incessant cycle of planting and harvesting from the sidelines. And so they live with the reality that they can only watch and touch but never claim.

Relatively speaking, the high socioeconomic group has fewer marginal comments since most of their comments are incorporated in the prototypical evaluations. The few comments that are out of the prototypical reveal their grasp of the explanations behind the agronomic properties cited as well as remedies for the perceived problems. Also observable is a tendency towards experimentation with new alternatives, e.g. 'IR 42 is dependable but we just switched to try IR 62,' something which is a market contrast from the closely-monitoring and rather conservative attitude of the middle class farmers towards new rice varieties.

With respect to gastronomic criteria, it will be seen from Table 11.2 that at times a rice variety such as IR 36 that was considered hard by the high

Table 11.2: 'Marginal' comments regarding major land-use options

| Land-use option | Socio-economic status | | | | | |
| | High | | Middle | | Low | |
	Male	Female	Male	Female	Male	Female
Malagkit sungsong			• good to plant so we won't have to buy anymore • lodges during the rainy season and when too much fertiliser is applied • tends to have empty chaffs	• better to plant during the dry season than during the rainy season	• cannot be consumed everyday, flavour is too rich • nice to watch, especially when the grains are ripening • first class, good enough for visitors	• suitable for making snacks • difficult to thresh, grains are difficult to detach from the panicle • looks very beautiful when grains ripen
Malagkit IRRI	• grains are hard when cooked				• commands a lower price than Malagkit sungsong but grains are heavier because they are bigger	• sends out a lot of shoots but is second class • seems to be mixed with non-glutinous rice
IR 36	• grains are comparable to C4 in quality but a little harder	• matures fast but if one is not conscientious about fertiliser application produces chaffs without grains	• satisfies easily because it is hard, one does not have to consume a lot to feel full	• expands when cooked so it is not expensive • one has to watch out for pests or there will be no harvest	• rice seeds are not difficult to find • easy to sell because the price is low • easier to care for during dry season	• not good cooking quality, too soft • not nice to watch

**Table 11.2: 'Marginal' comments regarding major land-use options
(continued)**

Land-use option	Socio-economic status					
	High		Middle		Low	
	Male	Female	Male	Female	Male	Female
IR 42		• 'sickly' when newly planted but takes only a short time to mature		• stalks are hard and rigid, so are the grains when cooked but they taste good	• yields better than IR 36 but grains are harder when cooked	• expands well; even when you cook just a little you end up with a lot • hard but good tasting
Super 42	• depend-able but we just switched so we can try IR 62		• called 'super' 42 because it tasted better than IR 42 • sends out a lot of shoots		• not resistant to flooding	
IR 62			• relatively new in Kabaritan; not as familiar as other IRs	• not yet tried, no problem anticipated but we will stick with IR 42 which is tried and tested	• not good to plant during the wet season	• rice plants have sharp leaves and spikelets and covered with pow-dery materials which are itchy
C40	• matures quickly • inviting to birds because panicle is tall and open and the grains smell good	• tends to have unfilled chaffs, that is why it is not recom-mended by bank officials		• difficult to cook (too watery) unless it has been aged for a year	• does not send out many shoots but the grains are first class	• the only drawback is when it is hit by a storm

▶

Table 11.2: 'Marginal' comments regarding major land-use options (continued)

Land-use option	Socio-economic status					
	High		*Middle*		*Low*	
	Male	*Female*	*Male*	*Female*	*Male*	*Female*
Sinando-meng	• takes only a short time to mature	• plants are 'sickly'	• so delicious that you end up eating too much, therefore, it is • wasteful	• cannot be eaten everyday, it gives a feeling of too much satiety • cannot be afforded by ordinary people	• full feeling does not last long, after a while you feel hungry again • too expensive, we just settle for IR 36	• almost like glutinous rice when cooked • not nice to cook because it is too soft
Taro	• we do not cultivate it because we have no more space-time for it	• we do not plant it because it is consumed by goats	• we do not cultivate this because people do not buy it	• just plant this and it grows, can also be served as a dessert but we have not more place for it	• can be planted during the wet or dry season, but do not have land	• should not be planted where the soil has poor drainage because the roots rot • good vegetable but we do not have land
Sweet Potato	• good as food as long as it does not develop ulcers (tanga)	• rich in Vitamin A	• at times this commands a good price, but it can be infested if planted at the wrong time	• good to plant so one does not have to buy it in the market	• cannot be fed to young children because it causes colic	• roots and young leaves are edible • the roots do not develop if you keep getting leaves

▶

Table 11.2: 'Marginal' comments regarding major land-use options (continued)

Land-use option	Socio-economic status					
	High		Middle		Low	
	Male	*Female*	*Male*	*Female*	*Male*	*Female*
Eggplant		• good vegetable for consumption and sale but we have no more space and time for it		• needs a lot of attention to make it bear fruit, otherwise it will just keep growing	• easily attacked by caterpillars • one has to water, week and apply fertiliser regularly so it will bear fruit	• vegetable, but we have no land on which to plant
Bell pepper	• easily destroyd by floods • we have no more time for cultivating this		• not strenuous to cultivate, not easily attacked by peasts, only problem is few people buy it.	• there is high demand for this only during fiestas and wedding	• nobody will buy this in Kabaritan • should not be fed to your children • we have no land for planting this	• seeds are hard to find, if we had seeds, we would plant this • during the dry season, the leaves get holes
Tomato	• would be nice to plant so we no longer have to buy from the store but we have no more space and time	• rich in Vitamin C • we have no more time for it	• needs greatest amount of care at start of flowering when it becomes suscep-tible to pest	• there are times when this com-mands a good price, but at other times the price is low	• good for fattening children but seeds should be removed	• bears a lot of fruit but not during the rainy season • would plant this if we had land and seeds

▶

Table 11.2: 'Marginal' comments regarding major land-use options (continued)

Land-use option	Socio-economic status					
	High		Middle		Low	
	Male	Female	Male	Female	Male	Female
Pisaray		• good decoration, should be protected from too much sun and smoke • cannot find good soil, no time left for this	• can be sold but sometimes there are no buyers • if planted at the wrong time, flowers will be very cheap	• we do not have enough time for cultivation and propagation • we have no more space for this	• good for gardens but should be protected from chickens because plant dies when scratched • one needs to know how to take care of them to make them flower	• can be sold but we have no more space for it
Aster			• other people won't share techniques of cultivation • if planted at the wrong time, flowers will be very cheap	• entails knowledge of how to cultivate, involved very intricate procedures • we have no more space for this	• attacked by caterpillars • one needs to know how to take care of them to make them flower	• one has to fertilise regularly and keep weeding so plants won't turn yellow
Tilapia			• not fussy, they eat anything, even leaves		• need to receive good care so they will lay eggs • presently there are few buyers	

▶

Table 11.2: 'Marginal' comments regarding major land-use options (continued)

| Land-use option | Socio-economic status | | | | | |
| | High | | Middle | | Low | |
	Male	Female	Male	Female	Male	Female
Carp			• difficult to introduce to lay eggs, won't grow well in fish cages	• we do not know how to take care of these	• one has to give it excellent care or it won't lay eggs	
Golden snail	• we do not eat this but some people do	• considered edible by some	• beneficial only to those who raise ducks and pigs • cannot be eaten by human beings because they are too slimy	• we do not eat this because it does not taste good	• edible but the problem is they eat newly planted rice	• we eat this but we do not culture it • not as delicious and firm as native variety • no longer cultured because they proved to be pests of rice

socioeconomic group was considered as too soft by the low socioeconomic group. Moreover, as one goes from higher to lower socioeconomic status, these is an increasing preference for rice that expands well (*mahilab*), feels heavier on the stomach (*mabigat sa tiyan*), and takes longer to digest (*matagal matunaw*). Highly-valued aromatic varieties like *Sinandomeng* and *Malagkit sungsong* which were considered the most delicious were also regarded as wasteful (*maaksaya*) because one tends to eat too much of it, too rich (*nakakaumay*) because of the strong flavour and aroma, too easily digested (*madaling matunaw*) because of its soft texture and, basically, too expensive for ordinary people.

The phrase, 'ordinary people', implies a sensitivity to the social hierarchy and awareness of their place in it. The salience of hierarchical ranking of categories is also evident in the preoccupation of informants belonging to the lower socioeconomic status with adjectives like 'first class' and 'second class' in referring to rice varieties.

As can be expected from the division of labour in the domestic unit, females were more concerned with cooking and keeping quality of rice, while males were more concerned with eating quality. However, comments of females also revealed a knowledge of agricultural production techniques and agronomic problems which could not have been obtained from a concentration in the housekeeping role or even from a casual and supportive role in farming as well as in marketing of farm produce.

In fact, results indicate that, compared to males of the same socioeconomic status, females have greater cognisance of cause-effect and constraint-consequence relationships in farming and marketing operations. This is evidenced by comments like 'tend to have unfilled chaffs that is why it is not recommended by bank officials', 'needs a lot of attention to make it bear fruit, otherwise it will just keep giving leaves', 'there is a high demand for this only during fiestas and weddings', and 'one has to fertilise regularly and keep weeding so plants won't turn yellow'. Yet, when male farmers in Kabaritan were asked if they take their wives' views into account in making agricultural decisions, they dismissed the prospect nonchalantly and replied that they usually say 'yes' to their wives' suggestions to avoid prolonged arguments but go ahead with what they think is right anyway.

In comparing the prototypical to the marginal observations, it appears that the former are more related to (1) the biological (including biochemical and agronomic) properties of the rice varieties, (2) the economic realities of the market, and (3) the cognitive predisposition of the high socioeconomic group. IRRI modern varieties have high amylose content and this property determines the hardness of boiled rice, particularly after cooling. More traditional varieties, in contrast, as well as C4, a modern variety, have intermediate amylose content, which give these rice varieties a moist, soft texture when cooked. As a direct offshoot of these properties, there exists a lower consumer demand, and consequently lower market price for many IR varieties. On the other hand, the IR varieties have been bred to be fertiliser-sensitive so that production can be increased without having to increase land area under cultivation. Therefore, compared with them, traditional varieties, which are taller and less fertiliser-dependent, were consistently viewed as prone to lodging during the rainy season and as a result of heavy fertiliser application.

With respect to other land-use options, there is a strong consensus that only land and time left over from what is required for rice cultivation and *tilapia* aquaculture should be devoted to vegetable gardening and cultivation of ornamentals. These are regarded as a good source of subsistence, particularly taro and sweet potatoes, and a welcome source of additional income, but never as a replacement for rice. Prototypical evaluation of vegetable crops revolves around their palatability and nutritive value, resistance to pests, wind, and floods, agronomic requirements, and economic potentials indicating the importance of these parameters to rural cultivators. Generally speaking, crops which require less care and have a more stable market were preferred over those which may command higher price but require too much work or involve too much risk.

More marginal comments deal with particular constraints faced by each group and the evaluation of the access price of diversification. Those informants belonging to the high socioeconomic status who do not engage in these options accounted for their not cultivating vegetables and ornamentals in terms of lack of space and time. High socioeconomic status females displayed greater awareness of specific nutrients contained in each vegetable than either males of corresponding rank or females of lower rank. Females, in general, demonstrated a working understanding of both the agronomic requirements and the market dynamics relevant to vegetable production.

Middle status farmers were more inclined than either high or low status ones to pay close attention to the presence and stability of a market for their products. For example, one reason given for not cultivating taro is 'because very few people buy it'. This is just one step short of saying that neighbours just ask for it. In the case of green pepper, they indicated that 'very few people buy it' because it is not regarded as everyday fare but reserved for special occasions. Tomatoes and ornamentals were likewise evaluated in terms of stability of market demand.

Informants belonging to the low socioeconomic group demonstrated knowledge of, and attention to, highly specific agronomic considerations, e.g. 'attacked by caterpillars', 'scratched by chickens', and 'eaten by goats' instead of just low resistance to pests or attractiveness to competitors. They also specified 'should be fertilised with chicken manure' instead of just fertilised. As can be expected, lack of land is perceived to be the biggest constraint and this is followed by inability to obtain seeds. Time, their only readily available resource, does not seem to be a matter of consequence to those belonging to the lower socioeconomic status as they evaluate major land use options. This is probably because time for them has very little opportunity cost.

The criteria used to compare two ornamental alternatives, aster and *pisaray*, are parallel to those used for evaluating two aquaculture alternatives, *tilapia* and carp. Both *pisaray* and *tilapia* were regarded as options which, comparatively speaking, have a more stable market, require less care, and on the whole are more reliable sources of income. Aster and carp, on the other hand, were evaluated as relatively new, high-income generating alternatives that demand too much work, require specialised knowledge, and for which the market demand is highly variable. Confronted with having to make a choice regarding appropriation of limited land, the people of Kabaritan opt for more stable, less strenuous, and less fastidious production regimes. This is shown by their evaluation criteria as well as the minimal amount of land devoted to aster and carp.

Unlike the local evaluation of vegetable and ornamental plants, lack of space and time was never cited as a reason for not engaging in *tilapia* aquaculture by informants belonging to the high and middle socioeconomic groups. Landowners, without exception, found the land and the time to divert to *tilapia* nurseries as soon as aquaculture proved to be a highly profitable venture. Only one informant, a female in the low socioeconomic group, cited lack of land as a constraint. All others did not consider land ownership as critical when it came to aquaculture.

Edible golden snails, which one household in Kabaritan experimented with in 1985 as another invertebrate which might be successfully cultured in aquatic nurseries proved to be voracious pests of young rice plants when they escaped from their nurseries into the surrounding rice fields during the 1986 flood. Although, strictly speaking, it is no longer considered as a feasible option now because of the extensive damage it has done and may continue to do, it is instructive to look at the marginal comments given to evaluate this strategy.

Going from the high to the low socioeconomic group, there is an interesting range of asides and excuses regarding culture and consumption of golden snails. High and middle socioeconomic status informants reported an aware-ness that the snails are edible but clearly distinguished between 'us' and 'them', the latter referring to those who, by choice or by necessity, eat snails. Informants belonging to the low socioeconomic status admitted eating the snails but made it clear that they do not culture it and they are aware of the damage it can do. They also referred to a local variety, the one they really prefer because its flesh was more firm and tasty, and correctly observed that upon the introduction of the new, imported variety there was extensive inter-breeding between the two such that now there are no more snails of the pure strain of local variety to be found in Kabaritan. The household that intro-duced the imported snails belongs to the high socioeconomic status.

Decision-making criteria in relation to class and gender

As is evident from Table 11.2, the high socioeconomic status informants have more empty cells for marginal comments than the middle and the low socioe-conomic status informants. The reason for this is that most of their evalua-tions of local land-use options were shared by all the other informants and thus integrated into the prototypical evaluations. It is tempting at this point to allude to the ideological hegemony created by elites, whether this be in spreading culture and consumption patterns from developed to underdevel-oped – at the level of countries within the world system, regions within coun-tries, or classes within region – or the institution of the dialect or world view of the dominant group as the national, or international, language or ethos.

According to Lakoff (1987: 68): 'There are concepts...that are based on a complex model in which a number of individual cognitive models converge, forming an experiential cluster. When the cluster of models that jointly char-acterise a concept diverge, there is a strong pull to view one as the most important.'

The results of this study provide some indication that even in an agricul-tural community of seemingly undifferentiated rural cultivators, the views of the higher socioeconomic group tend to be more dominant and shared. How-ever, because of the limited sample size, this conclusion may be premature and needs to be validated on a broader scale.

Another hypothesis which might be tested profitably in this connection is that proposed by Brown (1979) which revolves around the correlation between a culture's societal complexity and a progressively reduced reliance on detailed knowledge of specific plants and animals. From this perspective, another possible explanation for the observed paucity of marginal comments from the high socioeconomic group is that they have, in a sense, 'relegated' detailed knowledge to those in the lower socioeconomic groups who serve as their contract weeders or daily labourers.

Although farmers belonging to the high socioeconomic group are still very much involved in day-to-day agricultural activities, they have to 'make room' in their cognitive framework for economic and political relations which become increasingly complicated as modernisation progresses. One way of handling this complexity is by specialisation and a more sharply delineated division of labour between classes, which possibly translates to cognitive spe-cialisation as well. In sum, the matrix of local evaluation of major land use options in Kabaritan reflects intracultural variation predicated on socioeco-nomic and gender correlates.

Socioeconomic variables like land tenure, availability of labour and capital, access to knowledge and inputs, and social as well as sexual division of labour apparently shape the evaluation of options by influencing the perception of risk, benefits, and access price. The decision-making frameworks, processes, and outcomes of individuals reflect a vantage point which has been developed through a lifelong curriculum of socialisation embedded in social interactions. As Holy and Stuchlik (1983: 2) emphasised: 'The fickle and idiosyncratic activities of concrete individuals have to be studies in as much detail as possible, but what is important about them is not their individuality, but how they are patterned, how their existence can be explained in terms of society and its component groups and institutions, and how they, at the same time, manifest the existence of society and its component groups and institutions.'

In terms of agricultural decision-making, the results of this study confirm that the indigenous decision-making framework is not as homogeneous as it may seem but is greatly influenced by the decision-maker's position in the internal differentiation of society. Although there are basic similarities in desire for high yield, short maturation period, high resistance to biotic competitors and unfavourable environmental conditions, as well as good eating quality and market performance as reflected in the prototypical evaluations, there are perceivable patterns of variation in individual's evaluations.

Thus, while high socioeconomic households go for options which increase productivity, those of the middle status give priority to stability. On the other hand, low socioeconomic households, cognisant of their limitations, 'watch' and take note of various details in agricultural production and marketing. Also salient for them are experiences of moving around as hired labourers in others' fields. They take note of the sharpness of the leaves and spikelets, the itchiness of the pollens, and the density of shoots as well as the appetites of caterpillars, chickens, and goats.

While upper socioeconomic status informants look for flavour, aroma, and soft texture, those lower in the socioeconomic ladder down play the importance of these 'first class' qualities in favour of the grains' expanding, satisfying, and staying power. The latter also take note of the value of subsistence crops for feeding and 'fattening' their children and pay close attention to measures that should be taken to avoid unwanted side-effects (e.g. remove seeds from tomatoes so as not to induce appendicitis, feed only a moderate amount of sweet potatoes so as not to cause colic). Coping and survival are thus accomplished by substitution of less costly alternatives for highly valued commodities.

The foregoing account only goes to show that while basic elements of the decision-making criteria are shared by virtue of constant interaction, information exchange, and co-creation of meanings, individual decision-makers make elaborations on the basic theme – or, alternatively, internalise only certain portions of it – based on their position in the internal differentiation of society. Although every individual has some leeway for working the system to his or her minimum disadvantage, we cannot deny the 'boundedness' of the system in which day-to-day agricultural decision-making takes place, nor the fact that the ability to recognise the existence of alternatives and exercise choice is directly proportional to the individual's standing in the hierarchy of social and economic relations. This is so not only because access to resources is systematically skewed but even more so because the distribution of knowledge is socially patterned. It might be useful to keep the existence of systematic intracultural variation in mind when the scale-neutrality and gender-neutrality assumption rears its tempting head.

Note

1. The prototypical–marginal framework used here is adapted from the concept of categories as graded structures proposed by Rosch (1978). Following a parallel pattern, local evaluations of major land use options show a gradation from core values to peripheral ones such that it is possible to classify certain evaluations as 'prototypical' and the rest as 'marginal' to varying degrees.

12. Forest Gardens of Highland Sri Lanka – An indigenous system for reclaiming deforested land[1]

YVONNE EVERETT

Introduction

AGROFORESTRY, THE PRACTICE of combining annual and perennial crops, includes a wide range of techniques which can be ecologically sustainable and contribute to human welfare. Much of the research in agroforestry has been focused on the design of new systems using methods based on insights from forestry and agriculture in the North American and European temperate climates. Yet, sustainable agroforestry systems, many centuries old, are found throughout the tropics and represent generations of farmers' experience. An important component of developing systems for sustainable use of tropical forest resources is to study existing forest use and agroforestry to understand the ecological and sociocultural–cultural principles which govern their management. Such principles frequently offer more appropriate bases for understanding systems of sustainable tropical forest resource use than those derived from temperate experience.

The key to traditional agroforestry systems and their management is the farmer's knowledge. Many farmers understand the habitat and growth requirements of many species, seasonal yields, and compatibility with other species, and relate this information to the constraints of the microclimate, soils, and other site characteristics of the land they farm. This information is passed through generations, in family and village traditions, and through experiential learning. It is based upon the villagers' 'ecological theory' or understanding of nature. Such theory guides actions on the basis of anticipated outcomes. Little of this knowledge has been formally described, much of it may not ordinarily be verbalised, as well.

In 1985–6, I spent 13 months documenting the structure and composition of forest garden systems in a village in highland Sri Lanka (Everett, unpublished). This study presents initial efforts to understand farmers' ecological theory and management of these forest garden systems. The research is interdisciplinary, employing a combination of methods from landscape and vegetation ecology and ethnoscience.

Initially, forest gardens were inventoried using formal vegetation ecological theory and methods to gain an image of the structure and composition of agroforestry systems. Hypotheses as to expected patterns of vegetation development and change over time commensurate with formal theory were developed. Forest garden farmers were interviewed using various approaches from ethnoscience to elicit their garden management practices and the underlying principles guiding them. On the basis of the initial garden inventories, common understandings and divergences between formal ecological theory and farmers' theory (as well as the researchers' comprehension of the tacit knowledge of the farmers) were expressed in scientific terms and tested against the reality of existing gardens.

The relevance of forest garden research

This research was guided by the assumption that if it were possible to gain a clear understanding of the theoretical underpinnings of these systems, principles from their management should provide insight to the reforestation of degraded uplands in Sri Lanka and the provision of sustenance and cash income for immigrant farmers. The information could also contribute to the management of other areas in the highland tropics and transitional buffer zones around natural reserves.

The Uva Basin in the south central highlands of Sri Lanka is a microcosm of land-use problems in tropical highland areas. The basin is one-half of the watershed catchment for the Mahaweli, the largest river on the island, and the lifeline of Sri Lanka's lowland dry zone irrigation development projects. Protective forest cover on the upland watersheds is vital to ensuring a stable water supply throughout the year in the tropical monsoon climate. Yet, during the late nineteenth and early twentieth centuries, British colonial planters cleared many of the montane forests to establish coffee and tea plantations, often on slopes so steep or sites so marginal that they were soon abandoned (Tennent 1859; Werner 1984).

Natural forests were reduced to small remnants in inaccessible places. After independence, this deforested grassland scrub land called *patana* was claimed by the Government of Sri Lanka. Natural forests cannot regenerate on these sites due to grazing pressure from livestock from nearby villages and the frequency of fires in the dry seasons (Holmes 1951). The government forest department also has had great difficulty establishing and protecting forest plantations in the basin (Nanayakara 1980). Consequently, much of the land remains under grassland *patana* vegetation.

As population increases island-wide, immigrants from the lowlands, unfamiliar with hillside farming practices, are squatting on these government-owned lands. They grow lucrative annual cash crops, such as potatoes for one or two years of harvest, and then move on as the soil fertility declines, or as government officials evict them. These farming practices exacerbate soil erosion problems, reducing already marginal fertility in the highlands and increasing the silt load for dams in the irrigation projects downstream. A land use system for the deforested hills, which can provide upland watershed protection as well as land and income for immigrant small farmers, is needed. Forest gardens could be planted to reforest the grasslands while producing multiple crops for farmers.

The Sri Lanka forest gardens have been a dominant form of land use on the island for centuries. Similar agroforestry systems are known throughout the tropics (Fernandez *et al.* 1984; Kunstadter *et al.* 1978; Soemarwoto and Soemarwoto 1984). The gardens vary in structure and composition with climate and elevation. What little research has been undertaken on forest gardens in Sri Lanka has focused on the 'midcountry' Kandyan spice gardens, located below the 3,000-ft. elevation (Jacob and Alles 1987; Bavappa and Jacob 1981; McConnell and Dharmapala 1978).

Unlike traditional agroforestry systems in the forest or at the forest edge described, for example, in Indonesia (Christanty et al. 1986) and Mexico (Alcorn 1984b), the forest gardens in the largely deforested Sri Lanka highlands are begun on the degraded grassland hillsides.[1] In much of the Uva Basin, the A horizon of the primarily red-yellow podzolic soil has eroded away (Perera 1969; de Alwis and Dimantha 1981). Yet, as villages expand, the local farmers can create gardens of trees and shrubs on these very marginal sites in just a few years. As neighbouring gardens blend together, a village, seen from above, appears as a forest island in a sea of grassland. The 'village forest' provides vital refuge for native flora and fauna as the last remnants of natural forests in the highlands are decimated by illicit logging.[2] As the gardens provide wildlife habitat, they may be appropriate models for nature reserve buffer zone areas, providing a gradual transition from reserve to agricultural land use (for example, see Harris 1984).

The gardens, located immediately around the owners' homes, are commonly one component of the larger farming system which may also include rice paddies, vegetable fields and/or plantation crops such as tea. My research was undertaken in Mirahawatte, a slightly larger than average village of 600 households. The results reported here are based on a survey of 61 randomly selected households and forest gardens (Everett, unpublished).[3] In Mirahawatte, forest gardens account for nearly 50per cent of private land use. Throughout the year, they provide a wide variety of food, fuel, fodder, wood, medicinal and cash crops, including coffee, cinnamon and palm sugar (see the Appendix), as well as a cool and pleasant living environment.

Households gather 75–100 per cent of their fuelwood from their gardens (the remainder supplied by prunings from nearby tea plantations). The gardens produce such a surplus of jackfruit, a basic carbohydrate component of the villagers' diet, that 75 per cent of the fruit is left to rot on the trees (see also Moles and Wagachchi, unpublished). Individual timber and over-mature fruit trees are removed as wood is needed and various new seedlings are planted in their stead. The gardens are never clearcut and many predate living memory in the village.

On the average, the gardens are three-quarters of an acre in size, with over 250 individual woody perennials of 29 species. Key structural characteristics of the gardens, including their high density and species diversity, are comparable to measures from natural forests in similar elevations and climates. Such characteristics may be used as indicators of the vital functions of forest ecosystems, including nutrient cycling and watershed protection, suggesting that the gardens are a partial analog of natural forest systems (Everett, unpublished; Senanayake 1987).

The fundamental dynamics of forests and gardens alike are linked to the processes of regeneration and change of vegetation over time. The farmers' knowledge of these processes of change lies at the heart of their understanding and persistent ability to modify the surrounding landscape with such agroforestry systems. A clear grasp of the principles upon which farmers' action is based is prerequisite to further assessment of the potential of forest garden-like systems elsewhere.

Understanding the principles of forest garden management

The interdisciplinary research approach described earlier was applied in initial attempts to understand vegetation patterns in the gardens.

The vegetation ecological approach Succession is an important concept guiding the efforts of ecologists to understand the patterns in vegetation change. Succession, simply stated, is the establishment and progression of vegetation composition through time on a site. It has been studied, for example, in wildlands and old fields in the temperate climates of the United States and in forest fallows of shifting cultivators in the tropics.

As a concept for studying patterns of change, gap phase succession, a branch of successional studies which has recently gained much attention in forest ecology (Watt 1947; Pickett and White 1985), is useful in understanding complex perennial cropping systems. Regeneration of many species in tropical wet forest depends on the disturbance created by tree falls of scales ranging from single tree senescence to multiple tree blow-downs in hurricanes or other catastrophes (Brandani *et al.* 1988). This creation of gaps in the forest canopy allows seeds and seedlings access to otherwise unavailable resources, such as light, thus contributing to the process of successional change over time.

The degree to which the concept of succession, usually applied to non-managed, natural ecosystems, can be validly applied to a garden system continuously managed by people deserves discussion beyond the scope of this paper. In the following pages, I take the stance that people are one biotic factor affecting succession in a particular area, the Uva Basin. However, their influence may be different in scale and intensity than, for example, a roaming group of wild boar. Under human management, a garden begun on fire climax grassland of very poor site quality will support vegetation dominated by trees within a few years' time (Everett, unpublished). The process is not known to occur without human intervention protecting a site from fire. On the other hand, natural succession might progress, if there were no people in the Uva Basin, as many burns are caused by people, often using fire as a tool to influence vegetation composition. However, people are present and, for the purpose of this discussion, will be treated as part of the ecosystem. The degree to which the process of garden development from the grassland to the forestlike stage can be understood through conceptualisations of natural forest succession is of interest here.

Vegetation changes in 'stages of succession' or 'phases of regeneration' have often been defined through their species composition (Whittaker 1975; Watt 1947). Gaussen *et al.* (1968) describe the occurrence of native species of largely secondary, mid-elevation montane forests in Sri Lanka (1965). Several of the predominant species, such as *Neolitsea involucrata, Litsea spp., Garcinia echinocarpa, Achronychia pendunculata* and *Cinnamomum sp.* are common in forest gardens as well. Other species belonging to late successional stages of lower elevation forests, such as *Artocarpus integrifolia, Mangifera indica,* and *Caryota urens,* are among the most prevalent garden species.

Species of different stages along a successional continuum are identifiable in patches in natural forests. They can be categorised by life history and growth requirements. These categories can similarly be applied to the species composition of forest gardens. A table comparing partial species composition and succession categories in the remnant mid-elevation natural forest of the Uva region (Gaussen *et al.* 1965) and the species composition of the forest gardens of Mirahawatte is presented below (Table 12.1). Four groups or 'stages' were distinguished which fit phases in the forest development process described. The boundary lines of such 'successional stages' were drawn arbitrarily with borderline species fitting well within the upper and lower ranges of neighbouring stages.

The next step in applying the concept of succession to the forest gardens was to find out whether the stages of succession from the table were identifiable in patterns of species composition in the forest gardens, or whether species distribution within the gardens was random with respect to the succession categories.

In addition to five gardens from the original 61 garden survey which had been mapped in detail, ten gardens from the survey were selected. They were chosen to complement the five mapped gardens so a full range of age and most size classes of gardens were represented. The species placement in the ten gardens was sketched. Patches of species belonging to the different stages were found to be clearly distinguishable.

Figure 12.1 is a sketch of one garden delineating such mosaic-like patches of vegetation analogous in composition to the pattern to be expected from gap phase succession in a natural forest (Everett, unpublished).[4] To learn more about the vegetation patches and management leading to such patterns, farmers of the 15 gardens sketched and mapped were interviewed. Were there common management patterns based upon ecological knowledge?

Ethnoscientific exploration of the farmers' approach

In a pilot survey, 15 farmers were interviewed as to the compatibility of the fifteen species occurring most frequently in the gardens. Compatibility was defined as 'not affecting flowering, fruiting and growth in a negative way.' These questions were asked to better understand management practices and to test the idea for the proposed successional stages for species found in the gardens. It would be expected that species in the same or similar successional stages would be more compatible and more likely to be planted together than species of differing stages. The further apart the stages, the less compatible and less likely to be grown together. Farmer classification of compatibility resulting in similarly identifiable groupings would suggest ecological knowledge grounded in an understanding of species life form, growth habits and growth requirements through time.[5] The procedures and results are summarised in Table 12.2.

A pair-wise comparison of the 15 species was used to elicit information on species compatibility. Respondents were asked whether the species in a given pair were compatible if planted in close proximity. Each pair was given a '+' for compatibility or a '-' for incompatibility. The responses for each pair (9-15 each) were totalled and the proportion of positive or negative responses was noted.[6] If the majority of responses was positive, the pair was called 'compatible'; if the majority was negative, the pair was called 'incompatible'. If equal numbers of positive and negative responses were given, the pair was labelled neutral ('0'. Thus, 120 pairs with 9–15 responses each were tabulated.[7]

As a test of the successional stage delineations, each pair was then assigned to two stages one for each of its two species based upon the delineations from Table 12.1. Five stages and mid-stages (II, II/III, III, III/IV, and IV) were identified for this purpose. Thus, for example, *Musa sapientum* (banana), was in stage II as a short-lived early successional species, while *Artocarpus integrifolia* (jackfruit) was listed in III/IV, because it occurs in both stages III and IV. As a pair, they were listed as II, III/IV. All pairs were then compiled in sets, based upon their successional stages (*e.g.* all II, III pairs were one set). There were 15 possible sets. The number of compatible and incompatible pairs in each set was noted. A two-tailed Wilcoxon matched pairs signed rank test for small samples was applied to the compatible and incompatible pairs in the 15 groups. This non-parametric procedure is a common statistical procedure used to investigate differences among a set of n-matched pairs of observations. The null hypothesis states that no difference exists between members of a pair (Chiang, Selvin and Langhauser, unpublished: 14.6). At S=24.5 (n=15), the difference between sev-

Table 12.1: Succession of species in the natural forest of the Uva Region

Stage	Forest Succession	Species	Garden	Species Succession
I	Shade intolerant grasses, annual herbs, beginning perennial herbs	*Imperata cylindrica* *Cymbopogon nardus* *Themeda tremula* *Lantana aculeata* *Osbeckia spp.* *Microglossa zeylanica*	Annual vegetables, flowers, some herbs	*Brassica sp.* *Capsicum sp.* *Coriandrum sativum* *Cucumis sativus* *Ruta graveolens* *Tagetes sp.*
II	Shade tolerant grasses and herbs, shrubs and small quick-growing trees beginning to dominate	*Psidium guajava* *Ficus hispida* *Phyllanthus emblica* *Wendlandia notoniana*	Perennial herbs, some shade tolerant annual ornamental shrubs, short-lived trees and beginning seedlings of small fruit trees	*Ananas sativus* *Musa sp.* *Manihot esculenta* *Saccarum* *Psidium guajava*
III	Small trees and saplings domi-nate with shrubs and herbaceous ground below	*Calophyllum spp.* *Cinnamomum spp.* *Ligustrum walkeri* *Neolitsea involucrata* *Litsea ovalifolia*	Fruit trees, small woody shrubs and trees, vines, saplings of latter succession species	*Citrus sinensis* *Coffea arabica* *Annona cherimolia* *Persea americana* *Erythrina lithosperma*
IV	Mature trees with a closed canopy dominate; small tolerant trees and shrubs in under-story, herbs and leaf litter cover the ground	*Garcinia echinocarpa* *Elaeocarpus glandifuler* *Mangifera spp.* *Aleurites triloba*	Mature fruit and timber trees dominate, with shrub and small tree understory herbs and leaf litter on the ground; vines common	*Artocarpus integrifolia* *Caryota urens* *Cedrela toona* *Mangifera indica* *Michelia champaca*

eral stages was found to be significant at the .05 level (Table 12.2, Everett, unpublished).

The results indicate that farmers' classification of compatible and incompatible species is commensurate with the pattern predicted by forest succession theory. Thus, the patchy structure of forest gardens can be interpreted as a successional pattern, akin to gap phase succession, understood and managed by farmers, in part, on the basis of species compatibility.

Conclusion

This research is preliminary. It was undertaken with a partial list of species with a small number of farmers in one village. Nevertheless, it begins to indicate the depth of ecological knowledge held by forest garden farmers. If principles of

Table 12.2: Wilcoxon signed rank test of successional stage compatibility.

Pair	Stages	+	–	Difference	Rank	–Rank
1	II-II	3	0	3	8.0	
2	II-II/III	2	0	2	5.5	
3	II-III	6	3	3	8.0	
4	II-III/IV	0	12	-12	-14.0	-14.0
5	II-IV	0	2	-2	-5.5	-5.5
6	II/III-II/III	1	0	1	2.5	
7	II/III-III	5	0	5	10.5	
8	II/III-III/IV	4	1	3	8.0	
9	II/III-IV	0	1	-1	-2.5	-2.5
10	III-III	13	2	11	13.0	
11	III-III/IV	18	9	9	12.0	
12	III-IV	2	3	-1	-2.5	-2.5
13	III/IV-III/IV	21	1	20	15.0	
14	III/IV-IV	5	0	5	10.5	
15	IV-IV	1	0	1	2.5	
TOTAL						-24.5 -S

P (S+) or S(-) <25-.05 for n-15.

such knowledge can be crystallised through further interdisciplinary research at the individual garden as well as the village landscape level, they may give insights for reforesting the Uva watershed with forest-like systems that provide for the needs of incoming migrants, habitat for remaining flora and fauna and watershed protection for the downstream irrigation projects upon which the nation depends. In addition, they may contribute to efforts to reforest degraded land subject to population pressure elsewhere in the highland tropics.

Notes

1. The research was carried out in association with the NeoSynthesis Research Centre, a non-profit research organisation location in the Uva Basin of the south central highlands of Sri Lanka. I would like to thank the Centre's directors, Dr. Ranil Senanayake and Dr. Jerry Moles, and my advisers at the University of California, Drs. Jeff Romm, Arnold Schultz, and Louise Fortmann for all their support. Jeff Romm and Jerry Moles gave helpful comments on earlier versions of this chapter.
2. Historically, it seems likely that the gardens were situated at the edge of forests, but I have not found any references to this effect.
3. Seventeen per cent of the perennials in the gardens are semi-domesticates, self-seeded and left to grow by garden owners (Everett, unpublished). The primarily Buddhist villagers do not hunt, and birds and other species of wildlife thrive here (Senanayake 1987).
4. The survey was done with the help of a research assistant who spoke fluent English and Sinhala. For each household visited, garden structure and composition were inventoried, and the family was interviewed on species uses, garden management, land tenure, and general household information (Everett, unpublished).
5. The appendix lists the species found in the gardens, with their Sinhala names.
6. In addition to questions directed specifically at these problems of compatibility, ques-

tions concerning general garden planting, management, and yields were posed. The results will be discussed elsewhere.

7. In addition to these specific responses, other comments by farmers were noted, including general 'planting rules', 'such as avoid planting timber trees next to small fruit trees', and species specific comments regarding issues such as demands on soil and water resources.

Appendix

Garden perennials[a] of Mirahawatte

Latin	English	Sinhala	Use
Acacia sp.			
Acronychia laurifolia		Ankenda	F, M
Aegle marmelos		Beli	Fr
Agave sisalana	Agave	Hanna gass	M
Albizia lebbek		Mara	Fe, Fl
Albizza odoratissima		Suriyamara	F
Aleurites triloba	Candlenut	Telkakune	F
Alstonia macrophylla		Avarinuge	F
Anacardium occidentale	Cashew	Kaiu	F, Fr
Ananas sativus	Pineapple	Anasi	Fr
Annona cherimolia	Cherimoya	Anoda	Fr
Annona muricata	Soursop	Kathuanoda	Fr
Archontophoenix sp.		Dotulu	Or
Areca catechu	Areca nut	Puwak	N
Artocarpus incisa	Breadfruit	Del	Fr
Artocarpus integrifolia	Jackfruit	Kos	Fr, Fo
Averrhoa carambola		Kasmaranga	Fr
Azadirachta indica	Neem	Kohombe	M, Mu, Sh
Bambusa sp.	Bamboo	Una	T
Bixa orellana	Annatto	Rucon	P
Calophyllum inophyllum		Dambe	
Camellia tea	Tea	The	B
Carica papaya	Papaya	Papol	Fr, M
Caryota urens	Fishtail palm	Kitul	S, B, T
Cassia auriculata	Averie		Sh
Cassia spectrabilis		Mai	Fe, Sh
Casuarina equisetifolia	Casuarina		T
Cedrela toona		Toona	T
Cestrum nocturnum	Queen of the night	Rakumarima	Or
Citrus aurantifolia	Lime	Dehi	Fr
Citrus grandis	Grapefruit	Jambole	Fr
Citrus limon	Lemon	Lemon	Fr
Citrus nobilis	Mandarin	Naran	Fr
Citrus sinensis	Orange	Dodan	Fr
Citrus vulgaris	Bitter orange	Marmalade	Or
Cocos nucifera	Coconut	Pol	Fr, C, F
Coffea arabica	Coffee	Kopi	B
Coffea robusta	Coffee	Kopi	B
Crotalaria sp.			Mu
Cupressus knightiana	Cypress		T
Cupressus macrocarpa	Cypress	Cypress	T
Cyphomandra betacea	Tree tomato	Gasstakkali	Fr
Datura fastuosa	Datura	Atana	M
Dendrocalamus giganteus	Bamboo	Una	C
Diospyros discolor	Velvet apple	Mabulu	Fr

Elaeocarpus glandifuler	Ceylon olive	Weralu	Fr, T
Eriobotria japonica	Loquat	Lokat	Fr, Fe
Erythrina lithsperma	Dadap	Eramudu	Sh, Mu
Eucalyptus spp.	Eucalyptus	Terpentine	F, T
Eugenia jambos	Roseapple	Jambu	Fr
Eugenia michelii	Brazil cherry	Pitanga	Fr
Ficus fergusonii		Nuge	
Ficus hispida		Kotedimbule	
Ficus religiosa	Bo tree	Bodhi	R
Flacourtia ramontchi		Ugurasse	Fr, M
Garcinia echinocarpa		Kokatiya	O
Gliricidia sepium		Nangimorunga	Fe, Mu, Sh
Grevillea robusta	Silver oak	Sabuku	T, Sh
Heliconia brasiliensis	Lobster claw		Or
Hibiscus sp.	Shoeflower	Sapatumal	Or
Jacaranda mimosaefolia	Jacaranda		Or
Lawsonia alba	Henna	Morathondi	R
Leucaena leucocephala		Ipil-ipil	Sh, Mu
Ligustrum walkeri		Bora	F, Fe
Limonia acidissima	Woodapple	Divul	Fr
Litsea ovalifolia		Beeriya	F, Fe, T
Macademia ternifolia	Macadamia nut		N
Madhuca longifolia		Mi	O
Mangifera indica	Mango	Ambe	Fr
Manihot sp.		Rubber	Fe, F
Manihot ultissima	Manioc	Meioca	V
Melaleuca leucadendron	Cajeput	Lothsombul	O
Mesua ferra	Ironwood	Na	R
Michelia champaca		Sapu	T, F
Momordica charantia	Carilla	Karawilla	
Moringa oleifera	Horseradish tree	Morunga	S
Morus sp.	Mulbery		Fr
Muntingia calabura	Jam fruit		Fr
Murraya koenigii	Curry leaf	Karapincha	S
Musa sapientum	Banana	Kessel ghedi	Fr
Neolitsea involucrata		Kududawule	F
Nephelium longana		Mora	
Opuntia dillenii	Prickly pear	Katupatuk	O
Passiflora edulis	Passion fruit	Passiona	Fr
Persea americana	Avocado	Aligata peere	Fr
Phyllanthus emblica		Nelli	Fr, M
Pinus caribeae	Pine		T
Piper betel	Betel leaf	Bulath	Fo
Pithecoellobium saman	Rain tree	Paramara	O
Plumeria sp.	Temple flower	Arelia	O
Pongamia pinnata		Karanda	
Prunus persica	Peach	Peaches	Fr, O
Psidium cattleianum	Strawberry guava	Jam Peere	Fr
Psidium guajava	Guava	Peere	Fr
Punica granatum	Pomegranite	Delum	Fr, M
Puteria palmeri		Lawulu	Fr

Pyrus communis	Pear		Fr, O
Sambucus nigra	Elderberry		O, M
Santalum album	Sandalwood	*Sudhuhandung*	O, T
Semecarpus coriacea		*Badulla*	
Sesbania grandiflora			Or
Solanum indicum	Wild eggplant	*Tibatu*	V
Spathodea campanulata	Flame of the forest	*Jus mal*	Or, Sh
Syzygium fergusoni	False clove	*Walkarabu*	
Tamarindus indica	Tamarind	*Siambala*	S
Tecoma grandis Tectona	Teak		T
Tecoma sp.			Or
Tephrosia purpurea		*Pila*	Sh, Mu
Tithonia diversifolia	Mexican sunflower	*Titamal*	Fe, Mu
Toddalia aculeata		*Kurumiris*	
Vitex negundo		*Nike*	M
Vitis vinifera	Grape	*Waral*	Fr, O
Wendlandia notoniana		*Sawan widele*	Fe, F

a Perennials in this table are all species with growth periods exceeding 12 months, from planting to harvesting (i.e. banana, pineapple)

Use categories:
B = beverage
C = construction
F = fuel
Fe = fence
Fi = fibre
Fo = food
Fr = fruit
M = medicine
Mu = mulch
N = nut
O = oil
Or = ornamental
R = religious
S = spice
Sh = shade
T = timber
V = vegetable

Source: Purseglove, J.W., *Tropical Crops: Dicotyledons*, Essex, Longman Group Ltd (1968)

13. Indigenous Decision-making Systems – A key in understanding structural change in American agriculture[1]

ROBERT ZABAWA AND CHRISTINA H. GLADWIN

Introduction

WITH THE ADVENT of increasing numbers of development programs that use anthropological methods (such as international and domestic Farming Systems Research and Extension), a major question revolves around what theoretical paradigms can be employed to best explain 'traditional' behaviour and, in the process, enhance program efforts. Especially in applied work, most anthropologists agree that a description of cultural behaviour cannot be had via baseline surveys and statistical tests of factual data alone. Neither can quick and dirty reconnaissance surveys (*sondeos*) replace an adequate amount of participant observation, as has been suggested by Hildebrand (1981). An ethnographic description of a culture requires both in-depth participant observation as well as some acquisition of indigenous knowledge systems by the ethnographer (Brokensha, Warren and Werner 1980).

What applied anthropologists do not seem to agree on is the need for both *testable* ethnographic descriptions and a *link* between micro-level research of a group of individuals and macro-level structural description, alternately dubbed by some as 'regional analysis' (Smith 1976, 1978) and 'cultural materialism' (Harris 1979). In previous papers, Gladwin has argued for the use of testable ethnographic models of economic actors' decision processes in micro-level research (Gladwin 1975, 1976, 1979a, b, 1983). In this chapter, we argue for *both* testable models on the micro-level and structural analysis on the macro-level as necessary requisites for a more complete understanding of cultural systems.

To support our arguments, we describe the life-cycle decision processes of farmers in Gadsden County, North Florida, studied in 1981–2 by Zabawa (1984), using both participant observation and 'the ethnographic interview' (Spradley 1979). His intuitions and observations were then tested via ethnoscientific tools (Gladwin, Zabawa and Zimet 1984) and statistical tests. As the ethnography proceeded, it became clear that ethnoscientific tools *alone*, although invaluable, could not describe events in the last ten years in Gadsden. Neither were survey data, collected from individual farmers and verified by statistical tests, sufficient – on their own – to understand farmers' decision processes made in response to those events. An understanding of 'structural change' in the aggregate farming industry in Florida and the US was also needed, to understand Gadsden farmers' decision processes made in response to those macro-level changes.

Structural change

Structural change in the US food industry continues to result in fewer but larger farms producing most of the country's marketed food supply. Concentration in farmland acreage is now so extensive that farms of 1000 acres or more (7.2 per cent in 1982) represent more than half (61 per cent) of the land in farms (USDA 1982). Moreover, the USDA reports that, while the largest farms (with gross sales of $250,000 or more) represent only 4.3 per cent of the total farm population, they control 24 per cent of the land, produce 50 per cent of the gross sales and receive 59 per cent of the net cash income. Conversely, small farms (with gross sales of less than $40,000) represent 73 per cent of the farm population, but they control only 30 per cent of the land, produce only 11 per cent of the gross sales and receive only three per cent of the net cash income (USDA 1988).

Indeed, a recent transformation of census data into constant dollar categories shows that the so-called 'superfarms' with gross sales of more than $500,000 increased their share of net farm income from 25 per cent in 1970 to 48 per cent in 1982, while small farms decreased their share from 16 to zero per cent of net farm income in 1982 (Zulauf 1986). The other big change that occurred during the 1970s was the spread of part-time farming as a survival strategy from the small farm to medium-sized and large farms. Zulauf calculates that non-farm income is now more than half total family income for more than half the medium-sized farms with gross sales between $40,000 and $100,000 and for more than one-third the large farms with gross sales between $100,000 and $200,000. If present trends continue, more concentration of farm wealth and production, coupled with fewer farms with a full-time head, can be expected by the year 2000 (Lin *et al.* 1980). The total number of US farms will decline to 1.8 million. They will have a bimodal distribution, with many small, part-time farms (Tweeten 1983) and a few (less than one per cent) superfarms. Indeed, concerns about the disappearance of the small family farms have now been replaced with concerns about 'the disappearing middle'.

Affecting all size farms, but especially farms with a full-time head and/or low equity, are the macro-level economic forces causing concentration: inflationary increases in the cost of production inputs and credit during the 1970s which decreased farmers' profit margins, increased their level of indebtedness and caused negative cash flows (USDA 1981; Van Blockland 1981); inflationary increases in land values during the 1970s coupled with their sharp decline in the 1980s, which leaves beginning farmers without collateral to offset a negative cash flow; technological change which leads adopters to expand and leaves non-adapters behind (Cochrane 1979; Carter *et al.* 1981); monetary (as opposed to fiscal) policies which create an overly strong dollar and decrease exports (Schuh 1984; Tweeten 1984); and changes in international markets which may result in a minor squeeze or major collapse of the local market (Barkin 1983).

The materialist approach

Alternatively, some scholars have argued in support of a materialist approach to understanding structural changes in agrarian societies (Harris 1979; de Janvry 1981; Smith 1978). As de Janvry (1981: 7) forcefully points out 'There has been a tendency to look at the problems of agricultural production and the welfare of rural populations as separate issues that can be understood within the realm of the agrarian sector or even at the village or farm level. The monetarists have exposed the detrimental effect of market distortions on supply response without explaining their origins in the broader political economy. And the structuralists have concentrated on land tenure and farm size without questioning the broader class structure and economic systems in which they are inserted. We reject this approach and start our analysis...from the postulate that the problem is but a symptom of the nature of the class structure in the periphery and of the particular process of capital accumulation it undergoes.'

Whereas the neoclassical school 'has atomised society into rational self-seeking individuals whose actions are impartially reconciled into social optimality by the invisible hand of the market', (*ibid*.), de Janvry looks at the unequal development and resulting conflict between sectors, regions and countries which characterise the historical development of capitalism and accumulation of capital. As capitalism penetrates agriculture, it transforms existing social relations in ways that result in different class and land tenure patterns. One way this is done is via the 'farmer' or 'America' road of social differentiation, whereby peasants or small farmers gradually evolve into capitalist farmers and bourgeois landowners while the majority are transformed into proletarians (*ibid*.: 108).

Similarly, cultural materialists like Harris (1979) give highest priority to the formulation and testing of theories in which *infrastructural* variables (or changes in the mode of production at the aggregate or societal level) are the primary casual factors of change in a given society. Changes in the infrastructure then cause changes in the *structure* of a society (*e.g.* its political economy, division of labour and political organisations), which eventually bring about changes in the *superstructure* (*e.g.* a society's art, ritual, sport, science and belief systems). It is from this infrastructural basis that all causal factors and therefore investigation should start. Theories in which only structural variables are tested for causal primacy should be formulated only if investigation fails to identify causal factors in the infrastructure. Harris (1979: 56) stresses: 'Cultural Materialists give still less priority to exploring the possibility that the solution to sociocultural puzzles lies primarily within the behavioural superstructure; and finally, theories that bestow causal primacy upon the mental and emic superstructure are to be formulated and tested only as an ultimate recourse when no testable etic behavioural theories can be formulated or when all that have been formulated have been decisively discredited.' The present authors agree with the materialists that an understanding of the changes in US agriculture today should start with identification of infrastructural changes (or changes in the mode of production). Clearly, it is the capitalist penetration of US agriculture in the last century that is ultimately responsible for the macro-level changes threatening the existence of the medium-sized US family farm today (Vogeler 1981). With the spread of market forces into agriculture have come sweeping changes, which have been identified by de Janvry (1981) as the commoditisation of agricultural production (*i.e.* the change from primarily subsistence production to cash-crop production for the market) and the internationalisation of capital (*i.e.* the free flow of capital across national boundaries, the production of local goods for international instead of national or local markets). (See deWalt and Barkin 1987.) As part of a broader long-term picture, these changes in the mode of production are ultimately responsible for the macro-level economic forces identified by the neoclassicalists as causing concentration: fluctuating export markets, changes in monetary-fiscal policies, technological change and changes in farmers' production costs, indebtedness and cash flow (Cochrane 1979; Eginton and Tweeten, unpublished; USDA 1981).

Is that the whole story? We think not and we disagree with materialists who would model cognitive processes only as a last recourse, '...when no testable etic behavioural theories can be formulated or when all that have been formulated have been decisively discredited' (Harris 1979: 56). Instead, we see an interaction between infrastructural, structural and superstructural variables with feedback loops between them. As seen in Figure 13.1, the macro-level concentration forces impact on the individual farm family and affect their plans and decision processes (in this case their decisions to cut back production or quit farming altogether). To model this impact and the farmers' responses (*i.e.* superstructural changes), we use cognitive or ethnoscientific models of farmers' plans, scripts and decision processes. By making plans and decisions in response to concentration forces, farmers at the micro-level then go through a differentiation process and become either bigger farmers, smaller part-time farmers, or non-farmers (and proletarians). In the aggregate and at the macro-level again, (at the right hand side of the diagram), this differentiation process results in structural change in the agricultural sector as a whole.

The structure of farming in Gadsden County

For the better part of its agricultural history, Gadsden County's farming tradition has been based on shade, or cigar wrapper, tobacco. At its height, shade tobacco was planted on over 6,000 acres, produced over seven million pounds annually and 'represented a 100 million dollar industry of which 25 million dollars was invested in land, equipment, barns, packing houses and operating capital' in a four-county area in Florida and Georgia (Womack 1976: 98).

The development of the shade tobacco industry in Gadsden County was ideal for ecological, employment and financial reasons. Tobacco in general and shade tobacco in particular, is a land intensive crop. Because Gadsden's farmland is ecologically distributed among relatively small fields with rich soils separated by timberland, swamps, hills and other uncultivatable land (so that less than one-half of its land in farms is harvested), a labour-using, labour-saving crop was and still is, ideal for its geography. Economically, shade tobacco required a large number of person-hours in both fields and packing houses because the utmost care was needed to protect the individual leaves from the slightest damage. Shade thus represented a major source of employment and supplied nearly 18,000 skilled and unskilled jobs for Gadsden County alone (Korsching and Sapp 1976: 1).

Financially, shade tobacco was ideally suited for Gadsden's small farmers since the money to purchase production inputs was supplied by the buyer who established a formal 'forward contract' with the farmer. This relationship was established because shade tobacco required a large capital investment to produce: input costs increased from $1250 an acre in 1955 to $3000 an acre in 1968 to over $7000 an acre in 1977. To help reduce the tremendous financial burden on the farmers and insure their own investment, tobacco companies contracted ahead for a season's production and supplied up to 75 per cent of the input costs as an advance on the season's profits Shade tobacco was also a part of a more general farming strategy. Although shade tobacco received the most attention, other commodities (*e.g.* cattle and corn) were managed around the production of shade tobacco. Cattle were maintained for their manure that was added to the soil to maintain soil structure and augment the chemical fertilisers. Corn was produced mainly for cattle feed. While these two commodities had a direct economic effect on the production of shade tobacco, farmers frequently stated that the value of cattle and corn was associated only with their benefit to shade; in and of themselves, they were only break-even ventures.

During the decade 1967–77, however, a combination of factors led to the end of the shade tobacco tradition in Gadsden. These included: the escalating cost of

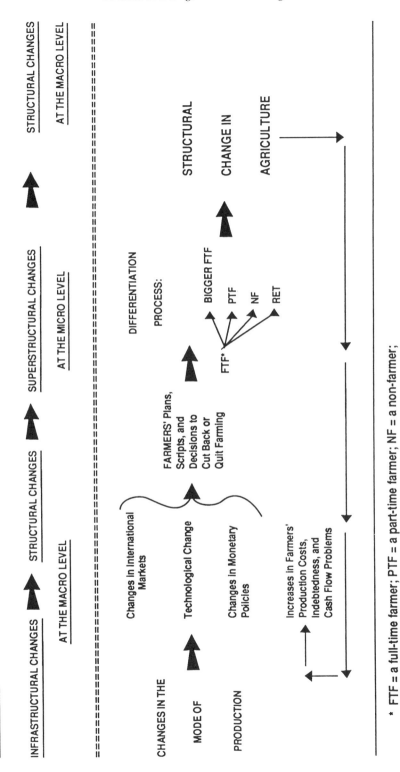

Figure 13.1: *Ethnoscientific, structuralist and materialist models: Complementarity of*

* FTF = a full-time farmer; PTF = a part-time farmer; NF = a non-farmer; RET = a retired farmer.

production and increasing competition from Central American production; advances in technology that led to the development of a homogenised or synthetic wrapper so that a natural leaf was no longer required to bind the cigar; and a decline in consumer demand for cigars (Plath 1970: 1–4; also see Zabawa 1984, 1987).

Farmers' responses

With the market demise of shade tobacco in 1977, farmers accustomed to forward contracts with tobacco companies had to look for new cropping strategies and in some cases completely new ways of making a living. The decision processes used by individual farmers in their search for new ways to make a living are modelled via decision-tree models and scripts.

The decision models assume that the farm family makes sequential, interrelated decisions of what crop to replace shade tobacco with (Figure 13.2) and whether or not to cut back production, given lack of a feasible substitute money crop (Figure 13.3). Interrelated logically with these decisions are subdecisions, for brevity presented elsewhere, which include the decision of how to cut back (Gladwin and Zabawa 1984), the decision to sell land and the decision to lease out land (Zabawa 1984).

The different options in each decision are seen in the set of alternatives (denoted by { }) at the top of each decision 'tree' model, which deterministically processes the information considered by each individual farm family (Gladwin 1980). In Figure 13.2 for example, farmers decide between the following crops as replacements for shade tobacco: staked tomatoes, nursery crops, flue-cured tobacco, pole beans and squash, row crops (wheat, corn, soybeans, grain sorghum, peanuts), cattle, or hogs. Alternatively, they may cut back farm production and sell or lease out their land.

The factors that enter into an individual's decision process are called 'decision criteria', aspects, or constraints and are denoted by the diamonds (< >) at the 'nodes' or the branching points of the tree. These criteria are the goals 'motivating' the decision, the aspects to be 'maximised' or ordered on, or the constraints that must be passed or satisfied.

For example, the second criterion in Figure 13.2 is: 'Do you want to grow a crop similar to shade in managerial style and use of resources: land, labour, equipment and capital?' If the farmer answers yes, the tree deterministically (with probability of 1) sends him – or more accurately his responses – down the left hand branch of the tree to consider crops very similar to shade. If the farmer answers *no*, the tree sends the farmer down the middle branch, to consider crops not so similar to shade (*i.e.* row crops). If the farmer cannot pass the constraints to row cropping, he is sent to the right hand branch to consider even more dissimilar cropping strategies such as livestock-centred farming systems. If the farmer fails this last list of constraints, he has no alternative but to cut back on the farm operations by hiring a manager, getting a partner, leasing, or selling. The latter decision is described at length elsewhere (Gladwin and Zabawa 1983, 1984; Zabawa 1984).

Criterion 2 is thus an ordering aspect in a 'stage two' decision process (Gladwin 1980) because crops *very similar* to shade are considered as shade replacement crops before crops *not so similar* which then precede crops *dissimilar* to shade. These same subsets of crops also share the same order on profitability: in general, tomatoes and nursery crops are more profitable than row crops (*e.g.*

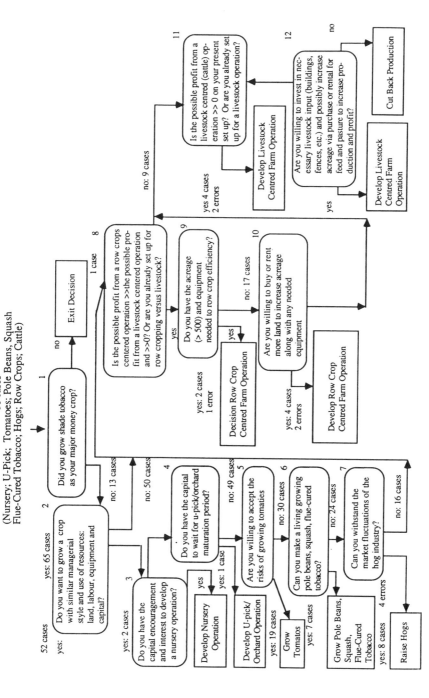

Figure 13.2: *The decision to change crops after shade tobacco (N = 66 cases of 44 farmers)*

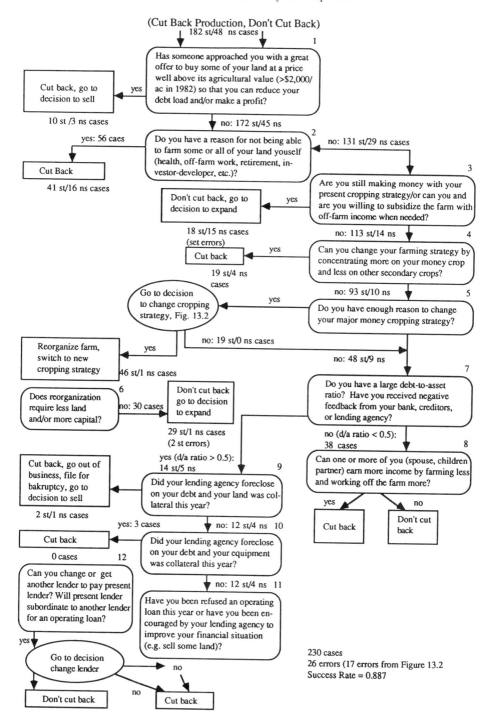

Figure 13.3: *The decision to cut back production (N=230 cases of 72 farmers)*

soybeans) which are more profitable than beef cattle. The ordering aspect in this decision can thus be either profitability or 'similarity to shade tobacco.'

Each subset of crops has its own set of constraints, which must be passed before a farmer proceeds to an outcome (denoted by ☐) specifying adoption of a particular crop. For example, nurseries have a high capital constraint due to the lag time between initial investment and first returns (criterion 3); while tomatoes have a high market risk factor (criterion 5); and row crops require equipment and at least 500 acres of land to be profitable.

The outcomes in Figure 13.2 show that, of the 65 cropping decisions made by 44 farmers who grew shade tobacco, there were 36 cases of farmers who chose very similar-to-shade cropping strategies of tomatoes, nursery crops, pole beans or squash and 6 cases of farmers who chose row crops and 4 cases of farmers who chose a cattle-centred farming system and 19 cases of farmers who decided to cut back on their farming operation altogether. (It should be noted that a farmer can enter the decision model more than once. This accounts for the number of cases exceeding the farmer sample size.)

The decision model is specified after personal interviews with a representative sample of farmers; it is then tested against actual historical choices of a second, independent sample of decision makers. In Gadsden, data from 30 farmers were used to build the model in 1982; while data from 72 farmers (51 ex-shade producers and 21 non-shade producers) were used to test the models in 1982–3. The samples were judged representative because the distribution of farms in the samples matched the distribution in the country by farmland acreage and gross sales based on agricultural census data. For brevity, results of the tests are summarised in the success rate shown on each decision tree.

Plans and scripts

How do farmers decide that a crop like staked tomatoes is *very similar* to shade tobacco, but a crop like beef cattle is *dissimilar* to shade tobacco? Simply, they use their 'indigenous knowledge systems' inherited from parents and grandparents and stored in their heads as plans or scripts. To understand the change of crops decision in Gadsden in the mid 1970s, then one must understand and elicit farmers' plans or scripts.

Instead of deciding how to do something every year, farmers develop a plan or inherit a plan already developed by their parents or grandparents. This plan, *How to do X,* is a sequence of mental instructions or rules that tell the actors who does what, when and for how long (Werner and Schoepfle 1987). To the insider or decision-maker, they are not decision rules, because he or she is not aware of having had to make a decision (Gladwin and Butler 1984). The decision is made so frequently, so routinely, that the decision rules become part of a pre-attentive plan or 'script,' like the script in a play that tells the actor what to say and do (Schank and Abelson 1977). By means of these scripts, the farmers do not have to make a million decisions; they know how and when to plant shade tobacco, probably because they were taught the script by their parents.

Eventually, this knowledge will be passed on to a new generation as a 'traditional' way of doing things. When the new generation of farmers is asked why they do the things the way they do, they may reply, 'It is the custom'. Some of them may even forget the original decision criteria; they only know that, for some reason, the traditional way is 'the best' way to do X, given the original constraints used or faced by their grandparents and parents. Examples of such inherited scripts or 'adaptive' strategies abound in the literature of economic and ecological anthropolology (Barlett 1980; Bennet 1969; Brush 1976; Cancian 1972; Chibnik 1981; Johnson 1971; Mayer 1979; Moran 1979).

The Gadsden farmers' plan or script for shade tobacco (Table 13.1) (Kincaid 1960) was quite similar to that for staked tomatoes (Table 13.2). For example, tobacco seed beds are planted and maintained in the same months when plastic is put out for rows for tomatoes. Tobacco seedlings and tomato plants are transplanted in a similar, labour-intensive way. In June and July, both tomatoes and tobacco are harvested by hand; and, in August, fields are cleaned up after harvests of both crops. Given the similarity of these plans, it is not surprising that many ex-shade producers decided to become staked tomato producers.

The decision to cut back production

Some of the cases which test Figure 13.2 are summarised in Table 13.3, which presents the cropping strategies chosen by the ex-shade farmers the year after they quit producing shade tobacco (column 1) and the strategies chosen by these same farmers in 1982 (column 2). From column 1, it is seen that at the end of shade tobacco production, the sample divided itself evenly into a subset of farmers who chose similar-to-shade alternatives (40.4 per cent), a subset who chose the cut back alternative (42.3 per cent) and a subset who chose the cutback alternative (42.3 per cent) and a subset who chose dissimilar-to-shade alternatives (17.3 per cent).

By 1982, the situation is changed. Although the number of similar-to-shade cases remains high at 32.7 per cent, the number of cases of farmers employing the dissimilar-to-shade strategies is significantly reduced to 3.8 per cent. Conversely, farmers who cut back have increased to 63.5 per cent of the sample. Because dissimilar-to-shade cropping strategies of row crops and livestock proved not profitable enough to support a large number of full-time farmers, many of them decided to cut back production further.

How did they decide? Failing criteria that must be passed in order to plant a similar-to-shade replacement crop, ex-shade producers enter the decision to cut back production[2] in Figure 13.3 at criterion 5. Other farmers, for example the non-shade producers, may enter Figure 13.3 at the top of the tree. Briefly, the tree model posits that the farmer must have at least one of the following reasons to cut back: a buyer appears with an offer that's too good to refuse (criterion 1); the farmer is not able to farm all of the land on his (or her) own for reasons of bad health, old age, widowhood, or off-farm work involvement (criterion 2); the farm is no longer making money and the farmer is unwilling or unable to subsidise it with off-farm income (criterion 3); the primary or secondary cropping system must be changed for some reason (criteria 4, 5); the farm business has a large debt to asset ratio and the farmer is now receiving negative feedback from a lender (criteria 7, 9, 10, 11, 12); and one or more family members have decided to increase their non-farmwork involvement (criterion 8).

Given a farmer's presence at any 'cut back' command, he or she (*i.e.* his or her data) proceed to the decision model of *how* to cut back, for brevity presented elsewhere (Gladwin and Zabawa 1984). If relatively painless methods to cut back (*e.g.* hiring a manager, getting a partner, cutting back land usually rented) are not feasible, the farmer then proceeds to the subdecisions to sell or lease out the farm (Zabawa 1984).

The model including all subdecisions was tested on 230 cases of possible cut-

Table 13.1: Gadsden County farmers' plan for shade tobacco

January 1	Plant seed beds.
January–February	Prepare soil, fumigate, and fertilise with manure and chemical fertiliser. Note: labour for shade tobacco was local, with the majority of the labourers being Black.
March	1. Harrow soil into rows four feet apart approximately three weeks before transplanting. 2. Install shade cloth shortly before planting.
Late March–early April	1. Transplant seedlings in the shade. 2. Water at transplanting at a rate of 10 barrels of water/acre. 3. Reset hills with missing or weak plants within a week. 4. Dust plants with insecticides on a seven-day schedule. 5. Plow the rows twice a week (discontinue near harvest time to prevent damage to the leaves).
April	String plants (starting when plants reach one foot), spirally from the stalk near the ground, to the overhead wire above the row. Continue to string, spirally between the leaves, once or twice a week depending on rate of growth.
May	Water when needed using overhead irrigation system.
June	'Top' plants to prevent budding if desired.
July	Harvest seven to eight weeks after transplanting. The harvesting procedure consists of: 1. Pick the desired leaves off each plant, *i.e.* 'priming' (there can be 2–5 leaves per priming and 6–10 primings per plant). 2. Place the leaves in the order picked and haul them to the tobacco barn. 3. String the tobacco in the barn. 4. Cure the tobacco in the barn (3–5 weeks). 5. Deliver the tobacco to the packing house.
August	Clean up and prepare for a fall crop (*e.g.,* polebeans) if desired.

Source: Kincaid 1960.

backs by 72 farmers, because farmers could decide to cut back more than once in the farm's history. Test cases included every time farmers actually cut back production or land use or *reported* that they *thought about* cutting back. The results are shown, on Figure 13.3. The model, including all subdecisions, correctly describes 89 per cent of the choices made. (Other results are reported in Gladwin and Zabawa 1984.)

Table 13.2: Gadsden County farmers' plan for staked tomatoes.

December–January	1.	Prepare the soil, lime.
	2.	Order plants.
		Note: Labour for the preparation, transplanting, staking, and stringing of the tomatoes is supplied mainly by local Black residents. Harvesting is performed mainly by migrant workers of Spanish descent from South Florida, Texas, and Mexico.
February	1.	Put plastic out on the rows (the plastic retains moisture, prevents leaching of the fertiliser, prevents weeds).
	2.	Fumigate, fertilise.
March	1.	Plants arrive.
	2.	Transplant into the fields around March 15th (plants are watered through trickle irrigation that is under the plastic; soil treatments are applied under the plastic as well; plant treatments are applied through overhead irrigation if available, or by portable sprayers).
	3.	Spray plant treatments on a five to seven-day schedule to prevent insects and disease.
April	1.	Stake plants approximately two weeks after planting.
	2.	Start horizontal stringing approximately two weeks after staking and continue on a two-week schedule for a total of four horizontal rows of string per row of tomatoes.
May	1.	Complete stringing.
	2.	Irrigate as needed.
June	1.	Start hand-harvesting the 'green' tomatoes using local and/or migrant labour and deliver the tomatoes to the packing house for shipment. (The harvesting cycle is to pick through one field, move to the next field, let the fields rest and the tomatoes mature, start picking again).
	2.	Start picking 'pink' tomatoes when they represent about 10% of the tomato population – approximately two to three days after harvesting begins (the 'pinks' are harvested by independent migrants who pay the farmer a flat rate per box of picked tomatoes and then sell the tomatoes at farmer's markets).
July	3.	Open fields for u-pick operation at the end of harvest and before clean-up operations begin (u-pick is saved for last to prevent damage to the plants and the spread of disease from other fields).
Late July–August		Clean up:
	1.	Burn the plastic string off the old plants with a 2-row propane burner.
	2.	Pull up the stakes and store them.
	3.	Mow the old plants down and harrow them into the ground.
	4.	Prepare for a fall crop (*e.g.* pole beans) if desired.

The transformation of full-time shade producers

The end result of repeated cut-back decisions by shade producers is that some of them sold their land and quit or retired; some of them became part-time farmers; while some of them decided not to cut back but expanded their farm operations and became even bigger full-time farmers. This transformation or differentiation of Gadsden shade farmers can be seen in the data of Table 13.4, which show the number of full-time farmers decreasing in the period from the mid 1970s to 1982.

During their last year of shade tobacco production, 98.1 per cent of the sample farmers were considered full-time farmers (defined here as those who perform an average of 40 or more hours per week of farm work) and only 1.9 per cent of the farmers were part-time (defined as those who farm at least 8 hours per week but less than 40 hours per week).

By 1982, full-time farmers represented only 36.5 per cent of the sample, part-time farmers represented 21.2 per cent of the sample and non-farmers (that is, those averaging less than 8 hours per week of farm work) represented 42.3 per cent of the sample. These data clearly show that there has been a move away from full-time farming; and a chi-square analysis finds this transition to be significant. Why? As noted above, the ex-shade producers, originally all full-time farmers during the good years of shade tobacco production, chose different paths in deciding on a shade replacement crop.

The results of farmers' cropping decisions seen in Figure 13.1 and Table 13.3 show that some farmers chose a similar-to-shade cropping strategy which allowed them to continue to be full-time farmers; some chose dissimilar-to-shade strategies which allowed them to be full-time farmers initially, but eventually caused them to cut back; and some chose to cut back and become part-time or non-farmers right away. The effect of this decision process has thus been a differentiation of the sample of full-time shade producers into subsamples of some full-time farmers, some part-time farmers and some non-farmers (Zabawa 1987) as postulated by Lenin's and de Janvry's 'farmer road' to unequal development.

Data in Table 13.5 show the result of this differentiation process, via a comparison of the financial position of farmers in the three different subsets: those who chose similar-to-shade cropping strategies, those who chose dissimilar-to-shade cropping strategies and those who cut back production. Their financial position is compared in the year following their last crop of shade tobacco (Table 13.5a) and again approximately seven years later, in 1982 (Table 13.5b). Results in Table 13.5a show that first, those farmers who continued with a similar-to-shade farming strategy (n=21) in the mid 1970s were in the best financial position of the three subgroups initially. They had the most owned acreage, the lowest debt, the lowest date-to-asset ratio and assets similar to those of the other subgroups in the year after their last crop of shade tobacco. Conversely, those farmers who cut back the year after their last crop of shade (n=22) were in the worst financial position, as might be expected. They had the smallest assets and owned acreage, the most debt, the highest debt-to-asset ratio and were the oldest in age.

Finally, those farmers who adopted a dissimilar-to-shade cropping strategy, while the youngest in age, struck a middle ground in having moderate debts, moderate debt-to-asset ratios and assets similar to those of the other groups.

Table 13.3: Change in crop choices of ex-shade tobacco producers over time

| | Year after shade production | | 1982 | |
	Number	Per cent	Number	Per cent
Similar:				
Nursery	2	3.8	3	5.8
U-Pick	0	0	1	1.9
Tomato	7	13.5	8	15.4
PB, FC, SQ[a]	5	9.6	2	3.8
Hogs	7	13.5	3	5.8
Sub-total		40.4		32.7
Dissimilar:				
Row crops	5	9.6	1	1.9
Cattle	4	7.7	1	1.9
Sub-total		17.3		3.8
Cut back:	22	42.3	33	63.5
Total		42.3		63.5
Total	52	100.0	52	100.0

a   Examples are pole beans, flue-cured tobacco, squash

Table 13.4. Transformation of full-time shade tobacco farmers

| | Last year in shade production | | 1982 | |
	Number	Per cent	Number	Per cent
Full-timers	51	98.1	19	36.5
Part-timers	1	1.9	11	21.1
Non-farmers	0	0	22[a]	42.3
Total	52	100.0	52	100.0

a   13 farmers retired
χ^2 = 44.96, P = 0.001

Table 13.5a: Financial position of ex-shade producers the year after the last crop of shade tobacco (N=52)

Strategy	N	Per cent Acreage	Owner ($)	Debts ($)	Assets (%)	D/A	Age
Similar	21	40.4 (n.s.)[a]	467 (n.s.)	24,650 (n.s.)	328,693 (n.s.)	9.7 (n.s.)	49.9
Dissimilar	9	17.3	372 (n.s.)	38,889 (n.s.)	359,811 (n.s.)	15.6 (n.s.)	44.1 (-1.46)*
Cut back	22	42.3 (1.37)*	284 (-1.33)*	53,015 (n.s.)	247,238 (-1.58)*	23.3 (n.s.)	51.5

Table 13.5b: Financial position of ex-shade producers in 1982 (N = 52)

Strategy	N	Per cent Acreage	Owner ($)	Debts ($)	Assets (%)	D/A	Age
Similar	17	32.7	476 (n.s.)[a]	187,036 (n.s.)	726,696 (n.s.)	33.2 (n.s.)	52.1 (n.s.)
Dissimilar	2	3.8	107 (n.s.)	150,000 (n.s.)	300,000 (n.s.)	37.5 (n.s.)	58.0 (n.s.)*
Cut back	33	63.5	246 (1.42)*	6,364 (2.50)**	263,026 (2.24)**	2.4 (3.43)***	51.5 (-3.20)***

a Numbers in parentheses are t-values of the difference between means. The t-values
   after the first row compare the similar and dissimilar strategies. The t-values after
   the second row compare the dissimilar and cut-back strategies. The t-values after
   the third row compare the similar and the cut-back strategies.
Significance levels of the one-sided t-test are:
* >0.05 and ≤0.10   ** ≤0.05   *** ≤0.01

By 1982, the financial positioning of these groups had changed significantly, as shown in Table 13.5b, which compares the financial position of the three sub-groups in 1982 and Table 13.6, which compares the 'before and after' financial positions of farmers who had adopted similar-to-shade cropping strategies with those who had cut back. Results show that the differences between the two sub-groups became magnified over time, as predicted by the materialist paradigm. Those farmers who were still in the similar-to-shade category in 1982 (n=17) continued to have most owned acreage and the highest assets. By 1982, they had significantly doubled their assets. In addition, however they had increased their debts by a factor of seven and their debt-to-asset ratio by a factor of three. In contrast, those farmers who cut back (n=33), whose numbers had increased by 50 per cent in 1982, had decreased their debts by a factor of eight and their debt-to-asset ratio by a factor of 10 by 1982. Those farmers who still were in the dissimilar-to-shade category in 1982 (n=2) had decreased their own acreage, had also quadrupled their debts and doubled their debt-to-asset ratio.

These results suggest that farmers' cut back strategies, although conservative, are allowing them to hold onto their assets and be a relatively stable group, a situation unpredicted and unexplained by the materialists! Clearly, the small, part-time farming sector in the US may be more than just a transitory semi-proletarian phase (Gladwin and Zabawa 1986).

Table 13.6: Change in financial position of former shade tobacco farmers over time.

	Similar strategy	*Cut back strategy*
After Shade	(N = 21)	(N = 22)
In 1982	(N = 17)	(N = 33)
Owned acreage after last year of shade tobacco	467	284
Owned acreage in 1982	476	246
t-value[a]	(0.05)	(-0.39)
Debts after last crop of shade	24,650	53,015
Debts in 1982	187,036	6,364
t-value	(2.23)**	(-2.42)**
Assets after last crop of shade	328.693	247,238
Assets in 1982	726,696	263,026
t-value	(1.97)**	(0.15)
Debt-to-asset ratio after last crop of shade (%)	9.7	23.3
Debt-to-asset ratio in 1982	33.2	2.4
t-value	(2.41)**	(-2.70)***
Age after last crop	49.9	51.5
Age in 1982	52.1	62.1
t-value	(0.66)	(4.26)***

a   t-value test difference between means. Significance levels of the one-sided t-test are: * >0.05 and ≤0.10, ** ≤0.05, *** ≤0.01

Conclusion

These data present a clear picture of what the shade tobacco farmers experienced in post-shade agriculture vis-a-vis the cropping alternatives open to them. First, farmers who adopted crops in the similar-to-shade category in the mid 1970s were in the best position to continue full-time. By 1982, however, these farmers experienced the financial consequences of adopting new, capital-intensive, high risk crops: they doubled their assets but tripled their debt-to-asset ratios. Second, because of the low income-generating potential of row crops and other dissimilar-to-shade crops, farmers who originally adopted dissimilar-to-shade strategies on a full-time basis had to eventually cut back. Finally, those farmers who did cut back and become part-time farmers, non-farmers, or retired farmers did succeed in reducing their debt significantly while at the same time retaining their assets. One wonders which category of ex-shade producers is now better off, those who are now farming full-time or those who have cut back and are now farming part-time.

We conclude that the case of Gadsden County shows how macro-level concentration forces (changes in international markets, technological change, increases in operating costs, monetary policies) affect farmers at the local, micro-level by forcing them to change their farming systems and in some cases to reorganise their farms. Farmers thus affected clearly undergo a differentiation process whereby a minority becomes either smaller part-time farmers or non-farmers. Furthermore, the Gadsden experience highlights the need for the collection of different yet complementary kinds of data and analysis in order to better understand a problem that has macro-level causes, micro-level processes and structural outcomes.

Notes

1. Major portions of this chapter were originally presented at the symposium on 'Minimum Standards for Ethnography' organised by Oswald Werner at the 1984 Annual Meetings of the American Anthropological Association. This research was funded by National Science Foundation Grants BNS 81124234 and BNS 8218894. The authors wish to acknowledge the help of the County Extension Service and especially the farmers of Gadsden County, Florida.
2. This model originally appeared in the *American Journal of Agricultural Economics* 1984 66 (5), reprinted with permission.

14. Indigenous Taxonomies and Decision-making Systems of Rice Farmers in South India[1]

BHAKTHAVATSALAM RAJASEKARAN AND *D. MICHAEL WARREN*

Introduction

RICE IS THE predominant staple crop in most parts of south India and is grown on 40.25 million ha in India. Tamil Nadu, the southern-most state of India, contributes to 11 per cent of the total rice production of the Indian sub-continent (Government of India 1988). The introduction of high yielding varieties through the Green Revolution movement increased the productivity of rice. However, many problems of resource-poor farmers were left untouched (Maurya 1989). In recent years, experience has shown the value of utilising the farmers' indigenous knowledge and decision-making systems in agricultural development projects (Warren, Slikkerveer and Titilola 1989). The identification and utilisation of indigenous knowledge on specific crop varieties can be highly useful in designing and implementing Farming Systems Research and Extension projects in developing countries. The purpose of this study is to explicate the relationship between indigenous rice taxonomies and farmers' rice production decision-making systems in south Indian agriculture.

The specific objectives of the study were:

○ to identify the local taxonomies of rice varieties in Tamilnadu State, India;
○ to analyse the decision making process of farmers in selecting rice varieties;
○ to explain the implications of local taxonomies of rice varieties to rice production;
○ to suggest suitable policy options regarding the use of local taxonomies in the formulation of recommendations by research and extension personnel, and
○ to develop strategies to train village extension workers in identifying and using local taxonomies of rice varieties.

Methodology

The indigenous categories of rice varieties used by the farmers in Chengalpattu District of Tamilnadu State were recorded during 1980–86 (Rajasekaran 1987). These records were used to identify the decision-making criteria of the farmers in selecting a rice variety from its alternatives. Data were also obtained from ancient Tamil traditions in a volume published in *Tamil Agricultural Heritage of the Tamils*, Kandaswami 1987. The taxonomy of rice varieties in Chengalpattu District was identified using a ethnoscientific methodologies. Taxonomies are hierarchical arrangements of categories of phenomena organised by the principle of class inclusion. A domain is the name given to the most inclusive category in the taxonomy. All terms in a given domain such as 'rice' share at least one semantic feature in common which differentiates them from terms in other domains. Each level of categories within the taxonomy is known as a contrast set. Segregates are categories within a contrast set which differ from one another by at least a single semantic feature. A monitoring and evaluation report on the utilisation of high yielding rice variety seeds during 1983–84 explored certain field-level constraints to the availability of high yielding varieties based on farmers' preferences (Department of Agriculture 1983). One policy option suggested in the report was the use of local taxonomies of rice varieties to determine seed preferences by small-scale farmers. Appropriate strategies to develop training programs under the Training and Visit (T&V) system of extension for Village Extension Workers (VEWs) were also formulated.

Results and discussion

Field-level constraints The farmer's body of knowledge used in selecting a rice variety for sowing could be incorporated into the dissemination and utilisation process of the T&V system of extension. This would help extension and research personnel to understand decision-making by small-scale farmers. Plant breeders and agronomists develop rice varieties suitable for different seasons and recommend these varieties to the extension personnel through the T&V system during the monthly zonal workshop. The Subject Matter Specialists (SMS) under the T&V system, in turn provide training to the VEWs on the package of practices for those recommended rice varieties during the following bi-weekly training programs. The VEWs are expected to disseminate information on the recommended varieties to the farmers during their field visits. Simultaneously, the Agricultural Officers responsible for seed centres are directed to multiply these recommended varieties at seed production farms. The multiplied seeds are stocked in the seed centres for distribution to farmers. Given this standardised sequence of steps, the farmers' preferences in selecting a variety can be overlooked by agricultural planners, extensionists and researchers. Chambers (1989: 186) noted: 'normal bureaucracy tends to centralise, standardise and simplify and agricultural research and extension are no exceptions.'

The top-down managerial approach can lead to other problems. Farmers, especially small-scale farmers holding less than 2.5 acres, might not obtain a preferred variety according to their choice since the seed varieties available in the seed centres were determined by research recommendations. The official release of of such varieties might prove unsuccessful when transferred to resource poor farmers (Maurya 1989). This could result in the stagnation of stocked seeds in the seed centres which gradually lose their germination potential and genetic capabilities.

As the personnel of the seed centres are made responsible for liquidating the undisposed seeds, they wait until farmers buy those varieties. When the farmers actually purchase and use these deteriorated seeds, the result is poor performance in the fields. Even respected VEWs who recommended those varieties can lose the trust of the farming community, resulting in resistance in the adoption of even viable technologies. This process could be more effective of extension workers understood better the indigenous knowledge used to choose a rice variety.

Lack of Multi-Locational Trials (MLT) for new rice varieties can result in uncertainties in rice production. For example, IR.50, a high yielding variety of rice recommended by research actually aggravated the problem of rice blast (*Pyricularia oryzae*), a fungal disease, in almost all of the rice growing regions of the Tamil Nadu State in 1984 and 1985. Further, the IR.50 rice variety served as the medium for spreading the disease inoculum to moderately resistant varieties such as CO.43 and ADT.27 which were grown in adjacent fields. This resulted in raising rice blast disease from minor to major disease status. Moreover, high yielding varieties released by the International Rice Research Institute (IRRI) in the Philippines, show a preference for well-drained soils because they were bred on such soils at the research stations in the Philippines (Harris 1977). In situations where similar drainage conditions are not available, these varieties do not perform well. Though Adaptive Research Trials (ART) are conducted in farmers' fields in evaluating the adaptability of a newly released variety, factors affecting farmers' decision-making systems are not usually given high importance. It is not sufficient to conclude that a variety is suitable to local conditions based on its performance in the ART. Farmers consider more than yield and pest resistance as positive indicators of performance for a particular variety. Inadequate feedback from the VEWs can also contribute to the lack of concern over the farmers' classification of rice cultivars. The feedback messages received from the VEWs are slowly diluted on their way between extension management and research functionaries. This paper focuses on how farmers classify rice varieties and what decision criteria they use to select a variety for cultivation.

During the study, it was observed that some farmers are not meticulous in differentiating the rice production for seed multiplication from that of production for consumption and market surplus. A considerable number of small-scale farmers were not aware of the fact that the high yielding varieties of seeds should be replaced with certified seeds once every three years in order to maintain their physical and genetic purity. There is a need to develop strategies to train VEWs to help farmers multiply seeds according to their own preferences.

Indigenous taxonomies of rice varieties

Indigenous agricultural knowledge is often based on many years of experience, and is passed on from one generation to the next. Many knowledge systems pertain to local environmental conditions (Thrupp 1988). The categories used to describe types of land, landscape, crops, and other natural resources are often based on functional criteria related to use, unlike the standardised criteria used by the physical and life sciences. The rice varieties cultivated in Chengalpattu District, Tamil Nadu, are classified into a taxonomy based on, source of water, cropping season, crop duration and time of sowing (Figure 14.1). This taxonomy is similar to Andean classification of potato varieties as recorded by Brush (1980). The first level of classification of rice varieties is based on the type of water source available for the crop. The rice varieties suitable for cultivation under rainfed conditions are classified as *manavari nel* (rainfed rice) and are entirely depends on monsoon rains for survival. Other rice varieties are grown initially using moisture available from the rain and the later part of the crop growth is taken care of by canal irrigation. The rice varieties with these attributes are referred to as *puzuthikal nel* (semi-dry rice). Rice varieties that are grown completely under irrigation are grouped as *nadavu nel* (wetland rice).

The second level of classification of rice varieties according to farmers of Chengalpattu District of Tamil Nadu State is based on the cropping season under which the rice varieties are grown. The varieties that are grown between Tamil months *puratasi masam* (September-October) and *thai masam* (January–February) are known as *samba nel*. *Navarai nel* refers to those rice varieties that are cultivated between *masi masam* (February–March) and *vaigasi masam* (May–June). The rice varieties that are grown between *vaigasi masam*

(May–June) and *adi masam* (July–August) fall under the category *sornavari nel*.

Length or maturation period crop varieties form the third level of classification. The varieties of rice that reach maturity within 145–160 days are classified as *Neendakala nel* (long duration rice). *Nadutharakala nel* (medium duration rice) rice varieties require 125–140 days before harvesting. The varieties that take 105–120 days for maturity are classified as *Kurugiyakala nel* (short duration rice). The final level of classification of rice varieties is based on time of sowing. *Mun vidaipu nel* (early sowing rice) and *Pin vidaipu nel* (late sowing) are the categories under time of sowing.

Implications of local rice categories for rice production

Local crop categories play a major role in the selection pattern of different varieties of a particular crop. Our understanding of the classification system greatly facilitates our comprehension of the agricultural systems associated with these crop varieties (Brush 1980). Though the literacy level of South Indian farming communities has increased significantly in recent years, the farmers continued to use their own cropping seasons based on Tamil months rather than adopting the English months used by the extensionists and scientists. Farmers' knowledge of weather and climate is usually valid and forms basis for farming decisions. For example, farmers expect rainfall between the third and eighth of *karthigai masam* (November) unless it is a drought year. Most of the rainfed farmers usually complete their sowing operations before this period. The farmers of the study area use their own rationale for using crop duration as one of the categories in the classification. For example, a farmer who wants to grow groundnuts (peanuts) followed by rice in samba season would prefer a short duration variety of rice (Figure 14.1).

On the other hand, a farmer who tends to grow either black gram or green gram will choose a medium duration rice variety. The farmers in dryland areas use different varieties for early sowing and late sowing; their decision on using either of the two depends on the onset of monsoon rains. For instance, if the monsoon is delayed, a dryland farmer prefers a variety from the category 'late sowing varieties'. The indigenous taxonomy of local rice varieties does not distinguish 'high yielding varieties' and 'local varieties'.

Decision-making systems of farmers

The folk taxonomy of rice varieties forms only part of the basis for the indigenous decision making system for rice farming. The process of making a decision to select a particular variety among its alternatives depends on the following factors: Cost of production, amount of risks involved, market demand for the surplus home consumption preferences (such as quality, taste, nutritional and social values), labour requirements, working capital, availability of seeds and other inputs, and cropping pattern. One can clearly understand from Figure 14.2 how farmers use their own body of knowledge in selecting a rice variety

Policy options

Based on the understanding of local taxonomy of rice varieties in Chengalpattu District, Tamil Nadu, India, there is a need to formulate certain policy of incorporating local taxonomies into the T&V system of extension.

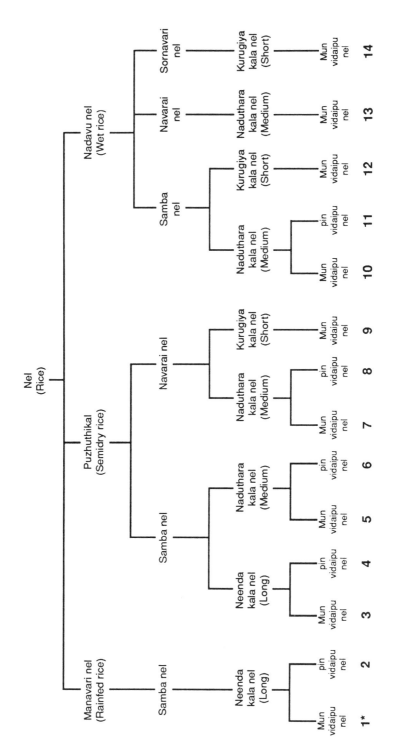

Figure 14.1: *Taxonomy of rice varieties in Tamil Nadu. (* The varieties that fall from 1 to 14 are listed in Appendix 14.1)*

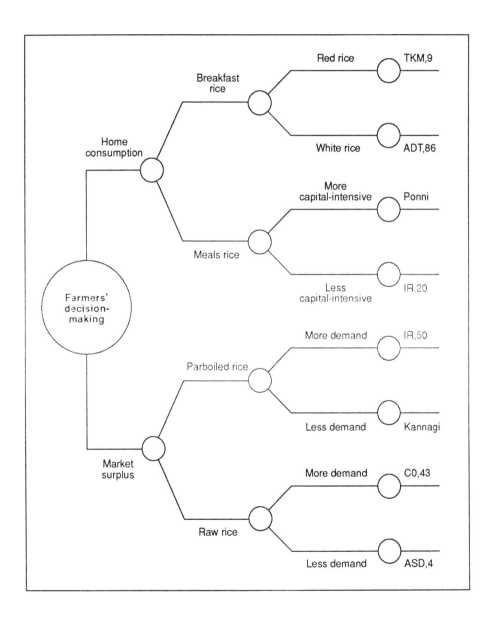

Figure 14.2: *Decision tree for selecting a variety*

1. Specific rice varieties should not be recommended to the farmers before the research and extension personnel understand the cognitive strategies of farmers which form the existing base for both local rice taxonomies and decision-making systems.
2. It is important that farmers' fields should not be used merely as a testing place for evaluating the genetic capacities of new rice varieties. A significant number of varieties released from the research stations have failed to perform well under farmers' field conditions. Apart from poor performance, some varieties have caused adverse effects.
3. The agronomists should use local taxonomies of rice varieties when developing technological recommendations for different varieties of rice.
4. The bi-weekly training sessions under the T&V system should be utilised to train the VEWs through team interactions in the identification of local rice taxonomies.
5. Since the seed distribution policy of the Department of Agriculture is to provide only twenty per cent of the seed requirement of the total cultivable area, VEWs must organise village-level seed farms to meet the demand for quality seeds.
6. The factors affecting decision-making systems of farmers should be given due priority while conducting adaptive research trials. Hence, collaborative client-oriented on-farm research trials involving local taxonomies and farmers' decision-making systems would yield results more acceptable to farmers' identified needs.
7. Understanding farmers' knowledge of soil types, soil fertility, topography and drainage capacity of the land before conducting trials and demonstrations of the varieties in farmers' fields is essential.
8. Evening meetings conducted under the T&V system are not only used as a place for presenting slide shows and discussions on recent technologies. These meetings could also include a decision tree game that can be played involving both contact and non-contact farmers in order to identify the factors affecting decision-making systems. This should be done well in advance of a cropping season to provide sufficient time to regulate the flow of information.

Training strategies for village extension workers

The Subject Matter Specialist (Information and Training) should train VEWs on the procedures to identify local taxonomies of rice varieties used by the farmers. This identification should be done separately for each VEW circle. The Agricultural Officer (T&V) should help the VEWs under his/her jurisdiction in this regard. This training program should focus on identifying major categories of rice varieties as classified by farmers based on indigenous linguistic terms (Warren and Meehan 1980); developing strategies to organise farmers' group discussion forums to identify the rationale behind their classification; and stimulating interest of farmers to participate in decision-tree games to identify factors affecting farmers' decisions in selecting a variety of rice from the available alternatives. This training effort is expected to provide the following outputs: a list of varieties that matches local conditions and farmers' preferences; a wide variety of choices for seed centre personnel to raise seed farms; timely procurement of seeds; and packaging of information for agronomists seeking to develop relevant technologies.

Apart from the biweekly training programs, VEWs and Agricultural Officers (T&V) should be provided with an institutional training on the production of quality seeds. This training would be highly useful for the VEWs to help farmers in organising their own seed farms. This training should be conducted by seed production scientists of the research system.

This training should focus on the following:

1. Use the local taxonomies of rice varieties as a base line for conducting the training;
2. Seed care and maintenance of seed purity at different levels:
   a. Nursery
   b. in field
      (1) Isolation
      (2) Rogueing
   c. Harvest
   d. Threshing floor
   e. Transportation and packing
   f. Storage
3. Field and seed standards;
4. Specifications for seed certification.

Conclusion

Rice remains the main source of food of Southern India. In addition, it contributes to the social and economic life of farmers in spite of a number of constraints. One of these constraints is the inadequate understanding by extension officers of the role of local taxonomies of rice varieties in the decision making process leading to farmers' selection of rice varieties. Choosing a rice variety depends on a number of decision-making factors. Specific cases collected from the field indicate that the extension and research systems could be improved significantly by understanding cognitive strategies and organised body of knowledge of the farmers in classifying and categorising rice varieties.

The village extension workers can be effectively used to reach the goal of distributing rice seeds based on farmers' preferences without deterioration of the physical and genetic purity of the seed. Well organised training programs for VEWs on strategies to identify local taxonomies of rice varieties and factors affecting farmers' decision-making systems is one of the means to achieve this goal. These training programs must be supplemented with specialised training on production of quality seeds at the village level. The entire effort is a multidisciplinary approach involving farmers, village extension workers, agricultural officers (T&V), subject matter specialists, agricultural officers (seed centre), agronomists, and seed technologists. This effort would certainly result in improving the subsistence living and market economy of the small-scale and marginal farmers of Tamil Nadu who form 82 per cent of the rural communities in the state.

Note

1. Paper presented at the Ninth Annual Farming Systems Research/Extension Symposium, October 9-12, 1989, Fayetteville, Arkansas.

Appendix 14.1: Rice varieties for categories 1–14

1
Vadan samba
Ottan samba
Mookan samba
Karunsooran

2
Kulla kar
Nettan samba
Karuna garan

3
Ottan samba
Kunguma samba
Vellai kar
Vennel

4
Kulla kar
kar arisi
Por sali

5
Arcot kichili
Gundan samba
ADT 26
ASD 4
IR 20
Ponni

6
Kichili samba
Kanchi
Karuna
Adi varagan
Kutralan
ASD 4

7
IR 20
Ponni
CO 43
Jaya
Vaigai

8
Kanchi
Vellai samba
TKM 6

9
IR 50
IR 56
IET 1444

10
IR 20
Ponni
IR 36
Kannagi

11
ADT 27
CO 40
IR 36

12
IR 50
TKM 9
AU 43/1
ADT 37

13
Jaya
ADT 36
CO 43
IR 20

14
TKM 9
IR 50
IET 1722

15. Expert Systems for Indigenous Knowledge in Crop Varietal Selection

SURESH CHANDRA BABU, D. MICHAEL WARREN AND
BHAKTHAVATSALAM RAJASEKARAN

Introduction

USING INDIGENOUS AGRICULTURE knowledge of farmers in developing appropriate technologies has been increasingly recognised as a method of attaining sustainability in agriculture and rural development programs (Warren *et al.* 1989). Identifying the indigenous knowledge systems for field applications in agricultural development projects is important in order to build upon the indigenous knowledge base.

For successful use of an Indigenous Knowledge System (IKS) in a development program, it is necessary to combine the identified knowledge base with existing modern agricultural practices. Evaluating agricultural practices based on indigenous knowledge individually, or combination with other newly introduced technologies, is essential for the sustainability of cropping systems. Fortunately, such a framework already exists in the form of Farming Systems Research (FSR) which is gaining importance as a successful method of evaluating agricultural technologies for their adaptability under conditions of local resource availability.

In general, FSR involves experts from different disciplines (biological and social sciences) to jointly analyse the existing farming situation and make judgments and recommendations for the betterment of farming community. This requires an enormous amount of human capital investment, which in general is a constraint in agricultural development of many developing countries. Hence, these countries often depend on foreign aid and foreign experts to design and implement FSR projects. The case with projects involving the identification, documentation and utilisation of indigenous knowledge systems is similar. Given these constraints, there exists a need to find alternatives to reduce the requirement for experts where this is possible, without disturbing the process of effective use of the identified indigenous technical knowledge to realise the fundamental goals of FSR. It may be possible to adopt indigenous knowledge that is identified and incorporated in FSR in a specific locality of a broader agro-climatic zone and recommend it to similar farming systems without involving additional research and testing.

This chapter discusses the development and use of IKS EXPERT, a prototype expert system for on-farm recommendations of indigenous technology choices within the framework of FSR. This system enables FSR scientists and Village Extension Workers (VEWs) to identify, document and recommend appropriate technology to the farmers based on farm-level indigenous information on soil type, rainfall availability, cropping pattern, consumption requirements and other resource constraints. The decision making knowledge base for the expert system is taken from indigenous knowledge systems that are already identified for a specific agro-climatic zone and are stored as a subshell in the expert system. Besides reducing the need for highly trained technical human resources, the advantages of the program include easy use with personal com-

211

puters and a spreadsheet data management system without requiring sophisticated programming skills.

The chapter is organised as follows: an introduction to decision making with the expert systems in agriculture with reference to IKS in FSR; a description of the components and use of IKS EXPERT; a case study to demonstrate the use of IKS EXPERT to choose indigenous technology using field-level information from South Indian rice farmers; concluding remarks.

Expert systems in IKS/FSR

'Expert systems' or 'knowledge-based decision support systems' are computer jargon referring to the provision of expert information to a decision maker, a procedure very familiar in the agricultural extension profession. Expert systems are becoming more widely used in agricultural decision-making and implementation. In general, expert systems are specific computer software applications that are capable of carrying out reasoning and analysis in a subject area with a level of proficiency close to the level of human experts (Coombs 1984). The advantage of an expert system is that once developed it can raise the performance of an average worker to the level of an expert. Expert systems technology is the ideal conduit of new knowledge from the agricultural scientists' laboratory to usage at the farm level (McKinion and Lemmon 1985). Expert systems are also ideal tools in several stages of field-level utilisation of IKS, namely identification, documentation and modification. Expert systems are also useful in Farming Systems Research, for diagnosing the present farming system, designing of improved systems, conducting experiment station trials, testing of improved systems and modifying the farming systems by extending the improved farming systems.

The use of expert systems in various stages of FSR and Extension is described in Figure 15.1. The documentation of IKS in agriculture, such as crop varieties, cultural practices, soil classification, principles of agro-forestry and local nutritional systems and conventions, are stored as a knowledge base using spread sheet programs for future retrieval. The stored IKS could be modified according to the local needs for the purposes of farming systems research trials at both the experimental station and farm. These are also used in expert systems. In general an expert system contains two major components, the knowledge base and the inference engine. The knowledge base contains the body of knowledge, rules of decisions and experience about a problem, while the inference engine interprets the rules of the knowledge base by logical deductions and manipulations (Nilsson 1980).

In applications of IKS in FSR, the typical knowledge base could be the information of the local knowledge of the farmers, local taxonomies, methods of classifying soil types, indigenous crop varieties, nutritional systems and natural resource systems. These could also be used along with the results of experiment station trials, results of on-farm trials that use IKS, feed back from the farmers on particular combinations and modifications of indigenous knowledge systems suiting local situations of resource availability and use. While there are several formats in which the knowledge base can be stored, specifying this information as conditional statements (to specify an action that is supposed to take place if certain conditions are met) is a common approach.

The development of Expert Systems in general requires special computer resources such as knowledge of computer languages like LISP or PROLOG.

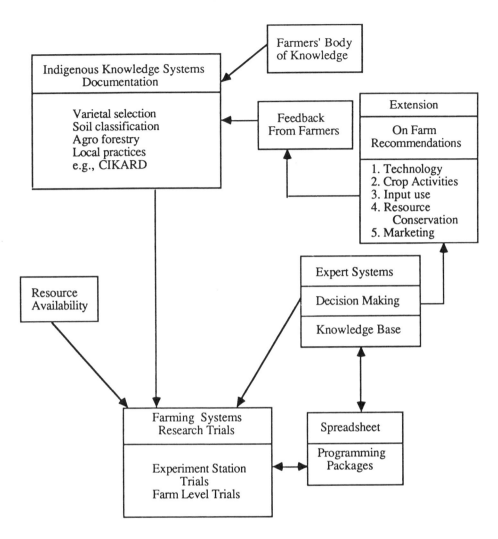

Figure 15.1: *Expert systems for utilising indigenous knowledge systems in FSR*

There is also a consensus among most expert systems developers that micro-computers do not yet have sufficient power to support the development of serious artificial intelligence systems (McKinion and Lenmon 1985). While this is true for large-scale artificial intelligence systems, as this paper exemplifies, many agricultural applications of expert systems could be handled by microcomputers at the farm level.

A case study using expert system for indigenous rice varieties in FSR

One of the fundamental roles that a FSR program could play is the identification of a crop variety suited for a particular location from a large set of cultivars with differing characteristics and specific uses. It is also important in that

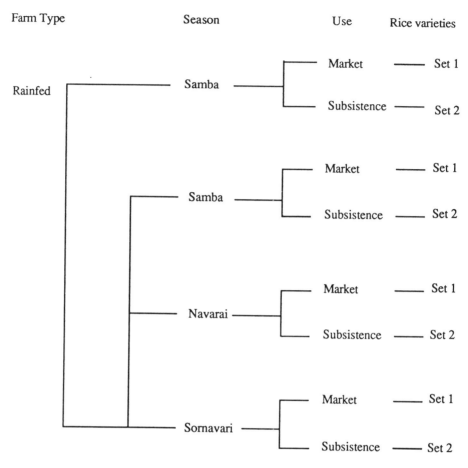

Figure 15.2: *Decision tree for crop varietal selection for farming systems research based on Indigenous Knowledge Systems*
**(Adapted from Rajasekaran and Warren, unpublished)

process to take into account the already existing local taxonomies of crop varieties in evaluating the varieties for their suitability at the farm level. The case study presented here enables the FSR personnel to choose a rice variety from a set of varieties based on the farmer resource availability (irrigation), seasons of crop growth and the final use of the output for local FSR trials. The knowledge base of IKS EXPERT comes from an already developed indigenous knowledge system of rice varieties from Chengalpattu District of South India by two of the authors (Rajasekaran and Warren, unpublished). While any IKS could be used in a similar fashion, the example of crop varietal selection is used here, since the above paper is also presented in this symposium so that it is easy to see how an indigenous knowledge classification could be used in expert systems.

A decision tree for rice varietal selection for FSR based on IKS is given in Figure 15.2, following Rajasekaran and Warren (unpublished). A knowledge structuring technique for IKS is also given in Table 15.1. This forms the knowledge base for IKS EXPERT which is operational at the local FSR or at the farm level as presented in the Appendix. The program has three major sections. The first one is the user interactive section (A1..J20) where the information from the farmer is input and the decisions on crop varietal section to be utilised in FSR projects as suggested by the knowledge base (Figure 15.2) are exhibited. The second section is the program which enables the user to code the raw information from the farmer in a fashion that is compatible with the rules of decision making. For example, the different types of farms are given different labels such as Rainfed=RF and Wetland=Wet and numerical codes for seasons and use of output are also used in decision making rules, such as Samba season=1, Navarai season=2 and Sornavari season=3; Subsistence use=1 and market oriented farming=2. The possible sets of rice varieties from the indigenous knowledge base are also presented in this section.

The program which selects the decision of a set of crop varieties based on the codes imputed by the user is given in section three. This is based on the forward chaining procedure in expert systems programming. The rules are written in such a way that given the availability of resources, irrigation in our case study, season of the crop growth and the final use of the crop output, the program selects the best combination of the rice varieties from which the farmer or FSR personnel could choose from a farming locality in a broader agro-climatic region.

This enables the VEW to provide on-farm recommendations of appropriate rice varieties and to enhance the decision-making ability of the farmers. The program could be modified according to the changes in indigenous knowledge systems due to updating and modification of original knowledge bases. It is also possible with this program to include the feedback information from the farm level trials in the program and evaluate different decisions that are appropriate for the local farming systems.

Conclusion

An expert systems program for utilising indigenous knowledge on rice varieties in farming systems research is developed in the chapter. It is shown that with the facilities of macro programming in LOTUS 123, it is possible to develop a rule-based expert system that is easily understood, and modified by the user with very little or no knowledge of programming languages (*cf.* Appendix). A case study of rice varietal selection from the local knowledge of the farmers for the FSR programs in Chengalpattu District in South India is presented to illustrate the use of the expert system. An added advantage of the procedure developed here is that since the program is written in a program LOTUS 123 worksheet, any optimisation program that utilises a data base from a spreadsheet could be used interactively with another program subroutine.

The knowledge-based systems in a similar fashion for utilising indigenous knowledge systems could be written for irrigation management, pest and disease control decisions, fertiliser mixing and application problems, soil classification and technology choices at the farm level. Some of the prototype expert systems which could be modified according to the needs of the user are available from the Centre for Indigenous Knowledge for Agriculture and Rural Development (CIKARD), Iowa State University (contact Dr. D.M. Warren). More complex programs which involve more input from farmers and other sources

Table 15:1: Knowledge structuring technique for Indigenous Knowledge Systems – rice varieties

Qualifiers	Situations						
	1	*2*	*3*	*4*	*5*	*6*	*7*
Farmer type	Rainfed	Semidry	Wetland	-	-	-	-
Seasons	Samba	Samba	Navarai	Sornavari	-	-	-
Duration	Long	Medium	Short	-	-	-	-
Use	Market	Subsistence	-		-	-	-
Grain type	Fine	Cource	-	-	-	-	-
			Options				
Combinations of	11111	12111	13111	11211			
Varieties	Set1	Set2	Set3	Set4	Set5	Set6	Set7

could also be developed using the above procedure for complete decision making at the farm level using indigenous agriculture knowledge. Also components of FSR such as household consumption and labour requirements could be handled with expert systems.

There are however some limitations in the application of IKS EXPERT in FSR and Extension. The initial investments in computer equipment could be high. Using expert systems also requires training of extension workers in basic computer operations at the local level. However, given the fast development of computer applications in several fields, it is to the advantage of the FSR community to take opportunities of such developments in utilising IKS where information dissemination plays a crucial role.

Appendix 15.1: Expert System for Indigenous Knowledge Systems Crop Varietal Selection

Alt P   To start
**

IR-50j
Farm: wet
Season: 3
Use: 2
Farm: Rainfed = RF, Wetland = Wet
Season: Samba = 1, Navarai = 2, Sornavari = 3
Use: Subsistence = 1, Market = 2
/wgrm/dqrq
{goto}C10⁻/x1ENTER THE FARM TYPE:~~
{goto}C11⁻/xnENTER THE CROP SEASON:~~
{goto}C12⁻/xnENTER THE USE OF OUTPUT:~~
/xiFARM='rf'~~/xcB33⁻{goto}B6⁻/xq
/xiFARM='wet'~~/xcB41⁻{goto}B6⁻/xq⁻
/xgB41⁻
/xiSEASON=1#and#USE=1⁻/CB55⁻E8⁻/xr
/xiSEASON=1#and#USE=2⁻/CB56⁻E8⁻/xr
/xiSEASON=2#and#USE=1⁻/cB63⁻E8⁻/xr
/xiSEASON=2#and#USE=2⁻/cB63⁻E8⁻/xr
/xiSEASON=3#and#USE=2⁻/CB63⁻E8⁻/xr
/cB55⁻E8⁻
/xiSEASON=1#and#USE=1⁻/cB57⁻E8⁻/xr
/xiSEASON=1#and#USE=2⁻/cB58⁻E8⁻/xr
/xiSEASON=2#and#USE=1⁻/cB59⁻E8⁻/xr
/xiSEASON=2#and#USE=2⁻/cB60⁻E8⁻/xr
/xiSEASON=3#and#USE=1⁻/cB61⁻E8⁻/xr
/xiSEASON=3#and#USE=2⁻/cB62⁻E8⁻/xr

Decision USE ONE OF ARCOT KICHILI, VADAN SAMBA, MOOKAN SAMBA, KUNGUMA

USE ONE OF KULLAKAR, NETTAN SAMBA, VENNEL, IVANANEL, AND KUNGUM
USE ONE OF SEMMILAGI, SENTHALAI, AND THIRUVARANGAN
USE ONE OF MADURANVANAN, SIRAIMEETAN, THIRAIKONDAN, AND KANJAN
USE ONE OF PANDI SAMBA, KONGARU SAMBA, AMIRTHAS SAMBA, ALAGU
USE ONE OF PUNUGU SAMBA, MANIKKA SAMBA, PAVALA SAMBA, OTTAN
USE ONE OF SALINEL, MUDANDAI NEL, IVANA NEL, TOPI NEL, KULA NEL
USE ONE OF ADT-27, ADT-31, IR-50, CO-43, TKM-9, AND KULA NEL
IN RAINFED ONLY SAMBA SEASON CAN BE CULTIVATED

Decision:
Use one of ADT-27, ADT-31,

16. *Como Se Cura*: Patterns of medical choice among working class families in the city of Oaxaca, Mexico[1]

MICHAEL B. WHITEFORD

Introduction

IN THE COOL of the early day Maria Valdenebro[2] shakes off the morning chill as she chats with her neighbours while they wait for the bus which will take them from their homes in Colonia Volcanes to the Abastos market, almost on the opposite edge of the city and a ride which will take her close to three-quarters of an hour. One of Maria's children is not feeling well and Senora Valdenebro is going to visit a *tisatera*, a herbalist who operated a stall in Oaxaca's main market, in order to get a botanical remedy for her daughter's raspy throat. She already thinks she will be told to prepare a tea from *hierbabuena* (*Menta piperita*) or *manzanilla* (*Matricaria chamomilla*), materials which she can get in the market and remedies which have produced successful results in the past, but she will defer to the herbalist's good judgement. Maria does not think the illness is serious, but notes that if her daughter is not better within a couple of days she will take the child to the Ministry of Health's hospital in the centre of town. She does not relish this prospect, as the waits are long and the treatment is frequently handled in a curt, brusque and impersonal fashion.

In another area of the Colonia Francisca Hernández is checking on her sleeping toddler Josué. The cough he had the previous day seems to have tone and he is sleeping soundly. Francisca notes that later in the day she will need to stop by one of the pharmacies in town to pick up some more of the penicillin which the druggist had sold her the day before. Then she and Josué will visit their neighbour Moncha Caicedo. She is a specialist in giving injections and administering *sueros* (elixirs of various kinds), who had diagnosed the illness and recommended that particular drug. Two visits were all that Dona Moncha felt would be necessary.

While of this is going on Ignacio Gónzales is gingerly getting out of bed. Several days before he had tripped down some stairs at work and had wrenched his right ankle. Thinking he had only a sprain, Ignacio had gone three times to a *sobador* (someone who cures through massage) for treatment. The ankle does not seem to be any better and now Senor Gónzales is convinced he had better go see a physician at the city's large social security hospital. Through his employer, Ignacio is eligible for this type of medical treatment and at his wife's urging he will go there later in the day.

Elsewhere in the Colonia Polonia Salcedo had just finished her breakfast and now, facing the small altar in her living room, she lights a votive candle in front of a glass-framed colour drawing of the Virgin of Guadalupe and whispers a prayer of supplication. Because it is Tuesday she can plan on spending around two hours that afternoon at Sister Imelda's, one of the spiritualists in the area. As she has for almost every Tuesday for the past year and a half, Polonia will go for a 'curing and cleansing' session in an effort to relieve the chronic rheumtism she has in her shoulders. For years prior to going to Sister Imelda, she had seen a number of physicians without getting much relief. She feels her current treatment is quite satisfactory.

This has been a difficult time for Rosalina Samboni. A woman in her late thirties, just that week she moved just to the Colonia with two of teenage children and her three-year-old son Francisco. They have come from Ixtepeji, a Zapotec community in the Valley, and while her children speak good Spanish, Rosalina is very uncomfortable with the language and somewhat overwhelmed with the move to the city. But her biggest concern is with Francisco who has not been feeling well for the past few days and has been vomiting with almost continual diarrhoea. Rosalina's sister-in-law, with whom they are staying, thinks the child has the evil eye, and suggests that it probable happened just before they left Ixtepeji. Both women know that this is a type of illness not recognised by physicians in the city and is something that will not respond to 'Western' medicine. The sister-in-law wants to take Francisco to see a *curandero,* a traditional folk healer or curer, and they discuss which of the several well-known and knowledgeable individuals they will visit.

The casual observer, trying to understand the medical world-view for many working class Latin Americans, would be dazzled not only at the plethora of factors which enter into concepts of disease causation, but also at the often subtle criteria used in determining which patterns of medical resort people eventually implement. For the outsider, who might believe that the primary causes of most maladies can be explained under the catch-all, quasi scientific patina or rubric of 'microbes', 'viruses', 'baceteria', with little or no room for anything else, that picture would be incomplete and inaccurate. Many of the residents of Colonia Volcanes associate concepts normally regarded as part of the 'Western' medicine paradigm as existing side-by-side with beliefs that illnesses are also occasioned by such things as 'fright', which causes the soul to separate from the body, or due to an imbalance in the metaphorical 'hot' and 'cold' qualities associated with food, drink, medicines, as well as emotional state and physical activities. Further, it is not unusual for illnesses to be brought about by such things as problems of interpersonal relationships, or the purposeful and unsavoury actions of others, or the intercession in one way or another by supernatural force.

Although on the one hand populations such as the residents of Colonia Volcanes might have what seems to be an almost unwieldily complex medical world view, on the other hand, as we shall see, there seems to be an orderliness and almost symmetry to their unspoken model. The purpose of this chapter will be to describe and place folk medical diversity and variation within a larger cultural framework of ethnomedical beliefs. A second and related component will be to describe the alternative curing strategies, or medical choices, practiced. The last thrust will be to present a model that predicts ethnomedical decision-making.

Background

Anthropology's interest in and fascination with Latin American folk illness, traditional medicine, or ethnomedicine has been standard concern of ethnographers at least since Redfield and Vila Rojas (1934) looked at curing practices in Chan Kom more than 50 years ago. Indeed, because traditional medicine permeates so many aspects of life, discussions of illness and curing, in one way or another, have constituted a common segment of studies of peasant life (*e.g.*

Reichel-Dolmatoff and Reichel-Dolmatoff 1961; Foster 1967). In the tradition of studying the community in a holistic fashion, it was not unusual to see discussions of illness and curing weave their ways through descriptions of agricultural practices, food preparation and consumption patterns and social organisation. Similarly, examination of local religious practices and beliefs were imbued with how the supernatural would be enlisted to keep body and soul healthy. As part of the theoretical thrust of acculturation studies that dominated anthropology from the mid-1930s until three decades ago, for a long time one of the particular concerns anthropologists had was trying to determine which aspects of folk medicine were Old World in origin and what components were indigenous to the Americas (*cf.* Foster 1953; Adams and Rubel 1967).

Humoral pathology

By the early 1960s and continuing up to the present, several distinct avenues of ethnomedical inquiry began to take shape. Perhaps no single folk medicinal subject was produced as many articles and discussion as the study of humoral medicine, often referred to as the 'hot–cold' syndrome (*cf.* Curier 1966; Foster 1953, 1979, 1984a, 1984b, 1987, 1988; Cosminsky 1977; Ingham 1970; Kay and Yoder 1987; M. Logan 1973, 1977; Mathews 1983; Messer 1981, 1987; Molony 1975; Tedlock 1987). Much of this discussion and interest focuses on the classification of food and medicinal substances into metaphorical categories of 'hot', 'cold' or 'neutral' qualities. The literature on this subject has been dominated by the examination of the 'principal of opposites', whereby people consciously attempt to symbolically 'balance' dietary intake, *e.g.* the well-balanced meal should more or less contain foods with opposing 'hot' and 'cold' qualities thus neutralising their metaphorical effects on one another. The healthy person was one who did not consume either 'hot' or 'cold' foods in abundance. The underlying philosophy was predicated on a concern that health was something depended on maintaining a dynamic equilibrium in all ingested items, as well as to other activities related to livelihood. In particular, the careful individual would thus avoid excesses of metaphorical and/or thermal heat and cold (Foster 1984b). In addition, M. Logan (1973) and others (*e.g.* deWalt 1977; Whiteford 1976; Higgins 1975; Press 1978) not only have looked at how individuals have classified illnesses and botanical remedies using these properties of 'hot' and 'cold' and how the curing process, but also how today in many areas ethnomedical beliefs have incorporated many pharmaceutical spectrum drugs (*e.g.* penicillin, tetracyclines, amoxicillins) into the curing system and are employing the same cognitive rules as locally grown botanical remedies.

Susto

A second major theoretical interest has been the etiology and treatment of the folk illness *susto* (*cf.* O'Nell and Rubel 1980; Rubel 1964; Rubel *et al.* 1984; O'Nell and Selby 1968; Uzzell 1974), or 'soul loss', a malady which is said to occur as a result of some frightening experience. While some of the initial work on the subject was primarily descriptive and dwelt on how cures were performed, much of the contemporary research has focused more on the epidemiology of *susto* as a measure of social stress or role failure (O'Nell and Rubel 1980; Rubel *et al.* 1984). Uzzell (1974) has looked at the 'strategic role' of deviant behaviour in the community setting, whereby the afflicted is excused from difficult situations or have a passive role. *Nervios* (nerves or anxiety) an ill-ness which in many respects resembles *susto*, has been described for Costa Rica (Barlett and Low 1980; Low 1981). In some instances, in fact, *nervios* can be caused by *susto* (Barlett and Low 1980). Much like *susto*, *nervios* is a culture-specific illness that embraces a rather wide range of symptoms. They are similar as individuals afflicted by both maladies have difficulties maintaining culturally acceptable patterns of behaviour and that public acknowledgement of the prob-lem is often a vital part of its treatment.

Health practitioners

A third significant anthropological focus in ethnomedicine has been on practi-tioners. Generally, these studies have asked the questions: how do individuals diagnose or have identified particular illnesses, and who is consulted during the curing process? Because historically the populations studies by anthropologists did not have direct or easy access to, could not afford, or maintained a medical world view (or any combination of these factors) at variance with western (or allopathic) healers, *i.e.* physicians and nurses and institutions (clinics and/or hos-pitals), the concern often has been on non-western indigenous curers and other traditional providers of health care. Past experience and finance considerations also enter into the decision-making equation regarding who should be con-sulted, for what reasons, and when. When illness or injury occur, often the first questions asked are how serious is it, who should treat it, and how. For many ailments home remedies are easily called up. In the countryside most families grow some medicinal plants, or have convenient access to them. Teas or poul-tices often are easily prepared for internal or topical problems. Treatment might also, and often does, include petitions to the supernatural, through prayer, the lighting of votive candles, or other hagiolatric efforts. When the situation requires consulting someone outside of the family, rarely does someone need look very far. Individuals with knowledge of an array of ailments and their cures can be found in most villages. They might range from the elderly woman next door, who claims no special expertise, but who from years of practice possesses an unsurpassed knowledge of the local botanical pharmacopoeia. Or it might be someone down the street who for a small fee gives injections of antibiotics, with-out necessarily having any strong understanding of medicine other than what types of actions are likely to produce results.

In addition to non-specialists, there exists a range of part-time folk medical practitioners, individuals acknowledged as possessing more than normal knowl-edge and power in identifying causes and illness and bring about cures. As a generic group, they may simply be known as *curanderos* (curers), although they may specialise in herbal or botanical cures, bonesetting, massage, or witchcraft. Many are generalists, knowing something about all of the above activities. Mid-wives are another important group of traditional practitioners (*cf.* Paul and Paul 1975; Fuller and Jordan 1981; Schwartz 1981). Spiritualist healers (*cf.* Finkler 1981, 1984; Kelly 1961; Press 1971) invoke the supernatural to deal with ail-ments which often are not felt to respond to western biomedical treatment. As indigenous healers, one common denominator is the belief these individuals have the ability to cure individuals from ailments not recognised by western practices. Illnesses felt not to respond to biomedical treatments are likely to include such maladies as evil eye, *susto* or witchcraft. While ethnomedical world views may believe that physicians and pharmaceutical drugs may not be effec-

tive in treating soul loss, under many circumstances 'modern' medicine is recognised as capable of producing miraculous results. Many folk practitioners have
no reservations about incorporating patent medicines, in conjunction with local
treatments.

Ethnomedical world-views increasingly incorporate the role of western medical personnel, along with those of indigenous practitioners. In many parts of
Latin America pharmacists (K. Logan 1983; Whiteford 1976: 100) enjoy an
almost exalted role for the knowledge and ability to dispense a wide range of
drugs. In contrast to their US counterparts, Latin American pharmacists have
considerable latitude in what they can sell without a physician's approval and as
a result particularly highly regarded pharmacists may enjoy quite a robust following.

A final group of health practitioners are the formal representatives of the
Western biomedical model, specifically individuals like physicians, nurses and
auxiliary health care promoters, all of whom generally share a common medical
world view. As representatives of the dominant official conveyors of health
care, they are almost always recognised as carriers of considerable knowledge,
as well as individuals who have access to a wide range of very important tools
and techniques for curing. These individuals, and what they represent, fit nicely
into the range of options for curing. The wise and judicious individual carefully
weighs the range of curing options available. Depending on the decision-making
criteria previously stated, different curing options may be consulted solely or in
combination with others (*cf.* Young 1978, 1980, 1981; Young and Garro 1982;
Woods 1977).

Research setting

The City of Oaxaca Urban life has existed in the Valley of Oaxaca for almost
2,500 years (*cf.* Blanton *et al.* 1981: 43; Winter 1989). For more than a millen-
nium the paramount city of the region was Monte Albán, which at its zenith had
a population of 25,000 inhabitants, an elaborate religious hierarchy and a pantheon of deities, and a complex political system which extended its influence
over the entire region. Today the valley is dominated by the city of Oaxaca,
home to approximately 300,000 individuals.

For most of the period before independence its existence was based on the
exploitation of the large and nearby Indian population which worked principally
in agricultural production. Most famous and lucrative of its products was
cochineal, the red dye made from the desiccated and ground insects which live
on nopal cacti. The textile industries in Europe could not get enough of the dye,
and the product served as a tremendous economic boom to the city (Murphy
and Stepick, unpublished). A local weaving industry, which make silk and cotton cloth, further contributed to the city's economic base. The years immediately following independence saw Oaxaca lose its economic position as it
became something of a backwater in the newly formed nation. In the aftermath
of the Revolution of 1910, Oaxaca's role in serving the surrounding region with
goods and services grew precipitously. Much of the commerce focused around
the city's central market, which served as the destination and distribution hub
for articles coming into and leaving the region. In addition to the items coming
from the outside, numerous smaller communities were linked to Oaxaca's market through a complex and systematic region 'solar' marketing system for which
the city of Oaxaca served as the apex (Waterbury 1970).

Today, in addition to serving its traditional functions, Oaxaca's market is a major tourist attraction. From many parts of the globe come the curious, not only to visit the region's many fascinating archaeological sites, but also to see the city's market where women in native dress of the valley, each denoting a different ethnic region, barter goods in a chorus of languages from Chonantec to Zapotec. In addition to selling fruits, vegetables, meat and poultry, items ranging from pottery made in Atzompa and Coyotepec and woven goods coming from Teotitlán del Valle, one finds live chickens, ducks, turkeys and the occasional bleating goats which are sold along with plastic shoes, racks of clothing, aluminium pots, religious icons, machetes, and cassette tape recorders.

Although its growth rate has been relatively slow, when compared to some of the nation's larger urban areas, like Mexico City, Guadalajara or Monterrey, its population has steadily increased in the years since the early decade of the century. From a population of just under 50,000 at mid century, the city has grown to its present population of more than a quarter of a million (Murphy and Stepick, unpublished). While some of the increase reflects a natural growth, aided by declines in infant and childhood mortality without an accompanying reduction in natality levels, most of the increase in due to in-migration from rural Oaxaca. Today only one-third of the city's household heads were born in the urban confines of Oaxaca. Countless others have come to the city in impressive numbers. Mainly the young, they have moved to the city of Oaxca from every region of the state, including villages quite close to the city. Individuals, who a year before were ploughing with oxen the same fields that their ancestors planted with a digging stick for hundreds of years, now make their living in an urban society, admire the way their children speak good Spanish, and see their decision to live in the city as unequivocally good.

Twenty or thirty years ago the attention of the first time visitor to Oaxaca focused on the stately baroque architecture of the city's churches and public buildings. The picturesque colonial appearance of the city of Oaxaca reminded outsiders of such urban areas as Guanajuato or Querétaro, Mexico or of Popayán, Colombia, other cities of adobe walls and the carefully sculpted stone fronts of churches, where tile roofs and the floral combinations of flaming red and purple bougainvillea with blue and mauve jacaranda in the downtown area gave an impression of cities where 'time stood still'.

Life seemed to centre on the heart of the city, around its central plaza or *zocalo*, where, in addition to locals, tourists, mainly Mexicans although North Americans, and Europeans made up a significant portion, would eat, or particularly in the mornings simply sit with their coffee and newspaper and admire the splendour of the city as they planned trips to outlying colourful Indian villages or archaeological ruins. While all of these things are still an important part of Oaxaca, the visitor to Oaxaca today, whether coming by air or road, is struck by a city that is rapidly growing. In all directions housing construction is taking place. Several small villages, such as the former indigenous community of Xochimilco, long ago were swallowed up by the city as its squatter settlements, occurring without government approval, others the result of public housing projects, and still others part of careful planning by private developers attest to the obvious: Oaxaca is a city of migrants.

Colonia volcanes

Research from which data for this chapter are drawn was conducted in a neighbourhood named Colonia Volcanes, an essentially working class community, located in the northeast edge of the city. Founded in the late 1960s, the colonia has approximately 8000 residents today. Like many of the inhabitants living elsewhere in the city, the majority of the household heads living in Volcanes were born outside the city (see Table 16.1), many arriving in the city of Oaxaca only within the past decade. Households are overwhelmingly nuclear in composition, perhaps reflecting an intentional migrant pattern of single individuals or young married couples leaving the countryside.[3] Families range in size from one individual to 12 persons, with a mean of 5.48 individuals and a mode of 5.00 occupants per dwelling. The focus of this study is to describe the medical world view and delineate strategies or patterns of medical choice among female household heads in this community. To achieve this objective, sample selection for this study was based on a two state process. Using very detailed (with a scale of 1:500) and June 1988 maps from the Officina de Obras Públicas, Obras de Recuperación, a random sample of one half of the total (N=88) blocks was obtained. From this sample of 44 blocks, approximately one-fourth of the female household heads (N=207) were selected in a random fashion and interviewed were using detailed interview schedule. Follow-up ethnographic interviews on an additional series of open-ended questions were conducted with 94 of these women. The women in the study ranged from 16 to 68 in age, with the mean aging being 38 and the mode 28 years old. Eighty per cent of them were born outside of the city of Oaxaca (as were comparably high per cent of their husbands). The most common pattern of education was completion of primary school, although the average women had just less than five years of schooling and almost a quarter of the women in the study had no formal education. Eighty per cent of the families are home owners, with the average dwelling being a three room, abode, with brick walls and a roof of laminated concrete sheet. Electricity exists in close to all (99 per cent) of the homes and periodically functioning city – supplied running water exists in most (80 per cent).

Table 16.1: Demographic characteristics of sample

Category	Per cent
Home tenancy	
Home owner	81
Renter	8
Free use/non-owner	11
Birth place	
Female household head	
Born in city of Oaxaca	20
Born outside city of Oaxaca	80
Male household head	
Born in city of Oaxaca	17
Born outside city of Oaxaca	83
Average age of female household head	
When left community of birth	17
When arrived in Oaxaca	22

Results

Illness and health From a series of open-ended interviews with 94 women a picture of how illness and health are defined, and the methods for addressing health-related problems begins to emerge. Although not necessarily explained in these terms, it appears that women in Colonia Volcanes envision states of well-being as positions along a metaphorical continuum ranging from being 'healthy' to 'ill'. Thus the sick person is not someone who has something or is infected with something radically different from the individual who is well, but rather, in contrast with a healthy individual, the sick person occupies a slightly different position on the gradient of well-being. For example, women use adjectives like 'active', 'good colour', 'eats well' or 'content' and (for children) 'likes to play' when talking about someone who is healthy. The sick person, on the other hand, is someone described as possessing one or more of the following characteristics: 'sadness', 'pain' or 'soreness', 'ill tempered', 'not sleeping', 'not eating' or as someone who 'does not feel like doing anything' or is 'too warm'. For those enculturated with a Western medical model, terms like 'fevers', 'chills', 'viruses' or 'bacterial injections' are conspicuously absent from this list of descriptors.

Staying well

The art of staying healthy appears to be based on the ability to maintain a delicate balance on the scale or continuum of health. Excesses of any kind are disruptive and will lead to illness. Thus one eats good food (with tortillas, beans, meat and egg commonly suggested), but not too much nor too little in quantity. Occasionally adherence to rules of balancing 'hot' and 'cold' qualities of foods were suggested and it is suspected that these notions are more widely practiced than spoken about. Several women mentioned that they told their children not to eat food prepared by street vendors, yet observations suggest that the vast majority of families are not really concerned about the ubiquitous peddlers of culinary delights. Women in Colonia Volcanes seemed concerned about the quality of their water, although there appeared to be some ambivalence about exactly what this meant. Several interviewees suggested boiling their water as a way to avoid problems, and indeed, more than a three-quarters of the households regularly boiled their water.

Another frequently submitted means for staying healthy was avoiding 'brusque changes in temperature'. Neither move quickly from a cool area to a hot one, nor vice versa as those actions will most certainly result in illness.

Patterns of medical resort

In spite of the best efforts to avoid sickness, illnesses are common occurrences in the daily lives of residents in Colonia Volcanes. For many families environment conditions, comprised in part of poor hygiene and inadequate resources to meet the nutritional and other health needs of members of their households, greatly exacerbate an already tenuous health situation. When women were asked what the three most common illnesses effecting their families were, diarrhoeal diseases, gastrointestinal problems and various types of 'colds' (coughs, runny noses, sore throats) comprised more than two-thirds of their responses. Other maladies ranging from such things as asthma, dengue fever, measles, skin lesions, *empacho* (surfeit), and evil eye were of concern as well. On a day-to-day basis women in Colonia Volcanes make a series of decisions that have a direct bearing on the health of family members. Often these decisions are pro-active, designed to keep individuals from becoming ill. These include such things as watching the diet, making sure behaviour is such as not to create potential problems, and in general, ensuring that the balance between illness and health is maintained. When this does not work out, actions need to be set into motion to correct the situation.

For women in Colonia Volcanes there are a wide range of options available to them for bringing these actions to fruition and they usually begin with an assessment of the problem; once the issue and its cause are determined, the next step in the curing process is to decide on a course of treatment. In about half (46 per cent) of the households, the woman makes these first evaluations herself. When this is not the case, slightly more than half (60 per cent) consult with their spouses and another one-third (33.5 per cent) will talk the matter over with friends or neighbours.

In presenting a hypothetical model of medical decision-making (see Figure 16.1), the following discussion attempts to summarise and synthesise what appears to occur in the lives of many residents of Colonia Volcanes when someone is thought to be ill. The first level of decision-making addresses the question of 'how serious' is the illness? Depending on that answer at least three choices are possible. The first series of contrasts simply establishes courses of action. If the illness is determined to to be 'serious' (such as sniffles, a mild cold or raspy throat), the family is likely to move quickly to the next dimension of the model which deals with financial matters. Should the family be strapped for cash, they are very likely to rely on home remedies. Many households grow herbs on their lots, or can obtain these medicinal items from neighbours.

They can also be found packaged in small cellophane envelopes and sold at modest prices in neighbourhood stores. If money is not a major consideration, the family still might take this course of action, or they may use various types of over-the-counter patent medicines. In particular, items like 'Vick's Vaporub' and 'Contact X', along with different brand names of aspirin-like compounds are extensively used, often in combination with herbal or other botanical remedies.

For illnesses that are regarded as moderately or gravely serious, another important dimension enters into the matrix: does the illness respond to western medical treatment and to patent medicines? On the one hand, while many residents recognise the efficacy of many new pharmaceutically based medicines and the wondrous powers for curing available to Western-trained health personnel, these same individuals, at the same time strongly believe that this medical system has certain limitations. In particular, maladies such as *empacho* (surfeit), *susto* (fright), or *mal de ojo* (evil eye) are felt not to be responsive to many patent medicines. However, residents realise that most physicians will not take people seriously who come into their consulting rooms saying they have one or another of these ailments. Residents often appear to be able to distinguish between etiology and symptomology.

Marcelina Bustamante explained that she often would patronise both systems by going to an allopathic physician for (or to confirm) a diagnosis, visiting a spiritualist in order to be cured, and often then returning to the physician for such things as 'X-rays to see if the problem is all gone'. Another respondent voiced a concern that folk curers are often more effective than physicians because they really need to understand illnesses and curing techniques and cannot simply depend on packaged drugs, many of which she volunteered had numerous, and often unanticipated, harmful side effects.

Of course not everyone is convinced of the value of some traditional medical beliefs and practices, and some individuals were very candid in expressing their

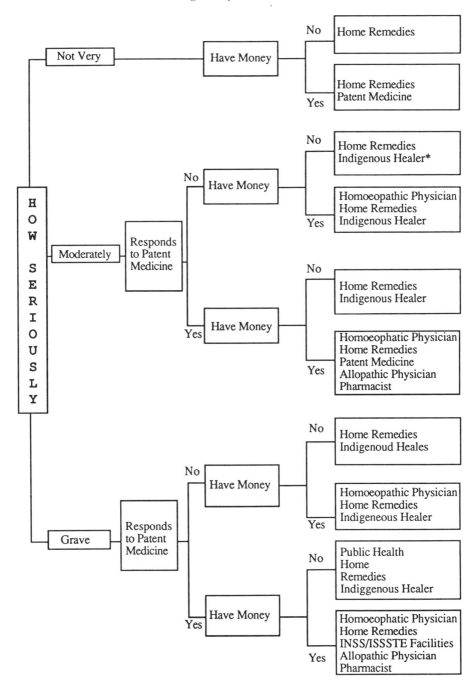

* *'Indigenous Healers' is a gloss referring to curers such as curanderos, herbalists, masseurs, tisateras, bonesetters, midwives and injectionists.*

Figure 16.1: *Hypothetical model of medical decision-making*

lack of 'faith' in such practitioners as *curanderos*. Still others sing the praises of important and highly knowledgeable curers whom they visit on a regular basis. After having an unpleasant experience with a physician who wanted to amputate her leg because of an infection, Alejandrina Fuentes went to see a *huesero* (bonesetter) who alleged to have performed a miraculous cure and to whom she now goes for treatment for a variety of ailments. Primitiva Garcia moved to Colonia Volcanes from the Zapotec community of Ixtepeji. All of her children were delivered by a traditional curer/midwife.[4] Although she now lives several hours by bus from her natal village, she still maintains contacts with a herbalist and a *curandero* and consults them when needed.

Thus, people with medical problems felt to be untreatable with western medical techniques have a variety of curing options at their disposal. Should the cost of treatment be a concern, home remedies or choices of indigenous healers[5] are often an inexpensive option.

Bridging the gap between illnesses felt to be unresponsive to western medicine are treatments offered by doctors of homeopathy. Because of their naturalistic approach, including the use of herbs and other botanical remedies in treatment, homeopaths seem to occupy a special niche in the medical world-view of residents from Colonia Volcanes. On the one hand, they are regarded as part of the professional, nationally recognised branch of medicine, and yet at the same time people feel that at least certain homeopathic physicians can be consulted for practically any type of illness. When residents talked about treatment and curers (folk and western), they were very clear in distinguishing what types of physicians they were talking about and used the terms 'alopata' (*alllopath*) and 'homeopata (*homeopath*) in the same manner as most North Americans would separate a medical doctor from a doctor of chiropractic. One of the differences in these analogies is that in the minds of these people allopaths and homeopaths were physicians of equal status, whereas many people in the United States probably would not say the same for MDs and DCs.

When illnesses are indeed felt to be responsive to patent medicines and where financial considerations do not loom as a major consideration, choices are quite varied and the course of action often involves convenience and personal preference as to the method of medical resort. In the city of Oaxaca alone there are over two dozen sanatoria, clinics and hospitals. Further, government workers and their families are eligible for free health care from the Instituto de Seguridad y Servicios Sociales de los Trabajadores del Estado (ISSSTE) facilities. The large Social Security (IMSS) Hospital, located on the Panamerican highway, which runs through town, is much used. Individuals participating in employer/employee pay-roll deduction plans have access to this type of care. For those without any insurance, the Ministry of Health operates a hospital in the city as well. In addition, individuals are able to tap into the services of an impressive number of allopathic physicians who have offices in the city. The most recent telephone book lists almost three pages of private practice physicians, with specialties ranging from endocrinology to otorhinolaryngology.

In Oaxaca pharmacies[6] play a much greater role in the diagnosing and curing process than do their counterparts in most US cities. In fact, throughout much of Latin America, as is quite common elsewhere in the developing world, drugs that in the United States are normally dispensed only with a prescription signed by a licensed physician, are easily obtainable in drugstores without restrictions. Indeed, indigenous curers, as well as friends and neighbours of a sick person may recommend powerful antibiotics which can then be easily purchased. One example of how patent medicines are recommended and used in conjunction with traditional cures comes from the case of Lola Martínez, a *tisatera* (herbalist) who operates a stall in the Benito Juarez market in Oaxaca. Her shop is tucked in among the vegetable vendors and from the stacks of dried herbs and other plants it is easy to see that her business consists principally of selling botanical remedies. In addition, she also sells religious paraphernalia (crosses, small votive metal replicas of limbs, drawings of saints and other supernatural entities), candles designed to bring good luck to the petitioner or misfortune to others, and various types of protective amulets and religious charms. While Lola primarily prescribes and sells botanical remedies, sometimes stopping to consult one of the several books she has on medicinal plants, she is not hesitant to suggest one of a number of antibiotics that her customers will purchase at one of the nearby pharmacies to take along with the recommended teas they will make.

Discussion

According to the most recent report of the Mexican Secretary of Health (Instituto Nacional de Estadística 1989: 24), acute respiratory infections, enteritis and other diarrhoeal diseases are the most commonly reported health problems for the state. These observations are corroborated in this study with data from Colonia Volcanes. Although only 20 per cent of the families interviewed stated they were discontented with their health situation or that of their families, coping with problems inherent in staying well is a continual process. The focus of this paper has been to look at and understand the strategies and decision-making patterns related to how female household heads determine what to do when members of their family become ill. What emerges from this discussion is the observation that, depending on how the health problem is diagnosed in terms of degree of severity, women are highly resourceful and often can pursue an amazingly wide range of options. Sometimes courses of action are simple and very straight forward. On other occasions, patterns of resort involve being able to choose from a rather mixed menu of alternatives. Whatever is accomplished is done in a fashion that often reflects a wider series of beliefs and values. Simply restoring the gentle equilibrium found in so many areas of daily existence requires this.

Notes

1. This chapter is based on research data gathered in Oaxaca, Mexico, between May and August 1989. I would like to thank Iowa State University for several small grants which assisted in carrying out this project. Special thanks go to Paola Sesia-Lewis, Alejandro de Avila and María Teresa Pardo at the Grupo de Apoyo al Desarrollo Etnico (GADE:) for personal institutional support in the field. Pedro Pacheco and Ruth Alden, graduate students from Iowa State University, were first rate research assistants and the data presented herein were collected by them along with our able assistants in Oaxaca: Zenón Ramírez, Lourdes Cornoa, Virginia Jurado, Julia Esther Rios, Catalina Solano, Alfonso Pacheco and Antoieta Solano. Most importantly, special thanks go to the women in Colonia Volcanes whose cooperation and participation made this project possible.
2. The names used in this chapter are pseudonyms. The anecdotal accounts described here are fictitious composites of activities largely based on ethnographic information.
3. The literature (*cf.* Butterworth 1971; Butterworth and Chance 1981) on Latin Amer-

ica suggests that the rural to urban migration process is selective in terms of which segments of the population are most likely to leave the countryside. Among them are the female household heads at the time of departure from their natal communities was just over 17 years (with a mode of 20 years of age). Clearly the process did not always result in their moving directly to the city of Oaxaca, as the mean age at the time of arrival was 22 years (and a mode of 20).

4. When asked where their youngest child was born, 75 per cent of our respondents replied the birth took place in a hospital or clinic. Ronald Spores, an anthropologist at Vanderbilt University who has worked in the Valley of Oaxaca for several decades, mentioned that he was surprised even 20 years ago when doing field work in a Mixtec community almost two hours from the city of Oaxaca that women made considerable effort, involving riding over tortuous roads, to deliver their children in clinics in the city. Often within the same day they would be back on the bus, with the newly delivered child tightly wrapped in a shawl, heading home (personal communication).

5. It should be pointed out that costs for visiting *curanderos*, herbalists, spiritualists and the like can range anywhere from simply a 'donation' to a rather expensive proposition. In general, however, this type of medical treatment can be quite inexpensive and respondents often mentioned that these curers were not doing their jobs in order to make money, but rather because they possessed special abilities or were responding to a 'calling'.

6. According to the 1989 telephone book for the state of Oaxaca, there are more than 100 '*farmacias, boticas y droguerias*' – all of which dispense medicines of one form or another.

17. Local Traditions and Community Forestry Management: A view from Nepal[1]

DONALD A. MESSERSCHMIDT

The underlying requirement...is to approach villagers as people who have something to teach as well as something to learn. The basic problem...is to understand the problem from the point of view of the local villagers and to develop relevant solutions in consultation with them.

(Gilmour, King and Fisher 1987:6–7)

THIS STUDY IS based on the premise that indigenous systems of natural resource management exist in many communities in the Himalayas. The indigenous knowledge systems in the Himalayas give planners and developers of resource conservation an unprecedented opportunity to pursue a dialogue with and assure participation of the local people. This existence puts a burden on socio-cultural and natural science researchers to examine and analyse further local resource circumstances. This would enable the researchers to integrate, more constructively, the facts of local life, the theories of modern science, and the practicalities of development action with a commitment to engage local people in participatory conservation planning and development.

A number of community forestry case studies are presented to illustrate a range of traditional systems of individual and community (user group) forest management in the Himalayas.[2] The case studies provide evidence of village people's concern for the resource. More important, they provide forest developers with an opportunity:

o to act constructively to enhance and implement existing people-oriented legislation;
o to put vision into development policy; and
o to pursue sensitive action that not only enables local people to be re-incorporated productively into long range development and management of forest resource but also encourages and empowers them to act in their own behalf.

The term 're-incorporate' is used purposefully, following the lead of Dr. K. Panday (personal communication 1986). This term is based on the belief that the right to benefit from natural resources, such as local forests, ultimately rests with the local people and that constructive and sustained management of the forests are, likewise, their responsibility. The people's rights and responsibilities are, in turn, backed up by government (*e.g.* state foresters), whose role is not so much to control but to facilitate and assist. Some foresters feel that management of the resource is a government responsibility to be carried out with the help of the people. Practically speaking, however, the inverse – that the people manage local forests with the help of the government – is far more realistic.[3]

Himalayan forests are many and are often small and scattered. The people who live there, within or adjacent to them, have intimate knowledge of forest conditions and know their own needs regarding the products of the forest. Their knowledge is derived from centuries of experience, often sustained by traditional management systems. The issue is not one of finally involving the rural people when faced with the problems of resource management, but rather of enabling their fundamental relationship with natural resources to re-emerge. The government forester's role now becomes one of technical assistance, a form of help that necessitates understanding the sociocultural definitions of the resource and practical needs of the people in addition to the practice of scientific forestry. The Forestry Master Plan of 1989 strengthens and institutionalises this approach (Nepal 1989).

We have much to learn from the people. Their customary knowledge and folk science have much to offer in the construction of scientifically-sound but humanistically-oriented theories and strategies for action. The object is to re-engage and re-involve the people, given that, in many instances of development in the Himalayas, they tend to have been ignored. It was through a combination of the rise of a technology-based forestry profession and the increasing unity and power of central governments that the local people became progressively disenfranchised from their existing control over the management and benefits of their forests.

In Nepal, for example, the people were disenfranchised before the 1950s, when the former Rana Government elites harvested the valuable forest products for their own profit. Following the nationalisation of Nepal's forests in 1957, the people's rights and responsibilities were further ignored. At that time, some people certainly forfeited those rights by wantonly destroying some forests, and as a consequence, considerable restorative action was necessary (see Bajracharya 1983a; Gilmour 1987; Mahat, Griffin and Shepherd 1986–7; Messerschmidt 1984). Comparable circumstances are documented in the history of India's forest policy in the Himalayas under British colonialism (Tucker 1982, 1984).

Fortunately, professional foresters and policy-makers in the Himalayan region are now recognising the need for re-engagement between the centre and the hinterland populations. Governments and development agencies are now acting with conviction through such exemplary programs as community forestry in Nepal and social forestry in India. The intent is to restore much of the responsibility for local forest management to the people through new policies and programs, such as the community forestry and decentralisation legislation in Nepal and the 'wasteland' development program in India.[4]

Conservation developers work with both the natural and the social resources – the forests and the people. If a resource is defined as: 'something to which one can turn for help or support or to achieve one's purpose' (Oxford dictionary), the question then, on the social side, must be 'What support or aid can the local people themselves provide in the face of the forest resource crisis? This is the principal question raised in this study. It will be discussed shortly, following a brief consideration of the resource crisis and its various causes and effects in the Himalayas.

The Himalayan resource crisis

Conventional wisdom has defined 'crisis' as massive degradation of the Himalayan environment, particularly evident in deforestation and soil erosion, resulting in disastrous downstream flooding in Northern India and Bangladesh.

Under further scrutiny, several parallel and progressively degrading events seem to be occurring in the Himalayas:

o increased population growth, leading to increased pressure on available resources (Macfarlane 1976);
o increased need for new agricultural land, leading to steadily greater incursions on forests and other marginal and fragile lands (Bajracharya 1983a, 1983b);
o increased tree cover loss, leading to mass wasting and accelerated soil erosion (Carson 1985);[5]
o ultimately, these events, taken together, lead to one result – increased sedimentation and flooding the heavily populated areas of the palins at the foot of the Himalayas (Eckholm 1975, 1976; Nichols 1982; *cf.* Hamilton 1987; Ives and Ives 1987).

The outcome of all these is that the people who live on the failing landscape, both upland and lowland, suffer inestimable hardship and deprivation. This – the people's welfare – is (or should be) the central issue in conservation development and resource management.

Inherent in the popular view of the crisis are the grounds for considerable controversy and contrary opinion. There is no doubt, for example, that deforestation in the Himalayas is accelerating at an alarming rate (World Bank 1979; WRI 1985; Nield 1985; Hamilton 1987). Questions have been raised about the relationship between the loss of uphill trees and the seriousness of downstream flowing and even of the increase in the incidence and natural severity of the flood phenomena. These topics are the subject of discussion and debate elsewhere (Hamilton and Pearce 1985; Gilmour and Applegate 1984; Gilmour, Bonnel, and Cassells 1987; Currey 1984; Ives 1984a, 1984b; Ives and Ives 1987; Ives and Messerli 1989). They are not pursued here other than to note their existence as the backdrop to concern about human impacts and inputs. But, lest the scientists and developers toss the proverbial 'baby-out-with-the-bathwater', it must be hastily said that despite current controversy and scepticism about the relationship between deforestation and disastrous floods, there is still a very real crisis. It is well expressed in contemporary shortages of fuelwood, fodder, and food, as well as in symptoms of landlessness, malnutrition, and the deleterious effects of human migration on an already overcrowded landscape.

This study does not intend to discuss the crisis so much as to address potential strategies for its amelioration. That, in turn, requires the examination of the social science or human-centred aspects of the debate. The critical question which links these two perspectives – the natural and the social – to the crisis is now the facts, myths, and misconceptions of each affect the other, particularly as those misconceptions guide and steer (or fail to guide and steer) contemporary conservation development. Jack Ives (1984a: 54) has said it well: 'Much of what we may call the theory of Himalayas-Indo-Gangetic Plains degradation is based, at least in part, upon a degree of myth – a quarter century of emotion and repetition of first impressions.... Is it really correct to assume that deforestation (human action) in the mountains causes soil erosion and landslides, with direct impacts all the way downstream to the Bay of Bengal, and to base development plans directly upon such a facile assumption?'

Human factors in the 'Himalayan Crisis'

There is a common belief that the people of the Himalayas are the fundamental cause of natural resource degradation. Bhattarai (1979: 30) refers to the human element as the source of an unprecedented *aggression against nature* in the Himalayas. Campbell (1979: 2-3) writes that: 'ecologically unsound agricultural practices have always been part of the economic strategies that Nepalese farmers use to maximise their productivity and that traditional systems of resource management...[are] usually concerned with rights of exploitation and distribution rather than with conservation.' Moddie (1981: 342) has concluded more grandly that 'in bygone ages the Himalayas seemed eternal; man's onslaught has rendered them among the most fragile ecosystems of the earth.'

These observations are partially correct, although local people are generally protective, not exploitative, towards specially designated community forests, as some of these same writers and I have noted elsewhere (Arnold and Campbell 1986; Wormald and Messerschmidt 1986). In fact, local prescriptions for managing forests tend toward protection, and the people have to be literally 'taught' concepts such as sustained yield management and rational utilisation. On the other hand, people do represent a sometimes exploitative and unwittingly destructive factor in the Himalayas, as they do in virtually all natural environments. Two points, however, must be made in defence of the local people.

First, as many contemporary observers have noted, people are not the sole cause of environmental degradation (Carson 1985; Hamilton and Pearce 1985). A negative interpretation of the contemporary human role in environmental degradation ignores certain historical, geological and other natural factors, as well as the extreme complexity of the issue. Humankind's effects on the naturally hazardous Himalayan landscape are relatively recent. While no less important in a holistic view of the problem, the people's disturbing effects on the ecosystem should not be overemphasised.

Human effects must be seen in relation to the entire process of natural mountain development and environmental stress. In defence of this position, Gurung (1982: 6–7) notes that extreme altitude and steep slope of the Himalayas create a *high energy environment*, observable in glacial scouring, landslides and soil erosion. The natural instability of the hills and mountains and the effects of the annual monsoon rains provide what he calls a natural *conveyor belt for material transport* to the plains (Gurung 1984). It is certainly true, however, that since the arrival of people on the scene, *i.e.* since at least the Neolithic Age, the condition of the natural resources has changed, sometimes with serious and detrimental consequences. The more advanced the economy and the greater the population, the more severe are the human pressures exerted on the environment (Cool 1983). Humankind's role in changing the natural landscape, however, is relatively brief and appears less formidable when compared to and contrasted with the time and temperament of the natural elements.

The second point is that the people are usually quite well aware of environmental problems particularly where they live, even if not often beyond the local neighbourhood, and that they have the ability to help ameliorate them (Bhattarai and Campbell 1983). In some instances, it is now becoming clear that they have understood the problem and have pursued individual remedial action, *e.g.* as farmers planting trees on private land (Gilmour 1987). In terms of community development however, they have, unfortunately, long been forgotten or ignored by policy-makers and planners. Re-engaging them now requires an extra effort to provide the opportunity and the means, through enabling legislation and ameliorative development strategies.

Johnson *et al.* (1982: 184–5) note that it is not the knowledge of cause and effect, but rather the means at the Nepali farmers' disposal which dictate farmer's action toward the environment. By providing villagers with the means for improvement, problems of environmental decline will be nearer solution: 'Many farmers distinguish between ideal measures which might be adopted given the availability of resources and feasible measures which are the ones they must select.... Farmers evaluate the options and, often, must choose the less effective one which is, however, the one within their means.'

Observing the negative results of farmers taking the 'less effective' but only available option has led some observers to predict disaster in the future of the Himalayas. Rieger (1978, 1979), for example, has described an interwoven set of environmentally-negative behaviours and concludes that the Himalayas are suffering the tragic consequences (see also critique by Messerschmidt 1984: 15 *ff.*). There is also a feeling of gloom and doom in the writings of such observers as Eckholm (1975, 1976, 1984) and Sterling (1976), and in the popular film *Fragile Mountain* produced by Nichols (1982, *cf.* Currey 1984).

Substantial evidence support the belief that, given a concerted effort on the part of developers to give people the means to express themselves in a rational and conservation-minded way, they will respond constructively and eagerly, with responsibility and foresight. Re-incorporation of positive local initiatives towards natural resources (much easier in the past, when negative pressures on these resources were comparatively less) is a key to the maintenance of a sustainable natural resource base in the Himalayas. Where villagers have been given the opportunity to be involved, they have shown remarkable care and constraint, working diligently to manage, improve and conserve the resources for the future. Developers, in turn, must take the opportunity to work with them.

A report from Nepal's innovative Community Forestry Development Project challenges the gloom and doom approach to peasant behaviours and resource degradation: 'Data from questions on local management of public forests challenges the now standard account of the demise of local forest protection since nationalisation. Over one-third (36%) of the ward leaders reported having systems for protecting some of their local public forests...the median numbers of years these forests have been protected is less than 20, while forest nationalisation took place over 25 years ago. This indicates that over a sixth of the villagers in hill Nepal have instituted some form of community management in spite of or perhaps even because of government nationalisation' (Campbell 1984: 24).

Recent observations throughout the Himalayas in Nepal document many examples of rural people who have established and maintained effective indigenous (non-government directed) management systems over forest resources and common forest properties, quite contrary to the negative behaviours and outcomes so often highlighted in the prevailing literature. The rest of this chapter highlights a number of positive local conservation practices in the Himalayas.

Human resource management conventions in Nepal

Established systems of community control and use-rights for forest resources and communal forest properties do exist in Nepal. They are found in the lowlands, the middle hills, and the high mountains, in ethnic and caste communities, among the rich and the poor. But what is their nature? What use-rights exist? What patterns in their design can be found and used? What features help explain their long-lasting success? Where, how, and why do they exist?

Research on these questions demonstrates two patterns of indigenous forest management systems in Nepal, individual (or private) and communal (or public). Both depend, to some degree, on influential local leaders who have both the foresight and the power with which to act, and ultimately on the village people to follow their lead. Some such systems are exclusively private. Others are conceived and operate on a community or user-group basis, are locally sanctioned, and are based on established and customary norms of groups behaviour.

Private initiatives. Recent observations in East Nepal, in the district of Ilam, confirm the importance and success of private forest plantations (*niji ban*).

Example 1: The private forest of Hari Kumar Parajuli, Sulubhang Panchayat, Ilam District

In 1954, Hari Kumar's father decided to convert approximately 1 ha of steeply-terraced, unirrigated hillside land (*bari*) on his farm to a variety of tree species for timber, fodder, fuelwood, and leaves for compost. Indirect benefits include an improved water source and wildlife habitat. At the time, the only nearby source of tree seedlings was a Government of India nursery located at Mani Banjhang in neighbouring Darjeeling District, in the State of West Bengal. The distribution of the seedlings to Nepalese nationals was, however, illegal.

Knowing the risk of arrest, but also considering the potential benefits of this 'crime,' Hari Kumar's father walked several days from his home near Sulubhang village in Nepal to Mani Banjhang. There, he bribed the nurseryman to fill his basket with seedlings. Then, travelling by night and using little known jungle paths to avoid detection, he slipped back across the border and returned home to plant his trees. Today, Hari Kumar proudly shows off the maturing and productive private forest. The species include poplar, alder, oak and associated species, with a crop of cardamon in the moist hillside draws (author's field notes of February 1986).

Example 2: Private forest beside the Ilam-Phidim road. Barabote Panchayat, Ilam District.

Not unlike the case above, is that of a Brahmin farmer whose house site next to the new Ilam Phidim road is reaping the benefits of a small 0.1 ha forest that his father planted three decades ago. Instead of taking seedlings from an established nursery, however, this man's father, in his youth, travelled to the high forest area (*lekh*) a day's walk above his home where he collected natural seeds and seedlings (poplar and oak associated species). He planted them for future fuel, fodder, and timber production and to serve as a windbreak to protect his house and property (author's field notes of February 1986).

It should be noted that since 1981, under Nepal's new Community Forestry Development Project (CFDP), a number of multi-species tree nurseries, tree plantations, and improved forests have been developed in Ilam District and in other hill districts across the nation. No longer do local farmers have to hike across the border or search the high forests for tree seedlings. While the CFPD's main emphasis is on community forestry initiatives, the project also encourages private tree planting. The private planting initiative has been hailed as a major success. To date, several millions of tree seedlings have been placed by farmers on private land throughout the country and about a million are now being planted each year.[6]

Communal resource management initiatives. Besides private forestry initiatives, anthropologists and others have documented numerous management systems of communal forest resource in the hills of Nepal. Most function in ways and for purposes similar to the cooperation and collective action that have previously been reported for Nepalese hill agriculture (Messerschmidt 1981).[7]

A number of forest management systems demonstrate the organisational richness and traditional public concern for conservation in the Nepal hills, even after forest nationalisation. Campbell (1979) has documented five systems of community forest conservation and mentions several others which either pre-date or are the result of their diffusion. They include examples of both group action dependent on strong and influential leaders (both natural and elected), and of government- and project-initiated action. Most of Campbell's examples support the conclusion that while local leaders are especially important in the initial phase of developing traditional (and project-inspired) systems: 'a people's eventual perception of the benefits they are receiving helps to insure their [ongoing] participation' (1979: 24).

More recently, Pelinck and Campbell noted that: 'The most important lessons to be learned from traditional management systems are that community management of forest resources is possible if the right social unit if self-selected, the objectives are widely understood and the benefits equitably distributed.' (1984: 5).

The following examples demonstrate the principle:

Example 3: Bagar village protected forest, Dhansuri Panchayat in the Dang Valley

A forest protection scheme was initiated in the early 1970s by a moderately wealthy Chetri caste landlord to save a community *sal* forest (*Shorea robusta*). It met with initial resistance from local people who were prevented from cutting trees and fodder in the forest. Eventually, seeing the long-range advantage of his conservation efforts, the villagers began to support his efforts, and ultimately established a system of paid watchmen, supported by household contributions. This system mimics, in some ways, pre-existing community-protected forest schemes in the vicinity, one of which is known to have been in existence since the early 1950s (Campbell 1979).

Example 4: Tika protected forest, Byaasi Village, Bhajang District

In 1970, three influential men of the Brahmin caste (the Vice Principal, the Assistant Headmaster, and the Accountant of the Byaasi village school), convinced their village neighbours to protect a degraded forest by prohibiting cutting and allowing for natural regeneration of the trees by coppice. The area selected was approximately five ha (100 *ropani*) in size. Villagers agreed to seek the necessary wood for fuel (*daura*) and fodder (*ghaas*) elsewhere, and to harvest only dead leaves for composting, and dead and dried twigs and branches (*jikra*) for fuel from Tika Forest. Limited cattle grazing was also allowed. Tika forest is comprised of oak and associated species. The local people consider this to be their own private village forest, unconcerned (or unaware) that such degraded forests were nationalised over a decade earlier in 1957.

Initially, they hired a forest watchman whom the householders paid annually in kind with grain. The positive results of closure are now self-evident and the villagers now practice self-restraint without a watchman. Seeing the successful and lush growth of tree stock in this small area, the Byaasi villagers are considering a similar closure of neighbouring scrubland, apparently willing to forego immediate gain and to seek their needs from further away (author's field notes, February 23, 1986).

Example 5: Banskharka Panchayat forest and nursery. Sindhu Palchok District

The local elected Panchayat Chairman, a Tamang, began a system of forest protection in the early 1970s. While his plans were initially resisted 'he managed to coax villagers into forming informal "protection committees", in which each participating family took turns in enforcing the forest restriction.' Over time, the forest regenerated dramatically and, as fodder production increased, a majority of villagers came to favour the scheme, supporting paid watchmen. 'Banskharka is now known to have the best forests in the area, and local people take considerable pride in their accomplishment.' Some neighbouring panchayats have more recently instituted their own forest protection schemes, have established nurseries (with project assistance), and are 'now actively competing with the Banskharka model' (Campbell 1979: 19-20).

The examples so far demonstrate that villagers are willing to pursue conservation in spite of forest nationalisation that effectively disenfranchised them from traditional management and control. They nonetheless embarked on systems of protection and limited harvesting of local forest products without outside support or assistance. In these and other cases, acceptance of restrictions on free and uncontrolled access to the forest is typically resisted in the beginning until positive results and benefits to the community are evident. These examples serve as 'models' of workable community management systems, the 'analysis of which increases our understanding of how community conservation activities can be fostered' (Campbell 1979: 18). Caution is, however, advised, in considering them as fixed formula to be applied indiscriminately in all contexts (Messerschmidt 1981).

In the mid- and late-1970s, new and enlightened forest legislation was promulgated in Nepal,[8] followed by the initiation of several donor-assisted community forestry efforts in the hills and lowlands.[9] The legislation and regulations allow previously nationalised forest tracts to be returned to village management. More recently, the Forestry Master Plan of 1989 has given further impetus and official sanction to local management of community forests by resource-user groups, backed up with technical assistance from professional foresters and developers. Some community forestry and other development projects have, in the meantime, begun building on pre-existing and traditional local resource management systems. It has taken time, however, to convince villagers and foresters alike to work together to design and implement community-based alternatives to uncontrolled deforestation and resource degradation.

Hawkins (1981) noted early in the hill Community Forestry Development Project (CFDP) that: 'The motivation of villagers for forestry activities is high. Before CFDP activities have started it is often difficult to evaluate the level of motivation. Once activities are underway villagers' motivation tends to develop. Forestry is a long term process, it requires several years before plantations and nurseries are a sufficient presence in an area to stimulate people's interest' (Hawkins 1981: 9. See also Arnold and Campbell 1987; Wormald and Messer-schmidt 1986).

Nepal's various government-sponsored community forestry projects have encouraged researchers to examine more closely the nature of traditional management systems. In 1981, Augusta Molnar, an anthropologist, conducted a study in project areas assisted by the United Nations and the World Bank. One case example from her findings will suffice to demonstrate the principle of individual influence followed by diffusion of ideas backed up by community support to continue.

Example 6: Singhana Panchayat private and community forest management systems, Baglung District

Several decades ago, a retired British Gurkha soldier in this community began planting trees on private land and set up a system of selective cutting and fodder collection. About 1961, following his example, neighbouring villagers closed a nearby forest area to grazing and hired forest watchers to prevent poaching or cutting of green trees. More recently, in the early 1970s, the Singhana Panchayat chairman, supported by villagers in his own ward, began to plant a patch of forest modelled on the original system. The villagers are willing to cooperate because they have seen the advantages of careful management. Previous knowledge of rapid depletion of forest resources and devastation of farmland caused by soil erosion 'also created enough concern to encourage village cooperation' (Molnar 1981: 4).

After examining the prevailing characteristics of local panchayats, forest utilisation, and other factors, Molnar notes that certain 'key factors,' such as leadership, available resources, land distribution, factionalism, and proximity to market tend to contribute to the success or failure of traditional forest management systems. She found both group-sponsored and individually-operated systems of managing the forest. The group systems of management involve preservation of existing woodlots or, in some instances, the rehabilitation of degraded forest areas. Historically, she notes, group systems are more prevalent in Western Nepal where they are based on clan, lineage, or village use rights. Individual management systems, on the other hand, appear more commonly in eastern Nepal, where they protect existing trees as well as to plant and transplant new trees or seedlings.

Molnar points out, however, that many group and individual systems have broken down in recent years, as soil erosion and deforestation have become more acute and as management difficulties, due to fodder and fuelwood shortages, have undermined local incentives for conservation (Molnar 1981: 2). The two main reasons are the negative effects of forest nationalisation and the pressures exerted on existing resources by increased population in the hills.

Examination of existing systems of forest management have also been encouraged in other resource development projects. Findings from the Resource Conservation and Utilisation Project (RCUP) illustrate the extent and nature of forest management systems among caste and ethnic groups in the Nepal hills. The following are four representative case examples.

Example 7: Tarke forest management system in Ward 1, Chhoprak Panchayat, Gorkha District

Since 1960, a settlement of 46 Brahmin, Chhetri, and artisan households, adjacent to a small and unfenced mixed deciduous forest in ward 1 of Chhoprak Panchayat, have maintained a watchman-rotation system (*ban palo garne*) on a daily basis. Each household sends a watchman (*pale*) by turn, so that there are regularly two watchmen on duty during the day and two at night. The forest is the source of the village water system, and home to a local tutelary goddess. Use rights to the forest include controlled access for firewood collection, fodder cutting and grazing, and timber for construction and repair of houses. There is no restriction on collecting dead or broken twigs (*jikra*) or on cutting grasses (*ghaas*) for fodder, even by non-participating villagers.

The user group meets annually to assign permits and regulate timing for cutting timber (*kaath*). Fines are levied against households that neglect to send a watchman during their turn and against intruders. Villagers say that they developed this system and maintained it in the 1960s and 1970s, despite forest nationalisation to protect their major resource. The initial and highly visible success of the Tarke Forest protection system has provided a model for the 45 predominantly Brahmin caste households in a nearby community to organise a reforestation and management effort in their own Gaire Forest.

Government foresters persuaded the villagers to turn Tarke Forest over as a Panchayat Protected Forest, as defined in forest legislation. They were promised fencing, reforestation measures, and watchmen. Some aspects of the original management system were retained. However, despite knowledge of pre-existing systems of control, there was minimal participation by the villagers in planning the new Panchayat Protected Forest system. Tarke villagers initially resisted government attempts to put barbed wire fencing around it. Meanwhile, neighbouring Gaire Forest was turned into a Panchayat Protected Forest (Report No. 5, Messerschmidt 1981–4; Shrestha 1982: 5–7).

Example 8: Big Pine protected forest, Ghatan Panchayat, Myagdi District

The predominantly Chhetri villagers of Galeswor attribute a local pioneer or visionary (*aguwa*), named Bala Badra Baniya Chhetri, with the development of their forest protection system approximately three generations ago. After fires which destroyed earlier natural forests in the area, this man rallied his neighbours to fence approximately 75 ha of land that had little value to agriculture, to allow it to regenerate as a pine forest. In time, the renewed forest was opened to controlled cutting of dead and fallen trees, for a small fee. The fees, plus small annual donations of grain from neighbouring households, paid for the watchman's services. The watchman was responsible for keeping the forest paths clear of pine litter and rallying villagers' help in the event of fire.

Despite forest nationalisation, this traditional management system was maintained until the 1970s, when the Department of Forests came under pressure to sell timber cutting permits to builders in the nearby district town of Beni. Local leaders, forestry officers, and American Peace Corps volunteers assigned to the RCUP project have been working on the management plans of the Panchayat Protected Forest to incorporate elements of the traditional management system (Field Report No. 7, Messerschmidt 1981–4).

Example 9: Forest management in Piple and Rakhu-Bhagwati Panchayats Myagdi District

Four small local forests in these two adjacent panchayats are managed by traditional protection systems, which includes planting and fencing by user group members and the employment of a forest watchman (*ban pale*). Each watchman is chosen from among the poorer families. A watchman's duties are to patrol the forest and to control access to firewood, building material, and fodder, according to rules set by the separate forest-user group committees. 'Typically, the rules allow for the collection of fodder once each year in the winter during the most critical fodder crisis period, cutting of thatch (khar) once each year during the festival time of Dasain in October and the cutting of wood for house construction on occasion. Only those households which are paid-up members of the village forest protection committee are allowed to use the forest in these controlled ways.' Fines are levied by the user group in the event of violations. A typical method of payment is for each user household to donate annually a specified amount of grain to the watchman. In one recorded example, the watchman collects seven *man* (about 310 kg) of grain annually, a boost to his household economy (Pandley 1983).

Example 10: Ramjang protected forest, Lete Panchayat, Mustang District

In the 1960s, the predominantly Thakali ethnic villagers of Ghasa and vicinity, in wards 1, 2, and 3 of Lete Panchayat, recognised that their local pine forest was rapidly being depleted by over-cutting, indiscriminate grazing, and general abuse. They closed off approximately five ha to allow regeneration. Access is controlled and the forest is patrolled by members of the community forest committee. Since 1974, access to sheep and goats has been strictly forbidden, although cattle, buffalo, horses and pack mules are allowed to graze. Cutting fuelwood and building materials by individuals is prohibited, although poles and timber may be cut for public use (*e.g.* school construction, bridge repair) by permission of the committee. Fines are levied by a panchayat committee for illegal entry or fuelwood cutting. The Mustang District Forest Office regulates the thinning of the forest and will allow permit cutting for large timber as soon as the second growth matures.

Annually, in mid-winter, each household is required to assist in debris and litter collection. Two persons from each of approximately 50 households are allowed to harvest five large basket-loads of pine needles and litter daily, over a nine- to ten-day period. This cuts down on the risk of forest fires, and the needles provide bedding for cattle. The forest is also home for a tutelary deity.

It was recommended that a management plan be prepared for designation of this forest as a Panchayat Protected Forest, but villagers have expressed concern that by changing their traditional management practices, they would lose control. This is a residual suspicion based on experiences regarding forest nationalisation and a distrust of the motives of government forestry personnel (Field Report No. 9, Messerschmidt 1981–4).

Conclusions

The examples presented above are selective. They represent a much wider universe of local group-managed forest resource management systems. They demonstrate the wealth and health of pre-existing and contemporary management actions with which the Himalayan villagers are familiar and, ultimately, most comfortable. They show the extent to which villagers are willing to go, provided that they are seriously concerned about the resource (for which there is considerable evidence), and are enabled and encouraged to do so (as, for example, by the Nepal government's commitment to community forestry). They also indicate to the sensitive developer some types of local individual and group commitments to the management of a resource upon which villagers depend so greatly for their livelihood and sustenance. This suggests that, far from display-ing little or no future orientation as argued by Rieger (1979), hill farmers fre-quently display a profound appreciation for the future.

Forest and other resource management systems quietly pursued in the moun-tain villages seem to be more prevalent than previously known or appreciated. However, many of the pre-existing individual or communal systems of forest management and user group cooperation in the Himalayas were developed under very different circumstances than exist today. Any use of such pre-exist-ing strategies must take current conditions into account. The resource crisis of today reflects a tremendous growth in population over the last half century. New economic opportunities brought about by the opening of new markets, the building of roads and improved transport and communication systems, new forms of off-farm employment, mass migration and organisation also create strains and put pressures on natural resources. Therefore, this calls for some outside help.

Changes, however, may lead to further alienation of the rural people from their traditions and may tend to cause further breakdown of existing manage-ment practices, unless the development interventions build on existing resource management systems. Success in addressing forest development and resource management depends on efforts that reflect continuity with and are guided by pre-existing forms of management, indigenous knowledge, local cooperation and popular participation.

In this study, I have argued the importance of local people's involvement in forestry development activities, grounding the observations in case examples and the findings of other investigators. But, while many foresters and social sci-entists agree that traditional systems of resource management have great promise for Nepal, voices of dissent and doom are still heard. Wallace (1987: 13) has recently written, for example, in *Community Forestry in Nepal: Too little, too late?*, arguing that existing forestry programs in Nepal 'just do not go far enough and are unable to keep up with the pace of deforestation.' The crisis, he says, is steadily growing, for which much more must be done and soon, if the Nepalese are to avoid the disaster of treelessness. Although Wallace expressed little faith in community forestry, he discusses several possible solutions, includ-ing the promotion of private planting and leasehold arrangements while expressing little faith in community forestry *per se*. But is Wallace asking the right question? Is this 'too-little-too-late' hypothesis of disaster accurate or even relevant? Does the problem lie with the concept and practice of community forestry?

In a study which contrasts greatly with Wallace's negative perspective, Gilmour (1987) points out that many critics and doomsayers have simply not seen the trees for the forest. Nor are the statistics they usually cite very trust-worthy. Even the definition of a 'forest' is controversial. Gilmour maintains that there are far more trees and a much stronger tradition of tree stewardship in the villages than many investigators have previously considered or attempted to document. The work of Gilmour (1987) and his colleagues in the Nepal–Aus-tralia Community Forestry Project (Gilmour, King and Fisher 1987; Griffin 1988; Malla and Fisher 1987) supports my contention in this study that the answer to Nepal's forestry crisis – if that is what it is – lies in re-engaging the people in the planning and implementation of forestry initiatives and in reconsidering in positive and progressive ways the socioeconomic facts and circumstances surrounding resource management in Nepal (see Messerschmidt 1988).

Re-engagement has to occur on both the individual or private level, as well as on the user group and community level. Fortunately, there are strong indications that this is happening; the lessons learned from recent experience under the community forestry initiatives with user group/community management and private plantings are being heeded. They are reflected, for example, in the new Forestry Master Plan of 1989 which strongly encourages decentralisation of forestry initiatives and more power and voice at the local community and district levels.

It can be said that the seeds to success in Nepal forestry are literally in the hands of the rural people, in the form of individual and indigenous knowledge and traditional management systems. They may need modification to meet contemporary and future circumstances and technical assistance and outside resources from professional foresters and development programs to be fully used. But they are there, like a great encyclopedia of practical experience waiting to be opened, studied, and put to work. Raising alarms of pending disaster does little more than point to the problem. Actively working to engage the local people in pragmatic actions allows a more positive approach to solutions. The international forester, Jack Westoby (1987: ix) said it all back in 1967: 'Forestry is not about trees, it is about people. And it is about trees only insofar as trees serve the needs of people'.

Notes

1. This article is a revised and shorted version of a 1984 monograph entitled *Using Human Resources in Natural Resource Managements: Innovations in Himalayan Development* prepared for the International Centre for Integrated Mountain Development in Kathmandu (ICIMOD Watershed Management Working Paper No. I/l). The author thanks the ICIMOD Director, Colin Rosser, and his staff for a congenial and inspiring atmosphere in which to work. Special thanks for their comments on this or earlier versions of the paper go to Binayak Badra, Deepak Bajracharya, Hikmat Bista, J. Gabriel Campbell, S. R. Chalise, John Cool, Anis Dani, Mark Fritzler, Jack Ives, and K. Panday.
2. The original work on which this article is based also included examples of indigenous systems of irrigation and drinking water scheme management (Messerschmidt 1984). For additional examples, see also Messerschmidt (1986, 1987).
3. Since this chapter was written and submitted for publication, two things have occurred in Nepal which encourage the people-centred approach espoused here. First, in 1989 His Majesty's Government formally promulgated the *Master Plan for the Forestry Sector*, Nepal (Nepal 1989). In the plan, fully 46 per cent of the energies and budget over the next two decades is devoted to community and private forestry. Community forestry in Nepal is now built upon the concept of the 'user group' as the vehicle for local resource management. Second, in 1990, Nepal underwent a relatively peaceful democratic revolution. Since then, participatory people-centred approaches to forestry, and to development in general, have been greatly enhanced. Readers should note that at that time, the former party-less *panchayat* form of government in Nepal was changed to a multi-party representative form. All references to the earlier form of government and development should be seen in their historic perspective.
4. Perhaps, a more precise term for the Indian government initiative is 'degraded land

development' instead of wasteland development. What is underutilised or 'waste' land in government foresters' eyes is not much wasted, but is frequently quite well utilised, even over-utilised, by local people (Subedi *et al.* 1992).

5. Mass wasting refers to the large-scale movement of fractured rock and other materials, including soil from a slope, as compared with soil erosion which refers principally to loss of topsoil due to rainfall or wind. Accelerated soil erosion is defined as that induced by human impact to the environment, as compared with natural or geologically-induced erosion and mass wasting (Carson 1985: 1).

6. Between 1980 and 1985, nearly three million tree seedlings from CFDP nurseries were planted by private initiative in the hill districts of the project – more than 300 per cent over the private planting target. A project report states that 'Seedling production is the most successful activity within the project.... People are now clearly aware of the project activities' (CFDP 1985: 10).

7. Not all observers agree that collective management has been so beneficial to resource conservation. Schroeder (1985: 39) states to the contrary, for example, that 'Communal management has been ineffective in conserving the agricultural land, and forest, pasture and waste land resources in Nepal.'

8. See the National Forest Law of 1976 and the Panchayat Protected Forest Rules of 1978 (amended 1980). The effect of the regulations are discussed in Arnold and Campbell (1987) and Messerschmidt (1987). Several categories of community forest were designated in this legislation. One category, called 'Panchayat Protected Forest' (PPF) was comprised of previously nationalised degraded forest tracts. Village Panchayat communities and 'user groups' could opt to restore and manage PPFs locally, through local forest committees (*ban samiti*). A Village Panchayat (*gaun panchaayat*) was the smallest unit of government in Nepal, comprising one or more villages, a population of between 3000 and 6000 inhabitants, in an area approximately 1000 to 6000 ha (Arnold and Campbell 1987; Manandhar 1982). Each Village Panchayat was divided into nine wards. In 1990, the Panchayat system of local government was changed. Now each former *gaun panchayat* is called a *gaun bikas samiti* (village development committee) and a Panchayat Forest is now called a *samiti ban* (Community Forest). (See note 3).

9. All subsequent donor-assisted and Nepal government-sponsored forestry projects reflect the progressive legislation of the 1970s. The largest of the donor-assisted projects of the early 1980s was Community Forestry Project (CFDP), housed in the Community Forestry and Afforestation Division of the Department of Forest, co-funded by the United Nations Development Programme (UNDP) and the World Bank and implemented by the United Nations Food and Agriculture Organisation (FAO). Other projects include the Nepal–Australia Community Forestry Project, the United States-assisted Resource Conservation and Utilisation Project and Rapti Integrated Rural Development Project, the German and Swiss government-assisted Tinau Watershed Development Project and the UNDP-, World Bank- and FAO-assisted Terai Community Forestry Development Project. These same donor agencies and others have continued in the spirit of the new forest policy to design community-oriented, user groups based forestry projects for implementation from the late 1980s well into the twenty-first century.

18. Indigenous Systems of Natural Resource Management among Pastoralists of Arid and Semi-arid Africa

MARYAM NIAMIR

Introduction

THROUGHOUT THE CENTURIES, pastoral societies have developed a diverse set of management systems, ranging from simple to complex, to coordinate and regulate the actions of individual members. These systems are based on an intimate and intricate knowledge of their physical and social environment. Their main objective is to maximise production in the long run while minimising risk. The simplest pastoral system is based on seasonal mobility between wet and dry season pastures (transhumance) that is regulated by climatic variability, the needs of their animals, and basic informal rules of occupation and tenure. The free-moving, chaotic 'nomad' is a myth. The most complex system regulates these movements by strict formal schedules, restrictions on numbers and types of animals, reserving or deferring pastures, assigning members to particular pastures and controlling the amount of time spent in one pasture. Thus, the organisational complexity varies greatly between different pastoral groups.

Although individual pastoral societies in Africa have been the object of numerous studies in this century, no systematic effort has yet been made to amalgamate the information to allow an analysis of the importance of indigenous natural resource management systems for the development process. This article is based on a study carried out for and published by the Food and Agriculture Organisation (FAO) of the United Nations that attempts to answer such a need (Niamir 1990). The study considers a wide range of issues centred around natural resource management, including environmental knowledge and management techniques, but only the institutional aspects are summarised here. These will be considered under three headings: informal and formal social controls over rangeland utilisation; natural resource tenure; and means of enforcement of rules and regulations.

Social controls on range use

Formal rules generally tend to be enshrined in communal codes and traditions which are recognised by all members of the group. These rights and regulations coordinate the actions of individual members at several organisational levels: the herding unit, a group of herding units, and the entire tribe. Many herding units have clear cut internal organisations for assigning chores and making communal decisions. These include range scouts, a headman and a council of elders, and regular daily or weekly meetings among all household heads.

Almost all pastoral groups place scouts ahead of the herd to monitor the range and to evaluate its quality, quantity and suitability for livestock. They will also report on disease, presence of other herds, and other information necessary for communal decisions. Some examples are the Rufa'a al-Hoi of Eastern Sudan (Ahmed, forthcoming: 47), the Somali nomads (Behnke and Kerven 1984: 39), and the Wodaabe of Nigeria, where the scouts are on horseback (Stenning 1959: 217).

Communal decisions are usually taken by a council of elders headed by a chief or elder statesman. The chief is often elected on the basis of his success in herd management, which is evident in the large number of livestock that he has (Wilson 1986: 33). But the chief has to have other important qualities. For example, the Dinka say that their elected headman has to be an arbiter, chairman, planner and enforcer of decisions. He appoints a deputy who manages daily affairs, such as assigning communal herding and other chores (McDermott and Ngor 1983: 11–13).

Communal meetings can also have different formats. For example, among the Wodaabe herding unit, an individual leader chairs the twice-daily council in which the information supplied by scouts are discussed and decisions on communal movements are made. Although the Wodaabe elders are respected and listened to, it is the opinion of young adults – the actual herders – which carries the most weight (Maliki *et al.* 1984: 258, 293, 308). In the Maasai herding unit there is no individual leader but a council of elders, who in the course of daily public meetings decide on range management strategies, and assign duties to herders and their supervisors (Jacobs 1980: 286).

Even though the herding unit is an organisation for communal decision making, each individual household is basically free to disagree with the decisions and leave the herding unit for other units. Such fluidity has been observed for example among the Dinka of Kongor Rural Council (McDermott and Ngor 1983: 13). Among the Turkana, detailed strategic decisions are made by each household, which allows them to make immediate responses to ecological and social change, but they follow the overall communal strategies agreed upon by the herding unit (Gulliver 1975: 372; McCabe 1983: 121). Such fluidity exists in principle, but in practice, most pastoralists prefer to use the areas they are familiar with and to stay close to relatives and friends. Thus, membership in the same herding unit and in rangeland use may be fluid in the short run but is fairly continuous in the long run. This fluidity may have to be mirrored by new structures, such as herder's associations and group ranches.

Herding units will at times join together into larger cooperating groups. This usually occurs in favourable seasons, and for sociocultural reasons, and a coordinating council made up of the elders of each herding unit will form to make communal decisions. These social gatherings are usually subordinate to ecological considerations, since large ceremonies are held only when and where there is enough pasture and water to support all attendants for the days required. This phenomena has been reported among the Somali (Behnke and Kerven 1984: 199), the Wodaabe (Stenning 1959: 53; Maliki *et al.* 1984: 302) and the Maasai (Jacobs 1980: 286).

Most herding units follow communal decisions laid down by a main tribal chief either on a year-round basis, or at specific times and places. For example, sets of laws and procedures (unfortunately not specified by the authors) have been reported for the Twareg of Gourma, the Berti of Sudan (Sandford 1984: 9), and the Somali (Rabeh 1984: 59). The council of tribal elders of the Il Chamus of Kenya enforces the grazing controls and coordinates movements of herding units through the members of the 18–30 year old male age set (Little and Brokensha 1987: 200). The Berbers of Morocco have a 'Chief of Grass' who is selected by the council of elders, and who makes final decisions concerning common grazing, such as the timing and location of movements, deferring grazing, and granting permission to outsiders (Artz *et al.* 1986). Among the Tswana, major decisions affecting a village and its several herding units, including allocation of grazing land, are made at the *kgotla* or public meeting (Schapera 1940: 72), and an overseer appointed by the chief is responsible for checking conditions of the rangeland assigned to each section, conferring with chiefs to move livestock if an area becomes overstocked, and allocating well digging sites and cattle posts according to a set of rules designed to avoid overgrazing (Devitt 1982: 18).

Within a pastoral group's territory, certain areas are often totally protected or reserved for certain periods of the year. These reserves may be exceptions rather than the rule in Sub-Saharan Africa (Sandford 1984: 6), but more pastoralists have reserves than was previously thought. Although no record was found of permanent range exclosure, many pastoral groups have temporary range reserves aimed at preserving forage for the dry season or drought years, preventing crop expansion, protecting timber, and regenerating degraded areas. The boundaries of the reserves follow prominent landscape features or are marked, like those of the Kikuyu (Middleton and Kershaw 1972: 52). Among the Northern Somali (Cerulli 1959 cited in Swift 1977: 284) as well as the Pokot (Schneider 1959 cited in Ware 1977: 187), the local chiefs could impose penalties on those who illegally entered the dry season reserves.

Apart from general all-year regulations, some social controls also are placed on certain times and places. The most renowned example is probably that of the Dina Code of the Macina Fulani. This Code regulated the movements of 15 Fulani and three Twareg clans into and out of the delta zone of the Niger River (Imperato 1972: 63). Before all herds and flocks could re-enter the delta in the early dry season, they would have to congregate at the border of the delta, waiting for the leader to permit them to cross (Wagenaar *et al.* 1986: 4). Other less well-known regulations also exist. For example, among the Tallensi of North-eastern Ghana/Southeastern Burkina Faso, only the chief has the right to set fire to bushland because of the danger of accidents (Fortes 1940: 259). Among the Rufa'a al-Hoi of Sudan, the tribal chief and his deputy confer with the sheikhs of the herding camps in order to coordinate the movement south at the end of rains. The coordinated movement is designed to avoid conflicts with the sedentary population and allow the farmers to finish harvesting the crops (Ahmed n.d.: 49). Finally, the Lozi King of Western Zambia would decide the date when cattle and people would have to leave the flooded area for higher ground (Gluckman 1951: 11).

Coordination among herding units occurs in most but not all cases. An exception is the Arab pastoralists of Central Chad, whose basic herding unit is made up of about 20 families. When these herding units join together in the rainy season, there is no higher level committee or cooperation in range management (Gilg 1963: 504).

In almost all cases, there is passive coordination, or 'choreography' of movements, where no formal agreements are made between tribes but where coordinated movements result from the wish to avoid other tribes, or seasonal niche specialisation due to differences in breeds and types of animals. Good examples are the Messeriya, Dinka, and Nuer of the Sudan (Niamir 1982), the Moors and Fulani of Western Africa, and the Fulani and Rufa'a al-Hoi of the Sudan (Ahmed, forthcoming: 54).

Informal rules, or principles of common sense, can be found among all pastoralists. Some rules tend to be common to all groups, such as 'first come, first served'. Pastoralists tend to avoid areas already in use, and will keep at a certain distance of others, although studies tend to be vague about what this minimum distance is, and how it varies with resource stress. In addition, they will avoid areas just recently vacated by others, but the time allowed to elapse before a campsite or pasture is reoccupied again varies among the groups.

A few groups have formal organisations for controlling and managing communal wells. Among the Wodaabe of Niger, wells are owned by lineage segments, but others are allowed to use them according to strict rules. In addition, dry season camps are dispersed and as far away as 70 km from the well, and are moved every 20–30 days around the well to avoid overgrazing (Maliki *et al.* 1984: 266). The Northern Somali manage communal wells through an elected committee of 3–20 people. The members of the committee are the water managers, and allocate water to the community and guests, guard the well, enforce and devise rules of use, charge fees if any, and maintain the well (Putman 1984: 169).

Each Borana clan of Southern Ethiopia has an elected water manager who supervises the well according to Borana laws. A council of elders supervises the water manager, and appoints a caretaker if he is temporarily absent. The users of the well also form a council and have ultimate authority over the water manager and the council of elders. A 'father of the watering order' appointed by the user council regulates daily use of the well by appointing two men to coordinate the action of the line of men and women (also chosen by the father of order) who draw water with containers and pass it along to a basin. This line can be 15–20 persons long. The basins are plastered with clay every morning, and the well maintained after every rainy season (Helland 1982: 251–2).

With the advent of deep, mechanised boreholes, the traditional systems for well management have been disrupted mainly because of the confusion in well ownership. Some groups actually prefer to return to their traditional wide-diameter wells. For example, the Rendille of Kenya prefer large diameter wells because they do not break down and have more minerals than boreholes (Oba 1985). A survey by the *Service de l'Animation* of Niger in 1972 among the Twareg, Fulani and Arabs showed that they prefer cemented wide-diameter wells to boreholes, because the former limit overstocking, are easier to learn about and maintain, and cause less weight loss in animals (since the rangelands are not overgrazed) (Monod 1975: 77).

These formal and informal rules are important in determining the principles that govern every-day decisions made by the herders. Their exercise results in an avoidance of the 'tragedy of the commons' syndrome. Unfortunately not enough studies have been done on this aspect, and its neglect has enhanced the myth of irrationality and irregularity among pastoralists. In addition, many of the rules, especially formal ones, are in the process of being destroyed or neglected. The causes are numerous, for example, population growth, crop expansion into rangelands, central government interventions into local political systems, and changes in local land tenure.

Natural resource tenure

The ownership of natural resources (land, water, trees, other wild plants and wildlife) has been the subject of many studies in recent years. These have helped create an awareness of the importance of ownership, in whatever form, for natural resource management. Resource tenure can be defined as the full and exclusive ownership of resources, or the right to use them without owning it (usufruct), or something between the two. Ownership includes the right to use the resource, and the right to determine the extent and nature of use by others. Resources can be individually or communally owned. Communal tenure implies that the enjoyment of rights is not exclusive to one individual, but is shared collectively by a community (Clauson 1953: 1). Not all types of tenure are communal, and not all resources are regulated by the same rights.

Rangeland tenure

One of the more enduring myths of our time has been that of the 'tragedy of the commons' first propounded by Hardin (1968). In its simplest form, it states that when land is communally owned, each individual has no incentive to reduce and restrict his use of it, thus leading inevitably to abuse of the resources. This concept was falsely attributed to communal property when it really refers to open access lands, *i.e.* where there are no communal and social controls over the land (Ciriacy-Wintrup and Bishop 1975: 713–27; Runge 1986: 626).

In most traditional systems all lands were claimed either privately or communally. The concept of 'vacant,' open access or unclaimed land has been introduced by colonial governments, and applied especially to range and forestlands, since maps of these areas were often based on surveys done only in one season, missing the pastoralists who were on transhumance (Noronha and Lethem 1983: 12). Some areas did appear to be vacant, in so far as there were no sustained claims to them, but they often were considered to be in the sphere of influence of certain tribes, or were the object of expansion and warfare between neighbouring tribes. For example the Twareg and Fulani of Northern Burkina Faso, in addition to having areas definitely divided between them, were continuously disputing rights to borderline areas (Barral and Benoit 1977: 103).

In general, natural resources are usually owned by the highest social level (*e.g.* tribe or kingdom) recognised in the group, and are then allocated down the hierarchy to lower levels of social organisation through intricate systems of distribution. At a certain sociopolitical level in the hierarchy natural resources are no longer distributed and are owned and/or controlled by the members of that level. This lowest sociopolitical level can be individual or communal and appears to vary considerably among pastoral groups, at least as far as transit routes and rangelands are concerned. The few records found on transit routes show that the lowest level can be subtribes, as among the Twareg of Niger (FAO 1972: 21) and Quaddai of Chad (Novikoff 1976: 57), lineages, as among the Bor Dinka of Kongor (Ahmed *et al.* 1976: 58), or herding groups. An example of the latter are the Arab pastoralists of Central Chad (such as the Khozam, Ouled Himet and Ouled Zioud.) where the herding units control transit routes which are several kilometres wide and include water points and markets (Gilg 1963: 502).

Some authors have generalised that rangelands (as distinct from transit routes) are usually allocated at the tribal or subtribal level, while water rights are at the clan or subclan level, because the latter require regular repair, are consistently used, and are more fiercely competed for (Hjort 1976a: 49). However, the records examined here show that rangelands are divided among so many different types of lower social units that it is impossible to make a generalisation. These levels can be kinship units (*e.g.* tribe, subtribe, segment and clan down to extended households and individual nuclear families), geographical and/or political associations, and contractual agreements with local land-owning farmers (Table 18.1). In almost all cases, the highest social level (*e.g.* tribe) retains formal ownership of the land, giving only rights of usufruct to the lower levels. In some cases, the tribe can theoretically change the land distribution pattern, but in most cases, the rights of the lower levels are known, constant, inalienable, and based on historical precedence.

Table 18.1: Examples of rangeland tenure among pastoralists in Africa

Type of tenure structure	Lowest socio-political level	Pastoral or agropastoral group
Kinship	Tribe	Lozi, Ila
	Sub-tribe	Hottentot, Shona
	Section	Dinka, Turkana, Nuer, Ait Ben Yacoub
	Clan	Samburu, Dorobo, Twareg, Zaghawa
	Lineage	Madi, Sere, Luo, Kikuyu, Mbeere
	Herding unit	Mbanderu Herero, Pokot, Maasai
	Household	Afar, Kasena, Ngwato Tswana, Kamba
Geo-political		Fulani, Lahawin, Ngoni
Contractual		Tonga/Twa, Fulani/Mossi, Fulani/Hausa

A few groups appear to recognise no formal tenure of rangelands. However, it is hard to tell whether the studies are referring to rights held at a level below the tribe, or to the existence of any kind of tenure. According to these studies, land use appears to be regulated on the basis of ownership of wells, such as among the pastoralists living west of the White Nile River in Sudan (Horowitz and Badi 1981: 19), and the Kel Adrar Twareg of Kidal (Mali) (Swift 1988: 8). In cases where the pastoralists tend to be recent arrivals to an area, rights to land are regulated by informal rules such as precedence and 'first come, first served', such as among the Twareg, Bella and Fulani of Northeastern Burkina Faso (Barral 1967: 28). In the case of the long-established Baggara and Kababish of Sudan, if there is not enough land, a strong local leader may try to arbitrate and assign rights, or even lots may be drawn, or ultimately wars will be fought, but these rights can be temporary (yearly) or permanent (Artz, unpublished: 5).

Many tribal territories are distinct, with boundaries often following prominent topographical features, and can be delimited precisely on maps. Examples can be found among the Toubou of Northern Chad (Gallais 1975: 71), the Shona (Holleman 1951: 367), and the Ait Ben Yacoub Berbers (Artz *et al.* 1986). However, in some cases the boundaries can be vague, except when they cover important points (wells, salt licks and ponds), such as among the Twareg of Niger (Gallais 1975: 71). In the case of the Samburu and Rendille, there is a deliberate, symbiotic overlap in territorial boundaries (Spencer 1965). The same kind of overlap can occur within a tribe. For example, among the Twareg, because of the quasi-feudal system and the vertical integration of castes, the territory of clans of the same caste and status do not overlap and are well separated, but the terrain of different castes do (Gallais 1975: 72). Even if the boundaries are clearly delimited and recognised, many groups tolerate a certain amount of trespass in either direction (Artz *et al.* 1986).

Tenure of trees, water and other resources

The ownership of trees on rangeland, like that on farmland, does not necessarily follow the same tenure patterns as that of the range itself. In other words, land tenure is not necessarily the same as tree tenure (Weinstock and Vergara 1987: 312). Very little has been written on the tree rights of pastoralists. In most cases each pastoralist is free to use any tree within the territory that he has grazing rights to. For example among the Shona of Zimbabwe, the use of trees is communal within the sub-tribe, but priority is given to the current user (Holleman 1951: 370). There are a few recorded cases of tree tenure at the family level. For example, among the Northern Turkana, both water and certain fruit and browse trees on the *ere* (or household's land) are exclusive to the household and passed down to sons (Barrow 1988: 4; Storas, unpublished: 15)). The Suiei Dorobo of Kenya recognise individual, exclusive, ownership of valuable trees in the bushland (Spencer 1965: 283). In some cases, ownership of trees in the bush may be *de facto*, not *de jure*. For example, the Fulani of Northern Senegal, say that trees in the immediate vicinity of a homestead 'belong' to the household (Diop 1987: 76).

The ownership of water points among pastoralists depends on the type of point. Natural ponds tend to belong to the social unit that owns the rangeland, be it tribe, section or clan. For example, use of natural ponds and springs on Jie and Turkana Territory is open to all members of the tribe on a 'first come, first served' basis (Gulliver 1970: 37). The Borana of Southern Ethiopia distinguish between two types of natural points: (1) *lola* or rainy season points are open to all unless they are close to settlements, in which case the local people have priority, and (2) *hara* or larger ponds that hold water into (but not all of) the dry season, and may be improved, belong to the clan (Helland 1982: 249). The volcanic mineral springs of Northern Cameroon are owned by different Fulani clans. The clan leaders have complete authority over their use, and will often close the springs temporarily. They also use the time when people use the springs to charge traditional taxes (Boutrais 1974: 162).

The ownership of wells is usually based on kinship units, but can also be geographical and/or political units, or a mixture of tenure types. The particular system often depends on the type of well (deep or shallow) and the amount of labour that is required to construct and maintain it. There is no record of tenure of wells at the higher sociopolitical levels, such as tribe or subtribe. Most wells are owned by subsections and clans, such as among the Maasai (Jacobs 1980: 284), the Zaghawa (Tubiana and Tubiana 1977: 46), and the Borana (Helland 1982: 250). However, in practice at least among the Borana, access to a well does not necessarily depend on clan membership, but on complex political negotiations based on contribution of human resources for the digging and maintenance of wells (Helland 1978: 80). Individual or household ownership of wells is also quite common, such as among the Jie and Turkana (Gulliver 1970: 37), the Twareg, Bella and Fulani of Northern Burkina Faso (Barral 1967: 28), and the Wodaabe Fulani of Niger (Sutter 1978: 29).

In many cases wells are owned by a mixture of tenure types. Deep wells dug through rock, or wells that need considerable money for structural support materials, are owned by larger groupings, such as clans and lineages among the Somali (Lewis 1961: 169; Putman 1984: 34–53), and villages or wards among the Bambara (Toulmin 1983: 10–12), whereas shallow wells dug through sand are owned by smaller groups.

As long as wells are owned by large social units the leaders can exert control over the number of wells that can be constructed in an area. When the wells are owned by a family or extended household then there is seemingly no system for regulating the spatial distribution of wells – men own the wells but not the aquifer. However, certain informal rules regulate the distance between wells, such as the desire to avoid intermingling of herds, and the fact that deep wells require considerable labour and will not be constructed by someone unless he is a regular user of the area.

The ownership of other resources, such as wildlife, wild cereals, fisheries and minerals, is usually open to all members within the land owned by the social unit. However, in a few cases, certain rules have been developed. Among the Lele of Western Burkina Faso, all members of the tribe are free to graze and cultivate in tribal lands without seeking permission, but its wildlife resources are owned by particular villages and any outsider, even a Lele, cannot hunt without permission (Barral 1968: 39). Although grazing land among the Suiei Dorobo is owned at the clan and subclan levels, each individual owns the trees and surrounding land that he uses for his beekeeping activities (Spencer 1965: 283).

Those pastoral groups that rely heavily on wild cereal gathering also have some form of tenure of the cereal growing areas. For example, the Zaghawa divide these areas among villages based on the rights of precedence first established by ancestors. Within each village, a woman does not have exclusive formal title to a cereal gathering area, but because of sustained use in the same spot every year, she has priority (Tubiana 1969: 61). The Teda of Tibetsi, divide the wadis where wild grains grow each year among the clans. There is no permanent continuity as among the Zaghawa, but there is more ritual and communal oversight (Tubiana and Tubiana 1977: 18).

In other cases, the tenure of land is different than the ownership of the wild cereals. For example, among the Twareg of Niger, rights to the harvest of *Panicum laetum* for food belongs to the household, groups or fractions that own the land, but *Cenchrus biflorus* grains can be harvested by anyone anywhere (Gallais 1975: 51), perhaps because the latter is more abundant and at the same time less valuable. The Tonga have no legal rights to honey or wild plants found on their private farmland (Colson 1951: 120).

There is usually no tenure associated with the harvesting of thatch for roofing. But in one case, that of the Tiv of Northern Nigeria, thatching grass can only come from one's fallow field (Bohannan 1954: 41). Finally, although resources may be open to all members of the social unit, not everyone has equal rights. In some cases, chiefs and kings tend to have priority. For example among the Tallensi of Northeastern Ghana/Southeastern Burkina Faso, all big fish and special portions of hunted or dead wildlife go first to the chief, then to the hunter. All stray animals, brass and copper found in the bush or farmland are also given to the chief (Fortes 1940: 258).

Analysis

Ownership and actual use are not necessarily synonymous. Whether the resources owned by a social unit will be used by its members depends on several factors. In the first place, although theoretically the land belongs to the social unit, a member's rights to its resources are based on continual exercise of those rights. If any area is abandoned then it reverts to the communal property of the social unit and can be used by any other member. Most people prefer to remain on the land they have come to know best, thus they tend to continuously occupy, and manage an area as if they owned it. Second, an area may belong to the social unit, but in any given year, only a small proportion of the members will actually use it, because of distance, availability of alternative resources and areas and changing needs. Thus, the actual pressure on the resources is lower than would be expected.

Ownership of resources exists and is recognised by neighbouring tribes, but in the absence of legal titles and/or formal agreements among tribes, it has to be continuously exercised and defended against intruders or usurpers. The degree of control over the resources depends on various factors. One is the value of the resource and the ease with which it is obtained. Second, rights are more strongly exercised and defended where the resources are more frequently utilised. This is especially evident in the recognition of a home territory around settlements. Third, control over territories depends on the political power of tribes, their relationships with neighbouring tribes, and their internal social organisation. Wars and raids force pastoralists to have tighter control over their territory, and may have resulted in more protection of the environment.

Finally, political alliances play an important part in determining grazing rights and land tenure. Good relations are maintained through paying tributes, taxes, and/or gifts to the local people. Intra-tribal boundaries are often more diffuse than inter-tribal ones, and the actual use of a piece of land will depend on the relations between neighbouring social units, and the degree to which the sociopolitical hierarchy can enforce rules. However, most pastoralists using or even seeking permission to use an area, will not do so if they know that they have bad relations and are likely to be refused access.

Because of the high variability of resources, every pastoralist will find that he has to enter another's territory sometime during his career. In most cases, outsiders must first ask permission, which is usually given when there are good relations with them, their livestock do not have contagious diseases, and there is ample forage and water for everyone. In times of stress, permission is rarely refused, but is accompanied by a tacit agreement that the outsider will leave as soon as he can. In some cases dues or fees have to be paid, or human resource contributed to the maintenance of wells and other improvements.

Means of enforcement of rules

Most pastoral groups do not have an internal police force, which raises the question of how the rules and regulations, discussed in the previous section, are maintained and enforced. Some of the rules on land use are so fundamental, that they appear to be taken for granted as inviolable, and are widely respected by all groups. These fundamental rules are 'first come, first served', rights of historical precedence, and rights of continual occupancy. These rules collectively can be described as a 'fairness ethic', and do not require formal enforcement since they are embodied in the moral culture of all groups, for example as shown by the Turkana (Storas, unpublished: 6), and the Fulani of Yatenga (Benoit 1979: 60). Their violation, when it does occur, is generally resolved by fights or wars.

More complicated rules require some form of informal or formal law enforcement procedure. Informal procedures are part of the social fabric of pastoral societies, where the kinship system and the rules and obligations set up by the culture provide the stabilising force. 'Rights must be respected, duties performed, the sentiments binding the members upheld, or else the social order would be so insecure that the material needs of existence could no longer be satisfied' (Fortes and Evans-Pritchard 1940: 14 and 20). The power of local traditions is so strong that no one would even dream of breaking them (Draz 1978: 101). Social ostracism is a powerful tool used by society to keep its members in line, and includes social rebuke, shame, or different degrees of social isolation. The society also uses praise and social rewards to reinforce positive actions. The belief in and use of curses can be a powerful tool for ensuring adherence to rules. In addition, rules of reciprocal obligations are daily reinforcers of regulations concerning tenure, consumption and protection of natural resources. Once the social order and the moral culture are destroyed, these social enforcement rules lose most if not all of their power.

Although rules and regulations exist in each group, they are rarely explicit, and need to be interpreted to fit each situation. Except for serious disputes which end up in front of traditional judges and courts, most rules are interpreted on a daily basis by the people involved, with the goal of establishing consensus among the parties. For example, the Turkana have general rules limiting access to certain pastures, but there is constant argument about where and when to apply these limitations, and who should apply them. They will use verbal persuasion and elaborate rhetorical arguments in order to influence communal agreement.

They often rely on arguments that stress the singularity of the situation to convince others of the need for change in the rules (Storas, unpublished: 3–4). Not all pastoral groups maintain such flexibility and individualism in the application of laws. Some, such as the Ait Ben Yacoub of Morocco, rigorously enforce the decisions laid down by the council and chief of grass (Artz *et al.* 1986). Another form of informal law enforcement procedure is the traditional relationship between the people and their leaders. In most cases, the political hierarchy is accountable and answerable to the people.

In other words, in most cases the people can abandon an oppressive, inefficient chief who does not perform well, is weak in enforcing rules, and does not respect his share of social obligations. The political power of the leader, and his ability to enforce rules, lies in the balance that he can achieve between power/authority and responsibility/obligations (Southwold 1964; Hjort and Ostberg 1978: 30).

Thus, the social structure defines the source of the power needed for enforcing rules. The means of enforcing rules vary among different groups. Some have an informal police force, such as a warrior caste, or official supervisors who monitor the activities of their people or of outsiders, such as the Twareg and the Il Chamus (Little and Brokensha 1987: 200). But most groups rely on the observations of each individual member to report transgressions and trespass. For example, among the Ait Ben Yacoub Berbers, trespass, whether tolerated or not, is easily detected by the herders who spend most of their time on the collective land and know who should use it.

Development experts and government agents insist on fences because they can't tell the livestock apart, and can't challenge a herder who claims to be of the collective (Artz *et al.* 1986). Some groups impose fees and penalties for transgression of rules. For example, among the Lowiili of Southern Burkina Faso, all stray animals (resulting usually from a lack of respect of rules by the herders), are said to belong to the earth shrine, and can only be redeemed into the owner's household upon sacrifices of grain and chickens (Goody 1956: 93). But the ultimate means of enforcement, often used when all else fails, is confrontation, fights, and in the case of inter-tribal disputes, warfare.

Conclusion

Through their observation and intimate knowledge of their physical environment, pastoralists have devised techniques for managing (harvesting, improving, protecting and regenerating) natural resources. Rules and regulations enshrined within the traditions of the society ensure the smooth functioning of the system by coordinating the activities of each member. It has been argued by some that the pastoralist does not improve or manage rangelands, and only uses it in a predatory way, but by keeping a low pressure on resources and high mobility and dispersion of his livestock, he is able to maintain an equilibrium (Bernus 1979: 125). This paper has shown that the pastoralist is much more of an active manager of his environment than implied by these authors, and that mobility and dispersion are just a few of the deliberate (rather than inadvertent) strategies that he relies on.

The discussion of the organisation of management and the means of enforcing rules leads to the obvious conclusion that the social structure defines the power base on which rules are enforced. As has been noted among the Maasai, the viability of the organisation rests on a system of mutual aid, information network, power lines that reinforce, reward and punishment and cooperation to eliminate competition and conserve energy (Jacobs 1980: 288). It also defines the way resource management techniques and rules will react to external forces, and how the society will adapt to new technologies and management strategies proposed by development workers. Thus, pastoral technologies should not be seen as isolated from their overall social framework.

Indigenous systems of pastoral production have undergone gradual change, as individual households faced with environmental and economic stress are forced to make permanent choices between production systems. Thus, in any group one finds those households who retain the old system, those that have completely abandoned it for crop cultivation, trade, and wage earning, and the vast majority of households that are somewhere in between. Many of these non-pastoral strategies were always used to deal with resource stress. In the past, the stress was usually of a temporary nature (droughts passed and local overstocking was alleviated with a move to fresh areas), and these strategies were eventually abandoned (Cassanelli 1984: 486).

However, in recent times, resource stress tends to linger on due to other cumulative factors, and many pastoralists find they cannot return to their pastoral system. It is an open question whether the traditional systems could be revived in their entirety if the current resource stress was relieved. An example that points to the affirmative can be found among the Rendille and Gabra of Northern Kenya who after the 1960s and 1970s droughts managed to return to their pastoral system by getting livestock loans from Missionary organisations (Lusigi 1984: 344).

Indigenous social controls and land tenure systems have generally eroded in recent years. Some contributing factors are crop expansion, social disintegration, increasing income gaps, decreasing resource capacity, and in many cases well-meaning development projects that have ignored traditional systems. However, this breakdown has not been homogeneous between tribes or even within tribes.

In general, local sociopolitical structures have lost much of their power and been partially replaced by an administration appointed by the central government. Thus, traditional leaders no longer have the power to enforce grazing controls. Although the knowledge of range principles and daily routines still lingers on, herding units, and even individual households are finding it necessary to abandon cooperation with others, to cut corners, and to strike out alone in search of decreasing and scarce resources. In general, formal rules have been the first to disappear because they rely on social cohesion and the power of local leaders to enforce rules. Informal rules are still viable, but are being modified to fit the requirements imposed by resource scarcity. However, some groups still retain their traditional structures and are able to enforce the indigenous regulations, such as the local chiefs in Lesotho (Bredemeier 1978: 90) and the Kaputiei Maasai (Hjort 1976b: 167).

In many cases, traditional land boundaries are no longer respected both by members of the tribe and by outsiders. Such a breakdown has been recorded in Botswana (Devitt 1982: 19), where land nationalisation had the overall effect of destroying communal management of land, and ossifying the income gap at one point in time, so that the rich remained rich and the poor no longer had recourse to the traditional sociopolitical system (Peters 1984: 33). Similar phenomena have been reported for the Twareg of Niger (Bernus 1981: 25), the Macina Fulani (Hiernaux and Diarra 1984: 201), and the Il Chamus (Little and Brokensha 1987: 201). Although the major cause of this has been the nationalisation and privatisation of land by the central Government, it alone is not a sufficient criterion. In general, if social cohesion and political authority have eroded, then communal cooperation for natural resource management is no longer possible. Thus, simply reinstating local tenure and formal control over natural resources, as some authors have suggested, will not automatically revive indigenous organisations, although it will help pave the way.

In a few cases the traditional tenure system is still *de facto* if not *de jure* alive, such as among the Mbanderu Herero of Northwestern Botswana (Almagor 1978 and Devitt 1981 cited in Devitt 1982), and the Fulani of Mubi (Gongola State, Nigeria) (Noronha and Lethem 1983: 3). In addition, in some cases communal tenure at the lower levels of sociopolitical organisation may have faded, but they remain intact at higher levels, such as among the Berbers of Morocco (Artz *et al.* 1986). In Kenya, where land privatisation is advancing at a fast pace, people have been laying claim to lands as close as possible to their traditional clan and lineage lands, thus effectively reestablishing traditional tenure structures (Jacobs 1980: 285).

In almost all cases, ownership of water points remains intact, even though the grazing lands around it may no longer be controlled by the group. For example, although traditional pasture rights no longer exist among the Wodaabe of Niger, clan ownership of wells still exists, and in practice contributes to a *de facto* recognition of traditional grazing lands (Wilson *et al.* 1984: 249). Government constructed water points have almost entirely been kept out of the traditional system. As a result they are open to all, and have contributed to a breakdown in the traditional resource tenure system, as among the Dinka of Kongor (Ahmed 1978: 12). However, some people are learning to fight back, such as the Illabakan Twareg of Niger who eventually forced the Government to close down some boreholes so that they could regain their control over the land when the outsiders left the area (Bernus 1974: 123), while others are taking advantage of the confusion in tenure rights to the detriment of their neighbours.

For example, some Somali lineages have constructed cemented hafirs with the Government's sanction in rival lineage or clan territories, leading to more confusion of grazing rights (Lewis 1961: 35).

Among those groups that had grazing reserves, very few still are able to restrict grazing according to traditional rules. Most groups have been forced to abandon the system due to increasing resource shortage, the construction of boreholes in the reserves by the government which then attracts outsiders, and crop expansion into the reserves. In addition, the breakdown of the sociopolitical system has eliminated the powers of enforcement that the leaders had. However, in at least one group, the people of Lesotho, indigenous reserves are still alive (Devitt 1982: 17; Odell 1982: 5), and among the Kikuyu sacred groves are still being protected even though they have lost their religious significance (Brokensha and Castro, unpublished: 20–21). In cases where the breakdown of the reserve has been due to resource shortage, closing off portions of the range to starving animals would be a waste, a practical impossibility, and cause further overcrowding and degradation on the remainder of the land. Other alternatives need to be found.

The situation in most parts of Africa is changing so fast, that what one concludes now may no longer be appropriate a few years later. Therefore, many of the studies already mentioned in this report may need to be revisited. This implies that any development project wishing to include indigenous systems into its design, must first conduct field surveys to validate and update its information on the systems.

Although some of the outmigration from the pastoral system is due to entire families leaving for other activities, some of it is also due to young men leaving for urban and industrial jobs, causing a serious human resource shortage in the remaining household. Greater incentives to keep the young on the range would help reestablish or create new grazing cooperation regulations. In addition, grazing coordination cannot be reinstated unless the underlying resource shortage is alleviated (through proper land use planning with enforcement to stop crop expansion, and/or range improvement techniques).

Project planning, design and implementation are often too inflexible in time and scope to properly take into account indigenous systems and popular participation. The experts, donor agencies, government officials and extension agents are often unwilling to consider the advantages of indigenous systems. The attitude of the local people, who are by now used to top-down projects, may also be a constraint.

19. A Socioecological Analysis of Balinese Water Temples

J. STEPHEN LANSING AND JAMES N. KREMER

*Because the Goddess makes the waters flow, those who do not follow
her laws may not possess her rice terraces.*
            Rajapurana Ulun Danu Batur, (Vol. II: 24 28 b.1)

Introduction

SIX DEGREES SOUTH of the Equator, towards the middle of the southern arc of
islands of the Indonesian archipelago, is the island of Bali. To the east of Bali lie
the arid and sparsely-populated islands of Eastern Indonesia. But Bali is a lush
volcanic island with ample rainfall, and an ancient system of rice terraces which
support a very dense population (estimated at 432 persons per square kilometre
in 1977). Wet-rice agriculture is very ancient in Bali, and irrigation tunnel
builders are mentioned in the very earliest Balinese inscriptions, dated 896 A.D.
(Goris 1954).

The Dutch conquered the island in a series of colonial wars, which began in
1846 and ended with the massacre of the court of Klungkung in 1908. As one
Balinese Kingdom after another fell under colonial rule, Dutch administrators
became involved in irrigation, as one of the principal sources of revenue for the
colonial Government (the other being the sale of opium). The colonial archives
overflow with theories and observations of Balinese irrigation systems, which
Dutch officials often described as engineering marvels. But colonial officials
were more interested in questions of taxation, and the role of the state in public-
work projects, than in the intricacies of traditional Balinese irrigation practices.

Recently, thanks largely to the work of Clifford Geertz (1972, 1980), Balinese
subak (local-level irrigation associations) have become celebrated examples of
decentralised irrigation control. But given the small size of the *subak* (usually
smaller than 100 ha) in comparison to the irrigation systems (up to thousands of
ha), questions still remain concerning whether some higher-level system of
coordination exists. Are the *subak* 'melons on a vine', each one drawing sufficient water from a constant river source? Or do seasonal fluctuations in river
flow force them to cooperate in a system of water sharing? Do the irrigation
requirements of upstream *subak* affect the availability of water for their neighbours downstreams? What are the actual technical requirements for managing
irrigation?

Part of the difficulty in obtaining a clear answer to such questions is due to
the kinds of conceptual models that have been developed to study irrigation systems. In the past, there have been two distinct approaches to this problem, one
created by social scientists and the other by engineers and hydrologists. Typical
of the social science approach are large-scale models like Wittfogel's (1957)
which are concerned with the long-term social effects of large irrigation systems
in arid regions. These models pay no attention to the physical or hydrological
characteristics of particular systems, but attempt to describe the common features of irrigation systems. Alternatively, there are very small-scale models

which have been developed for policy-oriented studies of local irrigation systems (*e.g.* Keller 1987; Gulati and Murty 1979, etc.). These models typically begin at the weir or main irrigation canal, and trace the system down to individual fields. Such models offer precise hydrological descriptions of *subak* sized systems, but leave untouched the questions of the relations between larger units, and the possible requirements for higher-level management of irrigation.

Over the past decade the authors, an anthropologist and a systems ecologist, have investigated the role of traditional Balinese 'water temples' in the management of irrigation (Kremer 1989; Kremer *et al.* 1989; Lansing 1978, 1983, 1986, 1987). Our attention was drawn to the temples by Balinese farmers, who complained that new development plans were ignoring the temple system, and creating unprecedented problems in water scheduling and pest control. Development agencies, however, were inclined to dismiss the water temples as a purely religious system, with no practical significance. Were the water temples really irrigation managers, as the farmers claimed?

To answer this question, we constructed a computer simulation model of the role of water temples along two adjacent Balinese rivers, the Oos and the Petanu. The model permits us to investigate relationships between physical, biological and social systems at the level of catchment areas, and thus to discover structures and relationships which would remain hidden from a purely sociological study of Balinese irrigation. In this chapter, we will try to explain the logic of our approach, and the results of our attempts to persuade development experts to explore new ways to think about water temples and ecological management. Since our approach is based on an ecological perspective, we begin with a brief introduction to the ecology of wet-rice terraces.

An ecological view of rice paddy management

Our approach is based on the observation that the role of water in traditional wet-rice paddies is quite different form that of other crops, like grains or vegetables, For most crops, irrigation is needed primarily to supply water and nutrients to the plant's roots. But in a rice paddy, water is used to create an artificial pond ecosystem, in which complex pathways link many species in synergistic relationships. Much of the work needed to support the growth of the rice is provided by the natural aquatic community growing at the base of the plants. Rice paddies are, indeed, unique among agricultural systems in that they can produce several tons of food per hectare per year indefinitely, with little or no added fertiliser.

The Balinese do not build irrigation tanks or storage dams, so irrigation is dependent on the seasonal flow of rivers and springs. About half of the 162 named streams and rivers on the island flow only during the rainy season, which lasts from November through April. Bali is a relatively ancient volcanic island, located in a region of heavy monsoons. Nearly all Balinese rivers to not flow at ground level, where irrigation would be easy, but in deep channels on the flanks of the volcanos. Gaining access to such rivers for irrigation poses a difficult engineering challenge. Most Balinese irrigation systems begin at a diversionary dam (or 'weir') across a river, which diverts part of the flow into a tunnel. The tunnel may emerge as much as a kilometre or more downstreams, at a lower elevation, where the water is routed through a system of canals and aqueducts to the summit of a terraced hillside. In the regions where rice cultivation is oldest in Bali, irrigation systems can be extraordinarily complex, with a maze of tunnels and canals shunting water through blocks of rice terraces. Since the volume of water in the rivers during the wet season can be ten times greater than the dry season flow, the irrigation systems have to cope with conditions ranging from a trickle to flash floods. Irrigation systems originating at different weirs are often interconnected, so that unused water form the tail end of one irrigation system may be shunted into a different block of terraces, or returned to a neighbouring stream.

The main crop produced is, of course, rice. In addition, the paddy also produced important sources of animal protein such as eels, frogs and fish. Most paddies also support a large population of ducks, which must also be carefully managed because they will damage young rice plants. After each harvest, flocks of ducks are driven from field to field, gleaning leftover grain and also eating some of the insects, like brown plant hoppers, which would otherwise attack the next rice crop. Traditional harvesting techniques remove only the seed-bearing tassel, leaving the rest of the stalk to decompose in the water, returning most of its nutrients to the system. Depending upon the danger from rice pests, the farmer may decide to dry the field and burn the stalks afterwards, thus killing most pests but loosing some of the nutritients in the harvested plants. Alternatively, he may flood the field and allow the rice stalks to slowly decompose under water.

As a method of pest control, the effectiveness of drying or flooding the fields depends on cooperation among all the farmers in a given block of terraces. For one farmer to try to reduce the pests on his own field, without coordinating with his neighbours is useless, because the pests will simply migrate from field to field. But if all the fields in a large area are burned or flooded, pest populations can be sharply reduced. Both kinds of fallow periods – burnt fields or flooded – are effective techniques for reducing the population of rice pests, but both depend on synchronising the harvest and subsequent fallow period over many ha. How large an area must be fallowed and for how long, depends on the species characteristics of the rice pests. Major pests include rodents, insects, and bacterial and viral diseases.

Until quite recently, rice scientists were unaware of the existence of this method of pest control. Studies of traditional Asian systems of wet-rice cultivation assumed that pest control research which was done on the sociological aspects of rice production focused not on the ecological effects of traditional systems of irrigation management, but on how to educate farmers in the effective use of agrochemicals. New agricultural policies based on these ideas were introduced in Bali in the 1970s, as a means to increase rice production. Farmers were required to plant high yielding varieties of rice, and very large quantities of pesticides applied to the fields, with disastrous results. A recent study by World Bank Officials (Machbub *et al.* 1988) concluded that pesticides have already *pervasively polluted the island's soil and water resource*. It is important to note that the social systems of water management which sustained the ecological productively of Balinese rice paddies for centuries do not function automatically. It is perfectly possible to grow rice with chemical fertilisers and pesticides, ignoring the biochemical cycles which sustain rice growth in traditional paddies. Indeed, on a short-term basis, extensive use of agrochemicals make it possible to dramatically increase crop yields, provided that sufficient water is available. Thus, the answer to the question of the type of social control required for irrigated rice production will differ drastically, depending on whether one approaches the question from the point of view of a biologist studying traditional farming systems, or an agronomist studying systems dependent on chemical inputs. From the latter perspective, all that is needed from the irrigation system is a sufficient supply of water. The timing of irrigation is not thought to have any influence on productivity. Instead, how much rice is grown depends on the rice variety and the amounts of fertiliser added. But for the systems ecologist, the timing of irrigation appears to be the key influence on the growth of the rice plants and other food species, maintaining the high productivity of traditional wet rice paddies.

Just as individual farmers manage their paddies by controlling the flow of water, so larger social groups control pest cycles by means of synchronised irrigation schedules. In summary:

1. In rice paddies, water is used to construct an artificial pond ecosystem, and not merely to deliver water to the roots of the rice plants.
2 The productivity of the paddy ecosystem is strongly influenced by the pulsing of water inputs, which affect nutrient cycles and pest populations.
3 The build-up of pest populations is affected by the regional coordination of fallow periods.
4. Irrigation management must therefore balance a suite of constraints, both physical and biological. Moreover, the physical and biological parameters are not constant, but vary seasonally and by elevation and topography.
5. Unlike natural aquatic ecosystems such as ponds, streams or oceans, rice terraces are under continuous human management. The nature of this management depends on the existing framework of social control.

Hence the need for detailed models of the socioecological system in specific watersheds.

Clearly, a social model of irrigation management which omits hydrology, or a physical model which ignores the biological effects of regional coordination and resource pulsing, will be of very limited value. To understand the kinds of human control needed to manage the rice terraces, we must move beyond generalised hydrological models, to a detailed analysis of the interaction of the physical, biological and social components of irrigation in specific watersheds.

The Bali model

Our simulation model was developed specifically to determine if there was an optimal spatial scale of coordination in cropping patterns to balance water use and pest control. For the simulation model, the most fundamental level of information is the geographical description of the area. The physical facts of hydrological interdependence dictate that the total watershed of a river is the appropriate scale of analysis. The Gianyar Region of Bali includes the watersheds of the Oos and Petanu Rivers (Map 19.1). In our approach, all information is organised in relation to the catchment basins and the hydrology that connects them.

Based on topographical maps, we divided the Oos-Petanu watershed into 12 sub-sections specifying the catchment basins for each of the dams for which hydrological data were available. For the 172 *subak* located in these basins, we specified their name, area, the basin in which they reside, the dam from which they receive irrigation water, and the dam to which any excess is returned. We also defined the real spatial mosaic connecting these *subak*. Thus, for each one we specified the neighbouring *subak* on all four sides, or if it is bounded by another kind of boundary, like a river, road or city.

Given his geographical setting, the simulation models computes the growth and ultimate harvest of rice. The computer programme consists of three sub-models: hydrology, rice growth, and pest dynamics. A full description of the model is inappropriate here, a brief synopsis must suffice. Based on historical data on rainfall by season and elevation, runoff to the rivers is calculated. The irrigation demand is computed each month from the cropping pattern specified in the model for each of the *subak*. Growth of rice depends upon the variety being grown and the available water supply, and the harvest is reduced if the supply form the rivers is insufficient to meet the demand. The level of pests in each *subak* depends on immigration from adjacent cropland, plus growth *in situ* if rice is being grown. At harvest time, the yield may be reduced by cumulative water stress and pest damage.

The key to the present application of the model is the choice of management scenarios. Seven choices are supplied that span a range of coordination among the 172 *subak* of the model, from all following the same schedule to 172 different schedules. These choices assume that the *subak* plant and harvest together in groups that parallel to various degrees the subdivisions of the temple hierarchy. The total watershed is divided into 13 *Masceti* temples and 26 *Ulun Swi* temples. All hydrological and biological results of each simulation run may be displayed for each catchment basin. For example, time series plots of the annual pattern of river flow, stage of rice growth and pest damage are shown below for four catchment basins in a simulation run where all 172 *subak* are assumed to plant three crops of a high yielding variety (HYV) rice with no local coordination (Figure 2). Despite the tendency for fallow periods to reduce pests in a single *subak*, notice that pest levels steadily increase overall in this run of the model, because of immigration from adjacent *subak* where rice is still being grown and pest populations remain high.

Simulation formally joins the ecological and social aspects of our conceptual model. It provides an internally consistent basis for comparing alternative scenarios. In the real world, we may speculate that water temple networks have evolved over centuries to optimise water sharing and pest control, but this thesis is simply unverifiable. In the model world, however, a series of runs may be done in which only the level of social coordination (*e.g.* via the temple hierarchy) is varied – all other ecological and physical variables are exactly the same. Specific results may change when different values of uncertain parameters are tried (*e.g.* pest spreading and damage rates, the maximum yields of rice varieties). Yet if the *patterns* of the results remain consistent across a range of runs with uncertain co-efficients, then we may safely conclude that this pattern is consistent with the conditions assumed in our conceptual model; these *comparisons* are valid even when their *absolute accuracy* is uncertain.

This by no means proves our assumptions – our model may still be incomplete, or even wrong – but simulation provides a rigorous quantitative procedure to evaluate the consequences of a certain conceptual model.

The Bali irrigation project

From the beginning, one of the goals of our collaboration was to provide scientific input into the controversy between Balinese farmers and development experts, over the role of water temples in irrigation management.

This controversy had its roots in the decision by the Asian Development Bank to modernise Balinese irrigation. Plants for the 'Bali Irrigation Project' were summarised in a Feasibility Study (Anon. 1981): 'The Bali Irrigation Project (B.I.P.) is the first large scale attempt in Bali Island to improve the irrigation systems. Past interventions by the Department of Public Works have been limited to isolated improvements, with negligible impact of the main improvements will concern:

- ○ river water sharing and subak coordination;
- ○ new O & M rules;
- ○ programmed cropping patterns;
- ○ use of measurement systems;
- ○ changes in cropping techniques;
- ○ yield monitoring systems;
- ○ taxes and water charges.'

'In consequence the Subak may lose some of its traditional facets, especially part of its autonomy' (Feasibility, Part 2, Bali Irrigation Project).

Map 19.1: *Map of the study site for the Bali model: The Oos and the Petanu rivers in the region of Gianyar, with the catchment basins, irrigation system and* subak *shown in relation to the water temples*

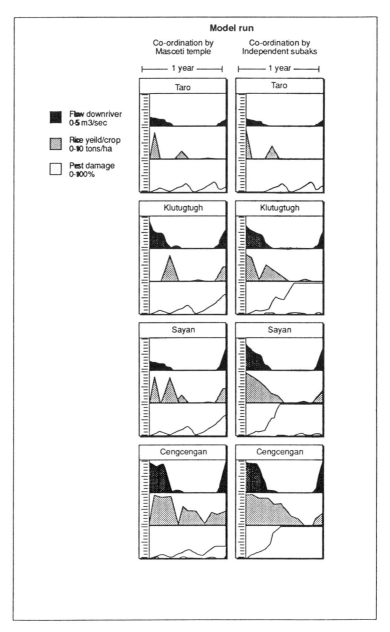

Figure 19.1: *Simulated annual patterns for river flow, rice yield and pest damage,*
comparing two runs of the model differing only by the scale of
coordination among the Subak. Each panel of three plots shows
average results for the catchment basins.
Note the increased levels of pest damage (up to 100 per cent loss of
crop) that result when all subak *plant and harvest independently.*
The downstream river is: Taro - > Klutugtug => Sayan =>
Cengcengan.

The principal emphasis of the Project was the reconstruction of 36 weirs and associated irrigation works, at an estimated cost of about forty million dollars. Since in most cases these *subak* improvement schemes' were not designed to bring new land into cultivation, economic justification for the project was largely based on a mandated change to continuous rice cropping for as many *subak* as possible. In the long run, according to project officials this would generate a minimum of 80,000 tons of additional rice production each year, which could be sold for export and thus provide the $1,300,000 per annum needed to repay the project loan from the Asian Development Bank. All of these estimates were later revised upward as the project added an additional 16 *subak* improvement schemes to the original 36.

The project assumed that each *subak* was an autonomous unit, and paid no attention to water temples. After meeting with various project officials, we learned that the Italian and Korean engineering firms which were supervising the project were unwilling to consider any changes in their plans without specific directives from the Bank. In 1984, Lansing wrote a report to the Irrigation Division of the Bank drawing their attention to the importance of water temple scheduling, especially with regard to pest control. The Director of the Irrigation Division replied that in his view the temples played no effective managerial role, and defended the enforced imposition of the new cropping patterns as follows (personal correspondence): 'Although these schedules do not allow for large ares to be fallow for a sufficient long time to minimise the pest population, the increase in local production makes it worthwhile to adopt these schedules. Pest control programmes are being carried out to reduce the pest population to reasonable levels.'

In 1985, the Bali Irrigation Project completed a survey of the results of the first four completed irrigation projects. The immediate effect of the first *subak* improvement schemes was an overall decline in rice production, which the project evaluation team attributed to an outbreak of rice diseases and pests.The ADB initially resisted our reports that water temples played an important role in higher-level ecological management. But when we began to use the ecological simulation model to demonstrate the rational basis for the long-standing success of the traditional system of water temples, the Bank began to pay attention.

Science and communication technology

It was not until the model was already functioning and we were faced with the need to communicate our results to development planners and Balinese farmers, that we began to consider the potential role of the computer model as a means for communicating our ideas. To develop this aspect of the computer programme, we relied upon the expert programming and design assistance of Tyde Richards of USC's Centre for Scholarly Technology and George Shearer of Biola University. The results of this collaboration was a software interface that visually presented the geographical context and the quantitative results of the computer model in three languages: English, Balinese and Indonesian.

As with the water temples themselves, it is essential to see the features of our computer system as an integrated unit (Figure 19.1). At the heart is the simulation model including hydrology, scales of social cooperation, rice growth and pest dynamics. The analysis depends on factual information for each of these parts, with different data required to build the model and to test and evaluate it. The HyperCard[1] software interface communicates these assumptions and

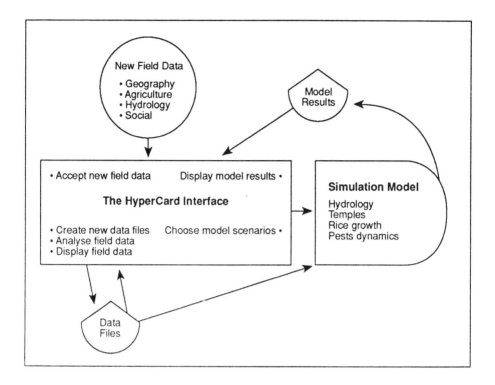

Figure 19.2: *Diagram of the design of the Bali project software package under development.*

results; this is the visible, usable part and it allows the complicated simulation to remain invisible for most people.

The HyperCard interface presently consists of three parts. Maps depict the two rivers in Gianyar (the Oos and the Petanu), the diversions and canals of the irrigation network, the *subak*, and the water temples. Given this geographical structure, the second part allows the specification of conditions to be explored in a run of the simulation model. Third, the results of model run may be displayed in tables, histograms, and time-series plots. Results of the runs are archived and automatically checked before running a newly specified scenario.

In future work we hope to improve the interface of this system allowing its application to other regions. This requires the input of newly gathered data, the presentation of these data to allow description and evaluation of the new study sites, and the translation of these data into the form required to support simulation. Finally, since much of the real data is similar to that predicted by the model (*e.g.* time series of flow rates, rice yields, pest levels), the same computer programme will display the real data and the model predictions and for direct intercomparisons. It is impossible to convey adequately in prose the features of the software, indeed it is the inadequacy of conventional, sequential text, figures, and numbers that makes it necessary. The emphasis is on graphics and visual clarity, while controlling data access and computations powerfully and flexibly. The approach communicated well enough to cause a flurry of attention in the public media – the point, according to an article in *Newsweek* magazine: 'is not that folkways never need fixing – they often do. It's that old and new aren't mutually exclusive. They can mix and merge, on the circuit boards of a computer.'[2]

Conclusions

One of our concerns was whether those to whom we demonstrated our model might misunderstand it, and expect to be able to use it as a predictor of real future crop yields. Yet this was rarely the case. Hydrologists at the Bali Irrigation Project readily saw the water budget computations of the model as a logical extension of their approach but on a larger scale, and saw this as desirable. Their appreciation of the practical importance of regional coordination was immediate and when it became clear that the temples actually serve this function, they for the first time sent delegated to discuss the common ground with the temple priest.

When shown the predictions of the model of water shortages in certain regions, the Jero Gde, the High Priest of the supreme water temple at Batur, suggested that we consult temple records. Village delegations are sent to the temple during times of water shortage or pestilence to pray and the Jero suggested that we should compare the tentative model results with the temples records of these visits. While such records are incomplete – which villages choose to send delegations and how severe the situations were are entirely uncontrolled – they may nevertheless will give some useful historical indication whether regional tendencies suggested by model results are valid.

When asked if he thought that such a tool as the MacIntosh model might be of use to him, the Jero Gde responded thoughtfully that it would indeed help him demonstrate to individual *subak* representatives the place their paddies occupied in the larger, interrelated system. By emphasising this conceptual side rather than the quantitative prediction function that might be erroneously expected from such a simple model as this, the Jero Gde demonstrated convincingly that he saw the true strengths and the real limitations of the model.

Recently, the Asian Development Bank (1988) formally acknowledged the importance of the water temples, and dramatically reversed their policy towards the 'traditional' Balinese systems of terrace management. The final evaluation of the Bali Irrigation Project concludes: 'The Project, being primarily concerned with the engineering aspects of irrigation development, had little control over the management of the systems or the cropping patterns adopted. However, it does appear that the Project Office and the Bank were convinced that the problems induced by changes in cropping pattern could be resolved by increasing commercial pesticide inputs for example. ...While administrators and subak have now returned to a lower rice cropping intensity and to a more coordinated rotation, the cost of the lack of appreciation of the merits of the traditional regime has been high. Project experience highlights that fact that the irrigated rice terraces of Bali form a complex artificial ecosystems which has been recognised locally over centuries. The system of [subak] makes decisions which manipulate the state of the system, at ascending levels in regional hierarchies. When they institute a fallow period to control a pest outbreak, they are in fact managing the regional terrace ecosystem, not just irrigation. Conclusions: Technological innovations in irrigation even when minimal in nature need to reflect local conditions and farmers should participate in that process. ...It also appears that belief in superior values and ritualisation of routine activities related to irrigated cropping are keys to sustained high performance. It is concluded that traditional value systems should be exploited for productive purposes even when technological innovations are introduced in irrigated agriculture, and the technological changes should not be introduced in isolation of rituals and traditions which have convincingly proven their contribution to sustained irrigated cropping.' (Project Performance Audit Report, May 1988; Bali Irrigation Project in Indonesia; Asian Development Bank Post Evaluation Office).

Notes

1 *HyperCard* is a software product for the Apple MacIntosh Computer.
2 Geoffrey Cowley, The 'Electronic Goddess', *Newsweek*, March 6, 1989, page 50.

20. Kpelle Farming through Kpelle Eyes

JOHN GAY

Introduction

PERHAPS I SHOULD say 'Kpelle farming through my eyes'. Obviously I have to begin with what I have seen and what I know, but the data allow me to move beyond my understanding of Kpelle farming to the way a community, comprising 131 households in a central village and 23 satellite hamlets in central Liberia, understands farming. A community is more than just the individuals which compose it; specifically it is an entity which has a corporate understanding, composed of the knowledge, the attitudes and the beliefs of the individual members. When a community is coherent, when it 'works,' then it is in a real sense an organism. When it becomes incoherent, then breakdown occurs, something dies, and something new and unexpected is born.

In 1974, when I lived in Gbansu-sulon-ma, on the edge of the rain forest, I belonged to a community still coherent enough to maintain itself. Gbansu was an organism in much the same way as Aunt Hillary in Douglas Hofstadter's book *Godel, Escher, Bach* (1980: 311–66). The image which Hofstadter used was that of an ant hill which had a life of its own, but which is made up of the individual ants, just as the brain (or a computer) has a mind which is more than the neurons or individual transistors which compose it. Gbansu was more than the individuals and households which made it up. In fact, the individuals and households complementing each other in such a way as to promote the well-being of the organism.

It had a corporate spirit like that described by Walter Wink (1986: 4–5) in his book *Unmasking the Powers*: 'The corporate spirits of IBM and Gulf and Western are palpably real and strikingly different, as are the national spirits of the United States and Canada.' The Gaia hypothesis urges us to consider communities as systems, and warns us against falling into the trap of reductionist science (Goldsmith 1988: 64–76).

In Hofstadter's book (1980: 319), Aunt Hillary was the greatest of friends with Anteater, despite the doubtless negative feelings of the ants themselves. Anteater said of himself: 'Far from being an enemy of the colony, I am Aunt Hillary's favourite companion... I grant you, I'm quite feared by all the individual ants in the colony – but that's another matter entirely.' It depends on the level of thought. Reductionist science insists on looking at the bottom level only, and sees the upper level as merely a conglomerate. I disagree.

Mistaken views of farming

There are two mistaken ways in which to look at farming in Gbansu. One would be to think only of the individual farmers, as in reductionism, in which case confusion results. The other is to fall into the trap of holism, which Hofstadter (1980: 319) shows to be the other side of the coin from reductionism. In this second form of error one has to invent an abstraction called The Kpelle Farmer. He (she? – the problem is, of course, that an abstract farmer can have no gender) is just as much a misconception as 'The Peasant' or 'The Capitalist', because nowhere do these beings exist.

269

What *does* exist, in my opinion, is a system, an organism, a whole which functions because of the parts and which provides the parts a reality within which to function. The individual farmers very much exist (and very much have gender), each individual with his or her own understanding of farming, an understanding which leads to action. In a community which is a system, an organism, these individual choices complement each other within the whole that they compose. Even what may seem to some members of the community as foolish or incomprehensible behaviour may be necessary to complete the whole pattern. I do not go so far as de Mandeville, who said, in his 18th century *Fable of the Bees,* that public benefit is made up out of private vice; nor do I altogether accept Adam Smith's idea of the invisible hand which guides the economy of a complex system. The system may in fact fail, things fall apart, and the whole becomes less than the sum of the parts.

The mistake that development 'experts' often make, a mistake which neither Aunt Hillary nor the organism that is Gbansu would make, is to generalise from economic and social averages to 'The Kpelle Farmer.' The experts then assume that each individual farmer is 'The Kpelle Farmer' (assumed to be a male), and invent strategies to help this person. I have seen this strategy fail in Liberia, Lesotho, Botswana, Tanzania, Uganda, Kenya and Ethiopia. It has to fail, because it deals with a mythical beast, and because it manages, quite remarkably, to commit simultaneously the errors of reductionism and holism.

A viable alternative is to deal with the community as an organism, realising that both the community and the individuals that compose it are real, living, and mutually dependent. It is in this sense that I say that community understands farming. If the system 'works', as it did when I was living in Gbansu in 1974, then the whole is distinctly greater than the sum of its parts, because the parts contribute to the whole in ways that no individual could by himself or herself imagine or predict.

The community as an organism

This is rather abstract so far. What is needed is to find out how the whole, in a specific situation, is both made up of, and gives reality to, the parts. It is easy to see how Aunt Hillary is more than the ants which make her up. It is even easy to see why Anteater is a friend to Aunt Hillary, even though not to the ants. With careful analysis of thoughtfully collected data, it is also not difficult to recognise and understand Gbansu as an organism, and then determine how the organism comprehends its task of self-maintenance.

I first explain my method for finding how the community understands farming. I then outline key points in Gbansu's view of farming, a view which is held by no single individual, but equally a view which is participated in by each individual. Clearly, such a communal understanding must have tensions within itself, disagreements which are reconciled within a larger agreement. Clearly only a schizophrenic individual could personally accept all that is implied by the system. Yet the complexities and inconsistencies must be held in creative tension by community leaders, who can see the system whole and thus benefit personally from it and hopefully lead the community into further growth.

My method starts by collecting information from as many individuals and households as possible. From these data I generalise – but not just to central tendencies and statistical measures of fluctuation. The mean and standard deviation are only starting points for understanding out how the community understands itself. What is needed is a way to see the distribution as a whole, where the deviant ideas are as necessary to the entire system as those which cluster about some kind of average.

Village and hamlet

I give an example which will play a key role in the rest of my analysis. Gbansu has one central village, a metropolis of 50 households, a place of endless fascination to the occupants of the 23 satellite hamlets. Similarly, the residents of the central place look on their country cousins as 'hicks', naive souls who go to sleep when it is dark and do not know how to behave when they dare to enter the 'nightclub' in the central village. The world-wide urban-rural contrast is repeated on a tiny scale in the 400 square km and 1106 individuals that compose Gbansu.

Diverse and contradictory as they are, the village and the hamlets need each other. Between them they compose a system that works well. Neither village sophisticate nor hamlet rustic is The Kpelle Farmer. Between and among them, Kpelle farming takes place. Of course, there is also no such thing as 'The City Slicker' or 'The Country Hick' in Gbansu. It would be quite inappropriate to present stereotypes for village and hamlet.

There is great diversity in each place, with individuals composing a functional system even at the family level. The diversity is needed to make the entire system, the entire organism, work. A profile of the way Gbansu understands agriculture has to include all of the diversity that is Gbansu. To make this profile, therefore, I had to question a wide range of people, and to find a way to represent the resulting wide range of answers.

Cluster analysis and multi-dimensional scaling

Two statistical techniques are useful here: cluster analysis and multi-dimensional scaling. Both techniques depend on obtaining answers to a range of questions within a framework that allows the answers to be presented in a two or more dimensional form, where spatial relationships correspond to cognitive or attitudinal connections. In contrast, normal statistical analysis only reports discrete facts or discrete relations between specific sets of facts.

I used several types of questions in order to obtain maps of knowledge and belief in the community. One approach was to use sentence completions. I set up 20 sentence introducers, *e.g. I know that...*, *I am sorry that...*, *I have heard that...*, *in the future...*, and *I wish that...* The people we interviewed were chosen from carefully selected population groups, so that we could get as nearly representative a sample as possible. We interviewed 8-to-11 year-old children, 18-to-21 year-old young adults, and 40-to-50 year-old adults. We balanced male and female respondents, persons who have been to school and those who have not, and in most cases also respondents from the central village and the outlying hamlets. Within each category, the respondents were chosen as nearly at random as possible, although true randomness was not possible.

The statements with which people completed these sentences were categorised and coded, so that statements which differed only slightly were lumped together as if they were the same. It was never necessary to use more than 65 different response categories in a particular set of interviews, and often the numbers of categories were less than 50. A cross-tabulation matrix was then set up indicating the number of times each response category was given to each sentence introducer. This matrix was the basis for rather complex mathematical manipulations performed by computer. A measure of similarity between each pair of responses was calculated, depending on how closely corresponding are the distribution of the two responses across the 20 sentence introducers. Responses which appeared in the most nearly similar ways across the sentence introducers were classified together, so that the farther apart were two responses in the diagram, the less similar they were.

This is exactly the same mathematical technique which is used in making computer-based taxonomies of biological species and varieties within species. In that case, the traits are matched with the species, the computer analysis is performed, and a taxonomy generated in which similar species find their place close to each other. The advantage of this technique for understanding the 'mind' of a community is that it allows all the statements of all the respondents concerning a particular topic to be organised into a cognitive system. No one individual would or even could make all these statements, but all the statements are included in the community's collective understanding. By interviewing as wide a spectrum of community members as possible, the entire universe of statements is elicited and organised into an overall framework which displays the intellectual system underlying the village and its activities.

Unprompted sentence completions

We began by asking respondents to complete the sentences on any topic they wished. The responses covered the whole range of experience in Gbansu. The most common response concerned making a farm, given in 7.6 per cent of the cases. Next in the list were responses concerning school attendance (4.5 per cent), God's goodness and helpfulness (3.5 per cent), the changes in today's world (3.2 per cent), having enough food to eat (3.1 per cent), not being able to go to school (2.9 per cent), needing more food (2.7 per cent), supporting oneself by hard work (2.7 per cent), being dominated by the modern world (2.7 per cent), and depending on animals and fish for food (2.7 per cent). There were another 60 less frequent responses. Even the most common answers show the diversity of the community. Some members rejoice in their education, while others worry about the lack of it. Some think about the modern world, while others look to the forest, with its farms, animals and fish to sustain life.

What is striking is how cluster analysis reveals a pattern wherein the universe of thought within the Gbansu community is rendered graphically. There is a sharp and dramatic split within the taxonomy between responses suggesting the modern urban world of money, government and school, and those based in the older rural world of rice farm, forest and spirits. Both sets of attitudes and values and ideas are present in the community, and they make a system that confirms the idea of rapid social change in Liberia. In this way Gbansu is a microcosm of the nation, and its collective consciousness reflects this split. The complete cluster analysis is given in the accompanying diagram (Figure 20.1).

Within each response category – modern and traditional – there is a further division between good and bad, favourable and unfavourable. The split between good and bad forms the basis for decision-making on actions to be taken, often very different actions by different individuals, depending on how the individuals and their actions fit into the entire organism that is Gbansu.

Farming finds its place close to medicine and witchcraft in the taxonomy.

Farming is not just a technical, scientific activity, as developers would have it, but is knit into the world of spirits, ancestors and supernatural powers.

Multi-dimensional scaling is another way of analysing sentence completions. The similarity function used for cluster analysis can be understood as a distance in multi-dimensional space. If there are as many dimensions as there are responses, then a perfect representation of the distance is possible. The test comes when dimensions are reduced to two, so that the responses can be placed in a flat plane. When there is a clear and consistent pattern, there is little distortion caused by reducing 65 dimensions to two. This was true with the sentence completions where no topic was specified. In this case the same two dimensions of modern-traditional and good-bad were clearly displayed, as shown in the accompanying diagram.

Clearly, farming is the major issue of people's lives. Almost a quarter of all the sentence completions concerned farming, positively or negatively. However, not everyone emphasises farming. Women, children and unschooled respondents uniformly had a higher level or interest in farming than men, adults and schooled people. Unfortunately, it is precisely the latter group that the development 'experts' want to think of as 'The Kpelle Farmer', even though members of this group turn their attention to government, modern life, education, morality, religion and money. Such non-farm issues are, of course, important to the well-being of Gbansu, and must form part of the collective mind. But, if the task is to improve farming, one should not preach to people for whom non-farm issues are paramount.

We applied the sentence completion technique to specific aspects of the farm cycle, to determine how the Gbansu community perceives and understands each of them. Topics for the sentence completions were forest, bush and swamp; rice, plants and trees; village, hamlet and *kwii* (the term used throughout Liberia to refer roughly to the educated, modern, white-collar person within the money economy); work, cooperative work group and market; and power and wealth. In each case the computer generated a representation of the Gbansu mind through cluster analysis and multi-dimensional scaling.

Obviously, I cannot in this short paper summarise each of these areas. What I will do instead is to give highlights which suggest the complexity and good sense with which these agricultural topics are viewed, and which confirm my hypothesis that Gbansu is indeed a coherent community which can be said to have a collective understanding of farming.

Forest, bush and swamp

I considered the types of land on which farming is done. The central village and hamlets of Gbansu are surrounded by secondary bush at various stages of regeneration. The fallow cycle ranges from 7 to 15 years, allowing enough time in almost all cases for the bush to mature before a new farm is established.

Within an hour's walk from Gbansu in most directions, but particularly to the north across the St. Paul River, there is uncut tropical rain forest. Scattered throughout the bush and the forest are numerous swamps, small and large. The ways in which the people of Gbansu understand and deal with the forest, bush and swamp are illustrated in the taxonomies of responses to these terms.

The primary statements concerning forest are that it can grow rice (14.7 per cent), that people work in the forest (12.2 per cent), that forest is good (7.8 per cent) and that people make farms in the forest (7.8 per cent). Further responses

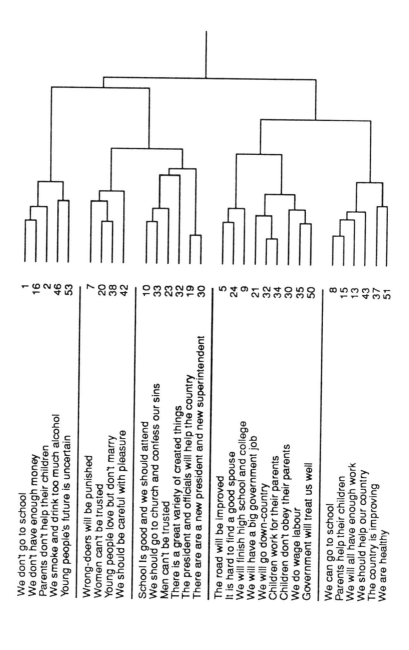

We don't go to school	1
We don't have enough money	16
Parents don't help their children	2
We smoke and drink too much alcohol	46
Young people's future is uncertain	53
Wrong-doers will be punished	7
Women can't be trusted	20
Young people love but don't marry	38
We should be careful with pleasure	42
School is good and we should attend	10
We should go to church and confess our sins	33
Men can't be trusted	23
There is a great variety of created things	32
The president and officials will help the country	19
There are a new president and new superintendent	30
The road will be improved	5
It is hard to find a good spouse	24
We will finish high school and college	9
We will have a big government job	21
We will go down-country	32
Children work for their parents	34
Children don't obey their parents	30
We do wage labour	35
Government will treat us well	50
We can go to school	8
Parents help their children	15
We will all have enough work	13
We should help our country	43
The country is improving	37
We are healthy	51

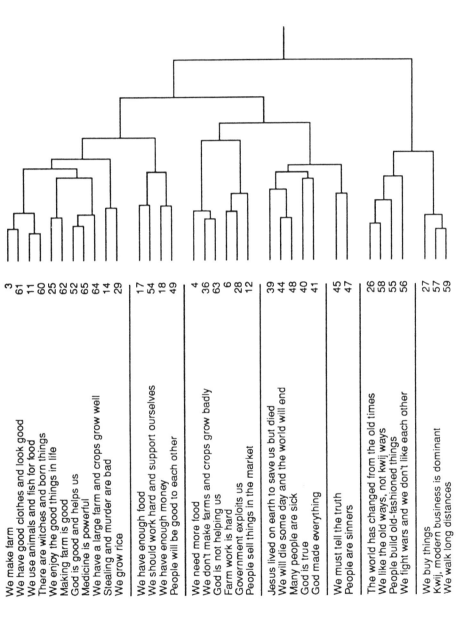

We make farm — 3
We have good clothes and look good — 61
We use animals and fish for food — 11
There are witches and born things — 60
We enjoy the good things in life — 25
Making farm is good — 62
God is good and helps us — 52
Medicine is powerful — 65
We have a large farm and crops grow well — 64
Stealing and murder are bad — 14
We grow rice — 29

We have enough food — 17
We should work hard and support ourselves — 54
We have enough money — 18
People will be good to each other — 49

We need more food — 4
We don't make farms and crops grow badly — 36
God is not helping us — 63
Farm work is hard — 6
Government exploits us — 28
People sell things in the market — 12

Jesus lived on earth to save us but died — 39
We will die some day and the world will end — 44
Many people are sick — 48
God is true — 40
God made everything — 41

We must tell the truth — 45
People are sinners — 47

The world has changed from the old times — 26
We like the old ways, not kwij ways — 58
People build old-fashioned things — 55
We fight wars and we don't like each other — 56

We buy things — 27
Kwij, modern business is dominant — 57
We walk long distances — 59

Figure 20.1: *Cluster analysis of unprompted sentence completions*

are that there are animals in the forest (3.8 per cent) which people hunt (3.8 per cent). More than half the responses are contained in these categories. Clearly, the forest is a great resource to the people of Gbansu, a resource which in the mid-70s they were managing quite well. The taxonomy of responses, according to cluster analysis, has two clear subgroups. In one, careful management of the forest is contrasted with destructive exploitation of the forest. In the other, the power of the forest, as a source of medicine and place of sacrifice, is contrasted with the dangers, natural and supernatural, to be found in the forest. Responses concerning the bush are somewhat similar, but with the main difference that people make their homes in the bush. The forest is sharply contrasted with human space, but the bush is a human place.

There were only two families who lived in the high forest across the St. Paul River when I was in Gbansu, and both families were considered to be strange. One was headed by a man who had been condemned to prison for murder, but who had been redeemed by the clan chief of the area and sent to live in the forest to produce rice for the chief. I visited his farm, and found it to be the most productive I had seen anywhere in Liberia. The other was a man who did not like the company of others. He had built his farm across the St. Paul River, and kept his canoe on the far bank. Visitors had to call across the river, and if he did not want to entertain them, he would refuse to send his canoe for them.

A further difference between forest and bush is that crops other than rice can be planted in the bush. High forest is cut down only to make rice farms. The act of cutting the forest reduces it to bush, which in the following years can be planted to groundnuts or maize or bananas, or perhaps to the cash crops of coffee and cocoa. By the act of cutting it down, forest is changed into bush and is thereby removed from the realm of the sacred and powerful. Multi-dimensional scaling, as applied to forest, reveals two major dimensions in the thought world of Gbansu people. One is the secular to the sacred, and the other is from observation to participation. In contrast, the dimensions in responses concerning the bush differ from those concerning the forest, namely, from traditional to modern and from nature to cultivation.

Gbansu people give more thought to understanding the bush than the forest. There is much more diversity in secondary bush than in the forest, even though there are, of course, many different species of trees in the high forest. But the high forest, having reached climax, has suppressed much of the undergrowth that makes the low and medium bush such a varied realm. I spent several days with an astute farmer in Gbansu surveying the types of primary and secondary forest. He identified 20 types of bush and forest for me, plus an additional six types of swamp land and six types of soil. He showed me how the different types of bush were suitable for different crops, from rice to bananas to sugar cane to garden crops such as cassava and groundnuts.

We asked people from the same population groups which provided sentence completions to tell us the first things they thought of when we named the different types of forest, bush, swamp and soil. The most common responses concerned rice farming, as might be expected, but there were also specific types of plants or specific activities related to particular types of bush and soil. There were also soil and bush types not at all suitable for cultivation.

In particular, Gbansu people considered the swamps in their area to be unsuitable for cultivation. More than half the farm households had some swamp on their family land, but most did not use it, even though they said they might use it in the future. Swamp is considered to be the last refuge of women who have no one to clear their land or of families whose upland farms have failed to burn properly in preparation for planting. Swamp farming is difficult and lonely, unpleasant, and likely to cause disease. Modern swamp rice techniques have been tried by a few, but have been found wanting. Year-round work, out of phase with the social cycle of the community, is required, and the results are uncertain. Almost half the responses concerning swamp stated or implied that the respondents would not work in such a place.

Vegetation and land

A further exploration asked people to give free responses to the various types of vegetation and land. Cluster analysis of these responses revealed a basic split between observed features of the physical environment and the uses to which they can be put. The environmental features included parts of trees, such as bark, leaves and fruit, and aspects of the landscape, such as type of vegetation or soil. The crops which can be planted on the different land types were traditional crops, including rice and the common garden and village crops, and modern cash crops, such as sugar cane, cocoa, coffee and citrus.

Of particular interest is the diagram which results from applying the multi-dimensional scaling computer program to the responses to land types. It shows two salient dimensions, one from natural to cultivated, and the second from difficult to easy access. The pattern is shown in the accompanying diagram. It is striking that the modern commercial crops, including swamp rice, are farther to the right on the cultivated dimension than the more traditional crops of upland rice and cassava.

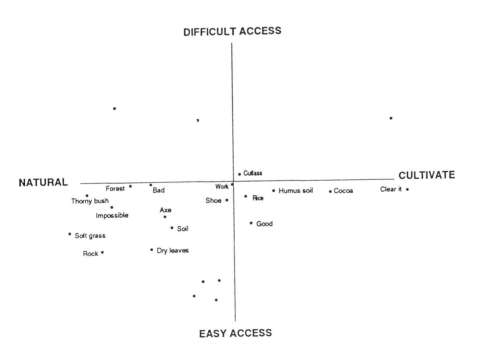

Figure 20.2: *Plot of multi-dimensional scaling*

On the vertical dimension, thick, tangled, secondary bush and swamps are far in the direction of difficult access, bush and forest are in the centre, and black soil (reputedly the best they have), young bush and sand are at the other extreme. At the very centre of the diagram, central on both dimensions, are rice, cutlass (*machete*) and work, which are in fact the centre of Kpelle life (Figure 20.1).A similar pattern is found if multi-dimensional scaling is applied to the types of forest, bush, soil and swamp themselves. Along one dimension, there is a contrast from the twisted mat of vines in thick bush to the open forest floor covered with dry leaves. Along the second is the contrast from the old farm site to the high uncut forest.

Attitudes toward forest and bush differ markedly among the population subgroups which we interviewed. As before, there is a real difference between men, young adults, schooled people and village residents, and their opposite numbers. Men look at the forest as a way to get rich, while women see it as a source of medicine. The schooled people see the forest as a place to exploit, and the bush as a home for animals, while the unschooled see both forest and bush as productive places in which to live and work. Young adults emphasise that work in the forest is difficult, and suggest that they prefer not to work there. Village residents speak of forest as a place that helps them by growing good crops, while the hamlet residents speak of owning the forest and working in it. The target group for development efforts clearly should not be those who hold themselves aloof from the forest and the bush, but should rather be the women, the children and the middle-aged, the unschooled and the hamlet residents.

The young, educated, male, village population is intent on dominating their environment to produce wealth. In contrast, the older, unschooled, female and hamlet residents have a symbiotic, respectful relation with their environment. The male villagers in particularly should be understood as managers, who take advantage of the hamlet people, regarding them simultaneously as ignorant country folk and as the source of the food and other forest and bush products that sustain the complex social life of the village. In the small compass of 131 households, the worldwide story of the exploitation of the periphery by the centre is told once again.

Rice

I applied cluster analysis and multi-dimensional scaling next to the all-important crop rice, and then to other plants. The Kpelle term for plant in practice implies cultivated crops other than upland rice (but including swamp rice) and tree crops.

Rice is the core of Kpelle agriculture and Kpelle society. There is the constant worry that there will not be enough rice, which is the most common answer to the sentence completions. Not everyone works hard to produce rice. In responses, the hamlet residents, females, children and unschooled persons stress the hard work that must be done to bring in a good rice harvest, while the village residents, men, young adults, and schooled persons emphasise buying, eating and having rice. There is a strong contrast between the producers and the consumers, a contrast which supports and reinforces the contrast mentioned above between labourers and managers.

When cluster analysis is applied to responses concerning rice, there are two significant sub-clusters. One sub-cluster brings together all the responses concerning the rice-growing cycle, from planting to harvest, and associates that cycle with the family and the cooperative work group. The other sub-cluster refers to the problems and difficulties which arise in growing rice. Particularly striking is the following group of responses: 'We don't make rice farms'; 'We work alone on the rice farm'; 'Schoolchildren don't make rice farms'; 'Some children make rice farm'; 'We buy rice' and 'We eat other foods besides rice'. When the traditional system breaks down, and the farm workers no longer produce enough rice for themselves and the managers, then people either work alone or are forced to buy their rice or eat other foods.

Multi-dimensional scaling of the responses to rice displays two major dimensions. The principal dimension is from shortage of rice to surplus, and the secondary dimension is from traditional subsistence cooperative rice farming to modern individualism. This offers further support to the contrasts noted in the cluster analysis.

There is a high degree of knowledge of rice and its varieties in Gbansu, but only among the producers, who are the people who care about rice farming. As might be expected from what has been said above, modernised, schooled, village males know almost nothing about rice varieties, as we found out by doing a simple test.

We had identified more than 100 different varieties by asking people to bring us as many different types of rice as they could. Our original intent had been to respond to a United Nations request to create a genetic bank of traditional varieties, so that in these modern days of monoculture the genetic diversity of traditional rice would not be lost. Once having collected these varieties, I designed a test to see how much ordinary people knew about the different types of rice. We found that females could name 50 per cent of the varieties, while males could name only 10 per cent. Older persons were better at naming varieties than young adults.

We then administered a second test in which two persons sat back to back on a mat. We put stalks of the same 25 varieties of rice in front of each person, and asked the first person to describe the varieties in such a way that the second person could make a correct choice. We then took an additional 25 varieties and reversed the direction of the test. We found that when the test was done by people whom villagers acknowledged to be experts in rice, they were correct in communicating the varieties in more than 70 per cent of the cases. However, when we asked people, almost always men, who admitted not knowing rice, the success rate in communication was essentially nil.

People who were successful at communicating rice varieties did so primarily by visible features, rather than by name. The most common feature was the husk colour, followed by the length of the hair at the tip of the grain. In third position after these two features came the name of the variety, followed by the hair colour, the seed colour, the seed length, the hair location, and the seed size. One reason the name was less important is that names varied significantly from hamlet to hamlet, and even from family to family. Certain varieties were easier to communicate than others, because people shared familiar descriptions, while other varieties were more difficult to describe because idiosyncratic descriptions dominated.

We asked people also to sort the 50 varieties of rice into groups which made sense to them, in other words, to create a taxonomy of the rice varieties. I subjected the results of this sorting exercise to cluster analysis, and found that the principal division among rice varieties was by colour of the husk, with a secondary split depending on the length or colour of the hair at the tip of the grain.

A similar pattern emerged from multi-dimensional scaling, with colour being the primary dimension, and hair length second.

Specific rice varieties were named for specific types of soil or bush. People, particularly older women who managed the family's rice store, were able to tell us which variety was good for which area. The best seeds were saved from the previous harvest, and used for planting in a similar area the next season. The men generally did not know which varieties should be planted where, because that is women's work. Women are producers, and men consumers!

In summary, expertise in rice is primarily the domain of women, and secondarily of unschooled older men who live in the hamlets rather than in the central village. And yet development experts prefer to deal with educated young men who live as close as possible to the main road and the modern world. A bigger mistake in development strategy can hardly be imagined!

Other crops

Rice is the principal crop, but not the only crop. As I said before, garden crops are planted, usually in the second year on an old rice farm, but also in the clearing around the family's farm shed where the rice is stored.

We interviewed people about the crops that are grown. I then did a cluster analysis of the types of crops named. They fell into two main categories: staple crops and the garden crops, which make the sauce to put on rice. Staple crops were divided into subsistence crops and cash crops. Subsistence crops were subdivided into farm crops, including principally rice, maize and cassava, and garden crops, including plantain, eddo and yam. Cash crops included cocoa, coffee, rubber, kola nut, groundnuts, beans, oranges and pumpkins. The small garden crops which go into the sauce include okra, bitterballs, pepper, eggplant and greens. Knowledge of crops was tested in much the same way as with rice varieties. We asked people to identify crops to each other without actually naming the crops. This task proved very easy for almost everyone. There was no uniform method of identifying the plants, with each plant having its own set of characteristics. Some plants were described by taste, others by the way they grow, their origin, or use. Two descriptions that I found interesting are as follows: 'There is something that we work for. We work for it very hard. We suffer for it. After you make the farm, you start scattering it. Can you tell me that thing, do you know it? That thing, after we have made the farm, the women start scattering it, as though we don't like it. They scatter it and start scratching it.'

The answer is clearly rice. It is described in such a way as to emphasise how necessary it is for survival, and how intense is the struggle to make it grow.

The other crop is described as follows: 'There is something. It came from the hands of the kwii people. They brought it here. It is what has broken our land. The leaves can get very long, and the tree can get very tall and very big. We have some around this village. They give us a knife to tap it. Do you know it?'

This is clearly rubber. The significant element in the description is that it has *broken our land*. By this the speaker refers to the fact that much good Kpelle forest land has been removed from cultivation and turned into rubber plantations. There is a poignancy in the comment, *They give us a knife to tap it*. The remote coastal elite referred to as *they* have profited from Kpelle land and labour, through planting rubber. The people of Gbansu are well aware that tree crops are a source of livelihood for them. Very few grow rubber, largely because of the difficulty in hiring tappers in such a remote area, and also because rubber is difficult to carry to market. Other tree crops fall into two categories. The first category consists of those which provide a traditional resource, such as kola nuts, plantain, banana, or piassava palm. One tree that is notably absent from this list is oil palm, because it is a gift of nature, not planted by people. The second category consists of cocoa, sugar cane, oranges, coffee and rubber, which are grown for sale to outsiders.

Leaders and workers

The next step in understanding the Gbansu view of agriculture is to analyse their approach to the allocation of labour. I have already pointed out the radical differences in attitude between men and women, village and hamlet residents, schooled and unschooled persons, and young adults as opposed to the older adults and children. I have also mentioned the fundamental split between central village and hamlets. These divisions are carried through and reach their logical culmination in the leadership and decision-making structures of the village. People who can avoid the hard and tedious work of making rice farms will do so, and there is a very clear recognition on the part of village people as to who belongs to the privileged elite.

An example of this was my friend and host, the village elder. He had long since given up doing any cultivation of his own. He had clients and wives and relatives to do his work for him. The village chief was in a similar position, although not quite so able to escape the hard work of the rice farm. He still had to show his solidarity with the community by occasionally working with his people on the farm.

We asked a set of 25 questions concerning village leadership, which gave insight into the way in which people assigned community tasks. The respondents were asked to name people who excelled in such categories as farm work, hunting, medicine, intelligence, strength, trustworthiness, wealth, friendship, modernisation, politics, and law. It is striking that more than 20 per cent of the total population of Gbansu, including both the central village and the hamlets, were named at least once. However, if I eliminated those named only once, I was able to reduce the list to 63 persons. It is important to realise that of these 63 persons only 10 were women. Gbansu is a male-dominated society. The village elder was named in 13.5 per cent of the responses and the chief in 8.5 per cent. Other important figures were the leading Muslim (6.2 per cent), the leading blacksmith (4.8 per cent), an influential farmer (4.7 per cent), a young wealthy farmer (4.5 per cent), a young storekeeper (4.1 per cent), and a young seller of medicine (4.0 per cent).

What was more significant than merely the list of important people was the way in which cluster analysis of the answers reveals the social structure of Gbansu. The accompanying figure shows the social system more clearly than I could have ever done during my eight months of observation. The central political leadership is the set of 21 persons I have called non-entrepreneurs, made up of 16 village leaders and 5 forest leaders. The village leaders include the central core of important office holders and a peripheral group of family heads and minor office holders. The contrast between village and forest leaders is quite sharp. The entrepreneurs are those who remain part of the traditional culture, but whose role is to make their living in exchange of goods, for example, the Muslim storekeepers who buy kola nuts to send to savanna areas in Ivory Coast, Guinea and Mali, and who then sell goods which come from those regions.

Those whose primary way of life is farming are not part of the main leader-ship group, as might be expected from the previous analyses. They are acknowl-edged for their skill and energy, but are not central. The other traditional group which is outside the main stream of day-to-day leadership consists of the elders. They have enjoyed power in the past, but have now moved to the status of elder, where they give advice and dispense traditional medicines. However, the elders are not expected to perform farm labour.

The modern group divides young modern adults from modern healers. The first subgroup contrasts those who are purely part of the modern world, and would never dirty their hands with farm work, with those who fill roles in both worlds, particularly the evangelist, the school teacher and the clan chief. The second subgroup parallels the elder category in the traditional sector, and con-sists of healers. There was no medical practitioner qualified according to west-ern standards in the village, and so these healers performed the role, selling injections of something which may have been penicillin and may have been condensed milk! I then subjected the questions themselves to cluster analysis, according to the similarity of distribution of persons across questions. In this case, as with the taxonomy of village leaders, there are two main categories: traditional and modern. Each category in turn is subdivided in the cluster analysis into subcategories reflecting power and knowledge. The same dimen-sions appear in the two-dimensional diagram produced by multi-dimensional scaling.

Traditional power is measured by physical strength, status in local politics, a large family, good crops and farm skills. Knowledge in the traditional sense involves medicine, the forest, secret matters, and the ability to give good advice in the affairs of the village. Modern power, on the other hand, extends to money, government affairs, education and the ability to decide court cases. Modern knowledge includes modern medicine, modern work and the ability to change old matters. Almost every one of the leading figures in power and influ-ence lives in the central village, as must be anticipated on the basis of the previ-ous analysis. The hamlet residents receive some grudging respect in terms of their knowledge of the forest, their ability to farm and the quality of their crops. But even in this case, the good farmers in the hamlets depend on their patrons in the central village. The person who wields power visits the hamlet from time to time to check on farming activities there, and may even have a hamlet that belongs to his immediate family, where he keeps his clients and their wives, but his main activities lie in the central village.

The relations between the central village and the farms are reflected in the layout of the central village itself and the trails to the farm areas. There are four main quarters in the central village, each with its quarter chief. The village chief and village elder belong to the principal quarter, while the other three quarters are more recent and are subordinate to the village chief's quarter. The central quarter was founded by the great-grandfather of the present village elder. This chief dominated the entire set of villages along the St. Paul River, and Gbansu was his central place. He contracted a series of marriages which define the rela-tions between the central quarter and the peripheral quarters. In particular, the Muslim community married into his family, and thus secured for itself a place in local society.

But wealth and political power are not strictly a matter of inheritance. The present leading figures acquired their influence and possessions through their own efforts, and especially through making advantageous marriages.

I.   Traditional leaders
A.   Middle-aged adults
    1.   Village-centred leaders
       a.   Non-entrepreneurs
          (1) Village leaders
            (a) Political leaders
                i.   Core leaders
                    (i) Chief and elder
                    (ii) Muslim leaders
                ii. Quarter chiefs
            (b) Family heads
                i.   Minor office holders
                ii. Wealthy family heads
          (2) Forest leaders
            (a) Secret society leaders
            (b) Good hunters
       b.   Entrepreneurs
          (1) Muslim storekeepers
          (2) Unscrupulous young men
    2.   Farm-centred leaders
       a.   Farm leaders
          (1) Cooperative work group leaders
          (2) Hamlet heads
       b.   Energetic farmers
          (1) Women
          (2) Marginal men
B.   Elders
    1.   Leading elders
       a.   Senior elders
       b.   Junior elders
    2.   Traditional doctors
II. Modern leaders
A.   Leading young adults
    1.   More modernised young adults
       a.   Active in the village
       b.   Residing outside the village
    2.   Less modernised young adults
       a.   Young farmers
          (1) Evangelist
          (2) Teacher
          (3) Clan chief
B.   Modern healers
    1.   Resident in the village
    2.   Resident in Monrovia

Figure 20.3: *Taxonomy of leading Gbansu citizens*

In Gbansu, marriage is a mechanism for social mobility, and often wives are transferred within leading families, or assigned to poor clients in order to build up one's own extended family. Through such a series of marriages and wife exchanges, the village chief and the village elder are able to claim as relatives essentially everyone in the community.

Each of the hamlets is in some way related to one of the leading residents of the central village, because these leading residents have located their clients and junior wives on farm sites which eventually became hamlets. Because of these linkages the spatial distribution of hamlets mirrors directly the spatial distribution of households within the central village.

I found it possible to reproduce a reasonable facsimile of the map of trails and farm areas and hamlets with respect to the central village by performing a multi-dimensional scaling and cluster analysis of the relation of each of 120 adults in Gbansu to the four quarters, to the hamlets, to the farming areas, and to the political leaders. The result is that the distribution of trails, farming areas and hamlets exactly matches the distribution of relations between households in the central village, expanded along radial lines which have their origin at the house of the village elder. Once again cluster analysis and multi-dimensional scaling demonstrate the integrity of the total community as an organism, albeit an organism with its own class structure and mechanism of exploitation of the periphery by the centre.

Development based on understanding

I return to the question: how does this organism which is Gbansu understand farming? In answer to this question, I summarise what I have said thus far. Rice cultivation is necessary to the maintenance of life, and provides the framework for all other activities. In order to grow rice, the community depends on a complex attitude to and knowledge of the land and its resources within the circumscribed territory at its disposal. It knows what varieties of rice, as well as what other crops, to plant on the different types of forest, bush and soil. And it organises the people of the community in a complex social system that allows its leaders to create and maintain the social structure that is supported by the producers of rice.

If aid experts wish to help the people of Gbansu, and all the many villages like it across Africa, they should begin by recognising the community for what it is. Gbansu is not a collection of replicas of 'The Kpelle Farmer'. It is not merely a conglomerate of individuals, with their own separate and differing identities. It is a living organism that has achieved over the centuries an understanding of its environment and thus knows how to sustain itself.

The only way to aid such a community is to help it – as a whole – to adapt to new and changing conditions. Were there world enough and time, Gbansu would make its own adjustment and would either continue to sustain itself, or would give birth to a new community. There is unfortunately little time and less world, as population grows and western society pushes into every corner of the globe. Thus a solution to the aid and development question must be found which makes the inevitable and ongoing intervention of the outside world into the affairs of Gbansu both humane and potentially successful.

Little has been done for or against the people of Gbansu in the period since I left it, except for the building of a motor road which is only open during dry weather.

There is therefore still the possibility that development aid to Gbansu can avoid destroying the organism that I have tried to describe in this paper. It seems clear that insensitive aid merely leads to destruction of the old without the aid agent being a thoughtful midwife to the new. What is needed instead is a development effort that grows naturally from within Gbansu itself, respecting the time-honoured lines of authority and the time-proven technology of living in balance with the rain forest.

Listening to what Gbansu knows is the right way to begin. And that means seeing the forest, the bush and the swamps through the eyes of the different strata in Gbansu society. It means knowing what rice means and how it works, and thus not insensitively imposing swamp rice technology on a community which has good reasons for not accepting it. It means working at each level of development with those individuals, families and social groups that already operate at these levels. It means understanding how the village and the hamlets stand in the relation of producer and consumer, labourer and manager. It means seeing the central village as a microcosm of the 400 square km of forest, bush, swamp, river, trail, farm, hamlet and village, and seeing the totality of the land as the central village writ large.

But above all it means seeing that all of these work together to form a living system. It is not possible to tinker with one part of the system without affecting the remainder. Thus the outsider intervenes with fear and trembling, unless he or she is intent on destruction. Far better is to approach Gbansu quietly and patiently, waiting until it shows where it is going and where it wants to go.

The Kpelle have a proverb: *Sitting quietly reveals crocodile's tricks.* The people of Gbansu are very good at applying that proverb to outsiders. Unfortunately, the crocodile that is the outsider world is too strong for the people of Gbansu to do more than simply adopt delaying tactics, which so far have worked reasonably well. If the outsiders wish to be more than the destructive crocodile, it is time for them to adopt the same strategy in reverse. Let them watch and wait, too, and between all concerned, a development strategy may emerge which respects the organism that is Gbansu.

21. Use of Local Knowledge in Managing the Niger River Fisheries Project[1]

THOMAS L. PRICE

Introduction

THE NIGER RIVER Fisheries Project evolved based on a premise different from most 'development projects' financed by bilateral or multilateral donors and executed in conjunction with national services. Although many contemporary projects assign at least superficial priority to local initiative, participation and responsibility, the technical interventions in agriculture, animal husbandry and health, are inspired by models external to local contexts. Little effort is devoted to adapting new techniques to local technologies or techniques; less effort is devoted to extension work inspired by local knowledge. National and foreign staff on the Niger River Project decided instead to root fisheries management in a dialogue between their technical services and fishermen organisation and knowledge. The economic, social and cultural characteristics of the fishing communities became central to project activity, rather than accessories for identifying constraints to introducing new technologies.

Niger fishermen have a profound knowledge of river ecology, that once served as the basis for their management of the fisheries. Project personnel solicited details of this knowledge and organisation from senior fishermen, complemented by information from biological, fish capture and socioeconomic surveys. They subsequently presented propositions for future management based on the resulting synthesis of scientific and local knowledge. Fishermen and fisheries agents debated the justifications, means of application, and effects of each management approach in a series of public meetings.

This procedure was a significant departure from the former practice of fisheries service. Fishermen responded quickly with interest in revitalising local practices based on a respect of their knowledge, in collaboration with government technical services. Project results suggest this approach is a genuine foundation for long-term development by and for local populations.

Historical background

Fishing is an ancient profession for specific groups along the Niger River. The *Sorko* fishermen and hunters have dominated the resource from Timbuktu in Mali to Lake Kainji in Nigeria, as have the Bozo and Somono in the Inner Delta. Ample documentary evidence attests to the predominance of this group in the region since at least the fifteenth century (Rouch 1950; Sundström 1972).

The *Sorko* are originally Songhay-speaking populations from around Bourem and Gao in the eastern bend of the Niger River. They have a central position in Songhay history. Their putative ancestor – Faran Maka Boté – founded the site for the imperial Songhay capital at Gao. During their movements between the Inner Delta and Kainji, they adapted local fishing techniques and spread their own knowledge throughout the region.

The *Sorko* were expert in hunting and fishing techniques for all aquatic fauna. Given the disintegration of the Songhay empire after the Moroccan invasion in the late sixteenth century, and the subsequent Fulani and Tuareg incursions until the early twentieth century, the *Sorko* limited the range of their movements. *Sorko* adopted the dialect or language predominant in their region, for example Songhay-Kaado in the river bend and Hausa around Kainji (these later populations became the *Sorkawa* in Hausa). In the early colonial period, these fishermen started travelling widely in the region, going as far as the Inner Delta, the Benoué River and Onitsha (Rouch 1950). The groups recognise common descent and share a common social organisation based on corporate patrilines. The *Sorko* historically regulated access and exploitation of the fisheries. For example, they specified fishing seasons, limiting fishing techniques by season or region, banned specific fishing techniques or gears, and selected sanctuaries for fish reproduction and growth. The senior fishermen based their authority on their knowledge and relationships with the water deities.

Another population putatively descended from the autochthonous riverine peoples (locally glossed as the *Gurma*) are important in the fishing communities. The *Do* ('water masters') maintain the religious prerogatives of their ancestors who propitiated the waters before the arrival of the *Sorko*. The *Do* remain central to the secular and ritual practices that regulate the resource. The senior *Sorko* and *Do* historically collaborated in local management.

The French colonial government radically affected the powers of the *Sorko* and the *Do*. Bodies of water became a common good regulated exclusively by the state for the entire population. The 'Waters and Forestry' (Eaux et Forêts) staff managed the fisheries for the colonial administration. Given an emphasis on European management models based on external information, the staff ignored local authority and knowledge.

The Niger government fisheries staff that inherited this administration at independence followed their predecessors' disregard for the fishermen's knowledge. The marginalisation of local authorities paralleled radical transformations in fishing gears and labour organisation. Manufactured nets imported from the coastal regions (such as Ghana) rapidly replaced locally produced nets, traps, harpoons and other gears, particularly after the Second World War (Sundström 1972). Dugouts carved in southern Nigeria – and later canoes built with imported planks – replaced canoes built using local woods. Outboard motors have completely replaced sails and oars on the large transport craft since the 1960s.

Work groups have become considerably smaller due to new gears, new techniques, and the ban on previous game and techniques. The fisheries service banned the collective hunting and fishing once common to the Niger River and her tributaries (such as the Sirba River). Many *Sorko* cooperated in hunting the large aquatic animals such as hippopotamus (see Rouch 1948). Large work groups, and periodically entire villages, assembled to exploit the traps, dams and other devices used seasonally.

The FAO Niger River Fisheries Project in Niger

The Nigerian Fisheries Direction (Direction des Faunes, Pêches et Pisciculture)[2] has initiated a new approach to Niger River fishermen since 1983. A multi-disciplinary team drawn from several institutions collaborated in developing this approach. An FAO-staffed and UNDP-funded fisheries project for Niger completed basic research on the river environment, fish populations, captures, and fishermen society and economy between 1983 and 1987. Peace Corps volunteers

Map 21.1: *Niger in Africa*
Source: Price (1987: 8)

and staff from the Department of Fisheries at Auburn University in Alabama participated in the research design, execution, and analysis. The research results served as the 'scientific' basis for a fisheries management plan.

The project staff and the fishermen started a dialogue in 1985 concerning the pre-existing organisation of the fisheries. The fishermen particularly emphasised the value of local management enforced by their own authorities. They blamed the lack of any effective replacement by the national fisheries service as a key cause in the decline of capture quantity and quality.

Project research detailed the dramatic condition of the fisheries often described by the fishermen. Average annual water flow has declined dramatically. Decreasing inundations of the floodplains essential to fish reproduction and growth, as well as closing extensive areas for irrigation projects (currently about 25 per cent of the floodplains), have seriously affected resource diversity and carrying capacity. Over ten fish species have virtually disappeared from the fisheries (Malvestuto, Meredith 1986a; Coenen 1987).

Human pressure has compounded the ecological crisis. Approximately 3000 fishermen dispersed among 240 riverside villages exploit the 550 kilometres of the Niger River in Niger. Fishermen have used fewer types of fishing gears and techniques over the last 30 years, which has paralleled the decreasing seasonal flood basin (Coenen and Price 1987).

The seasonal composition of locally manufactured traps, nets and other gears to micro-environmental conditions has yielded to the use of more 'efficient' industrial gears (Burtonboy 1987). Smaller work groups have tried to maintain their captures in spite of lower water levels by using increasingly selective gears. Average mesh size for nets has thus declined from 40 mm to 20 mm between the 1960s and the 1980s. Destructive gears, particularly seine nets and small-mesh cast nets used during the low water season, have become common in some areas.

These ecological and human factors have combined with dramatic effect. Annual production has fallen from 4500 metric tons in 1960 to 900 metric tons in 1985 (Daget 1962; Malvestuto and Meredith 1986a). Average daily capture by fishermen has also declined from 12.5 kg to 1.5 kg during the same period. By the late 1970s and early 1980s, the entire river was under heavy pressure with some regions extremely overfished. For the Gaya region, 80 per cent to 90 per cent of the capture for the 16 major commercial species was immature in 1985.

Under these circumstances, many fishermen, particularly in the heavily over-fished zones, cannot cover the recurrent costs for their equipment. Nigerian fishermen have moved to other fishing grounds (though Malian fishermen from between the Inner Delta and Gao have replaced these fishermen). Other fisher-men now rely on agriculture, animal husbandry, commerce and other activities until the fisheries improve (Price 1987). Given this crisis, the fishermen approached the project staff for possible alternatives to the continuing decline in the resource.

Developing management approaches

Project staff started from the basic premise that any effective approach to improving conditions in the Niger River fisheries must respect fishermen knowl-edge and authority. The research conducted on contemporary environmental and socioeconomic conditions served simultaneously as a means of gathering critical information and establishing a dialogue with influential community members key to future project success.[3]

The project approach corresponded fortuitously with the Niger government leaders' increasing emphasis on local initiative and responsibility as part of the 'Development Society' ('Société de Développement'). Groups organise on geo-graphical and professional bases in order to manage local development and exploit government technical services. In practice, the groups at least start to have a coherent voice at meetings with government administrators.

The fishermen expressed strong interest to project staff in starting their own professional associations ('Groupements Socio-Professionnels'). The fishermen established 11 associations at the district administrative level ('canton') covering the entire Niger River in Niger between 1985 and 1987. The governing commit-tees of each include senior local *Sorko* and *Do*. All fishermen are members of their local association, including 'foreign' fishermen from Mali and Nigeria.[4] Foreign fishermen are also represented in the governing committees, with eight to twelve members.

The regional government representatives ('chefs de canton', 'chefs de postes administratifs' and 'sous-préfets') formally recognised the creation of these associations. Although the groups correspond to national administrative divi-sions, the governing committees recognise the pre-existing zones of authority. The fishermen also plan to eventually constitute an overarching committee for the entire river drawn from the senior community members. The relevant minis-ter and the fisheries director first officially met with some of these senior officials in October 1986. The elaboration of the proposed management measures paralleled the birth of the fishermen associations. In effect, the measures furnish the basic content for the structure of the associations. Fishermen see the *raison d'etre* for the associations as the destruction of local authority, and thus local management. Discussions often focused on pre-existing forms of management and their justification. Forums, with 20 to 50 fishermen present for each association, then compared these practices with contemporary conditions and modern management approaches.

National laws include a number of regulations in order to prevent over-exploitation (Burtonboy 1986: Appendix). These regulations include prohibiting specific gears and regulating net mesh size by hydrological season. Although there are many similarities with pre-existing management practices, authority was uniquely invested in government technical services. The severely limited coverage of the river by a few fisheries agents, combined with frequent individual cases of these agents not enforcing regulations, have neutralised any enforcement of the legislation. In Niamey, some fishermen routinely catch fingerlings with 20 mm or even 10 mm mesh cast nets under the noses of the fisheries agents. Joint management furnished a viable alternative to the contemporary collapse in exercised authority.

The meetings between project staff and fishermen in 1985 specified the forms and historical transformations in local management. In early 1986, the project staff drafted their initial proposals for management measures based on these discussions and research results.

The resulting management plan evaluated the immediate and later impacts of effective measures in order to soften the implications for fishermen capture and income. The government fisheries service and the fishermen associations become joint managers for the resource, with primary responsibilities returned to the producers.

The fishermen and staff debated these proposals between April and September 1986. The project staff presented a final draft of the management plan to the Niger Government in late 1986. The FAO fish biologist and socioeconomist drafted a proposition for further project development while adapting the management measures to local reactions and circumstances through March 1987. The fishermen associations have since continued to coordinate their activities with the fisheries service as part of the gradual implementation of the management plan.

The measures

The fishermen associations are the primary enforcers of the management measures. The governing committees are responsible for regulating members' exploitation of the resource through individual counselling and public meetings, with final recourse to government agents when members continually refuse to observe restrictions. The fisheries remain open to both commercial and subsistence exploitation, though the associations are generally responsible for all management.

The discussions held between 1985 and 1987 inspired a series of propositions for fisheries management. Three kinds of measures are discussed in detail below:

Fishing sanctuaries. Fishermen have identified many locations along the river formerly restricted or forbidden for fishing. Local riverine authorities managed these points *(guntu)* by secular and religious regulations. *Do* and *Sorko* held annual and periodic ceremonies to the river deities at the *guntu*, including prayers, sacrifices and spirit possession dances. Fishermen violating local regulations were subject to public shaming, fines and eventually exclusion from regional fishing grounds.

The *guntu* generally correspond to particularly deep sections of the river that fishermen depict as critical for flora and fauna reproduction and growth. The water deities inhabit villages on the river bottom at these points. They control caverns where immature fish take refuge during the low water season. Other river fauna such as crocodiles and manatees also flourish in these areas. River bank and underwater shrines provided points of communication in order to insure the cooperation of these deities in the annual hydrological cycle.

Fishing in the *guntu* was therefore restricted seasonally or banned altogether in order to avoid compromising the entire resource. The loud sounds of outboard motors or of cast nets striking the river surface disturbed the deities. Nets drawn through the waters or scraping the river bottom drove all fauna deep into submerged caverns.

Although respect of these regulations has become sporadic, *Sorko* and *Do* can easily designate the *guntu* in their region. Project personnel suspected that these zones probably correspond closely to ideal sites for reserves and limited seasons. While awaiting a later biological study, the associations can identify the *guntu* in their jurisdiction and re-introduce local regulation. Some of the associations have already produced an itemised inventory for joint consultation with fisheries personnel (see Maps 21.2 and 21.3).

Fishing gears and techniques. During community meetings, *Sorko* and *Do* frequently emphasised the decline in the fisheries due to new gears and techniques. They particularly criticise the use of seine and small mesh cast nets. Seine nets scrape the bottom of the river, thus disturbing the deities and spirits inhabiting the river bottom.

The catastrophic effects of these nets is particularly marked when used at *guntu*. The fishermen emphasise that they exhaust the resource by eliminating all mature and many immature fish.

Cast nets used at low water have a similar effect. The technique of using small mesh cast nets during the low water season has become common among individuals of non-fishermen descent, with little capital investment in gears. *Bozo* fishermen with other traditions, and who recently arrived from the Inner Delta, spread bran on the water surface to attract small fish, which are gathered in the small mesh. They dry their capture to produce salted fish cakes for seasoning sauces. *Sorko* and *Do* concur that these techniques, and the progressive decrease in average mesh size for all nets, destroy the mature fish essential to reproduction. Average fish size at capture also declines, and thus capture value drops.

The governing committees of the associations proposed the ban of seine nets and small mesh nets, and seasonal restrictions on the use of cast nets. Subsequent debates aimed at developing measures administered by the associations, with the least dramatic effect on fishermen capture and income. The proposed measures finally included (Burtonboy 1987):

- banning all seine nets and small mesh cast nets;
- banning the use of cast nets during the low water season;

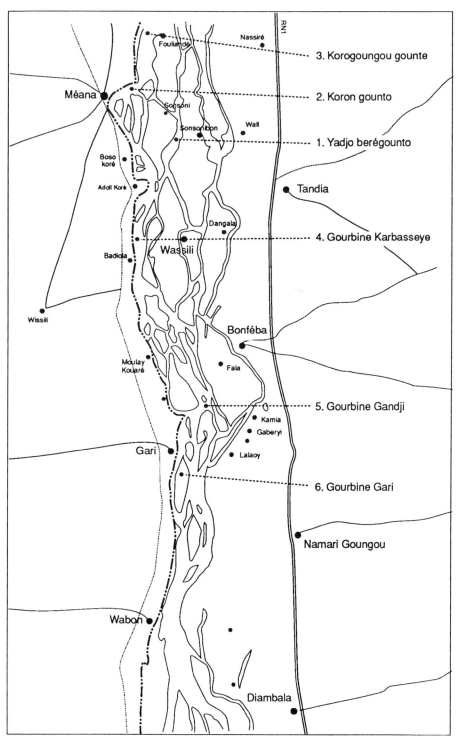

Map 21.2: *Inventory of Guntu*

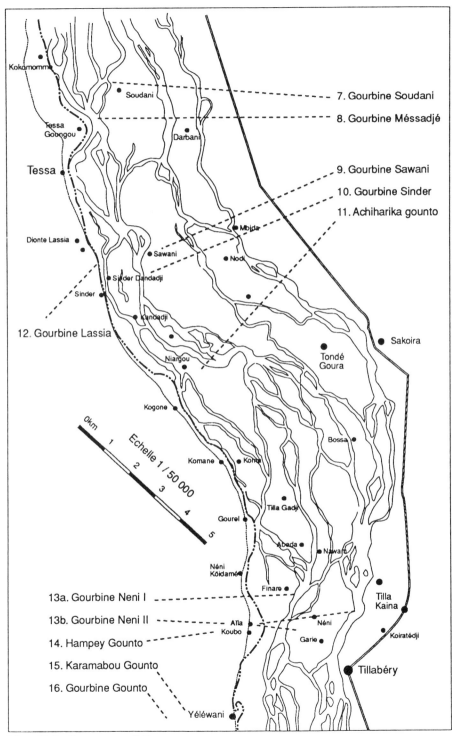

Map 21.3: *Inventory of Guntu*

○ banning trade or fabrication of mesh sizes of less than 40 mm. Fishermen can still use their nets with smaller mesh until discarded from normal wear. The many nets with 20 mm and 30 mm mesh sizes will disappear within one to two years given local use.

The fishermen associations will administer these regulations, with assistance from the national fisheries service upon request.

Fish growth and maturity. Sorko have an extensive vocabulary in Songhay and Hausa to distinguish the numerous fish species. The biological survey identified approximately 110 species currently in the Niger River in Niger (Coenen 1987). Fishermen categorise most fish using characteristics similar to European taxonomic classifications. Senior *Sorko* stress differences in fish species ('races', or *dumi* in Songhay) that are associated with important differences in behaviour and habitat. Fish are also ranked by their powers and putative seniority.

Sorko indicate major differences in average growth and size at maturity by species. They have stated that the indiscriminate fishing of all small fish depletes the stock of mature fish key to reproduction. Specific, diminutive species are normally captured as bait and by women and children as complementary relishes for daily consumption.

The project biologist developed a profile for size at maturity for the twenty major commercial species (Coenen 1987). This information served as the basis for illustrating the relationship between local and scientific notions of size at maturity. The governing committees have subsequently disseminated this information to the fishermen using the visual materials furnished to each association.

Conclusion

Associating local populations with natural resource management is not unique to fisheries in Niger. Contemporary programs in forest and wildlife management also rely on local interest and organisation, such as the Guesselbodi-managed forest for firewood near Niamey, and the new wildlife reserve in the Air Mountains. However, these programs are not yet rooted in indigenous knowledge of the environment and conceptions of human relationships with nature.

Although the management plan for the Niger River fisheries is not a reproduction of previous management, the process used to arrive at a regional approach respects local prerogatives. *Sorko* and *Do* recognise that the dramatic environmental and human transformations in the river basin have fundamental implications for all fishermen. They know that greater rainfall and higher water levels will not eliminate the effects of dams in Mali, or irrigated perimeters in Niger, or of denser riverside settlement. Information offered by the fisheries service on topics including fish biology and regional environmental change excites interest and discussion. Government fisheries agents thus provide technical advice and some regional services as the fishermen create new approaches to the fisheries inspired by local knowledge.

Notes

1 Based on applied research as an Institute for Development Anthropology Research Fellow for FAO on the Socioeconomic Study of the Niger River in Niger: GCP/NER/027/USA from August 13, 1984, to June 30, 1986. Subsequent participation on the project was sponsored by USAID/NIGER Contract No. 683-0230-C-00-

6025-00 from July 1 to September 30, 1986, and then through FAO TCP/NER/6652 (T) until March 31, 1987. Independent research has continued under Government of Niger Ministry of Education research permission number 00947 issued March 26, 1987.

2 The administrative organisation of the national fisheries service has changed several times. The incorporation of fisheries within 'Eaux et Forêts' ('Water and Forests') remained unchanged from the colonial through the national administration until 1981. Fisheries then became a separate administration – the Direction des Pêches et de la Pisciculture – within the Ministry of Hydraulics and Environment. In late 1987, fisheries was again reorganised to become the Direction des Faunes, Pêches et Pisci-culture within the Ministry of Agriculture and Environment. These administrative divisions reflect gradual improvements in technical training, increasing specialisation of government personnel, and national emphasis on environmental issues.

3 The genesis and development of the collaborative approach to fisheries management was only possible with the support of fisheries agents issue of river communities and – of course – the lively interest of the senior members of the fishing communities. Special acknowledgments are due to Mr. Adamou Harouna Touré, Lieutenant des Eaux et Forêts, Mr. Djibo Salou, Adjudant-Chef des Eaux et Forêts (deceased), Mr. Moussa Gado, Senior Sorko of Karey Kopto, and the governing committees of the Fishermen Associations of Sinder and the Sirba River.

4 All fishermen commercialising part of their catch are automatically active members of each local association. Individuals fishing strictly for their household consumption may participate in association meetings. Membership is – at least at present – open to new arrivals from other regions in Niger or abroad (a significant number of Malians from the Inner Delta and the Niger Bend have settled locally during the 1980s).

22. Farmers Who Experiment: An untapped resource for agricultural research and development

ROBERT RHOADES AND ANTHONY BEBBINGTON

Introduction

THROUGHOUT THE CHANCHAMAYO Valley of Peru's Eastern high jungle, he was known as 'El Loco,' the crazy one. He had migrated in 1978 to the Chanchamayo from the Highland Department of Huancavelica. Although his real name was Anchuraycu, he quickly acquired his nickname from a reputation of bold and sometimes comical experimenting. 'El Loco' was notorious for moving plants or seeds of important crops between extreme climates on the Andean slopes where temperature and climates change rapidly as one climbs from the jungle to the mountains. He uprooted potato seeds from their cool Highland home and carried them downhill to the hot, sultry jungle. With the banana, he carted it up the mountain to the point where he suspected it would not do well just to see what would happen. He was an incurable grafter, planter of many varieties, but above all an expert in home-designed agricultural experiments.

We first met 'El Loco' in 1980 while surveying possibilities of introducing the potato *(Solanum tuberosum)* into the hot, humid tropics (Rhoades and Recharte n.d.). The International Potato Centre had established an experimental station on the valley floor of the Chanchamayo at 800 m to conduct basic research in the development of a tropical potato. Our job as anthropologists was to explore the surrounding countryside to see if any farmers had attempted to grow potatoes. We stumbled upon 'El Loco' while he was cultivating a maize field. Our altimeter told us we were standing at around 890 metres, approximately a thousand metres below where potatoes can be grown satisfactorily. To our amazement, hidden and shaded among his maize was a beautiful stand of potatoes. 'El Loco' was obviously proud of this experiment, in a way reminiscent of our biological science colleagues. 'I'll castrate anyone who touches these potatoes', he scolded while waving a large machete. Experimentation for 'El Loco' was obviously serious business.

'El Loco' was one of the more extreme cases we encountered, but he was not the only farmer in the Chanchamayo who experimented with potatoes. In fact, our 1980 survey revealed that 90 per cent of all settler farmers of the upper Chanchamayo were avid experimenters. Perhaps some were more active than others, but virtually all conducted *pruebas* or trials, particularly with the potato. Although the Chanchamayo is an in-migrant zone, which links two major climatic zones and agricultural systems (highlands and lowland jungle) and therefore particularly conducive to farmer-based experimentation, evidence is now rapidly accumulating that small-scale producers of the Andes and elsewhere in the world are systematic, folk scientists in the creation of their own indigenous technologies or in the testing of introduced techniques (Chambers, Pacey and Thrupp 1989; Rhoades 1987).

The objectives of this chapter are three-fold:

○ to discuss farmer experimentation as revealed in the literature;
○ to analyse case studies of different kinds of farm experimentation with potatoes in Peru; and
○ to draw out the implications of this farmer-based research for scientists.

We will deal only slightly with the actual design, method and underlying episte-mologies involved in farmer experimentation. The data for this chapter were collected as a by-product of several independent studies of potato production in Peru, in particular, an agrarian ecological study of the Chanchamayo Valley and adjacent higher lying communities of Peru's *ceja de selva* (Rhoades and Recharte n.d.; Recharte 1981; Bebbington 1988). At the time of data collection, we were impressed by, but not fully aware of, the significance of widespread experimentation by farmers.

Farmers as experimenters: what the literature tells us

In the vast literature on agricultural development, almost no attention has been given to farmers as active experimenters or innovators in their own right (Rhoades 1987). Farmers have been primarily seen as adopters of technologies introduced from the outside, but not as creators of their own solutions (*see* the 1962 diffusion/adoption literature of the E. Rogers' School of Rural Sociology). The image we have come to accept is that peasant agriculture is stagnant and impetus for change must come from extraneous credit, education, and new tech-nologies (Schultz 1964). Peasants, although seen as rational actors in a con-strained circumstance, have been portrayed as shackled by low state investment in agriculture, by traditional culture, or by a marginal environment. Any innova-tions or technological breakthroughs made by farmers on their own were thought to be accidental and to have developed unsystematically through trial and error.

A small but growing literature challenges this view of the passive, small-scale producer in developing countries. Carl Sauer (1969) was an early proponent of the inventiveness of such farmers. He based his arguments both upon Latin American fieldwork and deductions about the origins of agriculture – deduc-tions that drew explicitly on the idea that proto-farmers with spare time would have been interested experimenters, who based their projects on their observa-tions of the local ecology. Also in the cultural-historical/cultural-ecological vein, discussions of the pioneer experience at the frontier have documented conscious experimentation by farmers encountering new environments (*e.g.* Thompson 1973). For Thompson such experimentation is part of the process of ecological adaptation (1973: 14–15). Turner (1961: 3) also implies that this process of learning a new ecology – as 'Little by little…[the colonist]…transforms the wilderness' – is part of the essence of the frontier experience.

A more explicit discussion of farmer creativity is offered in the seminal article of anthropologist Allen Johnson (1972). He points to discrepancies between his, Harold Conklin's (1957) and others' observations in the field and anthropologi-cal assumptions about culture-bound farmers who blindly follow the dictates of cultural traditions. Rather than pursuing time-tested rules, Johnson's evidence suggests that farmers act creatively and individually. He argues that, like biological evolution, cultural evolution (including agricultural change) also requires individual variation and adaptation (*see* also Denevan 1983). In a later article, Stephen Biggs and Edward Clay (1981) drew an important distinction between informal and formal research and development systems. In the informal system, farmers engage in indigenous experimentation and purposive selection in a continuous process of innovation. The advantage 'lies in the users of the technology innovating to meet their own needs by drawing on detailed knowledge of their environment and exploiting the opportunities offered by natural selection' (Biggs and Clay 1981: 325). The generator and user is therefore the same. The problems of communication and relevancy are greatly diminished.

In a workshop held in 1987 at the Institute of Development Studies (U.K.), the 'farmer as experimenter' was more fully developed in a series of papers (Rhoades 1987; Richards 1987; Box 1987; Edwards 1987). Rhoades (1987) and Richards (1987) argue that the archaeological and historical record show a long string of important agricultural technology breakthroughs made by farmers in traditional societies, although their rapidity and diffusion might have been slower than innovations in modern agricultural science.

Rhoades (1987) further posits that a scientific method, broadly defined, is followed by experimenting farmers. This notion was developed earlier in the writings of Claude Lévi-Strauss (1966: 14) who, in commenting on humankind's great achievements including the development of agriculture and domestication of animals, noted: 'Each of these techniques assumes centuries of active and methodical observation, of bold hypothesis testing by means of endlessly repeated experiments.' Lévi-Strauss readily admits that the peasants *science of the concrete*' as opposed to scientists' *science of the abstract*, as in the natural sciences, represent different levels of science. However, the science of the concrete is 'no less scientific and its results no less genuine. They were secured ten thousand years earlier and still remain at the basis of our own civilisation' (Lévi-Strauss 1966: 16).

Howes and Chambers (1979), in contrasting Indigenous Technical Knowledge (ITK) and Institutionally Organised Science, also stress that: 'the mode of ITK is concrete, not abstract' (see Farrington and Martin 1987). Indeed, conditions inherent in farm reality may limit the relevance of abstract 'basic' science while enhancing the power of concrete, 'applied' science. Potato scientists, for example, study 'how potatoes grow' (physiological changes, tuber formation, and nutrient uptake), but they may not know 'how to grow potatoes.' Furthermore, scientists, out of touch with farm reality, may not know how to transform their important knowledge of 'how potatoes grow' into practical knowledge of actually growing potatoes. Farmers, on the other hand, are often experts in growing potatoes, but could not necessarily explain scientifically the basis of that growth. However, they may advance lay explanations of crop performance. The trick is to link productively the two levels of 'science.' Dovetailing indigenous farmers' experiments with scientists' experiments is one option to improve the generation and transfer of appropriate technologies for traditional agriculture.

Given the paucity of research on how and why farmers experiment, this chapter attempts to examine from a critical perspective farmer's experimentation in three situations in Peru: (1) a traditional potato producing zone, the highlands above 2,500 m above sea level; (2) a hot, humid non-traditional potato zone, below 2,000 m above seal level, where the crop meets its environmental limits;

and (3) a district where farmer experimentation succeeded beyond scientific and governmental imagination. The third situation illustrates both the great potential as well as the risks inherent in indigenous farmer's experimentation. It further shows how the learning process stimulated through experimentation will be tested against and brought back in line with broader ecological and economic realities.

Farmer experimentation in two Peruvian potato production zones

Experiments in the traditional zone The mountains of the Peruvian Andes, flanked by a rainless arid coast on the west and the humid, Amazon jungle on the east, are one of the earth's ecologically-diverse regions. As one of the great centres of plant genetic diversity and crop evolution (Vavilov 1949), this region still sustains wild species and land races of the potato, sweet potato, lima bean, tomato, sea island cotton, papaya, and tobacco, along with dozens of minor crops. Over the centuries, Andean women and men have experimented with and manipulated these plants so that both plants and people are interdependent for survival (Gade 1975).

Among the world's most experienced potato farmers and consumers are found in Peruvian communities located between 2500 and 4500 m above sea level. Both cash income and household consumption depend on the hardy potato crop more than any other. Since the Andean potato production system is both ancient and well-defined, experimentation rarely takes on a radical character. Three kinds of experiments with potatoes can be identified:

○ curiosity experiments;
○ problem-solving experiments;
○ adaptation experiments.

Curiosity experiments Farmers, like most people, are curious. Indeed, Sauer (1969) identified such curiosity as a crucial factor in the original development of agriculture. He argues that populations, in stress-free environments and with time on their hands, would use that time to identify patterns of plant growth, experiment, and ultimately plant crops they had gathered previously. Farmers commonly set up a simple experiment to test an idea that comes to mind. These experiments may or may not have an immediate practical end. CIP anthropologist Gordon Prain (personal communication) tells of a farmer in the village of Chicche in Mantaro Valley who developed the hypothesis that cultivars expressing apical dominance would yield fewer but larger tubers, which would bring a better price, than cultivars without apical dominance, which have more shoots, but smaller tubers at maturity. To test this hypothesis, he has now planted two rows in his country yard garden: one row with apical dominance and the other row without. Although this experiment may ultimately have a practical end, it was stimulated fundamentally by curiosity.

Another example of the curiosity experiment is the planting of true botanical potato seed by farmers. Potatoes are almost universally planted using tubers or cut 'eyes,' and very rarely by true botanical seed produced by flowering cultivars. However, the authors have observed experimental plantings with true seeds along the shores of Lake Titicaca in Southern Peru. Farmers, and sometimes their children, who guard the fields over long periods, select out true seed balls, carefully separate the seeds, and then plant them in small, well-prepared beds near their guard huts. Such experimentation may arise out of boredom, but basic curiosity is the driving force. In similar vein, Christine Franquemont (1987: 3, 5) has described the experiments of *a highly skilled plant specialist*, Don Eugenio Aucapuma, of Chincheros, Cusco. Don Eugenio uses true botanical seed in experiments aimed at isolating new varieties of potato and improving existing varieties. One variety he developed has become widely used throughout Southern Peru. In fact, Carlos Ochoa (personal communication) posits that the continuing experimentation of farmers with true botanical seeds, which are sexually instead of clonally reproduced, explains in part the great genetic diversity of potatoes in the Andes.

Problem-solving experiments Farmers are keen to seek practical solutions to old and new problems through experimentation. In fact, propensity to experiment and try new ideas may be more pronounced in areas of diversified agriculture and poor extension services than in developed countries with less diversification and excellent research and extension facilities. Farmers' experimentation attempts to overcome recent perceived increases in insect damage in the Andean region provide cases in point. For example, increased attacks of the Andean weevil *(gorgojo de los Andes)* in improved potatoes led farmers to test effects of sunlight on seed. They spread potatoes to be used for seed in direct sunlight for short periods (Gordon Prain, personal communication). The effect was to drive the worm from the tubers. Tests are always done first on a small scale and later amplified if successful.

Farmers frequently develop ideas for experimentation that seem strange to scientists (Gupta 1987). For example, in adoption of diffused light potato stores, farmers often insisted that diffused light increased the incidence of the tuber moth pest *(Phthorimaea operculella)* in their stores. Since no scientific explanation for this observation had been developed, the suggestion was written off by scientists as absurd or more flippantly as 'now-they-can-see-the-tuber-moth, before-they-could-not.' However, scientists now suspect that the ecology of tuber moth may after all be tied to different intensities of light and darkness. After continued problems with tuber moth, scientific research verified farmers' observation that tuber moth does increase under diffused light conditions (Parker 1980–81: 35).

In the Guatemalan Highlands, farmers have difficulty with another pest, the aphid *(Myzus persicae)*. Through careful observation several farmers observed that aphids are attracted to green but not to red sprouts on potatoes. They were curious if colour attraction exists. Their pleas with local researchers to conduct experiments on this simple idea fell on deaf ears. So, farmers themselves designed experiments with small numbers of tubers. They insisted that their research showed the green aphid preferred green sprouts. The farmers concluded that one way to control aphids is to select red- or purple-sprouting potatoes (Rhoades 1986).

Farmers have two major advantages over agricultural scientists with regard to problem-solving experiments. First, due to the large numbers of farmers and their constant presence in the field, they have a greater opportunity to observe plants and the environment. On the contrary, most scientists spend much of their time at a desk or in a laboratory. Second, farmers are in a better position to determine which problems affect them directly and therefore to assist in guiding research directed toward solutions (Rhoades and Booth 1982; Lightfoot 1987; Ashby 1984). This advantage of farmers, when combined with the power of the natural sciences to trace connections and order data not visible to the human eye, can help us shape a new approach to experimental agricultural research (Richards 1985).

Adaptation experiments Adaptation experiments are conducted by farmers after they acquire a new technology, or after they have observed a new technology demonstrated elsewhere (for example, in another farmer's field, or in an extension service demonstration plot). Such experiments can occur in three contexts:

o when farmers are testing an unknown component technology within a known physical environment;
o when farmers are testing a known technology within an unknown environment, such as a zone of colonisation;
o when testing an unknown technology in an unknown environment.

Farmers expect experiments to answer such questions as:

o Does the technology work?
o How can it be fitted into the existing production-utilisation system?
o Is it profitable? (in cases of commercial markets)

Before they work out the economics, however, they must answer the first two questions.

Farmers' selection and use of new cultivars are a case in point. In the potato production zones of the Andes, the most intense interest in experimentation revolves around new cultivars. Planting of new cultivars, however, sets in motion a number of experiments on best use of the cultivars in specific locations (farmers generally plant in several agricultural zones and at different times in the production cycle). Because the Highland zone is where potatoes do best, experiments are aimed at discovering which cultivar does better than another, given the ever changing disease and climatic conditions.

Highland potato farmers realise that a broad genetic base of potatoes must be maintained, given the diversity of planting situations and potential risks (Brush *et al.* 1981). They do this through maintenance of individually-held 'germplasm banks,' generally consisting of six to seven varieties (Rhoades 1987). Whenever possible, either on trips or when government agronomists/extension personnel visit villages, farmers try to pick up an additional tuber or two. The 'reserve' potatoes are grown on a small-scale, while the majority of fields is sown to two or three 'proven' cultivars. Once a new cultivar is obtained, a few tubers are planted by farmers in a kitchen garden or a short row along a field boundary. This simple experiment they call a *prueba*, or trial.

Throughout the growing season, farmers monitor carefully the growth and performance of the new cultivar. If the farmer likes what he sees, then he amplifies production, restricted, of course, by the amount of seed available. Depending on the market and seed supply, they will put more and more of their land to the new cultivar. In the meantime, they maintain and replenish their 'germplasm' banks. Tubers will be counted, storability observed, processing qualities tested, culinary quality tasted, and so on. The storehouse of knowledge about cultivars is built up through such experimentation, giving farmers the ability to talk for hours about the pros and cons of different cultivars.

Another well-documented example of adaptation experiments by farmers is the well-known case of diffused light potato storage (Rhoades and Booth 1982). The basic principle that diffused light storage of potatoes, as opposed to dark storage, inhibits sprout elongation and improves overall seed quality was promoted by the International Potato Centre as a low cost solution to potato seed storage. Model demonstration stores were developed by over 25 national programs and introduced to thousands of farmers. Farmers exposed to the idea rarely copied the 'model'; rather, they adapted the principle of using diffused light to their own conditions, cultural preferences, and budgets (Rhoades and Booth 1982). Few farmers in the first year stored all of their potatoes in diffused light, preferring to test the idea on their own terms first. These initial experiments often consisted of placing a few tubers on a window sill just to see if the principle actually worked.

Experiments in the non-traditional potato zone

Peru's *ceja de selva* ('eyebrow of the jungle') is a tropical hill zone (also called the *montaña*), which links the high Andes with the lower Amazon Basin. Highland Indian and *mestizo* populations are colonising these lower elevations. Across Peru's high jungle zone, tens of thousands of settlers, such as 'El Loco,' the farmer we mentioned in the introduction of this chapter, carry out systematic experiments in an effort to define for themselves an appropriate land use and cropping patterns which will best provide for their needs. These experiments are similar in form to the literally thousands of experiments which have been conducted by farmers throughout the ages. Colonists of the high jungle bring with them their own agricultural systems/technologies and food habits to a new environment which must be understood and ultimately mastered. Experimentation, defined by Webster's Dictionary as: 'any action or process designed to find out whether something is effective, workable, or valid', is one of the fundamental strategies involved in the settlers' attempt to learn about and control their environment.

Two agroecological aspects of the Chanchamayo make it conducive for experimentation by farmers. First, the tropical hill zone is a major ecotone ('transition between two major biomes or vegetation communities') linking the Highlands and the Lowlands (see Rhoades 1978). This means that both Highland and lowland crops reach their effective limits around 1500 m (*i.e.* Highland crops, such as the potato, face more difficult growing conditions while lowland plants such as the banana or cassava face the same). Second, migrants from the Highlands come to the jungle area for land and the possibility of establishing a small plantation, primarily of coffee, tropical fruits, or coca. While their plantations are becoming established, farmers attempt, as much as possible, not only to grow their own subsistence food but also to replicate their Highland diets. Without potato, like bread in Europe or rice in Asia, the Highlander's meal is considered incomplete.

Because potatoes are relatively expensive in the local Chanchamayo market, farmers are keen to grow their own. For these reasons, experimentation with potatoes occurs on a widespread scale among Highland farmers inhabiting the ecological zone between 1000 and 1800 m. Virtually every farmer we interviewed in 1980 and living in this zone had experimented with potatoes over several seasons (Rhoades and Recharte, n.d.). Many had given up, but newcomers always tried their luck. Settlers from the Highlands, compared with farmers who have been in the area for many decades, did not initially carry with them the belief that potatoes could not be produced. In this regard, their innocence of possibilities is one of the positive points favouring creative experimentation.

Experiments in this transition zone are adaptation experiments with a crop or technology in a non-traditional environment. The challenge in this case is not to learn how a new technology fits a known system (*e.g.* new cultivars in the Highlands), but to adapt a known component or crop to an unknown environment and system. The immigrants have a knowledge of potato production but not of the new environment in which the new form of production is to take place.

The 15-member Colquechagua family, which resides in the high zone of the Colorado River, one of the tributaries of the Chanchamayo River, is a good example of how a household experiments. Among their subsistence goals is to produce enough vegetables on their land so they do not have to buy at the local market. Experimentation follows a 'start slowly, start small' pattern. They bring back from their Highland communities a few small sacks of the seed they want to try. In the first year, they brought approximately ten potato varieties: *Mariva*, *Revolucion*, *Renacimiento*, *Yungay*, *Huayro*, *Huamantay*, and several cultivars of a native type called *chaucha*. The first year they planted only a few kilos of each.

Gradually, they eliminated varieties which did not do well while doubling the amount of seed planted in the more adapted cultivars. During the first year, all *chaucha* varieties were eliminated due to their susceptibility to late blight *(Phytophtora infestans)*. In the second season, *Huayro* and *Huamantay* were eliminated. This left only 'hybrids' among which two varieties, *Mariva* and *Yungay*, yielded best. After four years of experimentation, they were relying mainly on the variety *Mariva*. Small-scale experiments continued each year with newly-acquired varieties.

In addition to cultivar testing, the Colquechagua family experimented with different periods of planting. They first tried the schedule of the *sierra* planting calendar; then, they shifted to the drier season schedule. Mental notes were kept on performance, attacks of disease, insects, and rotations. Over time and with experience, they learned where and when the crop performs best.

When farmers' experiments succeed: a case study of agricultural change

Indigenous experimentation reflects important areas of interest to farmers. However, experimentation is only one part of the on-going learning process required by the farming enterprise. Adaptation to the farming environment is a continuous process with no given end-point (Bebbington 1988; Ellen 1982).

The purpose of this last section is to place experimentation within this larger context of technological change. It illustrates how perception of the environment, individual innovation, and experimentation can interact to bring about rapid technological change. However, for an experiment to be successful, the resulting innovations must survive longer-term changes. The following case traces experimentation of farmers and its subsequent impact in Oxapampa, a district located just to the north of the Chanchamayo Valley in the same high jungle ecological zone, although slightly higher in elevation. Farmers from the Highlands, who are called *serranos*, have been migrating into Oxapampa, bringing with them their 'cultural baggage' which includes beliefs about what foods taste best and what they might be able to grow. Like the Chanchamayo, therefore, Oxapampa has been a zone of intense experimentation by in-migrants.

Located at an altitude of 1800–1850 m in the valley floor, the climatic and ecological context of Oxapampa is, however, peculiarly two-faced for potato cultivation. The high rainfall and warm temperatures are extremely conducive for late blight *(Phytophtora infestans)*, a fungus capable of destroying the crop within a couple of days after summer rains if fungicides are not applied immediately. This rainfall can also be very variable from year to year (1250–3000 mm) and from month to month, and summer drought can hinder production. On the other hand, warm conditions and relatively fertile soils mean that an adapted potato or one grown under environmentally altered conditions could produce high yields in a cultivation period a month faster than in the Highlands. Return on production investment could theoretically occur in a very short time and deliver high profits.

The idea for developing potato production in Oxapampa was fostered among the *serranos,* the ethnic group culturally disposed to the crop, but not among the older settlers of European descent or the native Amuesha Indians of the region. Unlike the latter, migrants from the *sierra* were not psychologically constrained in their image of what cropping patterns were possible. Before the 1970s, potato production had been largely confined to small gardens for home consumption, but, as more and more settlers arrived from the Highlands, experiments with the crop proliferated. As in the Chanchamayo, production failed and migrants returned to the Highlands after using methods, particularly the use of planting cycles, that were appropriate for the sierra but not the high jungle. Those who stayed, however, continued to experiment with different techniques to grow their beloved potato.

In the early years of innovation, information on the results of these experiments was constantly exchanged among these Highland settlers, although, as in the Chanchamayo, no set ideal on how to cultivate potato evolved. An important figure in these patterns of information exchange was one enterprising, experimenting Highlander who served as information broker for the idea of expanded potato production. He first became a district-wide source of expertise for Highland migrants and later for the established European settlers of the region. The farmers he advised experimented consciously with cultivars of seed, types and methods of fertilization and pest control, and devised agronomic strategies that gave notable increases in yields. Because the yield increases provided visible proof of the technical feasibility of commercial production, such experiments by farmers became an important forerunner to the rapid expansion of potato cultivation that was to occur in the 1980s.

Contacts between this Highland group and the earlier colonists of European and *mestizo* descent were, however, limited and during the initial stages of experimentation the exchange of information about potato cultivation remained confined largely to the poor in-migrant group which had little ability to expand production. This began to change as innovators more socially accessible to the wealthier farmers of *mestizo* and European descent helped promote the idea of potato cultivation among this group. One such innovating unit was one migrant and his German-descended Oxapampina wife who, after planting smaller experimental plots in 1981 and 1982, planted over 20 ha in 1983. Together, these yielded remarkable profits that helped them purchase a house, car and tractor.

This evidence of the potential profitability of the potato, along with the decision of the Peruvian Agrarian Bank to lend money freely for potato production and the visits of Lima wholesale merchants to purchase potato, removed psychological, credit and demand constraints to expanded production. In sum, this prompted an explosion of potato cultivation in 1984 (Figure 22.1). This increase reflected both the entry of new producers, and the expanded acreages of existing producers. The former lacked experience on crop production and the latter entered domains for which their experiments had not prepared them. All were building on accumulated stocks of knowledge generated from experience of the economic and ecological environment, as it had been encountered up to 1984. There was no reason to expect that this experience included all pertinent dimensions of environmental variability. Moreover, should problems arise, there was no strong institutional support and assistance outside the farmers' community. Staff of the extension services and the agrarian bank and local agro-chemical dealers had little experience regarding the crop, especially in the ecological context.

All this added up to a vulnerable regional production system about which prior experimentation, although showing the technical feasibility of potato cultivation, had not taught farmers everything – in particular, the constraints and complexities of the wider and longer term marketing and production environment in which they were operating. The events of 1984, however, did reveal these constraints and shattered this vulnerable system. Three particular problems, not experienced beforehand, arose that year (Bebbington 1988):

- A late rainy season and wet summer brought severe late blight and tuber-rot problems, fungicide costs soaring as a consequence;
- The labour supply required to apply fungicides to such a large area immediately after the rains was not available when needed;
- As production costs rose, potato prices in Lima collapsed unexpectedly .

In the end, farmers suffered the worst possible combination of high production costs, low prices, and reduced yields (BAP, 1984). Fields went unharvested and widespread bankruptcy occurred. The number of ha in potatoes dropped drastically (see Figure 22.1). Farmers subsequently shifted back to livestock management and lower input, lower risk crops such as maize and beans. Today, a vastly reduced number of farmers in Oxapampa still try to produce potatoes, but with a seasoned knowledge of the technical, ecological and economic context in which they operate.

The relevance of the Oxapampa potato experience lies in its warning that experiments are only a part of the larger learning process in agricultural change. Experiments are capable of altering how a human population perceives and acts upon a farming environment, but experiments alone cannot provide the knowledge needed to implement new innovations successfully. Experimentation occurs in an economic environment that exists beyond the farm gate. This environment not only has a temporality and variability that the farmer cannot control, but also takes on new characteristics as the innovation is more widely adopted. Furthermore, experimentation occurs in an ecological context, which also has dimensions of variability and whose periodicity exceeds the time during which initial experiments were undertaken.

This is equally true of experiments or demonstrations organised by agricultural research scientists. All too often, the experiment becomes, in formal research and development, both an end in itself or, if successful, a model upon which farmers and extension agents are expected to act. This, like potato production in Oxapampa, is 'risky business'. Experiments are the seeds of change but they are not the final harvest. Experimental research must be kept in this broader perspective.

Conclusions

Recent years have witnessed both academics and practitioners lauding and describing, farmers' knowledge (Brokensha *et al.* 1980; Barker *et al.* 1977;

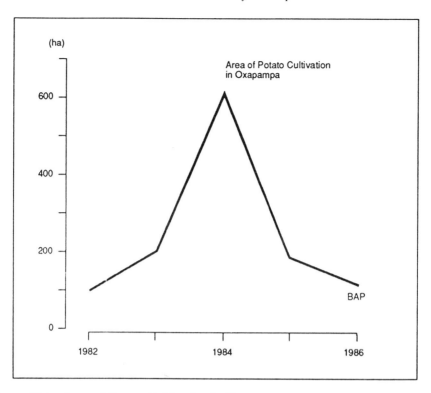

Figure 22.1: *Area of Potato Cultivation in Oxapampa*
          Source: BAP (Banco Agrario del Peru), various years.
          Note: 1986 area 10 July only.

Richards 1985), and making claims about the propensity of farmers to conduct experiments. However, the second claim has not been well-documented. In this chapter, we have offered empirical evidence of this propensity, and have suggested its almost ubiquity and irrepressibility.

Our extended examples have been taken from areas of considerable change ('adaptation experiments'), but we have also documented experimentation in more stable environments ('curiosity experiments' and 'problem-solving experiments'). This illustrates that such 'research' is not only the preserve of the colonist, migrant or recipient of a new technology.

The examples suggest that there is a thriving 'people's scientific community' 'out there,' parallel to the community of formal agricultural scientists. Not all – but definitely much – of the knowledge or endeavour of the 'people's scientific community' is necessarily useful. The knowledge, and the willingness and ability to pursue it, together constitute a great resource with which agricultural science should engage. With Lightfoot *et al.* (1987), we therefore suggest that scientists should conduct cooperative research with farmers on technical issues by letting farmers participate in and, in many cases, lead experimental strategies. This is what Biggs and Clay (1989) termed a *collegial* type of farmer participation.

We dealt little with the actual design of farmers' experiments, or comparisons between them and those of formal science. Unlike scientists, farmers show limited concern with statistical proof and complicated replication. In general, their social and ecological context does not allow this. While they will conduct comparative treatments in one season, they will deal with replication by conducting experiments across several seasons. Moreover, while scientists tend to think in terms of generalisable results and laws (Norgaard 1984), we suspect farmers are much more sceptical of extrapolation and their knowledge remains more location-specific. These comments raise questions about the relationship between material context, epistemology, and experimental method.

While the discussion has been pitched primarily at the level of the experiment itself, the example from Oxapampa shows clearly that experimentation should be seen conceptually as part of a larger process. It is by experimenting that farmers learn about new environments, changing environments, and new technologies. Experimenting is thus part of a goal-oriented adaptation strategy. Nonetheless, because the social, economic and ecological environment is always changing (sometimes due to the very process of experimentation), these goals are rarely reached, and never maintained for long. As environment changes, new experiments are conducted. Thus, experimentation is just part of a broader process of agricultural change. This is true of experiments conducted not only on the farm, but those at the research station as well.

Note

This chapter was first presented as a paper at the International Congress on Plant Physiology, New Delhi, India, 15–20 February 1988.

23. Phytopractices: Indigenous horticultural approaches to plant cultivation and improvement in tropical regions

YILDIZ AUMEERUDDY

Introduction

FOR GENERATIONS, FARMERS in tropical regions have selected plants from the wild and developed methods of cultivating and improving these plants. Phytopractice is the term used to refer to these indigenous horticultural methods which may improve, stimulate, regenerate, propagate, or preserve plants on an individual scale, either by mechanical manipulations on the plant or by microclimatic improvements. Post-harvest and pre-harvest conservation techniques are also taken into consideration when dealing with aspects related to intrinsic or micro-environmental characteristics of plant material. In all cases, the manipulations ensue from an empirical knowledge of the plants' intrinsic characteristics (morphological and physiological), as well as the micro-environmental needs of each plant (Aumeeruddy and Pinglo 1988). More specific aspects of microclimatic management of plants in tropical regions are described by Stigter based on the Tradition Techniques for Microclimatic Improvements (TTMI) project (Stigter 1985, 1986).

Why a horticultural approach to tropical crops?

The study of phytopractices shows a divergence between the traditional approach to plants by farmers in tropical regions and the modern technological approach used in temperate countries.

The latter, specially after the last world conflict, has evolved through sophisticated technologies and mechanisation towards an extreme control of cultivated plants and a reduction of the useful plant resources to a few high yielding varieties (Barrau 1983) thus leading to a highly productivist type of agriculture. Bergeret (1977) refers to this as a linear system, ignoring temporal forecasts beyond ten years or so. This may in the long term cause some ecological unbalance through the massive inputs of chemicals and the fragility of genetically homogeneous populations. This approach does produce impressive results in the regions where it has originated.

The transfer of this type of technology to tropical areas has had catastrophic results in some cases (Barrau 1983) and in general quite disappointing and short-lived results. More than 90 per cent of tropical farmers have less than 5 ha (Harwood 1979). Small-scale farmers often find high yielding varieties: 'irrelevant or unacceptable because they do not encompass the varied mix of crops and livestock that is his daily concern, and because they put him at the mercy of market forces he cannot control and probably does not understand' (Harwood 1979). He adopts more easily a flexible and dynamic system of production by using the different niches inherent in the structure of a multistoreyed agroecosystem. The use of shade is actually very typical of these systems (Wilken 1972). Shading influences the micro-environment of the garden as well as the use of such crops as tubers which are well adapted to shading conditions (Harris

1976). The farmers may also use successional stages analogous to natural succession in a garden having at the beginning a rather simple organisation (Hart 1980; Michon 1985). In the case of uni-storeyed agricultural systems in tropical regions, the genetic diversity maintained by farmers turns out to be also very high. Brush (1983) counts as many as 50 potato varieties preserved by farmers in their fields in the Andes. Boster (1983) describes a similar situation in the Jivaroan manihot (cassana) gardens in Peru.

In different situations described above, the farmer considers the garden as an association of individual plants or groups of individuals, arranged following an empirical knowledge of the environmental needs of each plant in terms of shade, humidity, and synergy or competition with other crop species.

This chapter reviews several indigenous plant manipulation techniques developed by farmers and based on their knowledge of the intrinsic characteristics of these plants.

A general approach to this problem – methods

Though the study of any technique or practice needs a good comprehension of socio-economical and cultural background (Sigaut 1985), we have decided through the study of phytopractices to consider the tropical regions as a whole for the following reasons?

o Indigenous knowledge in the tropics in general has been driven to a black-out situation, due to colonisation and a general acceptance by people in tropical countries that modern technology from temperate regions is more efficient compared to local technology.
o Though ethnological backgrounds are very different throughout the tropics, the convergence based on the natural environment is a very important link.
o Traditional practices have for ages been transmitted from parents to children, from neighbour to neighbour. Nowadays a total change in traditional structures due to demographic, economical and political problems enhances the necessity to find solutions from outside.

The following sample of phytopractices has been obtained during field research in Indonesia, Thailand, Congo, and Madagascar. Data are correlated with bibliographical research since many practices are sometimes mentioned in an anecdotic manner by some authors working on tropical crops. Some of the phytopractices are described in greater detail in Aumeeruddy and Pinglo (1988), a compilation of more than fifty practices.

Phytopractices viewed in the context of a home garden (Sumatra)

In South Sumatra, we have analysed the phytopractices and agroforestry techniques found on two home gardens. The home gardens studied are cultivated by Javanese people who have transmigrated in order to find new land for cultivation. Profile 23.1 illustrates the type of garden called *pekarangan* where coconut (*Cocos nucifera L.*, *Palmae*) is generally an important crop.

Saving plant diversity

Plant diversity is maintained by the farmer in order to promote diversity for the diet and as sources of income. An idea of this diversity is shown by the number of banana cultivars recorded in the small area of 100 m × 20 m, which is represented on the profile. The farmer actually grows different cultivars locally named: *pisang raja, pisang raja hijau, pisang raja nangka, pisang kelutuk, pisang ambon, pisang janten* and *pisang sereh*. Cultivars such as *pisang kelutuk* are valued for their leaves and inflorescences, whereas others are table fruits such as *pisang ambon* or *pisang sereh*, or used to make banana chips (*pisang raja*). All these cultivars are hybrids of two wild bananas: *Musa balbisiana* Colla. X *Musa acuminata* Colla. *Musaceae*.

Three species of bamboo are also cultivated in these gardens, *pring apus* (*Gigantochloa apus* (Schult and Schult) Kurz, *Gramineae*), *pring wulung* (*Gigantochloa atroviolacea,* Widjaya, *Gramineae*) and *pring legi* (*Gigantochloa atter* (Hassk) Kurz, *Gramineae*).

In saving plant diversity, the farmer contributes directly in saving crop genetic resources, thus decreasing crop vulnerability to epidemic attacks. In this way, the farmer's utilisation of local resources turns out here to be of immediate help in controlling pathogens and insect pests.

Managing the shade or the lack of shade

According to farmers very few species may grow in the shade of big bamboo clumps. For example the *Salak* palm (*Salacca edulis* Reinw. *Palmae*) which normally grows under the shade of most cultivated trees docs not thrive under bamboo shade. On the contrary, the farmer uses this specific niche to cultivate minor crops which are exclusively tuber crops, *ngarut* which combines two different species, *Canna edulis* Ker. *Cannaceae* and *Maranta arundinacea* L. *Marantaceae, mbuteh.* (*Colocasia esculenta* Schott. *Araceae*) and *suweg* (*Amorphophallus campanulatus* Blume *Araceae*). The knowledge of the effects of competition or tolerance between species enables the farmer to fill a niche otherwise empty because of too much shade or poor soil properties such as that underneath bamboo clumps as well as in competition with the bamboo's root system. Bahri (1984) discusses the use of this niche in agroforestry systems.

  ○ Banana plants usually grow well in wet conditions. In the home garden they are usually found in the understorey where the sun exposure covers an open area. The farmer compensates for the lack of humidity due to the absence of shade by planting the banana plants in big holes (Figure 23.1) filled with green manure. According to Halle (1986), this type of hole is also observed in Kenya[1]). They help to protect the banana plants from the wind, and also reduce competition between the banana plants' root system and the surrounding crops.
  ○ Young *salak* palms, normally grown in the undergrowth, are specially cared for when grown in an open area (Figure 23.2). Coconut envelopes (epicarp and mesocarp) are placed in a hole approximately 50 cm deep. This hole is filled with earth and the young salak palms are then planted on the top. These coconut envelopes are also placed at the foot of the young *salak* palms; they act as sponges and maintain humidity in the close environment of the young palm. A similar practice is used in Sri Lanka to maintain humidity in coconut plantations (Figure 23.3). It consists of putting coconut envelopes in holes situated between coconut rows. The holes may be one

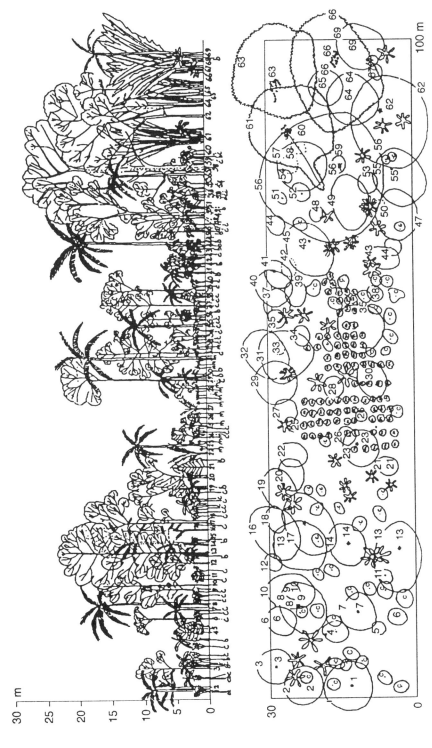

Profile 23.1: *Home garden in South Lampung (Sumatra), characterised by the cultivation of coconuts mixed with timber trees such as Pterospermum javanicum, Jungh Sterculiaceae and industrial crops (clove-coffee)*

metre deep. The coconut roots will normally grow outward to reach the humidity retained in these holes. This technique is very useful in regions where the soil is well drained and ground water inaccessible to the coconut roots. The Coconut Cultivation Board in Sri Lanka already uses and diffuses this practice (Personal communication Paul Luu 1989).

○ The Mukibat technique which has been very precisely described by Bruijn *et al.* (1974) is also used in terms of shade management. According to farmers, the graft of *Manihot glaziovii* Muell. (*Euphorbiaceae*), an arborescent manihot, on *Manihot esculenta* Crantz. (*Euphorbiaceae*) enables it to obtain good tuber production in shade conditions while *Manihot esculenta* would rot in the same conditions. Empirically farmers say that it is the latex contained in the tissues of *Manihot glaziovii* which protects the root from rot. This technique is actually a morphological manipulation of the plant resulting in an increase in tuber production due to the association of a tree and a shrub.

Phytopractices related to the propagation of plants

Preparation of seed or seedlings

○ Young coconut seedlings have fragile roots which are attacked by pests and break easily during transplantation. They also occupy an area on the ground which is space consuming. Farmers have solved this problem by hanging the seedlings in tree branches (Plate 23.1). The leaves will grow normally whereas the root system grows inside the fibrous mesocarp and, when breaking through the exocarp, becomes thick and coriaceous. When transplanted the roots will normally be more resistant to soil parasites. This is also a protection technique against animals, especially wild pigs.

○ To collect corn (*Zea mays* L. *Gramineae*) for sowing the farmer after the harvest period keeps one ear of corn from each plant. Leaves situated on each side of the ear are tied in order to protect it from the sun and direct rain. The seeds for sowing will come to maturity after one week. The ear is then harvested and hung to dry upside down for one month over smoke which protects the seeds from diseases caused by fungi and bacteria.

Vegetative propagation

○ Air-layering, locally called *cangkokan*, is often used to propagate most of the edible fruits in home gardens. In the home gardens visited in Sumatra, farmers recommend taking off the bark (2 to 3 cm) of the chosen branch and leaving the scar to dry for 2–4 days, in order to have a high percentage of success. This is then wrapped with earth rich in organic matter and with different materials such as coconut mesocarp (*sabut kelapa*), a bamboo internode (*tabung bamboo*), banana leaves or a plastic sheet.

The farmer chooses branches which are 'reiterated complexes.' When looking at the tree, one may distinguish a colony of small trees (De Castro e Santos 1980) inside the tree crown (Figure 23.4). These 'reiterated complexes', which are total or partial duplications of the tree's basic architectural model (Edelin

Figure 23.1: *Use of earth pits one metre deep for banana tree cultivation. The hole is filled with green manure to keep humidity and fertilise the tree. (South Lampung, Sumatra)*

Figure 23.2: *Young* Salaks *planted in holes filled with coconut mesocarps and earth. (South Lampung, Sumatra)*

Figure 23.3: *Earth pits filled with coconut mesocarps used to keep humidity in coconut plantations in Sri Lanka*

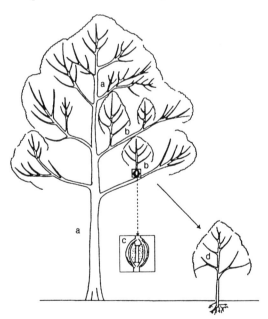

Figure 23.4: *Air layering of Rambutan (Lampung, Sumatra)*
a – Old Rambutan trees with colonies of small reiterated complexes
b/c – Layer wrapped with coconut mesocarps and earth
d – Younger layer which can potentially flower the next day
(Lampung, Sumatra)

1987), have the same morphogenetic potential as that of a seedling and hence can be considered as a little tree. Having already flowered in the tree crown, this part of the tree, after being air-layered and planted, will normally flower the following year. This method based on vegetative propagation also enables the farmer to preserve good varieties. Species already known to be propagated in this manner are *durian* (*Durio zibethinus* Murr. *Bombacaceae*) and *Citrus* sp (*Rutaceae*) (Aumeeruddy and Pinglo 1988). This technique has been recorded in the study area on other species such as *Rambutan* (*Nephelium lappaceum* L. *Sapindaceae*; Plate 23.2) and *Kenanga* (*Cananga odorata* Hook. *Annonaceae*).

Grafting is very commonly used for many different purposes. Early flowering may be obtained by grafting a bud from a branch which has already flowered on to a young seedling. The result is a dwarfed tree which fill flower in two or three years after the graft is made (Aumeerruddy and Pinglo 1988). Species newly recorded to be *Manggis* (*Garcinia mangostana* L. *Guttiferae*). *Petay* usually reaches 20 to 25 meters high and bears fruits five to ten years after planting (Soetjipto *et al.* 1981). A young grafted *petay* three years old has been recorded to already bear flowers.

Concerning *Manggis*, the method of top grafting on a seedling is recommended. A branch from an old tree is grafted onto the top of a young seedling. For the budding of *durian* it is recommended to graft the bud on the swollen part situated at the base of the seedling (Figure 23.5). Budding has already been tested on other fruit trees such as *Rambutan* (*Nephelium lappaceum* L. *Sapindaceae*), *Duku* (*Lansium domesticum* Corr. *Meliaceae*) (Aumeeruddy and Pinglo1988). Enquiries in the home gardens show that farmers have adopted these grafted fruit trees; the selling of young grafted seedlings is sometimes a source of income for skillful farmers.

Grafting may also be used to increase a plant's resistance to parasites. The aubergine (*Solanum melongena* L. *Solanaceae*) is grafted onto a wild species of the same genus, *Solanum torvum* Schwartz *Solanaceae*, locally named *takokak*. According to the farmers, this is also meant to give more fertility (*kesuburan*) to the aubergine plant through the scion. Felix has experimented with this type of graft on the tomato *Solanum torvum* in on-station trials and comes to the conclusion that two major diseases of tomatoes, bacterial wilt (*Pseudomonas solanacearum*) and nematodes (*Meloidogyne sp.*) can be controlled by using it. The type of graft used is the tongued graft method. The elimination of bacteria and nematodes from an infected soil is very expensive with chemical products. On the contrary the use of this grafting system is very efficient, achieving nearly a rate of 100 per cent of success.

Improving tuber yields Amorphophallus campanulatus Blume, *Araceae*, is an aroid locally named *suweg* or *suwak* and usually cultivated in Java where it is used only in periods of scarcity. In the region of Sukoyoso in the south of Sumatra, this plant is still cultivated and used for very specific dishes. The tuber must be two or three years old to be tasty. A unique cultivation practice is applied to this crop in order to increase the size of the tuber. This plant normally produces one big compound leaf; according to a precise rhythm these leaves will dry out and disappear. This is usually followed by the development of a unique inflorescence. The farmer prevents flowering by digging out the tuber which is approximately spheric, but slightly flatter on the top. This tuber is replaced in the gorund upside down. The farmer may repeat this operation

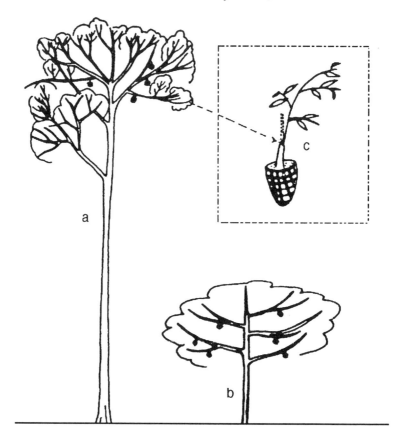

Figure 23.5: *a – Durian tree, 20–30 years old, approximately 25m high*
b – Grafted Durian, 10 years old, approximately 5m high
c – Detail of the grafted seedling. The bud coming from a
plagiotropic branch from the tree grown is grafted on the swollen
portion situated at the base of the seedling
(South Lampung, Sumatra)

Figure 23.6: *Taro planted in earth pits 20 to 50 cm deep in open fields, under*
direct sun light
(Region of Antanarivo, Madagascar)

several times during a few years, the result being an increase in the size of the tuber.

This plant flowers in a terminal position (personal communication Daniel Barthelemy) so that we may imagine that when the farmer blocks the expression of the flower, reserves in the tuber may on the other hand continue to increase. Following an internal rhythm, leaves will develop again, coming from buds situated around the central tuber. These buds will in turn develop into new tubers.

Convergence of practices adopted by farmers in tropical regions

Tree training In Western Sumatra (Maninjau) and Lampung (Liwa), coffee trees (*Coffea canephora* Pierre ex Frochner *Rubiaceae*) are trained in order to provoke an elongation of the lateral branches. The main stem is pruned at a person's height and all new coppice shoots are systematically pruned. As a consequence, the lateral branches grow in length much more than usual, some measuring up to two metres and more (Plate 23.3). A variation of this system consists of cutting the apex of the branch after it has produced three internodes. Two lateral branches will then grow which are also pruned after they have produced three internodes. The farmer thus obtains a small tree with a spreading crown.

This technique has also been recorded on *Ylang-Ylang* (*Cananga odorata* Hook *Annonaceae*) in Madagascar and Comoros, *Lucuma* (*Lucuma mamosa* Gaernt *Sapotaceae*) in Vietnam, *Terminalia* (*Terminalia catappa* L. *Combretaceae*) in Congo (Aumeeruddy and Pinglo 1988) and is also practiced in Indonesia on *durian* (*Durio zibethinus* Murr. *Bombacaceae*) and *sawa* (*Manilkara sapota* L. *Sapotaceae*). This enables the farmers to have dwarfed trees with fruits easily accessible for harvest. Dupriez (personal communication) has recorded the same phytopractice applied to the *baobab* (*Adansonia digitata* L. *Combretaceae*) in Africa. The baobab leaves are an important food source in some African regions. This practice thus makes the leaves more accessible for the harvest.

Propagation of trees by poles Propagation of trees by pole cuttings is widely used by farmers in most tropical regions. This technique consists of planting cuttings reaching two metres or more in height. It has been *Petay* (*Parkia speciosa* Hassk. *Leguminosae Mimosaceae*), an important legume tree in Malaysia and Indonesia, as well as *jambu air* (*Eugenia aqueum* Merr. *Myrtaceae*) are easily propagated by poles. *Peronema canescens* Jack., a *Verbenaceae*, usually known as *sungkai* is used in West Java for making live hedges. This tree, usually growing in secondary forests, is selected by the farmer for its multiple uses including firewood and medicine.

In Madagascar, startling results are obtained by farmers with species coming from the native bush, such as *Delonix adansonioides* (R. Vig.) R. Cap. *Leguminosae Caesalpinicideae* which grow by cuttings in very dry conditions, *i.e.* less than 500 mm of rain per year, on very dry sandy soil (Plate 23.4).

Use of earth pits The use of taro beds, planting taros in small pits in order to bring roots closer to ground water, is well known in Polynesia and Micronesia (Barrau 1961). This practice has also been recorded on the high plateaus of Madagascar (Figure 23.6). According to farmers, the lateritic soil is so hard that

Plate 23.1: *Coconut seedlings hanging to tree branches (South Lampung, Sumatra)*
Plate 23.2: *Air layering of a reiterated complex of rambutan (South Lampung, Sumatra)*
Plate 23.3: *Coffee trained to increase the growth of lateral branches (South Lampung, Sumatra)*

the tuber when growing tends to develop above the soil level. The holes thus provide good protection for these tubers and may be progressively filled by the farmers with manure and earth.

This practice is very close to what has been recorded for bananas in Sumatra and in Kenya (Halle 1986). Planting crops in natural or excavated pits as protection from the wind has also been reported from the Canary Islands and Easter Island (Wilken 1972). Effects of such pits may be connected to high radiation absorption together with windbreak effects.

Fruit protection: phytosanitary systems using plant insect interactions. Farmers in tropical regions often use mechanical systems to protect fruits from fruit flies or other insect pests. In Indonesia, fruit bags are placed over jackfruits or *nangka* (*Artocarpus heterophyllus* Lam *Moraceae*) but left open at the bottom leaving the fruit quite vulnerable to all fly attacks. Enquiries to the farmers and direct observation show that this system creates a shelter for ants which swarm over the fruit. The ants do not do any damage and according to the farmers, protect the jackfruit against fruit flies. In Malaysia, the same practice is used (personal communication. Dr. Chin See Chung). It is said that good fruit cannot be obtained without this kind of protection.

A practice used by Chinese citrus growers in South China consists of rearing ants of the species *Oecophylla smaragdina* so that the ants may keep away such insects as *Tesseratoma papillosa,* the stink bug insect which is very injurious to lychee and citrus fruits. The ant nests are collected in the wild and placed in the citrus trees; pieces of bamboo stems are placed from tree to tree so that the ants may cross. The usefulness of these ants is discussed by the authors from the point of view of their real economic value. In the author's opinion the ants do not destroy the scale insects and not always plant lice, which are also serious enemies of citrus trees. Yet, somehow they are very efficient against every other variety of ants or aphids which invaded the citrus trees. The farmers found by actual experience that when they do not have these nests in the trees very few fruits form.

Water stress to induce flowering of Citrus spp in Thailand: traditional techniques adapted to large scale agriculture In the Rangsit area situated in the region of Bangkok, farmers cultivate fields of *Citrus reticulata* Blanco (*Rutaceae*) in ancient paddy fields. The citrus plants are planted on high earth ridges surrounded by canals (Plate 23.5). In order to have a continuous production , the farmer takes out the water from the canals four or five times per year, each time during a period of approximately seven days. The fields are flooded when the leaves begin to droop showing signs of water stress. The citrus trees respond to this stress by producing new flowers. By this system the farmer may obtain 200 kg of fruits per tree and per year.

The use of water stress to increase production is well known since ancient days in North Africa where low trenches were made around date palms and filled with salt (Ibn al Awam XIIth century).

In India and Pakistan, the same technique is applied to Mango trees, accompanied by incisions on the root system (Coste 1983). The effect of water stress or defoliation has also been studied on guava by Shigeurea *et al.* (1975) and Chapman *et al.* (1979) who experimented with urea sprays. This resulted in an induction of defoliation which has been found to stimulate and synchronise bloom.

Plate 23.4: *Live hedges of* Delonix adansonioides *(R. Vig.) R. Cap*
          Cesalpiniaceae *with a phenomena of fusion of the pole cutting*
          (Bevaolavo, Madagascar, J.L. Buillaumet)

Plate 23.5: Citrus reticulata *Blanco* Rutaceae *planted on high ridges surrounded*
          by irrigation canals (Rangsit Area,Thailand)

Conclusion

This chapter identifies the farmer's reasons for using particular practices. The examples given in this review indicate how farmers use empirical knowledge of intrinsic characteristics of plants to achieve improvement by acting directly on the plant or on its micro-environment.

Creating a microclimate by the use of shade is in itself a wide field of investigation. The examples given illustrate the flexibility in shade management in relation to a plant's characteristics and the results desired by the farmers. Indeed, insufficient sunlight for photosynthesis or heating may be a problem even in the energy-rich tropics (Wilken 1972). In the case of the thick bamboo shade, the farmer has adopted the solution of filling this niche with minor crops. The use of organic mulches associated with the method of cultivation of bananas in earth pits is another example of the flexible use of plant materials. Whereas in high latitudes, straw and manure are used to protect plants from frost (Wilken 1972), in tropical areas mulches reduce evaporative losses and soil temperature, in the same way as trees are kept to protect the soil from overexposure.

Other examples given are directly or indirectly linked to the use of morphological or ecological characteristics of plants. The use of pole cuttings gives hints on the capacity of perennial crops to propagate vegetatively without external inputs, given the right mixture of variables such as the size of cuttings and period of propagation.

Some species also show better aptitudes than others. For example, in the Congo, *Safou* (*Dacryodes edulis* (G. Don.) H. J. Lam. *Burseraceae*) was found to be propagated by pole cuttings by farmers providing that the cutting is kept humid by a patch of leaves and earth which is fixed on the top of the cutting and kept permanently humid (Aumeeruddy and Pinglo 1988). On the other hand species such as *Spondias mombin* L.; *Anacardiaceae* may be propagated without needing any special care.

Concerning the phytopractice applied to *Amophophallus campanulatus*, a parallel may be established with a practice applied to the *Sago* palm by farmers in Papua New Guinea which consists in preventing the unique flowering of *Metroxylon rumphii* Mart. *Pamae* by the suppression of the floral bud. This results in an increase in the starch reserves accumulated in the stipe (Barrau 1959).

Finally, we may say that the preceding sample of phytopractices shows a tendency to horticultural manipulations in tropical regions which fits with the habit of establishing mixed forest gardens. Protection, care and an intrinsic knowledge of each plant on an individual basis are the main characteristics of this horticultural approach. Haudricourt (1962) talks of what he calls the 'friendship' between humans and plants, connected by the desire to restore to the plant the natural conditions necessary for its growth. Manipulations are restricted to mechanical interventions based on empirical knowledge of the morphological and physiological characteristics of plants as well as their micro-environmental needs. The economic importance of these practices should be carefully investigated. In our opinion they constitute a stock of indigenous technical knowledge concerning tropical crops which has not been exploited to its maximum capacity because of lack of information flow between tropical countries. Being inexpensive and generally readily available materials, their expanded use across countries in similar tropical ecozones could be invaluable.

Note

1. The practice of planting banana plants in big holes filled with green manure was introduced in Kenya by extension workers of the Agriculture Department around the 1960s (Editors' note, personal communication Dr. Bernard Riley)

24. Farmer Know-how and Communication for Technology Transfer: CTTA in Niger[1]

CONSTANCE M. McCORKLE AND GAIL D. McCLURE

Communication models in agriculture

THE EVOLUTION OF Western scientific thought regarding communication for technology transfer in agriculture across the past four decades can be summarised in increasingly sophisticated models of the linkages and communication flows among farmers (F), researchers (R), and extensionists (E). The earliest such model (Figure 1) was very simplistic, linear, one-way, hierarchical, and biased in favour of technology (Awa 1988; Coughenour and Nazhat 1985).

This model was originally elaborated to represent the US experience in Agricultural Research, Development and Extension (RD&E). Extension or transfer efforts under this approach were characterised by the source —> message —> channel —> receiver (SMCR) paradigm of communication (Berlo 1960), with F considered the receivers of agricultural messages, R the source, and E a principal channel. However, this formulation in fact failed to capture many of the essential ingredients that made for successful technology generation and transfer in U.S. agriculture (Lionberger *et al.* 1975; Rivera and Schram 1987).

Among other things (Rogers 1989), this model ignored the dynamic, interactive nature of grassroots, populist traditions in much of American agricultural communication patterns (Moris 1983), as well as Americans' optimistic belief in their ability to create and direct organisations on behalf of their own development. In the first half of this century, US farmers had a strong voice in agricultural RD&E. Both with and without the help of extension, farmer groups with strong mutual interests were formed, eager to share agricultural ideas and information, *i.e.* to communicate. These organisations, which in fact preceded establishment of the agricultural experiment station system, were able to influence

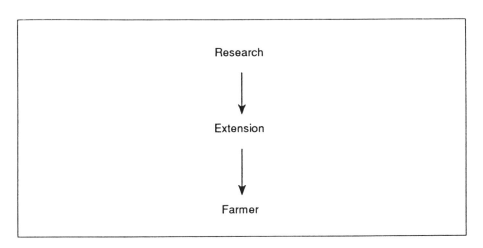

Figure 24.1: *First-stage model of communication for technology transfer*

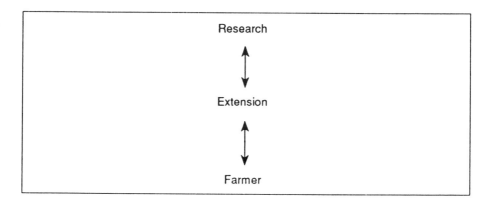

Figure 24.2: *Second-stage model of communication for technology transfer*

the scope and thrust of formal RD&E (Compton 1989a). Moreover, many researchers and most extensionists themselves came from farm families and often operated farms of their own. As a result, innovations tended to be developed and adapted locally rather than being externally imposed. In the US, the technology generation and transfer process was thus institutionalised in young, flexible organisations and agencies that were highly client-responsive and context-sensitive.

In short, the early model of Figure 24.1 greatly underrepresented the rich, multi-directional linkages among F, R, and E that promote successful technology generation and transfer. Unfortunately, this faulty model was the one initially exported to Third World countries, where it influenced much of development decision-making. As efforts to implement it met with repeated failure, however, the model began to evolve to include important communication concepts like feedback loops and interaction. Figure 24.2 schematises the resulting 'second stage' model of agricultural communication. Here, flows are still linear and basically hierarchical, but at least the communication process is expressed as a two-way interaction.

The third-stage model added a high-proximity network concept (Rogers 1983), positing the need for direct communication among the three major par-

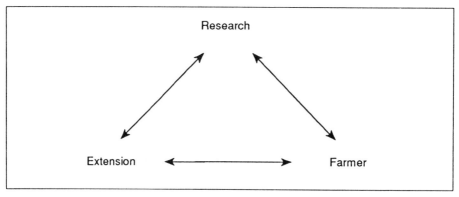

Figure 24.3: *Third-stage model of communication for technology transfer*

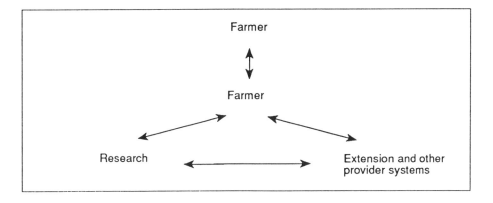

Figure 24.4: *The CTTA Niger model*

ties to the RD&E process (Figure 24.3). Recent Farming Systems Research and Extension (FSR/E) efforts work from models like this (*e.g.* Rhoades 1984). Such frameworks represent a major step forward in that they signal the importance of scientists' and extensionists' listening to farmers and diagnosing needs and problems from farmers' own perspectives (Chambers 1983). However, they still neglect critical F-F networks of communication – networks that can be of particular value in technology transfer. Also, they make no provision for other players in the agricultural technology system, such as private-enterprise suppliers of farm inputs and services.

Figure 24.4 depicts a more sophisticated model that emphasises farmer-to-farmer information flows and directs attention to the opportunities these offer for improved R and E. Moreover, this framework clearly assigns priority to F concerns. It makes *farmers* the focal point of RD&E, not researchers or extensionists and their respective institutions. Farmers are viewed as co-researchers, developers, and extensionists – colleagues who can provide crucial input in determining what problems to address and how to proceed (Chambers *et al.* 1989). This approach moves the intended beneficiaries out of the role of passive receivers so typical of early agricultural communication models into one of active participants. This was the model elaborated and applied by the Communications for Technology Transfer Program (CTTA) in its research on farmer innovation and communication in the developing African nation of Niger.

The CTTA concept and the Niger study

Drawing upon the historical lessons outlined above, the Communications for Technology Transfer in Agriculture Program (CTTA) stresses the need for close interaction among all components in the agricultural technology system. At the same time, CTTA acknowledges that many Third World nations lack the infrastructural and institutional resources to realistically expect that extension services alone can effectively implement all aspects of technology transfer. Consequently, transfer is more generally conceptualised as an interlocking set of communication/information/education processes rather than as the exclusive activity of a few, formal structures or entities.

In broad strokes, the concept behind the CTTA program is, building upon existing resources and realities, to put communication to work in creative ways so as to increase:

○ farmers' active participation in technology generation, adaptation, and transfer;
○ researchers' ability to design appropriate agricultural technology for Third World farmers; and
○ extensionists' effectiveness in transferring this technology to farmers.

To achieve these goals, CTTA employs an adaptive action model. (For details, consult Ray *et al.* 1986.) The guiding principle is that effective technology design and transfer in agriculture must begin and end with the low-resource producers who constitute the majority of Third World rural populations. Thus, CTTA projects and demonstration sites always start with a 'developmental investigation,' a field research activity in which the local people's practices, knowledge, and beliefs about the matter at hand are analysed within their specific agroecological, economic, sociocultural, and political context. Findings from the developmental investigation are then used to plan interventions that are sensitive to the needs and realities of the beneficiary population. This approach systematically incorporates the concerns of the end-user throughout the process of technology design and transfer.

The CTTA Niger study represented one such developmental investigation. Niger was selected as representative of the Sahel and many other parts of Africa in that, to date, few externally generated technologies have proven appropriate for low-resource farmers (Dommen 1988; Gakou 1987; Lele 1975). Also, by comparison to Asia and Latin America (Moris 1983), like most of Sub-Saharan Africa (*e.g.* Lebeau 1986), Nigerian research and extension institutions are poorly developed (CTTA 1988; DAI 1988).

At the same time, however, there is incontrovertible evidence that, drawing upon their own resources, African farmers have always been and continue to be great agricultural innovators and experimenters (*e.g.* de Schlippe 1956; Hill 1970; Johnson 1972; Richards 1983, 1985). Sahelian farmers in particular must constantly cope with rapid climatological changes in order to survive. To do so, they require a continuing supply of locally adapted technologies. The assumption behind the Niger study was that farmers are dynamic actors in the process of meeting this need. Indeed, there is some evidence that producers' propensity to experiment and innovate is greater in highly diversified and/or stressed environments where extension is poor or non-existent (Rhoades and Bebbington 1988). Much can therefore be learned from farmers. The Nigerian Sahel served as a natural laboratory in which to observe and analyse their adaptive, adoptive, and communicative behaviour.

The study also sought to explore the potential for integrating the farmer more fully into all phases of technology development and transfer, including planning, implementation, evaluation, and dissemination. Specifically, two basic questions were addressed. First, how can a better understanding of local agricultural experimentation, innovation, and communication help make R&E strategies more responsive to F needs and capabilities? Second, how can such improved strategies enhance the quantity and quality of farmers' own agricultural know-how?

To answer these questions, a CTTA research team conducted both *sondeo*-type surveys and in-depth research among Mawri and Zarma farmers in Southern Niger's Niamey and Dosso departments. Fieldwork was carried out in seven villages chosen to represent the diversity of rural communities in the region. Sites included villages with and without cooperatives, expatriate projects, and resident extension agents; and communities located on and off roads, and near to and far from urban areas. One team member surveyed all the villages, while the other conducted in-depth research in a single, remote community. Together, they interviewed several hundred men and women farmers.[2]

Farmer know-how

One of the major outcomes of this CTTA research activity was the compilation of twenty 'mini-case studies' documenting local farmers' experimentation with adaptation, and adoption (or rejection) of agricultural technologies that were new to them. In each case, the communicative routes by which knowledge of the new item or practice had been acquired were also traced. With the notable exception of rejected technologies (two cases), in the overwhelming majority of cases, the formal RD&E system in Niger had played little or no direct role in these indigenous processes.

A second major outcome of the CTTA Niger research was documentation of the wealth of local communication resources presently used for transfer of agricultural information and technology among farmers themselves, again with little or no direct support from the formal extension service. Other communication resources, both local and national, that could potentially be utilised to reinforce extension efforts were also identified.

Farmer experimentation and innovation The case studies include examples of successful experimentation and/or innovation in food and tree crops, irrigation and other water harvesting techniques, gardening, field and seed preparation, fertilisation, livestock nutrition, rodent and weed control, natural resource management, food storage, food processing, and market products and outlets. In sum, the cases span all four domains of agriculture: production, distribution, transformation, and consumption.

In the course of compiling the case studies, farmers were observed to manipulate such research-related concepts and techniques as the functional equivalent of a (necessarily oral) literature review before mounting field trials (akin to the interest and evaluation stages described by Lionberger and Gwin 1982), split plots and trial replications, experimental versus non-experimental variables, cost/benefit and risk assessments; team-like analyses of results, and hypothesis generation for future research.

A good example is Nigerians' own, on-farm trials with new short-cycle millet varieties under varying but controlled conditions, as they seek to confront the growing desiccation of their environment. Holding soil type and/or plot size constant, they are testing varietal performance with chemical fertilisation only, with manuring only, and with neither. The results are assessed across several years and across a large number of differentially-weighted parameters, including: the water requirements of each variety; its maturation time and, relatedly, resistance to parasitic weeds (see below); kernel size, candle length, and grain density; presence or absence of barbs to ward off birds; storability; ease of pericarp removal; speed of cooking; food colour, bulk, texture, and taste after cooking; and the rapidity with which a variety's desirable characteristics degenerate.

A related example is farmers' experimentation to solve the problem of striga (witchweed), a parasitic plant that chokes off their staple cereal crops at the root. Again through on-farm varietal testing, Niger producers are systematically selecting for short-cycle millets that can reach sufficient maturity by the peak time of striga attacks so that grain formation is little impaired. This approach is designed to complement another, longstanding indigenous strategy against striga wherein sesame is sown in the same seed pocket along with the food grain. The sesame works as a 'trap crop' to divert the striga's attacks.

Further examples are found in farmer innovations in fertilisation methods. Niger farmers have traditionally fertilised their fields by broadcasting manure; many today do likewise with chemical fertilisers, as per extension recommendations. With the growing shortage of the former and the rising price of the latter, however, farmers throughout Niger are avidly seeking more efficient and less expensive options.

For instance, one man is experimenting with a technique he learned of from a *marabout* (Muslim holy man). Before the rains begin, he digs his seed pockets, places manure directly into them, then re-fills them with earth. Termites help break down the manure, and time dissipates any 'burning' effects that the manure might have on the seed to be sown in the pockets. After the first rain, the sand above the prepared pockets is discoloured, making them easy to locate. The farmer then re-opens the pockets and plants dressed seed. The dressing wards off the termites at the same time that it ensures a high germination rate. This man believes his new manuring strategy is nearly as effective as chemical fertilisers and certainly much cheaper.

A farmer in another village has elaborated a calculated mix of seed, dressing, and chemical fertiliser to which he also adds small stones to control the proportions of the mix that fit into the fist of a child sower. The preparation is placed directly into the seed pocket at planting. This farmer proudly notes that his self-designed pre-mix simultaneously economises on costly chemical fertilisers, has a pre-thinning effect on the stands of grain, and is childproof.

Farmer communication Many further examples of these Sahelian farmers' vigorous experimentation and innovation could be adduced (see McCorkle *et al.* 1988). But it is also important to note that remote rural producers are equally 'inventive' when it comes to obtaining new agricultural information and technology in the first place. Instead of the thinly-spread and generally poorly trained field agents of the government extension service, farmers rely more upon, and place more credibility in, a wide range of informal communication mechanisms. The case studies attest to the wealth and variety of these informal sources of agricultural information.

As we have seen, Muslim holy men, who are typically widely travelled, can be one source of new ideas. Other sources documented in the case studies involving short-cycle millets were: village kin, neighbours, and friends; also, visits to and from kin and friends throughout Niger and bordering nations; market vendors and shoppers everywhere; and employers on farmers' temporary wage-labour jobs. In fact, in only one case was a new millet variety obtained more or less directly via the aegis of the extension service – from another farmer who was selling home-grown seed at a national agricultural fair. Additional informal sources recorded in others of the case studies included: petty bureaucrats who cultivate a plot in one's village; members of adjacent villages; passing pastoralists; and of course, one's own imagination and invention.

It should be noted that many of these sources can be accessed in two ways, either through conversation or merely through silent observation. Also noteworthy is the finding that, the greater the number of such informal sources and the greater the diversity of sources (whether informal or formal) that attest to the value and workability of a given innovation, the more likely it is to be tried out and adopted. None of the case studies revealed reports of anyone's testing or adopting an innovation based solely upon information derived from mass media or extensionists.

At a broader level, the CTTA Niger study delineated more general categories of communicators, contexts, and media through which Sahelian producers actually or potentially acquire new agricultural information and materials and exchange farming advice and opinion.

Three types of individuals who transmit such information and/or influence community opinion and action were identified: innovators, key communicators, and influentials, including a subtype of 'farmer paragons' – exceptionally adept cultivators or stockraisers who are frequently consulted by co-villagers for advice on practical farming matters.

A number of economic, biosocial, or religious groups were also found to play an actual or potential role in agricultural communication, including: cooperatives; women-centred cliques; *marabout* associations at both community, national, and cross-national levels; and the *samaria* or young people's association, a community-based civic and social group that is found among most sedentary Sahelian peoples. A great many contexts or locales in which people engage in 'farm talk' (Lionberger *et al.* 1975) were also documented, *e.g.* in market-places, mosques, and community gathering places akin to a 'village square'; at wells and shops; during social, civic, and ceremonial events; and while travelling or working away from home.

The CTTA study paid special attention to formal mass media[3] and extension. Findings indicated that both radio and television[4] play a prominent role in alerting people to new agricultural possibilities. But as noted earlier, interpersonal, peer, and group communication networks are far more active factors in farmers' actual adoption decision making. Extension received mixed reviews from interviewees; but the vast majority felt that both extensionists and researchers presently played little or no part in their agricultural communication networks or farming decision-making.

Moreover, they felt that the technologies and information currently offered by R&E were not relevant to their needs. One man echoed the views of many when he observed that: 'Everything the service brings us needs to be grown in fertiliser. But who can afford this?...The extension service is not "honest" because it refuses to work with the realities of our village.'

Conclusions and implications for agricultural development

The poor F-R-E linkages found in Niger and many other African countries in part result from fundamental communication problems. Although it is not possible to present all the findings from the CTTA Niger study here, as well as the detailed corpus of data upon which they are based, the major conclusions can be summarised as follows.

  o Sahelian producers manifest an indisputable thirst for fresh agricultural information and ideas, as farm families struggle to wrest a living from an ever-more-difficult physical and human ecology;
  o farmers endeavour to access such information through a multiplicity of

communication networks and channels, both informal and formal. But they rely more heavily upon informal sources in evaluating information and formulating decisions, because formal sources do not (and cannot by them-selves) fully meet farmers' need for credible and workable information;

- as part of their search for and validation of new agricultural information, Sahelian farmers design and conduct their own applied and adaptive research using 'concrete' (Rhoades and Bebbington 1988), empirical scientific methods. Much of this experimentation is explicitly impelled by what producers perceive as the inappropriateness of technology currently offered by formal systems of RD&E.
- There is a wealth of indigenous agricultural knowledge and expertise in the Sahelian countryside. With assistance from formal RD&E systems, some of this knowledge could be codified and disseminated to benefit low-resource producers throughout this ecozone;
- so long as farmers' own research efforts and their plethora of communication resources are ignored, much of donor investment in R&E institutions and projects will be wasted.

The last two points form the core of the CTTA concept. The shortcomings of earlier models of communication for technology design and transfer and the failed development efforts based on such models signal the immediate need to link local and scientific systems of agricultural RD&E. Ideally they should work together on mutually identified problems and opportunities. With relatively small inputs of donor assistance, this can be achieved through enriched, multi-directional F-R-E communication that simultaneously improves the relevance and effectiveness of formal R and E and increases the quantity and quality of F experimentation and diffusion.

Farmers and researchers   To illustrate in concrete terms, the Niger study found that farmers and researchers alike are worried about the problem of striga, which is rated *the major cereal pest in Niger* (CTTA 1988: 64) and indeed, is per-haps the most serious pan-Sahelian agronomic problem (Hendry 1987). In fact, agronomists in Niger were currently experimenting with trap crops for striga. But curiously, they were not investigating any of the cultivars normally grown in association with millet. Nor did they appear to have taken the trouble to dis-cover that Nigerian farmers have long used sesame as a striga trap. One can only speculate how much valuable research time and money might have been saved if scientists had first communicated with farmers about how farmers themselves approach this problem!

Also like farmers, scientists in Niger were experimenting with more efficient placement of fertiliser and with hardier, shorter-cycle millets (CTTA 1988: 48). But there was little indication that scientists had systematically consulted pro-ducers on the results of their own, informal experiments in these regards before setting formal research agendas.

Before committing massive amounts of scarce resources to a specific R&D thrust, scientists would be well-advised to first glean and sift through the pertinent information available from producers themselves (McCorkle 1989). To do other-wise is not only financially irresponsible; it is scientifically indefensible. It is note-worthy that a study of one of the world's major international agricultural research centres found that 90 per cent of the technologies currently being extended by the centre were elaborated on the basis of existing farmer practices (Goodell 1982, cited in Rhoades 1987: 9). Indeed, some experts suspect 'that much, if not all, of the technologies being promoted by agricultural development agencies the world over are derived directly or indirectly from farm people' (Rhoades 1987: 9).

The foregoing constitutes only one among many reasons why producers should be directly enlisted in the research enterprise and encouraged in their own on-farm experimentation. As the CTTA Niger study recommends, this can be achieved in a variety of ways. One is joint, on-farm mini-trials involving F, R, and E as a team, but with F taking an active rather than a passive role, particularly in the research design (*e.g.* choice of experimental variables, treatments and treatment levels, plot size and type planting densities). Another approach that has worked well is for F and R to jointly design experimental 'mini-kits' of seeds and inputs with which F can devise and conduct their own tests and then report their findings to R and E. Still other participatory research methods are detailed in Chambers *et al.* (1989).

Farmers and extensionists Like research, extension can draw upon indigenous systems to improve its performance, too. It can and should tap into informal F-F networks for transmitting agricultural information in order to stimulate the multiplier effect that is essential to successful technology transfer. Not even the most highly trained, motivated, staffed, and well-funded extension service in the world can single-handedly achieve this effect – much less the notoriously problem-ridden extension services of Sub-Saharan Africa.

As agricultural communication experts point out in no uncertain terms, even in modern-day America: '...communication provides most of the multiplying effect of local change-agent efforts in getting new information and innovations accepted and used... If all of the information from specialised agency sources had to flow directly to farmers, and if all the persuading had to be done by their representatives, acceptance would...be very slow indeed' (Lionberger *et al.* 1975: 7).

The CTTA Niger study made a number of recommendations for more tightly linking extension into farmers' interpersonal and other communication networks, as well as for increasing F, R, and E communication generally, whether in Niger or other Sahelian nations. A sampling of these recommendations includes the following:

o mobilise women's and young people's associations, cooperatives, and other local groups as major, multi-directional conduits of agricultural information, and involve them in the kinds of collaborative on-farm research described above;

o take advantage of natural fora like marketplaces and wells for extension of agricultural information;

o promote increased and geographically broader F-F communication of indigenous agricultural knowledge through interactive 'farm talk' radio and television shows;

o strengthen F, R, and E feedback loops through interactive media formats, with priority topics determined by F;

o explore the use of cassette tapes for disseminating agricultural information to and among F, and for collecting F commentary and opinion for transmission to R and E;

o investigate the possibility of extending printed matter through the major group of adult rural literates, the *marabouts*;

○ conduct in-depth research on the potentials of African folk media as additional, cost-effective channels for transmitting agricultural information.

In sum, the CTTA Niger research provides unequivocal evidence of widespread and systematic indigenous experimentation with and innovation in new agricultural technologies in the Sahel – just as farmers in all times and places have always done (Rhoades 1987). Likewise for rich and active indigenous networks for communicating about and transferring agricultural information. As Mundy and Compton (this volume) observe, the untapped extension potentials of such local and culture-specific communication resources are enormous. Along with Warren (1989a: 165), the CTTA Niger study can conclude only that 'In an era of scarce resources, it is more cost-effective to build development programs for agriculture...on indigenous decision-making organisations than to create new organisational structures that...have to be imposed from outside. It is also cost-effective to take the time and effort to delineate the indigenous agricultural technical knowledge...upon which...production practices are based...to understand...where convergence exists between the local and scientific systems, where communication...between the two...could be improved by working with and through the existing system.'

Notes

1 CTTA is funded under USAID Contract No. 5826-C-00-5054-00 with the Academy for Educational Development (AED). The program is jointly managed and supported by the Offices of Education, Agriculture, and Rural Development of USAID's Bureau for Science and Technology, in cooperation with the agency's Regional Bureaus and the country Missions in the nations where the program has operated (primarily Honduras, Indonesia, Jordan, and Peru). However, the views expressed here are those of the authors and do not necessarily represent official USAID policy.

2 Fieldwork was conducted during May 1988. It was preceded by several months of intensive literature review plus a preliminary in-country study of Niger's agricultural technology system (CTTA 1988). Fieldwork was followed by several months of analysis and write-up. For methodological and other details, see McCorkle *et al.* 1988.

3 Unfortunately, the tight field research schedule did not permit in-depth study of folk media as well. On this subject, consult Mundy and Compton (this volume) and the references therein.

4 Among Sahelian nations, Niger has an exceptionally well-developed television system which spans not only urban but also rural areas. In perhaps some 3800 villages, the government has installed a public television. For greater detail on these media, see McCorkle *et al.* 1988.

25. A Trans-local Adaptation of Indigenous Knowledge in Duck Farming in Indonesia

PATRICIA J. VONDAL

Introduction

THIS CHAPTER REPORTS on the successful application of local knowledge to the development of a commercial duck hatchery in South Kalimantan, Indonesia. It is also an example of farmer-to-farmer technology transfer from farmers in Bali to farmers in South Kalimantan. In an era of agricultural development characterised by a lack of sufficient appropriate and affordable new technology for small-scale farmers, and agricultural extension systems which often fall short, this case presents the elements of an alternative to current research, development, and diffusion models.

Duck farming has long been an integral part of the rural economy of many Southeast Asian communities. The Government of Indonesia has been seeking ways to intensify and commercialise this activity in order to increase both the income and domestic sources of protein of small-scale farmers. Yet most models for developing commercial poultry production are Western and rely on capital-intensive methods that only large-scale producers can afford. Furthermore, some animal scientists have questioned the availability of appropriate technology to raise poultry production at the household level of the small-scale farmer to a degree which would increase regional economies (Quijandria 1989; Hetzel, Sutikno and Soeripto 1981). The highly successful, native-developed and managed industry in the province of South Kalimantan serves as a possible model for achieving the goals of the Government of Indonesia in a small-scale farmer context. This presentation is based upon field research conducted on this industry between 1981 and 1983.[1]

The centre of this industry is Kabupaten (Regency) Hulu Sungai Utara, approximately 200 kilometres north of Banjarmasin, the provincial capital on the southern coast of South Kalimantan on the island of Borneo. It is a lowland region dotted with freshwater swamps, lakes, and ponds. It is intersected by two major river systems and their many tributaries flood much of the area between November and April (Vondal 1989). It is also an area of fairly high population density at approximately 200 persons per square kilometre. The majority of the population, which is dominated by Banjarese-Malay peoples, characterises themselves as small-scale farmers – their principal crop being rice – or as traders, most of whom engage in the trade and transport of agricultural products and articles of daily use. However, duck farming has been an integral part of this rural economy for well over 100 to 150 years. A regional industry based on commercial duck and duck egg production has been evolving for the past 80 years.

The Alabio duck *(Anas platyrhynchos borneo)* has been bred in this riverine and swampland region for more than a century. No one knows the exact origin of the duck or exactly how long it has been exploited for egg production by regional farmers. One theory is that it was originally from South India, and brought to South Kalimantan by the Javanese in the 15th century (Siregar 1982). Others propose that the duck was brought to South Kalimantan with the

333

Muscovy duck (*Carina moschata*) from Mexico via the Philippines or Malaysia (cited in Chavez and Ladmini 1978). Many farmers believe that the Alabio duck is indigenous to the area. It is said to be distinctly different from other ducks found in Indonesia (Robinson *et al.* 1977). Regardless, it is noted by both local duck farmers and scientists as a prolific egg producer, well suited to both foraging or confined management (caged) systems (Robinson *et al.* 1977; Chavez and Lasmini 1978; Kingston, Kosasih and Ardi 1978; Nawari and Ardi 1979). Furthermore, it has a low mortality rate, especially when compared to the native chicken, which is also used for egg production in villages throughout the province of South Kalimantan.

Duck eggs are produced by farming households which maintain flocks ranging on the average from 50 to 200 birds. They are sold on weekly market days to specialised egg traders, who in turn transport them to the provincial capitals of South, East, and Central Kalimantan. From these major markets, the eggs are bought by other traders and sold in secondary cities and small market towns throughout these three provinces. The industry has provided livelihood, then, for the farmers who hatch eggs for the production of ducklings, for farmers who produce eggs for the market, for the many large- and small-scale traders who transport eggs to market centres and consumers, and to other classes of traders who purchase the various duck feed components and transport them to the weekly markets where farmers bring in their duck eggs to sell.

Farmers who produce eggs for the market place have continually experimented with both feed and caging systems as a means of encouraging consistent productivity from their flocks. As a result of their experimentation and the steady consumer demands for eggs, many rural families have been able to specialise in egg production and gain their major livelihood from this endeavour.

The hatchery system and its commercial development

I have reported on the egg production segment of the industry elsewhere (Vondal 1987), but here I would like to focus on the hatchery operators who also play a crucial role. In response to the growing demand for ducks by commercial egg producers, and to opportunities for increasing their own incomes, hatchery operators have implemented a new technology which has increased the number of ducklings which could be hatched per cage, and has simultaneously decreased production costs.

Several villages in this region, reportedly in the 1940s, became highly specialised in the hatching of duck eggs. The resulting female ducklings were sold between the age of one to two weeks to farmers who manage flocks for production of eggs for consumers. Male ducklings were sold separately, the majority to traders who specialise in rearing them for eventual resale to restaurants throughout South Kalimantan.

Historically, ducklings were hatched either by mature broody hens, or by another breed of duck, the Muscovy. The Alabio duck, which is the actual egg producer in this industry, is not used. According to hatchery operators who still employ these methods, this is because the Alabio duck does not want to lay eggs any longer, after it hatches its first clutch of eggs. The Muscovy, in comparison with the Alabio duck, is a poor layer said to produce only 15 eggs a month, at the most. The Alabio duck itself can produce as many as 25–30 in the same time period. Thus, it makes sense to use the Muscovy duck for hatching purposes.

These ducks can be manipulated to maintain a period of brood for five to six consecutive months. One brood period is defined as the 28-day cycle necessary to hatch a clutch of eggs. Each duck can hatch between 20–30 eggs depending on its age and current state of broodiness (Kingston *et al.* 1978). Hatchery operators report that one Muscovy can hatch eggs for five years at the most, but may be sold before then as the body has less fat over time and thus becomes less suitable for hatching. Farmers stress the importance of warmth for hatching eggs produced from the duck's body heat.

Hatchery operators maintained flocks ranging between 20 and 300 ducks in special hatchery rooms constructed as lean-tos on the sides of their homes, or in separate cages next to their houses, depending on the flock size. They are family-run operations in which various household members are assigned the duties of purchasing fertile duck eggs, feeding and caring for the Muscovy ducks, caring for the newly hatched ducklings, and transporting these at the age of one week to the local markets for sale to other farmers.

Specialisation in hatchery operations centred in two closely located villages, but one of these became nationally known through a cooperative that was set up under the leadership of one of the residents. In 1971, this individual, who subsequently became the co-op president, received assistance from the local branches of the government-run Animal Husbandry Office and the Cooperative Office. The cooperative enabled its members to take out loans for enlarging hatchery rooms, buying Muscovy ducks and fertile eggs, as well as for home improvements.

In 1973, the central government's Animal Husbandry Office in Jakarta sponsored a National Poultry Contest and Exhibition in Java. The president of the new village cooperative was remembered by the Animal Husbandry Office and was invited to the exhibition to introduce the Alabio duck of South Kalimantan. In comparison with the other breeds of Indonesian ducks, the Tegal and Bali, the Alabio duck received favourable attention as a dual purpose bird. Egg production is high in the breed and the quality of meat was judged to be superior. Subsequently, news of the Alabio duck was spread throughout Indonesia with help from a government animal husbandry publication *(Media Peternakan)*. The co-op president began receiving requests to ship Alabio ducklings to Java. The first shipment was sent to Java in 1974 and, by 1975, 1000 ducklings a week were being sent out through the village co-op.

Growing demand for the ducklings began increasing nation-wide, and stimulated a new interest in the duck egg business locally in South Kalimantan as well, which placed a strain on the Muscovy hatchery system. Meanwhile, the co-op president had been impressed by the presentation of a hatchery operator from Bali at the 1973 Poultry Exhibition in Java. This farmer displayed an ancient technique utilised in Bali for hatching ducklings using discarded rice hulls instead of Muscovy ducks or hens. The method, which consists of packing empty rice hulls around and between layers of fertile eggs in cylindrical shaped containers, serves to generate as much heat as the Muscovy ducks do for hatching eggs in the same time period. The hatchability rate, at an average of 80–85 per cent, is the same as that derived using the Muscovy duck.

The advantages of the rice hull method are numerous. The problem of maintaining broodiness, which is the ability to hatch successive clutches of eggs, is eliminated. While some South Kalimantan farmers are able to maintain a 6-month period of broodiness from their Muscovy ducks, this had to be followed by a 4-month rest period. Furthermore, the cost and labour for feeding the Muscovy ducks is eliminated by using rice hull. An additional selling point is that rice hulls are free, and need replacement only every two years. Lastly, many more eggs can be hatched per given unit area.

However, the adoption of this new method did not come easily. It is a difficult method to master initially and requires considerable practice. Layers of eggs must be shifted consistently to maintain precise temperature control so that they receive sufficient heat during all stages of the hatching period. This is necessary so that the ducklings are able to develop properly and be able to peck their way out of the egg shells at the end of the 28 days.

When the co-op president first tried the method in his own hatchery, the attempt was a complete failure, as were his successive attempts. In 1975, he decided to finance, from his schoolmaster's salary, his own trip to Bali to study with the farmer who presented this hatchery method at the Poultry Exhibition. Upon returning to South Kalimantan, he tried the method and failed again, with a loss of 10,000 fertile duck eggs. After a second trip to Bali to study with the farmer, the result was another failure. The co-op president finally sold some of his rice lands and hired the Balinese farmer and his brother to come live with his family and teach the method until he could master it.

Other hatchery operators in the village reluctantly followed suit by studying with their leader after the Balinese farmer went home, but they were clearly worried about the high costs of mastering the technique themselves and the health of the resulting ducklings. Although the method was ancient and regularly practiced by Balinese duck farmers, it was a radical innovation to the Banjarese farmers of South Kalimantan. The savings in production costs and the clear profitability of the new system, and perhaps an unwillingness to be left behind in what was rapidly becoming the 'old' system, encouraged the other hatchery operators in Mamar to try.

All the Mamar hatchery operators experienced failures in their early attempts, but continued trials finally convinced them of the benefits of the new method. It was not a smooth transition. At the beginning, feelings ran high against the co-op president, a highly respected religious and academic leader in the village, but he prevailed in his strong belief that his innovation in hatching ducklings would ultimately be profitable. A further barrier was the reaction of duck farmers in surrounding villages who purchased ducklings from the hatcheries. They believed that ducklings hatched without the use of a brooding Muscovy duck or hen would be weak and even die, or if they survived, they would be poor layers. Locally, no one wanted to purchase the Mamar village ducklings. However, national demand for Alabio ducks had risen to a point where local perceptions about the viability of the resulting ducklings no longer prevented its adoption by Mamar's hatchery operators.

It took a three-year period before all the village hatchery operators successfully adopted the Balinese system. By using this technique, the operators were able to expand production of ducklings at a level equivalent to the rising level of both regional and national demand for Alabio ducks. By 1979, the co-op was exporting 5000 ducklings per week to Java. Many of the ducklings were hatched using the Balinese technique. The ducklings were sent to Semarang to a poultry feed store whose owners, in turn, shipped the ducklings to locations throughout Indonesia. The money from the sales in Semarang were wired to a local branch office bank in South Kalimantan and, from there, the earnings were distributed to the co-op members who had contributed ducklings from their hatchery enterprises. Each hatchery household in the village was purchasing an average of 1500 fertile Alabio eggs per week. This figure is three times the average number of eggs that were produced weekly by the same hatchery operators who used Muscovy ducks. The hatchery operators of Mamar began to prosper. Although the co-op stopped exporting ducklings by 1980 because of operational difficulties, the demand for ducklings by family-run commercial egg producers in South Kalimantan had, by this time, risen sufficiently to maintain profitability of hatchery production.

Of historical note is Adam Malik's visit to the cooperative and the village hatcheries in 1979. Malik, then the Vice President of Indonesia, said in his speech that the rice hull method was a 'modern' system; its costs are low and its production results are good. Malik declared that this system was beneficial for the economic development of the Alabio duck industry and for the people themselves. Representatives of foreign aid agencies, government officials, animal scientists, and university researchers from Indonesia, Australia, South East Asia, Europe and the US have since come to investigate the hatchery system and the duck egg industry itself.

The co-op leader informed me that a US official, impressed after visiting his hatchery in 1980, offered him a loan for purchase of an electric hatchery. By this time, though, he was convinced of the benefits of the rice hull method learned from fellow duck farmers in Bali, which he believed was ideal for his village. This ancient method is cheap, and has no need for electricity which, even today, is not a reliable commodity in any of the small villages and towns in the region. Local farmers also have fears about their ability to repay large loans. For these reasons, he turned down the offer. Electric hatcheries may someday be an alternative to the rice hull method, but with the unpredictability of a steady and reliable electric current, an owner could easily lose thousands of dollars in ruined eggs.

Factors that contributed to successful adaptation

What are the contributing factors in the successful adaptation of local knowledge? First was the role played by the village entrepreneur who help organise a cooperative and who was willing to experiment with a new technology. As a local leader of *Muhammadiyah*, a modernist reform branch of Indonesian Islam, he held a strong faith in the benefit of the rice hull method for both his community and the development of the industry. This modernist orientation and its associated willingness to institute change among *Muhammadiyah* members may have been a large factor in this and the propensity of other individuals to experiment and innovate. The role of *Muhammahiyah* in relation to commercial growth of the industry was not the focus of the original research. However, it was clear that other elements of Islam, irrespective of sectoral affiliation, did have an effect on the desire to profit economically to finance the pilgrimage to Mecca and to build local mosques and local religious schools.

Participation in this growing poultry industry was one way to help achieve some of these religious and social goals. South Kalimantan is noted as a centre of Islamic faith and devotion within Indonesia. The region's population is 95 per cent Moslem. Therefore, the innovativeness, determination, and leadership displayed by the Mamar Co-op President was central to the ultimate adoption of the Balinese technique. While the co-op president's personal story is impressive, he is not unique in the world of farmers. The literature on entrepreneurship, innovation development, and diffusion contains many cases of highly motivated individuals with varying and different incentives to risk experimentation.

The second factor was the role played by the technology itself – the Balinese rice hull hatchery system. The Muscovy system employed historically in South Kalimantan was fine for its time, but as the demand for Alabio ducks and eggs grew, it was not capable of higher levels of production. In this instance, local Banjarese knowledge was not sufficient. It is ironic that the low-resource Balinese hatchery technology, although not modern in the commonly-held meaning of the term, afforded the mass production methods needed to support the further commercial growth of the poultry industry. The technology involved has the additional virtue of being entirely appropriate for the rural economy of South Kalimantan, where rice hulls are abundant and electricity is still unreliable. Thus, this technology, based on local knowledge of the Balinese duck farmers, was incorporated into the already substantial knowledge base of duck production within the community of Banjarese hatchery operators in Mamar. Although the real fear of economic loss, as publicly experienced by the co-op president, and the time needed to develop the skill to employ the Balinese method were shown to be initial barriers to its adoption, the clear profitability and suitability of this technology won over its eventual adopters.

A third factor was the catalytic role unwittingly played by the Government. The local branch of the Animal Husbandry Office was helpful to the entrepreneur in this story. The village entrepreneur was assisted in setting up a village cooperative and, later, in marketing the Alabio ducklings hatched by the co-op members. The growth in national demand for these ducklings created a need for a more productive hatchery technology. The nationally-sponsored poultry contest and exhibition helped create that demand, but more important, played a key role in bringing successful breeders and entrepreneurs together which inspired the co-op president to try the rice hull technology from hatcheries in Bali. Clearly in this instance, local breeds of livestock and local technologies of management and production were given their day.

This is the kind of more limited role that governments should continue to play as a means of fostering communication and the introduction of suitable technologies between local experts and entrepreneurs. Exhibitions could be held more regularly to bring together local experts from different regions specialising in animal husbandry, horticulture, and other fields. Efforts could be made to identify local experts who would be willing to present their proven methods and low-cost technologies. The transfer of such knowledge from locale to locale across regions could thus be facilitated with minimal government investment.

Of course, not everyone has the resources of the entrepreneur in this story – a steady income from school teaching and rice lands to fund the cost of trial-and-error experimentation with a new technology over a period of several years. But again, a limited amount of support from national agricultural research centres could provide seed money to support such experimentation by willing entrepreneurs in a small-scale farmer context in villages. These individuals may be locally nominated or identified from their participation in national agricultural exhibitions.

Although not an alternative to traditional agricultural research, development, and extension, such support has the value of promoting legitimate technology development appropriate to both the resources and capabilities of small-scale farmers, building upon their local knowledge and expertise, and lessening the dependency on frequently inappropriate technology transferred from Western industrialised countries. Often, it can take a decade or more before an industrial technology is appropriately modified for small-scale farmers in radically different environments. These problems of technological inappropriateness and the lengthy periods of their development for local use are often compounded by ineffective extension systems in agriculture.

Other factors have likewise contributed to the success of the overall industry and this essay will not be complete without mentioning them. They include: a constantly growing demand for duck eggs and meat; extensive and well-established marketing networks for poultry products, poultry feed, and ducks run by Banjarese private sector traders; and the historically strong profit orientation and entrepreneurial spirit widely found among the Banjarese residents of South Kalimantan (Vondal 1984).

Moreover, the catalytic role played by the Indonesian Government at certain points in the development of this industry helped some of the local participants create a period of 'take off' growth by facilitating a highly successful case of trans-local transfer of technology. As a by-product, it contributed to the industry's further commercialisation and regional economic development from which many small-scale farmers, traders, and consumers have benefited. In the absence of funded research on commercial duck operations for Indonesia's small-scale farmers, the case history of experimentation in this native poultry industry contains many elements worthy of further study. Furthermore, as governments, international development banks and donor agencies now strive to strengthen and promote the commercial private sector as a means of achieving economic growth in developing countries, the limited role of the Government of Indonesia in the development of this industry in the 1970s could be adapted and used as a model elsewhere.

Note

1. This report is based upon research funded by the National Science Foundation under Dissertation Assistance Grant No. BNS-8107626, Cathay Pacific Airlines, and The Graduate School, Rutgers University, New Brunswick, New Jersey. In Indonesia, the research was sponsored by Universitas Lambung Mangkurat, Banjarmasin, and Lembaga Ilmu Pengetahuan Indonesia (LIPI), Jakarta.

26. Tinker, Tiller, Technical Change: Peoples' technology and innovation off the farm[1]

MATTHEW GAMSER AND HELEN APPLETON

Introduction

'INDIGENOUS KNOWLEDGE' IS beginning to be taken more seriously by the major players in the development process. However, there is a danger in such attention. If this knowledge, as it is popularised, is classified as a precious, but static commodity, to be appreciated and then incorporated (by Western-trained scientists) into research plans, then the bearers of such knowledge will be little better off for all the bother.

It is not enough to accept that poor people are not stupid. Their knowledge is dynamic, evolving over time as people constantly seek to improve their situation. Men and women not only know their environment, but also know how to work with it. In particular, they sense how different situations require different approaches to solve problems. Social, economic and cultural (including gender) factors affect the type of information people have access to, and determine the directions of their innovations.

Using this dynamic knowledge for development requires more than simply describing existing techniques and decoding classification systems in Western terms. It needs an understanding of the methods with which 'non-scientist' producers recognise and attack problems, and a consideration of how such methods and their practitioners can be incorporated into formal Research and Development (R&D) and technical assistance programmes. The real power of indigenous knowledge lies in people and their capacity to innovate, not in one or another product of their innovation.

Most work on indigenous problem-solving concerns farmers and primary production systems. This work is slowly increasing the acceptance of the importance of farmer participation in agricultural research. What is not recognised is that peoples' innovation is equally pervasive off the farm. While little from the billions of development dollars devoted to industrial assistance touches artisan innovators, it is these men and women who are keeping the poor majority fed, housed, and supplied with essential tools, and it is they who maintain these supplies throughout periods of extreme fluctuation in national economies and resource conditions.

Off-farm innovators and the ignored technological revolution

From the perspective of large and expensive 'technology transfer' projects, the history of technology in developing countries is a tale full of problems, and short on progress. However, from the perspective of poor people and the technologies they employ in daily life, recent history shows many dramatic innovations.

Such indigenous innovation, or 'peoples' technology' already plays a major role in national and regional economies. It is responsible for providing cassava food products to the vast majority of urban households in West Africa. It is delivering locally produced salt for Sierra Leone, thus saving foreign exchange. It has developed essential machinery for coffee processing in the small-holder-

340

dominated Tanzanian coffee industry. It is maintaining the livelihood of tens of thousands of artisanal fishermen in Bay of Bengal and Arabian Sea coastal communities. It is supplying essential agricultural tools and maintaining vehicles and machinery in Bangladesh. Where the informal sector is thriving, it is doing so not because of scientists, engineers, and foreign technical experts, but because of artisan innovators and the customers who advise them.

The *Tinker, Tiller, Technical Change* project seeks to raise awareness of the significance of 'peoples' technologies' for the poor of Asia, Africa and Latin America. Its investigators from 14 developing countries have produced case studies of 17 off-farm innovations, covering a wide range of technologies, cultures and environments. The studies examine the evolution of these innovations, their social and economic importance, and their limitations. Their examples, some of which are presented below, challenge perceptions of artisan innovators and of the industrial know-how of poor people and their communities.[2]

Cassava processing in Nigeria[3]

In the late 1970s, Nigerians subsisted on a diet of cheap imported wheat, rice and maize. The oil price crash brought dramatic economic decline, which led to a government ban on all food imports in the early 1980s. For a Western nation such food supply disruption would have been disastrous. Yet Nigeria has weathered this storm, largely through the efforts of informal sector, off-farm innovation.

Nigeria has been transformed from a country dependent on cereal imports for staple foods to one again reliant on locally grown, locally processed cassava during the last 10 years. This has been largely through the work of countless small-scale artisans, traders and farmers. These ordinary people increased cassava production, developed processing machinery, and organised processing enterprises to put *gari, fufu,* cassava flour, and other essential food products into millions of homes. From being a subsistence production operation carried out by individual households, cassava processing has become a major business, providing employment and income for both processors and the producers of processing equipment.

Cassava processing once was a completely manual operation, but today many of its components are wholly or partly mechanised. Grating, dewatering, sieving and frying machines have been developed by blacksmiths, welders, iron benders, mechanics and government R&D institutions. The most successful innovations in processing have come from small-scale artisan producers, who have responded most directly to local needs. Their rough and ready machines have been made from locally available materials, and are far more economical than imported 'sophisticated' technology. Also important has been the small-scale producers' ability to produce machines to meet specific customer needs, and to make modifications based on user experiences and suggestions.

Gari (processed cassava) production entrepreneurs are developing large and well organised networks of labourers to link the various components of cassava processing. They purchase peeled cassava in bulk from women farmers at special markets, and employ graters, pressers, and fryers. Some entrepreneurs are branching out into cassava harvesting and *gari* transport and distribution. Careful consideration is given to the selection of machines for processing, based on the entrepreneurs' calculations of labour costs and productivity. Unlike the larger, government-sponsored operations, their process development has not attempted to mechanise everything at once, but has sought to use machines where they have a clear advantage.

Both artisans and entrepreneurs carefully study technological problems and pursue innovative solutions through a trial and error basis. This process is effective, but slow. Low levels of literacy and scientific understanding limit the speed at which successes and failures can be communicated to others. Lack of basic tools and infrastructure (lathes, folding machines, electricity, credit) inhibits *technology* development work in small workshops. Lack of interaction with the formal scientific community makes it difficult to make progress in addressing important environmental questions surrounding cassava foodstuffs production and consumption (such as potential cyanin toxicity, and how it can be reduced).

Contrary to prevailing myths, women well understand the technical implications of *gari* production processes and contribute to further developments. Many technological innovations, for example the production of sturdier machines and more durable grater sheets, have been prompted by their demands. However, since few women own graters, mechanisation has meant that men have become more involved in *gari* production because they can access the capital which enables them to purchase the machines. Women may thus be losing control over a process which is traditionally theirs.[4]

Salt from silt in Sierra Leone[5]

Sierra Leone is another nation in which artisan innovation has been essential to maintaining food security during a period of dramatic economic decline. Despite hundreds of miles of coastline, Sierra Leone has relied on rock salt imports from Senegal for its national supply of this commodity. The country's economic decline and resulting foreign exchange scarcity are making such imports difficult to sustain. This makes import substitution essential. Large donor agencies have attempted to introduce solar salt extraction operations, but Sierra Leone's short dry season makes these impractical, and all have failed expensively.

Virtually unnoticed by the Government and development agencies, local artisan producers have adapted traditional salt filtration techniques, and now provide over 40 per cent of the national salt demand. Their production and market share continue to grow.

Artisans extract salt in one of two ways: boiling fresh seawater which is wasteful of wood and labour, or digging boreholes for brine collection in tidal estuaries where there are mud or clay soils. In the latter method, the seepage of sea water through the silts leads to a natural concentration of salt in the brine, which is then filtered by percolation, washed, evaporated by boiling and dried in the sun. The production process requires a percolation funnel, a stove, a spray/drainage unit for washing the salt crystals, and a wooden trough for collecting the brine during percolation. The women, who carry out the day to day operation of the technology, have already modified the stove design to be less wasteful of fuel, and it is this innovation which makes the 'salt from silt' process profitable. It is an invaluable source of income for the women who have to clothe themselves and their children and contribute towards school fees.

The setting up of production facilities utilises men's skills such as blacksmithing and masonry, and the production process utilises women's skills in boiling and percolation. Transfer of skills takes place informally by watching and doing, although more formal arrangements exist for women from outside the community who visit specifically in order to learn salt processing. Salt-from-silt technology could be extended to other areas through training of local people by the more skilled producers, and through developing larger scale filtration systems. The government is coming to accept that food security for this commodity lies in building upon local skills, and is examining how its research institutions can collaborate with artisan producers to expand production further.

Coffee pulping in Tanzania[6]

Although coffee has been one of Tanzania's main cash crops since the 19th century, Tanzanians were banned from involvement in the coffee industry during most of the colonial period. Farmers started growing beans only in the 1930s. Yet today, not only do Tanzanians possess substantial knowledge concerning coffee cultivation, they also control the technology required for coffee processing. Approximately 60 per cent of the country's coffee produced by small-holder growers is pulped using locally made machines.

The market price of pulped beans is on average about 10 times higher than that of unpulped beans. Hence most small-scale producers prefer to process their coffee at home. The first local Arabica coffee pulping machine was made by African artisans in the 1920s, with the material support and encouragement of German missionaries. The machine consisted of a pulping roller, made of wood, with the handle and other parts made out of metal. While there were a few imported coffee pulpers on settler farms even before the 1920s, coffee machines were imported on an appreciable level into Tanganyika from the mid-1930s on and were mainly bought by the rich farmers. Local farmers always have depended on artisan adaptations of these imported designs, which have evolved over time into more durable and efficient machines.

To the Tanzanian Government's credit, it has long appreciated the importance of artisan innovation, and has developed institutions to encourage further improvements at ground level. For example, the Centre for Agricultural Mechanisation and Rural Technology (CAMARTEC) in conjunction with a rural artisan, Wilson Msami, has made the roller out of concrete with wire rings. The smaller version of this machine is hand driven, and the larger version can be worked by hand or electric power.

Machine production skills are usually acquired by an apprentice attaching himself to a Master Artisan who gradually teaches him how to make the various parts and how to assemble the machine. The apprentice system, though informal and supposedly free of charge, has an in-built payment in kind for the knowledge by working on other tasks for the teacher, and the trainee is expected to donate several bunches of cooking bananas, or a goat or a calf at the end of his course.

Artificial reefs in Kerala State, India[7]

When artisanal fishermen in this Southern India State protested against the introduction of mechanised trawling in the 1950s, claiming that the fisheries resource would be decimated, scientists dismissed them as ignorant fools. For a few years catch levels increased, but from the 1970s yields have declined. From 1970 to 1980 total landings declined by 30 per cent. The share of this catch taken by artisan fishermen declined from 90 to 50 per cent.[8]

Not content with their environmental knowledge being proven superior, the fishermen also are leading in efforts to rehabilitate the fishery. The South Indian Federation of Fishermen's Societies (SIFFS) has supported a programme of artificial reef construction, building upon local techniques and experience. This programme is restoring the shallow water reef formations essential for fish populations.

The fishermen traditionally used wrecks and dump sites as reliable fishing grounds, and appreciated the importance of sea floor contours for fish aggregation and species diversification. Small experiments in artificial reef establishment had taken place since the 1920s. The fisheries environmental crisis caused a reappraisal and expansion of this activity. The fishermen redeveloped old reef sites, and explored ways to make these closer to real (but destroyed) reefs. They experimented with new reef formations to try to recreate the complexities and surfaces of natural reefs. They used new materials, such as stones packed inside coir or rope nets, painted stones, and tires fastened with concrete rings, to make the reefs more stable and attractive to fish. They modified reef designs to protect them from drift net entanglement. These and other artisan innovations (such as artificial bait design and use) have preserved the livelihoods of thousands of fishermen and their communities. The Kochuthope reef, built for Rs. 6000 ($400) by the fishermen's society, yielded Rs. 10,000 of fish for 100 fishermen in its first year of operation. The reef now supports 300 fishermen, all members of the local fishermen's society.

More important, the fishermen's work has earned the respect of the State Government and scientific community. The State has recognised the severity of the environmental problem it faces, and artificial reef establishment has been accepted as an essential part of its fisheries conservation effort. The latest State Five-Year Plan includes funding for the expansion of the fishermen's society reef building research programme. State fisheries research institutions, which formerly had little interest in the artisan sector, now collaborate with the society in monitoring fish populations on established reefs.

Blacksmiths in Bangladesh[9]

Though its workshops are small, blacksmith is a big business in Bangladesh. The country has approximately 10,000 blacksmithing enterprises, which account for five per cent of the country's gross output, nine per cent of value added, and 23 per cent of metalworking employment. Blacksmiths contribute 22 per cent of the total sales value of Bangladesh cottage industries, which in turn contribute 50 per cent of total manufacturing GD. Repairs by smiths keep Bangladesh' vehicles and industries in operation.

Blacksmiths in Bangladesh belong to an age old profession, traditionally the preserve of the Karmakar Hindu caste. Of late, groups of Muslim blacksmiths have begun to work in areas of the country with low Karmakar populations. Unlike in many countries, blacksmith is largely a full-time trade, with skills passed on within families. Blacksmiths develop close relationships with their customers, and most of their innovations arise from customer needs and comments on existing products.

A typical blacksmith's trade includes the production of 'traditional' and 'non-traditional' products. Traditional products are mainly agricultural tools, which have seasonal demand. Non-traditional products include carpentry tools, angle frames, machine parts, and rural housing hardware, in which demand is constant throughout the year. Blacksmith innovations are the product of interaction between artisans and customers. The learning process in this field is not a one shot affair. In Comilla and Brahmanbaria Districts artisans over time have become capable of producing blade hoes and rotavator blades for power tillers and tractors. Traditionally these parts would have been replaced with new imports, but by learning about the products through experiences in repairs the artisans were able to adapt their techniques to produce their own spares at half the cost of the imports.

Common supports and constraints on peoples' technology

The above examples only begin to demonstrate the significance of peoples' off-farm innovation and innovators to poor communities. Yet, the development process in most countries has marginalised poor people, their local knowledge, and their innovations. Technological development in most countries, dominated by imports of products and machinery from outside, especially hinders peoples' innovation. It puts formally trained scientists and engineers in front, and artisans and other 'informal' innovators at the back. As a result, poor people lose access to information, control over their local resources, and control over decision making that affects their future.

Paradoxically, this situation encourages peoples' technology development. Although Government actions put down local innovators and innovations, the worsening plight of the marginalised groups provides a greater motivation to innovate. Unlike research scientists, who innovate to satisfy their professional aspirations, peoples' technology innovators do so to survive . Increased poverty ensures increased growth of peoples' technologies. Products that evolve in these circumstances may not necessarily represent the best 'technical' solution to a problem, but they represent a logical solution that will keep working under local conditions.[10]

Peoples' technologies grow in different ways from 'transferred' outside technologies. The latter often are parachuted into a country in a fixed package. Their hardware and skills needs are set before their arrival, and may bear little relation to local skills and experiences. Their labour and management requirements are established in their countries of origin, and are based on those countries' social and cultural norms. Their natural resource requirements, too, are based on economic and ecological concerns at their points of origin.

Peoples' technologies, on the other hand, develop and diffuse slowly and steadily through a trial and error process. They rely on close communication between users and producers to identify the changes required to improve it and make it more widely useful. Because of this close consultation, the technologies develop in a way that retains and builds upon local skills. They show greater consideration of gender roles (their use is less likely to require men or women to do things that are physically, socially or culturally difficult or unacceptable). Because people do not like to pollute their own neighbourhoods, they tend to be more ecologically sound.

The spread of peoples' technologies is beset by many obstacles. Local innovation is not recognised by the formal scientific and industrial community . This denies it access to technical information, and to financial and communications channels open to the formal sector. Peoples' technology growth occurs in a 'horizontal' pattern, across groups of poor people, but prevailing social, political, and institutional structures place barriers against this sort of poor-to-poor interaction. Most peoples' technology users belong to groups that are traditionally marginalised – women, the landless, the rural poor – and that have both low profile and low social status. Where peoples' technologies have become widespread, a reorganisation and adaptation of these structures has taken place (often made necessary by economic, political, or environmental crisis).

How to support peoples' technologies

Recognition of the value of peoples' technology is the necessary first step towards strengthening the people and organisations behind it. The international agricultural research institutions are making a start at this for on-farm technologies. Little recognition of the value of off-farm innovation exists, but some developing country governments recently have taken promising steps. The Kerala State Government now supports artisanal fishermen's artificial reef investigations. The Government of Nepal provides credit to encourage adoption of artisan-developed watermill (hydropower) technology. Zimbabwe and Kenya have reversed Government policies of evicting artisan metalworkers from their squatter sites, and now provide permanent workplaces, water, and electricity for artisan cooperatives – encouraging innovation in various metal products and metalworking machinery. The Government of Nigeria may be taking the most radical step of all, bringing artisans into its polytechnics as partners in technical education.

Further policy reforms are needed to stop the reinforcement of the structures that are marginalising peoples' technology and its innovators. They should strengthen those peoples' organisations that exist and remove obstacles to their work in spreading information and ideas. Over time, they should build institutional bridges between these popular organisations and formal science, technology, and aid bodies, to combine the useful knowledge and experience developed in both.

At the same time, support for peoples' technology has to respect the informality under which it thrives. What is needed are policies that facilitate but do not 'bureaucratise', that ease access to credit, information, and markets, but that do not undo this through new regulations that accompany recognition. This is a tall order, and no global policy 'solutions' are in stock. The first steps have to be improving understanding of local innovations and innovators, identifying skills and needs, and fitting assistance into what is already going on. In Schumacher's words: *find out what people are doing, and help them to do it better.*

Notes

1 This chapter could not have been written without the advice and written contributions of 7 of the participants from the *Tinker, Tiller, Technical Change* project: Rakesh Basant of the Gujurat Institute of Area Planning, Priyanthi Fernando of ITDG (Sri Lanka), John Kadappuram of the *Programme for Community Organisation* (Kerala, India), Selina Adjebeng Asem of Obafemi Awolowo University (Nigeria), J.E.M. Massaquoi of the University of Sierra Leone, Guillermo Rochebrun of the Catholic University (Peru) and Flor de Maria Monzon of ITDG (Peru).

2. The full case studies and regional analyses are presented in Gamser et al. (1990). Shortened versions of the case studies and a brief overview of the research are found in the December 1989 issue of the *Appropriate Technology* Journal (available from Intermediate Technology Publications, 103–5 Southampton Row, London WC1B 4HH, UK).

3. For further details, see R.O. Adegboye, 'Cassava Processing in Oyo and Bendel

States, Nigeria', and S. Adjebeng-Asem, 'The Cassava Grater', in Gamser et al. (1990).

4. This important issue is examined in greater detail in the Adjebeng-Asem study (Gamser *et al.* in 1990).

5. From J.E.M. Massaquoi, 'Salt from Silt: A Viable Traditional Technology'', in Gamser *et al.* (1990).

6. From S. Nkonoki, 'The Coffee Pulper in Northern Tanzania', in Gamser *et al.* (1990).

7. From J. Kadappuram, 'Artisanal Fishing Innovations in Kerala', in Gamser *et al.* (1990).

8. Total marine fish landings for Kerala dropped from 393,000 tonnes in 1970 to 279,000 tonnes in 1980. Traditional sector landings declined from 840,000 tonnes to 144,000 tonnes during the same period (Data from Central Marine Fisheries Research Institute published statistics).

9. From M. Haque *et al.*, 'Blacksmiths in Bangladesh', in Gamser *et al.* (1990).

10. This issue is examined in greater detail in the study by Flor de Maria Monzon, 'Peoples' Innovations in Housing Construction in Huancayo, Peru', in Gamser *et al.* (1990).

27. Using Indigenous Knowledge Systems in the Design of On-farm Experiments – A Philippine case[1]

CLIVE LIGHTFOOT

Introduction

IF THE TECHNOLOGY that you have packaged is not being adopted, if your cooperation from farmers is poor, then Indigenous Knowledge Systems (IKS) may help. This was true for the Philippines Farming Systems Development Project - Eastern Visayas (FSDP-EV) in our work with shifting cultivators. Shifting cultivation is defined as: '...any system under which food is produced for less than 10 years from one area of land, after which that area is abandoned temporarily and another piece of land cultivated' (Greenland 1974). In the village of this example farmers produce crops for three to four years and abandon the land for ten to fifteen years (Pielago *et al.* 1987). However, this timetable is becoming harder and harder to follow with disastrous consequences.

Conventional wisdom holds that shifting cultivation is bad and that modern continuous cultivation farming must replace it. We experimented with high external input multiple cropping systems without success (FSDP-EV 1985). Our frustration at lack of farmer adoption of these systems caused us to turn to IKS for help. What follows illustrates how IKS helped us to understand better the farmers' problems so the right research questions could be asked. IKS helped us to search for better hypotheses and to implement better experiments and generate some innovations.

Basey is a hilly place in the Eastern Visayas. People are poor and environments are harsh. A typical farmer cultivates less than a hectare in the uplands which may be as much as one kilometre from home. Sloping landform, infertile acid alfisols and high erratic rainfall characterise these upland environments. Access to this land is restricted. Half of Basey's farming households own or lease their upland fields; the rest are tenants. Owners shun their distant fields in preference to tenanted but more·manageable and secure nearby plots. Many households supplement farm incomes from crop (maize, rice, taro) and livestock (chicken, pig) sales with off-farm jobs like carpentry, coconut sap (*tuba*) gathering, hired labour and mat weaving.

Farmers identify forty-four discrete steps in shifting cultivation. Table 27.1 gives the local term for each step described. Clearing a one to two metre wide boundary initiates the process and shows the work party the area. The next step consists of cutting shrubs, vines, bushes and small trees, felling large trees, and removing branches and treading down the vegetation. Burning must wait until the cut vegetation has dried. Unburnt trash is gathered, piled and burnt in the fourth step prior to planting the first crop. Farmers dibble maize as the first crop. Maize is chosen because it survives the dry season and grows well in newly opened land. Taro is interplanted into most maize crops. The first cropping is weeded three times to remove tree stumps and weed regrowth. After harvesting maize, farmers cut the stover, gather it up and burn it. Rice follows maize. Rice is dibble planted, weeded, interplanted with a seed crop of maize, and weeded

Table 27.1: Farmers' processes in shifting cultivation

1.	*Tahad/Ugba*	Clearing borders of land to be worked
2.	*Panaw*	Term for underbrushing-*pagharas*, cutting trees-*pagkahoy*, and branches-*panuso*
3.	*Sunog*	Burning of cut vegetation
4.	*Durok*	Gathering and burning of unburnt trash
5.	*Tanum*	First planting of maize
6.	*Gu-ad*	Planting of gabi as intercrop to maize
7.	*Tatap*	Weeding/cutting of stumps
8.	*Saksak*	Weeding 1st regrowth and uprooting stumps
9.	*Tagantan*	Weeding of 2nd regrowth
10.	*Panangi*	Harvesting of maize
11.	*Tatap*	Undercutting of maize stover
12.	*Popo*	Gathering and burning of trash
13.	*Pugas*	First planting of rice
14.	*Dalos*	First weeding
15.	*Halhag*	Planting of seed-maize intercrop to rice
16.	*Hagiwas*	Second weeding
17.	*Panangi*	Harvesting of seed-maize crop
18.	*Bari*	Harvesting of rice
19.	*Bagnas*	Weeding of maize stover and rice stubble
20.	*Gabot*	Harvesting of gabi
21.	*Tanum*	Second planting of maize (2nd year cropping)
22.	*Dalos*	First weeding
23.	*Hagiwas*	Second weeding
24.	*Panangi*	Harvesting of maize
25.	*Tatap*	Undercutting of maize stover
26.	*Pugas*	Second planting of rice
27.	*Dalos*	First weeding
28.	*Halhag*	Planting of seed-maize intercrop to rice
29.	*Hagiwas*	Second weeding
30.	*Panangi*	Harvesting of seed-maize crop
31.	*Bari*	Harvesting of rice
32.	*Bagnas*	Clearing rice stubble and maize stover
33.	*Tanum*	Third planting of maize (3rd year cropping)
34.	*Dalos*	First weeding
35.	*Hagiwas*	Second weeding
36.	*Dalos*	Spot weeding as may be required
37.	*Panangi*	Harvesting of maize
38.	*Tatap*	Undercutting of maize stover
39.	*Pugas*	Third planting of rice
40.	*Halhag*	Planting of seed-maize intercrop to rice
41.	*Dalos*	First weeding
42.	*Panangi*	Harvesting of seed-maize crop
43.	*Bari*	Harvesting of rice
44.	*Bagnas*	Clearing of rice stubble and maize stover

again before both crops are harvested. Removing the maize and rice stubbles and harvesting the interplanted taro crop completes the first year of cropping. This sequence of maize intercropped with taro followed by rice intercropped with seed maize is repeated for up to three more years, with attendant weeding cycles.

Given the human and physical conditions in Basey, it is hardly surprising that high input intensive cropping systems were not adopted. Our suggested three crops a year patterns were too expensive in fertiliser and pesticides, too demanding in labour, and too demanding on the fragile soil. Furthermore, farmers were not prepared to invest so much in this risky climate of typhoons and droughts. All was not lost, however, as some farmers did adopt some elements of the 'improved' technology (Alcober and Balina 1986). Modest adoption of a groundnut cultivar and taro spacing did not, of course, get to the heart of the shifting cultivation problem.

IKS helps understand the problem

Farmers complain that shifting cultivation no longer works because the land is not left long enough to rejuvenate. Farmers possess their own knowledge about land rejuvenation. Rejuvenated areas support a mini-forest (*kayaw*). Indicator species of rejuvenation include the fern *Pteridium aquilinum* (*lukdo*), a vine (*burakan*) and the tree *Anagasi*. Farmers identify rejuvenated soils by colour and texture. Fertile soils are creamy-brown (*matibulaw*) to blackish-brown (*mati-itom*) with a coarse granular texture (*gabhok*). On the other hand, less fertile soils are brown (*bulaw*) to reddish-brown (*matipula*) with a hard (*banti*) and sticky (*gasgas*) texture.

Interviewed farmers constructed the diagram shown in Figure 27.1 to summarise the biophysical and socioeconomic causes for shifting. Infertile soils along with rats, borers, mole cricket and birds cause low yields, but this is only one reason why farmers decide to leave the land. Obnoxious weeds and red ants are also key factors in the decision to shift. Difficult to control grasses, particularly *Imperata cylindrica* (*cogon*), thrive on the infertile soil and there is abundant *Imperata* seed in surrounding areas ready to take advantage of this. Moreover, *Imperata* emergence is hastened by cultivation practices that leave soils and seeds exposed. Red ants, whose bites soon lead to debilitating infections, exacerbate the weeding problem. These ants only nest in soil that has lost its structure.

Farmers said land and labour shortages constraining them from solving their problems with shifting cultivation (Figure 27.1). They rarely have enough cash to hire labourers to do the necessary land clearing or weeding at today's rates of one US dollar a day. Furthermore, conflicts occur when workers in labour pools leave for more lucrative cash jobs. Getting access to enough land to allow needed rejuvenation time is hard. Not only do too many people want land, but also tenurial arrangements and security problems in remote areas restrict their access.

When acceptable yields cannot be sustained and labour costs for weeding increases to intolerable levels, farmers abandon the area. But, nowadays farmers report that rejuvenated land supporting a mini-forest are getting much harder to find.

Thus they are forced into opening less fertile lands and a once sustainable system is no longer viable. We see the results of this as vast areas of denuded hillsides and brown silty streams. Clearly farmers do not seek high grain yield with high input technologies here. Rather farmers ask what will maintain crop yields for longer, reduce labour demand, and allow them to rehabilitate the hillsides and sustain the period of cropping.

IKS helps in the search for solutions

In our joint search for solutions farmers and scientists came up with many ideas that addressed the biophysical causes of shifting. Farmers told us that local poisons (*tuba, tubli, lagtang*) will kill red ants. They also burn or pour boiling water or waste engine oil on nest sites to kill the ants. They explained how intensive deep weeding with a cutlass controls *Imperata*. They had heard that herbicides and plowing controlled *Imperata* but had not tried them on grounds of prohibitive costs, excessive labour requirements and shortage of draught animals. Farmers knew that *Imperata* cannot tolerate shade, so planting shade crops like cassava and banana helps control it. Farmers also knew that shade protects the soil from being eroded away. Nevertheless these were not enough.

Indigenous knowledge about shade for controlling weeds and soil erosion provided a basis for exploring new technologies. We debated using contour-planted *Ipil Ipil* (*Leucaena leucocephala*) as a shade tree for weed and soil erosion control but rejected it because of land tenure. A cover crop like Tropical *Kudzu* as shade for weed control was rejected because farmers thought it would strangle their crops. The group suggested using a local small prostrate legume as a live mulch to keep the soil covered while the crops were growing.

Farmers expected a legume live mulch to sustain the period of acceptable yield and thereby increase returns to the heavy investments entailed in shifting by sustaining adequate yields over more years, maintaining soil fertility, reducing soil erosion, reducing labour in weeding, preventing red ant nesting, and reducing *Imperata* infestation.

Some scientific evidence supports these hypotheses. Scientists have known for some time now that cover crops reduce soil erosion (Lal 1974). Furthermore researchers in tropical Africa found that: 'Good maize yield was obtained in the live mulch in which weed competition was minimised by the legume cover' (Akobundu and Okigbo 1984). In addition, nitrogen transfer from legumes to other crops has been suggested by several researchers (Hanegraaf 1987). However, live mulch technologies have not been widely adopted. Most mulch species compete too much with the crop, and the techniques to reduce competition involve costly herbicides or weeding equipment.

IKS helps implement on farm experiments

The experiment required farmers to establish a nursery for *Desmodium heterophyllum,* the legume was chosen for its low prostrate creeping habit. Cuttings from the nursery would be planted out just before the first cropping at one meter square spacing and grown out to form a carpet of legume. Subsequent crops would be dibbled into the legume cover. Some farmers anticipated cutting back the legume to prevent it smothering the crop.

Farmers started learning and making changes from day one. The local *Desmodium* they had collected grew very slowly in their nurseries. Testing only resumed when we gave them a faster growing cultivated type. Slow growth happened again on some fields after transplanting. Farmers readily traced this to the fact that those fields had already been cropped for four years and were exhausted. The group learned that *Desmodium* had to be established on newly opened fertile land.

Managing the legume challenged farmers to generate many innovations. After one farmer experienced near failure in her maize crop, the group decided that ring clearing prior to maize planting was insufficient. Now farmers either clear wide strips or the whole area prior to planting maize. One particularly innovative farmer arranged the underbrushed *Desmodium* into contour strips. The barrier formed arrested soil movement and helped control erosion. After

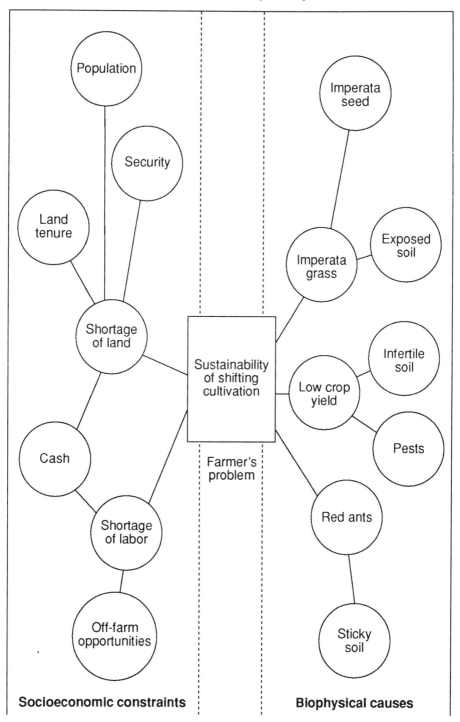

Figure 27.1: *Farmers' diagram of causal relationships in the sustainability of
         shifting cultivation*

crop establishment the *Desmodium* was free to grow back into the crop area. Unfortunately, keeping the legume off the maize takes time, but farmers are still evaluating this because they think that savings could be made in weeding. Rice does not demand so much attention be paid to the legume. Where legume cover is less than fifty per cent some farmers dibble rice directly into the live mulch. Rice is probably less sensitive to competition because its rapidly closing canopy soon shades out the legume and slows its growth. Except in the cases of legume competition, rice and maize yields have not changed appreciably. The group looks forward to constant or better yields, less erosion, and more fertile soils.

It is too early to tell whether our experiments will prove useful to farmers. But one potent sign, spontaneous adoption by neighbours, has started. In Basey not only have neighbours borrowed plant cuttings, but they have also successfully prevailed upon farmers and site staff to teach them about the technology.

Lessons learned

We, like others, have found that IKS enhances precision and relevance in the design of improvements (Ashby 1986), indigenous technologies can broaden the scope of experimental hypotheses (Richards 1986), and indigenous experiments can provide a basis for on-farm experimentation (Lightfoot 1987). The help that IKS gave in Basey has been evident in other project sites where IKS is being used in experimental design. A sequence of forage legumes is being tested to rehabilitate *Imperata* infested uplands (Lightfoot *et al.* 1988). A legume enriched fallow is being tested to restore soil fertility, control weeds, and reduce labour cost in cultivation of fallow rotation systems under coconuts (Repulda *et al.* 1987). IKS provides other important benefits, especially for scientists pursuing the participatory concepts of Chambers and others, and the holistic concepts of Farming Systems Research (Chambers and Jiggins 1987; Rhoades and Booth 1982; Norman 1980). These benefits go beyond purely practical matters like farmers' soil classification helping to put an experiment in the right place. Understanding indigenous farming systems widens the perspective of scientists. Eliciting indigenous knowledge increases farmer participation in the research process. Furthermore, the respect given to farmer knowledge puts the relationship between farmer and scientist on a correct footing, a footing that causes scientists to rethink convention. Shifting cultivation is not bad when done properly. Farmers are concerned about sustainability and environmental degradation. Indeed, as this case suggests when it comes to issues of environmental sustainability, IKS has a vital role to play.

Note

1. This work was conducted by the Farming Systems Development Project – Eastern Visayas, Department of Agriculture Region VIII, the Farm and Resource Management Institute, ViSCA, and Cornell University. Funding was provided by the US Agency for International Development and the National Economic Development Authority, Department of Agriculture, Visayas State College of Agriculture, The Philippines.

28. Taking Farmers' Knowledge and Technology Seriously: Upland rice production in the Philippines

SAM FUJISAKA

Introduction

FARMERS USE THEIR technical knowledge to develop technologies and strategies that solve problems. Other farmers in similar, but geographically removed environments may be interested in farmer-generated technologies because of their adaptability to real situations. This chapter describes a farmer-developed rice production system and how some of the innovations of that system are being introduced to farmers elsewhere for evaluation, adaptation, and possible adoption.

Crop production in Tupi, South Cotabato, The Philippines, was examined as part of research seeking to improve the productivity and sustainability of systems in which rice is a major component. Tupi farmers grow one upland rice crop and two to three maize crops a year. Although soils are favourable for rice and the gently sloping lands suffer little soil erosion, weeds, insect pests, diseases, and uncertain rainfall can seriously reduce rice yields. Tupi farmers have developed practices and technologies that respond to these local potentials and problems.

The upland rice production of these farmers features: (1) planting of separate parcels of traditional upland varieties which are stable-yielding, and modern lowland rice varieties, which are higher-yielding but disease-susceptible, (2) the *panudling*, a locally refined, five-tined, animal-drawn implement used for tillage, furrow opening, and interrow cultivation, (3) broadcast seeding, and (4) alternative strategies based on rice variety and management choices. The implements and management practices were determined to be an example of a technology with potentially wide applicability and are being introduced to farmers in other areas through farmer-to-farmer training.

Awareness of the need to understand and build upon the technical knowledge of farmers for sustainable agricultural development has increased over the last 30 years. This has led to the farmer-back-to-farmer model of technology generation (Rhoades and Booth 1982), a model followed in the case presented in this chapter. This awareness has also led to the recent creation of the Centre for Indigenous Knowledge for Agriculture and Rural Development (CIKARD) at Iowa State University (Warren and Cashman 1988).

Methods

Thirty-seven fields on 25 randomly selected rice farms in Tupi were monitored in 1987 and 1988. Farmers in this study include about an equal number of owner/leaseholders and tenants. Farmers were asked about crops and varieties, crop management, productivity, and locally-developed or refined production technologies. Crop cuts, along with observations of field operations,

354

were taken from monitored fields during the first or Wet Season (WS) in 1987, and from different rice fields of the same farmers in WS 1988.

A daily rainfall record from 1961 to the present was obtained from a Bureau of Plant Industry seed farm at Tupi. Soil samples were taken at 0–20 cm and 20–50 cm from monitored fields and were analysed by the Analytical Service Laboratory at the International Rice Research Institute (IRRI).

Tupi municipality

Tupi Municipality, which covers 286 km², is located at 275–300 m above sea level, and is linked by road to General Santos City and Koronodal (Map 28.1). A dormant volcano, Mt. Matutum, rises to 2293 m above sea level to the east, and the Roxas Range encloses the western and northern sections. Half of the area features gently undulating volcanic slopes which are shared by rice-maize farmers and a Dole pineapple plantation.

Annual rainfall averaged 1890 mm for 1961–88. The wet season starts March or April. Rains normally peak in June and decrease in November or December for the December-to-March dry season (Figure 28.1). The start of the wet

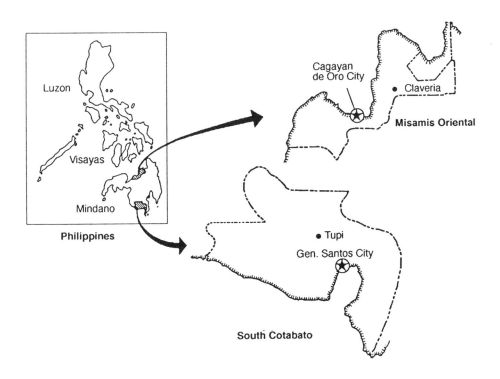

Map 28.1: *Locations of Tupi, South Cotabato and of Claveria, Misamis Oriental, the Philippines*

and dry seasons is variable and unpredictable each year. Rainfall also varies considerably in August during the critical rice reproductive phase.

Tupi soils are fine sandy loams with no features adverse to upland rice (Table 28.1). Cation Exchange Capacity (CEC) is relatively low, given a moderate organic carbon content of 2.3 per cent. Total nitrogen is moderate, available phosphorus very high, and exchangeable potassium high. Exchangeable aluminum is low and liming to zero aluminum saturation – although unnecessary for upland rice – would require only 500 kg./ha. (Neue, personal communication).

Table 28.1: Soil analysis in 25 upland farms, Tupi, South Cotabato (1987)

Analyses		Soil depth (cm)	
		0-20	20-50
pH 1:1 w/v H$_2$O		5.300	5.500
Organic C	(%)	2.250	2.170
Total N	(%)	0.177	0.171
Exchange cations K	(meg/100g ads[a])	0.499	0.530
Available P	(Bray 2; ppm ads)	129.000	107.000
Cation Exchange Capacity	(meg/100g ads)	10.010	10.340
Exchange Al	(meg/100g ads)	0.341	0.220

a   ads = air-dried soil

Farm size averaged 5.0 ha, which is divided into three parcels. For WS 1987, farmers had 1.7 ha of upland rice, 2.2 ha of maize, and 0.8 ha of perennials. Of the rice area, 0.7 ha had Traditional Upland Varieties (TVs) and 1.0 ha had Modern Lowland Varieties (MVs). MV seed is obtained from friends and relatives in nearby lowland areas. Farmers produce rice for consumption and sale, and maize for sale. The main cropping patterns are rice–maize–maize and maize–maize–maize or rice–maize and maize–maize. In 1987, 88 per cent of sampled farmers planted rice during the first season; 44 per cent followed the rice crop with maize–maize, while 36 per cent subsequently planted a single maize crop.

Farmers' practice and alternative strategies

This section describes the upland rice varieties, the upland rice crop management practices and technologies, the different strategies and respective costs and benefits, and the reasons underlying the Tupi farmers' choices among alternative strategies.

Upland rice varieties Farmers select rice varieties based on yield, eating quality, durable disease resistance, duration, lodging, and weed competitiveness. TVs, especially *Dinorado* and *Makaginga,* are selected for good eating quality, disease resistance, high milling recovery, high market price, and weed competitiveness. On the other hand, farmers dislike the susceptibility to lodging and the later maturation of these upland TVs. Tupi farmers are able to plant MVs developed for the lowlands because of favourable soil-water conditions. Varieties such as IR62 are selected for higher yield, good eating quality, early maturation, and resistance to lodging. Farmers, however, are wary of MVs because of the breakdown of their resistance to diseases, especially rice blast (caused by *Pyricularia oryzae*), brown spot *(Helminthosporium oryzae)*, and, possibly, leaf scald *(Rhynchosporium oryzae)*. Compared to TVs, MVs are also less competitive to weeds. In the past, farmers have dropped rice cultivars: upland TVs because of low yield and lodging, and lowland MVs because of diseases. In 1986, farmers quit planting IR36 and IR60 after widely adopting them, and then suffering up to total crop loss due to rice blast.

Table 28.2: Sequence of tillage and weed control activities and implements for upland rice production

Activity	Timing	Comments
Field clearing	start November-March	with bolo or inverted harrow
Tractor disking	start November-March	hired tractor
Harrowing *(karas)*	after tractor disking	animal drawn
1st ploughing[a] *(arado)*		perpendicular to tractor/harrow
Harrowing[b]		same direction as 1st ploughing
2nd ploughing		
Harrowing[b]		
Panudling[c]		45-degree angle to the ploughing
Panudling		perpendicular to 1st *panudling*
Panudling	if no rain but weeds present	perpendicular to 2nd *panudling*
Furrowing *(tudling)*	February-May range	with rains; original direction
Seeding	broadcast after furrowing	
Harrowing	next day	cover seed: 2x up and back
Harrowing	4 DAS[f]	same direction
Halod-hod[d]	8 DAS	shallow; in furrows
Panudling	12 DAS	
Halod-hod[e]	14 DAS	deeper
Panudling[e]	20 DAS	
Harrowing (weeding)	24 DAS	45-degree angle to rows
Panudling[e]	31 DAS	in furrows
Panudling	35 DAS	'opening'
Handweeding	after opening	several days work
Applying fertiliser	after weeding	broadcast mainly urea
Panudling	after fertilising	'closing'
Harrowing	intrarow cultivation	45-degree angle to rows
Applying fertiliser	50 DAS	optional
Panudling *(sera)*	after fertilising	'closing'
Handweeding	intrarow	and spot weeding as needed

a = Single-animal, steel single moldboard plough
b = Several types of steel or wood box harrows
c = Five Large blades for cultivation, furrowing and interrow weeding
d = Five Small blades or tines remaining after panudling blades removed
e = Some operations optional depending upon weeds
f = DAS = Days After Sowing

Upland rice crop management Although each farmer's calendar of rice crop operations depends on rainfall, available labour, and severity of weeds at different crop stages, a general sequence of the 28 field operations from land preparation to threshing can be described (Table 28.2); and rice production labour and labour costs were quantified (Table 28.3).

Most (86 per cent) fields are first prepared using both tractor and animal (*kerbau* or oxen). These fields are tractor-tilled either once (72 per cent) or twice (28 per cent), and then spike-tooth harrowed after each ploughing. Farmers use one of two animal tillage techniques, both using the moldboard plough. For 'conventional' ploughing, furrows are cut so that the slice is thrown onto the furrow made by the previous pass. A labour-saving alternative is 'furrow' ploughing (so-called because of resulting dead furrows), in which the distance between furrows is increased and slices do not overlap, but simply meet the edge of the previous furrow.

Weeds, especially *Rottboellia cochinchinensis, Eleusine indica*, and *Amaranthus spinosus* are a major problem. The stale seedbed technique is combined with final land preparation. As farmers wait for rains and enough soil moisture for seeding, the five-tined *panudling* is used up to seven times to destroy germinating weeds and to complete tillage. The *panudling* is drawn each time at an angle different to the initial ploughing to improve soil tilth.

When there is at least 10 cm of soil moisture, furrows are opened, again using the *panudling*. As another innovation, seeds are broadcast (about 100 kg/ha) and then harrowed by lightweight spike-tooth harrow to drop and cover the seed into the furrows. As a result, rice plants later emerge in the straight, equally-spaced rows established by the *panudling*.

Fields are harrowed one to four times in as many days after seeding, to remove emerging weeds. The five-wide *panudling* blades are removed, leaving narrow-tines. The resulting implement, the *halod-hod*, is used for shallow interrow cultivation (IRC). IRCs using *halod-hod* and then *panudling* follow at about four-day intervals. At 24 DAS, the field is harrowed at a 45 degree angle to the rows for intrarow cultivation. Harrowing causes some plant damage, but using relatively high seed rates compensates for losses.

The *panudling* is used again once or twice for IRC, followed by handweeding. Urea is broadcast at about 50 DAS and covered by *panudling*. The field is again harrowed diagonally to rows but at right angles to the previous harrowing. *Panudling*, handweeding, an optional application of urea, and diagonal harrowing are repeated.

Farmers applied inorganic fertiliser to both TVs in 14 of 15 fields and MVs in 15 of 17 fields at about the same rate: equivalent to 74 kg N, 6 kg P_2O_5, and 14 kg K_2O for the 29 fertilised fields. One to three handweedings are done from 30 to 50 DAS, with timing depending on TV or MV requirements. Up to 15 per cent of the fields are handweeded slightly late (after 50 DAS), due to labour constraints.

Pest management includes: two insecticide applications (monocrotophos or methyl parathion) to control leaffolder *(Cnaphalocrocis medinalis)*, grasshoppers *(Oxya sp.)* and *Locusta migratoria manilensis)*, rice bug *(Leptocorisa oratorius)*, and stemborer *(Maliarpha* or *Chilo suppressalis)*; one herbicide (pendimethalin) application; and one fungicide (edifenphos and benomyl) application.

Rice is harvested and threshed by hired labour paid in kind. For harvesting, women use panicle knives *(kayog)* and men use sickles *(garab)*. Use of the panicle knife requires more labour than sickle, but is preferred because threshing panicles takes less labour than threshing stalks. The same individuals do both harvesting and threshing.

Returns to alternative strategies Farmers choose among lowland MVs and upland TVs, between 'conventional' and 'furrow' tillage, and, to a lesser degree, among initial land preparation methods. Eighty-six per cent of rice fields first prepared by tractor and animal required a mean of 579 person-hours (phr) (Table 28.3) and or 4342/ha ($207/ha) to produce the crop (Table 28.4), including P1337/ha ($64/ha) for materials (fertiliser, chemicals, and seeds) (Table 28.5).

Based on crop cut samples from all 37 fields, WS 1987, yields averaged 2.8 t/ha, with MVs (3.3 tons/ha) significantly outperforming TVs (2.3 t/ha). MV yields were 3.6 t/ha for IR64, 1.2 t/ha for IR62 (due to blast damage), and 4.1 t/ha for the few, generally smaller fields of IR65, 'Los Banos' (UPLRi5), and 206. For TVs, the most widely-planted *Dinorado* yielded 1.6 t/ha, while *Makaginga* and *Himal-os* yielded over 2.0 t/ha (Table 28.6).

Use of lowland MVs rather than upland TVs resulted in higher returns above total variable costs ($156 versus $100), similar returns to labour, and higher returns to total material costs 3.9 versus 2.5). Furrow ploughing gave slightly higher returns to labour but lower returns to material costs than conventional ploughing; and, considering both tillage technique and variety, highest returns resulted from the use of furrow tillage plus MVs; and lowest returns resulted from the use of furrow tillage plus TVs (Table 28.5).

Strategy choice Farmers adopt a strategy of planting both MVs and upland TVs because of risks associated with MVs and because TVs are preferred for home consumption. Most important is the risk of disease losses. Several lowland varieties (IR36, IR42, IR60, and IR62) were adopted, performed well for three to four seasons, and then disease resistance was lost. Up to total crop losses resulted and the varieties were dropped. The productivity of TVs, although lower, has been much more stable.

In terms of tillage practices, conventional ploughing, practiced on 31 per cent of fields, contributed to a requirement of 659 phr/ha for all crop operations, while furrow was practiced on 69 per cent of the fields and required 543 phr/ha for all crop operations. Less labour and, more importantly, faster turn-around time underly farmer's choice: most of the 56 per cent of fields planted to three crops a year were furrow-ploughed, while more of fields planted to two crops were conventionally-ploughed.

With the arrival of rains, farmers must also decide how much rice and how much maize to plant. A major factor is the probability of adequate moisture during the reproductive phase of a crop. Figure 28.1 shows that rainfall is highly variable in the crucial month of August, and Figure 28.2 shows that the August rainfall (260 mm) was well above the 200 mm average in 1987, when sampled fields yielded an average of 2.8 t/ha, and was well below in 1988 (140 mm), when yields averaged 1.2 t/ha.

Farmers perceive a relationship between patterns of early and later season rains, and some may have anticipated adverse conditions for 1988. In 1987, 27 rice parcels accounted for 22 ha, and 16 maize parcels covered 25 ha. In 1988, the same area was divided into 19 rice parcels on 15 ha and 24 maize parcels on 32 ha. That is, the rice area decreased by 32 per cent while the maize area increased by 28 per cent for 1987–8.

Of the 27 rice parcels in 1987, farmers changed crops on 13 parcels and changed variety on 10 parcels the following year. Farmers claim that MVs and

TVs should be rotated on parcels to avoid diseases, and crops should be changed if necessary to avoid drought.

Another compromise strategy A few fields were initially prepared differently: two (five per cent) were prepared by tractor only (three diskings), and three (nine per cent) by animal only. Comparing animal alone, animal plus tractor, and tractor alone, mean yields and RAVCs were highest for tractor alone (3.2 t/ha, $235/ha) and lowest for animal alone (1.3 t/ha and $38). Data suggest that the 86 per cent of fields first tilled by tractor and animal represent a compromise between the higher cash cost of tractor only and the less effective and longer turn-around time resulting from animal alone.

Taking farmers' technology seriously

The Tupi farmers' use of both upland TVs and lowland MVs is rational although somewhat unusual. Rice research at IRRI to improve the farmer's chances against MV crop failure includes screening varieties for

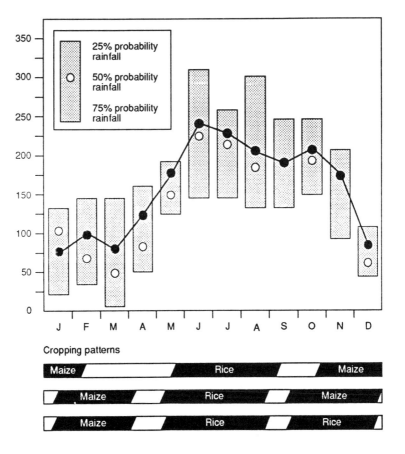

Figure 28.1: *Mean monthly rainfall (●———●); upper quartile 75 per cent and lower quartile (25 per cent) rainfall probabilities; and farmers' cropping patterns (Tupi, South Catabato, 1961–87)*

durable disease resistance and developing techniques for integrated pest management.

Furrow-ploughing was used by 22 of the 32 farmers who first prepared land by tractor and animal. Farmers planting maize after rice in a three-crop per year sequence usually only flatten rice stalk or leave stubble before furrowing for seeding maize. These techniques to reduce labour and speed up turn-around time can be tested in other upland areas. The five-tined tillage and weeding implement, the *panudling/halod-hod*, is, however, the cornerstone of the farmer-developed system.

Tupi settlers from Batangas, The Philippines, brought with them the wooden bladed *lithao* (Figure 28.3), the use of which has been described by rice researchers (De Datta and Ross 1975; Garrity 1976). In Tupi, farmers improved and adapted the implement to their slightly heavier soils. They first substituted steel pipe for portions of the wooden frame and replaced the wide wooden blades by steel tines and removable blades (Figures 28.4, 28.5). The implement is a *panudling* when the wider blades are bolted to the tines (making it similar to the *lithao*) and a *halod-hod* when the blades are removed and the remaining, narrower tines are used.

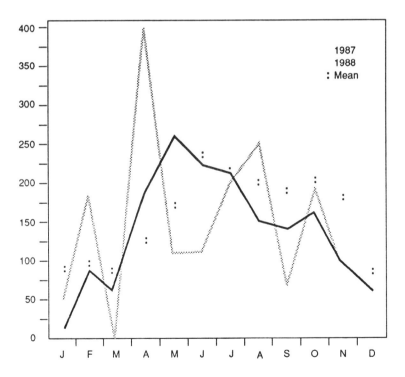

Figure 28.2: *Rainfall, 1987 (* ~~~~~~ *) and 1988 (* ▬▬▬ *), Tupi, South Cotabato*

Table 28.3: Labour (person-hours/ha) and costs (pesos/ha.)[a] for upland rice production, Tupi, South Cotabato, 1987

	Traditional		Modern		All	
	Hours	*P/ha*	*Hours*	*P/ha*	*Hours*	*P/ha*
Land Preparation						
0-1x field clearing[b]	12	46	9	30	11	40
2x animal ploughing[b]	39	241	33	209	36	224
1x tractor disking	2	362	2	352	2	357
2x harrowing *(karas)*[b]	23	145	21	142	2	143
2x harrowing *(panudling)*[b]	21	134	34	210	28	175
Seeding						
1x furrowing[b]	7	40	8	51	7	46
1x seeding[d]	4	14	4	12	4	13
1x harrowing (cover seed)[b]	6	37	6	34	6	36
Weed Control						
3x interrow *(karas)*[b]	17	103	19	117	18	111
2x interrow *(halod-hod)*[b]	14	89	10	61	12	73
2x interrow *(panudling)*[b]	20	117	23	142	21	131
2x handweeding[c]	87	327	146	547	117	440
Application of Fertilisers and Pesticides						
2x applying fertiliser	6	21	7	25	6	23
2x spraying insecticide	8	32	9	36	9	34
1x spraying herbicide	6	23	5	18	5	20
1x spraying insecticide and fertiliser	4	14	9	32	7	24
1x spraying fungicide	4	15	-	-	4	15
Harvest & Thresh[e]						
1x harvesting with *garab*	62	673	76	1193	69	935
1x harvesting with *kayog*	235	719	326	1233	278	790
1x threshing	46	982	45	1472	45	1273
Total Labour	530	3577	625	4820	579	4138

a = One U.S. dollar = 21 Philippine pesos
b = P50.00/day or P6.25/hour
c = P30.00/day or P3.75/hour
d = P25.00/day or P3.25/hour
e = Paid in kind, paddy valued at P3.50/kg.

Table 28.4: Labour for rice cropping strategies combining MV or TV, and furrow or conventional ploughing, and using tractor and animal for initial land preparation; 37 fields, WS 1987

	Modern Lowland Varieties			Traditional Upland Varieties			Overall
	All	*Furrow*	*Conv*[b]	*All*	*Furrow*	*Conv*[b]	
Number of farmers	17	11	6	15	11	4	32
Number of operations	23	23	24	22	20	27	23
Labour (person-hours/ha)	625	571	723	530	514	562	580
Cost of labour (P/ha)	4820	4490	5618	3577	3273	4413	4138
Cost of hired tractor	352	363	332	380	397	356	365
Cost of labour (imputed) [a]	4468	4127	5285	3197	2876	4057	3772

a = Imputed Cost of labour = Cost of labour minus cost of hired tractor
b = Conventional

Table 28.5: Costs (pesos/ha) for different rice cropping strategies

	Modern Lowland Varieties			Traditional Upland Varieties			Overall
	All	*Furrow*	*Conv*[a]	*All*	*Furrow*	*Conv*[a]	
Number of farmers	17	11	6	15	11	4	32
Cost of fertiliser	496	523	423	568	583	358	532
Cost of other chemicals	213	263	164	362	367	324	285
Cost of seeds	515	515	514	530	512	524	522
(Kg. seed/ha)	(103)	(103)	(103)	(106)	(102)	(106)	(104)
Total material cost	1224	1301	1101	1460	1462	1206	1339
Total variable cost	6044	5791	6719	5038	4735	4414	5477
Yield (kg./ha)	3004	2655	3967	2107	1920	2518	2571
Value of palay	10514	9293	13874	7375	6720	8813	8999

a = Conventional

Table 28.6:　Mean upland rice yields, Tupi, South Cotabato, 1987 and 1988 data from crop-cuts (tons/ha)

Varieties	Tons/ha	
	1987	*1988*
Modern varieties	3.3	2.0
IR64 (7-tonner)	3.6	2.4
R62	1.2	-
IR60	-	1.9
Others (Los Banos, IR65, 206)	4.1	-
Traditional varieties	2.3	1.3
Dinorado	1.6	1.5
Makaginga	2.8	1.2
Himal-os	2.3	1.6
Others	2.5	1.2
All fields sampled	2.8	1.2

Table 28.7:　Rice cropping strategies costs-returns ($US) per ha, 37 fields, 1987, Tupi, South Cotabato

Strategy	% of farmers	Labour cost	Material cost	TVC[a]	Gross returns	RAVC[b]	Returns to	
							Labour costs	Material costs
Tractor[c] + animal	86	207	64	306	429	123	1.8	3.5
2.6 123								
MVs	41	233	53	286	442	156	1.7	3.9
TVs	46	172	67	240	340	100	1.6	2.5
Conventional	27	247	54	301	432	131	1.5	3.4
Furrow	59	185	62	247	376	129	1.7	3.1
Conventional+MV	16	271	45	316	441	125	1.5	3.8
Furrow+MV	30	212	58	270	443	173	1.8	4.0
Conventional+TV	11	210	68	278	420	142	1.7	3.1
Furrow+TV	30	159	67	226	311	85	1.5	2.3

a = Total variable cost
b = Returns above total variable cost
c = One tractor disking + ploughing (72%) or two tractor disking + ploughing (28%)

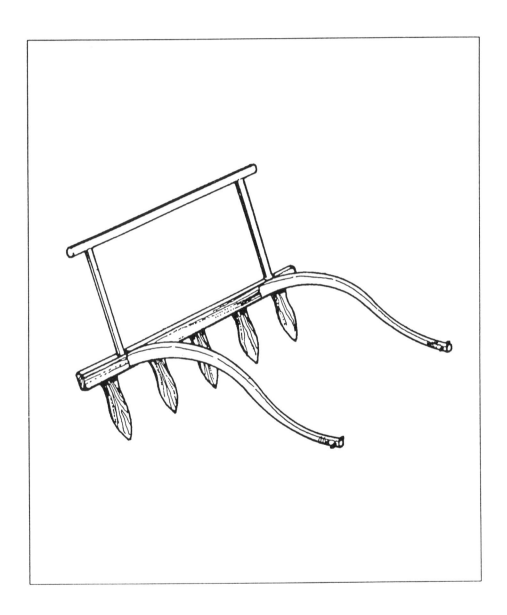

Figure 28.3: *The wooden* lithao *from Batangas, the Philippines*

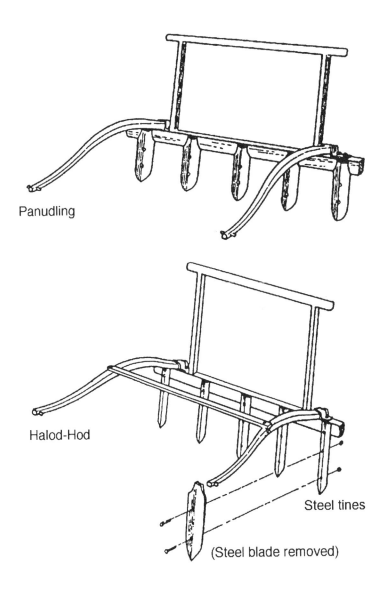

Figure 28.4: *The Tupi* panudling *and* halod-hod

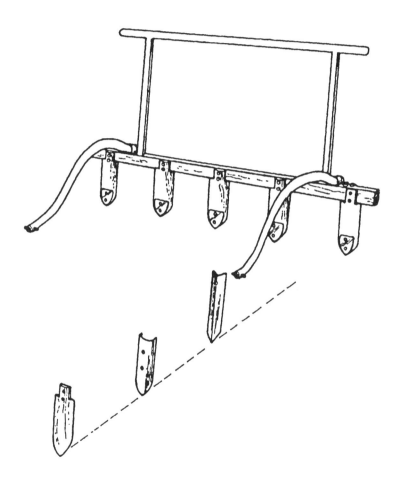

Figure 28.5: *Different* panudling *blade/tine attachments*

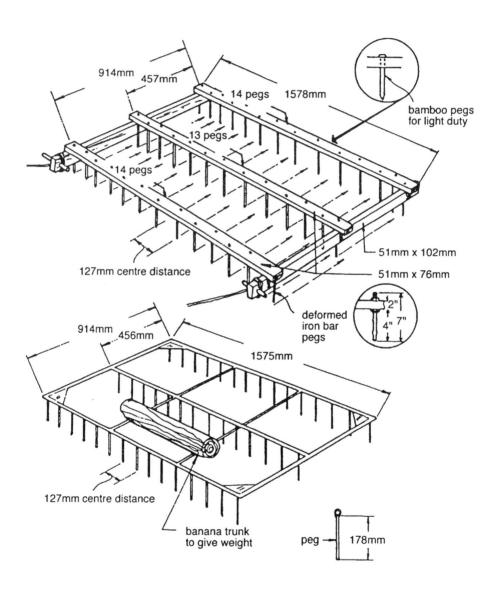

Figure 28.6: *Tupi harrows (Karas) used for intrarow cultivation*

The combination implement is used for secondary tillage, furrowing, IRC, and, as *halod-hod,* both IRC and intrarow cultivation when drawn at a diagonal to plant rows. Removable tines and blades match the implement to different needs and conditions over the crop season. Tupi farmers also employ two light-weight harrows with either bamboo or iron pegs (Figure 28.6) to drop and cover broadcast seed in the furrows and to intrarow cultivate when drawn at a diagonal to the plant rows.

Researchers at IRRI's upland farming systems site at Claveria, Misamis Oriental, The Philippines, tested the wooden *lithao* in weed control experiments (Elliot and Moody 1986). Farmers were interested in *lithao,* but it was difficult to control and tended to break easily in Claveria's clay soils.

Farmer-to-farmer technology transfer A group of Claveria farmers was taken to South Cotabato where several Tupi farmers provided a two-day, hands-on, lecture and field-demonstration training course on the *panudling/halod-hod*-based upland rice system. Claveria farmer-trainees are now (WS 1989) testing and adapting the system to local conditions. They first angled the blade-tine tips slightly forward to obtain better implement control and penetration in the heavier soils. One farmer constructed a *panudling* for about $25 (labour and materials). Such technology adaptation and adoption are being monitored.

Claveria farmers readily accepted the *panudling* as a furrow opener and interrow cultivator. Some, however, were hesitant to adopt broadcasting, preferring to drill their seeds. Another early adoptor/trainee, on the other hand, lacked a *panudling,* but furrowed by plough, made a light harrow, and then broadcasted and harrowed in the seed. His DS 1988 crop of IAC25 yielded over 3.5 t/ha. Farmers responded rapidly to these early technology demonstrations supplied by their neighbours. Twenty-five Claveria farmers are using the *panudling-halod-hod* in WS 1989.

Finally, Claveria and Tupi farmers are participating in a two-way farmer-to-farmer training experiment. Claveria farmers learned about the use of contour hedgerow systems to control soil erosion from farmers in Cebu, The Philippines, and have since been adapting the Cebu system to local conditions (Fujisaka 1989). Some of the Tupi farmers also plant rice on steeper slopes, and they were trained by Claveria farmers in contour hedgerow farming.

Conclusions

Tupi rice and maize farmers plant three crops a year while facing the problems of crop diseases, weeds, and uncertain rainfall. They plant maize, lowland MVs, and upland TV rice in the wet season, combine tractors and animals for initial land preparation, use a furrow secondary tillage technique, and developed the *panudling/halod-hod*-based broadcast seeding and weed control technology.

Returns were higher for MVs versus TVs, and for tractor versus either animal or tractor/animal primary tillage. Farmers choices, however, are systems-sound compromises that reduce risks (planting maize, and both modern and traditional rice varieties), reduce turn around time between crops (furrow ploughing), and optimise use of scarce cash resources (tractor-animal rather than only tractor).

For Tupi, rice research – to develop durable resistance to diseases, to test traditional cultivars, and to develop techniques for integrated pest management – is still needed. More important, the present effort to understand the problem-solving technologies and strategies used by Tupi farmers led to introducing and testing locally-developed technologies, such as the *panudling* and associated land preparation and weed control methods, in upland systems elsewhere. The training of Claveria farmers by Tupi farmers, and the technology-testing, evaluation, and adaptation by the former will be monitored. This will provide further insight into the potentials for wider applications of the knowledge and technology used by farmers.

29. Indigenous Soil and Water Conservation in Djenné, Mali[1]

ALISON AYERS

Introduction

IT IS INCREASINGLY recognised that adequate conservation of soil and water resources is a precondition for sustainable rural development in Sub-Saharan Africa (Rey 1987). Soil conservation constitutes any practice or technique which counteracts the processes which lessen the current and potential capability of the soil to produce goods or services. Water conservation is the physical control, protection, management and the use of water resources in such a way as to maintain crops, grazing and forest lands, vegetal cover, wildlife and wildlife habitat for maximum sustained benefit (FAO 1984d).

There are always strong links between measures for soil conservation and measures for water conservation. Many measures are directed primarily to one or the other, but most contain an element of both. For example, reducing erosion will usually involve preventing splash erosion or formation of crusts, or breakdown of soil structure, all of which will increase infiltration, and so assist the conservation of water.

Soil and Water Conservation (SWC) is generally classified as mechanical or biological. Mechanical or structural erosion control techniques concern all measures requiring earth movement, for example, terraces and bunds. They are generally constructed to reduce the steepness of a slope which permits better control of run-off. Biological erosion control techniques concern the management of vegetation (crops, trees and grasses) and animals, for example the establishment of a grass cover or increased crop density. The 1980s has witnessed a change in emphasis from solely mechanical forms of SWC, to increased attention and support for an integration of biological and mechanical forms of SWC.

SWC project and programmes

In some countries of Sub-Saharan Africa (SSA) major SWC programmes were established before their independence. However, colonial efforts to conserve the soil were often unsuccessful. In the British and Belgium administered areas the colonial authorities attempted to *impose* conservation, while in Francophone West Africa the colonial authorities undertook substantial research on land degradation but implemented little soil conservation.

Numerous soil and water conservation projects have since been initiated in SSA. However, in most cases the results of these programmes and projects have been disappointing. With few exceptions, SWC techniques have been introduced in SSA with little attention to the question of whether the local population could apply the techniques on their own fields. Experience shows that at the end of a project farmers seldom continued to expand application of the techniques to untreated fields. Furthermore, most conservation planners tended to assume that the local population would take responsibility for the maintenance of the structures built by a project. Practice shows that the local population seldom maintained structures, which usually degraded within a few years.

371

Table 29.1: Selected semi-permanent and permanent indigenous farming systems with prominent SWC practices in Sub-Saharan Africa

NO.	ETHNIC GROUP	COUNTRY	AVERAGE ALTITUDE (M.)	AVERAGE RAINFALL (MM.)	POPULA-TION DENSITY (KM2)	A	B	C	D	MAIN CROPS
1.	Dogon	Malli	200-500	550	20-50	x	x	x		Mi So
2.	Hausa	Niger, Chad	300-500	550	10-50	x		x		Mi Ni
3.	Mossi	Burkina Faso	200-500	650	100	x		x		Mi So
4.	Bobo	Burkina Faso	620	790	20-50		x			Mi Ya Ba
5.	Gurunei	Burkina Faso	620-1280	790	20-50			x		Mi Ya Ba
6.	Kamuku	Nigeria	620-1280	790	20-50			x		Mi Ya Ba
7.	Bauchi	Nigeria	620-1280	790	50-100			x		Mi
8.	Kassena	Ghana	200-700	800	100	x		x		Mi So
9.	Tigre	Ethiopia	1950-2750	610-990	100-150	x	x			Mi
10.	Bwa	Burkina Faso	200-700	800	100	x		x		Mi So
11.	Hausa	Nigeria	610-1280	790-990	120-250	x	x	x		Mi Gn Mn
12.	Batta	Cameroon	1020-1950	790-990	50-100			x		Mi Ya Ba
13.	Mandara	Cameroon	620-1500	800-110	50-200	x		x	x	Mi Be
14.	Kita	Mali	620-1200	990	10			x		Mi
15.	Malinke	Senegal Guinea	620-1200	990	10			x		Mi Ri Ma
16.	Gourma	Togo Burkina Faso	500	1000	45	x		x		Mi So Gn
17.	Dagari	Burkina Faso	100-300	1000	35	x		x		Mi So Ma
18.	Kofyar	Nigeria	300-1000	1000	100	x		x		Mi Ac Gn
19.	Sandawe	Tanzania	1010-1950	790-1190	10-100			x		Mi Ma Be
20.	Mbugu	Tanzania	1950-2570	790-1190	50-100	x	x			Mi Ma Be
21.	Konso	Ethiopia	1950	990-1190	190	x		x	x	Mi Ma Co
22.	Matengo	Tanzania	1280-1950	990-1200	30-100	x		x		Mi Me Mn
23.	Bano	Cameroon	1950-2570	790-1500	100-150	x	x	x	x	Mi Be
24.	Kiga	Uganda	1950-2570	790-1500	50-100	x	x			Ma Ba Be
25.	Kuru	Sudan	610-1280	990-1400	30-50			x		Mi
26.	Rundi	Burundi	1950-2570	990-1400	100-150	x	x	x		Ma Ba SP
27.	Ruanda	Ruanda	1950-2570	990-1400	150-200	x	x	x		Ma Ba SP
28.	Kinga	Tanzania	620-1950	990-1400	20-100	x				Ma Mi
29.	Baule	Ivory Coast	620	1190-1400	10-20			x		Ya Ba Ta
30.	Losso	Togo	620-1010	990-2000	50-100	x		x		Mi Ya Gn
31.	Kabre	Togo	1010-1280	1500	219	x	x	x	x	Mi Ri Ya
32.	Kipsigi	Kenya	1950-2570	1400-1800	50-100			x		Ma
33.	Wakara	Tanzania	1500	1600	209	x	x	x	x	Mi Mn Ri
34.	Gishu	Uganda	1200-2000	1700	240	x	x	x	x	Gn Ma So
35.	Chagga	Tanzania	1200-1850	1700	160	x	x	x	x	Mi Ba Cf
36.	Bamileke	Cameroon	700-1600	1500-2000	140			x		Ma Gn Ya

a = terraces and other structures; b = auxiliary irrigation; c = manuring; d = stall feeding, Mi = millet; So = sorghum; Ni = niebe; Ya - yams; Ba = banana; Mn = manioc; Gn = groundnuts; Be = beans; Ac = acha; Ma = Maize; Ta -= taro; Co = cotton; Cf = coffee; Ri = rice (after Ludwig 1968: 92-93; Reij 1987: Annex 29.1).

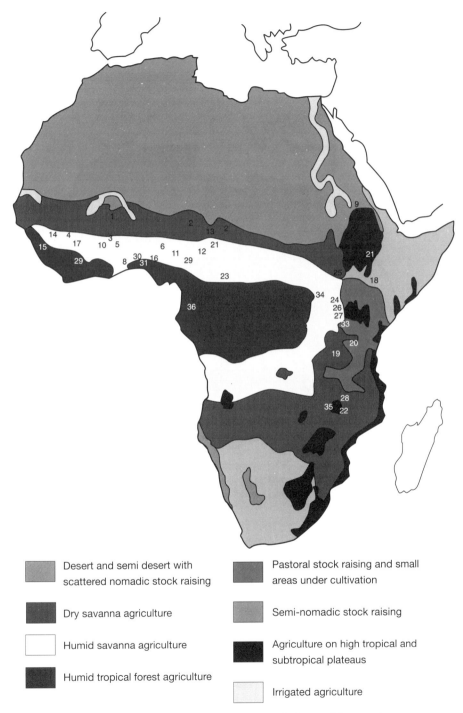

Map 29.1: *The location of selected African populations with prominent indigenous SWC systems.* (Adapted from Reij 1987)

Indigenous soil and water conservation

Indigenous SWC practices and techniques are used, maintained and expanded in many regions of SSA. However, despite the widespread use, variety and complexity of these practices, soil conservationists have almost without exception disregarded their existence and favoured modern SWC systems with which they are more familiar. Although modern SWC systems often look more spectacular, this does not mean that indigenous SWC systems are not important and have no role to play. In most areas indigenous techniques have been characterised by soil conservation 'experts' as rudimentary and have therefore deliberately neglected. Table 29.1 and Map 29.1 illustrate the extent of indigenous SWC systems in the many different farming systems of SSA. Furthermore, not only is indigenous SWC widespread but such systems are characterised by considerable variety and complexity. For example Pelissier and Diarra (1978) document the prominent features of indigenous SWC of the Mandara and Mafa of North Cameroon, which include extensive terracing, micro-catchments and mounds

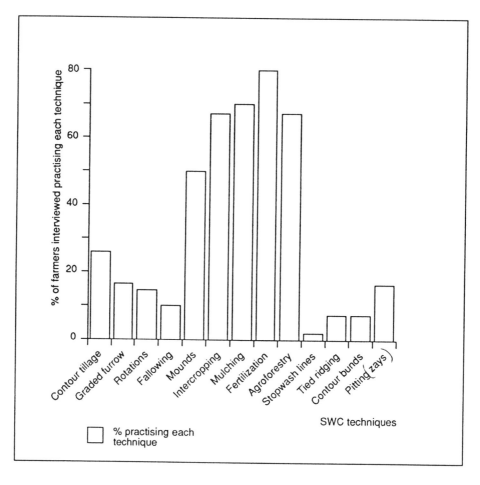

Figure 29.1: *Percentage of farmers practising each SWC technique*

for control of erosion by run-off, mulching, mixed cropping and rotations. Temple (1972) illustrates how the traditional ladder terraces of the Luguru of Tanzania are more efficient than the bench terraces proposed and enforced by the colonial authorities, while Basehart (1973) outlines the pit system practiced by the Matengo of Southwest Tanzania. The Konso of Southern Ethiopia construct extensive dry stone terraces and harvest floodwater (Hallpike 1972), while SWC practiced by the Gourma of the Tone Region of Northern Togo includes stone ridges along the contour, networks of drainage ditches, levelling of gully edges, mulching and fertilisation through green manuring (Spaanderman 1985).

These case studies exemplify the widespread nature and degree of sophistication of indigenous SWC, and thus demonstrate not simply the potential for basing SWC improvement on such indigenous techniques but the absurdity of ignoring them and attempting to enforce alien and, at times, inappropriate techniques. The following case study of SWC in the Circle of Djenné, Central Mali provides a more detailed account, description and analysis of indigenous SWC. It serves to illustrate and reinforce the value of indigenous SWC as a base for improved conservation of soil and water resources.

Indigenous soil and water conservation in the circle of Djenné

Background The administrative Circle of Djenné is located within the Fifth Region of the Republic of Mali. The Circle comprises two major ecological zones, the inundated areas of the Inner Niger Delta, and the rainfed, Upland Sahelian areas not prone to flooding. The principal economic activity within the Circle is agriculture, with millet and some sorghum, predominating in the rainfed upon areas, and rice being cultivated in the inundated areas.

Indigenous techniques of SWC Indigenous techniques of soil and water conservation identified in the Circle of Djenné were varied and at times demonstrated considerably levels of sophistication (Table 29.2). Although a wide variety of indigenous SWC techniques are practiced in the Circle of Djenné, considerable diversity exists with widely differing levels of application of each technique. Figure 29.1 presents the percentage of farmers interviewed practising each technique, and the subsequent sections describe and illustrate each of these practices.

Table 29.2: Indigenous soil and water conservation practices in the circle of Djenné

Biological SWC	Mechanical SWC
Contour tillage	Stop-wash lines
Farming on a grade	Tied ridging
Rotations	Contour bunds
Fallowing	Pitting/zays
Mounds	
Mixed cropping	
Surface mulching	
Fertilisation	
Agroforestry	

Biological SWC

Contour tillage Of the farmers interviewed 25 per cent, cultivated on the contour.[2] Of these, 96 per cent stated they did so in order to minimise run-off and hence erosion. In no cases were ridges used at right angles to the prevailing wind in order to control wind erosion, thus suggesting that farmers believe water erosion to present a greater problem. In all cases cultivation involved ploughing (*i.e.* ridging) and subsequently planting and cultivation on the contour rows.

In several cases farmers applied different methods within the same field, cultivating on the contour where the slope was gentle, and on the grade where the slope was steep. Furthermore, there was evidence of on-farm experimentation concerning the value of cultivation on the contour. For example, the children of one farmer had remarked that when ridging was parallel to the slope, humidity retention within the field was low. The farmer had therefore agreed to plough on the contour for the 1989 cultivation season in order to test the children's claim although he disputed their theory believing that heavy rains would break the ridges because of the reasonably marked slope within his field.

There were observed examples of cultivation on the contour where the slope was evidently too steep and thus storms and heavy rains had caused extensive overstopping and breaking of the contour rows and subsequently gullying and soil wash.

Farming on the grade Cultivation on the grade was practiced by 16 per cent of farmers. However, in only 19 per cent of these cases was it expressly stated that the objective was to convey excess water from the field and that the slope was too steep for contour ridges. In many other instances farmers ploughed on the grade to ensure run-off to low lying areas (*basfond*), where rice was invariably cultivated. While this may have ensured sufficient water for the rice and provided a second crop to the millet cultivated in the more elevated parts of the field, it was to the detriment of the soil – with evidence of soil wash (together with the increased likelihood on the silting-up of the *basfond*) – and thus cannot be regarded as a long-term sustainable strategy of production. (The cultivation of rice as a second crop is, however, a risk diversification strategy, with the farmer obtaining a good rice harvest in years of abundant rainfall and a good millet crop in years of lower rainfall. Thus, there could well be considerable resistance to any suggestions of altering the farming practice in order to reduce run-off and conserve the soil).

Of the remaining 59 per cent who neither cultivated the contour nor the grade, the great majority cultivated by hand and thus did not form ridges, while the 12 per cent who ploughed, actually stated that they cultivated without any regard to the slope of their land.

Rotations The use of crop rotation was not widespread within the Circle, with only 14 per cent of farmers undertaking any form of rotation. In 67 per cent of cases millet and sorghum were grown in rotation, generally after 2–3 years of each. In the remainder of cases millet and groundnuts followed each other.

Crop rotation is used for a number of reasons, including soil and water conservation, and also improved pest and/or disease control, shifting of resources and more reliable or improved crop yields. Improved soil conservation can be achieved by alternating high-residue producing crops with the growing low-residue producing crops. Millet and sorghum are both regarded as high-residue producing crops and thus the strategy cannot be regarded as applicable in this case. However, groundnuts are a very low-residue producing crop and the rotation of millet with the groundnut crop will certainly improve soil conservation.

Further objectives given for the use of rotation include: (1) improved crop yields through the alternation of millet and sorghum; (2) the choice of millet or sorghum according to the rain received in the early part of the rainy season –poor rains signalling the cultivation of millet; (3) the spreading of resources; and (5) according to taste – to provide a variety of cereals within the diet of the family. Thus, the use of rotation within the Circle cannot be regarded as practiced solely, or principally, for the objective of soil and water conservation.

Fallowing Fallowing was used to a very limited extent within the Circle, with less than 10 per cent of farmers permitting any fallow. Many of these stated it was only for a very limited period. Very little pattern emerged, with cultivation periods ranging from 3–8 years, and periods of fallow ranging from only 2–4 years. Land scarcity was stated to be a major constraint to production by 77 per cent of farmers, thus it seems likely that the extent of fallowing and the limited periods involved are a consequence of the low availability of the agricultural land within the Circle.

Mounds Mounds were constructed by 48 per cent of the farmers interviewed. These mounds were of varying specifications and materials and were formed for a variety of objectives:

- 65 per cent formed mounds between the seedlings at the time of weeding and subsequently when the millet or sorghum set seed placed the soil and decomposed vegetation at the base of the stalk. The majority of farmers would then seed on this mound the following year. There were three per cent (of this 65 per cent), however, who did not adopt this technique preferring to make small pockets in which they placed fertiliser, closed the hole and sometime later seeded within this pocket. The stated objectives for constructing mounds at the time of weeding and setting seed were: (a) support for the crop from strong winds; (b) water retention within the mound through increased infiltration; and (c) nutrient harvesting from the decomposed vegetation within the mound.
- A further 29 per cent formed pockets adjacent to mounds and generally seeded mid-way between the peak of the mound and the base of the pocket. The primary objectives were increased water infiltration and retention, several farmers stating they had commenced the practice because their soils had become compacted, and increased support and protection for the crop.
- The remaining six per cent seeded on mounds formed by decomposed vegetation from the previous season. That is, at the time of weeding, mounds were constructed between the seedlings and left to decompose *in situ* until the following cultivation season when they were seeded upon directly. The objectives of this technique appear to be nutrient harvesting and protection of seedlings from potential soil wash.

Mixed cropping Mixed cropping is widely practiced in the Circle with 64 per cent of farmers interplanting between two and five crops. The great majority of cases were a mix of millet and/or sorghum with haricot. While maize, okra, sorrel, groundnuts, rice, gourds, Bambarara earthnuts and fonio were also interplanted, although to a more limited extent.

Mixed cropping has the potential to reduce erosion by having a crop on the land for a longer period of the year. However, in this region the crops cultivated have widely similar growing seasons and thus the potential for this benefit is reduced. Nevertheless, the inclusion of legumes in the system may improve its nitrogen available for the cereal crops.

The stated objectives of the farmers interviewed about mixed cropping did not include an awareness of its potential for improved SWC. In the majority of case intercropping was undertaken as a strategy to hedge against risk, particularly where millet and sorghum, or millet and rice were cultivated. In other instances intercropping facilitated the production of commercial crops such as groundnuts together with subsistence crops, in areas where land availability was low. Finally, intercropping was practiced in order to obtain household foods, such as okro and cowpea, in addition to the cereal staples.

Surface mulching Of the farmers interviewed, 66 per cent used surface mulches on their fields, thus providing protective cover at a time when crop cover is not present, *i.e.* once the crop has been harvested. 97 per cent of farmers left crop residues *in situ* – primarily millet or sorghum stalks, while 12 per cent used dry branches, either in addition to, or instead of crop residues.

The benefit of a protective covering was widely appreciated, as was the improved infiltration rate afforded by the technique. A further stated objective was the addition of nutrients to the soil through the decomposition of the organic matter.

Analysis also revealed recent changes in practice. Several farmers stated that they had formerly burnt the crop residues and left the ash on the field as a means of fertilisation. While a few farmers stated that they still alternated this practice with the use of surface mulches, the majority claimed that the increasing prevalence of strong winds necessitated the use of a mulch.

Wider use of this practice may well be restricted due to the relatively small amounts of residue available and the competing uses which exist. For example, the use of residues as animal fodder was witnessed in many compounds within the Circle. Furthermore, the density of mulch viewed in many fields was below the level required to be most effective as a protective cover.

Fertilisation Fertilisation is especially important in areas of continuous cropping, in order to retain or augment levels of soil fertility. This importance is reflected in the very high frequency with which fertiliser was applied throughout the Circle, with 78 per cent of farmers interviewed applying one or more forms of fertiliser.

Inorganic fertilisers wee not used by any of the farmers interviewed. Most widely used forms were manure and humus which were transported to the fields during the dry season and in the majority of cases spread immediately. A few farmers stated that they also dug pits and composted the organic matter before spreading it on their fields. Other substances used for fertilisation were ash, household refuse which was buried, 'green' manuring (*see* section on agroforestry), and the use of cultivated areas as dry season pasture.

Agroforestry The use of agroforestry practices for SWC was not particularly widespread, except for the protection of naturally occurring species, which 64 per cent of farmers stated they undertook. The majority of farmers protected *Acacia albida* due to its nitrogen-fixing properties, but other tree species protected included *Butyrospermum parkii, Parkia biglobosa, Lannea microcarpa, Mitragyna inermis, Acacia sieberiana*, and *Tamarindus indica.*

Other agroforestry practices had extremely limited application. For example, less than two per cent produced tree crops in association with agricultural crops; this was a farmer who planted sorghum with his commercially-based mango and citrus fruit trees.

Less than two per cent planted wind breaks, despite the fact that more than 90 per cent of farmers stated that they encountered problems from strong winds, while only five per cent had planted trees, notably *Acacia albida,* but reported very low survival rates.

Mechanical SWC

Structures on the contour/stop-wash lines Only one farmer (less than two per cent of the interviewees) constructed a form of stop-wash lines. These consisted of earth ridges perpendicular in the slope and were constructed for the dual objectives of water retention and the prevention of soil wash. The farmer concerned stated that he had learnt the technique from his grandparents. The lines were not constructed of stones as stones are not available in the area and the farmer had not considered the piling up of crop residues to supplement the ridges.

Tied ridging Six per cent of farmers claimed to undertake tied ridging. Simple ridge and furrow were formed with the plough prior to sowing. Then, after germination of the millet or sorghum, farmers constructed the ties by hand. The practice was said to be limited to those parts of their fields where the gradient was relatively steep. However, no farmers who stated they formed tied ridges had at the time of the study constructed them and thus verification of the technique was not possible.

Contour bunds In four cases farmers had, or were planning to, construct contour bunds around the low-lying sections of their fields for means of water retention. While application of this technique is clearly very limited, the principle of bunds for water retention is nevertheless known in the region.

In two of these cases bunds were already in construction. The first was a termite bund, 50 cm high and 75 cm wide, constructed from broken termite mounds placed in two parallel lines and filled with soil. The slope was slight and plans were to construct the bund around the three low lying sides, principally to retain water but also to reduce soil erosion. The area covered 60 ha (although only 300 m had been treated). The land was formerly inundated but with the decline of the floods in the basin of the river Bani, the previous cultivators had abandoned it, and thus it had not been cultivated for 20 years except for a very small area of sorghum in 1988/89.

A group of seventy families from the town of Djenné had therefore approached the authorities to obtain permission to construct the bund and operate cultivation of the land as a collective. The operations had commenced in 1989 and each of the 70 families provided between one and three labourers to work on the bund each Sunday. The technique had been seen in an inundated area within the Region and members of the Collective believe that as the area is traditionally one of rice cultivation that the bund will permit, once again, the practice of rice cultivation through the retention of flood-water. The entire exercise appeared to be totally the result of local initiative and the Collective did not receive any technical support.

In the second case a termite and earth bund had been constructed around three sides of a field of approximately 1 ha at the base of the slope in order to

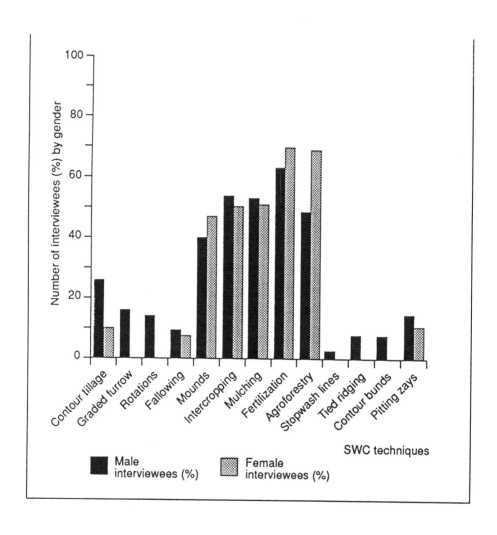

Figure 29.2: *Gender differences in SWC practices*

prevent removal of water from the field. The farmer had commenced the bund in 1987 having learnt the technique from his neighbour who had had a good harvest of sorghum and rice after implementation of a similar bund some years previously.

In the remaining cases, farmers stated they intended to constructed earth bunds at the base of the slope (*i.e.* at one side of their fields) in order to retain water but at the time of the study these had not been commenced and thus verification was not possible.

Zays/pitting Pitting, or zays, were practiced by 12 per cent of farmers. The stated primary objective in all cases was one of water retention. In the majority of cases zays were formed on degraded, principally crusted and compacted land. In each instance fertiliser was placed within the pit at the time of construction. In 44 per cent of cases farmers had commenced the use of zays since 1985 due to problems of compaction and thus reduced infiltration. Some farmers had observed the technique in other villages of the Region, while others claimed zays were an ancient technique which had generally been superseded by the plough. Many of these farmers had returned to the use of zays because of the problems of crusting and compaction and stated crop yields were higher from areas of zays than from areas of ridging with the plough, because of the improved water retention.

The application of zays appears to be strongly related to soil-type. The spacing of pits relates to the water-retention properties of the soil, illustrated by the wide spacing of pits on sandy soils but the more dense network of pits on the clayey soil. Furthermore, there were problems associated with the use of zays in areas of sandy soils. The latter being liable to silting or collapse as a result of strong winds and heavy rains. Another stated problem was the labour requirement of the technique, particularly in comparison with other traditional techniques such as mounds or pockets with mounds. Thus many farmers stated their application of pits would be restricted to areas of degraded, especially compacted and crusted, land where zays currently appear to offer the greatest potential.

Analysis of levels of SWC practiced

The preceding description demonstrates a wide variety of techniques, considerable levels of sophistication and the existence of indigenous experimentation and trials concerning techniques of SWC conservation. However, the extent and forms of SWC practiced varies considerably between farmers as illustrated below with reference to the variables of gender, ethnicity and class.

Differences in SWC practiced according to gender Figure 29.2 illustrates a significant trend in the levels of SWC practiced between the male and female farmers interviewed. Female interviewees appeared to concentrate on a selection of techniques which included mounds, mulching, fertilisation and intercropping. In only a few cases did women undertake the more 'sophisticated', high input techniques such as contour bunds, stopwash lines or zays. Several reasons are thought to account for this very marked difference. Firstly, the labour demands of the latter techniques are in themselves considerable.

Secondly women's fields tended to be secondary to the fields of the men where crops for family consumption were primarily cultivated. Thus few women had assistance from other family members on their plots and very few could afford to hire labourers, a marked contrast to the situation within the men's fields.

Thus labour represents a very real constraint. Furthermore, with reference to the SWC techniques which require ploughs, such as contour or graded furrows and tied ridging, the lower application of these techniques by the women reflects their lower access to animal traction. Finally, techniques such as contour bunds and zays appear to be either innovations, or possibly techniques which seem to be undergoing somewhat of a revival within the Circle. The male farmers interviewed appear to be rather more innovative regarding these SWC practices. This may be a result of the fact that women tend to travel less and thus do not have the opportunity to view other practices to discuss them to the same degree. It may also be due to the security of tenure of the women's land, many of their fields being under the customary tenure of their husband's family.

Correlation between SWC practices and ethnic origin of farmer The major production systems of the Circle were originally the exclusive province of different ethnic groups. Of the different ethnic groups included in the survey, the Bambara were dryland farmers, the Marka traditionally cultivated rice in the floodplain and the Songhai and Fulani kept livestock. Although these spheres of production are no longer relevant today – with the majority of producers being forced to spread their risks by moving into different forms of production – one might expect differences in farming practices according to ethnic origin. Yet, as Table 29.3 illustrates remarkably little difference appears to exist between the groups.

Table 29.3: SWC practiced according to ethnic origin (per cent)

Ethnic origin	Bambara	Fulani	Songhai	Marka
Contour tillage	26	33	-	27
Graded furrows	17	67	-	9
Rotations	9.5	67	-	27
Fallowing	5	33	-	26
Mounds	59.5	33	-	36
Intercropping	64	67	67	54
Mulching	69	33	67	54
Fertilisation	81	100	83	64
Agroforestry	67	33	33	73
Stop-wash lines	2	-	-	-
Tied riding	5	-	-	18
Contour bunds	5	-	16	9
Zays	12	33	50	-

Differences in SWC according to sociopolitical status Sociopolitical status is difficult to define and identify within a village. However, it represents a potentially important factor in analysing levels of SWC. High sociopolitical status was taken to include the *Chef du Village* or a close relation of the *Chef*, teachers, marabout, representatives of the village, such as the *Secretaire-Politique*, and those holding official positions within the village, such as President of a Village Cooperation.

Table 29.4 illustrates that very little correction exists between sociopolitical status and levels of SWC. Nevertheless, some patterns can be identified. A higher percentage of those lower status tended to practice the more traditional techniques, such as mounds, while those of higher sociopolitical status appeared more aware of the value of practices such as contouring. With regards to the more innovative practices such as stop-wash lines, contour bunds and zays, no correlation emerged. Two factors are probably responsible for this outcome. First, those of higher sociopolitical status tend to be more mobile and thus have a greater opportunity to observe and discuss SWC techniques. Second, low sociopolitical status frequently relates to low economic status. Those in the latter category may be forced therefore to consider and implement new or different practices as a response to declining yields. The survival of those of low sociopolitical and economic status may be less secure, thus increasing the pressure on them to innovate and invest to a greater extent in their land.

Table 29.4: SWC according to sociopolitical status (per cent)

Sociopolitical status	High	Low
Contour tillage	28	9
Graded furrows	-	19
Rotations	9	15
Fallowing	-	11
Mounds	47	54.5
Mixed cropping	45	68
Surface mulching	64	54
Fertilisation	67	81
Agroforestry	45	68
Stop-wash lines	-	2
Tied ridging	-	7.5
Contour bunds	9	6
Zays	18	13

Conclusions

A large number of varied and complex indigenous SWC practices were observed within the Circle of Djenné. These techniques included both biological and mechanical methods of SWC, although the former predominated in number of levels of application. The application of the SWC techniques is certainly dynamic. Examples of on-farm trials were witnessed, such as the farmer experimenting with cultivation on the contour. While considerable local initiative and innovation is also present, such as the contour bund currently being constructed by the Collective in the town of Djenné. Nevertheless, considerable differences exist in the levels of application of each SWC technique, as illustrated by the analysis of levels of application, according to the variables of gender, class and ethnicity.

As the preceding review of SWC projects in SSA revealed, many technological solutions that have been proposed have failed in the field because they have not taken into account the local culture and conditions, particularly the society's preferences, skills and knowledge. Indigenous systems exhibit considerable levels of sophistication. Indigenous SWC systems provide an excellent base on which appropriate SWC projects can be based. Where indigenous SWC is practiced, SWC projects should use these as *starting points*. Rather than introducing new techniques, the emphasis, wherever possible, should be on increasing the efficiency of indigenous techniques.

Notes

1. Information concerning SWC in the Circle of Djenné is based on three months research between June and September 1989, in association with the CARE International Agro-Sylvo-Pastoral Project in the Region, together with the International Institute for Environment and Development in London. For a more detailed account, see 'Indigenous Soil and Water Conservation in Sub-Saharan Africa in the Circle of Djenné, Central Mali' by A.J. Ayers, University of Reading, UK (1989), M.Sc. thesis (unpublished).

   The author would like to thank Dr. Camilla Toulmin at the International Institute for Environment and Development in London; Dr. Chris Reij at the Centre for Development Cooperation Services, Amsterdam; and the CARE International Project staff in Djenné, for all their assistance at various stages of the study.

   Thanks are also due to IIED; the Meyer Sassoon Scholarship at the University of Reading; the Gilchrist Educational Trust; the Balfour Charitable Trust; the Fund for Human Need; and the Radley Charitable Trust for their generous financial support.

   Finally, to the large number of farmers within the Circle of Djenné who so willingly and enthusiastically participated in the survey at what was such a critical period of the farming year, and without whose cooperation the study would not have been possible.

2. The concept of contours was unfamiliar to the majority of interviewees. The terms 'perpendicular' or 'parallel' to the slope were therefore used. Thus the practice can only be said to be very approximately on the contour.

30. Using Indigenous Knowledge in a Subsistence Society of Sudan

ROGER W. SHARLAND

Introduction

SUBSISTENCE PRODUCTION IS often seen as a problem by agriculturalists and other professionals seeking to introduce new technologies and ideas. This has led to a plethora of methodologies and techniques for transferring technology. Since subsistence societies are normally approached by professionals socialised within commercial sectors and societies, the development models used tend to reflect commercial values. Subsistence cultures have very different cultures and values, which although often difficult to appreciate from outside these cultures may be no less valid than those of the dominant commercial cultures (Sharland unpublished). The contrast in values may further be amplified by the marginal position in which most such societies find themselves within national and international economies.

The values and priorities of a subsistence society are rational responses to the environment in which they are located, being based on generations of experience and accumulated knowledge, solving problems, some of which the formal sector has yet to address. The details of the agricultural system and how it relates to the wild environment point to the need for a different extension approach, which accepts that the indigenous knowledge is a valuable resource that can be used in directed change, and that the society is open to change that relates to its values and priorities of production.

Recent thinking by those relating to resource-poor farming communities has highlighted the importance of indigenous knowledge (Chambers 1983; Richards 1985). The indigenous response to local conditions and production restraints has been seen as rational and locally adapted in a way formal knowledge is not. Although this knowledge is beginning to be used (Brokensha *et al.* 1980), it often remains marginal to extension efforts. This paper seeks to outline some ways in which change can be related to indigenous knowledge, based on a detailed study of, and work with, one tribe in Southern Sudan.

Although the writer spent twelve years working in the Moru area gaining background experience through participant observation, the specific insights in application of the knowledge were gained in a shorter time frame of about two years trying to incorporate recommendations based on the knowledge and needs of the farmers themselves into the extension system. The main methodology used was two way communication between the senior staff and field staff and field staff and farmers. This was greatly facilitated by the extension staff all being practicing traditional farmers themselves, having personal experience of both the indigenous knowledge and practical constraints of the farmers. A major tool used in developing solutions was the monthly meetings in which all field staff reported on problems encountered, and solutions were discussed in relation to both formal science and indigenous knowledge and practices. Many of the examples cited below were identified in these settings. In many respects the methodology used is similar to the Farmer-back-to-farmer model as developed by CIP in Peru (Rhoades 1984), although the four stages outlined by

Rhoades were not as clearly defined and tended to run together. The natural science and social science input were also combined in one person in the form of the writer, giving greater unity.

The Moru people

The Moru tribe has five major subdivisions which are unified by a common language, culture and a broadly similar agricultural lifestyle. They occupy the southern half of Mundri District in Western Equatoria Province of Southern Sudan. The means of livelihood and the associated cultural adaptations are strongly influenced by the ecology and climate of the area. The land is generally flat undulating open woodland savanna with low to moderate relief and narrow incised streamlines. The rains are medium length, most falling in 5–6 humid months. The 1200 mm. and 1300 mm isohyets pass through the Moru area, but the outstanding feature of the rainfall is its marked variability and unpredictability from one year to the next.

The country is now disrupted by civil war, but the study relates to conditions of peace, and the economic situation is described as such. Most Moru families are subsistence farmers depending on rainfed agriculture to produce food for their families. Surpluses are sold for cash or bartered for products that cannot be produced locally. The staple crop is sorghum which is central to the agricultural system, having strong cultural linkages, deeply rooted in the food system of the people. It is broadcast in association with sesame, cowpeas, bulrush millet and finger millet. The mixtures are not random but are relatively standardised into specific field types similar in principal to those identified among the Azande by De Schlippe (1956). A named field type has recognised ecological requirements, timings of activities and crop mixes and represents the key management unit of the agricultural system, which is heavily dependent on the judgement of the people. There are three major and a number of minor sorghum based field types, and a number of newer ones based on New World Crops. Risk is spread by diversifying and mixing both the crops and varieties of each crop. There are four major and a number of minor sorghum varieties each of which has a different growing season and climatic preference. Other important crops are groundnuts, maize, cassava, sweet potatoes, okra, pumpkins and various green vegetables. The eastern Moru have many sheep and goats, and a few cattle which have proved to have a degree of resistance to trypanosomiasis are still kept in one area. Poultry are kept by most households.

Since the population density is low the area cultivated is small relative to the surrounding bush. The garden immediately round the compound is used for crops that need the extra fertility provided by household waste or greater protection from wild animals. The main sorghum and sesame fields are traditionally grown away from the house in fields cleared for two to three years. These fields are cultivated with a number of members of the family having their own segments round a central point or *kätiri* (Catford 1951). Cooperation is important for social relationships although all production is individually owned. Interaction between the cultivated land and the wild bush is very important, and although the staple is cultivated many of the relishes are gathered from wild sources. Wild foods include vegetables, tubers, wild fruit, oil, salt from lye, fungi and insects, especially termites. Hunting for meat and fishing and honey collection are also important economic and social activities. The bush is also the source of building materials, fuel and fibres.

Using indigenous knowledge within extension

Study of the indigenous agriculture of the Moru points to a system which is finely adapted to the needs and restraints of the community. When the different values and priorities of a subsistence society are recognised, the question arises as to how to relate to such a society with directed change. Should all attempts at development intervention be dropped or should extension go ahead in a commercial mode ignoring the subsistence sector? Since subsistence is important neither of these reactions is relevant, rather extension must approach subsistence from within the values and knowledge of the subsistence sector. In this context the indigenous knowledge becomes a major resource, together with primary formal knowledge, for relating to the needs of the farmers and helping solve the problems.

Moru indigenous knowledge proved an invaluable resource for developing extension recommendations in Mundri District. From experience in the Moru situation, eight scenarios have emerged for using indigenous knowledge within a system of formal extension firmly based within the farm families, values and means of production, which include indigenous experimentation. These show considerable overlap with the six scenarios suggested by Warren and Cashman (1988), but also show significant divergence. Although it is believed these scenarios are widely applicable the illustrations given here are all drawn from experience with the Moru and the scenarios should be applied with sensitivity in a different situation.

Better communication and identification of needs

Studying indigenous knowledge can increase the effectiveness of communication in two major ways; by targeting the right section of the population and by using the proper vernacular terms in relation to explanations rooted in the formal knowledge sector.

Among the Moru the women are more vitally involved in agriculture than the men. They are involved in those parts of the agricultural cycle which require greater contact with individual plants and greater agricultural skill. They do the weeding, harvesting, selection of seed and frequently decide on land use. Moru women weed from a crouched position which involves close contact with individual plants. They also use the products in the kitchen. They therefore have more intimate and personal knowledge of the crops themselves and they are the ones who are involved in the key stages of production to which extension is directed. They are thus the largest source of indigenous knowledge and should also be the key focus of the main extension activities relating to subsistence production.

Correct use of vernacular terms has been important in many aspects of explanation. In some cases Moru terminology is more finely divided than English, in other less specific and in many cases just has different limits. For example many termite species are named in Moru and they are associated with different types of damage. If the wrong term is used when outlining control strategies, confusion results and undermines confidence in the outside input. Also the single word *Ä'di* in Moru describes many different conditions affecting the form of plants, including a number of parasitic plants, diseases and pests which result in a deformed appearance. The name helps identify a problem within one crop but is recognised as having the other meanings. Loose vernacular terms have been very helpful for describing formal scientific ideas. For example *ladra* meaning tongue in Moru is often used for buds, and gives clear linkages in the mind of the listener.

Moru soil names and ecological terms do not directly correspond to formal soil classifications. But, since they relate to specific agricultural conditions, such as water holding capacity, they have real practical value to the farmers and those seeking to help them. Their use is very specific to native speakers and can save much misunderstanding.

Understanding indigenous knowledge and perceptions can point to important ideas and practices that are necessary for subsistence, but are often overlooked by formal science, and can help in gaining understanding of farmers' perspectives.

Wild foods are a vital part of the total food production of the Moru but their value is often completely overlooked by professionals. Wild plants growing in the cultivated fields are not all 'weeds' to Moru women but many area valuable pot herbs, giving much better nutrition for less labour than introduced and formally recognised vegetables.

The reproductive instar of termites are a delicacy which are collected each year from termite hills, so conflict between the damage that permit workers do to the crops and the value of 'flying ants' for food is a practical factor. Without understanding the food value the needs of the crops may be put above the needs of the people.

Vertebrate pests such as baboons, monkeys, foxes and birds are far more limiting to Moru farmers than insect pests, but formal science has not easily related to them. Any innovation that does not take vertebrate pests into account can be disastrous. Strategies completely conceptually foreign to the formal sector have been developed by the Moru in relation to them. For example, the different Moru grain sorghums are adapted to different seasons. For each grain variety there is a corresponding sugar variety with a high sugar content in its stem, but the same growing season. When the grain is broadcast, seeds of the sugar varieties are always combined with the grain ones. As harvest time approaches it is essential that people are in the field to scare away birds, baboons and other mammal pests, so the sugar sorghums are selected to be ready for breaking and chewing as the grain harvest approaches.

As a result children, and even adults, are attracted to the fields, and are happy to stay there scaring the birds while they chew the sugar. A new short variety of sorghum introduced from Uganda with no corresponding sugar variety was rejected because of large scale bird damage. Helpful practices not thought of by formal science, such as the use of sugar sorghum, can to be identified and reinforced and possibly spread elsewhere.

The major concerns of the farmers are often highlighted through understanding the indigenous knowledge.

For the Moru the three most commonly cited problems are baboons, drought and foxes. If extension does not relate to these it cannot gain much credibility. Understanding of indigenous knowledge was used to develop control measures for vertebrate pests, and to communicate possible strategies on water conservation as a solution to an identified problem namely drought.

Factors in a new technology or idea that are of interest to farmers beyond the primary reason for introduction are often useful leads and can be identified and used in the extension effort.

When *Leucaena* was introduced as a wind break for citrus trees some farmers were attracted by its potential for planting ready for making sesame drying racks, a use solving a problem not previously identified from outside.

Indigenous knowledge can also be used to understand where a recommendation from formal knowledge may not be possible and compromise is needed.

Labour bottle-necks are an ever present part of subsistence production. Since these often involve the women's work they may be overlooked even though they make recommendations from formal science impossible. For example formal research recommended optimum planting dates for groundnuts and discouraged progressive planting. The reality of weeding for Moru women means that if all the groundnuts are planted at the 'optimum' time most of the crop will suffer from late weeding. Progressive planting helps deal with the problem of a heavy weeding burden and bottle-neck. The experienced farmer has a flexible work schedule so that what is done next is determined by what has happened already so far in the season. Management rather than rigorous timings gives the best results, and this depends more on indigenous understanding than research station wisdom.

Sharing of indigenous technology

Indigenous knowledge is often localised and restricted and there is much scope for sharing this knowledge more widely, or for adapting it to new uses. This can work in practice in a variety of different ways.

Technology already known and used in one context can be shared for use in another.

In relation to the problem of foxes eating newly planted groundnuts it was found that some Moru farmers use an infusion of mahogany bark as a seed dressing.

This infusion is bitter and makes the seed unpalatable so if the fox digs up several seeds and finds them unpalatable it leaves the field and looks for food elsewhere. Although not widely used as a seed dressing the technology of using mahogany bark is widely known for making a fish poison, and the technology for preparing it as a seed dressing is basically the same. Those farmers who do not know of using the bark as a seed dressing can easily be shown how to convert the technique used for making fish poisons.

Two technologies already used for seed storage by Moru women proved valuable for extending to the larger grain stores. When heads of grain kept for seed are hung from the roof of a hut, rats are kept away from them by threading half a gourd through the string above the seeds.

This is the same principle as the introduced idea of using rat guards on the legs of the traditional raised granary. Secondly wood ash is sometimes mixed with seeds when they are stored in a pot. Wood ash has also been shown as an effective way of protecting the food grain in the granary from insect attack.

It is sometimes possible to share technology already known and used in one location with another similar one. In some cases this interacts with transfer of technology from one use to another as with the mahogany bark for protecting groundnuts from foxes.

A good illustration of this sharing is a technology used for controlling termites. The neighbouring tribe to the Moru, the Morokodo, make a fairly technically sophisticated type of spring trap for snaring game, using a wooden bow sprung with a piece of hide. The wooden and leather parts are exposed to damage from termites. The Morokodo have developed an infusion made from a bulb called locally *Oboro* and the fruit of the tree *Catunaregan spinosa* which repels termites. The ingredients are pounded together with water into a concentrated pulp and poured over the traps. This same preparation was found to be very effective for protecting fruit trees from termites. The fruits of *Catunaregan spinosa* are available in the dry season when the termite problem on trees is most significant, and it is a time when heavy rain will not wash the mixture away. A tree may be treated for the first couple of years after which it is normally strong enough to resist the termites which only kill weak trees. The Moru do not have the same kind of game traps as the Morokodo, so do not know about this preparation. They are, however, familiar with plants as fish poisons and are familiar with the sources, methods of collection and methods of preparation, so the new technology can be easily borrowed from the neighbouring tribe and adapted to a new use.

Understanding that has been developed in relation to one area of life can also sometimes be used as a conceptual basis for clearer directed explanation in another.

The Moru recognise poor quality shrivelled seeds which they call *kye'be*. These are rejected from the seed used for planting. They do not normally select cuttings for cassava or sweet potato, since those plants propagated from cuttings are relatively new introductions, but the concept of *kye'be* understood in seed has been used to introduce the idea of selecting cuttings.

The bounds of male and female knowledge tend to be different and extension can sometimes help combine them for practical ends. Division of labour means that these sources of knowledge are kept separate within the culture and are only brought together when overlap is positively looked for.

For example, Moru men have more detailed knowledge relating to hunting and fishing. The women are more concerned with mammal damage such as foxes eating groundnuts. Male knowledge of mammal behaviour and fish poisons has been used positively to develop means of control for foxes, particularly in the way the groundnuts are planted by the women. Likewise, observations of baboon behaviour made by men while hunting enabled women to understand how to keep them from the gardens more effectively.

Existing knowledge that has stood the test of time often needs adapting for changing conditions in the same field and area. Traditional experimental procedures may be slow in effecting this adaptation. Extension can sometimes help the adaptation process when the indigenous knowledge is understood.

Moru shifting agriculture involves a detailed understanding of the relationship of trees to crops. This is manifested in the understanding of which trees need to be killed, which can be just cut and which can be left without interfering with the crop. These relationships can be developed for a more intensive stabilised system as a basis for formalised agroforestry.

Reinforcing indigenous technology with scientific basis

Traditional knowledge has a strong practical base but sometimes a weak theoretical foundation since it is limited to what can be observed with the naked eye, making wider application difficult for the practitioners.

Existing practices which are beneficial, but may be lost in a changing world, can be reinforced by the formal scientific sector by giving them backing that can relate to the growing schooled population.

The way trees are dealt with in the garden in relation to bush fallows can be brought into formalised agroforestry, and related to root structure and nitrogen fixation. Traditional practices that help conserve water in the soil can be reinforced and encouraged. This is particularly significant when the beneficial practice is actually done for a different reason than water conservation, necessitating a linkage to be made. When a Moru wants to chose a site for a new house he will dig a hole to check the soil depth. The main reason for this is not agricultural but to determine how easy it will be to dig graves. It has the unrecognised benefit however of ensuring a deeper agricultural soil which corresponds to greater water holding capacity.

Intertwining indigenous and formal scientific knowledge

Formal scientific knowledge is normally recorded in text books that are available to those educated in the formal scientific tradition. Indigenous knowledge is normally developed in the educational process of socialisation within an indigenous society. The two systems of knowledge are thus available to separate groups. Extension can be in a position to bring together these different types of knowledge for greater overall effectiveness not achieved by either one on its own.

Ideas that are already embryonic can be used in combination with scientific understanding to point to measures that are needed. This is particularly significant for weed and pest control.

An example of this is the weed, *Sorghum halpense*, called *ber.i* in Moru, a serious weed of cultivated sorghum when the cropping period is increased beyond the traditional two or three years. Since this slight intensification is a new practice resulting from recent concentrations of people the problem is not well understood. *Ber.i* is seen by, Moru women as originating from cultivated sorghum when it is winnowed near the field, reflecting that people already realise that it is worst in fields near the home (where winnowing takes place) which is where sorghum is most often grown for more years giving time for seed build-up. *Ber.i* builds up from year to year as sorghum is grown on the same land because the young plants are almost indistinguishable from the crop so are not weeded out and set seed before the crop is harvested. Since the relationship of *Ber.i* to the crop sorghum is made, there is an understandable starting point for explaining crop rotation. Teaching rotation in relation to nutrients or even diseases is difficult, but the known relationship of some weeds to particular crops makes a valuable starting point. The Moru also recognise a definite relationship between *Eleusine indica, Vigna luteola* and *Hyptis lanceolata* and the respective crops of finger millet, cowpeas and hyptis.

Cultivated tree crops are relatively new, so pests such as scale and aphids are not clearly understood. Scale are often identified by Moru as the eggs of the Red Fire Ant (*Oecophylla longinoda*). Although this relationship is not that understood by formal science it reflects an understanding of the link with ants. Sooty mold, which often indicates the presence of scale, is often seen on wild trees and widely recognised though not directly associated with a problem. Its importance as a diagnostic symptom of aphids or scale can be linked to the existing knowledge of the condition. Ladybirds congregate and breed where their food is abundant. Where there are many aphids or scales but few ants, ladybirds are often found in large numbers. Farmers often see the very noticeable ladybird larvae and sick looking trees and assume the ladybirds are the cause and ask for a spray to control them, rather than recognising that control is already underway. As trees are more widely grown, understanding of their pests will increase, meanwhile building on local perceptions the relationship with the ants can be explained and control of the ants (which leads to control of the scale and aphids) introduced. The indicative role of sooty mold and the value of ladybirds as a predator rather than pest bring together traditional observation with formal science.

Formal scientific reasoning can be applied to practices that are not well established or understood, and are controversial in the traditional setting.

Some Moru farmers expressed concern to their extension agents about the increase of worms eating their sweet potatoes. These were identified as being the larvae of the sweet potato weevil. One cultural recommendation for its control is deeper planting. While discussing possible control measures with farmers it was noticed that there was controversy among farmers as to whether it was better to plant the cuttings using a stick or by hand. The consensus of opinion was that planting with a stick was better, but at first sight this seemed an irrelevant belief. On further consideration it was noticed that planting with a stick increased the depth of planting. The local controversy of which method was better was used as the basis of encouraging deep planting.

Identifying harmful practices and explaining problems

Traditional knowledge has evolved within a specific set of constraints and conditions. Practices are sometimes continued with harmful effect because they are 'tradition' although the original reason and basis is no longer relevant. Formal science can help obtain understanding of the factors that become harmful in a changing situation, and can thus point to need for change once farmers recognise the problem in question.

Existing practices may become harmful under new conditions of a changing situation. Understanding indigenous knowledge can help point to these.

Some of the expedients that are applicable under extensive shifting cultivation or bush fallows, for example, can exacerbate drought and drying of the soil under even slight intensification. Burning of the rubbish is an important part of opening a garden from bush or after a fallow, and is an expedient that gives quick available nutrients with less time input at a season when labour demands are great. However when the fallows are reduced and land is used longer before returning to fallow, burning of the stubbles and regrowth can be a serious cause of soil drying. New practices are necessary and need for sensitive burning can be communicated in terms of the felt need that farmers already have in relation to drought, while recognising benefits and constraints in the traditional practices.

Some traditional practices have not been questioned or adapted because the farmers do not recognise a deleterious effect. For example, sweet potatoes are a relatively new crop to the Moru, and the method of planting involves using considerable quantities of vines. This makes it difficult to select cuttings, but the need to select cuttings has not been recognised. As sweet potato weevil becomes a greater problem, selection of cuttings is one of the preventative measures recommended. This is only made possible with more efficient use of cuttings and greater understanding of the nature of cuttings. The older practice of using excessive quantities of cuttings may thus be seen as harmful with new pest problems.

Misconceptions arising from misinterpretation of observation can sometimes be clarified using the limitation of farmers' understanding as the basis of new ideas.

Traditional understanding of factors such as pests and diseases depends on what can be seen with the naked eye. This can lead to assumptions that cause beneficial species to be mistaken as pests. One example is the way ladybirds are assumed to be the cause of the symptoms resulting from scale insects and aphids. Another widespread example is the way insectivorous birds are scared away from the crop as much as grain eating birds because they are not differentiated and the beneficial effect of such birds is not recognised. Complicated biological relationships, such as root nodules are often misinterpreted. They are often given the name *gbur.u* in Moru which is more commonly used for tumours, etc., so they are not associated as being beneficial and some people feel they are a symptom of disease. Clarification of relationships that are not obvious can prevent such misunderstandings, but will be seen as necessary only with understanding of the indigenous knowledge.

Identifying areas where solutions are needed from outside

Recognising the value of indigenous knowledge does not mean solutions from outside the traditional system are not beneficial or relevant. Understanding indigenous knowledge can point to gaps in local knowledge where outside ideas can be applied in a sensitive manner relating to existing conditions.

Solutions from outside are sometimes needed for problems that have been identified from within under changing conditions, but for which there is little understanding yet. This is again particularly relevant for problems resulting from causes not immediately observed with the naked eye, such as pests, disease and soil chemistry.

Since cassava mosaic virus affects all cassava plants grown by the Moru, it is not recognised as a diseased condition by most farmers so no measures are taken to reduce its incidence. Once it is recognised as a problem steps can be taken. Likewise leaf spot on groundnuts is seen as part of the natural aging process so is not perceived as a problem.

The parasitic weed *Striga* is a problem that has only become significant to the Moru where land is used for longer periods than traditionally. The concept of a

parasitic weed is new so no measures different from other weeds have traditionally been used. Understanding of the nature of the problem has led to recommendations for control.

Understanding indigenous knowledge can point to areas of knowledge which
are completely lacking what may be relevant for directed input. This may be
relatively unusual in the subsistence sector, although it is the approach most
extension favours.

Among the Moru few examples have been found. One may be the weed
Solanum incanum. The Moru have a clear concept of certain weeds being
related to crop plants but no concept of weeds being hosts for pests or diseases.
This weed can harbour pests and diseases of crops like tomato and eggplant, but
a new concept has to be explained to encourage its control.

Using indigenous change processes

Indigenous potential for change is an integral asset to extension.
Experimentation has increasingly been recognised as an essential ingredient
for survival (Johnson 1972; Box, unpublished), and can be a very positive
resource for directed change.

The Moru have responded to considerable change in their agricultural practices
and can assimilate more relevant changes if circumstances dictate. Moru women
are actively involved in experimentation every season, and particularly when
times get harder. The greatest experimental input is the testing of new varieties,
but new cultural techniques are also tried. Some Moru women have an insa-
tiable curiosity to try out new varieties or cultivars seen in another farmer's field
or when travelling in another tribal area.

A few seeds or cuttings are taken and tried in a corner of the field, and if they
show promise more and more are grown. This experimentation is not intrinsi-
cally risky but decreases risk as it increases the options. This adaptive research
has been observed to be far more efficient than formal research for the subsistence needs as it can easily assimilate subjective factors such as palatability or
reliability that are not easily measured. Farmer evaluation is very sensitive
though of a different nature from statistically based trials, it is denigrated and
ignored by the formal sector.

New varieties often need new cultural practices such as time of planting and
spacing and these are worked out on the farm and shared. One particularly clear
example is the dwarf okra variety, *Clemson spineless*, originally sent from
America. This proved a popular variety with farmers, so demand increased from
year to year. When it first arrived farmers grew it like any other variety of okra,
with one planting a year dispersed among the other crops, especially maize.
Clemson spineless is however a much smaller variety than the local ones and
although it yields quickly, it also ages quickly. Farmers adapted the practice of
okra planting so as to make up to three plantings a year, and planted the new
variety in either ridges around the groundnut fields or else in small plots specially given over to it. It did not replace the old varieties but added to them. The
method of cultivation was worked out by the characteristics.

The method of planting then became a standard recommendation and was
passed on from farmer to farmer informally and was eventually incorporated in
the extension recommendations.

Creation of an indigenous technical foundation

All the examples described in this paper, and much more that has been observed in relation to Moru agriculture and relationships with the wild environment contribute to the recorded sum of indigenous knowledge (Sharland, unpublished). Much of this has been shown to have use, but other knowledge of potential use also needs to be recorded in the same way as genetic material is kept in a gene pool. It may have potential use in the area where it is recorded or may include information relevant for solving problems in other areas. Unless it is recorded, however, much useful information is likely to be lost.

Several recommendations developed in relation to the Moru have had their foundation in the indigenous knowledge of other peoples. The use of wood ash, for example, in preventing insect damage in stored grain is well known in parts of West Africa, and has proved a useful technology for use in Moru granaries. If its use had not been recorded from West Africa its use would not have been tried among the Moru.

Indigenous technical knowledge is thus seen to be a very practical resource for use within the extension system, especially within a changing environment. It is a readily available source of information that even the poorest farmers can use. The main problems relate to how professionals can practically relate to this knowledge and use the wider world scientific foundation of knowledge to strengthen rather than weaken the indigenous foundation. The examples cited in this paper give an overview of ways it has been used in a specific situation and the scenarios outlined can be assumed to have wide applicability wherever extension seeks to relate to existing knowledge and practices. The Moru situation is one where agriculture is primarily practiced for subsistence purposes, and it is in this context that indigenous knowledge may have a particularly significant contribution in the future.

31. Kpelle Steelmaking: An indigenous high technology in Liberia[1]

GORDON C. THOMASSON

Kpelle steel and technological revolution

THE ABRUPT PHYSICAL transition from the savanna grasslands of the interior to the rain forests of Liberia marked the necessary beginning of an agricultural revolution as the Kpelle people mastered the upland cultivation of rice (*Oryza sativa*) in that new ecosystem. It also began a major Kpelle technological revolution, as is reflected in their metallurgy.

Ecology and industry Just as radically new agronomic knowledge and technology had to be discovered, experimentally developed, tested and adapted, so too manufacturing skills had to be invented and/or modified to fit the new ecological niche in which the Kpelle people found themselves. Tools that were sufficient for farming in the relatively more dry interior were not adequate for clearing the rank vegetation of the forest floor, let alone the triple tier forest's canopy of tall hardwoods, with their massive trunks and buttress roots. In the same way, if the Kpelle had and maintained an 'iron' manufacturing technology during their westward migrations, it would have had to be modified and adapted to the new constraints and opportunities which Liberia afforded. More accurately, like most traditional peoples, the Kpelle manufactured a carburised steel (*see* Goody 1971; Haaland and Shinnie 1985; Maddin *et al.* 1977; Muhly 1982; Van der Merwe and Avery 1982; Shinnie 1971), but with a difference.

Traditional Western perspectives on metallurgy

Basil Davidson, one of the most sympathetic researchers of and popular writers on African history and culture, nevertheless perpetuates views of traditional metallurgy that, like colonial views of indigenous agriculture, seriously undervalue the technology of peoples like the Kpelle. In a discussion of the consequences of the slave trade, after pointing out the incredible suffering of those who were enslaved and removed from the continent, Davidson and Buah (1967: 283-284) outline the impact on those who were left behind: 'Where, then, lay the main consequences of the slave trade for African life? These lay in the field of *production* and in the field of *politics* [emphasis in original]. The slave trade damaged the production of goods, the creating of wealth, in two ways. First of all, it obliged West Africa to export its most valuable raw material, which was human labour. Year after year, for more than three centuries, tens of thousands of African farmers and craftsmen were shipped away to work in American plantations, mines and cities. With their labour they created enormous wealth and profits, but seldom for themselves and never for Africa. All that Africa received in exchange were the manufactured goods of Europe; and this was the second way in which the slave trade damaged Africa. It is easy to see why. West Africa, like other parts of Africa, possessed its own craftsmen. Often they were highly skilled. They produced goods which were sold from one end of West Africa to the other. But they produced them by *old-fashioned hand-methods* [emphasis added]. Now they had to face the competition of much cheaper goods made by machinery outside Africa. Cheap foreign cottons, produced by Europeans or Indians forced to work for very low wages, began to ruin the market for cotton stuffs produced by self-employed and often prosperous African craftsmen. Cheap European metalware, machine-made, competed with the handwork of African metalsmiths. Understandably, African craftsmen suffered from this cheap competition. But they were not able to go over to European factory methods: they had neither the necessary money nor the knowledge, while their way of life kept them faithful to traditional methods. So the slave trade removed African labour from Africa, and did much to ruin the livelihood of African craftsmen.'

There are several typical assumptions made here. These include the idea that European goods displaced African manufactures by competition. From the capitalist view this took place through the workings of the 'free' market. Marxist dialectics see, on the other hand, that just as peasant agriculture must give way to industrialised agriculture, so too hand labour must be replaced by mechanisation and exploited industrial labour. Both systems of thought conclude that *old-fashioned hand-methods* (that are usually called 'primitive') are inferior and/or obsolete. As will be discussed below, however, at least in the case of Kpelle metallurgy, its problem was clearly *not* an inability to meet 'cheap competition,' nor were its products 'primitive' or inferior. Furthermore, it is not necessarily the case that converting to 'European factory methods' would produce either a cheaper or a better product in Africa, nor is the assumption justified that the demise of African technology came from peasant resistance to change or a 'way of life [that] kept them faithful to traditional methods.

Reconceptualisation metallurgy

The author's study of Kpelle metallurgy, as in the cases of his examination of their education and agriculture, has revealed that there was more than simply an 'appropriate' technology existing before conquest. Instead, it would be justified to speak of an optimum, but in no way static technology, in light of the available resource base that was part of the ecosystem in which Kpelle culture developed and existed, and which it still occupies today. Under careful analysis, it is obvious that this was a highly adapted indigenous knowledge system or complex of indigenous technical knowledge.[2]

Technological overview
There are significant impediments to any study of the Kpelle 'iron' industry, though much can yet be learned. Less is known about their bronze, gold and silver technologies. Historical and ethnographic approaches have their own problems, in part due to predictable and certainly not irrational patterns of secrecy found among guilds of metallurgists around the world. In fact, traditional metallurgical skills, such as those of the Kpelle cannot simply be committed to textbooks. The following description by Müller (1980b: 14) of a Tanzanian blacksmith's knowledge is typical (and could easily apply to a traditional smith almost anywhere around the world): 'The blacksmiths' knowledge is entirely based upon accumulated empirical experience, which has been "inherited" from one generation of blacksmiths by the next. This knowledge is part of the blacksmith's senses and cannot be separated from his [nor can it be abstracted into or learned from a textbook – it can only be learned through the formal education

of an apprenticeship]. If you give a blacksmith a piece of scrap, he will first test it. He weighs it a couple of times in each hand, heats it up in the furnace and observes how long it takes to reach a certain colour. Finally, he beats it and looks at the sort of sparks it gives, listens and feels how the iron "responds" and perhaps he will also smell the sparks. Meanwhile he mumbles,[3] as if he is talking to the steel. After testing it, he knows what sort of steel he is working with, furthermore, he even knows for which purpose this steel is best suited. He cannot convert his knowledge into the percentage of carbon content, but he "knows".'

In historic times some of the predecessors of the Kpelle in Liberia – specifically the Krahn – used pit furnaces with bellows for forced-draught smelting of iron,[4] as well as charcoal from the ubiquitous forest hardwoods. Charcoal is another industry in itself, which the immigrating Kpelle also developed in their own way.[5]

An archaeological problem Archaeological problems in studying the Kpelle in general are substantial. Nonprofessionals' expectations (including also the expectations of archaeologists without significant tropical experience) of the kinds of finds that will come from archaeology in hot, humid tropical areas, are usually based on the discoveries that come out of the near perfect preservation environment that constitutes much of the ancient Near East and Egypt. These hopes are totally out-of-touch with the reality of what we can expect to find in the rainy humid tropics. The same factors that so radically degrade tropical soil destroy artifacts. Everything from characteristically highly acid and bacterially hyperactive soils to virtually optimum temperatures for artifact destruction (too hot), couples with rainfall in huge amounts and falling with impacts at times exceeding twenty tons per square inch, work against finding very much at all.

Add to this the fact that if we equate the amount and sophistication of technique and data analysis, the ratio of serious work in the ancient Near East compared to tropical Africa is possibly 10,000:1, and what has been done usually involved techniques of recovery and preservation that had been developed in arid regions, and are often inappropriate to the point of being self-defeating. The disparity in sophistication of technology alone shows that dogmatic statement about the lack of evidence for some ancient civilisations in Africa are ludicrous. Moreover, some assume, for example, that an iron industry requires a large-scale infrastructure, but the material remains for such a technology actually may be quite inconspicuous (Gabel *et al.* 1972–4). For example, up into this century, before penetration by western technology, one traditional smelter built around a plantain stalk near a small village in what is at least now Kpelle territory (remains of the smelter are on the property of the Youth of Life Mission School, 6.5 kilometres east of Palala, Bong County), left behind a slag heap that measures approximately $3 \times 13 \times 50+$ m, which many nearby residents today do not even know exists.

The Kpelle ironworking tradition is one of several distinct technologies found in West Africa. In Liberia itself these mainly include the old Loma, Kpelle and Krahn traditions,[6] all of which involved some mining and smelting of iron as well as forging and, in the Kpelle case, possibly the casting of implements. One of the more well-known products of the extinct Loma industry is the so-called 'Kissi penny', a stylised arrow, bundles of which were part of a traditional bride price (and may have had a divinatory function, as well). These 'coins' are mentioned in the literature as early as 1687 AD (Schulze 1973: 153). Moreover, virtually all peoples of Liberia were active in working iron which they purchased from those who mined and smelted it. The mining and smelting of iron is still practiced among the neighbouring Senofu people of the Korhogo prefecture of the Ivory Coast (Jammes *n.d.*), but it is almost dead in Liberia.

Kpelle metallurgical technology, in contrast to the literature, as reflected in its material remains, and also in interviews with informants, was both sophisticated, quite distinctive and clearly not derived from neighbours, captives or slaves obtained as the Kpelle settled the area. Besides mining and smelting of iron alloys and brass, Kpelle smiths even may have made cast iron as well as forged tools; they did some types of welding and gunsmithing. Overall, while utilising what is often denigrated as 'primitive', or even appropriate technology, their knowledge was very advanced.

The Kpelle utilised an above-ground furnace that seems to have employed both bellows and convection-draught. The location of a smelter was consecrated or sacralised by the planting of one or more cotton trees (often reaching fifty meters in height), in the same way that traditional townsites were demarcated. The furnaces were built by covering a thick plantain stalk with termite clay (reportedly they were sometimes built on hillsides). Once the clay was more or less dry, the inner layers of the plant could be pulled out from the top (like rings out of a cut onion); after the clay was further dried (slowly, by periodic applications of palm oil), a fire inside the chimney that was thus created completed the drying and the hardening of the clay. Down- or up-slope winds probably had no significant role in the smelting process. On the other hand, the powerful suction created by the rising hot gases through the tall, tapering column could have combined with the bellows to make possible high smelting temperatures. It is noteworthy that plantain is not the most common savannah plant, though it may have been available to Kpelle blacksmiths prior to their arrival in Liberia's rain forests.

More problematic than the use of plantains for furnace building is that, given the relative scarcity of trees in the savannah, the technology for charcoal-intensive smelting of metals, if brought by the Kpelle from the southern Sudan, was maintained during their migrations at quite a considerable labour cost. Moreover, the ability to recognise new and diverse types of iron ore encountered as they moved from one into another of successive mineral environments is most astonishing.

Kpelle furnaces were charged with a mixed-charge of charcoal, possibly cork-wood, and ores, and at least one report holds that three days were the minimum time required to complete a run (Schulze 1973: 155). We do not know what sort of fluxes were used, but a silica flux in the form of grasses added to the charge is likely. Apparently continuous smelting was also practiced at times, recharging the furnace from the top and tapping the molten ore from the bottom. Several informants described the molten ore's flow through small trenches into holes (pigs?), suggesting that temperatures were high enough not just to extract blooms for the making of wrought iron, but to do casting. If this is true, it is unique in the ancient world. The percentage of metal extracted is undeterminable, but even if the technology were very inefficient (extracting, say, less than 20 per cent of the metal from the ore), the quantity of slag observable at some of the obviously more active sites indicates production would clearly have exceeded any possible domestic consumption.

The author also obtained reports from informants of the 'mixing' (alloying) of different types of ore (specifically referred to as 'rocks of different colours') to produce what informants consistently described as a high strength, rust-resistant

'Kpelle iron'. Unrelated interviewees in many distant areas reported that unlike *kwii* metals, 'Kpelle iron' did not rust away after acquiring a light surface patina. Close examination of museum pieces that had not benefited from any modern preservation techniques, let alone humidity and temperature control, confirmed these reports, as did less formal observation of the few pieces seen in the field. Further testing the reliability and validity of these claims was an essential task. The consistency of the reports from distinct sources gave some confidence, but the literature stood in direct contradiction. For example, Willi Schulze (1973: 155) noted that: 'The Kpelle furnaces were charged with one thick layer of charcoal on which roasted lateritic iron ore was heaped.'

Moreover, no one was willing to part with any old artifacts made of 'Kpelle iron'. The author was, however, able to collect both slag and laterite gravel (plinthite ore) from one Kpelle smelter site. This made possible empirical testing and verification of informants' verbal reports.

Laboratory perspectives X-ray fluorescence spectrometry revealed that slag samples from the Kpelle smelter contained (besides the predictable iron) silicon, sulphur and aluminum, significant residues of manganese, titanium and chromium, lesser amounts of barium, possibly traces of nickel and copper, and usual readings of calcium and potassium.[7] The significance of the tests is heightened by the fact that x-ray fluorescence spectrometry testing of the laterite gravel from the same furnace site revealed a composition of iron, a larger proportion of titanium and chromium than in the slag, some zirconium, and a trace of nickel, but, relative to the slag, almost no calcium or potassium, and most significantly, a comparative absence of manganese in the laterite gravel (roughly fourteen times more in the slag than in the ore).

The absence of manganese from the laterite gravel and its substantial presence in the slag shows that, contrary to what has been assumed in the past, laterite could not have been the Kpelle's only ore, because in and of itself, it could not account for residues in the slag.[8] Reports in the literature of the Kpelle simply smelting roasted laterite gravel ore, made by scholars who have not observed a smelter in operation, cannot be sustained by the evidence. The informants' reports of ores being mixed, on the other hand, tend to be confirmed. The superiority of 'Kpelle iron' is reflected in its surviving reputation among the older Kpelle and the reported demand for it from traders and neighbouring tribes (Schwab 1947: 136-146). One technical source (United States Steel 1957: 4), discussing iron in antiquity, noted: 'In some areas, the iron ores also contained some other metals beneficial to the properties of the iron with which they became alloyed during smelting (*manganese for instance*), and the metals produced from such ores were so superior as to become justly celebrated' (emphasis added).

The reputation of 'Kpelle iron' is unusual, then, not because of the metal's manganese content,[9] but due to the fact that, at least in this case, it was achieved by the conscious alloying of ores to obtain the desired characteristics. The reputation of Kpelle iron was well-deserved, and explains the, at times, high volumes of production reflected in some slag heaps, and its place in regional trade.

Blacksmithing and trade Among the Kpelle, tools were obtained from a blacksmith based upon an exchange of labour. *Kuu* (cooperative labour) groups and individuals would work on the blacksmith's farm a given amount of time, based upon the time a smith spent producing the goods received. But since, unlike farming, which is seasonal, smithing can be practiced year-round, surpluses were produced that could be exported. Thus, even more than leatherworkers, weavers, or those planting trees and occasionally harvesting kola nuts, smiths were engaged in commerce from a very early period. The blacksmith would have been one of the few people in Kpelle society who could offer sufficient goods in exchange for cattle that were brought into the rain forest areas from the savannah. It should be recognised that while not all blacksmithing groups are nomadic, the roles of smith and merchant are necessarily symbiotic, if not always synonymous, due to the durability and longevity of the goods the smiths produce. A traditional smith who does not engage in trade himself or through middlemen very quickly runs out of customers. The travelling smith and tinker are common to many societies. But the smith who mines and smelts as well as works metals is usually less mobile and more linked to travelling traders than those who only fabricate tools from metal that other produce. For people with an established smelting technology, leaving known ore deposits is a major step, since one cannot be assured of finding adequate sources elsewhere.

While virtually all their neighbouring tribes had smithing traditions, apparently only the Loma and Krahn were significant competitors in producing iron in the region, but, perhaps due to the Kpelle's metallurgical skills (alloying, etc.), 'Kpelle iron' was in higher demand. The Kpelle smiths and smelters kept their technology secret. They were, from all indications, not highly mobile, but were quite open to trade, especially through Mandingo (Malinke) who brought salt and other commodities in exchange for workable bars of 'iron' (steel – on other early African 'iron' trade see Morgenthau 1979: 109, Wilson 1979: 56–7, 62, Meillassoux 1965: 74–5, Miracle 1965: 289, and Bohannan 1964: 79–97). It is also possible that the Kpelle smelters supplied not just bar-stock, but smithing tools (especially anvil-hammers) to the blacksmiths of neighbouring tribes. Given the size of some slag heaps and the frequency of smelters around Kpelle villages it is reasonable to assume that trade carried 'Kpelle iron' throughout at least much of West Africa. Today, as will be discussed below, Kpelle smiths no longer mine and smelt their own iron, and are dependent on outside sources of *kwii* iron (old truck leaf springs, etc.), to make the tools they sell and exchange for labour.

Problems between Kpelle and Western metallurgy

Despite the obvious strengths of Kpelle steel manufacturing technology, that industry is at best moribund today. The author found only a rapidly diminishing number of old blacksmiths knowing anything about mining and refining iron ore. Toolmaking and repair have only a precarious status. Virtually every village still has at least one smith, but they are best described as underemployed, even though traditional-style tools are almost universally preferred over imported implements because of their functional utility. In every village studied, and in every interview conducted by the author with rural Kpelle under about forty years of age who were not blacksmiths, there was total ignorance that their ancestors had ever mined and refined iron. Even among Kpelle university students who had attended school at what is now the Youth of Life Mission School in Palala, where the largest known slag heap in the region is located, none was aware of that smelter's existence.

The older generation does not talk about the old iron industry, and some schoolteachers even ridicule blacksmithing as primitive and backward. Rather than there being anything wrong with the traditional industry, however, the reasons for the decline in smelting and making tools include, among other things, non-economic forces, changing patterns of trade, distortion of 'market' pricing, and disruption of traditional reciprocal labour relations. In the Kpelle case, however, it is not a sufficient explanation to argue that: 'The growth of this trade [with Europe] began to affect the structure of production in West Africa. Some previously economic activities – blacksmithing, iron smelting, even the mining of iron – declined, "ruined by the competition of cheaper and purer iron bars imported from Europe," as well as by increasing quantities of cheap European imports of iron basins, machetes, knives, hoes, wire and other metal goods turned out by the expanding mass production techniques of the industrial revolution.' (Wallerstein 1976: 36, quoting Flint).

'Free trade, mass production, and 'competition' with imported goods did not eclipse the Kpelle iron industry, nor was it displaced because it was an inferior technology linked to an obsolete form of social organisation. If it is in fact dead, it was killed by colonialism and monopoly capitalism, not because the product it produced was in any way inferior or overpriced in the marketplace.

Non-economic obstacles The suppression of traditional blacksmithing in favour of importers was not unique to Liberia, nor were the motives for destroying indigenous industries uniquely economic. Colleagues have verbally reported to the author cases of traditional smithing being suppressed elsewhere in colonial Africa for non-economic reasons, including preventing the manufacture of weapons (swords and spears, etc.). On the other hand, Müller's reports (1980b: 13) that 'During the colonial era [in Tanzania], blacksmithing was often actively suppressed in order to promote the use of imported goods, maximise the production of export crops, and prevent the manufacture of guns' have been rather carefully refuted by David Brokensha, who cites from colonial records from the 1930s to the 1950s to show that blacksmithing was recognised and valued by some officials in East Africa (Brokensha 1983: 90). Each case must be examined carefully.

Changing patterns of trade As certain imported consumer goods – pure refined salt, for example – became available at low prices in the interior, indigenous trading patterns began to evolve, but could have survived. While certain goods such as 'Kpelle iron' were still desirable, there were fewer indigenous products that African traders could offer of comparable value to the labour invested by the smiths, especially since the supposedly 'free' market prices had to match or be lower than those for non-African imported tools and scrap iron.

National boundaries, customs agents, bribes, and corruption also broke down traditional trading networks that had existed prior to these economically artificial barriers being interposed. Highly desired trade goods were more costly due to the new expenses and risks that resulted from governments redefining indigenous trade as crime (smuggling). As a result, 'legal' (coastal controlled) imports came to be substituted for the goods that moved through the indigenous system. This further enriched the dominant groups, while increasing the impoverishment of the indigenous majority in the long run. This is because the real, long term cost of substituting imports purchased through the sale of non-renewable resources for domestic manufactures is actually much higher than one could calculate from shipping invoices.

Distortion of market prices for goods The settler controlled Liberian government, throughout this century, actually subsidised the coastal merchants (largely themselves), to the long range destruction of indigenous industry, the economy and currency. From the initial incursion into Kpelle territory up through the first years of the Doe regime, this took place, in part, by putting artificially low ceilings with heavy penalties on the market prices of cutlasses and other implements manufactured by traditional smiths. While this resulted in traditional implements apparently costing less to buy than the imported tools, and therefore supposedly staying competitive with them, the controlled price (which was ostensibly a protection for indigenous industry), was always kept lower than what it actually cost for the smiths to manufacture the goods.[10] This made it impossible for the smiths to survive, and guaranteed a profit, first directly to the settler-Liberian merchants who imported metal tools, and later indirectly to themselves through Lebanese surrogates or other 'front-men'.

Accelerating through the Tolbert years, and getting even worse under the Doe regime, irrational subsidisation and price-distortion also takes place as the government allows merchants to spend costly 'foreign exchange' (*i.e.* U.S. dollars) on the importation of goods that could have been produced locally, to say nothing of the lost economic multiplier effect of domestic production and consumption. For instance, in 1982, depending on market prices and grade of ores or concentrates, from 3.5 up to as many as one-hundred long tons of Liberia's rapidly vanishing reserves of high-grade iron ore[11] had to be exported to generate the foreign exchange necessary to reimport steel in the form of a single Chinese or Brazilian machete (made from their own ore) that weighs approximately a pound. In 1982 such an implement cost US $4 in Kpelle country, and was inadequate to the task. In this type of exchange, the bulk of the profit goes to the more than generously licensed multi-national mining concessions, and again to the importers, who as quickly as possible ship their profits to banks outside Liberia. Neo-classical and monetarist 'free-market' theories are more than irrelevant when it comes to solving this kind of problem – they exacerbate it. Only domestic manufactures could reverse the situation.

Distortion of labour costs Another factor leading to the breakdown of the traditional industry was that it was based upon labour exchanges. There is nothing uneconomic or impractical about this type of reciprocity. From the extension of control by the coastal people over the hinterland, however, distortions in the 'market price' of labour again put blacksmiths at a disadvantage. *Corvée* labour was implemented on 'legal' and extra-legal bases from the moment that troops moved inland. Tribal peoples were first impressed as hammock carriers and bearers for the soldiers themselves and to carry their plunder. Then more *corvées* were established to build roads, create estates and plantations for district commissioners and other central government figures. Also the monetary 'hut tax' was imposed on the non-monetary rural economies. With ever greater frequency, the people's labour was forcibly diverted to uncompensated enriching of the dominant powers. Added to this were the quotas of labourers that chiefs were required to send to work on the million acre Firestone plantation (albeit at starvation wages) from 1927 onward into the 1950s, and the kidnapping by Monrovians of men that were sold into slavery and shipped to Spanish plantations on the island of Fernando Po and to Panama, which ended with the League of Nations censure in 1930.[12] Forced labour persisted in the Doe regime, with county superintendents and other military officers forcing entire villages to make enormous private rice farms for them without compensation of any kind.

Increasingly, schools have further depleted the traditional labour market, not just during class time, but throughout the lives of those who attend, both through the systematic denigration of the traditional system and the over-valuing of 'white collar' employment. The average school-leaver is accurately perceived in the village as 'lazy' – refusing to work in traditional ways, yet unfit for anything else in the almost non-existent westernised economy. All of these factors have artificially raised the cost (and availability) of labour to the point that the old exchange relationships are rarely viable, and farmers are forced to buy inferior imported goods while their neighbours cannot afford to produce implements that are worth buying, because of price ceilings.

Conclusion

Kpelle steelmaking was a viable economic enterprise, capable of producing a high quality product that was far better suited to the needs of local farmers in terms of functionality, strength, and rust resistance than are imports, at a far lower real cost to the nation. With minimal government cooperation, the author believes the industry still could be revived, better serving the nation's farmers, blacksmiths, and the economy as a whole, making Liberia self-sufficient in the production of iron hoes, axes, cutlasses, and etc., providing work for the blacksmiths and smelters, their children, and future generations, as may be happening in other parts of Africa (Müller, 1980a). Contrasted with mass-produced machetes, etc., the local smiths' products are far superior in many respects. As has been noted elsewhere (Müller 1980b: 11-13): 'As part-time farmers, the blacksmiths [of rural Tanzania] know local soil conditions, crops, and farmers' preferences. Therefore their *jembes* [heavy, more or less heart-shaped hoes] vary a great deal. The sizes and weights are determined by whether they will be used for digging or weeding. A different *jembe* exists for every crop and soil condition: some are heart-shaped, others are in the form of a dish; the former is for hard soil, the latter for soft...smiths are frequently asked to modify [hoes that are mass produced].'

The only real constraint would be the careful development and maintenance of 'woodlots' for charcoal production to prevent deforestation – a relatively easy task today. Kpelle steelmaking is indeed a high technology indigenous knowledge system which holds real promise for Liberia's future. It is also an endangered national resource that can become extinct with the death of its last practitioners.

Notes

1 This article was originally delivered at the Liberian Studies Association meeting, Santa Barbara, California, March 12, 1987. It is derived in part from chapter V (Kpelle Steel and Technological Revolution) of my Cornell University Ph.D. dissertation, 'Indigenous Knowledge Systems, Sciences, and Technologies: Ethnographic and Ethnohistorical Perspective on the Educational Foundations for Development in Kpelle Culture' (Ithaca, New York: 1987), which treats traditional agriculture, medicine, metallurgy, and education.

2 These themes are articulated today by a number of other scholars who somewhat parallel my approach, including Robert Chambers (1985, 1983), and his associates at

the Institute of Development Studies at the University of Sussex in publications such as *Rural Development: Whose Knowledge Counts?* (1979), David W. Brokensha, D. Michael Warren and Oswald Werner, in *Indigenous Knowledge Systems and Development* (1980), and William Foote Whyte and Damon Boynton in *Higher-Yielding Human Systems for Agriculture* (1983).

3. On the significance of such 'mumbling', compare my discussion of 'Ritual As a Mnemonic Strategy in Traditional Health-Care Training and Delivery' (Thomasson 1987: 274–84).

4. This technique is common in West Africa. Van der Merwe links it to Phoenician traders on the West Coast of Africa and dates it back as far as Nigeria in 400 BC (1982: 151).

5. Willi Schulze gives a good overview of what is known of migration patterns (1973: 45-49).

6. See the chapter on 'Mining: the Liberian iron ore industry' in Willi Schulze (1973: 153 ff.), and a discussion of Kpelle iron by the same author (1970-1971).

7. I am indebted to Fred W. Nelson, Radiation Safety Officer at Brigham Young University and an expert in doing such analyses in his own archaeological research, for conducting these tests. For technical details of the tests, see Thomasson (1987: 225-226 n. 11, 226 n. 12, and 226-227, n. 13).

8. This is certain, both because of the ease with which manganese melds with iron and its substantially lower melting point. If a furnace is hot enough to liquefy iron the manganese will already have melted. These factors combine to insure that Mg could not have resisted smelting and have become more concentrated in the slag than in the laterite. The trace of sulphur in the slag may have come in with the Mg-bearing ore. In the smelting process some Mg tends to fuse with S and float to the surface where it can be skimmed or otherwise removed and discarded, leaving a much better product.

9. Today manganese steels are known as high strength low-alloy steels of relatively lower ductility-perhaps this is a reason Kpelle blacksmiths did not generally water-quench their work. Due to the properties of the alloy it very possibly would have been too hard and brittle if quenched. See also my discussion of the Kpelle 'Well-Tempered Cutlass' (Thomasson 1987: 243–8).

10. As an example, a copy of the controlled commodities 'Price List' from the Liberian Ministry of Commerce, Industry and Transportation which I obtained in early 1982, gives retail price ceilings for locally made tools as follows:

No.	Item	Size	Wholesale price ($)	Retail price($)
104.	Cutlass	Large	2.50	3.00
105.	"	Medium	2.00	2.50
106	"	Small	0.75	1.00
108.	Ax	Large	1.25	1.50
109.	"	Medium	1.00	1.25
110.	"	Small	0.75	1.00
111.	Hoe	Large	1.25	1.50
112.	"	Medium	1.00	1.25
113.	"	Small	0.75	1.00

(Ministry of Commerce, Industry, and Transportation, *n.d.*)

11. From the Nimba range, the LAMCO concession exports raw ore that is up to 69 per cent pure iron, and soil fertility in the form of hardwoods from the vanishing rain forest. Latex (and therefore soil fertility) is exported in similarly enormous amounts with equally dismal returns to the nation. Firestone has, of course, refused for years to put a tire manufacturing plant in Liberia, in spite of the considerable market that exists there and throughout West Africa.

12. While apologetic historical revisionists today are tending to minimise the significance

of these events and the very uncomfortable image of settler-Liberian blacks enslaving tribal-Liberian blacks, the ethnohistorical perspective of Kpelle and other native informants recalling those events has been neglected. People interviewed by the author made clear distinctions between enslaving and being enslaved by neighbouring tribes on the one hand (where one might marry and live some semblance of a 'normal' life, however inferior one's status, or even be ransomed or rescued), and being carried away forever by the coastal peoples on the other. When asked if either condition was like dying, only the latter was so identified.

32. Survival under Stress: Socioecological perspectives on farmers' innovations and risk adjustments

ANIL K. GUPTA

Introduction

IT HAS BEEN suggested that it did not matter if the natural scientists did not interact with the farmers as long as they were developing technologies relevant for ecologically uniform and well endowed conditions such as irrigated plains areas. But, simulating on research stations conditions similar to the wide variety of production environments under which people try to survive in high risk environments is extremely difficult. As a result, most national and international centres of agricultural research recognise the need for on-farm research. Linking the context in which farmers' work, and the context in which scientists work –at station or at farmers' fields – requires precise understanding of the risk adjustment (RA) mechanisms evolved by different classes of rural producers.

We first present the socioecological paradigm in which household adjustment with risks can be studied in a multi-enterprise, multi-market context. In part two we discuss the institutional aspect of research on farmers' RA mechanisms. In part three we have presented a framework in which local/indigenous technical knowledge, and the experimental process of generating this knowledge, can be linked with formal research processes. Empirical examples drawn from historical studies in India, China and other parts of the world dating back to the second century BC are presented. Finally, a case is made for natural scientists to consider research on indigenous knowledge systems as a necessary complement of formal laboratory research. It is hoped that plant physiologists might find the innovations evolved by the farmers with regard to survival of crops/trees in high risk conditions worthy of formal testing before rejecting or accepting any innovation.

Farmers' experiments are not the only prime precursor of generating new technologies. The role of scientists in anticipating future needs of marginal farmers and generating technological options will always remain. However, indigenous knowledge can make in generating at least a few *new* relationships among *old* variables. Some ask. that if extraordinary contributions in farmers' own experimental repertoire, was so strong, why would there have been so many famines in olden times? Our reply is twofold: (a) famine induced distress was not always due to net decline in food availability, a thesis quite popular now; the political economy of 'entitlement', that people lose, may make all the difference. Thus famines may have been caused even when enough food existed; (b) over the years, the excessive emphasis the 'lab-to-land' approach has reduced the appreciation in the minds of the scientists of farmers' risk adjustment strategies. Moreover, massive relief-oriented policy of providing succour to drought affected people, also weakened their self-reliance. Instead of strengthening markets, public delivery systems and local R&D in such regions, we have relied on using famine prone regions as a cheap source of labour (NCDBA 1981). Arguments in this study should be seen in the light of mutual

407

learning, linking formal and informal R&D (Biggs 1981; Gupta, unpublished) rather than one substituting for another.

Part I: socioecological paradigm for household survival under risk

Several studies on the subject of farmers' adjustments with risks have shown a multi-market multi-enterprise approach to survival (Jodha 1975, 1979, 1985, Gupta 1981, 1986, 1987, Spitz 1979, Wisner 1986, Torry 1986, Turton 1985). These studies are reviewed elsewhere (Gupta 1984, 1987). Here we first define the terms and then discuss the socioecological perspective. The multi-market approach implies that farmers tried to adjust to the risks through simultaneous operations in factor and product markets. The factor markets imply land, labour, capital, and information, the product markets imply crops, livestock, and trees, including various technologies of land water use. The higher the amount of risk in the environment, the greater is the dependence between the decision made in one resource market with the other. Also these links are important in developed regions. The difference is that many imperfections in markets in the developedregions can often be offset through market mechanisms.

The multi-enterprise framework implies that farmers' adjustments with risks cannot be understood by concentrating on any one enterprise such as crops, livestock or trees at a time. The 'Four S model', linking Space, Season, Sector and Social stratification given below will further clarify the multi-enterprise focus. Each dimension can be dichotomised for ideal typing purposes. For instance, a 'space' can be dichotomised in terms of population density, or low lands and high lands, or undulated and plain topography. 'Sector' can be dichotomised as agriculture or industry; public or private; specialised or diversified; single crop or diversified crop region; cash crop or food crop.

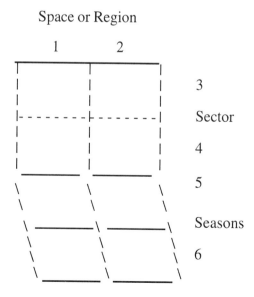

Figure 32.1: *The 'Four S model'*

'Season' can be dichotomised into uni-modal or bi-modal rainfall regions, arid or humid, low rainfall or high rainfall, low seasonality or high seasonality region.

Given any two parameters, the third can be anticipated. For instance, in a region with low population density and high seasonality (*i.e.*, low rainfall), the sectoral characteristics are expected to be intercrops. Likewise, household rather than being dependent on any one enterprise such as crops, livestock, trees or labour, may simultaneously pursue many of these activities at the same time. The social stratification in such regions is expected to be quite different compared to the regions with high population density, low seasonality and specialised sectoral activities involving only one or very few enterprises. In the former case, households may draw assurances from kinship and extended family networks in order to hedge risks. Thus we may find in high risk environments a preponderance of non-monetary exchanges, pooling of bullocks, and implements. In this manner the farmers try to deal with differential demands for draft power, or inputs in different villages or plots at different points of time due to the erratic nature of rainfall, through informal social and economic networks.

As we will see with the help of the socioecological paradigm illustrated in Figure 32.2, the interactions between space, season, and sector generate a range of choices which are not equally available to rich and poor farming households. Understanding of these differences may help natural scientists in developing technologies which will either be amenable to easy adaptation by farmers or will make minimum demands on the system in the short run. In developed regions no such constraint is needed to be taken into account because of strong market forces. Therefore, if a technology required several inputs simultaneously and in a particular proportion, it would not be difficult to organise that in well endowed regions.

The plant architecture cannot be divorced from social and institutional architecture evolved in a given region in a historical context The socioecological paradigm involves two assumptions: (1) ecology defines the range of economic enterprises that can be sustained in a given region; (2) the scale, at which different classes of rural producers manage each enterprise depends upon access of households to factor and product markets, kinship networks, public and other relief mechanisms, and common property resources (such as common grazing land, water tanks, and tree groves).

The asset portfolio is a mix of enterprises which evolved in a given ecological region and resulted in specific production conditions. These conditions could be understood with the help of a mean and variance matrix as shown below.

Households having portfolios with low mean productivity with high variance in output would be most vulnerable. Historically, the extent of poverty has often been most intense in regions, where low mean/high variance is the dominant characteristic of the portfolio. We will discuss in the third section the survival under such conditions of high risk through experimentation and innovation by the farmers.

Reverting back to the socioecological paradigm, we notice that the time frame and the discount rate chosen to appraise the investment choices depends upon (a) the portfolio characteristics, (b) the access to kinship networks, (c) access to intra and inter-household risk adjustments and (d) communal and public RA options. The time frame has a bearing on the sustainability of a technological choice. The shorter the time frame in which households or even the

	Low	Mean Return	High
Low	Low varieties of millets, cattles, long gestration multipurpose tree species, etc.		Mexican varieties of wheat, well adopted small scale vegetable cultivation
Variance			
High	Pulses, oilseed, crops, sheep herd, etc.		Crossbred cattle, hybrid varieties of millets, cotton, other cash crops, etc.

Figure 32.2: *The RA feedback mechanism*

scientists appraise their choices the less likely it is for technology to be sustainable. The discount rate indicates the way future returns from present investments would be converted into a net present value. The more uncertain the outcome, the higher may be the discount rate. The certainty itself may depend upon (a) the previous experience with a particular enterprise/crop, (b) immediate past experience, (c) successive losses or gains, (d) accumulated deficit or surplus in the household cashflow, (e) future expectations of returns, and (f) the complementarity between other assets/enterprises and the proposed investment.

The intra-household RAs include asset disposal, migration and modified consumption. Inter-household imply tenancy, credit and labour contracts. For further details see Jodha and Mascarenhas (1983). The communal RAs include reliance on common property resources. The public relief mechanisms include employment programs as well as aerial pesticides sprayed against pest or disease epidemics.

The result of various RA strategies available to different classes of households may reflect in some households having deficit/subsistence in the budget while others having surplus in the budget. This would have a bearing on the stakes different classes have in the sustainable ecological balance in the given region. This would finally feedback as shown in Figure 32.2 into the portfolios of economic enterprises evolved by different classes.

The purpose of the above discussion is to understand the macro (Four S model) and micro (Socioecological paradigm) context of household decision making in high risk environments. This will provide us with a basis for analysing the institutional contexts in which research on peasant innovation may or may not be done. This will also help us relate the principles of homeostasis as evolved in plant physiology and the socioecological systems.

Homeostasis

The plant physiologists generally define homeostasis at two levels, developmental and physiological. The former deals with adjustments made by plants at different stages of growth while the latter refers to the concurrent adjustments at any particular stage of growth. Likewise, farming households can make adjustments concurrently or over time depending upon the nature of contingency and their repertoire of risk adjustments.

Institutional contexts of research on farmers' risk adjustments

The detailed evidence with regard to this aspect is presented elsewhere (Gupta 1987a, b). We summarise here some of the most important findings which may be of interest to the natural scientists in so far as these may influence the future resource allocation in this direction.

In 1941 Saver recommended 'that the improvement of the genetic base of agricultural crops be predicated on an understanding of the relation of such work to the poorer segments of the society' (Oasa and Jennings 1983: 34). In India more than two decades ago Y.P. Singh pioneered two of the earliest studies aimed at unravelling the traditional farming wisdom regarding animal husbandry practices. A decade later, another study was initiated to understand indigenous dry farming practices (Verma and Singh 1969). Review of post-graduate theses in five disciplines from more than two dozen universities and colleges during 1973 to 1983 did not reveal any other research on similar subjects. Perhaps the contempt for farmers' knowledge is far too deeply embedded in the very structure of formal research institutions. Some of the important factors influencing perception of farmers' practices may be summarised here:

- o A considerable body of knowledge has accumulated on the linkage between formal and informal R & D (Biggs and Clay 1981; Gupta 1980, 1981; Richards 1983; Rhoades 1984; Chambers 1985, 1987; Verma and Singh 1967; Bush 1984). Still the formal scientific institutions consider research on farmers' practices/survival strategies as something non-glamorous. Perhaps the peer pressure, the monitoring system in the research bureaucracies, the norms of accountability of the scientists towards various constituents and the inability of a majority of the social scientists to act as a bridge between farmers and the natural scientists may all contribute towards this problem.
- o There has been an excessive bias in the technology generation process towards individual household oriented alternatives. The common property resource oriented solutions have generally been neglected. For instance, if cooperation in terms of sowing time of a crop could influence the pest build up and eventual intensity of crop damage, then research on such alternatives should take precedence over individual level pest control. Even otherwise, pests cannot be controlled at the individual level efficiently in the long term. Likewise soil and water conservation and consequent availability of moisture at critical stages of crops through common property resources such as farms, ponds, or other means of watershed management call for collective choice alternatives. Historically there are examples of such cooperation amongst farmers for a specific technological alternative.
- o Single disciplinary research could deliver some results when technologies for low risk and well endowed irrigated regions were to be developed.

However, the need for inter- and cross-disciplinary research for dry-farming areas does not need to be emphasised. The management principles which determined or influenced the formation of teams around riskier problems may not be the same as would be the case for easily predictable or less risky problems. How do we build teams to work on farmers' problems when division of responsibility cannot be very precise along disciplinary or functional boundaries?

o Another implication of crop-livestock-tree interactions is not only to have convergence in breeding, and other technological objectives, but also to take into account farmers' survival options while giving primacy to one or the other consideration. For instance, studies have shown that 'present trends in plant selection may be by-passing two important trade offs in the objectives of the farmers, i.e., fodder content of cereals or millets and lignin content of cereal stalks which affects bio-degradation in the soil and has implications for soil fertility' (McDowell 1986). Likewise recent studies have shown that most of the technologies even in dry farming areas are appraised only on the basis of grain yield rather than on the basis of both grain and fodder yield and quality. The data are collected on the entire biomass but are not used for the purposes of screening the lines.

o The purpose of extension in most agricultural universities has become merely to extend knowledge from lab to land rather than vice-versa. Our contention is that given the weak social science departments in most agricultural research institutions there is no substitute to direct interactions between natural scientists and the farmers. We also believe that biological scientists can learn social science concepts far more easily than otherwise.

o The socioeconomic class background of the scientists has some bearing on their perception of the farmers' problems. We do not suggest that scientists with low-risk backgrounds would not be competent to do research on problems of small farmers in high risk environments. However, there may be a tendency on the part of such scientists to consider basic problems as lying with the farmers, banks, and extension systems rather than with the technology itself. The implication is that reorientation of research priorities would require taking note of these worldviews so that alternative perspectives can be better argued. In general, far more scientists perceive farmers' innovations than the ones who decide to work on them.

The scientific context of research on farmers' innovations as are biased towards certain tools and techniques. As Richards (1983: 15) suggests, scholars are sometimes guilty of presenting peasant knowledge as practice without theory. In a historical account of Indian science and technology in the eighteenth century it was noted that many of the scientific discoveries being made in Europe were preceded by the actual farming practices based on the same principles in India (Walker 1820). What are the processes which snapped the link between technologies evolved by the farmers and the researchers who tried to derive a scientific basis for the same? Why did formal research systems in developing countries neglect their own reserve of ancient peasant knowledge? Is it not possible that farmers sometimes may do the right things for the wrong reasons? If so, how do we discriminate ritual from rationality? Is there no comparative advantage in tropical countries with so-called backward agriculture in high risk places?

In the next section we review some of the contemporary as well as ancient practices evolved by the farmers in high risk environments. This may help us in reinitiating a process of reverse transfer of knowledge and concepts. This may also help in building bridges between what farmers know and demand and what they do not know and therefore cannot demand. We have argued elsewhere (Gupta 1987a) that no farmers had demanded dwarf wheat simply because they never knew that such a plant type was possible. The role for supply side interventions by the scientists cannot therefore be ignored or under-played. At the same time what we are suggesting is that in high risk environments because of the complexity inherent in the farming systems the close interaction between scientists and farmers may be far more productive and efficient.

Perception of peasant innovations

In a recent paper (Gupta 1987c) we have tried to understand the barriers to scientific curiosity with regard to perceiving the peasant innovations but not subjecting them to scientific/formal scrutiny.

While arguing for transferring science and not just the technology to the farmers we have suggested the need for abstracting the science underlying farmers' practices. Any value added to such knowledge when transferred back would have far greater diffusion potential. The problems of classifying peasant innovations and building a theory of innovations for survival are beyond the scope of this article. We do however, review some practices which may hold the key to the issue of survival under risk through experimentation and innovation.

Chinese knowledge in the first century BC and the sixth century

An extremely rich account of farmers' knowledge existing in the first century BC (Sheng-Han 1963) and the sixth century (Sheng-Han 1982) provides instances where research on peasant innovations may extend the frontiers of science if pursued properly. We summarise some of these practices derived from these two sources.

○ To get drought tolerant plants the seeds of the cereals could be mixed with a paste of excrement of polyvoltine silkworms with melted snow; *after five or six days when the excrement becomes well softened rub it between hands* (Sheng-Han 1963: 13).
○ The treatment of seeds in extract of certain types of bones from which a decoction is obtained helps the seeds withstand stresses better. In case the described bones are not available the boiled steep of silk reeling basins may be used. When the rains fail in the sowing season of wheat, treatment with sour rice drink (lactic fermentation of cooked rice steep) may help the wheat to become drought resistant while bombyxine excrement may help in the wheat cold tolerance.

While commenting upon practices of these types Sheng-Han (1963: 59) suggests that high content of calcium carbonate in bombyxine excrements is mixed with lactic and acetic acids produced by fermentation of sour rice-grain.

These acids dissolve the calcium carbonate forming a solution of calcium salts of organic acids. Drawing upon the work of Henckel (of the Timiriazeff Institute of Moscow) it was found that wheat corn treated with a solution of $CaCl_2$ enhanced the drought resistance of wheat seedlings. The author has suggested the prescription by Sheng-Chih of treating wheat corn with organic calcium given in the first century BC might have the same effect.

The seed treatment rather than the soil treatment has been analysed from another angle. Excrement of the silkworm was very hygroscopic. While sowing the seeds of millets side by side with the excrement of silkworms, it was thought that the soil in the immediate vicinity of the seed might get enriched by moisture through vapour condensation from atmospheric air. This might improve germination ability. Further, bombyxine excrement contained quite a good amount of easily available potassium, nitrogen and phosphorous together with auxins and vitamins derived from mulberry tree leaves and a host of microbial action. Perhaps under suboptimal temperature and humidity such an inoculation of microbes and the nutrients of the darkness triggered the physiological activities. Perhaps the temperature and the moisture would then rise to the optimal level. The soil surrounding the seeds is expected to undergo changes favourable to the growth of the young radicals.

The author has critically analysed the significance of melted snow as a substitute for bone decoction while treating the seed. In arid Northwestern China, water from the river and particularly from the well was heavily charged by soluble salts present in the soils. Perhaps the sodium and magnesium salts available there might have some undesirable effect on the soil microbes and the seeds. The melted snow would obviously have a far lower content of salts and thus be devoid of harmful ions. The author has strongly recommended further experimental tests of these speculations.

o The bombyxine excrement when mixed with seeds of spiked millet is assumed to protect the millets from insects and other pests.
o To prevent the frost injuries in spiked millet it is advised to look at the night temperature 80–90 days after the sowing. If frost or white dew was suspected, two persons facing each other could drag a rope horizontally right through the crop to remove frost or dew. This should be stopped only after sunrise.

Interestingly, precisely this practice of taking a rope or even a bamboo pole through the nursery of paddy in the early hours of the day was noted in Bangladesh. The explanations offered were to protect the rice from the frost but more importantly to provide dew to the roots of the plant. It does not need to be mentioned that formal research on physiological aspects of such a practice had not been initiated in Bangladesh and for that matter in other countries as well.

o Drawing upon the work of Yao Shu compiling a sort of agricultural encyclopedia as of the sixth century, several suggestions have been given for linking the type of bone decoction to be used for treating the seeds *vis-á-vis* the type of soil. For instance for red hard soil the bone decoction of oxen has been suggested, whereas the decoction of the bones of hogs has been suggested for sowing in the clay soil. Research on the effect of gelatinous coats and the salts on moisture absorption and microbial activity remains to be seriously pursued.
o Extremely meticulous recipes have been given for preparing the shallow pit manure for growing melons and other crops.

In a study on indigenous knowledge of women around homestead production in Bangladesh we had found a similarly rich variety of manure compositions.

Chinese philosophical thinking very strongly underlined harmony of three cardinal factors, proper season, proper soil and proper human efforts, similar to our Four S model. While much more work remains to be done on the subject we will now review some of the practices noted in our own work in India.

The contemporary Indian experiene

We may add here, that there is a vast inventory of practices recorded from different parts of the country including both drought and flood-prone regions. These are a few examples to underline the importance of generating hypotheses from farmers' practices for formal research.

- o *Early planting of gram* During field work in 1985 in collaboration with Hiranand and Mandavkar as a part of our study on Matching Farmers' Concerns with technologists, Objectives in Dry Regions, we studied the issue of farmers' innovations and their recognition or lack of it by the scientists. In some cases we took examples of so-called irrational practices of the farmers from interviews with the scientists. And we pursued with farmers a more in-depth explanation of their rationality.

  Early planting of gram was reported to make it more vulnerable to wilt attack. Sowing was begun in the month of October and the main factor taken into account was soil temperature. The method of taking soil temperature varied in different villages at a small distance in the area of the study in Western Haryana. Soils in the village of Kasoli were predominantly loam rather than sandy loam. The soil temperature was noted by walking bare foot at noon time or by smelling the odour which emanated when water was dropped on the ground while drinking. In other villages another indicator, the rising of dust in the evening when animals returned after grazing, was investigated. Some other farmers felt that blooming of certain plants or sighting of certain birds could also indicate the appropriateness of the temperature. A farmer proposed a counter hypothesis about wilt attack and early sowing of gram. He felt that gram sown early might yield higher despite higher vulnerability to wilt attack because grain setting was completed by mid-February. By this time the strong winds or increase in temperature might affect the crop adversely.

  It is possible that none of the hypotheses mentioned above may be valid even if practice was still considered to be useful. The issue is not whether hypotheses derived by the farmers would prove superior to the ones generated by the scientists. The issue is, are there some relationships between biotic, edaphic, climatic and human factors important for survival of crops and the cultivators which people have derived intuitively even if not systematically. To what extent do these intuitive hypotheses deserve to be scientifically probed?
- o *PPST (Patriotic and People Oriented Science and Technology Foundation, Madras)* PPST recently brought out a bibliography on Indian agriculture and plant sciences (April 1987) which is a very rich reference source on the subject in the country. Perhaps the issue of linking formal and informal research cannot be delayed or ignored any further. The Academy of Development Science, Karjat, Maharashtra, and the Academy of Young Scientists, Chandigarh are other groups which are engaged in research on indigenous knowledge systems including plant sciences. If the community of plant physiologists consider some of these issues worthy of attention that they might consider initiating not only a formal dialogue but also

institutional innovations that can link knowledge that people have with the knowledge that they need to have to improve their livelihood systems.

Innovations from humid tropics: Bangladesh

The author recently had an opportunity of spending a year with agricultural scientists in Bangladesh, with specific reference to the development of methodologies and systems for on-farm research. One of the important objectives was to draw upon peasant innovations while developing a formal research agenda.

Some examples which might interest plant physiologists are mentioned here.

o When it was found that farmers were able to market tomatoes kept quite fresh even in the off seasons the agricultural administrators were keen to find out the reasons. Abedin and his colleagues were confronted with this problem. The best way to understand this problem was to ask the farmers themselves. Farmers uprooted the whole tomato plant before tomatoes were ripe and hung upside down in well-aired, shady places. The flow of chemicals responsible for ripening was impeded by this process. If this method has some validity, by adding modern scientific knowledge a useful technology could be developed as was done in the case of diffused light for the potato storage system.

o In case cucurbits, a widely found problem is the delayed transformation from the vegetative to the reproductive stage or sometimes excessive flowering without culmination into fruiting. Farmers in Bangladesh tried different methods to overcome this problem. They provided a vertical incision in the vine and inserted opium, tobacco, or just left it like that and found onset of fruiting.

o The jute capsularis seed abstract was used for controlling stem borer in paddy. The planking and laddering after 30–45 days in paddy and 20–25 days in wheat was found to have a positive effect on tillering of the crop.

o Women scientists who studied various household practices discovered several innovative strategies of risk adjustment which deserve further study. For instance it was noted that a banana plant grown in between four betelnut trees in north-west Bangladesh held in moisture available to the betelnut roots through banana suckers in stress periods.

There could be a large number of other practices which deserve to be studied systematically if for no other reason than to extend the frontiers of science.

Conclusion

We have suggested in this article that in the process of adjusting to risks various classes of household devise numerous risk adjustment strategies. At the macro level these could be studied with the help of the Four S model, which includes interaction between space–sector–season–social stratification. At the micro level, the socioecological paradigm could be of help. It essentially builds upon access of households to factor and product markets, and ecological and other resources; these include assurances available regarding risk (climatic, social *i.e.*, how would others behave given one's own behaviour, temporal *i.e.*, future returns from present investments), and abilities (skills) of the households to convert access to investments, given various assurances.

We have reviewed some of the institutional factors which influence perception of peasant innovations. Later we have drawn upon some of the specific examples of farmer experimentation in high-risk environments in China, India and Bangladesh. We have a far richer inventory of such practices than what has been presented in this chapter.

Our contention is that while in some cases rituals might dominate the rationality of peasant survival mechanisms, there are certainly many cases where peasant knowledge deserves to be systematically understood, analysed and built upon while generating new alternatives for technological development. In this process we would have not merely start to the process of transferring science, instead of only technologies, to the farmers, but also generate an alternative 'college of peers' involving poor farmers, pastoralists, and tenants who would collaborate in research and also validate knowledge so produced. There would still remain a case for some research being guided by scientists' own vision and imagination. What we are submitting is a small step, linking peasant science with modern science and technology in a manner that the knowledge generating systems in the rural areas are not converted into just the knowledge receiving systems. We believe that this is possible and would perhaps be pursued even by those who wonder whether we are not moving the wheel backwards!

Appendix 32.1: Upland research and development strategies

Methods \ Function	Prob. ident	Sel site	Plan	Diag	Under-stand	Screen tech	Inter-vene	Basic res	Vali-date	Extn	Moni eval.	Inst. Inno.
Socioecon. Survey	?	?	?	?	x	?			?		?	
RRA	x	x	x	?	?	?		?	////?///		?	
Sondeo	?	?	x	?	?	?		?	?		?	
Diagnostic			?	////x///	////x///	////x///			////?///			?
C.I.P.S.	?	?	x	?	?							
Farmers Expt.								////x///	////?///			
Agroecology	x	?	x	?	x	?		?			?	
Farm to Farm												
Ethnographic	?				x						////x///	
Transect	x	x		?	x						?	
Situation anal.					x						?	x
Benchmark Surv	?	x	?	?	?					x		
2' Data	x	////x///									////x///	
COBARMS	x	?	?	?	?	?				?	?	?
PDR			x		x						////x///	////x///
People Sch.										////x///		?
Demo/Pilot										?		
CPI/OFT						?	x	x				
T & V	?		?	?					?			
Lab/Stations						?		x	?			

Appendix 32.2: An example of farmers' risk diagrams:
BRGY SanVicente – Daram, Western Samar

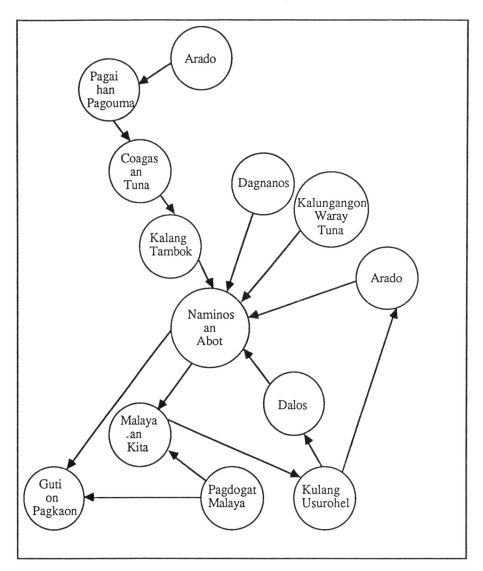

33. Transfer of Indigenous Knowledge and Protection of the Agricultural Environment in Eastern Africa

KEES J. STIGTER

If local knowledge is to be the key to participation and local development, it is the outsiders who have to be convinced, it is outsiders who will have to translate and exploit Indigenous Technical Knowledge in projects and programmes. (Michael McCall 1987)

Introduction

IN THEIR RECENT impact study of agricultural research in tropical Africa, Jahnke, Kirsche and Lagermann (1987) state that any beneficial role of International Agricultural Research (IAR), relates to the re-orientation of National Agricultural Research (NAR), the enhancement of scientific capital (including human capital) and the systematic elaboration of promising research areas in view of a slow but sure progress in agricultural production. The strength of NAR is the crucial problem for IAR success in tropical Africa. Despite severe shortcomings of NAR and its even negative effect on IAR impact, no substitute for NAR exists. For the fairness of argument, it should be added that IAR has had negative effects on African NAR as well. High priority should therefore be given to strengthening and improving appropriately the performance of African NAR (Jahnke *et al.* 1987; Stigter and Weber 1989).

This priority is one cornerstone of the rationale of the project Traditional Techniques of Microclimate Improvement (TTMI). The project started officially in 1985, after a successful trial of its approach in the early eighties at the University of Dar es Salaam, Tanzania. Another cornerstone is the belief in the content of McCall's (1987) statement used to introduce this chapter, with the explicit addition that the scientists participating from within Africa in NAR are or have become outsiders in this respect as well. A third cornerstone is the conclusion drawn from national (Stigter 1985) and international (Stigter 1988a) surveys that many traditional environmental management and manipulation techniques, especially those developed in harsh and marginal environments or under increasing intensity of land-use, are highly protective with respect to the agricultural environment.

A last cornerstone is the conviction that outside scientists could contribute to better understanding of Indigenous Technical Knowledge (ITK), thus to a more relevant assessment of its transferability. This could be done mainly by studying seriously and quantifying appropriately the endangered tropical environment of traditional farming to reveal parts of the cause and effect relationships (Howes 1980; Stigter and Darnhofer 1989; Stigter *et al.* 1989a).

Project strategy

The TTMI Project, internationally backstopped from The Netherlands, works with local PhD candidates, who are either junior staff members of local universities or of other local NAR institutes, supervised by teams of mainly local co-supervisors. The students do their theses on jointly-identified local problems of low external-input farmers. The theses involve the understanding and subsequent use of ITK of microclimate management and manipulation such as mulching, shading, wind protection, and other surface modification techniques. Such ITK principles may have been developed in the area concerned or transferred from experience obtained elsewhere. The ultimate aim of all PhD research is to develop a weather advisory system (Stigter and Weiss 1986). This may be defined as a production advisory regarding the use of manipulation of meteorological conditions in or close to the space occupied by crops and animals or their products to increase quantity and quality of these crops, animals and yields and their protection as well as that of the production environment.

The background ideas of TTMI, its first steps, the difficulties met, and some early results have been well-documented (Stigter 1987a, 1987b; Stigter *et al.* 1987a, 1987b, 1989b, 1989c, 1989d). Recently, such approaches as ours were independently advocated by Harrison (1987) and Moris (1988). In this contribution we want to discuss to what extent actual transfer of ITK and ITK principles is possible with respect to protection of the agricultural environment in Africa, the ultimate aim of the TTMI Project.

Transfer of indigenous technical knowledge

One of the outcomes of our surveys of traditional techniques confirmed earlier findings (Allan 1965) that ITK in East Africa was extremely local, and transfer apparently very limited (Stigter 1988a). East Africa is populated primarily by agro-pastoral societies. If aesthetics are culturally based, as Kamera and Mwakasaka (1981) state, then the East African creative and critical lore must derive from the sociocultural milieu in which indigenous East African move and have their being. By analysing East African folktales Kamera and Mwakasaka (1981) show that 'knowledge' is most often dealt with in the taboo sphere. In the Pare tale called 'Wisdom', this is strongly worded. 'Know how to keep your secrets. Even if you have a friend dearer than yourself, even if you have a wife you love more than your life, keep your secrets from them', an old man advises after having been asked for some words of wisdom. And when the man who was told this violates this rule, he loses his wealth, which he has wanted to trade for wisdom. The Chaga, from whose environmental management experience on the slopes of the Kilimanjaro so much may be learned (O'kting'ati 1984; Fernandes *et al.* 1984, Maro 1988), have a tale which with the tragic words of Morile 'Mother, I told you; Mother I warned you; don't feed me on taboos.' He meant that his mother should not have broken the food taboos of somebody else. Whether this is at least part of the explanation for the highly location-specific environmental management and manipulation of ITK in agricultural undertakings and the apparent lack of its transfer can only be speculated upon. However, the highly ethnic specificity of the knowledge that we collected in Tanzania points into this direction (compare Brokensha *et al.* 1980; Harrison 1987).

Differences in success to survive pressures of a dense population and the problems harsh environments pose are mainly due to the skill and diligence with which local groups in Africa apply themselves to the task of farming (Anthony *et al.* 1979) Knowing that population pressure will keep growing for quite some time and that this and other factors severely endanger the agricultural environment, we should assist in transferring, adapting, validating, and improving what were locally shown to be the most promising natural resource management techniques. Kusum Nair (1983) states that the capacity to provide back-up research to support and main high levels of productivity of improved practices and plant varieties that are available is very limited in Africa. In fact, even the methodology for tailoring technical packages to fit location-specific requirements has yet to be developed. This is particularly true when technical packages would be introduced from beyond Africa (World Bank 1981; OTA 1984; Elfring 1985; Wolf 1986).

However, only a decade ago, the studies of Brokensha and Riley (1980), Richards (1980), Belshaw (1980), Knight (1980), Howes and Chambers (1980), Howes (1980) and Warren (1980), to mention those most important with respect to the agricultural environment in Brokensha, Warren and Werner (1980), clearly demonstrated that the ethnoscientific approach was one way out of this dilemma and the more so in the present conditions of rapid change. However, this publication also showed that actual information was still widely scattered and relatively little used in rural development projects and programmes for low-input farmers. On the other hand, it provided a consistent picture of the value of ITK and the potential of its use, a picture completely different from what was generally portrayed in the past. The main question which remains is *Where do we go from here in practice?*

Proposals, as in the study of Howes and Chambers (1980), were setting the trends. Work of Richards (1985) and Chambers and Ghildyal (1985) started to provide the necessary details. Developments, as exemplified by the appearance of the ILEIA Newsletter (1985–90), showed that winds of change were starting to blow. More recently, McCall (1987) concluded from his own review of East Africa that ITK may act as both the means and the end in promoting rural peoples' participation as a condition in local development. A bibliography on ITK by the same author (McCall 1988), forms a strong foundation for the study of ITK and its principles in East Africa.

However, there remains a long way to go and over-optimism might be dangerous. Paul Harrison (1987), in his optimistic but inspiring chapter on 'The Secrets of Success' also takes participation as the key. He states that none of the successful projects he described involves any increase in the exposure to climatic risk. Indeed, many of them reduce risks and protect farmers and their crops and animals against the vagaries of the climate. Harrison assesses that agroforestry is arguably the single most important discipline for the future of sustainable development in Africa. However, compared to our TTMI experience, he oversimplifies matters by noting that the basic principles of alley cropping are so straightforward they can be put across in six simple drawings with one-sentence captions.

With this warning against oversimplification, we will next discuss the difficulties we met in our project strategy. We seriously tried to contribute to the transfer and use of ITK and ITK principles, in some well-defined priority areas of microclimate management and manipulation.

Examples of success and failure

Alley cropping We read about the successes obtained with alley cropping, an alternative to shifting cultivation. The latter aspect is now endangering the agricultural environment. Alley cropping is based on indigenous knowledge of combining crops and trees (Kang, Wilson and Lawson 1984). Therefore, we joined the Dryland Agroforestry Research (DAR) Project set up by several Kenyan NAR Institutes, advised by the Agroforestry IAR Institute ICRAF, at Machakos, 70 km. east of Nairobi. DAR studied on-station an alley cropping system of the local staple maize, grown between *Cassia siamea* trees. After seven seasons maize can be planted twice a year in this area (Coulson *et al.* 1989; Mungai *et al.* 1989; Stigter *et al.* 1989d). We concluded that this particular system should not be recommended to farmers. Only in average and especially in above average rainfall seasons, the maize between the trees, of which prunings are used as mulches to sustain soil fertility, yields better. In below average rainfall seasons, when the conditions for reasonable yields are most difficult, the trees compete too much. The maize yields between the Cassia become even less than on the unmulched soil without the trees.

The conclusion must be that it was wise not to have trials of this system on-farm, as the risk was too high. Apparently we do not understand alley cropping under semi-arid conditions sufficiently for the right choices yet to be made. But what to do now? As in all applied scientific research, there are some options. Did we make the wrong choice? Do we continue the maize/Cassia system in other management options? Would the system have been more beneficial, because more protective, under higher rainfall run-off conditions in the plots without trees? Do we try other systems? Can the farmer wait for us? Or did we only contribute just one more stone to the ivory tower (Knight 1980)? We would like to conclude that, given the small pieces of relevant knowledge we have collected over these four years, we should continue this on-station work. We should learn how to design systems of trees and crops that take their water and nutrients from different horizons, so compete less. Also we should look closer into the long-term sustainability of yields for these systems (Moris 1988). But we have also to conclude with Nair (1983) that development of 'effective technical packages' for each region and each farming system could take not a few years but decades. Even though we based ourselves on transfer of ITK principles. Again Harrison (1987) might be too optimistic here. He states that given modest extra resources and guidance, African farmers will be capable of rapid advances that could transform Africa's food outlook within a decade.

Shelterbelts At the regional University of Gezira in Wad Medani, Central Sudan, our local co-supervisors and one of the local PhD candidates identified an urgent desertification problem in the north-western part of the Gezira. It is part of a huge one million ha gravity irrigated, low external input, water management scheme that derives its water from the Blue Nile. We decided to take up the challenges to understand how a shelterbelt of irrigated Eucalyptus succeeded to keep the sand out of the canals and fields. It had been established by the National Forest Department and FAO over five km. long and 200-500 m. wide. The ultimate aim would be to give indications on design criteria. The farmers had to get interested by paying special attention to the arguments they normally use against the large scale introduction of trees in the Gezira. We quantified wind fields and sand transport in front of and within the belt edge. After four year we have largely understood the mechanisms, although we are still surprised by the survival power of the trees in the front lines, after deposition of two meters of sand (Stigter *et al.* 1989a, 1989b, 1989d). The use of trees for this purpose of keeping sand out of irrigation schemes appears to be traditional in Egypt. It was developed there by the farmers themselves and therefore not much written evidence of such establishments could be detected. An Egyptian consultant of one of our local funders confirmed their existence (M.H. El-Lakany, personal communication, 1986). Our PhD candidate at present participates successfully in the attempts of the local Forest Authorities to plan, together with the tenants, more of these belts and other tree plantings within the scheme. A series of objections had been demonstrated to apply less to our trees as long as they get their minimum share of irrigation water (A. El-Tayeb Mohamed, personal communication, 1989). Also the visibly encroaching sands in the area have certainly contributed to convince farmers that something should be done. Their need for wood products and the general scarcity of fire wood and poles are other arguments that count. Again, as in the first example, transfer of ITK principles more than of well articulated ITK *per sé* took place. But it had appreciable more success in this case. One could argue that the urgency of the problem of protecting their agricultural environment more than the applicability of ITK principles has caused the change of mind among the tenants. But certainly their participation in the arguments about the disadvantages and advantages of trees in the Gezira has played an important role, as well as the fact that those scientists/administrators involved wanted to understand and react to their objections.

Trees and, again, trees It is certainly not accidental that two other TTMI subprojects, both tackled by the same Tanzanian Ph.D. candidate, use ITK on trees. Trees have many protective functions in the agricultural environment (Stigter 1988b). These two sub-projects are on wind protection. The first one has been designed to obtain basic information in an actual tropical savannah woodlot edge condition on wind reduction by scattered trees with a density that a crop could easily be grown between them. This work was taken up because of the almost complete absence of any quantification of this method of wind protection. Our surveys indicated it to be an excellent example of African ITK (Stigter 1984). At the same time we obtain highly useful information as countervailing power to the cutting of trees in the Sahelian and other parts of Africa that increasingly suffer from wind erosion problems (Baldy 1986; Baumer 1987). The measured wind reductions at two heights within the tree space, in the order of 50 per cent over less than 100 m of trees, are indeed impressive (R.M.R. Kainkwa, personal communication 1989).

The second project was based on straight local ITK. The Director of the Agricultural (formerly Coffee) Research Station in Lyamungu near Moshi in Kilimanjaro Region (North Tanzania) had pointed out to us that local farmers do not want to follow the extension advice to cut shade trees above their coffee. They believe in their wind protection function for the coffee bushes (D.L. Kessy, personal communication 1986). Several years of experiments have shown the farmers to be right. The umbrella type of trees appear to offer protection against occasional but devastating high vertical winds just before and during violent showers. The horizontal winds that we quantified were slightly increased by a tuneling effect. High horizontal winds do not occur in most of this area, contrary to the region where the first experiment was carried out (R.M.R. Kainkwa, personal communication 1989). In the shade trees above coffee example one cannot talk about transfer of ITK, because the example is rather location specific. But the value of local ITK was once more demonstrated and could be used as a countervailing power. In the savannah woodlot edge case, quantitative knowledge about important ITK is now available for transfer and has already drawn attention from within West Africa.

An example of farmer-induced change The last of our first four ITK inspired TTMI PhD studies nearing completion is again one in the Gezira, Central Sudan. A very different one, again identified for study by local co-supervisors in the TTMI Project. Traditional tenants in the Gezira scheme have over the past years, especially since independence, slowly abandoned their traditional labour intensive ways of irrigation *angaya by angaya*, as you find it still applied directly along the borders of the Nile (Mohammed and Tiffen 1986). The main reasons appear to be economical in nature, with respect to paid labour for such management. These days water is applied continuously in the day-time, and sometimes illegally at night, leaving standing water on the soil for some longer time. They apply in general more water per unit of time and land and cause some soil erosion near outlet pipes. It is the feeling of the administration and some intervening international organisations in structural adjustment programmes that water is wasted this way. But nobody actually came forward to support or disprove these arguments. We are therefore trying on-farm, with the immediate participation of local tenants, to compare water-use efficiency of sorghum and groundnut under the former traditional labour intensive approach and the present unattended *laissez faire* modes of irrigation. The preliminary trend of the results points towards an appreciably higher water use efficiency. Only groundnuts give also more actual yield with the traditional method.

A host of other factors, such as intercrop yields, are as important as the method of irrigation (A.A. Ibrahim, personal communication, 1989). The soil erosion concerned appears minimal but there is more risk of groundnut failures in the unattended mode. We also attempt to compare remaining 'wastage of water' with other losses from the canals, when the water is on its way over one hundred and more kilometres, and from Lake Sennar that supplies the system. In the latter investigation we surprisingly could prove that the present calculations of evaporation of Lake Sennar are much too high. The result could have appreciable consequences for the distribution of Nile water between Egypt and Sudan (Ibrahim *et al.* 1989; Abdullai *et al.* 1990). In this example it was the participation of local tenants in the evaluation of the change from traditional ITK to modern ITK that made all the difference, but they insisted on being compensated for lost yields, if any, in applying their traditional methods again.

Final remarks

The above examples prove the variety of ways in which ITK and transfer of ITK and its principles come into the picture in our different sub-projects in the three East African countries concerned. This is confirmed by our numerous more recent attempts to mount new sub-projects on the same footing (Stigter *et al.* 1989d). This first and foremost proves the enormous variation in the kinds of problems of the agricultural environment locally identified as priorities for study at the PhD and MSc levels. It also shows the necessity for interdisciplinarity of any attempt to contribute to the solution of such problems.

Our work confirms many of the problems that occur in the earlier inventories in Brokensha *et al.* (1980). It has gone already a long way in obtaining new credit for the ethnoscientific approach by just throwing itself into the water and being forced to swim. Rereading such procedures as brought forward by Belshaw (1980) for participatory research, we get the strong impression that such rules may fit better in relatively simple interventions such as the introduction of a new variety of farm implement (Jahnke *et al.* 1987). They are less rigorously applicable to the environmental issues we work on. We nevertheless conclude (compare Moris, 1988, for an identical reasoning) that our less strict project strategy has contributed, using ITK and/or ITK principles, to the solution of problems. Problems that were locally felt, by the farmers as well as the scientists concerned as agricultural environment protection priorities. They could be tackled within the limits of NAR. What else can we want for the future in IAR than getting ever closer to the best problem identification and the best solutions with ever more powerful NAR that put an ever growing confidence in ITK?

Acknowledgments

Co-supervisor, PhD candidates and MSc students, local authorities and not the least local farmers and tenants are thankfully acknowledged for sharing so many of their ideas among each other and with me over the past five years of the TTMI Project. The Netherlands Ministry of Foreign Affairs, DGIS/DPO/OT, is acknowledged as the core funder of the TTMI research.

34. CIKARD: A global approach to documenting indigenous knowledge for development

D. MICHAEL WARREN AND GERARD McKIERNAN

Indigenous knowledge and development

THE CENTRE FOR Indigenous Knowledge for Agriculture and Rural Development (CIKARD) was established in 1987 at Iowa State University. CIKARD is dedicated to interdisciplinary research, training, and extension activities that will assist domestic and international development agencies and practitioners to reduce poverty, enhance equity, reduce environmental degradation, help rural areas work toward self-sufficiency and self reliance, and provide mechanisms to improve local participation to the development process. CIKARD focuses its activities on documenting and preserving the indigenous knowledge of farmers and other rural people around the globe, and making this knowledge available to development professionals and scientists.

Indigenous Knowledge (IK) is local knowledge – knowledge that is unique to a given culture or society. This is in contrast to the international knowledge system generated through the global network of universities and research institutes. IK is the basis for local-level decision-making in agriculture, health care, food preparation, education, natural resource management, and a host of other endeavours in rural communities. By documenting these systems, we can compare and contrast them with the international knowledge systems. It is impossible to identify those aspects of the indigenous knowledge systems (IKS) that are beneficial as well as those that could be improved using technologies available through the international system. Development professionals increasingly are recognising the value of indigenous knowledge in helping them work more effectively with local communities to solve their agricultural and environmental problems.

Indigenous knowledge is important if development activities are to be successful. If it has not been documented, it remains largely inaccessible to development workers seeking solutions to locally defined problems. Solutions offered through a development project may fail because they do not fit in well with the local knowledge system. The success of a development project often depends on local participation. Familiarity with indigenous knowledge can help change agents to understand and communicate more effectively with local people, enhancing the possibilities for participatory approaches to development and sustainablity of these efforts. This enables project staff and local people to work as partners in planning and implementing development activities.

The role of CIKARD

The mission of CIKARD involves the development of cost-effective mechanisms to facilitate participatory and sustainable approaches to domestic and international agricultural and rural development. CIKARD's activities are based on the following objectives:

o to act a clearinghouse for documenting, collecting, and disseminating information on indigenous agricultural and rural development knowledge;
o to develop improved methods for documenting this knowledge;
o to conduct training courses on indigenous knowledge for extension and other development workers;
o to support interdisciplinary research on indigenous knowledge systems; and
o to promote the establishment of regional and national indigenous knowledge resource centres.

CIKARD currently concentrates its efforts on documenting and disseminating information on these indigenous systems and structures:

o the knowledge systems themselves (such as local soil taxonomies);
o the decision-making systems based on this knowledge (such as what crops grow best on which soils);
o the organisational structures through which decisions are made and implemented (such as farmers' problem-identification groups); and
o innovations and experimentation that lead to acceptable changes (such as new approaches to crop pest management).

The structure of CIKARD

The Director of CIKARD reports to the Dean of the College of Agriculture and, through the Dean, to the Provost of Iowa State University. Three Associate Directors coordinate the activities for the Documentation Unit and Library, the Research Unit, and the Training and Consultancy Unit. Three Regional Coordinators maintain communications with regional and national centres in Asia, Latin America, and Africa. CIKARD is guided by an interdisciplinary Internal Advisory Committee composed of Iowa State University faculty and administrators as well as State of Iowa community leaders. An international External Advisory Board is comprised of a network of individuals committed to indigenous knowledge and development from the USA, Costa Rica, Great Britain, Sudan, Peru, The Philippines, Nigeria, India, The Netherlands, China, Kenya, Finland, Mali, and Japan. Members of the External Board are called upon to provide policy guidance, identify possible funding sources, and assist in the establishment and support of regional as well as national indigenous knowledge resource centres. The External Board also provides an international communications network linking CIKARD to other comparable programs and institutions.

CIKARD activities are carried out by research associates, an interdisciplinary and international group of faculty and graduate students at Iowa State University and sister institutions. Currently the CIKARD research associates represent the academic fields of journalism and mass communications, development anthropology, community and regional planning, agricultural education, agronomy, soil science, rural sociology, international development studies, forestry, library science, veterinary medicine, and agricultural economics. They include citizens of Bolivia, Nepal, the USA, China, Korea, Kenya, Taiwan, Mexico, Burkina Faso, Nigeria, Zimbabwe, Germany, The Netherlands, Great Britain, India, Dominican Republic, Costa Rica, and Malaysia.

The CIKARD Documentation Unit and Library of Indigenous Knowledge

In the fall of 1988, a Documentation Unit and Library of Indigenous Knowledge was formally established as part of CIKARD. It serves the centre in its efforts to document, analyse, and use indigenous knowledge for agriculture and rural development. The identification, organisation, and management of the literature of indigenous knowledge, as well as documents which record the application of such knowledge, are primary activities of the unit. Although there has been increased awareness of the potential value of indigenous knowledge for development, particularly in the developing nations, access to the literature related to this interdisciplinary topic has been inadequate. The nature and characteristic of this literature are among the reasons for this situation.

As a field of study, research on indigenous knowledge potentially can encompass many aspects of a variety of disciplines. A high portion of the literature can be found in anthropological, economic, sociological, and agricultural sources. Although medical, technical, and biological publications also contain a significant number of relevant titles. Comprehensive access to this literature has been severely limited as a result of its wide distribution and multidisciplinary nature.

Access

Few indexes or abstracts cover the range of subjects in the field, and fewer still cover the subject in sufficient depth to provide access that is adequate, appropriate, and relevant. Although free-text searching of on-line databases does permit identification of additional titles, lack of appropriate indexing terms and inconsistent policies and practices in these and other finding aids restrict access to all potentially appropriate publications. In many instances, the aspect relating to indigenous knowledge is not represented directly but is included under a broad heading, represented differently in different records in the same index, abstracting service, or database; in a significant number of instances it is ignored completely.

Although indexing vocabularies, policies, and practices have a direct effect on identifying relevant publications in any field, adequate and appropriate acquisition and coverage of the literature by indexing and abstracting services is fundamental to identification. A significant portion of the literature of many disciplines is covered by commercial indexing and abstracting services in printed and machine-readable formats, yet an equally significant portion of the literature of every discipline is not covered by most services, namely its 'grey literature.'

Grey literature

Long considered of limited use in scholarship, 'fugitive,' or 'non-conventional' literature, as it is also known, has become recognised over the past several years as a valuable resource for research. Indeed, several studies have concluded that non-conventional literature can constitute from 40 per cent to 60 per cent of the literature of certain disciplines or publications of particular countries. Special studies, reports, proposal, and conference papers are common examples of fugitive literature. In view of of the diversity and the availability of the literature relating to indigenous knowledge, and as a result of an expressed need on the part of research personnel worldwide, CIKARD has established an International Documentation Unit and Library of Indigenous Knowledge.

The Centre will manage and provide appropriate access to this important resource and assist regional and national centres in the establishment of a similar resource pool to serve their interests and needs.

Collection policies

Although CIKARD has a general interest in all areas related to indigenous knowledge and its application, its main interests are ethnoscience and indigenous technology and their relationship to agricultural and rural development. CIKARD is actively involved not only in the development and use of methodologies for recording indigenous knowledge, but also with the incorporation of indigenous knowledge and its inherent aspects into formal and informal education and economic-development programs.

CIKARD is also interested in approaches that have been demonstrated as effective in creating appropriate and sustainable development. Programmes, methods, and techniques that encourage local participation in local projects, as well as those that promote self-reliance and self-sufficiency are also of interest. Traditional and appropriate methods that meet the basic needs for food, clothing, and shelter are of particular concern, as are practices that enhance the sustainability of these methods. Modern scientific methods that can augment traditional indigenous methods and practices and that are appropriate for use by indigenous people are of particular interest.

Collection development

At present, the centre holds a significant number of key papers and reports in these areas. Although its holdings are significant, they represent only a portion of the literature and descriptions believed to exist. In order to enhance its present library collections, CIKARD actively seeks the donation of relevant papers, reports, studies, and descriptions from personnel associated with local, regional, national, and international organisations and associations involved in areas of interest to the centre.

CIKARD is interested in all sources that contain information related to indigenous knowledge and its mission. Although its collection consists primarily of 'fugitive' literature, CIKARD has, in recent months, acquired a significant number of journal articles and monographs as a result of major literature reviews on ethnoveterinary medicine and indigenous tree management. The latter commissioned by the Food and Agriculture Organisation of the United Nations.

To fully develop its collection, CIKARD plans to cooperate with future regional and national centres to systematically review all appropriate abstracts and indexes in the life and social sciences to identify additional publications relevant to its mission and interests.

Acquisitions and accessions

Upon receipt, documents are marked with the centre's stamp. Each is then reviewed to determine the general nature of the document for cataloguing purposes. Accordingly, each is then placed in a file folder with a standard cataloguing workform appropriate to the document. The item is then assigned an accession number designating the year received and the next available number in a sequence of item numbers (*e.g.* 90–604, 90–605, 90–606). The author, title, current date, and accession number are recorded in an accession log and provide preliminary access to the library's collection. The document, cataloguing workform, and file folder are stamped with the identical accession number.

These procedures provide the necessary physical control as the document is processed and simple, effective bibliographic control as it is used. Accessioned documents in their folders are then filed in accession number order in an appropriate file cabinet for subsequent descriptive cataloguing and indexing. File cabinets and folders are the most appropriate means of storage for the collection at this time, as it consists mainly of reprints, papers, reports, manuscripts, and similar types of documents.

Descriptive cataloguing

After accessioning, individual documents are described in accordance with standardised cataloguing procedures. Current library cataloguing rules serve as guidelines to assure consistency and uniformity. The author, title, pagination, place of publication, publishers, and date are among the types of cataloguing data extracted from each document. Analogous cataloguing elements can be identified and assigned to original field descriptions or documents that summarise specific examples of indigenous knowledge or its application. Within limits, the full text of field notes also can be input along with cataloguing data.

To facilitate the descriptive cataloguing of the documents, we use PRO-CITE, a bibliographic software package from Personal Bibliographic Software, Inc., of Ann Arbor, Michigan. PRO-CITE offers twenty different types of cataloguing workforms appropriate to specific types of documents, most notably journal articles, reports, conference proceedings and papers, monographs, and manuscripts. Each workform solicits cataloguing information specific and appropriate to the document, as well as information common to all items, including notes, call numbers, index terms, and abstract.

Indexing

To provide comprehensive and appropriate access to the content and subject of each catalogued document, each will be fully indexed. Documents can be indexed by using the identical PRO-CITE software used for descriptive cataloguing.

We have adopted an indexing vocabulary consisting mainly of terms used to index the literature of agriculture, agriculturally related subjects, and rural development, that of the Commonwealth Agricultural Bureaux International (CABI). As we begin to actively index the collection, the CABI base index will be enriched by terms from other appropriate indexing vocabularies in the areas of development, ethnography, and science. Concepts not expressed by standard indexing terms will be represented by appropriate terms from the body this of literature and from specific ethnographic descriptions. Each catalogued document will receive indexing terms that reflect its content at both the specific and broad levels to assure the highest precision as well as the highest recall for retrieval.

After considerable discussion within CIKARD, we have decided that several categories are necessary and appropriate for indexing this literature. Among these are relevant ethnic groups, plant and animal species, geographic and political areas, and material culture. Popular as well as scientific names will be assigned, if provided. Ethnic names used are those adopted by the source group itself. To assist in the preparation of a network directory, we also plan to note named individuals and organisations. For each specific subject term assigned to a document, a general term also will be assigned to provide an appropriate level of retrieval.

Recently, several CIKARD associates began indexing publications in their areas of interest or specialisation with assistance from the coordinator of the documentation unit, by using the guidelines noted previously. Fully accessioned, catalogued and indexed documents in their respective folders are filed in a separate bank of file cabinets and constitute the active collection of the documentation unit and library. Abstracts or annotations can be provided for each document by using the same PRO-CITE software, and CIKARD plans to provide these after the collection is fully indexed.

Reference services

One of the future plans of CIKARD is to provide reference services to local, national, and regional government officials and to development agencies, students, and researchers.

PRO-CITE, as an integrated bibliographic software package, not only facilitates cataloguing and indexing, but information storage and retrieval as well. This function permits a search of the file of catalogued and indexed documents by any common data element. This search capability permits the retrieval of relevant citations for any appropriate inquiry from the centre's collection. For descriptive cataloguing, indexing, and retrieval, we use the version of PRO-CITE for the Apple Macintosh computer. This version offers a number of advantages for all operations at various skill levels. It is menu-driven software with drop-down menus, icons, and user friendly display formats and screens.

Publications

When a majority of the collections is properly catalogued and indexed, CIKARD plans to publish a series of bibliographies on indigenous knowledge and rural development. The PRO-CITE software will be used to generate these bibliographies from the catalogued and indexed documents in the PRO-CITE database. Bibliographies and series devoted to specific subject areas or geographic areas can be generated on a regular basis, provided on demand to users for this database.

Until recently, the centre has published a newsletter, *CIKARD News*, describing activities of the centre and describing significant new acquisitions in the library. At the start, the quarterly newsletter was sent to nearly 2000 individuals and organisations in 120 countries. In view of the close collaboration with the Leiden Ethnosystems And Development Programme (LEAD) of Leiden University, *CIKARD News* was soon jointly published, and sent to an fastly increasiung number of individuals and institutions around the world.

By 1993, as the number of recipients worldwide had augmented up to over 3,500, the Centre for International Research and Advisory Networks (CIRAN) of the Nuffic in The Netherlands, as the third Global Centre of the International Network on Indigenous Knowledge and Development agreed – together with CIKARD and LEAD – to further institutionalise the communication and networking activities among participants in this newly-developing field, and publish the *Indigenous Knowledge and Development Monitor.*

Regional and National Resource Centres

Another of CIKARD's major objectives is coordinating the establishment of regional and national indigenous knowledge resource centres within selected host institutions around the globe. Staff associated with the international documentation unit at Iowa Sate University will participate in providing the necessary training and assistance for staff at these centres to identify, acquire, and manage the literature and ethnographic descriptions of indigenous knowledge available from a region. With the appropriate funding, the international centre also intends to offer copies of significant literature to national and regional centres when acquisitions from sources outside of a region are relevant to their interests.

In recent months, several institutions have formally agreed to serve as regional resource centres or have expressed interest in serving as national indigenous resource centres. In Africa, the Nigerian Institute of Social and Economic Research (NISER), Ibadan, has agreed to serve as the site of the African Resource Centre for Indigenous Knowledge (ARCIK). It will function both as the Nigerian Indigenous Knowledge Resource Centre and the African regional support unit to facilitate the establishment of national centres in other African countries. Staff from several institutions in Botswana, Malawi, Tanzania, and Zimbabwe already have expressed interest in serving as hosts for future national centres. ARCIK will be housed physically within a new library facility currently under construction for NISER.

In Asia, a proposal for a new regional program to promote indigenous knowledge recently was prepared by staff associated with the International Institute of Rural Reconstruction (IIRR), Silang, the Philippines. The proposed Regional Program for the Promotion of Indigenous Knowledge in Asia (REPPIKA) is designed to achieve several objectives.

First among these is the promotion and utilisation of indigenous knowledge in the design and implementation of development programs within Asia.

A second objective is the establishment of a regional resource centre for indigenous knowledge to catalyse, support, and link efforts of different groups and individuals within the region to promote and use local knowledge in development projects.

A dialogue between CIKARD and several Latin American institutes is expected to result in the establishment of a regional and several national indigenous knowledge resource centres in the near future.

The CIKARD Research Unit

CIKARD research associates, in cooperation with colleagues, have written a variety of research proposals, most of which are in the review process. We are particularly interested in exploring the dynamic nature of indigenous knowledge systems. We are expected to initiate research on the adaptability of indigenous systems to conditions involving rapid population growth, environmental degradation, and agricultural policies that promote cash cropping based on high external inputs. This will include research on indigenous strategies for managing renewable natural resources in different types of constraining circumstances, such as agriculture changing from extensive to intensive approaches, movement to marginal lands, and deforestation and desertification due to population pressure. Of particular interest is variability in indigenous knowledge components into development projects.

Indigenous knowledge often represents ways people have dealt successfully with their environment. Because most indigenous knowledge has never been documented, it is being forgotten as it is replaced by modern education and technology. Scientists are trying to preserve the world's rich plant genetic diversity in gene banks. It is equally important to do the same for the world's indigenous knowledge as it applies to the broad range of issues related to biodiversity.

CIKARD has supported several efforts to explore the role of nineteenth century social science and colonialism in generating the popular belief that indigenous knowledge is primitive and unworthy of investigat4Jiggins 1989, Slikkerveer 1989, and Warren 1989b). A major review of all research documents dealing with ethnoveterinary medicine was recently published (see Mathias-Mundy and McCorkle 1989). A review of indigenous knowledge related to the private-sector management of trees and tree products in developing nations is currently being conducted by CIKARD research associates for FAO.

Research projects currently conducted include an analysis of the indigenous agricultural knowledge systems for the Old Order Amish in Iowa and an analysis of indigenous knowledge related to soils and rice varieties in the Philippines. New proposals being developed include gender analysis of Maasai ethnoveterinary medicine, indigenous concepts of nutrition in China, indigenous irrigation-management systems in Taiwan, and indigenous natural resource management systems among several Native American groups.

The CIKARD Training and Consultancy Unit

The Training and Consultancy Unit has sponsored or co-sponsored a wide variety of lectures,workshops, and seminars. Training materials have been developed and introduced into existing courses and workshops at Iowa State University. Workshops, conferences and seminars have been held in Amsterdam, Washington, DC, the University of Notre Dame, and at Iowa Academy of Sciences.

CIKARD Inaugural Lectures were delivered by Paul Richards (University College, London), L. Jan Slikkerveer (Leiden University), and Adedotun Phillips (Nigerian Institute of Social and Economic Research) (see Richards *et al.*, 1989).

CIKARD seminars and lectures have been conducted at sister institutions in Wales, Nigeria, Kenya, the Netherlands, the Philippines, Japan, and several universities in the USA. Professional staff representing the new regional resource centres for Africa (ARCIK) and Asia (REPPIKA) are currently at CIKARD to learn the various methodologies for documenting the indigenous systems in their own regions. They will play key roles in training and consultancy when they return home.

A training manual is being developed at CIKARD for use by regional and national centres in conducting workshops on indigenous knowledge at the local level. It is anticipated that this will be of use by many development agencies.

35. LEAD: The Leiden Ethnosystems And Development Programme

L. JAN SLIKKERVEER AND WIM H.J.C. DECHERING

Introduction

IN THE COURSE of the seventies, a new perspective on the practical implications of of socioeconomic development theories in the Third World gradually evolved in Anthropology and Sociology of Non-Western Societies at the Institute of Cultural and Social Studies of Leiden University in The Netherlands. Much earlier, the 'Leiden traditions' of Applied Development Sociology of Van Lier (1971, 1977) and Structural Anthropology of J.P.B. de Josselin de Jong (1935) and P.E. de Josselin de Jong (1977, 1980) had already laid the foundation for such a new orientation, in which sociohistorical and anthropological concepts of particular communities had branched into a renewed, ethnoscience-based perspective on Development Studies. This perspective, further operationalised in emic-oriented fieldwork in *i.a.* Ethiopia (Slikkerveer 1978, 1982, 1990; Buschkens and Slikkerveer 1980), Kenya (Slikkerveer 1989), Ivory Coast (Van den Breemer 1984), Sri Lanka (Dechering 1986) and Indonesia (Holtzappel 1987), was further expanded by the end of the eighties with regard to Cameroon (Geschiere 1989, 91); Senegal (Bergh and Van den Breemer 1991), and Kenya (Leakey and Slikkerveer 1991)

Meanwhile, in 1986, the *Leiden Ethnosystems And Development Programme* (LEAD) had officially been established at the Institute. Several in-depth studies were carried out in different sectors of Third World countries as these transpired from a closer collaboration of a group of anthropologists and development sociologists from Leiden working in policy-based projects with local perceptions, practices, skills and ideas, and their underlying cosmologies in the context of processes of socioeconomic development. It included extended research in sectors such as human health, agriculture, botany, social forestry and ecology. Later on, the LEAD Programme has gradually been extended with the work of associated members such as colleagues of sister-institutions, PhD fellows and visiting scholars involved in the study of indigenous knowledge and development in adjacent sectors of ethnomedicine, ethnohistory, local credit organisations,indigenous natural – and aquatic resource management, and ethnolinguistics.

The 'Ethnosystems Approach'

Central in the LEAD programme has been the concept of *ethnosystems*. Such systems encompassing local people's indigenous knowledge and practices based on long-standing experience and wisdom in particular sociocultural settings over generations. Such systems possess many dimensions, including linguistics, education and socialisation, health and healing, agri- and horticulture, animal husbandry, artisan skills, ecological knowledge and practice, and kinship and social structures. Ethnosystems, moreover, go beyond the general system of knowledge to include local, culture-specific concepts, beliefs and perceptions that form the praxis of daily livelihood and survival – often referred to as 'indigenous knowledge' – as well as local channels of communication and decisionmaking systems.

Theoretically, the concept of 'ethnosystems' broadens the perspective on culture, allowing the study of the cognitive and behavioural components of particular communities in a rather holistic way. Furthermore, it enables the elaboration of the classical – often static – definition of culture in a more dynamic way of historical processes in which not only acculturation and transculturation between different cultures have occurred – 'Great' versus 'Little Traditions (Redfield 1956) – but in which the interface and interaction between local systems and (inter)national systems (or between *ethnosystems* and *cosmosystems*) can be assessed in a more balanced mode (*cf.* Leakey and Slikkerveer 1991; Slikkerveer 1993). Under such a definition, the term 'ethnosystems' becomes an articulation of a particular culture, describing the often unique systems of Indigenous Knowledge (IK) and Indigenous Technology (IT) characteristic of local populations or groups in the Third World as well as of similar groups in Western nations.

Departing from the 'classical' ethnoscience studies of language, cognition and behaviour as part of the prevailing culture, this new approach aims at designing practical models of integration of indigenous and cosmopolitan knowledge systems with a view of more balanced processes of development and change in the tropics. In this way, the LEAD Programme seeks to contribute to the recent development of a new field of Indigenous Knowledge Systems Theory and Practice, focussed on the study, documentation, analysis, and ultimate incorporation of such ethno-specific systems of knowledge and technology into a fundamentally new paradigm of sustainable development among local communities. Within the development-related social sciences, and in particular in development anthropology and sociology, few studies of the concept of Indigenous Knowledge Systems have so far tended to focus on the interaction between local structures of perceptions and practices on the one hand, and outside forces of innovation, development, and social and cultural change on the other (Slikkerveer 1992). Gradually, the study of 'ethnosystems' has come to encompass at least five major aspects:

o the (pre)historical assessment of a particular community or society in its natural and cultural setting;
o the culture-specific or culture-bound reference of the term;
o the holistic approach towards the inclusion of a range of sub-systems of knowledge and technology in sectors such as medicine, agriculture, environment, education, and so on;
o the more dynamic assessment of the concept of 'culture' in terms of a configuration of interacting Western and Non-western knowledge system;
o the comparative – instead of a normative, western-inspired – orientation towards the development process.in certain regions or 'culture areas'.

If we regard such a theoretical concept of ethnosystems within the historical processes of sociocultural change and technical innovation, the dynamic character of culture not only becomes apparent, but more important, the interaction between ethno- and cosmosystems then enables us to widen our research interest to include the behavioural component of the innovation and development processes. It is indeed such a behavioural component that has given rise to a 'neo-ethnoscience', as previously the initially promising efforts of classical ethnoscience and cognitive anthropology during the fifties and sixties in terms of well-documented studies of sophisticated ethnolinguistic material on language, and ethnopsychological data on beliefs and attitudes had run the risk of walking into a scientific *cul de sac*.

The past decade of this so-called 'second generation' of ethnoscience, initiated by the pioneering work of Brokensha, Warren and Werner (1980), took a most promising path into the direction of a rather behaviouristic approach to innovation and development, in which the acting individuals within the prevailing ethnosystems were chosen as the primary source for *development from below*.

The 'Leiden Traditions' in anthropology and sociology

In line with this new orientation, the LEAD Programme at Leiden University was based on two fundamental assumptions, derived from the borrowings from Leiden's scholarly traditions in Cultural Anthropology and Development Sociology. First, Development Sociology provides a most valuable *Historical Dimension* (HD) to the orientation towards long-term development processes and practical situations in the Third World. Second, Structural Anthropology contributes two significant concepts which have been brought within the scope of the LEAD Programme: a) the concept of the *Participants' View* (PV), and b) the concept of the *Field of Ethnological Study* (FES).

The consideration to include from the beginning the target population's or *participant's view* into the policy planning and implementation process of innovation and development has encouraged a new relativist's look on other cultures and societies. Through this method of observing, describing and analysing a particular sociocultural system, the individuals' *subjective* perceptions and attitudes evolve, as it were, into an *objective* social system that represents an additional, most important and valuable component in the study of ethnosystems: people's indigenous cosmologies, perceptions, and decision-making systems. This approach links up with the *emic* view of cultures from *within*, as contrasted to the *etic* view from *outside*, and enables a non-normative assessment of local and regional cultures in the Third World most critical in the context of development and change.

In 1935, one of the early 'structural anthropologists' from Leiden, Van Wouden developed the concept of *Field of Ethnological Study* during his fieldwork in Indonesia. Starting from the linguistic configuration in which – alongside the original *lingua franca* of Pasar Malay (derived from Classical Malay) – a whole range of regional languages existed over the entire Archipelago, he observed and described in what he called the 'Field of Ethnological Study of Indonesia' certain pan-Indonesian features that characterised and delineated the entire cultural and geographical area. Other studies documented similar cultural traits such as kinship classifications, patterns of social organisation, ornaments on bronze kettle-drums, patterns of woven cloths, and perceptions and practices in indigenous medicine. Van Wouden's (1935) concept – later on elaborated and operationalised by J.P.B. de Josselin de Jong (1935) and P.E. de Josselin de Jong (1980) – can be compared with Hunter and Whitten's (1975) recent concept of 'Culture Area'.

In the case of study and analysis of complex configurations, albeit in medicine, religion, agriculture, ecology or languages, the strict contemporary-oriented approaches have virtually failed – as so many development projects have experienced -- to highlight the dynamics of origins and development processes, which have led to present-day complexes. Particularly in transcultural settings, such as *e.g.* the Horn of Africa, a historical and pre-contemporary analysis of acculturation and migration over the past has facilitated the comprehensive reconstruction of political, medical and agricultural systems (*cf.* Markakis 1987; Slikkerveer 1990), Indeed, the processes which have evoked the significant Agricultural Revolution in the culture area of the Horn of Africa, and the subsequent pre-Columbian, colonial and post-colonial complexes of indigenous and imported systems of agri- and horticulture are still under-documented. This situation has been hampering both the adequate analysis of present-day problems and questions in agriculture and extension, and the improvement of agricultural policy planning and implementation in the area.

Recently, a number of studies have focussed on the history of African technology and field systems, highlighting the early development of indigenous agriculture, indigenous irrigation and cultivation techniques, and contributing to the development of a history of indigenous agriculture and cultivating of natural resources in Sub-Saharan Africa (Sutton 1989; Adams 1989; Leakey and Slikkerveer 1991; Wigboldus 1991). However, with such interest in the reconstruction of early agriculture *vis-à-vis* a wide range of studies of contemporary agricultural systems dominated by an attention for problems of 'imported agriculture' and 'agribusiness', the significant intermediate period of time of pre-contemporary processes equally runs the risk of neglect. As far as Eastern Africa is concerned, the recent studies of Wigboldus (1991a), Waaijenberg (1991), Rossel (1991) and Quené (1991) are bridging the gap.

LEAD and the global network on IK

In 1987, the LEAD Programme, chaired by Dr. L. Jan Slikkerveer officially joined the Centre for Indigenous Knowledge and Agricultural Development (CIKARD) Global Network on Indigenous Knowledge and Development of Iowa State University (ISU) in the U.S.A. under the Directorship of Dr. D. Michael Warren. Since then, LEAD has closely worked within the Network as a sister-institute of CIKARD at the global level to collaborate and contribute to the production of *CIKARD News*, and a variety of Monographs and Bibliographies of ISU's *Technology and Social Change Series*. As is further elaborated on in the next chapter 36, the Network has recently been extended with the entry of the Centre for International Research and Advisory Networks (CIRAN) in The Hague at the global level, supporting the networking activities, and facilitating the transformation of the rapidly expanding *CIKARD NEWS* into the *Indigenous Knowledge and Development Monitor,* an international bi-annual journal with one additional 'special issue' per annum serving over 3500 institutes and individuals around the world.

Meanwhile, the LEAD Programme has also been supporting development activities based on the study and practice of indigenous knowledge in Kenya, including the recent establishment of the Kenyan Resource-Centre for Indigenous Knowledge (KENRIK) at the National Museums of Kenya in Nairobi in collaboration with Kenya Wildlife Service in Nairobi under the Directorship of Dr. Richard E. Leakey. The Programme is also supporting the newly-established Indonesian Resource-Centre for Indigenous Knowledge (INRIK) at the Universitas Padjadjaran in Bandung, Indonesia (Dr. Kusnaka Adimihardja, Director).

The practical implications of the LEAD Programme are most manifest in the implementation and evaluation of this approach in terms of models, methods and technologies for understanding and revitalisation of indigenous knowledge and technology in several research and training projects particularly in *i.a.* the *Mediterranean Region*, and the two specific Leiden 'areas of specialisation': *Sub-Saharan Africa* and *Indonesia.*

Since the early 1980s, a number of research and training activities have been executed within the LEAD Programme in several sectors. These include the following studies:

- o 'Semiotics and Ethnobotany' (Van den Broek 1980)
- o 'Ethnomedicine and Primary Health Care in Ethiopia' (Buschkens and Slikkerveer 1981; Slikkerveer 1982, 1991)
- o 'Indigenous Artisans' Technology Development in India' (Brouwer 1984)
- o 'Farming Systems and Innovation in Ivory Coast' (Van den Breemer 1985)
- o 'Low-Cost Housing in Senegal' (Bergh 1986)
- o 'Demographic and Health Development in Sri Lanka' (Dechering 1986)
- o 'Indigenous Agricultural Knowledge Systems in East Africa' (Leakey and Slikkerveer 1991)
- o 'Primary Health Care in Ghana' (De Bekker 1992, 1993; Bosch 1993)
- o 'Indigenous Herbal Medicine *Jamu* in Indonesia' (Slikkerveer and Slikkerveer, this volume)
- o 'A New Measurement Model for Age Corrections in Pakistan and Egypt' (Niemeijer and Dechering 1993)
- o 'The Impact of Environmental Factors on Infant Mortality on Estates in Sri Lanka and its Prevention'. (Dechering and Gurunathan 1993)
- o 'The Expert Sign: Semiotics of Culture; Towards an Interface of Ethno- and Cosmosystems' (Slikkerveer and Van den Broek 1993)
- o 'Local Credit Unions in Ghana' (Gheneti, in progress)
- o 'Comparative Traditional Customs in Child Health in Irian Yaya, East Africa and Crete' (Voorhoeve, in progress)
- o 'Sociopolitical Development and Change in Cameroon' (Geschiere, in progress).
- o 'Plural Medical Systems in Rural Crete' (Slikkerveer, Lionis and Voorhoeve, in press)
- o 'The Multimedia Approach towards Indigenous Medical Knowledge and Primary Health Care in Crete' (Dechering, in progress)

LEAD: internationalisation and interdisciplinarity in the study of IKS

Following these ongoing LEAD activities in the context of Development Studies, new initiatives for similar projects on indigenous knowledge and development have recently been explored in collaboration with colleagues from related disciplines, such as *i.a.* in:

- o the field of wildlife management on 'Roots and Shoots: Chimpanzee Community Conservation and Local Peoples' Perspectives in Gombe, Tanzania' (in collaboration between Dr. L. Jan Slikkerveer, Drs. Ignaas Spruit of Pro Primates Foundation, Leiden, and Dr. Jane Goodall, Director of Gombe National Park)
- o the field of human ecology on 'Halimun Ecology and Development in West Java, Indonesia' (in collaboration between Dr. L. Jan Slikkerveer, Dr. Kusnaka Adimihardja, and Dr. Oekan Abdoellah, resp. Director and Secretary of INRIK)

○ the field of multimedia development on 'CD ROM: New Challenges for IKS Documentation and Analysis in The Tropics' (Dr. Wim H.J.C. Dechering).

○ the field of human health: 'Communication Doctor-Immigrant (CD-I) for General Practitioners in the EEC' (in collabor·tion between Dr. Wim H.J.C.Dechering and Dr. Augusto Pinto, Instituto Superiore di Sanita, Rome)

In addition to the strong and steady support of LEAD from the Institute of Cultural and Social Studies. the Office for International Cooperation, and the Bureau for Internal and External Relations of Leiden University, a formal co-operation programme for education and training in this field with regard to rural Crete and Sub-Saharan Africa has financially been supported by the ERASMUS Programme of the European Commission in Brussels since 1987. In this cooperation programme between the University of Crete, the Health Centre of Spili (Greece) and LEAD, post-graduate fieldwork training and research activities have been acrried out in rural Crete. The African Studies programme has been extended in 1991 with the Centre of African Studies of the University of Edinburgh (Scotland). Furthermore, the LEAD Programme has recently received financial support as well as advanced electronic equipment from Philips Medical Systems in the Netherlands, and support from UNESCO in Paris with regard to the Leiden-Nairobi Project on 'Indigenous Agricultural Knowledge Systems in Kenya, East Africa', that officially has been acknowledged as a Project of the *World Decade for Culture and Development 1987-1997* (WDCD).

As further described in chapter 47, the recently granted substantial support of the European Union in Brussels for the Leiden-Nairobi-Bandung-Chania three-year project on 'Indigenous Agricultural Knowledge Systems' has not only meant a true break-through for the study of indigenous agricultural knowledge and practice in the context of development cooperation, but – more importantly – for the international acknowledgement of a major donor agency of the significance of the potential role of indigenous knowledge systems in achieving agricultural food production in a more sustainable mode.

As LEAD gained a more central position in the further study and analysis of Indigenous Knowledge Systems in the context of development in different sectors, the social scientists involved have been joined by a number of natural scientists such as biologists, ecologists, soil scientists, and physicians paving the way to a future interdisciplinary programme of Indigenous Knowledge and Sustainable Development in The Tropics.

36. CIRAN: Networking for indigenous knowledge

GUUS W. VON LIEBENSTEIN, L. JAN SLIKKERVEER
AND D. MICHAEL WARREN

Growing interest

INTEREST IN THE ROLE that Indigenous Knowledge (IK) can play in truly participatory approaches to development has increased dramatically during the early
nineties. This interest is reflected in a myriad of activities generated within communities that are recording their knowledge for use in their school systems and
for planning purposes, within national institutions where indigenous knowledge
systems are now being regarded as an invaluable national resource, and within
the development community where indigenous knowledge provides opportunities for designing development projects that emerge from priority problems
identified within a community and build upon and strengthen community-level
knowledge systems and organisations.

Widening the scope

Interest in indigenous knowledge has been expressed in a growing number of
academic disciplines. Ten years ago most of the academics working in the area
of indigenous knowledge represented anthropology and geography. Today
important contributions to our understanding of indigenous knowledge and
decision-making also being made in the fields of ecology, soil science, veterinary
medicine, forestry, animal science, aquatic resource management, botany,
zoology, agronomy, agricultural economics, rural sociology, mathematics,
management science, agricultural education and extension, fisheries, range
management, information science, wildlife management, and water resource
management.

International policy forums

The United Nations Conference on Environment and Development in Rio de
Janeiro in June 1992 highlighted the urgency to development mechanisms to
protect the earth's biodiversity. Many of the documents signed at UNCED also
reflect the urgent need to protect the human knowledge of the environment that
is also being lost in many communities. The complementarity of cultural diversity and biodiversity is being highlighted at a growing number of forums, many
of which provide opportunities for representatives of communities – including
those of indigenous peoples – to interact with persons from universities and
academies as well as from national and international development agencies.
Within the relatively short period of time of 1992/1993 international symposia,
workshops, and seminars on the role of indigenous knowledge in sustainable
development have been held in Kenya, Indonesia, the Philippines, Canada,
Zimbabwe, Germany, the Netherlands and the USA.

Since the Earth Summit in Rio de Janeiro, Canada's International Development Research Centre (IDRC) broadened its mandate as an Agenda 21 Organi-

sation to emphasise even more than before sustainable development issues. The Centre, now in a process of readjusting policy to its new identity, has shown an explicit interest in indigenous or local knowledge and development, in particular in relation to biodiversity and natural resources management.

IDRC has funded conferences on IKs and Development in Third World countries (*e.g.* the International Conference 'Indigenous Knowledge and Development' in Silang, The Philippines, 20–26 September 1992) and in Canada (Seminar on IKs and Development in Ottawa, October 1992). Another international agency that recently acknowledged the relevance of indigenous knowledge for development is UNDP. This member of the UN family supports the establishment of a Sustainable Development Network (SDN) in order to strengthen capacity building to sustainable development using information and communications. The Sustainable Development Network is an important tool to help develop national plans for Agenda 21 to promote sustainable development. Indigenous knowledge is considered to be of high relevance as one can read in the draft report of the Sustainable Development Network (SDN) Workshop that was recently organised by UNDP (New York, September 1992) that '...Indigenous, traditional and local knowledge needs to be better integrated in decision making. SDN need to facilitate increased use of locally available knowledge and expertise or experience for sustainable development...'

National resource centres

Efforts to recognise the immense value of indigenous knowledge for development activities if we are to achieve the potential of participatory approaches to sustainable development are now being carried out by a growing number of formally established Indigenous Knowledge Resource Centres. Presently, about *twenty* centres have been established around the globe. In addition to the three Global Centres the United States, and in the Netherlands, (CIKARD, LEAD and CIRAN), Regional Centres encompass ARCIK in Nigeria and REPPIKA in The Philippines. National Centres include BRARCIK in Brazil, BURCIK in Burkina Faso, CIKO in Cameroon, GHARCIK in Ghana, INRIK in Indonesia, KENRIK in Kenya, MARCIK in Madagascar, NIRCIK in Nigeria, PHIRCSDIK in the Philippines, RIDSCA in Mexico, SARCIK in South Africa, SLARCIK in Sri Lanka, URURCIK in Uruguay, and VERSIK in Venezuela.In addition, a number of centres are in the active process of being established in Benin, Namibia, Zimbabwe, Crete, Costa Rica, Colombia, Peru, Bolivia,Tanzania, Nepal, Thailand and Australia. These centres provide opportunities for committed persons in these countries to record indigenous knowledge so it can be used to facilitate development activities. They also provide the means to recognise the contribution of a nation's citizens to human knowledge and to protect the knowledge in the best interests of a country and its citizens.

National indigenous knowledge resource centres are in the process of strengthening their capacity for a variety of important functions. These include national and international networking and information flow, documentation of the indigenous knowledge systems existing within a country, research on the impact of new constraining circumstances on these systems and the role that extension could play in helping small-scale farmers to move through difficult transition periods, design of training materials for use in national extension training institutes and universities so that more nationals have access to the methodologies for recording indigenous knowledge systems, and the establish-

ment of documentation units where recorded systems are accessioned and
stored for use by development practitioners.

Creating a global network

The most cost-effective way that indigenous knowledge systems can be recorded
for use in development activities is through a global network of national centres.
Most countries now have at least a limited number of individuals scattered
across the institutional landscape who are involved in research on indigenous
knowledge as it relates to development. National centres provide a networking
function that both unites and expands this group of individuals who tend to be
isolated by artificial institutional and sectoral barriers. The networking function
allows for a more effective pooling and exchange of experience and information
on indigenous knowledge both among practitioners within the country as well as
between centres.

Centres also provide a national data management function where published
and unpublished information on indigenous knowledge are systematically maintained for use by development practitioners. Establishing a national centre indicates that a country has recognised the fact that although its indigenous knowledge may have been ignored or overlooked in the past, it now regards its knowledge as a national resource. By recording and evaluating its indigenous knowledge, a national centre can protect its intellectual property rights for knowledge
that could be exploited economically for the benefit of the country. A national
centre can also provide the mechanism to recognise and acknowledge the contributions to knowledge generation by its own citizens.

As the existing Global Network of Indigenous Knowledge Resource Centres
becomes linked by a common electronic communications system, indigenous
knowledge and technologies found to be effective in dealing with small-farm circumstances in an agro-ecozone in one part of the globe can be transferred for
consideration to a centre in another part of the world where a similar agro-ecozone exists. Examples of this transfer of technology already exist. The use of
vetiver grass for soil and water management and the use of neem tree seeds as a
biopesticide are both technologies discovered by farmers in South Asia many
generations ago. These technologies have now been adopted by small-scale
farmers in many other parts of the world through networking mechanisms provided by the World Bank and other development agencies.

Organising the global network

In May l992 a Memorandum of Understanding was signed by the three Directors of the three centres at the global level of the IK&D Network. This Memorandum of Understanding underscored the role of CIKARD, LEAD and
CIRAN, in facilitating the activities of the regional and national centres through
global networking, information exchange, and backstopping in the establishment of standard approaches to documentation and databanking. A proper
functioning of the Global Indigenous Knowledge and Development Network
requires active national and regional networks. Various instruments are available to promote the active functioning of these networks. One of the most common instruments used by networks for the dissemination of information is the
newsletter. It is often the first activity that is undertaken. However, a newsletter
is only supportive to the functioning of a network; it is not networking in itself.

The amount of networking a newsletter can generate depends on the extent to which the receivers of the newsletter interact. When the network members are spread over the globe, a newsletter can be a powerful communication instrument. A newsletter can also provide a platform for debate, an instrument for needs assessment, and a forum for information on recent developments and publication etc. A newsletter can equally provide a network with information on activities beyond the narrow range of its members.

IK&D Monitor: an instrument for networking

The *Indigenous Knowledge and Development Monitor*, which absorbs CIKARD News has been produced by CIRAN in close cooperation with CIKARD and-LEAD, and all the other national and regional indigenous knowledge resource centres, Published three times a year in two regular volumes and one special issue, it provides a major forum for the established centres to interact with all other persons and institutions interested in the role that indigenous knowledge can play in participatory approaches to sustainable development. Also, the IK&D Monitor allows the centres to maintain a closer working relationship with several other institutions and associations working in the area of indigenous knowledge, but with more specialised focuses. These include the Information Centre for Low External Input and Sustainable Agriculture (ILEIA), the International Programme for Traditional Ecological Knowledge (TEK), the Honey Bee Network, the Network of the Association of Farming Systems Research-Extension (AFSRE), the Sustainable Development Network of the United Nations Development Programme (UNDP), and the International Institute for Environment and Development (IIED).

Since the principle task of the Monitor in facilitating the exchange of information and promoting active networking has been highly appreciated in- and outside the Global Network, it is envisaged to develop a future marketing strategy for a sustained basis for continued publication and distribution through a system of funding, which enables free subscription for recipients, in particular those from the developing countries.

Note

Further information on the *Indigenous Knowledge and Development Monitor* can be obtained from: CIRAN/NUFFIC, P.O. Box 29777, 2502 LT The Hague, The Netherlands

37. IUCN and Indigenous Peoples: How to promote sustainable development

JEFFREY A. McNEELY

Introduction

CONSERVATION IS LINKED in the public mind with wildlife. But humans have occupied this planet very thoroughly for thousands of years, and few 'natural' habits remain. Instead, the Planet Earth consists of a number of more-or-less anthropogenic habitats, occupied by people who have developed cultural approaches to managing the resources of their local ecosystems in a sustainable fashion.

These indigenous people are the repository of understanding lost by urban and industrial societies. They illustrate the sorts of life that are sustainable through the judicious use of renewable resources. Depending almost totally on the resources available from within their own ecosystems, they have a far greater awareness of the importance of conservation than any urban-dweller, no matter how conscientious. Therefore, those interested in conserving biological diversity must be equally concerned about conserving cultural diversity, and marshalling that diversity to the benefit of forms of development which are sustainable.

For those who are not familiar with IUCN – for I fear that we too often work under the cloak of anonymity – we are the Third World Conservation Union, consisting of 400 NGOs, 60 states, and 130 government agencies in 120 countries. IUCN is the largest professional body in the world that is working to care for the soil, lands, forests, waters, wildlife and air of our planet – the essential natural resources without which there can be no human future.

In 1980 IUCN, in partnership with the United Nations Environment Programme (UNEP) and the World Wildlife Fund (WWF – now the Worldwide Fund for Nature) and in collaboration with UNESCO and the Food and Agriculture Organisation of the UN (FAO) published the World Conservation Strategy. The WCS has been hailed as the most important conservation manifesto of the 1980s. Its central theme is that development – action that alters the environment so that it caters more effectively for human needs – is essential if the World is to be free from poverty and squalor, but that such development must be based on resources that regenerate naturally and can meet our needs indefinitely. Destruction of tomorrow's foundations in order to satisfy today's needs is self-evident folly.

Within sustainable development we must find room for wild nature, which is both a spiritual enrichment and in a very practical sense the foundation of our lives. It is the processes of wild nature that renew the oxygen in the air, maintain the cycles of essential elements, sustain the fertility of the land, and regulate the flow of rivers. We turn to wild nature for new crops and new drugs, as well as for the beauty that enriches life. The World Conservation Strategy emphasises that conservation and development are not opponents, but are inseparable one.

IUCN has an abiding interest in the relationship between traditional peoples and the conservation of ecosystems. At present our Commission on Ecology is supporting a Task Force on Traditional Knowledge, our Plants Programme has a Working Group on Ethnobotany, our Species Survival Commission has a Specialist Group on Ethnozoology, and our Commission on National Parks and Protected Areas is working on improving the relationship between indigenous people and protected areas. Recent IUCN publications particularly relevant to this field include *Culture and Conservation* (1985), *Traditional Life-Styles, Conservation and Rural Development* (1984) and *People and Protected Areas in Hindukush-Himalaya* (1985). We also number several indigenous peoples' organisations among our membership, including the International Indian Treaty Council, the Inuit Circumpolar Conference and the Inuit Tapirisat of Canada.

Many of IUCN's activities are of direct relevance to indigenous people. For example, we annually issue a statement to the International Whaling Commission. In a recent year our statement read in part: 'IUCN recognises the justifiable use of whales for aboriginal and subsistence purposes under the moratorium, provided that it is truly aboriginal and relies on an irreplaceable subsistence resource and does not cause population decline or significantly retard the recovery of depleted populations.'

In assisting FAO and the World Bank to develop guidelines for implementing the Tropical Forest Action Plan (TFAP), we issued the following statement: 'The interests of forest-dwelling indigenous peoples should be addressed by TFAP. In particular: representatives of indigenous peoples' organisations, and of government ministries or other agencies responsible for their welfare, should be involved in national TFAP exercises; TFAP forest sector reviews and national exercises should document and evaluate the natural resource management practices and traditional ecological knowledge of indigenous peoples, or encourage their study where unknown; the impact of existing forest policies and projects on the practices and livelihood of indigenous forest peoples should be evaluated; and TFAP project and policy preparation should involve and take full account of indigenous peoples, their economic development, health, welfare, and legal and traditional rights.'

This chapter briefly presents IUCN's perspective on the major problems affecting indigenous peoples and conservation, outlines how we suggest the problems be addressed, and make some specific recommendations about how IUCN can collaborate more closely with other organisations concerned about traditional knowledge.

IUCN's perspective on traditional knowledge and development

First of all, IUCN wholeheartedly accepts the principle that cultural diversity and biological diversity need to be conserved together if either is to prosper. It is no surprise to us that indigenous people know that business – these cultures have been surviving for thousands of years by harvesting their wildlife on a sustainable basis. Traditional cultures – unlike modern industrialism – have stood the test of time. In the fairly recent past, most human populations depended primarily on the natural resources that could be harvested from the surrounding region. Cities were small, trade was limited, energy systems were relatively simple and people were thinly scattered across the landscape.

But in the past few decades, people everywhere have profoundly changed the way they relate to their environment. Indications are that the rate of change will continue to accelerate and emerging technologies such as gene splicing and breeder reactors could bring even more profound changes in the near future. One result could be even more widespread and complete relinquishment of the kind of contact with nature that indigenous peoples retain. Another will almost certainly be a change in the values of the organised majority, which because it controls the means of production, trade and communication, will inevitably be imposed on others. The seeds of these changes have already been planted. Today's urban populations certainly do not depend on their local ecosystems for sustenance, instead exploiting the entire globe and drawing on energy and other resources from distant shores. We have become part of what is truly one world.

The ecological interdependence among nations is often viewed as basically desirable, and indeed the World Commission on Environment and Development has called for greatly expanded interdependence through enhanced flows of energy, trade and finance. On the other hand, some have suggested that such interdependence – making the world a single global system – is the ultimate source of the global depletion of resources. As the distinguished ecologist Ray Dasmann pointed out over a decade ago, when we are all part of one system connected by powerful economic forces, it becomes very easy to over-exploit any part of the global system because other parts will soon compensate for such over-exploitation. The damage may not even be noticed until it is too late to do anything to avoid permanent degradation. Perhaps worse, global interdependence enhances the domination of the economically powerful, yet requires a support structure which in itself can be very fragile – the impacts of changes in oil prices and interest rates demonstrate the point.

The system of trade which has enabled the entire globe to be exploited primarily for the benefit of urban populations, has led to great prosperity for those who have been able to benefit from the expanded productivity, but it has often led to devastation of local ecosystems. And what happens to the local people who remain dependent on the now-depleted living resources and indeed had developed ways and means of using these resources sustainably, without depleting them?

The World Commission on Environment and Development provided an answer: growing interaction with the larger world is increasing the vulnerability of these isolated groups, since they are often left out of the processes of economic development. Social discrimination, cultural barriers and the exclusion of indigenous people from national political processes makes them vulnerable and subject to exploitation. Many groups become dispossessed and marginalised and their traditional practices disappear. They become the victims of what could with justice be described as cultural extinction. This is not a trivial problem. 'It is a terrible irony that as formal development researches more deeply into rain forests, deserts and other isolated environments' says the WCED, 'it tends to destroy the only cultures that have proved able to thrive in these environments.'

Fortunately a growing number of people are beginning to doubt the desirability and durability of the present situation and various major impacts of exploiting the environment – such as the greenhouse effect and possible changes in climate – suggest inevitability of profound changes in the way humans relate to the environment. The exact direction of these changes is unpredictable – the ecological niches of human communities could take any of a large number of forms in the coming years. One possibility would be a series of local adaptations to locally-available resources, with distant resources being consumed only to the extent that such use is sustainable. This need not necessarily mean a radical reduction in quality of life, but social, economic and environmental conditions will surely be fundamentally different than they are in today's 'consumer society' and perhaps will come to increasingly represent traditional cultures.

Examples of ecologically and culturally sensible interactions between people and their environment can be found in all parts of the world. Such traditional communities, says the *World Conservation Strategy*, often have profound and detailed knowledge of the ecosystems and species with which they are in contact and effective ways of ensuring they are used sustainably. Cultural diversity, which is provided above all by the great variety of indigenous cultures in all parts of the world, provides the human intellectual 'gene pool', the basic raw material for adapting to the local environment.

IUCN concludes that indigenous people who live in intimate contact with their major resources could provide much of the intellectual raw material for such a shift to sustainable societies. The challenge is applying this knowledge and, where appropriate, transferring associated techniques and thinking to conservation management systems appropriate to today's circumstances. What can be done? IUCN suggests six major steps that can be taken.

o First, *give appropriate value to traditional rights, knowledge, and skills.* The wisdom of indigenous peoples is an asset from which all humanity should benefit. One way of using this asset is to ensure that the rights, knowledge and production systems of traditional people are properly valued in economic assessments of development projects. Development agencies and others should support the formation of associations of traditional peoples for conservation and sustainable development based wherever possible on indigenous institutions; and existing associations of traditional peoples should be involved in organisations working for sustainable development.

o Second, *take special measures to protect the rights of traditional people.* Many, even most, indigenous communities are already practicing sustainable development and should not be disrupted by value systems that are looking increasingly outmoded. In the context of the needs of conservation and sustainable development, a basic report needs to be prepared on the status of the world's traditional peoples and their knowledge systems. Governments should provide support for communities which choose to continue their traditional lifestyles; experience gained from protected areas where resident communities continue their traditional lifestyles should be documented and assessed. IUCN should compile the basic policy statements of its State Members on traditional peoples, together with summaries of relevant development programs. Multilateral development banks should be encouraged to report specially on the role of traditional peoples in development projects which they fund. In all of these activities, the guiding principle should be to ensure that any such special measures be designed and applied locally. Local communities need to be given their rightful responsibilities for managing the biological resources upon which they depend.

o Third, *provide information on traditional management systems.* We need to work together to compile information on traditional cultures which are particularly good examples of productive relationships between people and the environment, including the use made of species. An inventory should be compiled on traditional knowledge systems which are endangered. Educational agencies should be assisted to introduce elements of traditional conservation knowledge and practice into appropriate curricula, and educational activities should be undertaken which encourage interest in traditional knowledge and its practitioners. To the extent possible, indigenous people should be used to demonstrate the value of traditional management systems.

o Fourth, *design and implement research programs aimed at promoting the application of traditional wisdom to modern resource management.* An exchange of knowledge and methodologies would foster greater mutual understanding between indigenous peoples and conservation scientists and managers. To facilitate such consultation, indigenous peoples may need training in the approach and techniques of conservation science. Scientific investigators and researchers should include indigenous co-investigators in all phases of their research design and implementation, with the objective of establishing networks for the long-term exchange of information and learning. Financial and technical resources should be made accessible to enable indigenous peoples to conduct their own research. The aim should be to create an indigenous scientific community that includes both traditional expertise and acquired scientific skills and procedures.

o Fifth, *design projects which benefit indigenous people.* On the basis of the above, opportunities should be identified for projects to demonstrate how traditional knowledge can be combined with science to design systems for sustainable use of resources, and to develop such projects for external funding. Based on a review of various development projects which have related to indigenous people, workshops should bring together a number of experts who have had experience in such projects to develop guidelines which can be used by development agencies to enhance the design, implementation and monitoring of their projects.

o And finally, *design projects which benefit from traditional knowledge.* To promote the idea that traditional knowledge and practice are still relevant for contemporary natural resource management, professional groups should be presented with the rationale of examining traditional knowledge and rules – such as customary law – with a view to the scientific insights which such knowledge can provide. Traditional land tenure arrangements should be used as a basis for planning and executing conservation projects and those more directly concerned with food and materials production. Marine conservation and inshore fisheries development programs should be based on established rights and tenure systems and make good use of local ecological and management knowledge. Where traditional tenure systems appear to be inadequate for markedly changed circumstances, such as greatly increased human population or resource degradation, new systems should be adopted on the best of the old foundations.

IUCN shares with many other institutions a serious concern about the loss of human cultures and of traditional wisdom about the environment. We are well aware that part of the richness of human life around the globe is due to the inter-relations between people and their local environments. The loss of cultures, or of traditional knowledge within cultures undergoing rapid change, is a problem which is at least as serious for humanity as is the loss of species. All who follow will share the loss of traditional knowledge about the local environment. Crucial knowledge about how that environment might be used to provide benefits on a sustainable basis may be lost forever, along with the species that have supported human welfare for thousands of years.

IUCN seeks opportunities to work together with other organisations to find new opportunities for achieving sustainable development with the close participation of traditional peoples and with the help of their knowledge of ecosystems, species and sustainable resource use.

Acknowledgments

This chapter has benefited from contributions by Graham Baines (Chair of the Ecology Commission Working Group on Traditional Knowledge), Paul Wachter, Delmar Blasco, Martin Boldgate and David Munro.

38. International Institute for Environment and Development (IIED) and Rapid Rural Appraisal for Indigenous Sustainable Agriculture

JENNIFER McCRACKEN

IIED

THE INTERNATIONAL INSTITUTE for Environment and Development was established in 1971 with the aim of promoting sustainable development, that is, development which is sensitive to the cultural mores of the human communities it is meant to serve, and to the realities of the natural resource base from which those communities derive their stability and ultimately their prosperity. It has since followed this objective by means of policy advocacy, research, fieldwork, training, and information. The work is conducted through a number of coordinated programs – including forestry and land – use, economics, sustainable agriculture, human settlements, and drylands. The Institute has offices in London, Buenos Aires and an associate office in Washington, DC, and is funded by private and corporate foundations, international organisations, governments, and concerned individuals.

With the surge of interest in sustainable development and environmental issues, the IIED is now complementing its earlier concern with advocating sustainable development by playing a role in trying to translate the concept of sustainability into concrete action on the ground, and tackling such questions as 'What does sustainable development mean to farmers, foresters, fishermen, town planners, and economists?', 'What examples are there of sustainable use of natural resources?', 'What donor and government policies are compatible with promoting sustainable development?', and 'How can the local people (including women and the poorest members of the communities) become involved in the decision-making stages of local development work?'. These and other issues have been investigated and directed at aid agencies, governments in the North and South, and through the IIED's independent publishing house, Earthscan, to the general public.

On this agenda, IIED cooperates with many local NGOs in the South, with European agencies such as IUCN and WWF, and with bilateral and multilateral aid agencies.

The Sustainable Agriculture Programme

Based in the London office of IIED, staff of the Sustainable Agriculture Programme work to promote research and disseminate information on agricultural development which is socially, economically and ecologically sustainable. Key activities of the Programme are:

- keeping development agency decision-makers abreast of recent 'key' topics in sustainable agriculture, by producing (Gatekeeper) briefing papers to inform and advise them on such issues as pesticide hazards in developing countries, trees as security for the rural poor, and use of indigenous knowledge for sustainable agriculture;

451

o researching sustainable agriculture topics, such as agricultural pollution, pastoralist systems in patchy environments, and participatory mechanisms for sustainable agriculture;

o developing Rapid Rural Appraisal (RRA) methodologies and techniques for use in a wide variety of situations, through both fieldwork and training;

o producing a journal, RRA Notes, to allow the worldwide network of practitioners to share their experiences of the approach quickly and informally;

o producing RRA training materials for use in workshops or in the field;

o jointly with the Institute for Development Studies of the University of Sussex (IDS), organising Review Workshops on RRA, where practitioners can discuss recent developments and consider future developments of the methodology.

Rapid Rural Appraisal in sustainable agriculture

The RRA component of the Programme's work has expanded recently as interest in the approach has grown immensely and demands for testing the applicability of RRA and training local staff in the methodologies have increased accordingly. The methodologies being developed at IIED, including Agro-ecosystem Analysis, centre around a modified systems approach, where not only is the productivity of the system taken into account, but also the stability, sustainability and equitability of that production. The inevitable trade-offs between these four properties are made explicit through the techniques employed, and opportunities for development activities are assessed partly on their impact on these properties.

A key feature of RRA as developed at IIED is the use of diagrams as tools of information-gathering, analysis, conflict resolution and presentation. Maps, transects, seasonal calendars, time trends and Venn diagrams are among those used to investigate particular aspects of the system. These diagrams are often drawn in the field, with local people, and have been used successfully in village meetings where the findings of the RRA are brought back to the villagers for feedback discussions.

One current focus of the methodological development concerns the extent to which RRA can be participatory – *i.e.* how much the local people can be involved in the work. Advances have been made in adapting the interviewing and diagramming techniques to encourage more participation, but there is still much experimenting to do. Another new development is the potential for non-agricultural applications of RRA. While maintaining its primary focus on sustainable agriculture, the Programme is, through RRA, beginning to explore the links with urban, forestry, economics, health, and other sectors.

All of the RRA work which the Programme undertakes in the field is by request of an NGO, Government Ministry, donor agency, or University in the particular country. Generally there is also a training objective of the work, as well as a goal of getting useful information for planning development work. One or two members of the Programme usually work with 15–25 local staff. These staff range from field level extension workers or researchers, or farmers, to planning and decision-making HQ staff. The work is conducted in teams, which split up into small groups for the field investigations. In the field, local people often accompany the team in its work and participate in various stages throughout. Emphasis is given to the need to train future trainers, by involving a core number of local staff in several RRA exercises, and supporting them with training materials specially adapted for their area of work and occasional visits to review their progress. This means of passing on the training role to the local staff members while still in its early stages is proving very successful as a means of institutionalising and fine-tuning the RRA approach.

The Programme has conducted RRA fieldwork/training exercises in Indonesia, India, Thailand, Pakistan, Zimbabwe, Ethiopia, Kenya, Sudan and Senegal, and RRA training workshops in Europe, Scandinavia and North America.

To take one example of an RRA training exercise, two members of the Programme recently conducted RRAs in Wollo, Ethiopia, with local staff of the Ethiopian Red Cross Society, who are working in a disaster prevention project. Working in two teams of ten people from different disciplines, the participants spent ten days investigating issues of tree management and hillside closures in two Peasant Associations. The team discussed these sensitive topics in several focus group sessions with various different sections of the community, and then held a meeting on the final day, attended by representatives from the focus groups. In this way, the conflicts of interest and the different opinions of these groups were brought into the open, and at least to some extent compromises were reached to develop a more equitable management plan for the Peasant Associations. Implementation of the ideas which were brought forward was left as the responsibility of the community and the Ethiopian Red Cross Project. As several of the participants had taken part in a previous RRA training exercise with IIED, they were able to get a better grasp of the approach, and are now available as resource persons for future RRA work in the project.

39. Agricultural Development with a Focus on Local Resources: ILEIA's view on indigenous knowledge

BERTUS HAVERKORT

Introduction

ILEIA STANDS FOR Information Centre for Low External Input and Sustainable Agriculture. It was established in 1982 by the ETC Foundation and has mainly been funded by the Netherlands Ministry of Development Cooperation. ILEIA's long-term objective is to contribute to a situation in which Low External Input and Sustainable Agriculture (LEISA) is:

○ understood in its theoretical aspects and its practical applicability;
○ recognised as a means to balance locally-available resources and local knowledge with modern technologies requiring inputs from elsewhere; and
○ widely accepted and adopted as a valid approach to agricultural development, complementary to the approach where the level of use of external inputs is high.

ILEIA is reaching its objectives by its documentation centre, the publication of a quarterly news magazine, bibliographies, readers and reference books, and through the organisation of international workshops and support to regional networks on LEISA in the Third World.

Low External Input and Sustainable Agriculture is agriculture which makes optimal use of locally-available natural and human resources, such as climate, landscape, soil, water, vegetation, local crops and animals, labour, local skills, and indigenous knowledge. Furthermore, for it to be sustainable, it needs to be economically feasible, ecologically sound, culturally adapted, and socially just. The use of external inputs, such as mineral fertilisers, pesticides, hybrid seeds, machineries, and external advisers is not excluded, but is seen as complementary to the use of local resources and has to meet the four criteria of sustainability.

LEISA can be characterised by its three sources of knowledge, *i.e.*:

○ traditional agricultural practices;
○ indigenous knowledge;
○ scientific insights as developed in agroecology;

Traditional agriculture practices refer to agricultural production where technologies being used depend completely on local resources and has, over time, developed a wide range of site-specific technologies embedded in the culture of the people in a certain area. Indigenous knowledge is the actual knowledge of a certain farming population which reflects the experiences based on traditions and includes more recent experiences with modern technologies.

This knowledge is far more than technical methods and cultivation practices of farmers. It entails many kinds of insights, wisdom, perceptions, and practices related to people's resources and environments. It is not static. Experimentation and screening and integration of knowledge are activities of farming, as much as

454

tilling of the soil. But indigenous knowledge also has its limitations and short-comings, especially in disrupted situations.

ILEIA, therefore, sees indigenous knowledge as the major articulation point for agricultural development. This knowledge should not be treated as something that could be collected, frozen in models or expert systems, stored for future use by scientists, or as something that could be easily transplanted to other regions. Such knowledge is generated and continues to develop in specific cultural and ecological systems and cannot be seen independent from these systems. The complementarity between indigenous knowledge and science-based knowledge keeps promise for successful innovations for the development of sustainable agriculture. Development workers, agricultural researchers, and extension workers may, therefore, have to play an important role in supporting and further developing indigenous knowledge.

One serious option for agricultural development support is to help farmers to become more effective technology developers. These activities can be seen as a neglected area of technology development for tropical agriculture which has its place next to on-station research, farming systems research, and farmers' participatory research. In these approaches, it is the researcher who conducts the process of technology development and who allows or seeks a certain level of participation of the farmers in their activities.

In Participatory Technology Development (PTD), it is the farming community that develops technologies with the support of development workers. The task of the development workers is then the strengthening of the capacity of local communities to experiment and innovate technologies that are relevant for local agriculture. In 1988, ILEIA organised a workshop on operational methods of PTD. It was concluded that, especially for complex, diverse, and risk-prone rain-fed agricultural systems, PTD is a necessary condition for site-specific and appropriate agricultural development. Methods for PTD were identified on the basis of existing experiences.

ILEIA published proceedings of this PTD workshop as well as an issue of its news magazine in PTD (Volume 4, Number 3, 1988). The Centre also has a theme issue on the role of indigenous knowledge in agricultural development (Volume 6, Number 1, 1990). A reader on practical cases of PTD (*Joining Farmers' Experiments*) and a more elaborate reference book on LEISA *(Farming for the Future)*, with ample attention on PTD, have been published. Two bibliographies have been published by the Centre: *Understanding Traditional Agriculture* (1986) and *Towards Sustainable Agriculture* (1988).

ILEIA supports existing or emerging networks on LEISA in the Third World. This may exist as support for documentation of innovations of farmers, regular meetings of non-governmental organisations (NGOs) or governmental organisations (GOs) engaged in agricultural development, training of field staff or farmers in PTD, and the initiation of newsletters.

A closer look at indigenous knowledge and farmers experiments

It is presently widely acknowledged that farmers are generally arriving in experimentation and accumulation of experiences and thus modify and develop farming practices. Insight in the exact ways farmers carry out their experiments is, however, limited. Rhoades and Bebbington (1988) distinguish three kinds of experiments as they are being carried out by potato growing farmers in Peru: curiosity experiments, problems solving experiments and adaptation experiments. It is often suggested that farmers follow a linear pattern of experiment-ing: identification of a problem, assumption about better options, design and implementation of an experiment and assessment of the results and finally wide-spread communication and adoption.

This 'model' for experimentation suggests the use of a logic which comes close to the Western scientific concept, where a direct cause-effect relationship between different biophysical variables is assumed.

Other authors challenge the evidence of such a linear experimental practice and elaborate the influence of the cosmovision on the experimental practices. The concept of 'cosmovision' was introduced by Pratec (1991) and van den Berg (1991) in the context of the indigenous Peruvian culture. This culture is pre-sented as a holistic world view or cosmology; it takes into its perspective not only the world, but the totality of the cosmos. In this view, the whole of nature is conceived as a living being like an animal in which all its parts are interre-lated, man being one of them. In this scheme of things, nature does not belong to man, but man to nature. Thus, human society does not stand in opposition to nature, rather, man works in and communicates with nature. There is no static conception of the world, but a dynamic one in which there is a continuous trans-formation of the environment.

The concept of cosmovision thus refers to the way a certain population per-ceives the world or cosmos: It includes the assumed interrelationship between spirituality, nature and mankind. It describes the roles of the superpowers, the way natural processes take place, the relationship man–nature and it makes explicit the philosophical and scientific premises on the basis of which interven-tion in nature (as is the case in agriculture and health care) takes place.

The cosmovision thus has a major influence on the scientific concepts philoso-phy and morale of the population. It leads to assumptions on cause-effect rela-tionships, chance and synchronicity. It frequently indicates a hierarchy in divine beings, spiritual beings (including ancestors), natural forces (such as climate, diseases and floods), soil, vegetation, animals and men and women. This hierar-chy has given rise to several rituals in which the elders men (and women) of wis-dom, priests, soothsayers play prominent roles and which prescribes the way experimentation can take place. The cosmovision determines the way the peo-ple go about knowledge and technology development. In its turn cosmovision and knowledge system determine how the society is organising itself and how effective it is in achieving its goals.

Thus knowledge about the cosmovision of a people is a first requirement for any outsider wanting to cooperate with this population in developing technolo-gies or in modifying the knowledge system. This notion has far reaching implica-tions for field methods such as Participatory Technology Development (PTD). The case descriptions on PTD generally have been based on the assumption that farmers use a 'Western logics' in their experimentation.

The evidence of anthropological research (Van den Berg 1991; Huizer 1991; Van den Breemer 1991; Persoon 1991) and agroforestry research (Chandrakant *et al.* 1990 and Adzobu *et al.* 1991) suggests that the cosmovision demands a much wider range of variables to be taken into account than the straightforward cause-effect relations between biophysical factors only.

Studies of Indigenous Knowledge Systems result in a number of different reactions: conventional anthropology tends to describe the folk sciences and sci-entific artifacts; conventional missionaries tend to study the indigenous faiths as a way to enhance their missionary activities; conventional agriculturalists till recent have rather neglected ethnosciences. Its recent discovery and the development in biotechnology and pharmacy has led to important debates about intellectual property rights, concern about missing of the riches of indigenous knowledge and the possibilities and difficulties for 'just compensation' of the use of Indigenous Knowledge by commercial industries.

In many Indigenous Knowledge Systems and cosmologies, the women have a different position from the men. Women generally have their own socioeconomic position and thus tend to have their own subculture, own networks, knowledge systems and own interpretations of the cosmologies. In many cases it has been found that women have more knowledge on food production, quality of food and interrelationship between food and health. They also attach more value to maintaining agricultural productivity and cultural values, whereas men tend to be more included to focus on short term benefits, production for the market and 'Westernisation'.

At present ILEIA aims at identifying cases where indigenous knowledge and formal knowledge have been integrated in a synergistic way, at learning from these experiences and at supporting these initiatives in its further development. We assume that such an approach would lead to a greater diversity of cultures and agricultural systems. We think that the greatest challenge is to develop systems of cooperation between Indigenous Knowledge Systems and formal knowledge systems.

Since 1984 ILEIA has been engaged in documenting and studying forms of agriculture where low levels of external inputs are being used. A global network of development workers, NGOs and researchers is exchanging experiences and tries to come to grips with the concepts of sustainable agriculture and conditions for developing them.

In this process the ILEIA network has gradually broadened its attention from a focus on technologies, to also include aspects of methods of and criteria for technology development. In its reflection on agricultural development ILEIA has come to a point that the primary of Western concepts is being questioned and that the need is felt for an approach where the non-Western concepts of science and development are taken serious. Such an approach would lead to a multitude of sources of knowledge and a diversity of development options fitting the specific sociocultural and ecological situation.

The ILEIA *Newsletter* functions as a means of exchange between field workers. This network is made up of more than 3000 persons, based mainly in the Third World and actively engaged in ILEIA and PTD. The magazine contains experiences and reflections on specific themes, such as use of natural pesticides and local genetic resources, and management of nutrients and microclimate. The articles are generally brief and emphasis is on the experiences gained by farmers or development workers or both.[1]

Note

1. Third World readers may apply for a free subscription. ILEIA's address: ILEIA. P.O. Box 64, 3830 AB Leusden, The Netherlands.

40. The Latin American Consortium on Agroecology and Development (CLADES) – Fostering rural development based on indigenous knowledge

MIGUEL A. ALTIERI AND ANDRES YURJEVIC

AS IN MANY parts of the Third World, agricultural development in Latin America was influenced by two dominant views:

- that hunger and rural poverty were the result of high population growth and low agricultural yields, and
- that this population/food resources gap could only be closed by modernising agriculture through the transfer of high-input technology from the North.

Local traditional farming techniques were discussed to be 'primitive' and inappropriate to boost productivity. This assumption proved misleading in guiding small farm development in the region, as technologically-intensive approaches by-passed the peasantry, compounding a legacy that links rural poverty and environmental degradation.

This failure not only prompted an intensive critique of top-down agricultural research and development by agroecologists, but also stimulated an active search for new kinds of agricultural development and resource management strategies that, based on local participation, skills and resources, enhanced productivity while conserving the resource base. Local farmers' knowledge about the environment, plants, soils and ecological processes regains unprecedented significance within this new agroecological paradigm. Understanding the ecological and cultural features of traditional agriculture, such as the ability to bear risks, biological folk taxonomies, the production efficiencies of symbiotic crop mixtures, and the use of local plants for pest control, is crucial for obtaining useful and relevant information to guide the development of appropriate agricultural strategies more sensitive to the complexities of agroecological and socioeconomic processes and that are also tailored to the needs of specific peasant groups and regional agroecosystems. The idea is that agricultural research and development should operate on the basis of a 'bottom up' approach, starting with what is there already: local people, their needs and aspirations, their farming knowledge and their autochthonous natural resources.

Although the above argument has penetrated most circles engaged in international research and development, the topic has remained largely an academic one, rarely transcending the boundaries of seminars, conferences, books and articles. This is not the case, however, for a large group of non-government organisations (NGOs) which emerged in Latin America and that are challenging the notion that development can only be done 'top-down' from the state. NGOs in Latin America have actively promoted the idea of alternative development. They represent a step forward in technological innovation and new development styles, more connected to the cultural traditions and resource endowment of each region and/or country.

Some NGOs involved in rural development programs (RDPs) have demonstrated a unique ability to understand the specific and differentiated nature of small farm production and have promoted successful experiences in generation and transfer of peasant technology. The programs of these NGO's are guided by four main concerns:

- o the progressive deterioration of the natural resource base of the peasantry;
- o the precarious subsistence level of the peasant family;
- o the growing loss of identity of peasant groups; and
- o the limiting factors that inhibit the peasant accumulation process as well as the lack of incentives for peasants to improve their poverty conditions.

Even though there exists a large variety of RDPs promoted by NGOs, there is a consensus that there are specific components that cannot be ignored if one hopes to effectively combat the social exclusion, environmental degradation and impoverishment experienced by the peasantry. One of these components is the organisation of the peasantry, therefore a dominant trait of NGO activities is the awakening of a determination for social change within the peasantry. Social organisations can take the form of unions and federations organised around labour, or they can be community based. Although these organisations may be motivated by technically-productive questions, the efficiency of peasant activities is directly dependent on the quality of their organisations and the creation of leaders.

The question of peasant identity is another aspect that RDP's consider when confronting rural poverty, especially when dealing with indigenous communities. In these communities, NGOs' popular education programs always have the development of a social consciousness and the reinforcement of the ethnic identity of the peasantry as an objective.

A strong emphasis of these programs is the defence and rescue of the traditional peasant productive rationale and culture. These programs are implemented at the community level and seek to strengthen community institutions such as collective work and natural leadership hierarchies, as well as to fortify the subsistence economy. Although many of these programs have been criticised as idealising a past world, and of not understanding the dynamics of capitalist modernisation and of the development process, several NGOs have transcended conventional wisdom by integrating social and technical aspects involved in rural development into a single strategy.

The starting point has been to define a new agricultural approximation of the peasant production process based on agroecological principles. The agroecological approach is culturally compatible since it does not question peasants' rationale, but actually builds upon traditional farming knowledge, combining it with elements of modern agricultural science. The resulting techniques are ecologically sound because they do not radically modify or transform the peasant ecosystem, but rather identify traditional and/or new management elements that, once incorporated, lead to optimisation of the production unit. The objective is to develop a peasant productive rationale which can give place to a process of reconstruction of autochthonous values and indigenous culture.

Even though NGOs that have been influenced by this new perspective are a minority in Latin America, they are clearly the ones which are projecting a growing image of creativity and realism. It is this group of eight Latin American NGOs (see Appendix I for a description of the member NGOs and their activities) that, convinced of the need of a new institutional arrangement to foster a

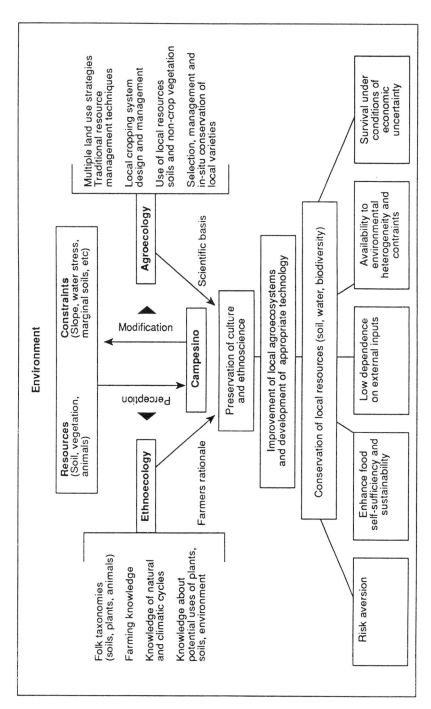

Figure 40.1: *An agroecological and ethnoecological paradigm that integrates traditional knowledge and Western science in the search of sustainable agricultural strategies*

more in-depth development of agroecology and its application in rural development, created the *Consorcio Latino Americano sobre Agroecologia y Desarrollo* (CLADES – Latin American Consortium on Agroecology and Development) January 1989 in a meeting in Santiago, Chile. The central objective of the Consortium is the development and diffusion of technological options for peasants based on an agroecological approach and the training of professionals and technicians associated with institutions committed to sustainable agriculture. Thus, the Consortium will serve as an institutional axis to coordinate a research, training and information exchange between the member NGOs, which in turn will extend the Consortium's contributions within their own national and regional spaces.

CLADES' approach to preserve and strengthen peasants' productive rationale is through programs of popular education and training using demonstration farms that incorporate both traditional peasant techniques as well as new viable alternatives. In this way farmers' knowledge and environmental perceptions are integrated into schemes of agricultural technological innovations that attempt to link resource conservation and rural development. If a resource conservation strategy that is compatible with a production strategy is indeed to succeed among small farmers, the process must be linked to rural development efforts that give equal importance to local resource conservation and food self-sufficiency and/or participation in local markets. Any attempt at soil, forest or crop genetic conservation must struggle to preserve the agroecosystems in which these resources occur. It is clear that preservation of traditional agroecosystems cannot be achieved isolated from maintenance of the ethnoscience and socio-cultural organisation of the local people. It is for this reason the CLADES emphasises an agroecological–ethnoecological approach as an effective mechanism to link farmers' knowledge with Western scientific approaches in the search of an agricultural development that matches local needs, constraints and resource-base (Figure 40.1).

Appendix 40.1: Non-government organisations comprising the Latin American Consortium on Agroecology and Development (CLADES):

Servicios Multiples de Tecnologias Apropiadas (SEMTA), Casilla 20410, La Paz, Bolivia.
For 10 years SEMTA has been devoted to the development of appropriate technologies for rural areas in the central altiplano (highland plain) of Bolivia. Their agricultural work emphasises organic potato production, crop protection through biological pest suppression, vegetable production in greenhouses appropriate to the Altiplano, and small scale irrigation. They also have a strong medicinal plants program built upon the ethnobotanical knowledge of the Kallawaya Indians.

Projeto Tecnologias Alternatives (PTA), Rua Bento Lisboa 58, 3° Andar, Catete, CEP 22221, Rio de Janeiro, RJ, Brasil.
This organisation promotes alternative technologies to support small farmer organisations. They provide technical assistance to organisations and communities of small rural producers in the areas of production, marketing and labour organisation. Their approach is to enhance solidarity among farmer groups, distributing technological innovations to allow people to collectively confront production limitations. Presently, they work within twelve states through a network of documentation centres, centres of alternative technology (for experimentation, training and demonstration), publications and training courses for PTA technicians and rural promoters. FASE regularly publishes the magazine *Proposta,* which, among other things, describes PTA activities. FASE/PTA also intermittently publishes a series entitled *Boletin do Projeto T.A.* which describes organisation activities, upcoming events, and current projects and technologies.

Centro de Education y Tecnologia (CET), Casilla 16557, Correo 9, Santiago, Chile.
CET is devoted to the search for alternative forms of agricultural development among the rural and urban poor, building upon the resources available to these sectors. They have developed programs in six regions of Chile reaching approximately eighty communities. In their research/training centres they have trained technicians from about one hundred and sixty Chilean and Latin American institutions on alternative farming techniques. They publish the series *Somos Capaces* in which they describe their model organic peasant farm and intensively managed homegardens, which have proved to sustain productivity and provide diet diversity relying only on local resources. Associated with CET is the *Comision de Investigacion de Agricultura Alternativa (CIAL),* which is a group of professors from the schools of agriculture of the University of Chile, Catholic University Santiago, and Quillota Campuses who conduct and sponsor research in collaboration with CET on alternative agriculture. Although each professor emphasises a particular research area (organic soil management, biological pest control, agroforestry and livestock production), they collaborate in on-farm case studies and also direct student theses on topics that reinforce CET's community training work

Centro de Tecnologia Campesina (CETEC), Avenida 5 Norte #20-37, Cali, Colombia.
CETEC concentrates its efforts in the southwestern part of the Cauca Valley. In the realm of agriculture its training and technical assistance efforts are targeted to provide low-input technologies tailored to the needs of small cassava producers and to enhance the food self-sufficiency of sugarcane labourers and their families through the establishment of intensive home gardens. CETEC has established working relationships with other Colombian NGO's (*i.e.* FUNDAEC, IMCA) engaged in technological development for campesinos.

Centro Andino de Accion Popular (CAAP), Apartado 173-B, Quito, Ecuador.
Established in 1977, CAAP implements rural development activities among the peasants and indigenous peoples of the North and Central Sierras of Ecuador. The aim of their agricultural project is to rescue traditional knowledge in order to conceptualise the productive rationale of Andean peasants. CAAP tries to strengthen this productive rationale by supporting peasants in their quest for appropriate technologies and a connection to local markets. Through demonstrative and experimental farms, CAAP adds to the Andean technology. CAAP also supports traditional health systems based on existing traditional medical practices and agents through their health program. Both programs are integrated through social organisation strategies based on social affinities particular to each group. CAAP has an active publications program which includes three series: *Cuadernos de Educacion Popular, Cuadernos de Discusion Popular* and *Cuadernos de Capacitacion Popular* (popular education, discussion and training). In addition, they publish *Ecuador Debate* of which some issues are devoted to rural development and the peasantry.

Centro de Promoción Campesina de la Coordillera (C.P.C.C.), Dr. Pino 1975, Caacupé, Paraguay.
CPCC is an institution administered by a peasant organisation that promotes farmers' participation in alternative development programs emphasising agroforestry, apiculture, food production and commercialisation. Their activities concentrate in an area of minifundios about 50 km. from Asunción

Centro de Investigación, Educación y Desarrollo (CIED), Apartado 11-0104, Lima II, Perú.
CIED initiated its education and promotion activities in 1973 to support the peasants of the Altiplano, especially in the areas of Lima, Puno, Arequipa and Cajamarca. For example, CIED's Equipo de Desarrolla Agropecuario (EDAC) in Cajamarca centres its activities on: a) soil and water conservation in micro-watersheds of Porcón and Chonta, b) diversification of Andean crop production for subsistence and marketing through appropriate technologies, revolving credit and seed banks, c) animal husbandry for income generation, d) marketing; e) crafts, f) health and nutrition, and g) social organisation.

Centro Ideas, Apartado 11670, Lima 11, Perú.
Centro Ideas is interested in reversing several of the problems affecting rural areas of Cajamarca (i.e. soil erosion, disappearance of Andean crops, crop monocultures leading to protein-poor diets, etc.). Their alternative production schemes are based on organic agricultural principles. They have developed improved crop rotations and associations in a model-demonstration farm, which includes crops such as lentils, quinoa, and lupins. A research component has been added to quantify yield trends in each proposed rotation. Preliminary results show yield increases as well as monetary gain. They also emphasise small animal husbandry (goats, cuyes), planting of native fruit trees, medicinal plants, insect repellent plants, and soil conservation practices. Their women-children program features mixed home gardens, food preparation and basic health education.462

41. Traditional Ecological Knowledge and UNESCO's Man and the Biosphere (MAB) Programme

MALCOLM HADLEY AND KATHRIN SCHRECKENBERG[1]

Introduction: the MAB context

THE MAN AND the Biosphere (MAB) Programme was launched by UNESCO in the early 1970s. Its overall aim is to help develop the basis within the natural and social sciences for sustained resource management and improved land use planning. The program is rooted in national efforts, promoted and sponsored through more than a hundred MAB National Committees, with technical and financial support from UNESCO and collaborating international organizations. Among the underlying principles of action are the consideration of conservation as an integral part of management and the linking of basic and applied research with efforts for education, training, and the dissemination of information for different user groups. Further background on the program is available in a variety of UNESCO reports (*e.g.* UNESCO 1987, 1988, 1989) and a twice-yearly newsletter InfoMAB.

Given the overall objective of MAB, it would be somewhat surprising if the program did not include studies on indigenous peoples and their decision-making and resource use systems. Work has been carried out by national participating institutions, in a variety of ecological and socio-cultural settings. This work has encompassed such topics as traditional medicinal plants in islands of the Caribbean (Weninger and Robineau 1987) and the Mediterranean (Giani 1987), the attempted recreation of historical grassland management in the mid-latitude biosphere reserve, Vassertal in the German Democratic Republic (Seidel 1988), the use of a traditional community gathering – the Maori Hui – for discussing research and development plans in a coastal marine area in New Zealand (Simpson *et al.* 1987), leadership, channels of communication and decision-making processes among pastoralists in Northern Kenya, as ingredients for shaping extension programs (Lusigi 1984), biosphere reserves and the conservation of traditional land use systems of indigenous populations in Central America (Houseal and Weber 1989).

In the following paragraphs, we provide an idea of the flavour and content of MAB studies on traditional ecological knowledge, by drawing on examples from the inter-tropical belt. We group these insights under two headings: field studies on traditional resource use systems, and efforts to synthesize and diffuse information on traditional ways of using natural resources in the humid tropics. Activities have touched on technological and cultural characteristics of tropical forest societies and the various ways of using natural resources and obtaining food, including food gathering, swidden cultivation and settled agriculture.

Field studies on traditional resource use

Understanding and adapting traditional agricultural systems in Mexico One example within MAB of scientists seeking to understand a traditional agricultural system and adapt it to present-day development needs is afforded by the Mexican 'chinampas' project (Gómez-Pompa and Venegas 1976, Gómez-Pompa *et al.* 1982, Morales 1984). In Mexico, as in most developing countries, a priority problem is to find inexpensive ways of increasing food output using systems that take advantage of the characteristics of the local environment and that can be sustained without the need for large-scale inputs in terms of fertilizers, capital, and equipment. The promising approach to this problem developed by scientists from the Institute for the Study of Biological Resources (INIREB) in Jalapa, stemmed from the recognition of the special nature and success of a traditional agricultural system, the chinampa, and the possibility presented by this system to create a new method for meeting food needs.

In the chinampa system, raised beds of soil and organic matter were built above the water surface and were maintained by cultivation of a great diversity of aquatic plants and crops. This system fed the Aztec city of Tenochtitlan and from archaeological evidence was widespread throughout the Americas. However, it is thought that the system persisted only in the vicinity of Mexico City to modern times. Analysis on the chinampa has showed it to be a low-capital, labour-intensive, sustainable system of farming, with the potential of being combined with small-scale forest industries to produce multiple products from farm and forest. The system has been tried out in four rain forest areas in Mexico. One of these areas, in Tabasco state, consisted of a combination of semi-evergreen rain forest and swamps. Another very different site was chosen in tropical rain forest at Chiapas – traditionally farmed by shifting, slash-and-burn methods. Here, chinampas were built near a river which provided the irrigation water, with the organic mulch for the chinampa plots being obtained from the litter of the adjacent rain forest.

Satisfactory results have been obtained from the mixed agropiscicultural systems that have developed on a pilot basis. Tree crops such as papaya and banana have been successfully combined with vegetable crops and poultry, pig and fish production. Systems of recycling plant residues and animal wastes have been refined and high sustained yields of tree and vegetable crops have been recorded. Progress has also been achieved in promoting the use of native tree species in reforestation and agro-forestry programs, following studies that demonstrated the adaptability of the species to a variety of soils and climates, their rapid growth, the use of leaves for forage, the nutrition value of fruits (particularly seeds) for human and animal food, the commercial potential of wood.

The research of the INIREB team was closely linked with training and demonstration at various levels, and these activities lay at the heart of the success achieved. Formal graduate and undergraduate courses were regularly offered by the researchers themselves, in which theoretical knowledge was combined with field practice. Seminars and workshops were organized on specific subjects for scientists and technicians. Students came from a number of disciplines, both in the natural and social sciences, training for careers ranging from bio-ecological field research to social work, marketing management, and planning. Another successful innovation in the training and information activities of the chinampas and integrated farming projects was the organization of field training seminars for and by the peasant farmers, based on their own knowledge and experience and reinforced by their active participation in field work.

Follow-up work by Mexican researchers has included ecological analysis of Maya agriculture (Gómez-Pompa 1987, 1989) and the combination of traditional tree and crop species in managing the secondary vegetation in the Uxpanapa area of Veracruz State (del Amo 1989). The Veracruz studies, for example, have entailed comparison of corn field two-year old orchards and nine- and twelve-year-old secondary forest. Elucidation of recovery processes has aimed at identifying ways and means of managing and accelerating the succession towards more useful and productive stages. Clearance of some plants and enrichment with others are among the experimental treatments, which have sought to take advantage of knowledge about traditional systems of horticulture (Mayas), multiple use of land (Lacandones), and the use of different ecological habitats (Chontales, Nahuas) in Mexico. Data include rates of biomass and nutrient accumulation during the fallow, and chemical interactions between and among the naturally occurring and introduced plant species. Management insights generated by the study include ways of introducing valued species with different ecological strategies into the successional sequence, and the imitation to the extent possible of the 'natural' structure of the various successional stages.

People-forest interactions in East Kalimantan, Indonesia Integrated social and biological research at several tropical forest locations in the Indonesian province of East Kalimantan has indicated variation among farmers in their reasons for practicing shifting cultivation, the extensiveness of their farming, and the amount of forest damage they cause. The research was undertaken within a MAB project headed by Kuswata Kartawinata (a botanist who was formerly head of the Bogor Herbarium and is now regional adviser in ecology at the UNESCO office in Jakarta) and Andrew Vayda (an anthropologist at Rutgers University). In providing information about people's response to changing economic opportunities in East Kalimantan, the researchers hoped to show (a) the range of people's forest-related knowledge, (b) their repertoire of forest-related activities, (c) the variety of situations in which decisions to engage in those activities or to change them are made, and (d) the environmental and social effects that the activities have (Kartawinata *et al.* 1981).

Three main locations for the research were selected, a remote interior plateau, a down-river resettlement area and the environs of the provincial capital. The remote Apo Kayan plateau, the homeland of several thousand Kenya people who live in long-house communities and practice forest-fallow shifting cultivation, has been the site of part of the study. The Kenya people are not reckless destroyers of the forest. Rather, they maintain, tend and re-use sites and, throughout the last couple of hundred years at least, there has been a fairly persistent conservative pattern of forest exploitation. In the Apo Kayan, the Kenya have converted the virgin forest into a mosaic of secondary forest of different ages, plus unfelled reserves where they can harvest products which are rare or not to be found in secondary forest.

Most swiddens (sections of forest cleared for agriculture by cutting and burning) are made on more fertile soils, on slopes of intermediate grade, and in secondary forest that is eight to twenty years old, with primary forest reserves maintained close to the villages.

Results of studies on the seed bank (the seeds actually present in the soil), of sampling of one to four-year-old fields and of surveys of secondary forest, provide consistent evidence that shifting cultivation at Apo Kayan is a forest-maintaining agricultural system. Those tree species common in secondary forest appear early in old field succession and seem to be particularly well adapted to regeneration after shifting cultivation because they resprout or their seeds survive burning.

The situation is somewhat different at Telen River, the downstream area where settlements of migrants from the Apo Kayan were established prior to the post-1967 timber boom. Despite the hopes of some planners that 're-settled' shifting cultivators could be induced to use more intensive agricultural methods, shifting cultivation is more, not less, extensive than at Apo Kayan. Moreover, it is being practiced mainly in primary rather than secondary forest.

This is not due to any backwardness on the part of the migrant farmers, but results from the promotion by extension workers of inappropriate methods (such as irrigated rice cultivation) and from economic circumstances which both encourage extensive agricultural production and make the clearing of large areas of primary forest relatively easy because of the ready availability of chain-saws, outboard motors and fuel. A related factor is the low inherent fertility of soils in the area which precludes intensive sedentary agriculture.

Market-oriented production systems in the Peruvian Amazon Many of the cyclic agroforestry systems studied to date in the tropics have been those practiced by relatively remote tribal groups that are largely outside the chain of active commerce. This has tended to suggest that such systems of resource management are suited only to subsistence production. However, recent investigations carried out by a number of independent researchers indicate that they can also be important cash producers.

One study, sponsored by US–MAB and local Peruvian institutions, examined a market-oriented system practiced by farmers at Tamshiyacu, Peru (Padoch *et al.* 1985, Denevan and Padoch 1988). The Tamshiyaquinos are a non-tribal group some 2000 strong, of mixed Amazonian and European ancestry, living about 30 km south-east of the regional market centre of Iquitos. They engage in a large number of agricultural and extractive activities, exploiting a wide variety of the land and water resources available to them. The techniques used by the Tamshiyaquinos include the farming of upland sites under both high forest and fallow growth of varying ages, the cultivation of seasonally inundated, low-lying sites, as well as fishing, hunting and the extraction of a variety of forest products. Foods, fibres, handicraft materials and charcoal are among items obtained from the fields and forests of Tamshiyacu that appear on the local market and the urban market of nearby Iquitos.

The agroforestry cycle begins with cutting of the standing vegetation. In secondary forest areas, the slash is not burned in the manner typical of shifting cultivation. Instead, the larger woody vegetation is often converted into charcoal. After clearing, a variety of annual and semi-perennial crops are planted. Some of these crops are re-planted during the second year. A number of perennials – most of them tree crops – are also planted in the second year.

Annual crop production is gradually phased out after an initial two-to five-year period. Perennial tree crops become the most important source of income from the plot and production may continue for 25–50 years if the fields are maintained and protected from cattle. The plot is cleared several times a year while annuals and semi-perennials predominate, but this is gradually reduced in frequency to once or twice a year just before the harvest of the Umari, the most important tree crop. As soon as production drops significantly – after between about 25 and 50 years – the larger items of vegetation (the Umari and the Brazil-nut trees) are cut and converted into charcoal.

Following this second round of charcoal-making, the field is generally left to lie fallow for six years or so. Secondary growth invades the plot and, according to local farmers, begins to restore it so that another production cycle can be set in train. Most households have several agroforestry fields operating at any one time. Since these fields are in different stages of the production cycle, farmers tend to obtain an income from the sale of a variety of resources. This strategy limits the risks inherent in specialization, spaces out the need for often scarce labour and assures households of some cash flow throughout the year.

The limited observations so far made indicate that, thanks to the cyclic agro-forestry production method, the Tamshiyaquinos enjoy some of the highest average annual incomes to be found among rural dwellers of the region. In one survey of thirteen villages in the Iquitos region, some Tamshiyacu households were found to have gross yearly incomes of nearly $5000, although the mean for village households was a more modest, but still above average, income of some $1200.

Synthesis and diversification of technical information

From state-of-knowledge reports to slides and posters Complementing support of field projects are efforts to synthesize and diffuse scientific information for different audiences. Such past synthesis activities relating to the humid tropics have incorporated components on traditional resource use. Thus, one of the three main sections of a 683-page state-of-knowledge report on tropical forest ecosystems prepared by UNESCO, UNEP and FAO (UNESCO 1978) focussed on human populations and patterns of use of tropical forest ecosystems, includ-ing indigenous resource use. A slide tape program on Man and the Humid Tropics (UNESCO 1979) addressed traditional agricultural use in these regions, among other issues. One of the posters in a 36-poster exhibit entitled 'Ecology in Action' (UNESCO 1981) was devoted to learning from traditional resource use (Illustration 41.1). A three-stage, five-country study of shifting cultivation in Asia included profiles on indigenous resource use in five countries (UNESCO 1983). More recently, in 1989, two semi-popular reports have addressed two aspects of traditional resource use in the humid tropics – one concerning a sur-vey of traditional crop improvement techniques, the other the relations of African forest-dwellers with their equatorial environment.

Survey of traditional crop improvement techniques Phytopractices, after 'phyto-pratiques' in French, is a term of recent origin that describes all those treat-ments which may improve, select, propagate or preserve plants on an individual basis. Included are a range of plant manipulation techniques and practices which are applied with care to each plant or a few associated plants, in order to improve the quality and quantity of the products that can be obtained from those plants. Also included are techniques for selection, preservation or propa-gation. Though a great variety of techniques are involved, a common thread is the culture of plants as individuals. Two examples are illustrated in Figures 41.1 and 41.2.

Considerations of phytopractices take into account the inherent characteris-tics of each plant (morphology, physiology, and biological cycle) as well as its micro-environmental conditions (soil, sunlight, and influence of neighbouring plants). Skill, a keen sense of observation and judicious timing, contributes to the successful application of such practices. Most practices are simple, inexpen-sive and call upon materials that are readily available. As such, they provide a complementary approach to genetic techniques for improving biological perfor-

Illustration 41.1: *Coloured poster on traditional resource use from the ecology in action exhibit (UNESCO 1981, actual size 120×80 cm)*

Figure 41.1: *Cover design from a preliminary survey on phytopractices in tropical regions (Aumeeruddy and Pinglo 1989), showing stages in moulding square-selected bamboo, for use as building materials, scaffolding ornamental columns.* Artwork by Jill Courbet

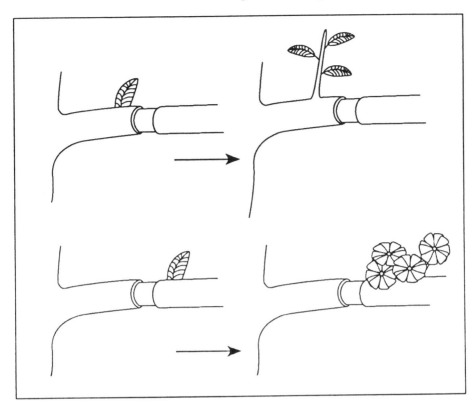

Figure 41.2: *Effect of ringing on the growth of flowering or vegetature buds. An incision made above the bud (i.e. between the bud and the end of the branch) favours the development of vegetature sprouts. An incision below the buds blocks sap circulation. Photosynthesis by-products accumulate in the distal part, thus favouring flowering.*
From Aumeeruddy and Pinglo (1989)

mance. They also represent one response to a certain dissatisfaction with a number of the development approaches that have been promoted in the tropics over the last few decades.

The large-scale transformation of tropical forests, the transfer of sophisticated technologies developed elsewhere and the use of high input agriculture can indeed produce impressive results, given the right mix of ingredients. But often results are disappointing and progress short-lived, for a variety of technological, environmental, economic and cultural reasons. Hence the search for approaches which consider the needs and concepts of tropical farmers, and which build on the mixed cropping systems which have long been a feature of tropical environments. It was within such a context that a preliminary survey of traditional crop improvement techniques in tropical regions has been prepared, as one of several collaborative efforts in the field of tropical ecology of UNESCO–MAB and the Laboratoire de Botanique Tropicale in Montpellier, France (Aumeeruddy and Pinglo 1989).

The aim of the report is threefold: first to present a compilation of traditional techniques of plant manipulation in tropical regions, as a contribution to current efforts to improve agricultural production in these zones; second, to invite comments and suggestions for modifying and completing the present test; third, to encourage new initiatives of research, synthesis and application geared to sustained development in the tropics, which is in tune with the ecological and socio-cultural characteristics and constraints of these regions. While both trees and herbaceous species are reviewed, the survey concentrates on techniques used for woody plants. Notations are used to signify those methods that have been tested scientifically, are in need of further testing, or are original but lack adequate scientific study.

This report is, admittedly, very much an incomplete compilation, a working tool, an invitation for readers to react, and those who have knowledge and experience with other traditional methods of crop propagation and improvements have been encouraged to contribute to this working document. Depending on the reaction to the compilation, the intention is to produce a revised version of the report in about two years' time, and/or to transform and adapt the information into different forms, (*e.g.* individual 'fiches' or 'cards' for specific practices), for particular purposes, regions, groups of techniques. In the immediate term, attention is being given to further testing and demonstration of particular groups of techniques under field conditions. An example is within a project geared to integrated rural development in the Mayombe region of the Congo, where a roving rural orientation seminar in December 1988 brought together some 150 peasant farmers and other local people around the theme of fruit tree phytopractices (Koyo *et al.* 1989).

Food and nutrition in the African rainforest The complex relations between traditional forest-dwelling peoples, their natural environment and its resources, has been well reflected and recorded in a multidisciplinary research project on the feeding and food anthropology of populations of the humid tropical zone of Africa. The research was carried out by a research team of the French Centre Nationale de Recherche Scientifique, working in collaboration with local research institutions in Cameroon, Central African Republic, Congo, Gabon and Zaire. Involved in the project were about a dozen researchers, specialists in ecology, anthropology, human ecology, ethno-ecology, psychophysiology and nutrition. In addition to individual reports and articles in the scientific press, the results of the research team have been presented in a poster exhibition originally displayed at the Maison des Sciences de l'Homme in Paris in October–November 1987.

These origins are reflected in the many graphics which embellish a semi-popular report subsequently compiled and edited by the three coordinators of the project, Claude-Marcel Hladik, Serge Bahuchet and Igor de Garine (Hladik *et al.* 1989). Published as a joint venture of CNRS Research Team 263 ('Anthropologie Alimentaire Différentielle') and UNESCO–MAB, in collaboration with the French Ministry of Cooperation and Development, the report comprises five substantive sections which reflect the sorts of interests and concerns that contribute to a biocultural study of resource use in the humid tropical zone. Thus the five sections deal with:

o the dense equatorial forest and its hunter-gatherer populations (structure, production and products of the forest, the Aka pygmies of the central African forest, the art of trapping animals in the forest);

- forest-dwelling farmers (the history of cultivated plants in Central Africa, agricultural strategies which complement hunting and fishing, seasonality of food, seasonal hunger and the yearning for meat);
- preparation, conservation and consumption of food (forest recipes, products of the oil palm, measurement of food consumption);
- physiological and biomedical aspects of nutrition (energy balance and nutritional adaptability, tasting perceptions, biomedical surveys, feeding of vulnerable groups); and
- sociocultural dimensions of nutrition (organization of meals, values attributed to foodstuffs and socio-economic structures, nutrition and traditional medicine, feeding of the weaning mother, food taboos and nutritional concepts).

The reports attempt a synthesis of a fair amount of original scientific information, much of it as yet unpublished or not widely available, in a form understandable by the non-specialist. The study has for example confirmed that human beings can subsist solely from the natural resources of the equatorial forest. Here the wild ignames (tuberous plants originating in the dense African rain forest) constitute a critically important resource, with more than five tonnes of tubers permanently available in the 50 km^2 area corresponding to the gathering area of a small group of pygmies (Hladik *et al.* 1989). Qualitatively, a potentially important discovery has been that by Van der Wel *et al.* (1989) of non-glucose sugars in a climber Pentadiplandra brazzeana, which offers possibilities for use by the food processing industry. Research has also confirmed previous findings on seasonal hunger, which appears to be a widespread phenomenon in tropical Africa though culturally specific (Pagezy 1988). It can be linked to a shortage of basic calorie-providing foodstuffs or to a lack of a particular culturally esteemed food like game or fish. A survey of four ethnic groups in southern Cameroon has shed new light on the different food strategies adopted by different ethnic groups, through. New results have also been obtained on the energy expended in various daily and seasonal tasks, based on oxygen consumption measures.

The report was published in its original French version in September 1989. An English language version of the report is under preparation, under the working title 'Food and Nutrition in the African Rain Forest', with an anticipated publication by UNESCO in late 1990. Among the planned follow-up activities is an international scientific conference on the general theme of biocultural dimensions of resource use in the humid tropics.

Conclusions

Many groups of researchers, from a wide range of disciplines, have a contribution to make to the search for sustained production systems in the tropics. Many approaches can contribute to this process, including research on traditional knowledge of local farmers and other resource users. Much of this knowledge remains unrecorded and unexploited. Every year sees part of this knowledge being lost with the transformation of ecosystems and local cultures. Yet recording and applying this traditional ecological knowledge provides one approach to making more effective use of the biological wealth of our planet.

Indeed, studies on traditional ecological knowledge and people-forest interactions reflect clear but cautious optimism concerning the future of tropical forest lands as summarized in some of the overall findings of some twenty field studies supported by a consortium of institutions under the auspices of US–MAB during an eight-year period in the late 1970s and early 1980s (Lugo *et al.* 1987). Tropical forest-dwelling farmers often have a profound knowledge of their highly varied environments which could be better tapped in assessing the agricultural potential of their home regions and in shaping schemes for the settlement of migrants. There is evidence that many tropical forest inhabitants are progressive, permanent-field farmers producing surpluses despite a growing population and without destroying forests. Moreover, many tropical forest zone inhabitants are eager to accept change, but at their own pace and on their own conditions. Planners should take the pace of adaptation into account when proposing changes such as the adoption of new crops or switching from land-extensive to land-intensive forms of agriculture.

In sum, the results of people-environment studies highlight a way forward in the search for an improved basis for ecologically sound development in the tropics – that of integrating the resource-based knowledge of local people (in such domains as multiple-cropping, manipulation of swidden fallows, etc.) with modern technological know-how, in flexible ways that are capable of adapting and being adapted to changing social and economic circumstances.

Note

1. The views expressed in this contribution are the authors' and not necessarily those of UNESCO.

42. Sustainable Development and Indigenous Knowledge Systems in Nigeria: The role of the Nigerian Institute of Social and Economic Research (NISER)

ADEDOTUN O. PHILLIPS AND S. OGUNTUNJI TITILOLA

Introduction

IT IS INCREASINGLY evident that past approaches to development which neglected local knowledge systems and institutions were unlikely to be productive in solving developing countries' problems. These approaches are not likely to be in the long-term interest of these countries in view of recent revelations, especially in agriculture about the effects of such development paradigms on the environment and sustainability of development in general (Wolf 1986).

As a result of this and in view of the recent strides in biotechnology development, emphasis is now being devoted to the study of local agriculture systems because of their usefulness in enhancing biotechnology research and also in the preservation of gene pools which are essential to the advancement of such research efforts.

The current emphasis of development in Nigeria concentrates on the rural areas where a majority of Nigerians reside. What the local people know and want for improvement must be fully understood and used to develop a participatory development model. In this case, indigenous knowledge becomes the key to local level development.

Agricultural development and local knowledge systems

In the last ten years, an increasing number of publications supports the argument that farmers in developing countries have a wealth of knowledge about their environment, have developed skills to rationally exploit their environment and are very active and creative in their use of the environment for reaching their goals. Prominent advocates of this new line of thinking are Richards (1985), Dommen (1988), Chambers (1985), Chambers *et al.* (1989), Warren and Cashman (1988) and Ruthenberg (1985). Institutions such as the United States Agency for International Development (USAID), Consultative Group for International Agricultural Research (CGIAR) (York 1988), and the United States Congress Office of Technology Assessment (OTA) (1984) have similarly endorsed this view. This line of reasoning calls for conceptual and fundamental changes, in the ways agricultural researchers, extension workers, and international agricultural development donors, they see and relate to farmers and their perceived problems. For instance, in a USAID evaluation program report of past development efforts in less developed countries, it is explained that 'the farmers in developing countries are knowledgeable about the environment, i.e. soil and climate, in which they operate more than the researchers working at the national or regional level' (AID 1983).

In a study of the grasshopper (*Zonocerous variegatus*), the findings of the ethno-ecological investigation corroborated those of the scientific study. The farmers described in great detail the behaviour of the grasshopper in ways similar to the findings of the scientific study (Chambers 1980).

In 1988 NISER began conducting an in-depth examination of Nigerian Indigenous Grain Storage Techniques in order to identify, describe and characterise the socio-economic factors which influence their utilisation. In addition, the study seeks to identify factors which may have constrained their further development, and to assess the viability of promoting their enhanced utilisation (Phillips,1989).

As a result of ineffective attempts to introduce agricultural technologies to many developing countries, experts in agricultural development assistance have become interested in analysing traditional agricultural systems, viewing these systems as valuable resources for agricultural development. This change of attitude reflects efforts to understand indigenous agricultural practices and scientific research results that show that traditional farming systems often represent efficient responses to meeting multiple objectives with meagre resources (OTA 1984; Dommen 1988). According to Paul Richards (1985), indigenous knowledge is the single largest knowledge resource not yet mobilised in the development enterprise. Recently agricultural scientists have begun to recognise that many farming systems that have persisted for many years exemplify competent management of soil, water, and nutrients (Wolf 1986).

The role of NISER

NISER, a Nigerian federal government institution plays an important role in the promotion of social and economic development in Nigeria through its specialised studies of issues pertaining to development, its seminars, conferences, workshops and training programs. The Institute's research output has been an important component in the development of Nigeria National Plans.

Currently, the issue of the use and importance of indigenous knowledge systems in development is assuming an important dimension in Nigeria. In the past, development agencies have too often neglected the use of local knowledge in development models. Instead there has been a tendency to rely mainly on modern technology. The agencies often forget that technologies are products of science (knowledge) and human value systems of the society generating the technologies.

Technology is like genetic material in that it carries with it the code of the society which conceived it. Hence technology well-suited to one sociocultural environment may not be ideal to another society with different value systems, unless the technology goes through the process of indigenisation.

Indigenous technical knowledge is an important aspect of the culture and technology of a society that has generally been overlooked. Warren and Cashman (1988) characterised such knowledge as the sum of experience and knowledge for a given group which forms the basis for decision-making in regard to familiar and unfamiliar problems and challenges. Another definition by Altieri (1988) however characterised such knowledge as accumulated knowledge and traditional technological skills of the local people. This knowledge is derived from the direct intervention of humans and their environments. Successful adaptations are preserved and passed on from generation to generation through oral and/or experimental means.

Indigenous knowledge is a valuable national resource which has been overlooked in development efforts. Most of today's developed countries have at one time or another relied on their local knowledge in addition to knowledge from outside sources. The importance of indigenous knowledge includes the following:

o It encourages participatory decision-making and formation and effective functioning of local organisations;
o It is a practical concept that can be used to facilitate communication among several people; and
o It helps to assure that the end users of specific development projects are involved in developing technology appropriate to their needs.

By working with and through existing systems and institutions, change agents can facilitate the transfer of technology generated through the international research network in order to improve local systems.

Program development and implementation

To assure that valuable knowledge is identified and applied towards the improvement in the living conditions in Nigeria, the Nigerian Institute of Social and Economic Research (NISER) in collaboration with similar institutions worldwide is in the process of establishing two related institutions, (a) The African Resource Centre for Indigenous Knowledge (ARCIK), and (b) The Nigerian Resource Centre for Indigenous Knowledge (NIRCIK)

These centres have the following broad goals and objectives:

A. Promote the incorporation of indigenous knowledge in the design and imple mentation of development programs within Africa and Nigeria.
   1. Identify individuals and institutions who are involved in or wish to become involved in applied development studies of indigenous knowledge in such areas as agriculture, health, forestry, nutrition, aquaculture, natural resource management, credit, and decentralised decision-making.
   2. Carry out activities such as conferences, workshops and targeted publications to develop a greater awareness, understanding, and appreciation of indigenous knowledge and its actual and potential role in development.
   3. Facilitate the development of skills for identifying, recovering and utilising indigenous knowledge in development programs.
   4. Facilitate a cross-institutional and inter-African sharing of perspectives, experiences and skills in the incorporation of indigenous knowledge in development programs.
   5. Facilitate the establishment of national resource centres in each African country with documentation, training/consultancy and research functions.

B. Establish an African resource program for indigenous knowledge at NISER. The regional program would function to enhance NISER's role as a catalyst for an African regional effort to use indigenous knowledge in improving development programs. It would also
   1. Establish a well-defined organisational structure and leadership for an IKS program within NISER.
   2. Develop the capacity of the NISER staff for handling research, training and consultancy activities in IK in the African region.
   3. Document NISER's past and existing efforts to assess, record and utilise indigenous knowledge in a number of problem areas.

4. Identify and establish working relationships with individuals and groups in the African region who are involved and interested in IKS.
5. Facilitate region wide sharing of knowledge, strategies and methods for recording and incorporating IKS into development programs through conferences, workshops, seminars and publications.
6. Provide training and consultancy services to other agencies in the region in the following areas:
   (a) Skills in the use of methods for identifying, recording, assessing, storing, retrieving and using indigenous knowledge.
   (b) Develop the capability and the will among rural development workers to facilitate rural people's learning from each other.
   (c) Develop strategies and methods for incorporating IK to facilitate improved interaction among scientists, development workers and rural people.
   (d) Develop documentation capability within national and subregional settings.
   (e) Design and implement formative and summative evaluation strategies which assess the impact of IK on selected development programs.

C. Integrate a regional program for indigenous knowledge into the global network of regional and national resource centres for IK.
   1. Participate in the global documentation services and assist in developing a unified system for information sharing.
   2. Participate in international conferences aimed at furthering the science and art of incorporating IK into development.
   3. Write scholarly and popular papers on IK for publication and/or distribution throughout the world. Establish an African regional newsletter.
   4. Participate in the worldwide resource pool of expertise in the sharing of training and consulting services.
   5. Serve as an advocate for the global effort to promote the effectiveness and efficiency of IK in development efforts.

ARCIK has been located within the new library building at NISER, while NIRCIK has been housed at the Institute for Agricultural Research. Both centres have a full-time program director who will be assisted by a core of relevant staff. The new centres became operational in late 1990.

Conclusion

Although indigenous agricultural knowledge systems hold important potentials for improving agriculture in development countries, it is equally important to know that not all aspects of such knowledge systems will be functionally relevant. It is therefore important that we understand the dynamics of the systems before recommending changes that are likely to have positive effects on local conditions. Neither modern Western agriculture with its cost implications, high energy demand and environmental disregard nor indigenous traditional agriculture with its low yields are exactly what will be needed and desired by small scale farmers. The challenge for agriculture research is to endeavour to improve agriculture in ways to retain the strength of traditional agriculture while meeting the needs of changing times.

43. The Regional Program for the Promotion of Indigenous Knowledge in Asia (REPPIKA)

JUAN M. FLAVIER, ANTONIO DE JESUS AND CONRADO S. NAVARRO

Rationale

DEVELOPMENT AGENCIES HAVE too often neglected the use of indigenous knowledge (IK) in designing their development paradigms. It is not uncommon for them to brush aside the people's indigenous knowledge systems and folk beliefs as mere 'superstition,' 'backward ideas' and 'pagan practices.' Instead, there is tendency to rely solely on modern technological inventions. While there is no doubt that modern science has contributed a lot to the human race through technologies such as oral rehydration therapy (ORT) or improved seed varieties, the heavy reliance on technology has also had negative effects.

One can cite the problems brought about by ecological damage, the high cost of modern technology, the problem of project sustainability and the over-dependence on certain product inputs. These effects plus mounting pressures on the environment from pollution, population increases and shifting weather patterns have motivated some quarters to press for a reassessment of present-day development strategies.

This rethinking has brought about renewed interest on indigenous knowledge. Recent studies on ethnoscience have dismissed as unfounded the allegations that indigenous knowledge is irrational. Techno-economic innovations based on indigenous knowledge have been tested through time. Indigenous knowledge is a science that is user-derived and not scientist-derived, and its utilisation with development efforts could provide long-term advantages that would complement and enhance the contributions of modern-day inventions.

What is indigenous knowledge? Indigenous knowledge is basically local knowledge that is unique to a given culture. It is the information base for a society which facilitates communication and decision-making. Indigenous information systems are dynamic, and are continually influenced by internal creativity and experimentation as well as by contact with external systems. Indigenous knowledge systems include those defining the social, natural and physical environments, as well as cognitive and ideational systems. Indigenous knowledge systems form the basis for indigenous decision-making, which is operationalised through indigenous organisations. They provide the foundation for indigenous innovations and experimentation.

Why is indigenous knowledge important?

Indigenous knowledge is a valuable national resource. It exists and can be a source of pride and ownership in development. It is also a useful tool. It encourages participatory decision-making and the formulation and effective functioning of local organisations. Indigenous knowledge is a practical concept which can be used to facilitate communication among people coming from different backgrounds such as researchers, extension workers and beneficiaries. Familiarity with indigenous knowledge helps change agents understand and communicate with clientele groups by facilitating participatory approaches to decision-making. Indigenous knowledge helps to assure that the end-users of specific development projects are involved in developing technologies appropriate to their needs. By working with and through existing systems, change agents can facilitate the transfer of technology generated through the international research network in order to improve local systems. Indigenous knowledge is cost-effective since it builds on other development efforts aimed at sustainability and capacity-building.

Some knowledge systems are at risk due to Western-oriented educational systems and loss of biodiversity. Thus, there is a strong need to retrieve and protect these threatened knowledge systems.

Why a program for indigenous knowledge?

Although there is a very rich resource for indigenous knowledge, it is dispersed in various local entities. Also, it has to be retrieved from obscurity because of past efforts to deny its role in development. Thus, there has to be a systematic program that would identify, analyse, systematise and promote indigenous knowledge. A program for indigenous knowledge would cater for these needs.

Why Asia?

Asia is the world's biggest continent, both in land size and population. Asia's inhabitants amount to about 60 per cent of the world's population. In this vast land, the traditional and still dominant basis of livelihood is agriculture. Thus, the farmers constitute an overwhelming force in the region. Asia is also one of the world's cradles of ancient civilisation. Historically, Asia has played an important part in spreading knowledge to other parts of the globe. Thus, Asia is a gigantic resource area where indigenous knowledge could be retrieved and applied for the over-all human development.

Approach to program development

To ensure that valuable indigenous knowledge within the Asian region is identified, recovered and documented, shared and applied towards the improvement of the living conditions of the peasants, the International Institute of Rural Reconstruction (IIRR) has proposed to establish a Regional Program for the Promotion of Indigenous Knowledge in Asia (REPPIKA). REPPIKA has been officially inaugurated during the international symposium on 'Indigenous Knowledge and Sustainable Development' held at IIRR in Silang, Cavite, The Philippines, from 21–25 September 1992

Goals and objectives

A. Promote the incorporation of indigenous knowledge in the design and implementation of development programs within the Asian region.
   1. Identify individuals and institutions who are involved in or wish to become involved in applied development studies of indigenous knowledge in such areas as agriculture, health, forestry, nutrition, aquaculture, natural resource management, credit, and decentralised decision-making.

2. Carry out activities such as conferences, workshops and targeted publications to develop a greater awareness, understanding and appreciation of indigenous knowledge and its actual and potential role in development.
3. Facilitate the development of skills for identifying, recovering and utilising indigenous knowledge in development programs.
4. Facilitate a cross-institutional and inter-regional sharing of perspectives, experiences and skills in the incorporation of indigenous knowledge in development programs.
5. Facilitate the establishment of national resource centres in each Asian country with documentation, training/consultancy and research functions.

B. Establish an Asian resource program for indigenous knowledge at IIRR, building on the existing strengths and traditions of the IIRR as a rural development organisation. The regional program would function to enhance IIRR's role as a catalyst for an Asian regional effort to use indigenous knowledge in improving development programs.
1. Establish a well-defined organisational structure and leadership for an IKS program within IIRR.
2. Develop the capacity of the IIRR staff for handling research, training and consultancy activities in IK in the Asian region.
3. Document IIRR's past and existing efforts to assess, record, and utilise indigenous knowledge in a number of problem areas.
4. Identify and establish working relationships with individuals and groups in the Asian region who are involved and interested in IKS.
5. Facilitate region-wide sharing of knowledge, strategies and methods for recording and incorporating IKS into development programs through conferences, workshops, seminars and publications.
6. Provide training and consultancy services to other agencies in the region in the following areas:
   (a) Skills in the use of methods for identifying, assessing, recording, storing, retrieving and using indigenous knowledge.
   (b) Develop the capability and the will among rural development workers to facilitate rural people's learning from each other.
   (c) Develop strategies and methods for incorporating IK to facilitate improved interaction among scientists, development workers and rural people.
   (d) Develop documentation capabilities within national and sub-regional settings.
   (e) Design and implement formative and summative evaluation strategies which assess the impact of IK on selected development programs.

C. Integrate a regional program for indigenous knowledge into the global network of regional and national resource centres for IK.
1. Participate in the global documentation services and assist in developing a unified system for information sharing.
2. Participate in international conferences aimed at furthering the science and art of incorporating IK into development.
3. Write scholarly and popular papers on IK for publication and/or distribution throughout the world. Establish an Asian regional newsletter.
4. Participate in the worldwide resource pool of expertise in the sharing of

training and consulting services. Add IK components to established IIRR training modules.

5. Serve as an advocate for the global effort to promote the effectiveness and efficiency of IK in development efforts.

Why is IIRR interested in this program and what could it contribute?

There are a number of reasons why IIRR feels that this is an appropriate program for it to undertake. Among these are the following:

1. For the past seventy years, IIRR has been involved in a continuous generation of knowledge in rural development. Through the 'social laboratory approach,' which its founder, Dr. Y.C. James Yen, pioneered in China in the 1920s, it undertakes field operational research projects in selected rural villages of the Third World through which it 'learns by doing.' It generates knowledge on how to effectively enable peasants to improve their lives by actually undertaking rural development work with them in their own villages. In this way, IIRR is able to acquire knowledge in development work that is simple, practical and adaptable because they were developed in partnership with the peasants themselves. This is the same process involved in the identification of indigenous knowledge.

2. Dr. Yen himself was a pioneer in the use of indigenous knowledge. It was in his first 'social laboratory' in Ding Xian in North China that the concepts of the 'barefoot doctor' and 'farmer scholar' were born between 1929 and 1939. These were the progenitors of today's 'indigenous specialists' who utilise and share indigenous knowledge.

3. Learn by doing is just one of several development principles which guide IIRR's work. These principles are found in the following 'Credo of Rural Reconstruction':

Go to the People
Live among the People
Learn from the People
Plan with the People
Work with the People
Start with what the People know
Build on what the People have
Teach by showing
Learn by doing
Not a showcase but a pattern
Not odds and ends but a system
Not piecemeal but integrated approach
Not to conform but to transform
Not relief but release.

'Learn from the people', 'start with what they know', 'build on what the people have' – these are precisely what indigenous knowledge promotion is all about.

4. IIRR's mission statement mandates it to share knowledge in rural development with other development institutions and organisations throughout the world through a two-way process whereby it learns from others even as others learn from it. This is the same spirit behind the concept

of REPPIKA: a two-way process of sharing between and among various institutions and organisations in the Asian region who have an interest in the identification, recovery, documentation, sharing and application of indigenous knowledge.

5. The operationalisation of IIRR's sharing mission is facilitated by the existence of a network of national rural reconstruction movements and alumni associations throughout the Asian region which are affiliated with IIRR. This network includes the Philippine, Indian and Thailand Rural Reconstruction Movements; the South Asia Rural Reconstruction Association (SARRA), a sub-regional association of IIRR's training alumni in India, Nepal, Bangladesh and Sri Lanka; the Rural Reconstruction Alumni and Friends Association (RRAFA) of Thailand; and a number of still-to-be-organised alumni in China, Pakistan, Indonesia, Malaysia, Kampuchea and Laos, all of whom are potential collaborators in the proposed REPPIKA.

6. REPPIKA will require capabilities in research, appropriate technology, documentation, training and communication. All of these capabilities now exist in IIRR. It has entire divisions devoted to Field Operational Research, Appropriate Technology Research and Development, and International Training and Communication. Among its staff are highly trained and experienced individuals from different academic disciplines and work backgrounds. This staff includes anthropologists, sociologists, agriculturists, environmentalists, economists, health specialists, appropriate technology experts, communicators, trainers, and management practitioners.

7. More important, the identification, recovery, documentation, sharing and application of indigenous knowledge is not new to IIRR. In the past, it has undertaken projects which identified and utilised indigenous knowledge (and organisations) in the fields of health, education and culture, livelihood development and community organisation, albeit in a less systematic manner than that proposed under REPPIKA. In the field of health for instance, it has extensively made use of indigenous knowledge in herbal medicine that exists among traditional village healers. It has also identified and made use of indigenous knowledge in nutrition, rehydration, diagnosis of illnesses, maternal and child care, and family planning. In family planning, it has gained renown for its work in the identification and collection of indigenous agricultural concepts and terms which describe and help people understand analogous family planning concepts and terms. (IIRR is currently undertaking a project that trains groups in several countries in the identification of their own indigenous concepts and terms to describe analogous family planning and health concepts.) In education and culture, it has made use of traditional folk media as vehicles for educating people in rural reconstruction. It has also made use of folk music as an instrument for organising communities, even bringing together 'warring' political factions in a village. In livelihood, it has utilised indigenous work groups to facilitate the planning and implementation of projects. It has also made extensive use of farmers' indigenous agricultural knowledge in its appropriate technology research and development program. Examples of these are the identification and promotion of plant-based animal health care products; the use of botanical pesticides in lowland rice production; and the propagation within agroforestry projects of useful tree species 'discovered' by the farmers themselves. Of course, IIRR has also long used a 'farmer- to-farmer' method

of technology transfer (ever since Dr. Yen pioneered the 'farmer scholar approach' in Ding Xian days.

REPPIKA can build upon this wealth of experience while at the same time strengthening IIRR's capability in this field, particularly in terms of systematising its process of identifying, recovering and documenting indigenous knowledge.

Implementation strategies

Inventory of what is known From its seventy years of practical experience in working with rural development problems, the IIRR has a wealth of experience on which to draw. Intuitively and informally, IIRR staff have always incorporated indigenous knowledge into their programs. It has been part of its operating philosophy of starting with the people. The IIRR has a wealth of experience from which to codify the experience of using IK in rural programs. In addition to documenting as well as possible this previously accumulated knowledge, an initial step would be to reassess past experience and document in a more systematic way the various indigenous knowledge bases with which it has been working.

An early effort would also be needed to identify key rural development problems and issues and determine the primary knowledge systems related to each. Assigned IIRR staff would develop their abilities to understand and use a wide range of effective techniques and methods recording and otherwise documenting IK. Examples of important methodologies include taxonomies, decision trees and matrices, paradigm models, visual illustrations, and dictionaries. As a result of this field work, IIRR would develop a documentation unit using standardised recording formats and computer software.

IIRR would stage an initial regional conference aimed at facilitating a sharing of knowledge concerning IKS recovery strategies and methods among individuals who are already involved in doing this type of work. The purpose of such a conference would be to augment the knowledge of methodologies at IIRR as well as to encourage or facilitate the work of other individuals participating in the conference.

Training and consulting services

IIRR will offer effective training and consulting services by segmenting various audiences (such as scholars, government officials and field workers). They will determine the specific nature of the interests and needs of these audiences or groups regarding their own role in IK development efforts and tailor services to meet their needs.

IIRR staff would work to develop and refine methods for designing, testing and promoting the incorporation of IK into existing problem-focused programs and on-going institutional structures and systems by working with and through the type of individuals mentioned above.

Research program

A major effort would be made to establish a viable research program aimed at impacting on the development process through the development, testing and refinement of models for using IK in development programs. This would entail work on each of the stages of identification, assessment, recording/codifying, storing, retrieving and utilising IK. The results of this research would be circulated to appropriate target audiences ranging from those in academic institutions, donor agencies, government agencies, consulting firms and interested individual scholars. The results of this research would also be used to facilitate a continuous effort to further refine the documentation, training and consulting services.

An additional effort would be made to foster the formation of problem or sector focused Regional Training Networks (RTN's) as peer-based psychological support systems. For instance, individuals interested in and working with social forestry, aquaculture, women in development and many other areas could benefit from such peer-based working groups.

An important consideration in integrating IK into development programs will be to incorporate evaluation strategies to measure the impact of IK on actual programs. Early in program planning phases, evaluation designs should be considered, both formative and summative. In many instances, evaluation efforts have been minimal because of limited resources and lack of planning. The IK program at IIRR will emphasise the development of strong evaluation skills. Even with limited resources, a selected, yet fairly comprehensive scheme of evaluating the impact of IK on programs will be used.

Regional activity

IIRR will strive to cooperate and participate with other centres and programs within the region which would stand to benefit from involvement in and the results of the IK program. This would include existing networks such as the Southeast Asian Agricultural Universities (SUAN), the Association of Asian Agricultural Colleges and Universities (AAACU), Asian Cultural Forum on Development (ACFOD), Southeast Asian Regional Consortium on Agriculture (SEARCA), the Asian Non-Government Organisations Coalition(ANGOC), the South Asian Rural Reconstruction Association (SARRA), Centre for the Development of Human Resources in Rural Areas (CENDHRRA), and others, especially the ecologically oriented ones. These networks will be utilised to access the interest and involvement of others in establishing national centres for IK.

IIRR as a regional network or program will work to stimulate and facilitate the development of national centres and programs. Its staff will serve as consultants in conducting pre-training reconnaissance workshops and seminars and post-training trouble-shooting. It will develop communication technologies appropriate for facilitating the effective functioning of national centres and other regional networks. This will entail providing professional and technical support for the establishment of computerised data collection, maintenance and access capabilities.

Standardised formats for recording, reporting, storing and retrieving documented knowledge will be sought and promoted. Explorations will be made and prototype models developed for the use of video, audio cassettes, radio, facsimile, and other emerging technologies in the regional and global effort. A special effort will be made to develop and promote the use of video, capturing the process dimensions of indigenous decision-making, indigenous organisational behaviour, and the educative process for promoting a lateral transfer of indigenous knowledge across groups and populations.

Phases of Implementation

The program has been implemented in 1993 to encompass a five-year period that is divided into three phases.

Phase I (Year I, 1st Semester)
Organisation and training of program staff to include identification and documentation of local (Philippines) IK as part of the capability-building process.
Phase II (Year I, 2nd Semester through Year V)
Establishment/implementation of country-specific applied IK research and promotion of programs in 4–5 countries within the region in collaboration with individuals/institutions with interest in or working with IK. This would include provision of training and consultancy services to collaborating individuals/institutions, and establishment of National Centres for the Promotion of Indigenous Knowledge (NACPIK).
Phase III (Year II through Year V)
Provision of support (*e.g.* training, consultancy services, linkages with CIKARD) to national networks/centres for IK research and promotion in participating countries.

At the end of the fifth year, there will be an Asian Regional Congress on the Promotion of Indigenous Knowledge. Participants from the various countries will share their experiences with development leaders and practitioners, as well as with representatives of donor agencies, in order to gain more adherents to the cause of using indigenous knowledge in rural development.

Linkage with CIKARD

To ensure consistency with the overall philosophy behind the promotion of indigenous knowledge, to facilitate the exchange of information with other regional IK programs/centres, and to benefit from expertise in the promotion of IK already existing elsewhere in the world, the REPPIKA program staff will maintain a continuing and working linkage with the Centre for Indigenous Knowledge in Agriculture and Rural Development (CIKARD) at the Iowa State University (ISU), and through it, with the other regional IK programs/centres and other institutions involved in similar endeavours.

More specifically, the Director of CIKARD and members of its External Advisory Committee will be invited by IIRR to serve as advisers/consultants to REPPIKA, particularly during its formative years (first 3–5 years). The services/assistance of CIKARD will also be solicited in the matter of training the REPPIKA staff in their functions, and in providing backstopping to this staff when they actually begin performing those functions, again especially during the first few years.

Program management

REPPIKA has been implemented by a special program unit to be created within IIRR's Field Operational Research Division (FORD). This division is responsible for carrying out IIRR's mission to generate knowledge in rural reconstruction, hence it is the logical 'home' for REPPIKA.

A full-time Program Manager will be appointed to head REPPIKA. This person will be assisted by a small core staff consisting of the following:

o a Research & Documentation Coordinator;
o a Training and Consultancy Coordinator;
o an Administrative Assistant;
o a Program Secretary.

The Program Manager and staff will work closely with the rest of IIRR's staff, particularly its research, appropriate technology, training and communication personnel who will actually undertake the research, technology adaptation, training and communication activities of REPPIKA, under the direction/coordination of the REPPIKA program staff. To ensure that the participation of IIRR's staff in REPPIKA is assured, this will be built into IIRR's annual plans and the staff members' work programs at the beginning of each year. For REPPIKA activities which extend beyond one year, these will be built into the three-year IIRR plans and the staff member's three-year work programs.

Physically, REPPIKA is housed in a suitable office space within the IIRR campus. However, to ensure that it does not have to compete for the use of IIRR's limited office equipment and facilities, it will have to have its own microcomputers, photocopier and audio-visual equipment. For external communication purposes, it may share IIRR's telephone, telefax, and telex facilities.

44. Ethnoveterinary Medicine and Development – A review of the literature[1]

EVELYN MATHIAS-MUNDY AND *CONSTANCE M. McCORKLE*

ETHNOVETERINARY MEDICINE DEALS with indigenous knowledge, beliefs, skills, methods, and practices relating to the health care of animals. As a named and recognised area of academic study, it has a relatively short history, with significant systematic research beginning only in the mid-1970s (McCorkle 1986). Before then, descriptions of folk veterinary medicine were mostly byproducts of ethnographic or other disciplinary studies (*e.g.* De St. Croix 1972; Evans-Pritchard 1940; Merker 1910).

Veterinarians and other biological scientists have often deprecated local veterinary knowledge (*e.g.* Leparc 1947; Marucchi 1950). More recently, however, scientists and international development specialists have begun to view ethnoveterinary medicine as a valuable potential source of new pharmaceuticals and ideas with applications in both the First and the Third Worlds, as well as a factor in the maintenance of biodiversity and as a lesson in low-input sustainable agriculture (McCorkle 1989c).

This chapter provides a brief review of much of the existing literature pertaining to traditional veterinary medicine worldwide and indicates some of the immediate applications of systematic efforts in the field to international agricultural development. The chapter represents a summary of information detailed in an extensive bibliography with nearly 250 annotated entries spanning five continents and seven decades (Mathias-Mundy and McCorkle 1990).[2]

Recording ethnoveterinary knowledge

Collecting, recording, and understanding indigenous disease taxonomies and other folk veterinary knowledge require an interdisciplinary approach involving biological and social scientists (Lozano-Nathal and López-Buendía 1988; Martínez and Miguel 1988; McCorkle 1986, 1989b; Sollod 1983; Sollod and Knight 1983; Sollod *et al.* 1984). To provide a basis for comprehensible communication between stockowners and Western-trained veterinarians and other scientists, local disease concepts and practices (including etiologies, symptoms, treatments, and prophylaxes) must be 'translated' into Western scientific terms. This is not an easy task because modern medicine classes diseases according to etiological (causal) information, while folk disease distinctions may rely on clinical signs, epidemiological observations, or supernatural explanations (McCorkle 1986).

Various researchers have tackled this translation task. For example, Ba (1982, 1984) details the clinical signs, treatments, and possible Western diagnoses for 72 livestock ailments recognised by Fulani pastoralists of Mauretania. Disease classifications among other Fulani groups have been studied by Bah (1983), Bonfiglioli *et al.* (1988), Ibrahim (1986), Maliki (1981), Sollod *et al.* (1984), Wolfgang (1983), and Wolfgang and Sollod (1986). Ohta (1984) describes 37 livestock diseases recognised by the Turkana of Kenya. Schwabe and Kuojok (1981) summarise indigenous knowledge of livestock diseases and detail the clinical signs, pathological changes, and local beliefs and practices for five ailments recognised by the pastoral Dinka of Sudan. For Andean agropastoralists, McCorkle (1982, 1983, 1988, 1989a, 1989b) compares both emic and etic information on supernatural ills, parasitic and non-parasitic diseases, and plant poisoning in herd animals. Rangel and Felipe Ortiz (1985) report on more than 30 ailments of cattle, horses, pigs, sheep, donkeys, and poultry in two P'urhé communities of Mexico. Perry *et al.* (1984) and Primov (1984) present assessments of the importance of livestock disease to farmers in Zambia and Brazil respectively. Morvan and Vercruysse (1978) provide local terms for disease names among the Mbororo and Foulbé, two Fulani groups in Central Africa; Fulcrand (1983) and Huanca (1985) do likewise for Quechua Indians in Peru.

Researchers from a variety of disciplines provide guidelines on how to collect these and other kinds of ethnoveterinary information (Aguilar 1988; Grandin 1985; Ibrahim 1986; Martínez and Miguel 1988). Also, a computer database program (HERVET) is available to facilitate the systematisation of ethnobotanical data (López Buendía *et al.* 1988).

Ethnoetiologies and ethnoveterinary healers

A people's beliefs about the causes of human disease typically apply to animals, too. Since the third century BC in Sri Lanka, Ayurvedic medicine has been administered to horses, elephants, and other animals, as well as to human beings (Anjaria 1987). In traditional Thai medicine, the theory that the body is composed of four elements (earth, water, wind, fire) holds for both people and animals; if these elements become imbalanced, illness ensues (FAO 1984b). Latin-American hot/cold explanations of disease causation rely upon a cognate tradition deriving from Greco-Roman humoral theories. In classical Chinese medicine, the balance between *yin* and *yang* forces and other elements dictates diagnoses and choice of treatment for both human and animal ills; and oriental acupuncture techniques have long been used on livestock as well as people (Metalie 1984).

Many supernatural ethnoetiologies also apply to both human and livestock health, *e.g.*: the evil eye (Jones 1984; Shanklin 1985b), witchcraft and transgressions of taboos (Maliki 1981); evil winds and spirits, ancestors and genies; punishment from deities for wrongdoing or incorrect propitiation; and more (Carter and Mamani 1985; Chavunduka 1976; Ibrahim 1984; Kimball 1985; McCorkle 1989a; Ohta 1984; West 1981; Wolfgang 1983; *see* section on magico-religious practices).

Given such correspondences, it is little surprise that healers of human ailments also often treat animals, employing the same herbs, drugs, techniques, magical therapies, and so forth. Such specialists include the Arab *toubib* (Curasson 1947), Nepali *ayurveda* (FAO 1984a), Masai *laibon* (Forde 1968), Brunei Malay *dukun* (Kimball 1985), Amerind horse doctors (Lawrence 1988), Dinka *atet* (Schwabe and Kuojok 1981), and Quechua *altu misayuq* (McCorkle 1982). It is rare to find that, as Ibrahim notes of Nigeria, 'The veterinary and human aspects of traditional medicine are quite distinct from each other in terms of their practitioners, concepts, materials and the methods employed.' (1986: 191).

In addition to the specialists cited above, healers may consist of a particularly adept stockowner-neighbour or a Western-style veterinarian (*e.g.* Bonfiglioli *et al.* 1988; Brisebarre 1984b; Rangel and Felipe Ortiz 1985; Waters-Bayer 1988). However, since virtually all stockowners everywhere know at least some traditional treatments, they generally call upon a veterinary specialist only in complicated cases or only for certain species. For example, sheep farmers in Ireland seldom consult a veterinarian, whereas cattle owners frequently do so (Shanklin 1985a). And when no veterinary services are available – as during several months' long annual transhumance undertaken by Cevenol shepherds in France (Brisebarre 1978), or as in many remote parts of the Third World – stockowners must depend entirely upon their own resources for curing their animals and protecting them from disease.

Ethnoveterinary techniques and practices

Pharmacology Pharmacology is probably the most extensively studied aspect of ethnoveterinary medicine. Worldwide, a great variety of herbs and plants is used. For example, approximately 140 such plants in Nepal have been identified (FAO 1984a), 150 in Thailand (FAO 1984b), 250 in India (FAO 1984c), and 92 in Nigeria (Nwude and Ibrahim 1980). Other studies with information on herbs and drugs used to treat animals include Anjaria 1986; Aubert 1988; Bazalar and McCorkle 1989; Cerrate de Ferreyra 1980; Chavunduka 1976; Esquivel Mendoza 1982; FAO 1986; Fernández 1988; Gourlet 1979; Kerharo and Adam 1964; Khanna *et al.* 1978; Law 1973; López Buendía 1988; Lozano Nathal 1988; Maydell 1986; Minja 1984, Moscoso Castilla 1942; Soukup n.d.; Sumano López *et al.* 1988; Teit 1930, and Wahua and Oji 1987.

Laboratory and field tests have confirmed the efficacy of many folk pharmaceuticals. In Nigeria, experiments on six plants used by Fulani herders showed significant activity against *trichostrongylus* in rats (Ibrahim 1984, Ibrahim *et al.* 1984). In India, *Leptadenia reticulata*, a traditional galactagogue, has been experimentally demonstrated to improve milk production in cows, buffaloes, and sheep (Anjaria 1986, 1988). Research on medicinal plants employed by Mauretanian Fulani recommends ten such plants for treating eight livestock diseases (Niang 1987). Esparza B. (1988) lists 25 general applications of herbal therapies that are practical in veterinary medicine.

Examples of traditional remedies from Latin America with proven efficacy include *Aspidium Filiz-mas* against hepatic distomatosis (liver fluke) in sheep (Cáceres Vega 1989), *Minthostachys andina* (*muña*) against ectoparasites of livestock (Caballero Osorio 1984a, 1984b; Roersch and Van der Hoogte 1988), and *Lupinus mutabilis* (*tarwi*) against ectoparasitic manges in alpaca (Avila Cazorla *et al.* 1985a, 1985b; Jiménez J. *et al.* 1983; PRATEC 1988b; Sánchez n.d.; Tillman 1983). Likewise for a dip of *Nicotiana paniculata* L., a sylvan Andean tobacco, against *Melophagus ovinus* (Bazalar and McCorkle 1989); artichoke leaves and *jaya-shipita,* an unidentified Andean plant, against liver fluke in sheep (*ibid.*); *Senecio spp.* and seeds of the squash *Cucurbita maxima* Duch against gastrointestinal parasites of sheep (*ibid.*); a traditional remedy for bronchitis in dogs (Vásquez Manríquez *et al.* 1988); the root of *Helopsis longipes* against *E. coli, Staphylococcus aureus,* and two species of fly that parasitize horses and sheep (Romero Ramírez *et al.* 1988); *Helenium quadridentatum* against saprolegniasis, a fungal disease of fish (Auró Angulo and Sumano López 1988); ground garlic against internal parasites in fish (Peña Haaz *et al.* 1988); and still more.

Different plant parts are used and prepared in many different ways, depending upon the active ingredient to be extracted and the route of administration. Andean stockowners use an eyewash of *manzanilla* (*Helenium quadridentatum*) against contagious keratoconjunctivitis in their sheep (Fulcrand 1983) and an infusion of *Trichocereus* sp. against bloat in their cattle (Lindo Revilla 1982). To relieve swelling of the udder in lactating cows, they apply a decoction of *hinojo* (PRATEC, 1988a), probable genera *Myriophyllum*. Modes of administering medicines to animals span drenches (forced ingestion of liquids), inhalation of smoke or vapours, ointments, massages (Bonfiglioli *et al.* 1988), intranasal application (Ba 1982; Evans-Pritchard 1938; Lawrence 1988; Wolfgang and Sollod 1986), and bouquets of medicinal plants hung in animal quarters and other places (Brisebarre 1984a, 1985, 1987).

Vaccination

Many African pastoral societies have indigenous vaccinations against infectious diseases. The Fulani (Ba 1982; De St. Croix 1972; Wolfgang 1983), Masai (Schwabe 1978), WoDaaBe (Maliki 1981), and Somali (Mares 1951, 1954b) have developed similar techniques of vaccinating against bovine pleuropneumonia by inserting a piece of infected lung in an incision in the nostrils or the bridge of the nose. The Fulani and Somali also have effective vaccinations against rinderpest. (In contrast, according to Herbert 1974, 18th century European inoculations of cattle against rinderpest reportedly were rarely successful.) It appears that, when properly done, all these indigenous techniques are effective, although they may produce undesirable side effects such as swellings and inflammation.

Russian cossacks and Arab and Indian camel keepers successfully innoculate their camels against pox, *variola* (Curasson 1947). In India, an effective homemade vaccine prepared from the scabs of naturally infected camels is administered. Bantu peoples of Kenya mix the blood of animals that have died of blackleg with pounded roots; they then sprinkle the mixture over their healthy cattle (Wagner 1970). This can be beneficial insofar as cattle often have skin wounds or other portals of entry for such preparations (Schwabe 1978).

Surgery

Wounds Most societies have developed methods of wound care for their animals. Plants and other substances used as dressings include sterile cattle-dung ashes and cow's urine (Schwabe and Kuojok 1981); mud (Schulz-Weidener 1961, cited in Schinkel 1970); *Piper angustifolium* R and P and *P. elongatum*, commonly known as *matico* (Alarco de Zadra 1988); aloe juice and *capulí*-wood ash with alum and sulphur (Moscoso Castilla 1953); *Haploppapus spp.* (Farga and Lastra 1988); a mixture of resin, wax, and sheep butter (Kopczynska-Jaworska 1961); and soot, cattle dung, spider webs, and herbs (Timaffy 1961). Indigenous materials used to suture wounds include: thorns held in place with tendons (Schwabe 1978); the strong tail hairs of giraffes and the softer tail hair of cattle (Schwabe and Kuojok 1981); and sinews of antelopes, jackrabbits, and elks (Lawrence 1988).

Cauterisation and bloodletting These seem to be routine, multi-purpose techniques among stockowners around the world, but especially among African pastoralists. The following publications all mention cauterisation: Ba 1982; Bonfiglioli *et al.* 1988; FAO 1984c, Maliki 1981; Marx 1984; Marx and Wiegand 1987; Ohta 1984; Peña Bellido 1975; Schwabe 1978; Wolfgang 1983, and Wolfgang and Sollod 1986. Descriptions of bloodletting are found in Allan 1965; Dahl and Hjort 1976; Dupire 1962; Evans-Pritchard 1937; Forde 1968; Hartmann 1869 (cited in Schinkel 1970); Lawrence 1988; Leakey 1977, Marx 1984; Marinow 1961; McCorkle 1986; Schwabe 1978, and Wagner 1970.

Castration Naturally, castration is a universal surgical practice. Methods include open surgery, as with a knife; biting off the seminal duct from outside without damaging the scrotum itself, as practiced by early US and Australian shepherds; striking the cord with a mallet, stones, or other blunt objects; and cauterisation (Bernus 1979; De St. Croix 1972; Elmi 1984; Evans-Pritchard 1937; Lawrence 1988; Mares 1954a; Marx 1984; Ohta 1984 and 1987; Schwabe and Kuojok 1981; Schram 1954; West 1981; Wolfgang and Sollod 1986). Mauretanian Fulani have a way to temporarily 'castrate' small ruminants. They push the testicles towards the inguinal channel and lodge them latitudinally under the abdominal skin. In the breeding season the testes can be let down again and the animals regain their virility (Ba 1982). Castration in female livestock is reported only from China (Wagner 1926).

Other surgical techniques These include rumen trocarization in cases of bloat (Ba 1982; Brisebarre 1978; Maliki 1981; Schwabe and Kuojok 1981; Wolfgang and Sollod 1986) and bone-setting (Ba 1982; Schwabe 1978; Wolfgang 1983; Wolfgang and Sollod 1986). Aymara Indians treat fractured bones in both animals and humans with a hot plaster of seven plants ground together with lime and water (CEDECUM 1988), while stockowners in the Peruvian altiplano apply a hot poultice compounded of a local loco weed (*Astragalus spp.*), human urine, dried snake flesh, and coarse brown sugar (Proyecto de Tecnologías Campesinas-CEPIA 1988).

Many authors describe both surgical and non-surgical treatments for footrot (Ohta 1984; Pompa 1984; PRATEC 1989; Primov 1984; Wolfgang and Sollod 1986). In China, for severe lameness in mules and camels, the coronet (or other areas, depending on the case) is pierced with a long needle (Wagner 1926). Obstetrical procedures include episiotomy, embryotomy, and operations to correct uterine prolapse (Ba 1982, Schwabe and Kuojok 1981). Intricate cosmetic surgery is performed on the horns of bulls by the Samburu of Kenya (Jones 1984) and the Dinka (Schwabe 1984, 1987). Bulgarian (Marinow 1961) and Hungarian (Bene 1961) herders surgically remove the parasitic cysts of coneurosis from the brains of sheep thus afflicted.

Management practices

Pest and parasite control Virtually all stockraising societies have ways to control insects and parasites that plague their animals. Fumigation and smudge fires are common techniques for driving off pests, whether in Malaysia (Kimball 1985), Hungary (Timaffy 1961), Nigeria (De St. Croix 1972; Ibrahim *et al.* 1983), North and South American Indian cultures (Bolton and Calvin 1985; Dobie 1950; PPEA-PRATEC 1989), Siberia (Forde 1968), Sierra Leone (Bah 1983), or

Sudan (Evans-Pritchard 1938). Seasonal herd movements among nomadic pastoralists are often guided as much by the need to avoid disease-bearing livestock pests as to find forage and water (*e.g.* Elmi 1989; Hussein 1984). Pest control is also one reason for seasonally burning rangelands ('Fulahn' 1933).

Other methods of pest and parasite control include washing with fly-repellent liquids (Dalziel 1937; cited in Ibrahim 1986; Law 1980; Pompa 1984); manual removal of ticks or avoidance of infested areas (Bah 1983; Lira 1985; Marx 1984; Wolfgang 1983; Wolfgang and Sollod 1986), and innumerable home remedies against ecto- and endoparasites (Bazalar and McCorkle 1989; Bustamante 1982; Bustinza Choque and Sánchez Viveros 1985; de Carlier 1981; Casaverde 1985; Córdova 1981; Evans-Pritchard 1938; Herrera 1941; Lira 1985; Marchand 1984; Mares 1954b; Marinow 1961; Marx 1984; McCorkle 1982 and 1989a; Moscoso Castilla 1953; Palacios Ríos 1985 and 1988; Proyecto de Tecnologías Campesinas-CEPIA 1988 Valdizán and Maldonado 1985; Wagner 1926).

Range and forage management Pastoralists everywhere have highly detailed knowledge of forage flora and poisonous plants (*e.g.* Ba 1982; Bonfiglioli *et al.* 1988; Hobbs 1989; Hussein 1984; Ibrahim *et al.* 1983; Mares 1954a; McCorkle 1982). Loco weeds of *Astragalus* spp., for example, are a major problem for shepherds throughout the Andes (West 1981). Antidotes to *Astragalus* poisoning are drenching with an infusion of *Psoralea glandulosa* (Salcedo 1986) or a solution of salt and ash made from the same plant (Choquehuanca 1987), and feeding large amounts of roughage (McCorkle 1982). The weed can also be rubbed on horses' lips to condition them against eating it (Valdizán and Maldonado 1985). Bell (1928) reports a similar practice among Chumbi Valley Tibetans to prevent aconite poisoning in their herd animals.

Dietary supplementation Livestock often receive supplementary minerals, digestible earths, special feeds, or tonics. These are designed to ward against illness, promote growth and fertility, increase production of milk, meat, and fibre, or enhance still other desirable qualities. Examples are found among Nigerian Fulani (Waters-Bayer 1988), the Gende of New Guinea (Hughes 1977), Thai farmers (FAO 1980, 1984b), and West African horse owners (Law 1980). To fatten their animals, Peruvian smallholders mix *beleño negro* seeds into horse rations (Málaga 1988) or sulphur into livestock water (Moscoso Castilla 1953); they feed other seeds to their guard dogs to make them fierce (Lira 1985). Somali stud camels receive extra rations of ghee and sesame oil to enhance their virility (Hussein 1984).

Both Somali and Tuareg camels are regularly provided salt, whether by grazing them on salty forages or in salty areas, feeding them rough salt, or watering them at salty wells (Bernus 1979; Hussein 1984; Mares 1954a). Salt feeding is also mentioned in Ba 1982; Barfield 1981; Bonfiglioli *et al.* 1988; Maliki 1981; Marx 1984; McCorkle 1983; Schinkel 1970, and Walker 1986.

Calf care and weaning In India, buffalo calves that have difficulty digesting their dam's milk are given opium or a preparation of barberry root juice, bean leaves, salt, and butter (Hockings 1980). Almost everywhere, stockowners know many tricks to make a dam or another cow accept a calf, and many specialised techniques for keeping cows in milk (*e.g.* Ba 1982; Elmi 1989; Hussein 1984; Evans-Pritchard 1937; Schinkel 1970; Walker 1986). When a newborn calf dies, a common practice is to dress another calf in its hide or present the hide in other deceptive forms to the dam (Casimir 1982; De St. Croix 1972; Elmi 1984; Evans-Pritchard 1937; Hermanns 1948; Maliki 1981; Mares 1954a; Ohta 1987).

Stockraisers have likewise developed a variety of weaning methods. These serve to protect the dams' health if they soon become pregnant again or to harvest more milk for human consumption. In Mali, for example, pastoralists dab dung on the dam's teats, immobilize the offspring's tongue, or affix thorns to its muzzle so that suckling pricks the dam (Ngwa and Hardouin 1989). Still other weaning practices are described in Comisión Organizadora de Criadores de Alpaca 1985; Elmi 1989; Hussein 1984, and Monod 1975.

Magico-religious practices

As in human ethnomedicine, magic and religion form an integral part of ethnoveterinary medicine (McCorkle 1986). An overview of the literature clearly indicates that supernatural practices often accompany naturalistic ones (*e.g.* Dubois 1984; Dupire 1962; Lawrence 1988; Maliki 1981; McCorkle 1982 and 1989a).

Magico-religious practices range from complex healing, protective, fertility, and management-related (*e.g.* castration, ear-notching) rites to simple actions such as magical or religious incantations and recitations and suspension of amulets or bouquets on animals or in their quarters. Examples of recitations include those employed by the WoDaaBe (Maliki 1981) and Brunei Malays (Kimball 1985). Navajo and Apache (Lawrence 1988), Quechua and Aymara Indians (numerous references cited in McCorkle 1983, 1989a) have songs and/or complicated ceremonies for the increase and protection of their herds. To ward against accident, straying, predation, rustling, witchcraft, and other evils, many culture employ magical prophylaxes like talismans, bells, and festish bundles (*e.g.* Abu-Rabia 1983; Dupire 1957; Van den Berg 1985).

Catholic farmers in Ireland may sprinkle holy water on cattle bought from a Protestant, as a precaution against any religious impurity associated with the exchange (Shanklin 1985a). French stockowners still make pilgrimages and/or pray to a pantheon of 'veterinary saints ' to promote their herds' well-being; and French, Belgian, German, and Dutch stockowners hang pictures of such saints in their stables (Brisebarre 1984b; Dubois 1984; Leparc 1947; Millour 1984; Villemin 1984).

Sympathetic magic, based on the principle of 'like affects like', is a common feature of ethnomedical systems worldwide. Also known as the 'doctrine of signature' (FAO 1980) or 'law of signatures' (Nwude and Ibrahim 1980), an example is the Quechua custom of setting smoke fires or casting alcohol into the air to combat or propitiate aerial spirits (McCorkle 1982). Another example is the Indonesian practice of giving *Curcuma sp.* to animals with jaundice, because of the plant's yellow colour (FAO 1980). Among African pastoralists, many plants with thick, juicy leaves or milky sap are employed to increase lactation because of their resemblance to the udder or to milk (de St. Croix 1972; Ibrahim 1986; Nwude and Ibrahim 1980). The same principle lies behind the French custom of hanging strong-smelling bouquets in livestock quarters to combat malodorous diseases (Brisebarre 1985).

Supernatural interpretations of disease etiology can nevertheless lead to effective management or therapeutic practices (Mathias-Mundy and McCorkle 1989). Examples are: in the Andes, keeping herds away from cold, windy places or, as a result of supernatural stipulations, using the cleanest available water when treating certain ailments (McCorkle 1986, 1989a, 1989b), in France, feeding saint-blessed salt and bread to livestock (Brisebarre, 1984b), and in New Guinea, rubbing mineral-rich earths into the skin of domestic animals (Morren 1975).

Ethnoveterinary medicine and development

Of course, not all ethnoveterinary practices provide effective or ideal solutions to animal health problems – no more than does Western veterinary science. Ethnoveterinary therapeutic and prophylactic compounds may be inconvenient to prepare or administer;[3] their ingredients may be available only seasonally; without (and even with) the necessary social and political controls, they may be ineffective against infectious epidemic diseases; as in any medical system, in the absence of correct diagnoses, ethnoveterinary treatments can be inadequate; and some appear to be harmlessly mistaken or even dysfunctional (Mathias-Mundy and McCorkle 1990). Detailed, contextualized studies on specific practices within ethnoveterinary medicine are needed to delineate which techniques are of practical use in agricultural development.

Nevertheless, an overview of the literature clearly indicates that many domains of ethnoveterinary medicine have ready development applications. In our opinion, these include ethnopharmacological and other treatments for certain skin diseases and internal parasites; indigenous vaccinations, especially for poxes or where Western alternatives are unavailable; wound and fracture care; basic surgical procedures such as castration, trocarization, and obstetrical operations; dietary supplementation; and certain treatments for hormonal imbalances and physiological malfunctions.

In short, ethnoveterinary medicine offers many techniques that work, that are cheap and readily available, and that are pre-adapted to Third World human and physical ecologies. A classic example is the proven effectiveness of *tarwi* (*Lupinus mutabilis*) water in the Andes in curing and preventing manges. A critical food plant in the indigenous diet, *tarwi* also constitutes a superbly cost-effective alternative to purchased pharmaceuticals – particularly since none of its value as human food is lost in extracting the ectoparasiticide (Avila Cazorla *et al.* 1985b).

An excellent illustration of how such knowledge can be put to work for the benefit of Third World stockowners is offered by the Small Ruminant Collaborative Research Support Program (SR-CRSP) in Peru. There, teams of stockowners and social and biological scientists have worked together to test and enhance traditional herbal therapies and prophylaxes for herd animals, so that people can prepare even more reliable home remedies – thus freeing themselves from alien, uncertain, and impossibly expensive external sources of veterinary inputs (Bazalar and McCorkle 1989; Fernández 1986; McCorkle 1989a, 1989b; Mathias-Mundy 1989). As Anjaria (1987), Sumano López *et al.* (1988), and others have pointed out, such initiatives can also give rise to new rural industries or reinforce existing ones.

Of course, in any medical system, prevention should take precedence over curing. Much of the ethnoveterinary literature stresses this point (*e.g.* Aguilar *et al.* 1988; Chavunduka 1984; Halpin 1981). In preventing disease, good management is critical (Schillhorn van Veen 1984). Here, too, ethnoveterinary medicine has something to offer. Many traditional practices reflect sensitive environmental adaptations that contribute to disease prevention. Examples given earlier include pest control, herd movements, and dietary supplementation; still others, like housing types and grazing strategies, are detailed in Mathias-Mundy and McCorkle 1989. Local husbandry practices should be thoroughly studied and, wherever valid, offered as alternatives or complements to Western management dogma in livestock development programs – as Verma and Singh (1969) urged two decades ago.

Another useful strategy is instructing indigenous healers in key techniques of Western veterinary medicine and supplying these individuals with basic drugs such as antibiotics. Work in medical anthropology has clearly demonstrated that cooperation between traditional and Western-trained medical professionals can make for more effective delivery of human health care (*e.g.* Cosminsky and Harrison 1984; Harrison and Cosminsky 1976; Warren *et al.* 1982). The same is true for veterinary services. Many authors suggest ways to do this through the recruitment of local healers like the Dinka *atet* and/or stockowners themselves as animal health workers (Almond 1987; Grandin 1985; Halpin 1981; Sandford 1981; Sollod *et al.* 1984). These authors argue that clients have greater confidence in such individuals because of their firsthand familiarity with local languages, cultures, and ethnoveterinary beliefs and practices. Conversely, these native 'paravets ' are more at ease with clients and their lifeways because, to paraphrase Almond and Halpin, *they are not afraid of the bush* .

Furthermore, as Schwabe and Kuojok (1981) propose, in addition to providing basic veterinary care, trained paravets can serve as an intelligence network to assist livestock services in epidemiological surveillance. To test this idea, Zessin and Carpenter (1985) conducted a cost-benefit comparison of a conventional mass vaccination campaign in Sudan versus an animal-disease surveillance system that would combine existing formal veterinary resources (slaughterhouse and field personnel, foreign donors, laboratory and other facilities) with traditional healers. These authors found that such a surveillance network would not only be economically superior to mass vaccinations, but would also gradually improve the veterinary infrastructure by better linking healers and stockowners in the field with government veterinary institutions.

A good example that combines many of the foregoing applications is a participatory ethnoveterinary program established by Heifer Project International (HPI) in Cameroon. Triggered by 'frustrations over the high cost and erratic supply of "modern" veterinary drugs…and over the inadequacy and unreliability of "modern" veterinary services' in the country (Nuwanyakpa 1989: 2), a highlight of this initiative is the successful creation of an Association of Traditional Veterinary Doctors. Along with livestock-service and HPI personnel, these indigenous professionals hold seminars and discussions on the relative advantages of traditional and modern veterinary techniques plus demonstrations on methods of collection, preparation, storage, and administration of ethnoveterinary medicines. A five-year plan is being constructed for cross-training of traditional and modern veterinary workers. Meanwhile, the program is systematically collecting information on animal, mineral, and vegetable materials (including taxonomic identification of 100 plant species) traditionally used to treat 29 economically important cattle ailments, plus ethnodiagnostic data on these ailments.

To summarise, concrete recommendations for improved utilization of ethnoveterinary medicine include identification of traditional medicinal plants, laboratory and clinical evaluation of these plants' pharmacological activity and effectiveness, participatory field testing of improved home remedies, integration of traditional veterinary medicine into formal veterinary services, and training in ethnoveterinary medicine for both stockowners and veterinary students and professionals (*cf.* FAO 1980, 1984a, 1984b, 1984c, 1986; among many others of the references cited). Also useful are local-language publications on indigenous health and husbandry practices, such as those by Jallo (1989a, 1989b) in Fulfulde.

As indicated by efforts like those of the SR-CRSP, HPI, and earlier, the NRLP (Niger Range and Livestock Program; *cf.* Sollod, 1981; Wolfgang 1983; Wolfgang and Sollod 1986), increasing numbers of experts in international agriculture have begun to appreciate the usefulness of understanding, respecting, and applying local concepts and practices in development. (For additional cases related to livestock development, see *e.g.* Gilles 1982; Grandin 1985; Schillhorn van Veen 1986.)

In ethnoveterinary medicine, this includes understanding not only local terminology and technology, but also the cultural and social systems pertaining to animals. In many societies, the health care given to livestock does not depend solely upon their market value. For example, Andean stockowners view illness and death among their beloved llama and alpaca not just as economic or natural phenomena but rather as signs of cosmological turmoil or the anger of powerful supernatural beings. Many Andean veterinary and husbandry strategies are dictated by these perceptions, rather than by purely profit-oriented motives (Greslou, 1989).[4] Development experts must take care not to insult or denigrate local ideologies and attitudes. Otherwise, their veterinary or other livestock interventions are likely to be rejected. Worse still, through an imperfect understanding of the sometimes vital etic correlates of emic aspects of animal husbandry, developers' ignorance can even imperil the very existence of the people they seek to serve (Lawrence 1982, 1985; McCorkle 1989b).

Simply put, a 'knowledge of indigenous knowledge 'facilitates communication and information exchange between development practitioners and their clientele, and enables project planners to design socioculturally, economically, and technologically appropriate assistance measures (Mathias-Mundy and McCorkle 1990; McCorkle 1989c) – and with them, more successful development programs.

Notes

1. Preparation of this chapter was supported by Iowa State University's Centre for Indigenous Knowledge for Agriculture and Rural Development (CIKARD) and by the Title XII Small Ruminant Collaborative Research Support Program under Grant No. AID/DAN/1328-SS-4093-00 through the SR-CRSP Sociology Project, housed in the Department of Rural Sociology at the University of Missouri-Columbia (MU). Additional support was provided by MU. The authors wish to thank Paul Mundy for his editorial assistance and computer-science savvy in preparing the chapter and the annotated bibliography on which it is based. Thanks are also due to SR-CRSP Sociology Project Intern and Information Officer DeeAnna Adkins for her copyreading and editorial contributions to the bibliography.</p>

2. The Bibliography is No. 6 in Iowa State University's Series of Bibliographies in the Technology and Social Change. It is available for purchase by writing to CIKARD, 318 Curtiss Hall, Iowa State University, Ames, Iowa, 50011, USA. Readers should note that the bibliography includes precise page citations for all of the ethnoveterinary practices, findings, opinion, etc. here cited only by author(s) and date. Moreover, the bibliography is cross-referenced and/or indexed by author, general subject

matter, plant or animal species, disease, modes of treatment, country, ethnic group, and still other variables.

3. However, Third World stockowners often level the same complaints against commercial pharmaceuticals (McCorkle 1986).

4. In the Andean case, this is because camelids are in many ways viewed 'as people, too' and certainly as highly social beings (McCorkle, 1983). This perception is somewhat akin to the way North American, French, and other cultures relate to their domestic pets, but with far more profound historical, functional, and cosmological (as versus merely psychological) underpinnings. For an overview of studies of human–animal relationships and the symbolic/ideological importance of domesticated animals worldwide, see Shanklin 1985b.

45. Indigenous Knowledge as Reflected in Agriculture and Rural Development

S. OGUNTUNJI TITILOLA AND DAVID MARSDEN

THE PIONEERING WORK of Brokensha, Warren and Werner in 1980 serves as a point of departure for this bibliographical essay. A number of hitherto disparata fields of interest were brought into closer alignment through that publication; the concerns of ethnosientists and anthropologists were married with those of development administrators and agricultural economists. This alignment has been considerably strengthened over the intervening decade.

The links between agriculture, rural development and indigenous knowledge are not new. They have been at the heart of the anthropological enterprise since its inception. The evolving relationship between anthropology and other disciplines concerned with development has a more recent history. It reflects wider developments in the social and natural sciences which increasingly emphasise cross-disciplinary cooperation in an era when disciplinary specialisations themselves are being torn down. As the social sciences become more reflexive and interpretative, the old axioms no longer hold.

The reflexive search for alternative moves centre stage; alternative forms of development, alternative means of interpretation and alternative evaluations of the meaning of development which require the elaboration of alternative mechanisms for the execution of development policies. In addition, the political ideologies which clearly separated left from right and entrenched thinking behind dogmatic boundaries, are being radically re-thought.

A number of themes have become dominant in development discourse and underpin thinking across a broad spectrum of interests. All focus on a clearer understanding and intensified utilisation of indigenous knowledge systems. These include:

○ Participation and decentralisation of decision-making;
○ Encouragement of the private and the voluntary sectors associated with the retreat of the state;
○ A focus on the poor and on disadvantaged minorities; and
○ An increased concern with gender issues.

Development initiatives are prefaced with calls for 'reversals' – to put the last first, to empower the 'hitherto excluded', to break down the professional and technical barriers that mystify rather than clarify the development process, to put farmers themselves centre stage in the planting and execution of development project (Chambers 1985; Chambers and Jiggins 1987; Chambers *et al.* 1989). The problems of rural development are no longer seen to reside in the 'traditional' cultures of under-developed people, but rather in the partial and biased understandings that have emanated from the unreflexive application of a western scientific rationality, and in the results of a rapacious and selfish capitalism that has exacerbated rather than reduced inequalities. Indeed 'traditional' cultures are now seen as containing the bases for any effective development.

For all these reasons there is a heightened awareness of the central importance of indigenous knowledge systems in the construction of sustainable strategies for rural development. These should be developed from where people are rather than from where the disqualified 'experts' would like them to be. The 'blue-print' approach is giving way to a negotiated, situation-specific approach which demands a dialogue between the different parties to the interventions that are constructed in the name of development, and which recognises the important, often crucial, knowledge that the traditional recipients of development aid have to offer.

Much of the literature in this area has stressed the importance of anthropological knowledge and the use of much more qualitative methodologies as the 'top down', 'high technology' approaches to rural development are challenged (see Barlett 1980). An attempt is made here to highlight what are perceived by the authors as key texts in this realignment of interest. It is impossible to do justice to the wide variety of material that has been published over the last dozen years which bring together agriculture, rural development and indigenous knowledge systems. The present volume provides extensive proof of the richness of the research effort. It is difficult also to categorise the various contributions into discrete compartments as much of the work is cross-disciplinary and comes from a wide variety of sources – the academic community, multilateral organisations such as the World Bank and the various UN bodies, and non-government organisations, but the isolation of a number of major themes, might help in this endeavour.

Two sorts of analysis might be identified which underpin discussion of these different themes. Firstly there are those analyses which are rooted in particular disciplinary pre-occupations and which emphasise indigenous technical knowledge. Soil scientists (see Guillet, this volume), agronomists (Thurston and Parker, this volume), agroecologists (Altieri 1983), agroforesters (Gomez-Pompa 1976) and range management experts (Niamir, this volume; 1990) are utilising local knowledge to overcome problems of rural development, and devising more appropriate natural resource management methods, supported by a variety of institutions concerned with raising agricultural productivity. Their efforts build on and are supplemented by that of ethnoscientists (Juma 1988). Indigenous knowledge systems are being recovered for the elaboration of more effective irrigation management systems (Lansing 1987), for developing more effective credit systems for resource poor farmers (Moseley 1989; Cashman 1988) and for developing less harmful systems of pest control (Thurston and Parker, this volume). Secondly, there are those analyses which emphasise the construction of what has been termed 'people's science'. these latter analyses call for fundamental 'reversals' in the ways in which development projects and programs are conceived and executed. They tend to be more holistic in their interpretations and to focus on indigenous knowledge systems.

The two sorts of analyses are not mutually exclusive but, rather, proceed from different understandings of the research process and from different intellectual traditions, rooted in the natural and social sciences respectively. The former tends to be instrumental, development from a positivist western scientific tradition. The latter tends to be more interpretative, developed from a changing appreciation of the nature of knowledge and the processes surrounding its acquisition and use. It tends to be rooted in a more reflexive understanding of the partiality of the western intellectual tradition and serves as a basis for rethinking the whole nature of the development task.

As Thrupp (1989) has argued, in the legitimation of local knowledge there is a danger of 'scientising' it; merely incorporating it into pre-existing and unquestioned frame of reference and thereby enhancing the ability to appropriate it and use it as an instrument of oppression and exploitation. If the interpretive understandings of local knowledge are to be developed then this means a fundamental re-alignment of the interests of donor and beneficiaries. The recovery and utilisation of local or indigenous knowledge becomes a major instrument in the empowerment of local people (1989: 138). This is also reflected in the work of the United Nations University (see Programme on Indigenous Intellectual Creativity and Marji-Liza Swantz 1987).

Bringing the instrumental and the interpretative types of analysis into closer alignment has been a major pre-occupation of much work in the last ten years; building the links between natural and social scientists and between outsiders and insiders. This has not been easy and, although one would have thought that the systematic use of indigenous agricultural knowledge would have been regarded as a pre-requisite for the design and implementation of rural development project, this has seldom been the case.

Many efforts have been made over the last decade to address this problem, some with more success than others. Multi-disciplinary teams have attempted to construct common frames of reference that will allow them to learn from each others specialisations and there are many examples of the ways in which the incorporation of indigenous cultural values might enhance development efforts. These range over a wide variety of fields and involve a whole variety of different organisations.

In the field of Social Development, a recent compilation (Cernẹa 1986), serves as an introduction to the ways in which an understanding and incorporation of different cultural values and indigenous knowledge based on them can enhance the design and implementation of rural development projects. Social Development has continuously stressed the needs to take such values into account. Some early general works (Conyers 1982; Hardiman and Midgeley 1983; MacPherson 1982; Rondinelli 1983) stand out as contributions to this effort, as does the seminal article on Counter-development by Galjart (1981). The work of the Dag Hammerskjold Foundation through its Journal Development Dialogue and the dossier produced by the International Foundation for Development Alternatives have consistently provided ammunition as well as fora for those struggling to redefine the nature of development.

More recently the work of Uphoff (1986) and Korten (1987) has focused on the utilisation of local human resources and organisations as the basis for building effective development strategies. Westview and Kumarian Press have been instrumental in the publication of many works which reflect new thinking in the integration of rural development strategies with local knowledge systems.

Perhaps, the most widely known work in this general area is that of Robert Chambers and his colleagues (Chambers 1983; Chambers and Jiggins 1987) based at the Institute of Development Studies in the University of Sussex. Attempts to institutionalise reversals in thinking by putting the last first, by the application of Rapid Rural Appraisal techniques, by the development of Farming Systems Research and appropriate extension methodologies are reflected in this work. They are all underpinned by an appreciation of the importance of understanding the knowledge systems and values of the different actors in the project community.

Building on this base, the work of the International Institute for Environment and Development stands out with its sustainable agriculture programme and its Rapid Rural Appraisal Notes and its Gatekeeper series. The Agricultural Administration, Social Forestry, and Pastoral Networks established by the

Overseas Development Institute in London have provided opportunities for the publication and dissemination of much relevant research material at often early stages in its development. It has been particularly useful in disseminating the results of Farming Systems Research (see Farrington and Martin 1987).

The Development of a 'people's science' is advocated in the influential work of Paul Richards (1985). It draws on a 'populist' tradition within the social sciences while eschewing the gross over-generalisations of both the modernist and the materialist perspectives in favour of an analysis of the many ways in which sustainability has been enhanced through local experimental responses to changes in both the natural and the cultural environment. Earlier interests in what came to be known as 'eco-development' are reflected in the work of I. Sachs (1984).

The eco-development movements of the seventies extended the holistic insights derived from ecosystems research into the social world and crystallised in a concern for integrated approaches to rural development which stressed the interconnected nature of activities within the rural environment. The ecodevelopment movement has been transformed in the eighties with the growing interest in environmental issues. This is highlighted through the report of the World Commission on Environment and Development (the Brundtland Report, 1987) and the adoption of its recommendations by the World Bank in its 1988 Annual Report (Vanek 1989).

These interests take a variety of forms but all feed into a growing appreciation of the importance of indigenous knowledge, either in conserving the diversity of genetic resources, natural and cultural, or in creating the pre-conditions to enhance sustainability (Klee 1980, McNeely and Pitt 1985; Marten 1986; Riley and Brokensha 1988). Several manuals have appeared in the 1980s designed to provide the foundations for the development of sustainable human settlements which recognise the negative effects of modern intensive production methods and the complexities of natural ecosystems that are being disrupted by current practice (see Mollison's comprehensive manual on Permaculture, 1988). Central to these strategies is the commonsense knowledge of everyday interaction with the environment which is the hallmark of indigenous knowledge systems.

Recent work on sustainable agriculture focuses on the utilisation of fewer external inputs and on utilising the traditional knowledge of farmers on the assumption that their methods, having been tried and tested over generations, represent the best fits under circumstances which are often marginal, but also under conditions in which the concentrated use of chemical fertilisers, pesticides and herbicides is causing concern for human health and the long-term sustainability of agricultural practices and the environment generally. A major recent study by the National Research Council (1984), draws attention to these dangers and advocates taking advantage of naturally occurring beneficial interactions rather than relying heavily on off-farm input in the interests of greater diversity and of increased long term profitability. Traditional agricultural resource management is dealt with in the work of Carlier (1987), Dommen (1988) and Niamir (1989).

A major impetus to the utilisation of local knowledge in the development of rural areas has been given by the work of the various non-government organisations. For a variety of reasons their work has expanded considerably in the last decade and organisations like Oxfam, the Intermediate Technology Development Group (ITDG) (Gamser, this volume), and ActionAid have produced important information on ways in which the rich resources bound up in indigenous knowledge systems are being and might be more effectively utilised in the search for self-reliant and self-sustaining development. A major focus of this effort has been on enhancing participatory strategies. This focus is represented in the contributions to be found in *The Greening of Aid*.

It is complemented by the work of a number of UN organisations. The International Labour Office for example as well as the Food and Agriculture Organisation (People's Participation Programme) and the International Fund for Agricultural Development have all initiated major programmes which emphasise local self-sufficiency and the utilisation of local human resources and organisations. The Man and the Biosphere programme of UNESCO has also done important work in this area.

An associated area of work has related the whole issue of culture to that of conservation, recognising that external inputs reduce diversity and increase risk (Redclift 1984; Blaikie 1985). People themselves are the best indicators of what will or will not work, what can be sustained and what cannot.

While the language they use to express this knowledge may not be that of the western scientist, their often emotional and sometimes visionary responses to changes over which they feel they have little control need to be interpreted as significant interventions in the planning process (see *The Hidden Voice*, ZED Press).

This focus has been given a sharper edge through a concentration on gender issues and an increased recognition of the singular contributions that women make to agriculture. The hitherto ignored contributions that women have made to agricultural development is gradually being recognised and the distinctive knowledge that they have of the local environments in which they operate finally is being recognised (Moser 1979; Norem 1983; Jiggins 1986; Illich 1985). In addition gender issues are gradually being incorporated into farming systems research as more attention is given to the family as a unit of production and consumption, and attention is shifted from the farm to the people who provide the definition for that 'farm'.

An impetus to the incorporation of indigenous knowledge in research and development strategies has been given by a number of the different International Agricultural Research Centres, in particular CIMMYT, CIP, and IRRI and by ISNAR. Their work has provided the foundations for a systematic incorporation of the rich natural resources that remain part of a largely oral tradition into the international research effort aimed at maintaining diversity, developing flexible varieties for higher productivity, and building on the often complex methods and techniques employed by farmers in their pursuit of livelihood strategies (see Rhoades 1984; and the work of the Office of Technology Assessment, US Congress 1984).

In the field of agricultural extension, the seminal work of Paulo Friere in the seventies has sensitised many extensionists to the top-down nature of much extension activity and of the need to incorporate the different local and cultural perceptions of risk and acceptability into any extension scheme. A recognition that the extension process is not the one way exchange that was traditionally accepted allows for the incorporation of people's knowledge through a dialogue which enhances the development of locally conceived and locally specific solutions to problems of rural development (see Röling and Engel 1989; Compton 1989b).

Appendix 45.1: Indigenous knowledge systems and agriculture and rural development

○ Indigenous knowledge systems and soil taxonomies
○ Social forestry
○ Seed types
○ Food crops
○ Range management
○ Water conservation
○ Irrigation management
○ Pest control

46. From Ecology through Economics to Ethnoscience: Changing perceptions on natural resource management

OLIVIA N. MUCHENA AND ERIC VANEK

Introduction

THIS ESSAY EXPLORES emerging literature dealing with the role of indigenous knowledge in natural resource conservation. A flourish of recent publications by environmental protection and international development agencies, as well as by biological and social scientists, has addressed this topic. Realising that consumptive growth is limited by the earth's capacity to support it, these authors have considered that non-industrial people may know about saving the resources of their local environments to afford cultural fulfilment and longevity.

A watershed for literary exegesis on enlisting the minds of non-industrialised people in creating sustainable patterns of consumption is the report of the 1972 United Nations conference on the human environment. This meeting in Stockholm, Sweden, was attended by delegates from 113 countries. Also represented were U.N. agencies such as the Educational and Scientific and Cultural Organisation (UNESCO), World Health Organisation (WHO), Food and Agriculture Organisation (FAO), together with the World Bank and many intergovernmental and international non-governmental development organisations.

In its list of declarations, the conference proclaimed: 'A point has been reached in history when we must shape our actions throughout the world with a more prudent care for their environmental consequences. Through ignorance or indifference we can do massive and irreversible harm to the earthly environment on which our life and well-being depend. Conversely, through fuller knowledge and wiser action, we can achieve for ourselves and our posterity a better life in an environment more in keeping with human needs and hopes... Man must use knowledge to build, in collaboration with nature, a better environment. To defend and improve the human environment for present and future generations has become an imperative goal for mankind – a goal to be pursued together with, and in harmony with, the established and fundamental goals of peace and world-wide economic and social development.'

This statement by the UN General Assembly called for a popular global effort to cultivate a new environmentally-sensitive wisdom for the 'creation of a good life.' Indeed, less-industrialised people were invited to participate in this enlightenment. They were, however, cast in the role of active students, rather than that of innovators and teachers. Scientists, themselves educated in the universities of industrial nations, were proclaimed as the prophets of 'rational management of resources and thus improve the environment.'

Scientific research and development in the context of environmental problems, both national and multinational, must be promoted in all countries, especially developing countries. In this context, the free flow of up-to-date scientific information and transfer of experience must be supported and assisted to facilitate the solution of environmental problems.

With exhortations based on the paradigms of ecology, scientists answered the

international community's call for guidance in natural resource management-
ment.

Conservation through ecology and economics

The basic precepts of ecology had been defined by European biologists as early
as the 1930s (see Tansley 1935), and were in common use in the natural sciences
by the 1950s (see Odum 1953). In 1956, for example, a standard English textbook in introductory biology, *Modern Biology*, included in its glossary the term
'ecology,' defined broadly as 'a study of the relations of living things to their
surroundings (Moon, Mann, and Otto 1956: 725). Today, as it was then, ecologists have been trained that 'the living world maintains a natural balance'
through harmonious and continuous cycles of consumption and regeneration.
According to this conviction, therefore, it follows that people understand the
cycles of nature to work with them to ensure human welfare (Moon, Mann and
Otto 1956: 74–5).

The specific study of human settlements and their relations to the organic,
inorganic, and socio-cultural components of their surroundings was coined
'human ecology.' The challenge of human ecology, as clarified at the 1975
UNESCO- and WHO-sponsored international meeting on human ecology, was
to explain the '...balance that must exist between man and his environment in
order to ensure his well being, which concerns the 'whole man' not only his
physical health but also his mental health and the optimum social relations
within his environment' (Macuch 1976: 12).

Natural resource conservation became an important subject of human ecology. General ecology had been used in natural resource management for some
time and, of course, many of the principles were recycled through human ecology. For example, the definition of conservation, as conceived by ecologists, was
acceptable to human ecologists. Moon *et al.*'s definition 'the preservation and
wise use of natural resources' (1956: 724) could continue to be used. The criterion constituting 'wise use', however, was in need of clarification.

Early ecologists/conservationists had come to justify their recommendations
monetarily. This is understandable, as natural resource conservation in the West
requires the cooperation and support of industry. Businesses needed to be convinced to employ ecology in moderating their use of resources, therefore, limiting immediate production and profit, rather than pursuing lucrative short-term
gains. Hence, conservation through the principles of ecology was touted for
being economically wise.

This marketing of conservation ecology obscured its original goal, which,
regardless of its economic merits, is to balance patterns of human consumption
with the regenerative cycles of nature (Moon *et al.* 1956: 65-76). To illustrate,
Benton and Werner published in 1958 a seminal work on conservation entitled
Principles of Field Biology and Ecology. The volume deals with conservation of
forests, soil, and water.

Taken from a section of that book dealing with wildlife conservation, the following quote shows how ecologists were obliged to sell themselves to industry
(Benton and Werner 1958: 186): 'The value of wildlife is rather difficult to
appraise, for it must include other factors besides the actual monetary value of
the animals as food. The aesthetic value of wildlife in terms of human enjoyment, cannot readily be measured in dollars and cents... In any case, wildlife is
of economic worth and is sufficiently important to warrant the time and money

spent by biologists in their efforts to learn about natural history, conservation, and management.'

By the 1960s, the economic correlates of ecological principles was beginning to be taken for granted. Industrial managers were applying them routinely to their operations. *The Ecosystem Concept in Natural Resource Management*, a volume prepared in 1969 as a reference book for international resource management courses, is clear evidence that ecology and industrial economics were becoming isomorphic (Spurr 1969: 3–7): 'Management is defined as the manipulation of the ecosystem by man. Beneficial management involves manipulation to maximise the returns to man, while exploitation is management that results in the reduction of the productivity of the ecosystem to mankind over a period of time. The ecological principles of natural resource ecosystems are generally applicable regardless of the particular natural commodity. So, too, are the tools of management and the basic rules governing their application.'

Eventually, during the mid- to late seventies, the proponents of human ecology , who began to express their views during the early seventies, took issue with this notion of equating wise use of natural resources with the economic concerns of industry. In 1974, Simmons addressed the agents of progress in his book *The Ecology of Natural Resources*: 'If material wealth is seen as the natural and proper goal of man's activities, then mastery of man over nature (and the pre-eminence of economic thought over ecological thought) becomes a fulfilment of human destiny. The perspectives of ecology are different from those of economics, for they stress limits rather than continued growth, stability rather than continuous "development", and they operate on a different time scale, for the amortisation period of capital is replaced by that of the evolution of ecosystems and of organisms.'

Simmons reaffirmed the edicts of ecology by advocating that people understand their environment to adapt themselves to it, rather than using ecology as a means to adapt the environment to people's industrial concerns (Simmons 1974: 29): 'It appears healthier for man to regard the planet less as a set of commodities for use and more as a community of which he forms a part... Such an attitude will mean the abandonment of the central theme of our intellectual heritage and especially of its religious accompaniment, its anthropocentricity. To do that requires a revolution in thought, involving essentially the realisation that our survival as a species is dependent upon non-human processes.'

In developing his models for solving the complex problems of ecology and conservation faced by natural resource managers, Simmons elevated the role of people in non-industrial societies. He made a radical departure from the position established by the 1972 US Human Environment Conference. He suggested (1974: 33) that non-industrial societies could actually teach sound principles of natural resource management rather than only be converted by them (Simmons 1974: 33): 'Before the advent of Western culture, some "primitive" groups had been notably successful in adapting to extreme environments in which there appears to our eyes to be a paucity of resources. The Bushmen of the Kalahari desert are an often quoted example: to them the recognition of sources of moisture in their arid surroundings is the critical element. Thus, all manner of plants and animals are used for food and some of these probably largely as sources of moisture. The people become adept at spotting the traces of delicacies such as buried ostrich eggs, for example, which add valuable elements to their diet.'

Simmons extolled the merits of a locally 'preferred limit' to natural resource use. This, he wrote, is the most hopeful way of coming to grips with 'man's most fearsome problems' (Simmons 1974: 375-376): 'The containment of population, the management of energy flows, the development of stable ecological and political orders, and the formulation of a coherent political and ethical doctrine for human behaviour in relation to natural systems, and furthermore one which neither attempts the unforeseeable nor commits the irrevocable. Bringing this about is a task of immense difficulty, because it can only be made meaningful to diverse groups of men in terms of the lineaments of their own culture: success is unlikely if new ways are imposed internationally or by foreign-educated governors. But because of the accelerating rush to instability brought about by the exponential growth of number of people, consuming materials and energy, and subsequently discharging waste, all men should recognise that ecological instability is their common enemy, one which will not distinguish between rich and poor, black, white or brown, PhDs and peasant farmers.' (Emphasis added)

In 1980, the Independent Commission on International Development Issues, otherwise known as the Brandt Commission, published the book *North-South: A Program for Survival.* The report, as its title suggests, analyses the constraints to human development and makes urgent recommendations for their resolution, including ecological restoration and conservation. UN Secretary-General Kurt Waldheim and Robert S. McNamara, president of the World Bank, had shown great interest in the formation and findings of this independent commission.

The membership of the Brandt Commission, like that of the 1972 Conference on the Human Environment, had a significant contingent representing the so-called 'Third World' or 'Southern' nations. Unlike the 1972 group, however, the commission did not advocate scientific imperialism from the industrialised 'North' in international conservation efforts. Rather, its recommendations were based on the premise popularised by human ecologists, like Simmons, which call for using locally appropriate indigenous knowledge systems in natural resource management (*North-South. The Report of the Independent Commission on International Development Issues* 1980: 23): 'We must not surrender to the idea that the whole world should copy the models of highly industrialised countries. One must avoid the persistent confusion of growth with development... There is fierce discussion about how to progress from here – with different technologies, with a less wasteful way of life. Ideologies of growth in the North (and not only the West of the North) have had little concern for the quality of growth. A people aware of their cultural identity can adopt and adapt elements true to their value system... There is no uniform approach; there are different and appropriate answers depending on history and cultural heritage, religious traditions, human and economic resources, climatic and geographic conditions, and political patterns of nations. But there is a common notion that cultural identity gives people dignity.'

Conservation through indigenous knowledge

Several approaches to the cultural/human dimension of conservation have emerged with the increasing awareness and interest in indigenous natural resource management. These approaches range from the idealistic and romantic view of indigenous peoples and their knowledge and attitudes to nature, to the role of various disciplines in designing conservation strategies.

Torres' writing on 'The Andean Native Peoples in the Conservation Planning

Process', advocates a 'splendid isolation' type of strategy on the premises that traditional societies of the Andean region of Peru, Chile, Bolivia, and Ecuador have such agroecological knowledge and practices that they should live in a protected area corresponding to a territory of a particular people or in native-owned lands. These types of settlement would protect the endangered native culture and knowledge about ecosystems, plants, and weather prediction (see McNeeley and Pitt 1984).

Bennett (1984: 306) in points out the naivete of such romantic views: 'In the early ecology movement, the fact that some subsistence-tribal societies were represented as approximating ecosystemic homeostatic properties was the occasion to recommend similar behaviour for modern society, ignoring the fact that modern society operates on entirely different principles of resource use and with differing social and economic magnitudes.'

Pearson (1989: 13), challenges the romantic view that indigenous people possess ecological wisdom which form their basis for the respect and conservation of natural resources. 'Almost every culture has restrictions, religiously or socially sanctioned, on the use of certain plants, animals, or limitations on hunting and gathering activities by particular groups or during certain periods throughout the year, resulting in limited resource exploitation. In fact, the formally called "natural religions" are to a large extent to be viewed as religiously based forms of native conservation. Therefore, it has also been suggested that native conservation and indigenous life-styles are more or less synonymous.'

The idealism of the early indigenous peoples' ecology movement is giving way to challenges of the role of indigenous knowledge in present-day efforts to design conservation strategies that have a cultural basis. The basic theoretical concern for Bennett (1984: 293) is whether or not human factors can be incorporated in balanced and sustained ecosystems. The important question he raises is '...are humans part of ecosystems in the sense that their needs can be satisfied without running down the system?'

According to Leff (1985: 260) ethnobotany and anthropology provide inter-linkages between nature and culture, and the implications for conservation strategies: 'Every culture, although identified by its traditions, is transformed through an historical process of influence from external social systems. Our historical option is to conceptualise an alternative strategy of development, based on the articulation of nature and culture and on a new paradigm of eco-technological productivity that would promote a sustained and diversified process of production of the means of well-being of different societies, while preserving their fundamental ecological structures and cultural traits for the reproduction of their natural resources.'

Leff's views contrast sharply with the simplistic return-to-tradition or the imposition of Western natural resource management models. The cultural diversities and dialectical nature of societies and natural environments become central in any proposed conservation strategy. For the process of conceptualising alternative strategies, anthropology provides the analysis of mythical representatives, religious beliefs, and unconscious behaviour of societies. Ethnobotany unveils the historical process of the constitution, conservation, and destruction of natural resources through transculturation.

Leff (1985) illustrates the contributions of various disciplines to the understanding of the interlinkages between nature, conservation, and culture. Ethnology and anthropology provide the theoretical tools for understanding the complexity of cultural organisation. Enthnobotany is useful for reconstructing inter-actions between cultures and their natural recourses. According to Jacques Bar-rau (cited by Leff: 264), ethnobotanics address the following questions:

o How men...see, understand, and use vegetal environment; how do they participate and how they recognise, name, classify their elements?
o What is the cultural significance of vegetals?
o What are the origins, the uses, and properties and the economic value of these plants?

Emerging literature confirm the above as key questions in indigenous knowl-edge systems and conservation (see also Makina 1981, Posey *et al.* 1983, Bro-kensha *et al.* 1980).

The universality of religious beliefs and practices as a conservation method has been illustrated by Pei (1985) in southwest China, Schultes (1974) in north-west Amazon, Ayensu (1980) in the Amazonia, Barrow (1988) in Kenya, Guha (1985) in India, and Maydell (1986) in Africa. The common element in the above literature is the reverence and protection of physical phenomena, such as certain trees, forests, pools, animals, or birds for religious purposes. Leff (1989: 266) points to the importance of these religious/conservation practices when he states that '...in as much as the ethnobotanic study deals with the cultural signif-icance and religious beliefs of the community, it should be supported by an anthropological study about the mythical representations of the people, as much of the rationality of their perception and use of their resources is 'hidden' in their ideological formations.'

Conservation and ownership

Ownership as a means of conservation and protection of resources is also a topi-cal issue in the literature on indigenous management of natural resources (see Fortmann and Bruce 1988; Weinstock and Vergara 1987; Barth 1975; Saussay 1987). Rights and responsibilities, *vis-a-vis* communal or common property, led to Hardin's (1968) notion of the 'tragedy of the commons,' *i.e.*, resources held in common will inevitably be overexploited and degraded. Bromley and Cernea (1989: 6) reject Hardin's notion because the latter confuses 'an open access' (free-for-all) with a common property regime (in which group size and behav-ioural rules are specified)

Among the Vugusi and Logoli of Western Kenya, the checks and balances of common property are described by Wagner (1970: 83): 'Trees growing on sur-plus clan lands are looked up as clan property. On such lands, clansmen and *avamenya* (those who stay on the land) of long standing may fell any trees which they need for building – large and conspicuous trees and those that marked boundaries between clan territories were formerly under the protection of the *eligutu* (clan head) and could only be felled with his consent... The sacred grove where tribal sacrifices are offered twice a year to Agoma is likewise protected.'

What is evident from the management practices based on cultural beliefs and magico-religious practices is that common property in these societies was not equivalent to open access as Hardin implied.

However, the situation is changing, as Bromley and Cernea (1989: 17) sug-gest: '...compliance, protected and reinforced by an authority system, is a neces-sary condition for the viability of many property regime When authority breaks down for whatever reasons, then the management or self-management of resources use cannot be exercised...and for all practical purposes, common property (*res communis*) degenerates into open access (*res nullis*).'

In summary, recent literature indicates a dynamic shift in emphasis from matters purely ecological and economic to an increasing concern with the human and cultural dimensions of natural resource management. The search for effective policies and strategies has led to an analysis of the human dimension of conservation. According to Roy (1987: 159), 'social aspects of resource management – patterns of development – demand equivalent attention to technical aspects.' The editors of *Sustainable Resource Development in the Third World* give a fitting conclusion in the postscript when they indicate that: 'When policies and projects fail, insufficient attention to the social and institutional context of environmental concern is frequently the cause.'

47. INDAKS: A bibliography and database on indigenous agricultural knowledge systems and sustainable development in the tropics

L. JAN SLIKKERVEER

Introduction

OVER THE PAST decades, among scientists, planners and extension workers, the concern on the progress of modern, Western-oriented programmes and projects of socio-economic development in many Third World countries has gradually increased, and a general awareness has emerged that, if present trends will continue, humankind will soon face the virtually certain prospect of a global collapse. As widely experienced in many sectors of society, such as human health, agriculture, forestry, fishery and natural resources management, the model of Transfer-of-Technology from Western to non-Western countries has too often led to overexploitation, depletion of resources and a general threat of extinction of species.

In response to the general call for alternative approaches encompassing a more sustainable mode of development, a renewed interest in the role of local farmers, medical practitioners and women's groups in the management of their environment and natural resources has emerged, bringing indigenous knowledge and skills firmly into the international debate. Indeed, in addition to the significance of biodiversity conservation, the interest in the role of cultural diversity in terms of indigenous peoples' various systems of knowledge and practice has generated a totally new, interdisciplinary field of indigenous knowledge systems theory and practice.

Departing from the results of early ethnoscientific studies which have shown the efficacy and appropriateness of alternative, locally oriented approaches towards development projects, the first true break-through in this field took place by the end of the seventies, when at the *International Conference on Primary Health Care* of WHO in Alma Ata (1978) the role of traditional medicine was purposely introduced into the global effort to attain the objective of 'Health for All by the Year 2000'. Partly engendered by promising examples of local and regional medical systems which proved to be more effective and less costly, and – perhaps even more important – partly by the increased assertiveness and political consciousness of client and patient groups, traditional medicine has come to be generally accepted and officially integrated in most health care delivery systems around the world (*cf.* Kleinman 1980; Bannerman, Burton and Ch'en Wen-Chieh 1983; Leslie 1988; Slikkerveer 1990). The inductive processes of involving indigenous medical knowledge and practice 'from the bottom' into national health care systems has not only led to a more realistic attitude of national health planners and administrators, but also to an increased awareness among international donor agencies. of the importance of participatory orientations in the health sector.

Later on, during the 1980s, a second break-through in the recognition of indigenous knowledge and practice in the international development effort took place in the related sectors of agriculture and environment. Indeed, in the West, the environmental movement gained such public weight that soon ecological issues came to dominate the political agendas of many nations.

In the developing world, an increasing number of countries – particularly in Sub-Saharan Africa – became faced with rapid environmental depredation and declining agricultural production which soon led to the widely acknowledged 'Crisis in African Agriculture'. As Mazur and Titilola (1992) rightly note, natural resource degradation encouraged by population pressure, poverty and the implementation of inappropriate technology are generally considered to cause adverse trends in crop production and productivity. Particularly in agriculture, the combination of massive external inputs of costly fertilizers, herbicides, fungicides and pesticides has not only been unable to maintain adequate production levels, but has created an alarming situation of near-bankruptcy and pollution in both the economical and ecological sectors of developing countries.

By consequence, an international call for 'alternative agriculture' which could lead to 'Sustainable Agriculture and Rural Development' (SARD) has prompted the current resort to sustainable approaches in agriculture. As such reorientation seems to require a fundamentally new paradigm of sustainable development in which indigenous agricultural knowledge and practice plays a central role, anthropologists and development sociologists have come to join agronomists, botanists and soil scientist to document, study, analyse and re-integrate local farmers knowledge into the overall agricultural development efforts.

Since the interest in indigenous knowledge systems has virtually emerged from experiences of the practical setting of the applied, development-oriented sciences in the tropics, the theoretical and methodological aspects of the newly-developing field of agricultural knowledge systems theory and practice have so far remained in the background. Among the few theoretical orientations are the innovative studies from the extension sciences related to knowledge, information and agricultural development by Röling (1986, 1988a; 1988b), Röling and Engel (1989), from the cognitive sciences concerning knowledge creation, exchange and utilisation by Beal, Wassanayake and Konoshima (1986), and from anthropology and development sociology, focused on knowledge, cognition and culture by Pearce (1988), Warren, Slikkerveer and Titilola (1989), and Leakey and Slikkerveer (1991). As a result, the study of indigenous knowledge systems in relation to the development process has largely remained outside the academic arena. By consequence, the conceptualisation of such systems and their components certainly need further clarification. Not only for the full understanding of what in fact encompasses indigenous – or local – knowledge and practice, but even more so, of what changing connotations are currently connected to the term 'indigenous'?

Indigenous Knowledge Systems (IKS) have been defined as systems of knowledge and practice, developed over generations in a particular field of anthropological study, and as such unique to a specific culture or region. Sometimes referred to as systems of 'local knowledge', 'traditional knowledge', or even 'commonsense knowledge', these systems have mainly evolved outside – or in contrast with – Western-oriented, 'scientific', or 'modern' systems of knowledge and technology generated through universities, research institutes and industries. Indigenous Knowledge (IT) has formed the basis for local-level decision-making in sectors of the society such as human and animal health, agriculture and food production, natural resources management and fisheries (*cf.* Warren, Slikkerveer and Titilola 1989; Warren 1991; Slikkerveer *et al.* 1993)

Apart from 'Western' or 'scientific' knowledge which has developed on a rather separatist, monodisciplinary basis, Indigenous Knowledge encompasses a strong interdisciplinary orientation towards practice and experience. As there are both similarities and differences between 'traditional' and 'Western' knowledge, it is interesting to note, that from an anthropological, cultural-relativist's point of view, as Bronowski (1978) stresses, the practice of science, including belief and magic, forms a fundamental characteristic of all human societies. The implication of such position pertains to the conclusion, that both Western and indigenous science are the result of the same general, intellectual process of creating order out of disorder. Since such adaptive knowledge and practices are often passed down the generations through the oral tradition, these systems are – in contrast with some Western stereotyping of the past – not 'simple', 'static', 'old-fashioned' or even 'archaic', but rather dynamic with elements of both continuity and change, embedded in their adaptive capacity, selection mechanisms and appropriate use (*cf.* Jiggins 1989, Slikkerveer 1989, Warren 1989). In this context, the term 'indigenous' should not be confused with former concepts with strong negative connotations from the colonial past including Dutch terms such as *inheems* or *inlands*, or the Eng;lish terms *primitive*, *native* or *aboriginal*.

On the contrary. While these terms previously indeed tended to refer to 'rurality' and 'backwardness' often in connection with particular ethnic groups, the designation 'indigenous' has lately come to highlight the uniqueness, the artisan and the rich heritage aspects of specific cultures and communities in their particular locality. It is therefore not surprising, that recently, partly out of a resentment or even rejection of Western, often materialistic life-styles, several cultures around the globe have proudly adopted the term 'indigenous' to stress the values, attitudes and life-styles underlying their own cultural identity and uniqueness in a world that seems to glide to globalization and Westernization.

The revaluation of local cultures in terms of 'indigenous' providing an expression of their own cultural heritage was recently strongly encouraged by the Official United Nations 'Year of the Indigenous Peoples' of 1993, enhancing the process of 'reculturation' or 'indigenization' *(indiginismo)* of many cultures around the world. While the specific conditions of indigenous systems show a vast variety over different regions, nations, culture areas, and continents, distinct *principia media* could however be identified at the theoretical level, providing the preconditions for the advancement of the newly-developing field of IKS & D.

Particularly in the agricultural sector, as a result of failing Western knowledge and technology inputs by the beginning of the 1990s, national governments and international donor organisations and development agencies seem finally prepared to acknowledge the importance of so far largely ignored local people's empirical knowledge and experience, as well as of their values, perceptions and practices in the development process: the 'cultural dimension of development'. Although for a long time, the concept of culture has been regarded as an 'obstacle to change' by development experts and extension workers, often directly linked with stereotyped labels of 'rurality' and 'traditional life-styles', now its potential for facilitating the development process seems finally to undergo a significant reorientation.

The INDAKS project

While during the early 1990s a number of donors still were unable to completely disengage from a post-colonial syndrome of regarding indigenous knowledge as 'non-scientific', a major first step was taken in 1993 by the European Community in Brussels providing substantial support to the ongoing scientific collaboration in the field of indigenous agricultural knowledge systems between the National Museums of Kenya in Nairobi (NMK), the Universitas Padjadjaran (UNPAD) in Bandung,, Indonesia, the Mediterranean Agronomic Institute of Chania (MAICH) in Crete, Greece and Leiden University (LEAD Programme) in The Netherlands (*cf.* Slikkerveer 1989).

The joint project on 'Indigenous Knowledge Systems for Sustainable Agriculture in Developing Countries' focusses specifically on indigenous knowledge and practice in agriculture and food production. Its primary objective is to provide a contribution to both the further theoretical and methodological development of the study of indigenous agricultural knowledge systems, and its applicable principles in sustainable agriculture and rural development. As such, the project seeks to develop a comparative analytical model of Indigenous Agricultural Knowledge Systems (INDAKS) in relation to sustainable development, based on cross-cultural research in different areas. The project includes the execution of four tasks:

  o the study, analysis and documentation of INDAKS in specific research areas of Kenya and Indonesia;
  o the evaluation of the potential contribution of INDAKS to achieving sustainable development programmes;
  o the development of a practical model of integration of INDAKS into the SARD strategy;
  o the strengthening of the existing research and training capacities among the counterparts, as well as its linkage with the Global Network on IK&D.

Despite the progress, recently made in the field of agricultural knowledge systems, particularly with regard to its role in socio-economic development in tropical areas, a coherent body of knowledge does hardly exist (*cf.* Tillmann *et al.* 1991). Indeed, as an accumulation of case studies, practical experiences and project reports fragmented in different (sub)disciplines, does not necessarily represent such 'body of knowledge', an attempt is made to provide a clarification of the field by defining INDAKS, categorising its different components and factors, and provide an inventory of existing research within related disciplines such as anthropology, agronomy, ecology and natural resources management.

Using a systems perspective in the definition of Indigenous Agricultural Knowledge Systems (INDAKS) facilitates the introduction of a dynamic aspect to the conceptualisation of indigenous knowledge and practice with regard to agriculture. Following the culture-bound conceptualisation of Beal *et al.* (1986), who rightly regard 'knowledge' as the primary cognitive part of any given culture, indigenous agricultural knowledge systems, then, could be defined as encompassing both immaterial *and* material phenomena of any given agricultural system.

Such definition refers to a system of local perceptions, practices, technologies, artefacts and cosmologies with regard to agriculture, developed over generations in a particular field of anthropological study, and as such unique to a specific culture or region. Here, the relativist cultural significance of knowledge – North/South, Eastern/Western, or for that matter Developing Countries/Developed Countries – gains a new meaning.

Since indigenous agricultural knowledge systems, on the one hand, have – that is until recently – largely been left outside the academic area of interest, and on the other hand, have mainly been recorded as a 'side-line' in 'scientific' agricultural research, often in a fragmented way in various sub-disciplines, a first literature survey has been set up under the auspices of the project. It includes the compilation of a bibliography, specifically focused on INDAKS in developing countries, including local knowledge and practice in *i.a.:*

- agriculture/agronomy;
- agro-ecology, including traditional ecological knowledge (TEK);
- agro-forestry and wild plant utilisation;
- ethnobotany;
- agro-aquaculture;
- soil science;
- natural resource management;
- water management and irrigation; and
- ethno-biotechnology including food processing and storage.

In addition to the review of existing books, scientific journals and – most important – research reports, generally referred to as 'grey' or 'fugitive' literature, a bibliographical computer search on related keywords is being carried out, including AGRICOLA, CAB, CHRIS, GEO INDEX, TROPAG, and AGRIS. Closely related to the bibliography on INDAKS, a computerised data base is presently being designed at LEAD in Leiden, specifically developed for the collection and documentation of indigenous knowledge systems in agriculture in the tropics: the INDAKS/LEAD Data Base. In this context, further joint efforts will be undertaken among the four counterparts in the Programme, and in conjunction with CIRAN (The Hague in The Netherlands) and CIKARD (Ames,Iowa in the USA), to facilitate further information exchange and utilisation in this particular field.

In this respect, it is the implicit objective of the project through the exchange of its information and research results, to provide a contribution to strengthening the R&D capacity of the counterpart institutions in Indonesia and Kenya, and for that matter elsewhere in the developing world.

Note

The author would like to express his gratitude to Dr. Wim H.J.C. Dechering,, Ms. Drs. Margot Starkenburg. Ms. Drs. Jacqueline Smak Gregoor, Ir. Bert Keizer, Ms. Diana Bosch for their contribution to the project as part of the LEAD Programme of Leiden University.

Bibliography

Abadi, S.L.M. (1983a) *Pengobatan Tradisional Resep-Resep Obat, Barat, Timur dan Cina,* Pekalongan, Bahagia.

— (1983b) *Mengenal Apotik Hidup (Obat Asli Indonesia),* Pekalongan, Bahagia.

Abdulai, B.I., C.J. Stigter, A.A. Ibrahim, A.M. Adeed and H.S. Adam (1990) *Evaporation Calculations from Lake Sennar (Sudan): A Search for a Meteorological Minimum Input Approach, A Synopsis.*

Abu-Rabia, A. (1983)*Folk Medicine among the Bedouin Tribes in the Negev,* Ben-Gurion University of the Negev, Sede Boger Campus, Israel, Social Studies Centre, The Jakob Blaustein Institute for Desert Research.

Adams, R.E.W., W.E. Brown Jr. and T.P. Culbert, (1981) 'Radar Mapping, Archaeology and Ancient Maya Land Use', *Science,* 213, pp. 1457-1463.

Adams, R N. and A.J. Rubel (1966) 'Sickness and Social Relations', in M. Nash (ed). *Handbook of Middle American Indians* VI: Social Anthropology, Austin, University of Texas Press.

Adhikary, S. (1981) 'The Togo Experience in Moving from Neem Research to its Practical Application for Plant Protection', in H. Schmutterer, K.R.S. Ascher and H. Rembold (eds.) *Natural Pesticides from the Neem Tree,* pp. 215-222, Proceedings, 1st International Neem Conference, Rottach-Edern, 1980, Schriftenreihe der GTZ, Deutsche Gessellschaft für Technische Zusammenarbeit (GTZ) GmbH.

— (1985) 'Results of Field Trials to Control the Diamondback Moth, *Plutella xylostella* L, by Application of Crude Methanolic Extracts and Aqueous Suspensions of Neem, *Azadirachta indica* A. Juss, in Togo', *Zeitschrift für angewandte Entomologie,* 100, pp. 27-33.

Adimihardja, K. (1990) 'The Concept of Jamu: Perception of the Local People of West Java', Paper presented to the Third International Congress on Traditional Asian Medicine (IASTAM), Bombay.

Advisory Committee on the Sahel (1983) *Agroforestry in the West African Sahel,* Washington, D.C., National Academy Press.

AFGRO (Agency to Facilitate the Growth of Rural Organisations) Contract AFR-0000-0-00-9028-00.

Aguilar C., C. Abigail, M.A.A. Martínez, V. Argueta, J. Dorantes and H.B. Esparza (1988) 'Mesa Redonda: Perspectivas de la Herbolaria Medicinal en la Medicina Veterinaria', in L.L. Nathal and G.L. Buendía (eds.) *Memorias: Primera Jornada sobre Herbolaria Medicinal en Veterinaria,* pp. 178-189, México DF., Universidad Nacional Autónoma de México, Facultad de Medicina Veterinaria y Zootecnia, Coordinación de Educación Continua.

Ahmed, A.G.M. (1978) *Integrated Rural Development: Problems and Strategies: The Case of the Dinka and the Nuer of the Jonglei Project Area in the Sudan,* Republic of Sudan, Executive Organ Development Projects in Jonglei Area, Report 8.

— (n.d.) 'Nomadic Competition in the Funj Area', Sudan *Notes and Records,* Khartoum.

Ahmed, A.G.M. *et al.* (1976) '*Jonglei Socio-Economic Research* Team Interim Report', Republic of Sudan, Executive Organ, Development Projects in Jonglei Area.

Ahmed, S. and M. Grainge (1986) 'Potential of the Neem Tree (*Azadirachta indica*) for Pest Control and Rural Development', *Economic Botany,* 4, pp. 201-209.

Akobundu, I.O. and B.N. Okibo (1984) 'Preliminary Evaluation of Ground Covers for Use as Live Mulch in Maize Production', *Field Crops Research,* 8, pp. 177-186.

Alarco de Zadra, A. (1988) *PERU el Libro de las Plantas Mágicas: Compendio de Farmacopea Popular,* Gráfica Bellido for CONCYTEC (Consejo Nacional de Ciencia y Tecnología), Lima, Peru.

Alcober, D.L. and F.T. Balina (1986) 'Farmer Co-operators and their Response to the FSDP-EV Introduced Farm Innovations at Villaba and Jaro Sites', *FSDP-EV Project Paper 44,* Tacloban, The Philippines, Department of Agriculture.

Alcorn, J.B. (1981) 'Factors Influencing Botanical Resource Perception Among the Huastec', *Journal of Ethnobiology,* 1, pp. 221-230.

— (1984a) *Huastec Mayan Ethnobotany,* Austin, University of Texas Press.

— (1984b) 'Development Policy, Forest and Peasant Farms: Reflections on Huastec-managed Forests', Contributions to Commercial Production and Resource Conservation', *Economic Botany,* 34 (4), pp. 389-406.

— (1988) *Making Use of Traditional Farmers' Wisdom,* Paper presented at Common Futures: An International Forum on Sustainable Development, Toronto, Canada, June 1988.

— (1989a) 'Process as Resource: The Traditional Agricultural Ideology of Bora and Huastec Resource Management and its Implications for Research', in D.A. Posey and W. Balee (eds) *Resource Management in Amazonia,* pp. 63-77, Bronx, New York Botanical Garden.

— (1989b) 'An Economic Analysis of Huastec Mayan Forest Management', in J.O. Browder (ed) *Fragile Lands in Latin America: Strategies for Sustainable Development,* pp. 182-206, Boulder, CO, Westview.

— (1990) 'Indigenous Agroforestry Systems in the Latin American Tropics', in M.A. Altieri and S. Hecht (ed.) *Agroecology and Small Farm Development,* pp. 195-210, Boca Raton, FL, CRC Press.

— (in press) 'Indigenous Agroforestry Strategies Meeting Farmers' Needs', in A. Anderson (ed.) *Alternatives to Deforestation,* New York, Columbia University Press .

Allan, W. (1965a) *The African Husbandman,* Edinburgh, Oliver and Boyd (Reprinted in 1977 by Greenwood Press, Westport)

— (1965b) *The African Husbandman,* New York, Barnes and Noble.

Almond, M. (1987) 'A Para-vet Programme in South Sudan', *Pastoral Development Network Paper* 24c, Agricultural Administration Unit, Overseas Development Institute (ODI), London, U.K., Regent's College, Inner Circle, Regent's Park.

Altieri, M.A. and D.K. Letourneau (1982) 'Vegetation Management and Biological Control in Agroecosystems', *Crop Protection,* 1, pp. 405-430.

Altieri, M.A. (1983) *Agroecology: The Scientific Basis of Alternative Agriculture,* Boulder, CO, Westview Press.

— (1984) 'Towards a Grassroots Approach to Rural Development in the Third World', *Agriculture and Human Values,* 1 (4), pp. 45-48.

— (1988) 'Why Study Traditional Agriculture?', in C.R. Carrol *et al.* (ed.) *The Ecology of Agricultural Systems,* New York, Macmillan Press.

Ameeruddy, Y. and F. Pinglo (1989) *Phytopractices in Tropical Regions: A Preliminary Survey of Traditional Crop Improvement Techniques,* Paris, UNESCO.

Amo, S. del (1989) 'Management of Secondary Vegetation for Artificial Creation of Useful Rain Forest in Uxpanada, Veracruz, Mexico – An Intermediate Alternative between Transformation and Modification.', in A. Gómez-Pompa, T.C. Whitmore, and M. Hadley (eds) *Rain Forest Regeneration and Management,* Man and Biosphere Book Series, Paris, UNESCO/Carnforth, Parthenon Publishing.

Anderson, A.B. (in press) 'Extractivism and Forest Management by Rural Inhabitants in the Amazon Estuary', in A. Anderson (ed.) *Alternatives to Deforestation,* New York, Columbia University Press.

Anjaria J.V. (1986) *Indigenous Drug Research – A Brief Review*, Paper presented at Inservice Training Course of Veterinary Surgeons in Traditional Veterinary Medicine, Veterinary Research Institute, Gannoruwa, Peradeniya, Sri Lanka, October 1986.

— (1987)*Traditional (Indigenous) Veterinary Medicine Project (Ayurvedic Veterinary Medicine)*, Final Report SL-ADB Livestock Development Project, Veterinary Research Institute, Gannoruwa, Peradeniya, Sri Lanka.

— (1988) 'Herbs in Therapy of Milk and Reproductive Disorders', *AYU*, pp. 16-30.

Anonymous (1981) 'Bali Irrigation Project Feasibility Study', Jakarta, Republic of Indonesia, Ministry of Public Works, Directorate General of Water Resources Development.

Anthony, K.R.M., B.F. Johnston, W.O. Jones and V.C. Uchendu (1979) *Agricultural Change in Tropical Africa*, Ithaca, NY, Cornell University Press.

Argueta Villamar, A. (1988) 'Medicina Popular, Animales de Traspatio y Etnozoología en México', in L.L. Nathal and G.L. Buendía, (coord.), *Memorias, Primera Jornada sobre Herbolaria Medicinal en Veterinaria*, pp. 164-177, Universidad México DF, Nacional Autónoma de México, Facultad de Medicina Veterinaria y Zootecnia, Coordinación de Educación Continua.

Armillas, P. (1971) 'Gardens on Swamps', *Science*, 174, pp. 653-661.

Arndt, H.W. (1983) 'The "Trickle-Down Myth"', *Economic Development and Cultural Change*, 33.

Arneson, P.A. (1971) *Guia para la Producción de Mani (Cacahuate) en Nicaragua*, San Pedo Sula, Honduras, Departamento de Investigaciones Tropicales, United Fruit Company.

Arnold, J.E.M. and J.G. Campbell (1986) 'Collective Management of Hill Forests in Nepal: The Community Forestry Development Project', *Common Property Resource Management*, pp. 425-454, Washington, D.C., National Academy Press.

Artz, N.E. (1984) 'A Critique of the "Tragedy of the Commons" Paradigm in Pastoral Development Policy', Draft paper.

Artz, N.E., B.E. Norton and J.T. O'Rourke (1986) 'Management of Common Grazing Lands: Timahdite, Morocco', in BOSTID (ed.) *Proceedings of the Conference on Common Property Resource Management*, pp. 259-280, Washington D.C., National Research Council.

Ascher, K.R.S. (1981) 'Some Physical (Solubility) Properties and Biological (Sterilant for *Epilachna variestris* females) Effects of a dried Methanolic Neem, *Azadirachta indica* Seed Kernel Extract', in H. Schmutterer, K.R.S. Ascher and H. Rembold (ed.) *Natural Pesticides from the Neem Tree*, pp. 63-74, Proceedings, 1st International Neem Conference, Rottach-Edern, 1980, Schriftenreihe der GTZ; Deutsche Gessellschaft für Technische Zusammenarbeit (GTZ) GmbH.

Ashby, J.A. (1984) *Participation of Small Farmers in Technology Assessment*, Alabama, IFDC.

— (1986) 'Methodology for the Participation of Small-Farmers in the Design of On-Farm Trials', *Agricultural Administration*, 22, pp. 1-19.

Asian Development Bank (1988) *Project Performance Audit Report, Bali Irrigation*, Project PE-241/L352-INO, Manila.

Aubert, I. (1988) 'Antecedentes Históricos de Algunas Plantas Medicinales Utilizadas como Antidiarréticos en Animales Domésticos', in L.L. Nathal and G.L. Buendía, (coords.), pp. 12-22, *Memorias: Primera Jornada sobre Herbolaria Medicinal en Veterinaria*, México DF, Universidad Nacional Autónoma de México, Facultad de Medicina Veterinaria y Zootecnia, Coordinación de Educación Continua.

Aumeeruddy, Y. and F. Pinglo (1988) *Phytopractices in Tropical Regions:*

Preliminary Survey of Traditional Crop Improvement Techniques, Paris, UNESCO Laboratoire de Botanique Tropicale (Montpellier).

— (1989) *Phytopractices in Tropical Regions: A Preliminary Survey of Traditional Crop Techniques*, Paris, United Nations Educational, Scientific and Cultural Organisation.

Auró Angulo, A. and H.S. López (1988) 'Uso de la Manzanilla (*Helenium quadridentatum*) para el Tratamiento de la Saprolegniasis (*Saprolegnia spp.*) en Tilapias (*Tylapia mossambica*): Estudio Comparativo con la Acriflavina', in L.L. Nathal and G.L. Buendía, (*coords.*), *Memorias: Primera Jornada sobre Herbolaria Medicinal en Veterinaria*, pp. 90-95, México DF., Universidad Nacional Autónoma de México, Facultad de Medicina Veterinaria y Zootecnia, Coordinación de Educación Continua.

Avila Cazorla, E., V.B. Choque and S. Jiménez (1985) 'Estracto [sic] Etanólico del Tarwi (*Lupinus mutabilis*) en el Tratamiento de la Sarna de Alpacas', in V. Bustinza Choque *et al* (eds) *Proyecto Piel de Alpaca: Informe Final*, pp. 85-89, Puno, Peru, Universidad Nacional del Altiplano (UNA), Instituto de Investigaciones para el Desarrollo Social del Altiplano (IIDSA), Convenio UNA-NUFFIC.

Avila Cazorla, E.V., B. Choque and R. Sapana (1985) 'Alternativas de Tratamiento de la Sarna de Alpacas', in V. Bustinza Choque *et al.* (ed.) *Proyecto Piel de Alpaca: Informe Final*, pp. 90-98, Puno, Peru, Universidad Nacional dell (UN), Institute de Investigations par El Social dell (IUDs), Confine UN-NUFFIC.

Awa, N.E. (1988) *Communication at the Grassroots: Towards a Communication Strategy for Mobilising Human Resources for Rural Development in the Third World*, Keynote Address to the International Seminar on Agricultural Communication and Rural Development, Ilorin, Nigeria, Agricultural and Rural Management Training Institute, 21-24 June.

Ayensu, E.S. (ed.) (1980) *Jungles,* New York, Crown Publishers.

Ba, A.S. (1982) 'L'art Vétérinaire des Pasteurs Sahéliens', *Environment Africain, Série Etudes et Recherches*, 73, pp. 82.

— (1984) *L'art Vétérinaire en Milieu Traditionnel Africain*, Paris, France, Imprimerie Express Tirages for Agence de Coopération Culturelle et Technique.

Bah, M.S. (1983) *Observations on Disease Problems and Traditional Remedies Relating to the Use of Work Oxen in the Karina Area*, Report on a Pilot Study of Preparation for the Research Project 'The Health and Management of N'Dama Cattle in Sierra Leone, with Special Reference to the Use of Work Oxen in Village Conditions', Freetown, Sierra Leone, Sierra Leone Work Oxen Project.

Bahri, S. (1984) *Plantes Utiles de Sous-bois une Perspective en Agroforesterie Tropicale*, D.E.A., USTL, Montpellier, 52.

Baier, S. (1976) 'Drought and the Sahelian Economics of Niger', *African Economic History* 1.

Bajracharya, D. (1983a) 'Deforestation and the Food/Fuel Context: Historico-Political Perspectives from Nepal', *Mountain Research and Development*, 3, pp. 227-240.

— (1983b) 'Fuel, Food or Forest? Dilemmas in a Nepali Village', World *Development*, 11, pp. 1057-1074.

Baldy, Ch. (1986) *Agrometeorologie et Developpement des Regions Arides et Semi-Arides,* Paris, INRA.

Banco Agrario del Peru (1984) *Bancoeru Agrario del Perú – Oxapampanca Brh. Quarterly Reports*, Oxapampa, Banco Agrario del Peru.

Bannerman, R.H., J. Burton and Ch'en Wen-Chieh (ed.) (1983) *Traditional Medicine and Health Care Coverage; A Reader for Health Administrators and Practitioners*, Geneva, WHO.

Barfield, T.J. (1981) *The Central Asian Arabs of Afghanistan: Pastoral Nomadism in Transition*, Austin, Texas, USA, University of Texas Press.

Barker, D., J. Oguntoyimbo and P. Richards (1977) *The Utility of the Nigerian Peasant Farmer's Knowledge in the Monitoring of Agricultural Practices*, MARC Report 4, London, Chelsea College.

Barkin, D. (1983) *Global Proletarianization: An Alternative Approach to the New International Division of Labour,* Paper presented at the Workshop on the Americas in the New International Division of Labour, Gainesville, FL., University of Florida, Centre for Latin American Studies.

Barlett, P.F. (ed) (1980) *Agricultural Decision Making: Anthropological Contributions to Rural Development,* New York, Academic Press.

Barlett, P.F. (1976) 'The Structure of Decision Making in Paso', *American Ethnologist*, 4 (2), pp. 285-307.

— (1980) 'Adaptive Strategies in Peasant Agricultural Production', *Annual Review of Anthropology*, 9, pp. 545-573.

Barlett, P. and S. Low (1980) 'Nervios in Rural Costa Rica', *Medical Anthropology* ,4 (4), pp. 523-564.

Barral, H. and M. Benoit (1977) 'Nature et Genre de Vie au Sahel, L'annee 1973 dans le Nord de la Haute-Volta', in J. Gallais (ed) *Strategies Pastorales et Agricoles des Saheliens durant la Secheresse 1969-1974*, pp. 91-112, Bordeaux, CEGET/CNRS.

Barral, H. (1967) 'Les Populations D'eleveurs et les Problemes Pastoraux dans le Nord-est de la Haute-Volta, 1963-1964', *Cahier ORSTOM Serie Sciences Humaines*, 4 (1), pp. 3-30.

— (1968) 'Tiogo: Etude Geographique d'un Terroir Lela (Haute-Volta)', *Atlas des Structures Agraires au Sud du Sahara*, 2, Paris, ORSTOM.

Barrau, J. (1959) 'The Sago Palms and Other Food plants of Marsh Dwellers in the South Pacific Islands', *Economic Botany*, 13 (2), pp. 151-163.

— (1961) 'Subsistence Agriculture in Polynesia and Micronesia', *Bernice P. Bishop Museum Bulletin, 223*, Honolulu, Hawaii, B.P. Bishop Museum.

— (1983) 'Les Hommes et Leurs Aliments: Esquisse d'une Histoire Écologique et Ethnologique de l'Alimentation Humaine', *Temps Actuels*, 378, Paris.

Barrera, A., A. Gómez-Pompa and C. Vázquez-Yanes (1977) 'El Manejo de las Selvas por los Mayas', *Biotica* (Mexico), 2 (2), pp. 47-61.

Barrow, E.G.C. (1988) 'Trees and Pastoralists: The Case of the Pokot and Turkana', *Social Forestry Network Paper* 6b, London, Overseas Development Institute (ODI).

— (1988) *Trees, People and the Dry Lands: The Role of Local Knowledge,* Institutional invited Paper presented to the Second Kenya National Seminar on Agroforestry, International Council for Research in Agroforestry, Nairobi, Kenya, 7-16 November, 1988.

Barta, A.L. and A.F. Schmitthenner (1986) 'Interaction Between Flooding Stress and Phytophthora Root Rot', *Plant Disease* ,70, pp. 310-313.

Barth, F. (1975) *Ritual and Knowledge Among the Baktaman of New Guinea,* Oslo, Norway, Universitetsfarlaget/New Haven, CT, Yale University Press.

Basehart, H.W. (1973) 'Cultivation Intensity, Settlement Patterns and Homestead Forms Among the Matengo of Tanzania', *Ethnology* , 12 (1), pp. 57-75.

Baumers, M. (1987) *Agroforesterie et Desertification*, Ede, CTA.

Bastien, J.W. (1987) *Healers of the Andes,* Salt Lake City, University of Utah.

Bavappa, K.V.A. and V.J. Jacob (1981) 'A Model for Mixed Cropping', Rome, *CERES, FAO Review*, May/June, pp. 44-46.

Bazalar, H. and C.M. McCorkle (ed.) (1989) *Estudios e Enoveterinarios en Comunidades Altoandinas del Perú*, Lima, Peru, Lluvia Editores.

Bebbington, A. (1988) *Farmer Strategies in Regional Agricultural Change: The Case of Commercial Potato Production in Oxapampa*, Social Science Working Paper, Lima, Peru, International Potato Centre.

Behnke, R.H. and C. Kerven (1984) *Herd Management Strategies Among Agro-Pastoralists in the Bay Region, Somalia*, Somalia, Bay Region Socio-Economic Baseline Study.

Bell, C.A. (1928) *The People of Tibet,* Oxford, Clarendon Press.

Bell, M. (1979) 'The Exploitation of Indigenous Knowledge or the Indigenous Exploitation of Knowledge: Whose Use of What for What?', *IDS Bulletin*, 10 (2), pp. 44-50.

Belshaw, D. (1980) 'Taking Indigenous Knowledge Seriously: The Case of Intercropping Techniques in East Africa', in D. Brokensha, D.M. Warren and O. Werner (ed.) *Indigenous Knowledge Systems and Development*, Lanham, MA, University Press of America.

Bene, Z. (1961) 'Die Schafzucht und die Verarbeitung der Schafmilch auf dem Gebiet des Cserehat (Nordostungarn)', in L. Földe (ed.) *Viehzucht und Hirtenleben in Ostmitteleuropa: Ethnographische Studien*, pp. 559-579, Budapest, Akadémiai Kiadó, Verlag der Ungarischen Akademie der Wissenschaften.

Bennett, J.F. (1969) *Northern Plainsmen: Adaptive Strategy and Agrarian Life*, Chicago, Aldine.

Bennett, L. (1983) *Dangerous Wives and Sacred Sisters: Social and Symbolic Roles of High-Caste Women in Nepal*, New York, Columbia University.

Benoit, M. (1979) 'Le Chemin des Peuls du Boobola', *ORSTOM Travaux et Documents* , 101, Paris, ORSTOM.

Benton, A.H. and W.E. Werner (1958) *Principles of Field Biology and Ecology*, New York, McGraw-Hill Press.

Berg, H. van den (1985) *Diccionario Religioso Aymara*, Iquitos, Peru, Talleres Gráficos del CETA (Centro de Estudios Teológicos de la Amazonia) with IDEA (Instituto de Estudios Aymaras).

– (1990) *La Tierra no da Asi no Mas. Los Ritos Agricolas en la Religion de los Aymaros-Christianos*, Amsterdam, CEDLA.

Bergeret, A. (1977) 'Des Systèmes de Production Écologiquement Variables; Illustrations dans le Domaine de l'Agriculture, Nouvelles de l'Éco-Développement 3-Suppl. à MSH Informations', pp. 3-26, *Critique dans Environnement Africain*, 3 (2), pp. 102-106.

Berlin, B., D.E. Breedlove and P.H. Raven (1974) *Principles of Tzeltal Plant Classification: An Introduction to the Botanical Ethnography of a Mayan-Speaking People of Highland Chiapas*, New York, Academic Press.

Berlo, D.K. (1960) *The Process of Communication*, New York, Holt, Reinhart and Winston.

Bernard, H.R. *et al.* (1986) 'The Construction of Primary Data in Cultural Anthropology', *Current Anthropology,* 27 (4), pp. 382-396.

Bernard, H.R., P.D. Killworth, D. Kronenfield and L. Sailer (1984) 'The Problem of Informant Accuracy: The Validity of Retrospective Data', *Annual Review of Anthropology,* 13, pp. 495-517.

Bernus, E. (1957) 'The Natural Regeneration of the West and Dry Evergreen Forests of Ceylon', *Ceylon Forester* , 2 (4), pp. 153-164.

— (1974) 'Possibilites et Limites de la Politique Hydraulique Pastorale dans le Sahel Nigerien', *Cahier ORSTOM Serie Sciences Humaines,* 11 (2), pp. 119-126.

— (1979) 'Le Contrôle du Milieu Naturel et du Troupeau par les Eleveurs Touaregs Sahéliens', *Pastoral Production and Society/Production Pastorale et Société,* pp 67-74, Proceedings of the International Meeting on Nomadic Pastoralism/Actes du Colloque International sur le Pastoralisme Nomade, Paris 1-3 December 1976, Cambridge and Paris, L'Équipe Écologie et Anthropologie des Sociétés Pastorales, Cambridge University Press and Editions de la Maison des Sciences de l'Homme.

— (1981) 'Range Management Traditionnel et Planifie: Remarques a Propos des Eleveurs Nigeriens', in P.C. Salzman (ed.) *Contemporary Nomadic and Pastoral Peoples: Africa and Latin America*, pp. 23-30 Williamsburg, College of William and Mary, Studies in Third World Societies 17.

Bhattarai, S. (1979) 'State of the Environment in Nepal: Environment Management Project', *Publication 2*, Kathmandu, Department of Soil Conservation and Watershed Management.

Bhattarai, T.N. and J.G. Campbell (1983) 'Plantation Survival, Private Planting, Improved Stove Use and Increase in Knowledge in Community Forestry: Results of On-Going Evaluation Surveys 1982-1983', *Misc. Doc.* 15, Kathmandu, Community Forestry Development Project.

Biggs, S.D. (1989) *Resource Poor Farmer Participation in Research: A Synthesis of Experiences from Nine Nahoral Agricultural Research Systems,* OFCOR Comparative Study Paper 3, The Hague, The Netherlands, International Service for Nahoral Agricultural Research.

Biggs, S.D. and E. Clay (1981) 'Sources of Innovation in Agricultural Technology', *World Development* , 9, pp. 321-36.

— (1984) *Agricultural Research: A Review of Social Science Analysis,* Discussion Paper 115, U.K., University of Anglia, SDS.

Bisilliat, J. (1983) 'The Feminine Sphere in the Institutions of the Songhay Zarma', in C. Oppong (ed.) *Female and Male in West Africa*, pp. 99-106, London, George Allen and Unwin.

Blaikie, P. (1985) *The Political Economy of Soil Erosion*, London, Longman.

Blanton, R., S. Kowalewski, G. Feinman and J. Appel (1981) *Ancient Mesoamerica: a Comparison of Change in Three Regions*, New York, Cambridge University Press.

Blockland, P.J. van (1981) 'Trends in Agricultural Finance with Reference to Florida', *Florida Food and Resource Economics Newsletter,* 38, Gainesville, University of Florida, Department of Food and Resource Economics.

Bloemen-Waanders, P.L. van (1859) *Aanteekeningen omtrent de Zeeden en Gebruiken der Balineezen, inzonderheid die van Boeleleng*, Batavia, Kolff and Co.

Bohannan, P. (1954) *Tiv Farm and Settlement*, Colonial Research Studies 15, London,

— (1964) *Africa and Africans,* Garden City, New York, The Natural History Press.

Bolton, R. and L. Calvin (1985) 'El Cuy en la Cultura Peruana Contemporánea', in H. Lechtman and A.M. Soldi (ed.) *La Tecnología en el Mundo Andino: Runakunap Kaw-sayninkupaq Rurasqankunaqa, Tomo I: Subsistencia y Mensuración*, pp. 261-326, México DF, Imprenta Universitaria de la Universidad Nacional Autónoma de México.

Bonfiglioli, A.M., Y.D. Diallo and S. Fagerberg-Diallo (1988) *Kisal: Production et Survie au Ferlo (Sénégal)*, Oxfam, Dakar, Senegal, Rapport Préliminaire.

Bontekoe, C. (1689) *Korn. Bontekoe; Al Zijn Philosophische, Medicinale en Chymishe Schriften*, Amsterdam.

Booth, R.H. (1977) 'A Review of Root Rot Diseases in Cassava', in T. Brekelbaum, A. Bellotti and C.J. Lozano (ed.) *Proceedings: Cassava Protection Workshop*, Cali, Colombia, Centro Internacional de Agricultura Tropical (CIAT).

Boster, F. (1983) 'A Comparison of the Diversity of Jivaroan Gardens with that of the Tropical Forest', *Human Ecology*, 11 (1), pp. 47-68 (84-166).

Boutrais, J. (1974) 'Les Conditions Naturelles de l'Elevage sur le Plateau de l'Adamaoua (Cameroun)', *Cahier ORSTOM Serie Sciences Humaines*, 11 (2), pp. 145-198.

Box, L. (1985) *Cultivation and Adaptation: An Essay in the Sociology of Agriculture,* pp. 161-187, Wageningen, Agricultural University Wageningen.

— (1987) *Experimenting Cultivators: A Methodology for Adaptive Agricultural*

Research, Paper for the workshop on Farmers and Agricultural Research: Complementary Methods held at the Institute of Development Studies, University of Sussex, July 26-31.

Brandani, A., G. Hartshorn and G. Orians (1988) 'Internal Heterogeneity of Gaps and Species Richness of Costa Rican Tropical Rain Forest', *Journal of Tropical Ecology*, 4 (2), pp. 99-199.

Brandstadt Report (1987) *Our Common Future*, World Commission on Environment and Development.

Brass, L.J. (1941) 'Stone Age Agriculture in New Guinea', *Geographical Review*, 31, pp. 555-569.

Bredemeier, L.F. (1978) 'Socio-political Practices Hinder Improved Range Management', in D.N. Hyder (ed.) *Proceedings of the 1st International Rangeland Congress*, pp. 90-91, Denver, SRM.

Breemer, J.P.M. van den, H. van der Pas and H.J. Tieleman (eds) (1991) *The Social Dynamics of Economic Innovation*, Leiden, DSWO Press.

Brisebarre, A-M. (1978) 'La Médecine Vétérinaire Traditionelle du Berger de Transhumance en Cévennes', *Le Courier de la Nature*, 75, pp. 4-12.

— (1984a) 'A Propos de l'Usage Thérapeutique des Bouquets Suspendus dans les Bergeries Cévenoles', *Bulletin d'Ethnomédecine*, 32 (4), pp. 129-163.

— (1984b) 'Le Recours à Saint Fleuret, Guérisseur des Bestiaux, a Estaing (Aveyron)', *Ethnozootechnie*, 34, pp. 59-76.

— (1985) 'Les Bouquets Thérapeutic en Médecine Vétérinaire et Humaine-Essai de Synthèse', *Bulletin d'Ethnomédecine*, 35 (3), pp. 3-38.

— (1987) 'Pratique et Insertion Sociale d'un Berger-Guérisseur Cévenol', *Bulletin d'Ethnomédecine*, 39 (2), pp. 135-151.

Brokensha, D. and A.P. Castro (1988) 'Common Property Resources', Paper presented at *FAO Expert Consultation on Forestry and Food Security*, (15-20 February), Rome, FAO.

Brokensha, D. and B.W. Riley (1980) 'Mbeere Knowledge of their Vegetation and its Relevance for Development', in D. Brokensha, D.M. Warren and O. Werner (eds) *Indigenous Knowledge Systems and Development*, pp. 111-129, Lanham, MD, University Press of America.

Brokensha, D. (1983) 'Review of Jens Müller: Liquidation or Consolidation of Indigenous Technology: A Study of the Changing Conditions of Production of Village Blacksmiths in Tanzania', *Africa Studies Review*, 26 (2), pp. 90-91.

— 1987 'Development Anthropology and Natural Resource Management', *L'Uomo*, 11 (2), pp. 225-249.

Brokensha, D., D.M. Warren and O. Werner (ed.) (1980) *Indigenous Knowledge Systems and Development*, Lanham, MD, University Press of America.

Bromberger, C. (1985) 'Identité Alimentaire et Alterite Culturelle dans le Nord de l'Iran: le Froid, le Chaud, le Sexe et le Reste', *Identité Alimentaire et Alterite Culturelle*, 6, pp. 5-34, Recherches et Travaux de l'Institut d'Ethnologie, Neuchatel, Université de Neuchatel.

Bromley, D.W. and M. M. Cernea (1989) *The Management of Common Property Natural Resources*, World Bank Discussion Paper 57, Washington, D.C., World Bank.

Brundtland Report (1987) *Our Common Future*, World Commission on Environment and Development, Oxford, Oxford University Press.

Bruijn, de G.H. *et al.* (1974) 'The Mukibat System, a High Yielding Method of Cassave Production in Indonesia', *Neth. J. Agric. Sci*, 22, pp. 89-10.

Brush, S.B. (1976) 'Introduction to Cultural Adaptations to Mountain Ecosystems', *Human Ecology*, 4 (2), pp. 125-133.

— (1980) 'Potato Taxonomies in Andean Agriculture', in D. Brokensha, D.M. Warren and O. Werner (eds) *Indigenous Knowledge Systems and Development*, pp. 37-48, Lanham, MD, University Press of America.

— (1983) 'Agricultural Change and Genetic Erosion in the Andes', *Biology International*, 10, pp. 2-5.

Brush, S.B., H. Carney and Z. Huanar (1981) 'Dynamics of Andean Potato Agriculture' *Economic Botany*, 35 (1), pp. 70-88.

Burgel, J.C. (1977) 'Secular and Religious Features of Medieval Arabic Medicine', in Ch. Leslie (ed.) *Asian Medical Systems; A Comparative Study*, pp. 44-63, Berkeley, University of California Press.

Burke, R.V. (1979) 'Green Revolution Technologies and Farm Class in Mexico', *Economic Development and Cultural Change* , 28, pp. 135-54.

Burkhill, I.H. and M. Haniff (1930) 'Malay Village Medicine', *The Garden's Bulletin*, 6 (April).

Burtonboy, A.H. (1987) *Développement des Pêches et Etude Socio-Economique de la Pêcherie du Fleuve Niger; Niger: Conclusions et Recommendations des Projets*, Rome, FAO, FI, DP/NER/79/018 and GCP/NER/027/USA.

Bush, L. and W.B. Lacy (1984) 'Sorghum Research and Human Values', *Agricultural Administration* , 15, pp. 205-222.

Bustamante, J. (1982) 'La Gallina de los Huevos Verdes', *Minka*, 8, pp. 9.

Bustinza Choque, V. and C.S. Viveros (1985) 'Formas de Tratamiento Tradicional de la Sarna de Alpacas', in V. Bustinza Choque *et al.* (ed.) *Proyecto Piel de Alpaca: Informe Final*, pp. 80-84, Puno, Peru, Universidad Nacional del Altiplano, Instituto de Investigaciones para el Desarrollo Social del Altiplano, Convenio UNA-NUFFIC.

Butler, B. E. (1980) *Soil Classification for Soil Survey*, Oxford, Clarendon Press.

Butterworth, D. (1971) 'Migración Rural-Urbana en América Latina: el Estado de Nuestro Conocimiento', *América Indígena*, 31 (1), pp. 85-105.

Butterworth, D. and J. Chance (1981) *Latin American Urbanisation*, New York, Cambridge University Press.

Butterworth, J.H. and E.D. Morgan (1968) 'Isolation of a Substance that Suppresses Feeding in Locusts', *Journal of Chemical Society, Chemical Communications,* pp. 23-24.

Caballero Osorio, A.A. (1984a) 'Efecto del Aceite Esencial de Muña en el Control del *Haemotopinus suis*', in A.A. Caballero Osorio and M.A. Ugarte (eds) *Muña: Investigación y Proyección Social*, pp. 17-19, Cuzco, Peru, Instituto de Investigaciones UNSAAC-NUFFIC.

— (1984b) 'Uso del Aceite Esencial de Muña en el Control de la Sarna de Alpacas (Géneros *Sarcoptes, Psoroptes*)', in A.A. Caballero Osorio and M.A. Ugarte (ed.) *Muña: Investigación y Proyección Social*, pp. 20-25, Cuzco, Peru, Instituto de Investigaciones UNSAAC-NUFFIC.

Campbell, J.G. (1979) 'Community Involvement in Conservation: Social and Organisational Aspects V (Mb)', *Resource Conservation and Utilisation Project*, Kathmandu, Agricultural Projects Services Centre.

— (1984) 'People and Forests in Hill Nepal, Preliminary Presentation of Findings of Community Forestry Household and Ward Leader Survey', *FDP Project Paper* 18, Kathmandu: Community Forestry Development Project.

Cancian, F. (1972) *Change and Uncertainty in a Peasant Economy,* Stanford, Stanford University Press.

Carlier, H. (1987) *Understanding Traditional Agriculture*, Leusden, The Netherlands, Information Centre for Low External Input Agriculture (ILEIA).

Carrier, L. (1923) *The Beginnings of Agriculture in America*, New York, McGraw-Hill Press.

Carson, B. (1987) 'Erosion and Sedimentation Processes in the Nepalese Himalaya', *ICIMOD Occasional Paper* 1, Kathmandu, International Centre for Integrated Mountain Development.

Carter, H.O., W.W. Cochrane, L.M. Day, R.C. Powers and L. Tweeten (1981) *Research and the Family Farm: A Paper Prepared for the Experiment Station Committee on Organisation and Policy,* Ithaca, NY, Cornell University.

Carter, W.E. and P.M. Mamani (1982) *Irpa Chico: Individuo y Comunidad en la Cultura Aymara*, Empresa Editora Urquizo S.A., La Paz, Bolivia.

Casaverde, J. (1985) 'Calendario Alpaquero', *Minka*, 16 (March), pp. 18.

Cashman, K. (1987) *Seeing the Forest for the Trees: A Participatory Approach to Sustainable Food Production*, Paper presented at the Farming Systems Research Symposium, Fayetteville, AR, 18-21 October 1987.

— (1988) 'Promoting the Fertiliser Bush Among Nigerian Farmers', *VITA News*, (July/October), pp. 7-10.

Casimir, M.J. (1982) 'The Biological Phenomenon of Imprinting – Its Handling and Manipulation by Traditional Pastoralists', *Production Pastorale et Société*, 11, pp. 23-27.

Cassanelli, L.V. (1984) 'Historical Perspectives on Pastoral Development', in P.J. Joss, P.W. Lynch and O.B. Williams (ed.) *Rangelands: A Resource Under Siege, Proceedings 2nd International Rangeland Congress*, pp. 483-487, Adelaide, Australia.

Castillo, G. and J.W. Beer (1983) *Utilización del Bosque y de Sistemas Agroforestales en la Region de Gardi, Kuna Yala (San Blas, Panama)*, Turrialba, Costa Rica, CATIE.

Catford, J.T. (1951) 'Katiri Cultural in the Moru District of Equatoria', *Sudan Notes and Records*, 32.

Cáceres Vega, E. (1989) *Fasciola Hepatica: 'Enfermedad y Pobreza Campesina*, La Paz, Bolivia, Imprenta Metodista.

CEDECUM/Proyecto de Tecnologías Campesinas/CEPIA (1988) *Tecnología Aymara: Revaloración del Saber Campesino*, Serie Eventos Campesinos, Lima, Peru, Servicios Editoriales Adolfo Arteta.

Centlivres, P. (1985) 'Hippocrate dans la Cuisine: Le Chaud et le Froid en Afghanistan du Nord', *Identité Alimentaire et Alterite Culturelle*, 6, pp. 35-57, Recherches et Travaux de l'Institut d'Ethnologie, Neuchatel, Université de Neuchatel.

Cernea, M. (1986) *Putting People First: Sociological Variables in Rural Development*, Oxford, Oxford University Press.

Cerrate de Ferreyra, E. (1980) 'Plantas que Curan las Heridas del Hombre y los Animales', *Boletín de Lima*, 3-4, pp. 1-12.

Chambers, R. (1980) 'The Rural Farmer is a Professional', Rome, *CERES, FAO Review*, 13 (2), pp. 19-23.

— (1983) *Rural Development: Putting the Last First*, London, Longman.

— (1985a) 'Putting Last Thinking First: A Professional Revolution', *Third World Affairs*, 1985, pp. 78-94, London, Third World Foundation for Social and Economic Affairs.

— (1985b) *Rural Development: Putting the Last First*, London, Longman.

— (1989) 'Reversals, Institutions and Change', in R.A. Chambers, A. Pacey and L. Thrupp (ed.) Farmer *First: Farmer Innovation and Agricultural Research*, 182, London, Intermediate Technology Publications.

Chambers, R. and B.P. Ghildyal (1985) 'Agricultural Research for Resource-Poor Farmers: The Farmer-First-and-Last Model', *Agric. Administr.*, 20, pp. 1-30.

Chambers, R. and J. Jiggins (1986) *Agricultural Research for Resource Poor Farmers: A Parsimonious Paradigm*, Discussion Paper 220, University of Sussex, Institute of Development Studies.

— (1987) 'Agricultural Research for Resource-Poor Farmers, Part II: A Parsimonious Paradigm' *Agricultural Administration and Extension*, 27, pp. 109-128.

Chambers, R. and M. Leach (1987) 'Trees to Meet Contingencies: Savings and Security for the Rural Poor', *Institute of Development Studies Discussion Paper*, 228, Brighton, UK, Sussex University.

Chambers, R., A. Pacey and L.A. Thrupp (eds) (1989) *Farmer First: Farmer*

Innovation and Agricultural Research, London, Intermediate Technology Publications/New York, Bootstrap.

Chan, P. (1985) *Better Vegetable Gardens the Chinese Way*, Pownal, VT, Garden Way Publishers.

Chandler, R.F. (1981) 'Land and Water Resources and Management', in D.L. Plucknett and H.L. Beemer, Jr. (ed.) *Vegetable Farming Systems in China*, pp. 9-18, Boulder, CO, Westview Press.

Chandrakanth, M.G. *et al.* (1990) 'Temple Forests and India's Forest Development', *Agroforestry Systems*, pp. 199-211.

Chapin, M. (1988) 'The Seduction of Models: Chinampa Agriculture in Mexico', *Grassroots Development,* 12 (1), pp. 8-17.

Chapman, K.R., J. Sarannah and B. Paxton (1979) 'Induction of Early Cropping in Guava Seedlings in a Closely Planted Orchard Using Urea as a Defoliant', *Aust. J. Exp. Agric. Anim. Husb,* 19, pp. 382-384.

Chavez, E.R. and A. Lasmini (1978) *Comparative Performance of Native Indonesia Egg Laying Ducks,* Bogor, Centre for Animal Research and Development, Report 6.

Chavunduka, D.M. (1976) 'Plants regarded by Africans as being of Medical Value to Animals', *Rhodesian Veterinary Journal,* 7 (1), pp. 6-12.

— (1984) 'Delivery of Animal Health and Production Services- General Aspects', in D.L. Hawksworth (ed) *Advancing agricultural production in Africa*, pp. 262-266, Arusha, Tanzania, Proceedings of CAB's First Scientific Conference, February 1984.

Chen, A. (1987) 'Unravelling Another Mayan Mystery', *Discover,* (June).

Chiang, C.L., S. Selvin and C. Langhauser (1974) *Biology and Public Health Statistics*, Berkeley, University of California, Course Reader, BIOENV 130A and B.

Chibnik, M. (1981) 'The Evolution of Cultural Rules', *Journal of Anthropological Research*, 37 (3), pp. 256-268.

Choquehuanca Rodríguez, S. (1987) 'Principales Enfermedades en Ovinos y Alpacas y Tratamientos en Uso en la Comunidad de Quishuara', in Editoriales A. Arteta for CIID, ACDI and PISA, *Anales del V Congreso Internacional de Sistemas Agropecuarios Andinos*, pp. 414-415, Lima, Peru.

Christianity, L., O. Abdullah, G. Marten and J. Iskandar (1986) 'Traditional Agroforestry in West Java: The *Pekarangan* (Home garden) and *Kebun-Talun* (Annual-Perennial Rotation) Cropping System', in G. Marten (ed.) *Traditional Agriculture in South East Asia,* pp. 132-158, Boulder, CO, Westview Press.

CIKARD (1988) Centre for Indigenous Knowledge for Agriculture and Rural Development, Brochure, Ames, IA, Iowa State University.

Ciriacy-Wintrup, S.V. and R.C. Bishop (1975) 'Common Property as a Concept in Natural Resource Policy', *Natural Resources Journal,* 15, pp. 713-727.

Clark, C. A. and J.W. Moyer (1988) *Compendium of Sweet Potato Diseases*, St. Paul, MN, American Phyto-pathological Society.

Clauson, G. (1953) *Communal Land Tenure*, Rome, FAO Agricultural Studies 17.

Clay, J.W. (1988) *Indigenous Peoples and Tropical Forests*: *Models of Land Use and Management for Latin America*, Cambridge, Massachusetts, Cultural Survival Report 27.

Clifford, J. (1983) 'On Ethnographic Authority' *Representation,* 1 (2), pp. 118-146.

Cochrane, W.F. (1979) *The Development of American Agriculture: A Historical Analysis, Minneapolis*, University of Minnesota Press.

Coe, M.D. (1964) 'The Chinampas of Mexico', *Scientific American,* 211, pp. 90-98.

Coenen, E. and T.L. Price (1987) 'Projet Développement des Pêches – Phase

Transitoire', TCP/NER/6652 (T): Tapport Technique Manuscript (to be released by Rome, FAO, Fisheries Department).

Coenen, E. (1987) *République du Niger: Résultats des Etudes Ichtyo-Biologiques sur le Niger, Rapport préparé pour le Projet de Développement des Pêches*, Rome, FAO, FI, DP/NER/79/018.

Colson, E. (1951) 'The Plateau Tonga of Northern Rhodesia', in E. Colson and M. Gluckman (ed.) *Seven Tribes of British Central Africa*, pp. 94-162, Oxford, Oxford University Press.

Comisión Organizadora de Criadores de Alpaca de la Provincia de Caylloma (1985) *Alpaqueros de Caylloma: Problemas y Alternativas*, Lima, Perú, DESCO – Centro de Estudios y Promoción del Desarrollo.

Compton, J.L. (1973) *The Indigenous Nonprofessional: A Theoretical Basis for a Practical Strategy of Rural Reconstruction*, Silang, Cavite, The Philippines, International Institute for Rural Reconstruction, (Mimeo).

— (1980) 'Indigenous Folk Media in Rural Development', in D. Brokensha, D.M. Warren and O. Werner (eds) *Indigenous Knowledge Systems and Development*, pp.317-319, Lanham, MD, University Press of America.

— (1984a) 'Knowledge Creation-Diffusion-Utilisation: Problems and Prospects for a College of Agriculture' *AAACU Newsletter*, 12, pp. 22-28, Pasay City, The Philippines, Asian Association of Agricultural Colleges and Universities.

— (1984b) 'Linking Scientist and Farmer: Rethinking Extension's Role', in M. Drosdoff (ed.) *World Issues*, pp. 79-84, Ithaca, NY, Cornell University International Agriculture Program.

— (1989a) 'The Integration of Research and Extension', in J.L. Compton (ed.) *The Transformation of International Agricultural Research and Development*, pp. 113-136, Boulder and London, Lynne Rienner.

— (1989b) 'Strategies and Methods for the Access, Integration and Utilization of Indigenous Knowledge in Agriculture and Rural Development', *Indigenous Knowledge Systems: Implications for Agriculture and International Development*, Studies in Technology and Social Change Series 11, pp 21-32, Ames, IA, Iowa State University.

Conklin, H.C, (1957a) *Hanunoo Agriculture: A Report on an Integral System of Shifting Cultivation in the Philippines,* Forestry Development Paper 12, Rome, FAO.

— (1957b) *Hanunoo Agriculture A Report on an Integral System of Shifting Cultivation in the Philippines*, Northford CT, Elliot's Books.

Conroy, C, and M, Likvinoff (eds) (1988) *The Greening of Aid: Sustainable Livelihoods in Practice*, London, Earthscan.

Conyers, D, (1982) *An Introduction to Social Planning in the Third World*, New York, John Wiley and Sons.

Cook, R.J, and K.F, Baker (1983) *The Nature and Practice of Biological Control of Plant Pathogens*, St, Paul, MN, American Phytopathological Society.

Cool, J.C, (1983) 'Population Growth and Unequal Access to Resources in Asia', in A.M, Shrestha (ed), *Agriculture, Environment and Rural Development*, Kathmandu, Agricultural Projects Services Centre.

Coombs, M.J. (1984) *Developments in Expert Systems*, London, Academic Press.

Corbett, J. (1988) 'Famine and Household Coping Strategies', *World Development*, 16 (9), pp. 1099-1112.

Cosminsky, S. (1977) 'Alimento and Fresco: Nutritional Concepts and their Implications for Health Care', *Human Organisation,* 36, pp. 203-207.

Cosminsky, S. and I.E. Harrison (1984) *Traditional Medicine II: Implications for Ethnomedicine, Ethnopharmacology, Maternal Health and Public Health – An Annotated Bibliography of Africa, Latin America and the Caribbean*, Garland, New York.

Coste, E. (1983) 'Traumatismes Destinés à Améliorer la Production des Arbres Fruitiers Tropicaux', *Diplôme d'Etudes Approfondies d'Ecologie,* Montpellier, France, U.S.T.L.

Coughenour, C.M. and S.M. Nazhat (1985) *Recent Changes in Villages and Rainfed Agriculture in Northern Central Kordofan: Communication Process and Constraints,* 4, International Sorghum and Millet Collaborative Research Support Program, Lexington, KY, University of Kentucky, Department of Sociology.

Coulson, C.L., D.N. Mungai, C.J. Stigter, P.W. Mwangi and D.M. Njiru (1989) *Studies of Sustainable Crop Yield Improvement through an Agroforestry Intervention, Involving Postgraduate Training, Methodology and Appropriate Equipment Development: The Collection of Data and General of Weather Advisories through a Multidisciplinary Integrated Approach,* Paper presented for the Amelioration of Soil by Trees, Agroforestry Programme Review Meeting, ICRAF, Nairobi, Commonwealth Science Council.

Cowley, G. (1989) 'The Electronic Goddess: Computerising Bali's Ancient Irrigation Rites', *Newsweek,* (March 6), pp. 50.

Córdova, P. (1981) 'Así Curamos el Ganado en el Canipaco', *Minka,* 5 (January), pp. 11.

Cramer, H.H. (1967) 'Plant Protection and World Crop Production', *Pflanzenschutz Nachrichten,* 20 (1), pp. 524.

Covarrubias, M. (1986) *Island of Bali,* London, Kegan Paul International.

Crozier, R.C. (1977) 'The Ideology of Medical Revivalism in Modern China', in Ch. Leslie (ed) *Asian Medical Systems; A Comparative Study,* pp. 322-341, Berkeley, University of California Press.

CTTA (1988) *Identification and Assessment of Stage of Readiness for Diffusion to Farmers of Agricultural Technologies and Technology Systems in Senegal and Niger,* Washington, D.C., AED.

Curasson, G. (1947) *Le Chameau et ses Maladies,* Paris, Vigot Freres.

Currey, B. (1978) 'The Famine Syndrome: Its Definition for Relief and Rehabilitation in Bangladesh' *Ecology of Food and Nutrition,* 7, pp. 87-98.

— (1984) 'Fragile Mountain or Fragile Theory', *ADAB News,* (November-December), pp. 7-13.

Currier, R. (1966) 'The Hot-Cold Syndrome and Symbolic Balance in Mexican and Spanish American Folk Medicine', *Ethnology,* 5, pp. 251-63.

Curwen, E.C. and G. Hatt (1953) *Plow and Pasture: The Early History of Farming,* New York, Collier.

Cutler, P. (1984) 'Famine Forecasting: Prices and Peasant Behaviour in Northern Ethiopia', *Disasters Journal,* 8, pp. 48-56.

— (1986) 'The Response to Drought of Beja Famine Refugees in Sudan', *Disasters Journal,* 10, pp. 181-188.

Cutler, P. and R. Stephenson (1984) *The State of Food Emergency Preparedness in Ethiopia,* London, International Disasters Institute.

D'Andrade, R.G. (1974) 'Memory and the Assessment of Behaviour', in H. Blalock (ed) *Measurement in the Social Sciences,* Chicago, Aldine.

Daget, J.M.A. (1962) *Rapport au Gouvernement du Niger sur la Situation et l'évolution de la Pêche au Niger,* FAO/Rome, PEAT Rapport 1525.

Dahl, G., A. Hjort (1976) *Having Herds: Pastoral Herd Growth and Household Economy,* Stockholm Studies in Social Anthropology 2, Stockholm, Sweden, University of Stockholm, Department of Social Anthropology.

DAI (Development Alternatives Inc.) (1988) First External Evaluation of the Agricultural Support Project in Niger, Washington, D.C., DAI.

Daryanto (1981) *Kumpulan Jamu Tradisional,* Semarang, Aneka Ilmu.

Dasmann, R.F. (1973) *Ecological Principles for Economic Development,* New York, John Wiley and Sons.

— (1980) 'The Relationship Between Protected Areas and Indigenous Peoples',

in J.A. McNeely and Miller, K.R. (ed.) *National Parks, Conservation and Development: The Role of Protected Areas in Sustaining Society,* pp. 667-671, Washington D.C., IUCN/Smithsonian Institution Press.
— (1985) 'Achieving the Sustainable Use of Species and Ecosystems' *Landscape Planning,* 12 (3), pp. 211-220.
Davidson, B. with F.K. Buah (1967) *The Growth of African Civilisation: A History of West Africa, 1000-1800,* (second edition), London, Longman.
De Alwis, K.A. and S. Dimantha (1981) *IRDP Nuwara Eliya Sri Lanka Netherlands Project Land Suitability, Evaluation and Land Use Study,* Colombo, Government of Sri Lanka, Land Use Division, Irrigation Department.
De Carlier, A.B. (1981) *Así Nos Curamos en el Canipaco: Medicina Tradicional del Valle del Canipaco, Huancayo, Perú,* Huancayo, Producción Gráfica Color Jesús Ruiz Durand.
De Datta, S.K. and V.E. Ross (1975) Cultural Practices for Upland Rice, *Major Research in Upland Rice,* Los Banos, The Philippines, International Rice Research Institute.
De St. Croix, F.W. (1972/1945) *The Fulani of Northern Nigeria,* Westmead, Farnborough, Hants, England, Gregg International.
De Waal, A. (1987) *Famine that Kills,* London, Save the Children Fund, (U.K.), Internal Report.
De Waal, A. and M. el Amin (1986) *Survival in Northern Darfur, 1986-1986,* Nyala, Sudan, Save the Children Fund, (U.K.), Internal Report.
De Walt, R. and D. Barkin (1987) 'Seeds of Change: The Effects of Hybrid Sorghum and Agricultural Modernisation in Mexico', in H. Russell Bernard and P. Pelto (ed.) *Technology and Social Change,* pp. 138-165, (second edition), Prospect Heights, IL, Waveland Press.
De Walt, B. and K. de Walt (1980) 'Stratification and Decision Making in the Use of New Agricultural Technology', in P.F. Barlett (ed) *Agricultural Decision Making: Anthropological Contributions to Rural Development,* New York, Academic Press.
De Walt, K. (1977) 'The Illnesses no Longer Understand: Changing Concepts of Health and Curing in a Rural Mexican Community' *Medical Anthropology Newsletter,* 8 (2), pp. 5-11.
— (1983) *Nutritional Strategies and Agricultural Change in a Mexican Community,* Ann Arbor, University of Michigan Press.
De Castro e Santos, A. (1980) 'Essai de Classification des Arbres Tropicaux Selon Leur Capacité de Réitération', *Biotropica,* 12 (3), pp. 187-194.
De Janvry, A. (1981) *The Agrarian Question and Reformism in Latin America,* Baltimore, MD, The Johns Hopkins University Press.
De Lattre, A. and A.M. Fell (1984) *The Club du Sahel,* Paris, OECD.
De Schlippe, P. (1956) 'Shifting Cultivation in Africa: The Zande System of Agriculture', London, Routledge and Kegan Paul.
Denevan, W.M. (ed) (1986) *The Cultural Ecology, Archaeology and History of Terracing and Terrace Abandonment in the Colca Valley of Southern Peru,* Technical Report to the National Science Foundation, Madison, University of Wisconsin.
Denevan, W.M. (1970) 'Aboriginal Drained-Field Cultivation in the Americas', *Science,* 169, pp. 647-654.
— (1983) 'Adaptation, Variation and Cultural Geography', *Professional Geographer,* 35 (4), pp. 399-406.
— (1985) 'Peru's Agricultural Legacy', *Focus,* (April), pp. 16-29.
Denevan, W.M. and C. Padoch (ed.) (1988) *Swidden-Fallow Agroforestry in the Peruvian Amazon,* Advances in Economic Botany, 5, New York, NY, Botanic Garden.
Denevan, W.M. and J.M. Treacy (1987) 'Young Managed Fallow at Brillo

Nuevo', in W.M. Denevan and C. Padoch (ed.) *Swidden-Fallow Agroforestry in the Peruvian Amazon*, 8-46, Bronx, NY, New York Botanical Garden.

Denevan, W.M. and B.L. Turner II (1974) 'Forms, Function and Associations of Raised Fields in the Old World Tropics' *Journal of Tropical Geography*, 39, pp. 24-33.

Department of Agriculture (1976) *Monitoring and Evaluation Report*, Madres, Agriculture Unit Press.

Devitt, P. (1982) 'The Management of Communal Grazing in Botswana' *Pastoral Network Paper,* 14d, London, ODI.

Dewey, K.G. (1981) 'Nutritional Consequences of Transformation from Subsistence to Commercial Agriculture in Tabasco, Mexico', *Human Ecology*, 9, pp. 151-187.

Diaz Bordenave, J. (1975) 'The Role of Folk Media: A Point of View' *Instructional Technology Report,* 12, Informational Centre on Instructional Technology, Washington, D.C., Academy for Educational Development.

DFDP (1985) *Project Progress Report* 1/7/84-15/7/85, Kathmandu, Community Forestry Development Project NEP/80/030.

Diop, A.T. (1987) *Les Resources de l'Aire Pastorale de Tatki: Inventaire et Etude du Mode d'Exploitation, Proposition de Plan d'Amenagement et de Qestion Rationnelle,* Dakar, Institut Senegalais de Recherche Agricole (ISRA)/Laboratoire Nationale d'Elevage et de Recherche Veterinaire (LNERV)/FAO.

Dobie, J.F. (1950) 'Indian Horse and Horsemanship' *Southwest Review,* 35, pp. 265-275.

Dolva, H. and R. Renna (1989) 'Indigenous Soil Classification: A Study Among Small-Scale Farmers in the Northern Province of Zambia', MS. Thesis, Norway, Agricultural University of Norway, Department of Soil Science.

Dolva, H., B. Mwale, R. Renna and C. Simute (1988) 'Preliminary Report', in C. Kerven (ed) *Indigenous Soil Classification in Northern Province of Zambia,* Misamfu, Zambia, Adaptive Research Planning Unit, Soil Productivity Research Project, Soil Survey Unit.

Dommen, A.J. (1988) *Innovation in African Agriculture:*, Boulder and London, Westview.

Doob, L.W. (1961) *Communication in Africa: A Search for Boundaries*, New Haven, CT, Yale University Press.

Dorm-Adzobyu, C., O. Ampudu-Agyei and P.G. Veit (1991) *Religious Beliefs and Environmental Protection: The Malshegu Sacred Grove in Northern Ghana*, Washington, D.C., WRI.

Dove, M.R. (1984) *Government Versus Peasant Beliefs Concerning Imperata and Eupatorium: A Structural Analysis of Knowledge, Myth and Agricultural Ecology in Indonesia*, Honolulu, HA, East-West Centre.

— (1987) 'The Practical Reason of Weeds in Indonesia: Peasant vs. State Views of *Imperata* and *Chromolaena, Human Ecology,* 14, pp. 163-190.

Draz, O. (1978) 'Revival of the Hema System of Range Reserves as a Basis for the Syrian Range Development Program', in D.N. Hyder (ed) *Proceedings of the 1st International Rangeland Congress,* pp. 100-103, Denver., SRM.

Drewes, G.W.J. (1929) 'Verboden Rijkdom: Een Bijdrage tot de Kennis van het Volksgeloof op Java en Madura', *Djawa*, 9, pp. 133-158.

Dreyer, M. (1984) 'Effects of Aqueous Neem Extracts and Neem Oil on the Main Pests of *Cucurbita pepo* in Togo', in H. Schmutterer and H. Rembold (eds) *Natural Pesticides from the Neem Tree*, pp. 435-443, Proceedings, 2nd International Neem Conference, Rauisch-Holzenhausen, 1983, Schriftenreihe der GTZ; 161, Deutsche Gessellschaft für Technische Zusammenarbeit (GTZ) GmbH.

— (1987) 'Field and Laboratory Trials with Simple Neem Products as Protectants against Pests of Vegetable and Field Crops in Togo', in H.

Schmutterer and K.R.S. Ascher (eds) *Natural Pesticides from the Neem Tree (Azadirachta indica A. Juss) and Other Tropical Plants,* pp. 431-448, Proceedings, 3rd International Neem Conference, Nairobi, Kenya, 1986, Schriftenreiche der GTZ 206, Eschborn.

Dubois, D. (1984) 'Quelques Saints Vétérinaires de Picardie-Nord, Special issue entitled La Médecine Vétérinaire Populaire' *Ethnozootechnie* 34, pp. 77-85.

Duchhart, I., F. Steiner and J.H. Bassman (1989) 'Planning Methods for Agroforestry' *Agroforestry Systems,* 7 (3), pp. 227-258.

Dunn, F.L. (1977) 'Traditional Asian Medicine and Cosmopolitan Medicine as Adaptive Systems' *Asian Medical Systems; A Comparative Study,* pp. 133-158, Berkeley, University of California Press.

Dupire, M. (1957) 'Pharmacopée Peule du Niger et du Cameroun' *Bulletin IFAN,* 19 (3-4).

— (1962) *Peuls Nomades: Étude Descriptive des WoDaaBe du Sahel Nigérien,* Paris, Musée de l'Homme, Institut d'Ethnologie.

Durrenberger, E.P. (1977) 'Lisu Etiological Catagories', *Bijdragen tot Taal-, Land- en Volkenkunde,* 133 (1), pp. 90-100.

Eckholm, E.P. (1975) 'The Deterioration of Mountain Environments' *Science* 189, pp. 764-770.

— (1976) *Losing Ground,* New York, W.W. Norton.

— (1984) 'Nepal: A Trek Through a Forest in Crisis' *New York Times,* New York, NY, February 14: C1 and February 21: C2.

Edwards, R. (1987) 'Mapping and Informal Experimentation by Farmers: Agronomic Monitoring of Farmers' Cropping Systems as a Form of Informal Farmer Experimentation' Paper for the workshop on Farmers and Agricultural Research: Complementary Methods held at the Institute of Development Studies, University of Sussex, July 26-31.

Eginton, C. and L. Tweeten (1982) *Impact of National Inflation and Entrance and Equity Growth Opportunities on Typical Commercial Farms,* Paper presented at the Annual Meetings of the Southern Agricultural Economics Association, Atlanta, GA.

Elfring, C. (1985) 'Africa Tomorrow – If We Act Today', *Bioscience,* 35 (7), pp. 400-402; 407.

Ellen, R. (1982) *Environment, Subsistence and System,* Cambridge, Cambridge University Press.

Elliot, P.C. and K. Moody (1986) *Weed Control Studies in Upland Rice-based Cropping Systems,* Paper Claveria Cropping Systems Annual Review, Cagayan de Oro, The Philippines, International Rice Research Institute (unpublished).

Elmi, A.A. (1984) 'Observations on the Browsing and Grazing Behaviour of the Vamel', in M.A. Hussein (ed.) *Camel Pastoralism in Somalia: Proceedings from a Workshop held in Baydhabo, April 8-13, 1984,* 115-136, Camel Forum Working Paper 7, Mogadishu, Somalia/Stockholm, Sweden, Somali Camel Research Project.

— (1989) 'Camel Husbandry and Management by Ceeldheer Pastoralists in Central Somalia' *Pastoral Development Network Paper* 27d, London, UK., Regent's College, Inner Circle, Agricultural Administration Unit, Overseas Development Institute (ODI).

Elshout, J.M. (1923) *Over de Geneeskunde der Kenja-Dajak in Centraal Borneo in Verband met hunnen Godsdienst,* Amsterdam, J. Muller.

Endra, W.S. (1980) *Obat-Obatan Ramuan Asli,* Surabaya, Usaha Nasional.

Erickson, C.L. (1985) 'Applications of Prehistoric Andean Technology Experiments in Raised Field Agriculture', Huatta, Lake Titicaca, 1981-1982, in I.S. Farrington (ed) *Prehistoric Intensive Agriculture in the Tropics,* pp. 209-232, Oxford, B.A.R. International Series 232.

Esche, D. (1987) *Pedoman Untuk Memanfaatkan Apotik Hidup,* Samarinda, TAD.

Esparza, H.B. (1988) 'Consideraciones sobre la Aplicación de la Herbolaria a la Medicina Veterinaria', in L.L. Nathal and G.L.Buendía, (coord.), *Memorias: Primera Jornada sobre Herbolaria Medicinal en Veterinaria*, pp. 108-123, México DF, Universidad Nacional Autónoma de México, Facultad de Medicina Veterinaria y Zootecnia, Coordinación de Educación Continua.

Esquivel Mendoza, G. (1982) *Pensamiento Mágico-Religioso de un Grupo Nahua del Estado de Guerrero con Respecto al Origen y Tratamiento de las Enfermedades de sus Animales*, Thesis, México, Facultad de Medicina Veterinaria y Zootecnia, Universidad Nacional Autónoma de México.

Evans-Pritchard, E.E. (1937) 'Economic life of the Nuer: Cattle', *Sudan Notes and Records*, 20, pp. 209-245.

— (1938) 'Economic life of the Nuer: Cattle II', *Sudan Notes and Records*, 21 (1), pp. 31-77.

— (1940) *The Nuer: A description of the mode of the livelihood and political institutions of a Nilotic people*, Oxford, Clarendon Press.

Everett, Y. (1987) 'Seeking Principles of Sustainability: A Forest Model Applied to Forest Gardens in Sri Lanka', Master's Thesis, Berkeley, University of California (unpublished).

Ewel, J. (1986) 'Designing Agricultural Ecosystems for the Humid Tropics', *Annual Review of Ecology and Systematics*, 17, pp. 245-271.

Fabrega, H. (1977) 'The Scope of Ethnomedical Science', *Cultural Medical Psychiatry*, 1, pp. 210.

FAO (1972) *Report on the FAO Expert Consultation on the Settlement of Nomads in Africa and the Near East,* Cairo, 4-12 December 1971, RP 20, Rome, FAO.

— (1984) 'Tillage Systems for Soil and Water Conservation', *FAO Soils Bulletin*, 54, Rome, Italy.

— (1986) 'Tree Growing by Rural People' *FAO Forestry Paper*, 64. Rome, FAO.

FAO (based on the work of C.G. Sivadas) (1980) *Preliminary Study of Traditional Systems of Veterinary Medicine,* Bangkok, Thailand, FAO Regional Office for Asia and the Pacific.

FAO (based on the work of D.D. Joshi) (1984a) *Traditional (Indigenous) Systems of Veterinary Medicine for Small Farmers in Nepal,* Bangkok, Thailand, FAO Regional Office for Asia and the Pacific.

FAO (based on the work of P. Buranamanus) (1984b) *Traditional (Indigenous) Systems of Veterinary Medicine for Small Farmers in Thailand,* Bangkok, Thailand, FAO Regional Office for Asia and the Pacific.

FAO (based on the work of J.V. Anjaria) (1984c) *Traditional (Indigenous) Systems of Veterinary Medicine for Small Farmers in India,* Bangkok, Thailand, FAO Regional Office for Asia and the Pacific.

FAO (based on the work of M. Maqsood) (1986) *Traditional (Indigenous) Systems of Veterinary Medicine for Small Farmers in Pakistan*, Bangkok, Thailand, FAO Regional Office of Asia and the Pacific.

Farga, C. and J. Lastra (1988) *Plantas Medicinales de Uso Común en Chile* I, Santiago, Chile, Soprami Ltda.

Farnsworth, N.R. (1983) 'The NAPRALERT Data Base as an Information Source for Application to Traditional Medicine', in R.H. Bannerman, J. Burton and Ch'en Wen-Chieh (eds) *Traditional Medicine and Health Care Coverage: A Reader for Health Administrators and Practitioners*, pp. 184-193, Geneva, WHO.

Farrington, J. and A. Martin (1987/8) *Farmer Participatory Research: A Review of Concepts and Practices*, Discussion Paper 19, Agricultural Administration (Research and Extension) Network, London, Overseas Development Institute.

Fernandez, E.C.M., A. Oktingati and J. Maghembe (1984) 'The Chagga Home

Gardens: A Multistoried Agroforestry Cropping System on Mt. Kilimanjaro (Northern Tanzania)', *Agroforestry Systems*, 2 (2), pp. 73-86.

Fernández, M.V.G. (1988) 'Rescate, Valorización, Mejoramiento y Devolución de la Medicina Veterinaria Folklórica en el Seno de la Comunidad', *Ladera,* 5, Cajamarca, Universidad Nacional de Cajamarca, Boletín Informativo del Grupo Polivalente de Proyección Social Chim-Shaullo de la Universidad Nacional de Cajamarca (September).

Fernández, M.E. (1986) *Participatory-Action-Research and the Farming Systems Research Approach with Highland Peasants,* SR-CRSP Report 75, Columbia, USA., University of Missouri-Columbia, Department of Rural Sociology, Small Ruminant Collaborative Research Support Program.

Feuerhake, K.J. (1985) 'Unterschungen zur Gewinnung und Forumlierung von Sameninhaltssoffen des Niembaumes (Azadirachta indica A. Juss) im Hinblick auf ihre Verwendung als Schädlingsbekämpfungsmittel in den Entwicklungsländern' (Investigations on the Production and Formulation of Seed Ingredients of the Neem Tree (*Azadirachta indica A. Juss*) with regard to their Use as Pesticides in Developing Countries), Ph.D. Dissertation, Giessen, FDR, Universität Giessen.

Feuerhake, K.J. and H. Schmutterer (1985) 'Development of a Crude Standardised and formulated Insecticide from Crude Neem Kernel Extract', *Zeitschrift für Pflanzenkrankheiten und Pflanzenschutz,* 92, pp. 643-649.

Finkler, K. (1981) 'A Comparative Study of Health Seekers: or, Why do Some People go to Doctors rather than to Spiritualist Healers?', *Medical Anthropology,* 5 (4), pp. 383-424.

— (1984) The Nonsharing of Medical Knowledge among Spiritualists Healers and their Patients: a Contribution to the Study of Intra-Cultural Diversity and Practitioner-Patient Relationship, *Medical Anthropology* 8 (3), pp. 195-209.

Fisher, R.J. (1987) 'Guest Editorial on Social Science in Forestry', *Banko Janakari,* 1 (3), pp. 1-3.

Fleuret, P. and A. Flueret (1980) 'Nutrition, Consumption and Agricultural Change', *Human Organisation,* 39, pp. 250-260.

Food and Agriculture Organisation (1980) *Preliminary Study of Traditional Systems of Veterinary Medicine* (based on the work of C.G. Sivadas), Bangkok, FAO/UN, Regional Office for Asia and the Pacific, RAPA 43.

— (1984)*Traditional (Indigenous) Systems of Veterinary Medicine for Small Farmers in Nepal,* Bangkok, Food and Agriculture Organisation of the United Nations, Regional Office for Asia and the Pacific, Regular Programme, RAPA 81.

Forde, C. D. (1968/1934)) *Habitat, Economy and Society: A Geographical Introduction to Ethnology,* London, Methuen.

Fortes, M. and E.E. Evans-Pritchard (eds) (1940) *African Political Systems,* London, Oxford University Press.

Fortes, M. (1940) 'The Political System of the Tallensi of the Northern Territories of the Gold Coast', in M. Fortes and E.E. Evans-Pritchard (eds) *African Political Systems,* pp. 238-271, London, Oxford University Press.

Fortmann, L. and J. Bruce (eds) (1987) *Land and Tree Tenure in Humid West Africa: A Bibliography,* Addis Ababa, Ethiopia, International Livestock Centre for Africa.

Foster, G.M. (1953) 'Relationships between Spanish and Spanish American Folk Medicine' *Journal of American Folklore,* 6, pp. 201-19.

— (1967) *Tzintzuntzan: Mexican Peasants in a Changing World,* Boston, Little, Brown and Company.

— (1976) 'Disease Etiologies in Non-Western Medical Systems', *American Anthropologist,* 78, pp. 773-782.

— (1979) 'Methodological Problems in the Study of Intracultural Variation: The

Hot/Cold Dichotomy in Tzintzuntzan', *Human Organisation,* 38, pp. 179-183.

— (1983) 'An Introduction to Ethnomedicine', in R.H. Bannerman, J. Burton and Ch'en Wen-Chieh (eds) *Traditional Medicine and Health Care Coverage: A Reader for Health Administrators and Practitioners,* pp. 17-25, Geneva, WHO.

— (1984a) 'The Concept of 'Neutral' in Humoral Medical Systems' *Medical Anthropology,* 8, pp. 180-194.

— (1984b) 'How to stay Well in Tzintzuntzan', *Social Science and Medicine,* 19 (5), pp. 523-33.

— (1987) 'On the Origin of Humoral Medicine in Latin America', *Medical Anthropology Quarterly, International Journal for the Cultural and Social Analysis of Health,* 1, pp. 4 (NS), pp. 355-394.

— (1988) 'The Validating Role of Humoral Theory in Traditional Spanish-American Therapeutics', *American Ethnologists,* 15 (1), pp. 120-135.

Fowler, M.L. (1969) 'Middle Mississippian Agricultural Fields', *American Antiquity,* 34, pp. 365-375.

Fox, J. (1975) 'On Binary Categories and Primary Symbols: Some Rotinese Perspectives', In R. Willis (ed), *The Interpretation of Symbolism,* London, Malaby Press.

Frake, C. (1961) 'The Diagnosis of Disease Among the Subanum of Mindanao', *American Anthropologist,* 63 (1), pp. 113-132.

Franquemont, C. (1987) *Potato Breeding in High Altitude Environments in the Andes,* Paper presented at the 10th Annual Conference of the Society for Ethnobiology, Gainesville FL, March 6.

Fransella, F. and D. Bannister (1977) *A Manual for Repertory Grid Technique,* New York, Academic Press.

Freire, P. (1971) *Pedagogy of the Oppress(ed),* New York, Herder and Herder.

— (1973) 'Extension or Communication', in Freire, P. (ed.) *Education: The Practice of Freedom,* London, Writers and Readers Publishing Cooperative.

— (1978) *Cultural Action for Freedom,* Harmondsworth, Penguin

Fritz, V.A. and S. Honma (1987) 'The Effect of Raised Beds, Population Densities and Planting Date on the Incidence of Bacterial Soft Rot in Chinese Cabbage', *Journal of the American Society Horticultural Science,* 112, pp. 41-44.

FSDP-EV (1985) 'Review of Research Methods and Findings', *FSDP-EV Project Paper 33,* Tacloban, The Philippines, Department of Agriculture.

Fujisaka, S. (1988a) *Rice Agroecosystems, Farmer Management and Social Organisation in Kampuchea,* IRRI Research Paper Series (IRPS) 136.

— (1988b) *Towards Farmer-Appropriate Soil Nutrient Management Research in Madagascar's Central Highland,* IRRI-Economics (unpublished mimeo).

— (ed) (1988c) *Laos: Rice Farming Systems and Rice Research* (unpublished).

— (in press) 'A Method for Farmer-Participatory Research and Technology Transfer: Upland Soil Conservation in The Philippines', *Experimental Agriculture.*

Fujisaka, S. and D.P. Garrity (1988) *Developing Sustainable Food Crop Farming Systems for the Sloping Acid-Uplands: A Farmer-Participatory Approach,* Paper presented at the 4th SUAN Research Symposium, Khon Kaen, Thailand.

Fulcrand, T.B. 1983/1978) *Enfermedades de los Ovinos y su Tratamiento,* (second edition), Cuzco, Peru, Centro de Estudios Rurales Andinos 'Bartolomé de las Casas'.

Fuller, N. and B. Jordan (1975) 'Integrative Aspects of Folk and Western Medicine among the Urban Poor of Oaxaca' *Anthropological Quarterly,* 48 (1), pp. 31-37.

— (1981) 'Maya Women and the End of the Birthing Period: Postpartum

Massage-and-Binding in Yucatan, Mexico', *Medical Anthropology*, 5 (1), pp. 35-50.

Furbee, L. and J. Sandor (1990) *Articulation of Folk and Scientific Classifications of Soils in the Colca Valley, Perú*, Paper presented at the 18th Midwest Conference on Andean and Amazonia Archaeology and Ethnohistory, Chicago, Illinois, February 1990.

Furbee, L. (1989a) 'A Folk Expert System: Soils Classification in the Colca Valley, Perú', *Anthropological Quarterly*, 62 (2), pp. 83-101.

— (1989b) 'Preliminary Version of Cognitive Soils Management Expert System', in D. Guillet (ed.) *Cognitive, Behavioural and Agronomic Studies of Soil Management in the Colca Valley, Perú*, Technical Report to the National Science Foundation, Anthropology Program, Washington, D.C., Catholic University, Department of Anthropology.

Gabel, C., R. Borden and S. White (1972-4) 'Preliminary Report on an Archaeological Survey of Liberia', *Liberian Studies Journal*, 5, pp. 2, pp. 87-105.

Gade, D. (1975) *Plants, Man and the Land in the Vilcanota Valley of Peru*, The Hague, W. Junk.

Gadgil, M. and V.D. Vartak (1981) 'Sacred Groves of Maharashtra: An Inventory', in S.K. Cain (ed.) *Glimpses of Indian Ethnobotany*, pp. 279-294, New Delhi, Oxford and IBH Publishing Co.

Gakou, M.L. (1987) *The Crisis in African Agriculture*, London, Zed Books.

Galjart, B. (1981) 'Counterdevelopment: A Position Paper', *Community Development Journal*, 16 (2).

Gallais, J. (1975) *Pasteurs et Paysans du Gourma: La Condition Sahelienne*, Paris, CEGET/CNRS.

Gamser, M. *et al.* (ed.) (1990) *Tinker, Tiller, Technical Change*, London, Intermediate Technology Publications.

Garaycochea, Z.I. (1985) 'Potencial Agricola de los Camellones en el Altiplano Puneño', *Andenes y Camelones en el Peru Andino: Historia Presente y Futuro*, pp. 241-251.

Garrity, D.P. (1976) *A Test of Potential Cropping Patterns for an Upland Rice-growing Region of The Philippines*, MS Thesis, Los Baños, University of The Philippines at Los Baños.

Gaussen, H., P. Legris, M. Viart and L. Labroue (1968) *Explanatory Notes on the Vegetation Map of Ceylon*, Colombo, Ceylon, Government Press.

Geertz, C. (1972) 'The Wet and the Dry; Traditional Irrigation in Bali and Morocco', *Human Ecology*, 1, pp. 34-39.

— (1976) *The Religion of Java*, London, Phoenix Press.

— (1977) 'Curing, Sorcery and Magic in a Javanese Town', in D. Landy (ed) *Culture, Disease and Healing; Studies in Medical Anthropology*, pp. 146-154, New York, Macmillan Press.

— (1980) *Negara: The Theatre State in Nineteenth-Century Bali*, Princeton, NJ, Princeton University Press.

Giani, S. (1987) *Le Piante Medicinali delle Isole Eolie*, Pungitogo, Marina di Patti.

Gilg, J.-P. (1963) 'Mobilite Pastorale au Tchad Occidental et Central', *Cahiers d'Etudes Africaines*, 3 (12), pp. 491-510.

Gilles, J.L. (1982) 'Planning Livestock Development: Themes from Indigenous Livestock Systems', *Agricultural Administration*, 11, pp. 215-225.

Gilmour, D.A. (1987) 'Not Seeing the Trees for the Forest: A Re-Appraisal of the Deforestation Crisis in Two Hill Disctricts of Nepal, *Nepal-Australia Forestry Project Paper* August, Kathmandu, NAFP

—_ (1988) 'Not Seeing the Trees for the Forest: A Reappraisal of the Deforestation Crisis in Two Hill Districts of Nepal', *Mountain Research and Development*, 8, pp. 343-350.

Gilmour, D.A. and G.B. Applegate (1984) Community Forestry as an Option for Containing Environmental Degradation: A Case Study from Nepal, Paper prepared for the IUFRO Symposium *Effects of Forest Land Use on Erosion and Slope Stability* at the University of Hawaii, Honolulu.

Gilmour, D., M. Bonell and D. Cassells (1987) 'The Effects of Forestation on Soil Hydraulic Properties in the Middle Hills of Nepal: A Preliminary Assessment, Mountain *Research and Development* , 7 (3), pp. 239-249.

Gilmour, D.A., G.C. King and R.J. Fisher (1987) 'Action Research into Socioeconomic Aspects of Forest Management', Paper prepared for the IUFRO Symposium on *The Role of Forest Research in Solving Socio-Economic Problems in the Himalayan Region*, Peshawar, Pakistan, October 17-27.

Gladwin, Chr.H. (1975) 'A Model of the Supply of Smoked Fish from Cape Coast to Kumasi', in S. Platner (ed.) *Formal Methods in Economic Anthropology,* pp. 77-127, Washington, D.C., American Anthropological Association.

— (1976) 'A View of the Plan Puebla: An Application of Hierarchical Decision Models' *American Journal of Agricultural Economics,* 58 (5), pp. 881-887.

— (1979a) 'Cognitive Strategies and Adoption Decisions: A Case Study of Nonadoption of an Agronomic Recommendation', *Economic Development and Cultural Change,* 28 (1), pp. 155-173.

— (1979b) 'Production Functions and Decision Models: Complementary Models', *American Ethnologist* , 6 (4), pp. 653-674.

— (1980) 'A Theory of Real-Life Choice: An Application to Agricultural Decisions', in P.F. Barlett (ed) *Agricultural Decision Making: Anthropological Contributions to Rural Development,* pp. 45-85, New York, Academic Press.

— (1983) 'Contributions of a Decision-Tree Methodology to a Farming Systems Program' *Human Organisation,* 4 (2), pp. 146-157.

Gladwin, Chr.H. and J. Butler (1984) 'Is Gardening an Adaptive Strategy for Florida Family Farmers?', *Human Organization,* 43 (3), pp. 208-216.

Gladwin, Chr.H. and R. Zabawa (1983) *The Effects of Concentration on the Full-Time Farmer in Gadsden County, North Florida: His Strategies to Survive and Preserve His Farmland,* Paper presented at the Annual Meetings of the Society of Economic Anthropology, Iowa City, IA.

— (1984) 'Microdynamics of Contraction Decisions: A Cognitive Approach to Structural Change', *American Journal of Agricultural Economics,* 66 (5), pp. 829-835.

— (1986) 'After Structural Change: Are Part-Time or Full-Time Farmers Better Off?', in Joseph Molnar (ed) *Agricultural Change: Consequences for Southern Farms and Rural Communities,* pp. 39-59. Boulder, CO, Westview Press.

Gladwin, Chr.H., R. Zabawa and D. Zimet (1984) 'Using Ethnoscientific Tools to Understand Farmers' Plans, Goals, Decision Processes and Farming Systems', in P. Matlon, R. Cantrell, D. King and M. Benoit-Cattin (ed.) *Coming Full Circle: Farmer's Participation in the Development of Technology,* pp. 27-40, Ottawa, Canada, International Development Research Centre.

Glaeser, B. (ed) (1984) *Ecodevelopment: Concepts, Projects, Strategies,* Oxford, UK, Pergamon Press.

Gliessman, S.R. (1987) 'Ecology and Management of Weeds in Traditional Agroecosystems', in M.A. Altieri and M. Liebman (ed.) *Ecology of Weed Management,* Boca Raton, FL, CRC Press.

— (in press) 'Ecological Basis of Traditional Management of Wetlands in Tropical Mexico', in M.L. Oldfield and J.B. Alcorn (eds) *Biodiversity: Conservation and Development of Biological Resources Under Traditional Management,* Boulder, CO, Westview.

Gluckman, M. (1951) 'The Lozi of Barotseland in North-Western Rhodesia', in E. Colson and M. Gluckman (eds) *Seven Tribes of British Central Africa*, pp. 1-93, Oxford, Oxford University Press.

Gómez-Pompa, A. (1976) *Investigaciones sobre la Regeneracion de Selvos Altos en Vera Cruz, Mexico*, México DF.

— (1978) 'An Old Answer to the Future', *Mazingra*, 5, pp. 51-55.

— (1987) 'Learning from Traditional Ecological Knowledge: Insights from Maya Silviculture', in A. Gómez-Pompa, T.C. Whitmore and M. Hadley (ed.), *Rain Forest Regeneration and Management*, Man and Biosphere Book Series, UNESCO, Paris and Parthenon Publishing, Carnforth.

— (1987) 'On Maya Silviculture.' *Mexican Studies/Estudios Mexicanos*, 3 (1), pp. 1-17.

Gómez-Pompa, A., H.L. Morales, E.J. Avilla and J.J. Avilla (1982) 'Experiences in Traditional Hydraulic Agriculture', in K.V. Flannery (ed.) *Maya Subsistence: Studies in Memory of Dennis E. Puleston*, pp. 327-342, New York, Academic Press.

Gómez-Pompa, A. and R. Venegas (1976) *La Chinampa Tropical*, INIREB Informes, Comm. 5. Xalapa, Instituto Nacional de Investigaciones sobre Recursos Bióticos.

— (1989) 'Biosphere Reserves and the Conservation of Traditional Land Use Systems of Indigenous Populations in Central America', in W.P. Gregg Jr., S.L. Krugman and J.D. Wood Jr. (ed.) *Proceedings of the Symposium on Biosphere Reserves*, pp. 234-241, Fourth World Wilderness Congress, Estes Park, Colorado, USA, 14-17 September 1987, Atlanta, Georgia, US Department of the Interior, National Park Service.

Good, C.M., J.M. Hunter, S.H. Katz and S.S. Katz (1970) 'Componential Analysis and the Study of Meaning', *Language*, 32 (1), pp. 195-216.

— (1979) 'The Interface of Dual Systems of Health Care in the Developing World, Toward Health Policy Initiatives in Africa' *Social Science and Medicine*, 13D, 141-154.

Goodell, G. (n.d.) 'Communication from Farmer to Scientist', (unpublished manuscript).

Goody, J.R. (1956) *The Social Organisation of the LoWiili*, Colonial Research Studies 19, London, Her Majesty's Stationary Office.

— (1971) *Technology, Tradition and the State in Africa*, London, Oxford University Press.

Gordon, B.L. (1982) *A Panama Forest and Shore*, Pacific Grove, California, Boxwood Press.

Goris, P. (1954) *Prasasti Bali, Bandung, Lembaga Bahasa dan Budaya*, Universitas Indonesia, Jakarta, Masa Baru.

Gould-Martin, K. (1978) 'Hot Cold Clean Poison and Dirt: Chinese Folk Medical Categories', *Social Science and Medicine*, 12 (1B), pp. 39-46.

Gourlet, S. (1979) 'Les Plantes en Médecine Vétérinaire Populaire', Doctoral Thesis, Toulouse, France, Veterinary Science, Université Paul-Sabatier.

Government of India (1988) *Agricultural Situation in India*, New Delhi, India.

Grandin, B.E. (1985) 'Towards a Maasai Ethnoveterinary', International Livestock Centre for Africa (ILCA), Kenya (unpublished paper).

Greenland, D.J. (1974) 'Evolution and Development of Different Types of Shifting Cultivation', *Shifting Cultivation and Soil Conservation in Africa*, FAO Soils Bulletin, 24, Rome, FAO.

Greenwood, D.J. (1973) *The Political Economy of Peasant Family Farming: Some Anthropological Perspectives on Rationality and Adaptation*, Rural Development Occasional Paper 2, Ithaca, NY, Cornell University.

Greslou, F. (1989) *Visión y Crianza Campesinas de los Animales Andinos*, Lima, Peru, PRATEC (Proyecto Andino de Tecnologías Campesinas).

Griffin, D.M. (1988) *Innocents Abroad in the Forests of Nepal: An Account of Australian Aid to Nepalese Forestry*, Canberra, Anutech.

Guha, R. (1985) 'Scientific Forestry and Social Change in Uttarackhand', *Economic and Political Weekly*, 20 (45-47), pp. 1939-1951.

Guillet, D.W. (1979) *Agrarian Reform and Peasant Economy in Southern Peru*, Columbia, MO, University of Missouri Press.

— (1989a) 'A Knowledge-based-systems Model of Native Soil Management', *Anthropological Quarterly*, 62 (2), pp. 59-67.

— (1989b) 'Native Soil Management in the Colca Valley, South-western Perú', in D. Guillet (ed) *Cognitive, Behavioural and Agronomic Studies of Soil Management in the Colca Valley, Peru*, pp. 61-97, Technical Report to the National Science Foundation (Anthropology Program), Washington, D.C., Catholic University, Department of Anthropology.

Gulati, H.S. and V.V.N. Murty (1979) 'A Model for Optimal Allocation of Canal Water based on Crop Production Functions', *Agricultural Water Management*, II.

Gulliver, P.H. (1970) *The Family Herds: A Study of Two Pastoral Tribes in East Africa, The Jie and Turkana*, Westport, Negro University Press.

— (1975) 'Nomadic Movements: Causes and Implications', in T. Monod (ed) *Pastoralism in Tropical Africa*, pp. 369-386, London, Oxford University Press.

Gupta, A.K. (1980) *Communicating with Farmers,* IIPA, New Delhi, mimeo.

— (1981) *Viable Projects for Enviable Farmers – An Action Research Enquiry into the Structure and Processes of Rural Poverty in Arid Regions,* IIPA, New Delhi and IIM, Ahmebabad.

— (1983) *Impoverishment in Drought Prone Regions,* SDC/NABARD/IIMA, Ahmebabad, mimeo.

— (1984) *Small Farmer Household Economy in Semi-Arid Regions,* CMA, IIM, Ahmebabad, mimeo.

— (1985) 'Socio-Ecological Paradigm to Analyse Problems of Poor in Dry Region', *Eco-Development News*, 32-33, pp. 68-74.

— (1987a) *Organising the Poor Client Responsive Research System: Can the Tail Wag the Dog?,* Paper for the workshop on Farmers and Agricultural Research: Complementary Methods held at the Institute of Development Studies, University of Sussex, July 26-31.

— (1987b) *Organising and Managing the Poor Client Oriented Research System: Can Tail Wag the Dog?,* First draft presented at the workshop on Farmer Participatory Research Complementary Methods at IDS, Sussex, July 1987, Revised and enlarged version presented at the Advisory Committee Meeting and Workshop on On-farm Oriented Research, ISNAR, The Hague, October 1987.

— (1987c) *Scientific Perception of Farmers' Innovations in Dry Regions: Barriers to the Scientific Curiosity,* Paper presented at IDS workshop on Farmers Participatory Research, Sussex, IIM, Ahmebabad.

Gupta, A.K., N.T. Patel and R.N. Shah (1987) *Matching Farmers' Concerns with Technologists' Objectives in Dry Regions: An Exploratory Study of Scientific Goal Setting,* CMA, IIM, Ahmebabad, mimeo.

Gurung, H. (1982) *The Himalaya: Perspective on Change,* Kathmandu, New ERA.

— (1984) *Nepal: Dimensions of Development*, Kathmandu, Sahayogi Press.

Haaland, R. and P.L. Shinnie (ed.) (1985) *African Iron Working- Ancient and Traditional,* Oslo, Norwegian University Press.

Halle, F. (1986) 'Un Système d'Exploitation Ancien, Mais Une Interface Scientifique Nouvelle: l'Agroforesterie dans les Régions Tropicales', in Chavelin and Riou (ed.) *Milieux et Paysages*, pp. 37-53, Masson, Paris.

Hallpike, C.R. (1972) *The Konso of Ethiopia: A Study of the Value of a Cushitic People*, Oxford, Clarendon Press.

Halpin, B. (1981) 'Vets – Barefoot and Otherwise', *Pastoral Network Paper, 11c,* London, UK, Regent's College, Inner Circle, Agricultural Administration Unit, Overseas Development Institute (ODI).

Hamilton, L.S. (1987) 'What are the Impacts of Himalayan Deforestation on the Ganges-Brahmaputra Lowlands and Delta? Assumptions and Facts', *Mountain Research and Development,* 7 (3), pp. 256-263.

Hamilton, L.S. and A.J. Pearce (1985) 'What are the Soil and Water Benefits of Planting Trees in Developing Country Watershed?', A paper prepared for the International Symposium *Sustainable Development in Natural Resources in the Third World,* Columbus, Ohio, Ohio State University and Argonne National Laboratory.

Hanegraaf, M. (1987) 'Nitrogen Transfer from Legumes' *ILEIA,* 1 (3), pp. 8.

Hansen, A. (1986) 'Farming Systems Research in Malawi: Limited Utility of High Yielding Varieties', in R. Jones and B. Wallace (ed.) *Social Sciences and Farming Systems Research,* pp. 145-169, Boulder, CO, Westview Press.

Hansen, D.O. and J.M. Erbaugh (1987) 'The Social Dimension of Natural Resource Management', in D.D. Southgate and J.F. Disinger (ed.) *Sustainable Resource Development in the Third World,* pp. 81-94, Boulder, CO, Westview Press.

Hardestry, D.L. (1977) *Ecological Anthropology,* New York, John Wiley and Sons.

Hardiman, M. and J. Midgley (1982) *The Social Dimensions of Development,* John Wiley and Sons, Chinchester.

Hardin, G. (1968) 'The Tragedy of the Commons', *Science,* 162 (13), pp. 1243-1248.

Hardjono, J. (ed) (1991) *Indonesia; Resources, Ecology and Environment,* Oxford, Oxford University Press.

Harris, D.R. (1976) 'The Origins of Agriculture in the Tropics', in R.L. Smith (ed.) *The Ecology of Man: An Ecosystem Approach,* New York, Harper and Row.

Harris, J. (1977) 'Implications of Change in Agriculture for Social Relationships at the Village Level: The Case of Randam', in B.H. Farmers (ed) *Green Revolution? Technology and Change in Rice Growing Areas of Tamilnadu,* London, Longman.

Harris, L.D. (1984) *The Fragmented Forest: Island Biogeography Theory and the Preservation of Biotic Diversity,* Chicago, University of Chicago Press.

Harris, M. (1979) *Cultural Materialism,* New York, Random House/Vintage Press.

Harrison, I.E. and S. Cosminsky (1976) *Traditional Medicine: Implications for Ethnnomedicine, Ethnopharmacology, Maternal Health and Public Health- an annotated Bibliography of Africa, Latin America and the Caribbean,* New York, Garland.

Harrison, P. (1987) *The Greenings of Africa: Breaking Through in the Battle for Land and Food,* New York, Penguin Books.

Haryadi, J. (1986) 'Pendapat Dr. Leendert Jan Slikkerveer: Tentang Jamu dan Pengobatan Memakai Cara Traditional' *Pikiran Rakyat* , (October), Bandung.

Hart, D.V. (1969) *Bisayam Pilippino and Malayan Humoral Pathologies: Folk Medicine and Ethnohistory in Southeast Asia,* Data Paper 76, Ithaca, NY, Cornell University, Department of Asian Studies.

Hart, P. (1980) 'A Natural Ecosystem Analog Approach to the Design of a Successional Crop System for Tropical Forest Environments' *Biotropica – Suppl,* 12 (2), 72-83.

Harwood, R.R. and D.L. Plucknett (1981) 'Vegetable Cropping Systems', in D.L. Plucknett and H.L. Beemer, Jr. (ed.) *Vegetable Farming Systems in China,* pp. 45-118, Boulder, CO, Westview Press.

Harwood, R.R. (1979) *Small Farm Development Understanding and Improving Farming Systems in the Humid Tropics,* Boulder, CO, Westview Press.

Haudricourt, A.G. (1962) 'Domestication des Animaux, Culture des Plantes et Traitement d'Autrui', *L'Homme,* 2(1), pp. 40-50.

Haverkort, B., W. Hiemstra, C. Reintjes and S. Essers (1988) 'Strengthening Farmers' Capacity for Technology Development', *ILEIA,* 4 (3), Leusden.

Hawkins, T. (1981) 'Community Forestry Development in Ohaulagiri Forest Divison 1980-1981', *CFDP Miscellaneous Document,* 6, Kathmandu, Community Forestry Development Project.

Hayuningrat (n.d.) *Resep Pengobatan Traditional Jamu Jawa,* Bintang Usaha Jaya.

Helland, J. (1978) 'Sociological Aspects of Pastoral Livestock Production in Africa', in D.N. Hyder (ed) *Proceedings of the 1st International Rangeland Congress,* pp. 79-81, Denver, SRM.

— (1982) 'Social Organisation and Water Control Among the Borana', *Development and Change,* 13 (2), pp. 239-258.

Hendry, P. (1987) 'In Africa, Weed Control Takes Aim at Parasitic Striga', Rome, CERES *FAO* Review, 116, 29 (2), pp. 4-5.

Herbert, W.J. (1974) *Veterinary immunology,* Oxford, Blackwell Scientific.

Herklots, G.A.C. (1972) *Vegetables in South-east Asia,* New York, Hafner.

Hermanns, M. (1948) *Die A Mdo Pa-Grosstibeter: Die Sozial-wirtschaftlichen Grundlagen der Hirtenkulturen Innerasiens,* Freiburg, Philosophische Fakultät der Universität Freiburg.

Herrera, F.L. (1941) *Sinopsis de la Flora del Cuzco: Tomo Ia y Tomo Ib, Parte Sistemática,* Supremo Gobierno del Perú.

Hetzel, J., I. Sutikno and Soeripto (1981) 'Beberapa Pengaruh Aflatoksin Terhadap Pertumbuhan Itik-itik Muda', *Proceedings of the Seminar Penelitian Peternakan,* pp. 400-404. Bogor.

Heyzer, N. (1986) *Working Women in Southeast Asia: Development, Subordination and Emancipation,* Philadelphia, Open University Press.

Hidding, K.A.H. (1935) *Gebruiken en Godsdienst der Soedanezen,* Batavia, Kolff and Co.

Hiernaux, P. and L. Diarra (1984) 'Is it Possible to Improve the Traditional Grazing Management in the Flood Plain of the Niger River in Central Mali?', in P.J. Joss, P.W. Lynch and O.B. Williams (ed.) *Rangelands: a Resource Under Siege. Proceedings 2nd International Rangeland Congress,* pp. 201-204, Adelaide, Australia.

Higgins, C. 'Integrative Aspects of Folk and Western Medicine among the Urban Poor of Oaxaca', *Anthropological Quarterly* 48 (1), pp. 31-37.

Hildebrand, P.E. (1981) 'Motivating Small Farmers, Scientists and Technicians to Accept Change', *Agricultural Administration,* 8 (6), pp. 423-432.

— (1982) 'Historical Forces that Have Shaped World Agriculture', in R. Haines and R. Lanier (eds) *Agriculture, Change and Human Values,* pp. 14-28, Gainesville FL, University of Florida, Humanities and Agriculture Program.

Hill, P. (ed) (1970) *Studies in Rural Capitalism in West Africa,* Cambridge, Cambridge University Press.

Hill, P. (1984) 'The Poor Quality of Official Socio-Economic Statistics Relating to the Rural Tropical World with Special Reference to South India', *Modern Asian Studies,* 18, pp. 491-514.

Hiroko, Horikoshi-Roe (1980) 'Asrama: An Islamic Psychiatric Institution in West Java', *Social Science and Medicine,* 14B (3), pp. 157-167.

Hjort, A. (1976a) 'Traditional Land Use in Marginal Drylands', in A. Rapp, H.N. Le Houerou and B. Lundholm (ed.) *Can Desert Encroachment Be Stopped,* pp. 43-53 Stockholm, Ecological Bulletin (Stockholm) 24, UNEP/SIES, NFR.

— (1976b) 'Regional Studies and Proposals for Development: Kenya', *Ecol. Bull.* (Stockholm), 24, pp. 165-169.

Hjort, A. and W. Ostberg (1978) *Farming and Herding in Botswana*, Swedish Agency for Research Cooperation with Developing Countries R, 1.

Hladik, C.M., S. Bahuchet and E. de Garine (eds) (1989) *Se Nourir en Forêt Equatoriale,* Anthropologie Alimentaire des Populations des Régions Forestières Humides d'Afrique, Paris, UNESCO.

Hobbes, J. (1989) *Bedouin Life in the Egyptian Wilderness*, Austin, Texas, University of Texas Press.

Hockings, P. (1980) *Sex and Disease in a Mountain Community*, New Delhi, India, Vikas Publishing House.

Holleman, J.F. (1951) 'Some 'Shona' Tribes of Southern Rhodesia', in E. Colson and M. Gluckman (ed.) *Seven Tribes of British Central Africa,* pp. 354-395, Oxford, Oxford University Press.

Holy, L. and M. Stuchlik (1983) *Actions, Norms and Representations: Foundations of Anthropological Inquiry,* Cambridge, Cambridge University Press.

Hornik, R.C. (1988) *Development Communication: Information, Agriculture and Nutrition in the Third World*, New York, Longman.

Horowitz, M. and K. Badi (1981) *Sudan: Introduction of Forestry in Grazing Systems,* Rome, FAO/SIDA Forestry for Local Community Development Program, GCP/INT/347/SWE.

Horton, D.E. (1984) *Social Scientists in Agricultural Research: Lessons from the Mantaro Valley Project, Peru,* Ottawa, IDRC.

Howe, L.E.A. (1984) 'Gods, People, Spirits and Witches: The Balinese System of Person Definition', *Bijdragen tot Taal-, Land- en Volkenkunde*, 140, 2, (3), pp. 193-223.

Howes, M. and R. Chambers (1972) 'Individuality and Experimentation in Traditional Agriculture', *Human Ecology*, 1 (2), pp. 448-459.

— (1979) 'Indigenous Technical Knowledge: Analysis, Implications and Issues in Rural Development: Whose Knowledge Counts?' *IDS Bulletin*, 10 (2), pp. 6-11.

— (1979) 'Indigenous Technical Knowledge: Analysis, Implications and Issues' *IDS Bulletin,* 10 (2), pp. 5-11.

— (1980) 'Indigenous Technical Knowledge: Analysis, Implications and Issues', in D. Brokensha, D.M. Warren and O. Werner (eds) *Indigenous Knowledge Systems and Development*, pp. 329-340, Lanham, MD, University Press of America.

Howes, M. (1979) 'The Uses of Indigenous Technical Knowledge in Development', *IDS Bulletin*, 10 (2), pp. 12-23.

— (1980) 'The Uses of Indigenous Technical Knowledge in Development', in D. Brokensha, D.M. Warren and O. Werner (ed.) *Indigenous Knowledge Systems and Development*, pp. 329-340, Lanham, MD, University Press of America.

Huanca, T. (1985) 'Sanidad de Alpacas', *Minka,* 16 (March), pp. 24-25.

Hughes, I. (1977) *New Guinea Stone Age Trade: The Geography and Ecology of Traffic in the Interior*, Terra Australis 3, Canberra, Australia, Australian National University, Department of Prehistory, Research School of Pacific Studies.

Huizer, G. (1991) *Indigenous Knowledge and Popular Spirituality: A Challenge to Developmentalists*, Paper for the International workshop Agricultural Knowledge and the Role of Extension, Bad Boll, University of Hohenheim.

Hussein, M.A. (1984) 'Traditional Systems of Camel Management and Husbandry', in M.A. Hussein (ed.) *Camel Pastoralism in Somalia: Proceedings from a Workshop held in Baydhabo, April 8- 13, 1984*, pp. 37-48, Camel Forum Working Paper 7, Mogadishu, Somalia/Stockholm, Sweden, Somali Camel Research Project.

Ibn Al Awam (12th Century) *Le Livre de l'Agriculture,* Bouslama, Tunis, Translated from Arabic.

Ibrahim, A.A., H.S. Adam, A. Adeeb and C.J. Stigter, with the collaboration of B.I. Abdulai (1989) 'Evaporation from Sennar Reservoir, Paper presented at the Conference on Irrigation', *Management Studies, Report 11RC 2.,* Wad Medani, Ford Foundation/HRS.

Ibrahim, M.A. (1984) *Evaluation of the Activities of some African Traditional Anthelmintic Herbs against Nippostrongylus braziliensis in Rats,* MS Thesis, Zaria, Nigeria, Department of Veterinary Physiology and Pharmacology, Ahmado Bello University.

— (1986) 'Veterinary Traditional Practice in Nigeria', in R. von Kaufmann, S. Chater and R. Blench (eds) *Livestock Systems Research in Nigeria's Subhumid Zone,* pp. 189-203, Proceedings of the 2nd ILCA/NAPRI Symposium held in Kaduna, Nigeria, 29 October-2 November 1984, Addis Ababa, Ethiopia, International Livestock Centre for Africa (ILCA).

Ibrahim, M.A., N. Nwude, R.A. Ogunsusi and Y.O. Aliu (1984) 'Screening of West African Plants for Anthelmintic Acitivity', *ILCA Bulletin,* 17, pp. 19-22.

Ibrahim, M.A., N. Nwude, Y O. Aliu and R.A. Ogunsusi (1983) 'Traditional Concepts of Animal Disease and Treatment among Fulani Herdsmen in Kaduna State of Nigeria', *Pastoral Development Network Paper* 16c, London, UK: Regent's College, Inner Circle, Agricultural Administration Unit, Overseas Development Institute (ODI).

Ibrahim, C.S. (1986) *Obat-Obatan dan Larutan,* Jakarta, Bhratara Karya Aksara.

IDS (ed) (1987) 'Farmers Knowledge, Innovations and Relation to Science', in R. Chambers, A. Pacey and L. Thrupp (eds) *Farmers First: Farmer Innovation and Agricultural Research,* pp. 31-37, London, Intermediate Technology Publications.

ILEIA (1985-1990) 'Information Centre for Low External Input Agriculture' *Newsletter,* 1-5, Leusden, ILEIA.

Illich, I. (1985) *Gender,* London, Marion Boyers.

Imperato, P.J. (1972) 'Nomads of the Niger', *Natural History,* 81 (10), pp. 61-68, 78-79.

Ingham, J. (1970) 'On Mexican Folk Medicine', *American Anthropologist,* 72 (1), pp. 76-87.

Institute of Development Studies (1979) 'Rural Development: Whose Knowledge Counts?' Special Issue, in Robert Chambers,(ed) *IDS Bulletin,* 10 (2).

Instituto Nacional de Estadística, Geografia e Informática (1989) *Información Estadística: Sector Saludy Seguridad Social,* Cuadro 6, México DF, Instituto Nacional de Estadística, Geografia e Informática.

International Institute of Tropical Agriculture (1976) *Annual Report 1975,* Ibadan, Nigeria, International Institute of Tropical Agriculture.

International Rice Research Institute (1989) *IRRI: Toward 2000 and Beyond,* Manila, International Rice Research Institute.

Ives, J.D. (1984a) 'Current Approaches to Research and Development in the Hindu-Kush-Himalayan Region', in *Mountain Development: Challenges and Opportunities, Proceedings of the First International Symposium and Inauguration of the International Centre for Integrated Mountain Development* (ICIMOD), pp. 54-56, Kathmandu, ICIMOD.

— (1984b) 'The Himalaya-Ganges Problem in the Context of Peace and Resource-Use Conflict Management, Mountain Chronicles', *Mountain Research and Development,* 4, pp. 363-365.

Ives, J.D. and P. Ives (ed.) (1987) "The Himalaya-Ganges Problems: Proceedings of a Conference', *Mountain Research and Development,* 7 (3), special issue.

Ives, J.D. and B. Messerli (1989) *The Himalayan Dilemma: Reconciling Development and Conservation,* London, Routledge.

Jackson, A. (1975) 'The Descent of Man, Incest and the Naming of Sons', in R. Willis (ed.) *The Interpretation of Symbolism*, London, Malaby Press.

Jacob, V.J. and W.S. Alles (1987) 'The Kandyan Gardens of Sri Lanka', *Agroforestry Systems*, 5, pp. 123-127.

Jacobs, A.H. (1980) 'Pastoral Maasai and Tropical Rural Development', in R.H. Bates and M.F. Lofchie (eds) *Agricultural Development in Africa: Issues of Public Policy,* pp. 275-300, New York, Praeger.

Jacobs, P. and D. Munro (ed.) (1987) *Conservation with Equity: Strategies for Sustainable Development.*, Gland, IUCN.

Jacobson, M. (1986) 'The Neem Tree: Natural Resistance Par Excellence', in M.B. Green and P.A. Hedin (ed.) *Natural Resistance of Plants to Pests: Roles of Allelochemics*, pp. 220-232, Washington, D.C., American Chemical Society.

— (1987) 'Neem Research and Cultivation in the Western Hemisphere', in H. Schmutterer and K.R.S. Ascher (ed.) *Natural Pesticides from the Neem Tree (Azadirachta indica A. Juss) and Other Tropical Plants,* pp. 33-44, Proceedings, 3rd International Neem Conference, Nairobi, Kenya, 1986, Schriftenreiche der GTZ, 206, Eschborn.

— (1988) 'Pharmacology and Toxicology of Neem', in M. Jacobson (ed) *1988 Focus on Phytochemical Pesticides, I, The Neem Tree,* pp. 133-154, Boca Raton, FL, CRC Press.

Jahnke, H.E., D. Kirschke and J. Lagermann (1987) 'The Impact of Agricultural Research in Tropical Africa' *CGIAR Study Paper* 21, Washington D.C., The World Bank.

Jalaluddin as Syuthi (n.d.) (reprint) *Therapi Alamiah Yang Cespleng; Resep-Resep Specialis Ketabiban*, Solo, Aneka.

Jallo, Y.D. (1989a) *The Life of the Fulbe in the Ferlo, II: Cattle Diseases (in Fulfulde), Ndakaaru, Dakar, Senegal, Goomu Winndiyankoobe Demde Ngenndiije*, Groupe d'Initiative pour la Promotion du Livre en Langues Nationals.

— (1989b) *The life of the People of Ferlo, I Their Social System , Their Strategies of Herding, Their Knowledge about Agriculture (in Fulfuldee), Ndakaaru, Dakar, Senegal, Goomu Winndiyankobe Demde Ngenndiije,* Group d'Initiative pour la Promotion du Livre en Langues Nationals.

Jammes, O. (n.d.) *Les Forgerons Du Pays Senoufu,* (Publication date probably around 1980).

Janzen, J.M. (1978) *The Quest for Therapy in Lower Zaire*, Berkeley, University of California Press.

Jarvis, D.C. (n.d.) *Pengobatan Tradisional dengan Madu and Apel*, Bandung, Pionir Jaya.

Jaspan, M.A. (1969) *Traditional Medical Theory in South-east Asia*, Hull, University of Hull Publications.

— (1977) 'The Social Organisation of Indigenous and Modern Medical Practices in South-west Sumatra', in Ch. Leslie (ed.) *Asian Medical Systems; A Comparative Study*, pp. 227-243, Berkeley, University of California Press.

Jiggins, J. (1986) *Gender, Related Impacts and the Work of the International Agricultural Research Centre*, Washington, D.C., World Bank.

— (1989) 'An Examination of the Impact of Colonialism in establishing Negative Values and Attitudes toward Indigenous Agricultural Knowledge', in D.M. Warren, L.J. Slikkerveer and S.O. Titilola (eds) *Indigenous Knowledge Systems: Implications for Agriculture and International Development*, pp. 68-78, Ames, IA, Iowa State University.

Jiménez J.S., A.T. de Jiménez, A.V. Muñiz and C.M. Gonzales (1983) 'Los Alcaloides del Lupinus Como Pesticidas en el Control de Ectoparásitos', *Ciencia y Pueblo: Revista de los Institutos IIUN-IIDSA-NUFFIC* 1, pp. 107-125.

Jiménez-Osornio, J.J. and S.R. del Amo (1988) 'An Intensive Mexican Traditional Agroecosystem: The Chinampa', in P. Allen and D. van Dusen (eds) *Global Perspectives on Agroecology and Sustainable Agricultural Systems* II, pp. 451-455, Agroecology Program, Santa Cruz, University of California.

Jochim, M.A. (1981) *Strategies for Survival. Cultural Behaviour in an Ecological Context*, New York, Academic Press.

Jodha, N.S. (1985) 'Population Growth and the Decline of Common Property Resources in Rajhastan, India', *Population and Development Review*, 11, pp. 247-264.

— (1986) 'Common Property Resources and the Rural Poor in Dry Regions of India' *Economic and Political Weekly*, 21 (27), pp. 1169-1181.

Jodha, N.S. and A.C. Mascarenhas (1979) *Some Dimensions of Traditional Farming in Semi-Arid Tropical India*, ICRISAT, EPPR 4.

— (1983) *Adjustment to Climatic Variability in Self Provisioning Societies: Some Evidence from India and Tanzania*, ICRISAT, EPPR 48.

Johannes, R.E. (1978) 'Traditional Marine Conservation Methods in Oceania and their Demise' *Annual Review of Ecology and Systematics*, 9, pp. 49-64.

— (1982) 'Traditional Conservation Methods and Protected Marine Areas in Oceania', *Ambio*, 11, pp. 258-261.

Johnson, A.W. (1971) 'Security and Risk-Taking Among Poor Peasants', in G. Dalton (ed.) *Studies in Economic Anthropology*, pp. 143-178, Washington, D.C., American Anthropological Association.

— (1972) 'Individuality and Experimentation in Traditional Agriculture' *Human Ecology*, 1 (2), pp. 149-159.

— (1974) Ethnoecology and Planting Practices in a Swidden Agricultural System, *American Ethnologist*, 1 (1), pp. 87-101.

— (1980) 'The Limits of Formalism', in P.F. Barlett (ed) *Agricultural Decision Making*, pp. 19-43, New York, Academic Press.

— (1983) 'Machiguenga Gardens', in R.B. Hames and W.T. Vickers (ed.) *Adaptive Responses of Native Amazonians*, pp. 29-63, New York, Academic Press.

Johnson, K., E.A. Olson and S. Manandhar (1982) 'Environmental Knowledge and Response to Natural Hazards in Mountainous Nepal', *Mountain Research and Development*, 2, pp. 175-188.

Johnston, S.A. and J.K. Springer (1977) 'Pepper: Phytophthora Blight Cultural Control Test', *Plant Pathology Leaflet*, pp. 104, New Brunswick, NJ, Rutgers State University.

Jolin, D. (1985) *La Méthode Chorotega de Multiplication des Arbres par Boutures Hautes*, pp. 18, Traduction du Mémoire Présenté au 9éme Congrès Forestier Mondial de Mexico.

Jones, D.K. (1984) *Shepherds of the desert*, London, Elm Tree Books/Hamish Hamilton Ltd.

Jones, P.S., S.V. Ley, E.D. Morgan and D. Santafianos (1988) 'The Chemistry of the Neem Tree', in M. Jacobson (ed) *1988 Focus on Phytochemical Pesticides* I, *The Neem Tree*, pp. 19-45, Boca Raton, FL, CRC Press.

Jones, W.O. (1959) *Manioc in Africa*, Stanford, CA, Stanford University Press.

Jordaan, R.E. (1982) 'Tombuwan in the 'Dermatology' of Madurese Folk Medicine', *Bijdragen tot Taal-, Land- en Volkenkunde*, 138 (1), pp. 9-29.

— (1985) *Folk Medicine in Madura*, Ph.D. Dissertation, Leiden, Leiden University.

Jotwani, M.J. and K.P. Srivastava (1981a) 'Neem Insecticide of the Future I: As a Protectant against Stored Grain Pests', *Pesticides*, 15, pp. 19-23.

— (1981b) 'Neem Insecticide of the Future II: Protection against Field Pests', *Pesticides*, 15, pp. 40-47.

— (1981c) 'Neem Insecticide of the Future III: Chemistry, Toxicology and Future Strategy', *Pesticides*, 15, pp. 12-15, 19.

— (1984) 'A Review of Neem Research in India in Relation to Insects', in H. Schmutterer and H. Rembold (eds) *Natural Pesticides from the Neem Tree*, pp. 43-56, Proceedings, 2nd International Neem Conference, Rauisch-Holzenhausen, 1983, Schriftenreihe der GTZ; 161, Deutsche Gessellschaft für Technische Zusammenarbeit (GTZ) GmbH.

Juma, C. (1988) *The Gene Hunters*, London, Zed Press.

Jurion, F. and J. Henry (1969) *Can Primitive Farming be Modernised?*, Publication de L'Institut National Pour L'Etude Agronomique du Congo.

Kandaswami, L.S. (1987) *Agricultural Heritages of the Tamils*, Coimbatore: Kalaiselvam Publication (in Tamil).

Kamera, W.D. and C.S. Mwakasaka (ed.) (1981) *The Compliment, East African Folktales* Arusha, East African Publications.

Kang, B.T., G.F. Wilson and T.L. Lawson (1984) *Alley Croppings: A Stable Alternative to Shifting Cultivation*, Ibadan, IITA.

Karim, W-J.A. (1981) 'Mak Betisek Concepts of Humans, Plants and Animals', *Bijdragen tot Taal-, Land- en Volkenkunde*, 137 (1), pp. 35-61.

Kartawinata, K., S. Adisoemarto, S. Riswan and A.P. Wayda (1981) 'The Impact of Man on a Tropical Forest in Indonesia', *Ambio*, 10 (2-3), pp. 115-119.

Kat Angelino, A. de (1909) *Mudras op Bali: Handhoudingen der Priesters*, Den Haag, Adi-Pustaka.

Kay, M. and M. Yoder (1987) 'Hot and Cold in Women's Ethnotherapeutics: the American-Mexican West', *Social Science and Medicine*, 25 (4), pp. 347-355.

Keesing, R.M. (1987) 'Models, Folk and Cultural: Paradigm Regained?', in D. Holland and N. Quinn (eds) *Cultural Models in Language and Thought*, Cambridge, Cambridge University Press.

Keller, A. (1987) *The USU Unit Command Area Model, Water Management Synthesis II* , Project Report 71, (December), pp. 43-45, Logan, Utah, Utah State University.

Kelly, G. (1955) *The Psychology of Personal Constructs*, I and II, New York, W.W. Norton.

Kelman, A. and R.J. Cook (1977) 'Plant Pathology in the People's Republic of China: Annual Review' *Phytopathology*, 15, pp. 409-429.

Kerharo, J. and J.G. Adam (1964) 'Plantes Médicinales et Toxiques des Peul et des Toucouleur du Sénégal' *Journal d'Agriculture Tropicale et de Botanique Appliquée*, 11 (8-9), pp. 384-444.

Kerven, C. and P. Sikana (1988) *Case Studies of Indigenous Soil and Land Classification in Northern Province,* Misamfu, Zambia, Adaptive Research Planning Team.

Khanna, B.M., Y.P. Singh and R.P. Singh (June 1978) 'Veterinary Therapy in Hissar Villages: Digestive and Respiratory Disorders', *The Haryana Veterinarian*, 17 (1), pp. 42-51.

Kidd, R. (1982) *The Popular Performing Arts, Non-Formal Education and Social Change in the Third World: A Bibliography and Review Essay*, Bibliography 7, The Hague, Centre for the Study of Education in Developing Countries (CESO).

Kimball, L.A. (1979) *Borneo Medicine: The Healing Art of Indigenous Brunei Malay Medicine*, Ann Arbor, University Microfilm International.

— (1985) 'Brunei Malay Traditional Ethnoveterinary Practices', *Borneo Research Bulletin*, 17 (2), pp. 123-150.

Kincaid, R. (1960) 'Shade Tobacco Growing in Florida' *University of Florida Agricultural Experiment Station Bulletin* 136, pp. 5-41.

King, F.H. (1926) *Farmers of Forty Centuries*, New York, Harcourt Brace.

Kingston, D.J., D. Kosasih and I. Ardi (1978) *The Use of the Muscovy Duck for Hatching of Alabio Duck Eggs in the Swamplands of Kalimantan*, Report 7 , Bogor, Centre for Animal Research and Development.

Klayman, D.L. (1985) Qinghaosu (Artemisinin): An Antimalarial Drug from China, *Science* 228 (4703), pp. 1049-1055.

Klee, G. A. (ed) (1980) *World Systems of Traditional Resource Management*, New York, John Wiley and Sons.

Kleinman, A. (1978) Concepts of a Model for the Comparison of Medical Systems as Cultural Systems, *Social Science and Medicine* 12 (2B), pp. 85-93.

— (1980) *Patients and Healers in the Context of Culture*, Berkeley, University of California Press.

Kleiweg de Zwaan, J.P. (1914) 'Denkbeelden der Inlanders van onzen Indischen Archipel omtrent het Ontstaan van Ziekten', *Onze Kolonien*, 7, pp. 1-40.

— (1931) 'Bijgeloof in den Indischen Archipel inzake Krankzinnigheid', *Tijdschrift Koninklijk Nederlandsch Aardrijkskundig Genootschap*, 48, pp. 609-638.

— (1933) 'Over de Invloed van Hemel – en Natuurverschijnselen op den Gezondheidstoestand van den Mensch: Opvattingen der Inlanders van den Indischen Archipel', *Mens en Maatschappij*, 9, pp. 411-428, 513-526.

Kloppenburg-Versteegh, J. (1934) *Wenken en Raadgevingen betreffende het Gebruik van Indishe Planten, Vruchten, enz.*, Semarang, Van Dorp and Co.

Knight, C.G. (1980) 'Ethnoscience and the African Farmers: Rationale and Strategy', in D. Brokensha, D.M. Warren and O. Werner (ed.) *Indigenous Knowledge Systems and Development*, pp. 203-230, Lanham, MD, University Press of America.

Knowles, P.F. and M.D. Miller (1965) *Safflower*, California Agricultural Experiment Station Extension Service Circular, 532, Davis, CA, University of California.

Kopczynska-Jaworska, B. (1961) 'Das Hirtenwesen in den Polnischen Karpaten', in L. Földe (ed) *Viehzucht und Hirtenleben in Ostmitteleuropa: Ethnographische Studien*, pp. 389-438, Budapest, Akadémiai Kiadó, Verlag der Ungarischen Akademie der Wissenschaften.

Korsching, P.F. and S.S. Sapp (1976) *People and Jobs for Gadsden County.* Gainesville, FL, University of Florida, Centre for Rural Development, Institute of Food and Agricultural Sciences.

Korten, D.C. (ed) (1987) *Community Management: Asian Experience and Perspective*, West Harstford, CT, Kumarian Press.

Koyo, J.P., V. Doulou and J. Sénéchal (ed.) (1989) 'Stage sur les Phytopratiques en Arboriculture Fruitière', *Les Saras*, 10-17 Décembre 1988, République Populaire du Congo/PNUD/UNESCO, Projet des Recherches et de la Planifications du Mayombe PRC/88/003, Rapport 2, Paris, UNESCO.

Kremer, J.N. (1989) *The Formulations of the Bali Model*, Technical Report of the Bali Rice Ecosystem Simulation Model.

Kremer, J.N., S. Lansing, T. Richards and the Project Jefferson Team (1989) *The Bali Notebook (Version 1.0)*, Ecological Simulation Model Software developed by Centre for Scholarly Technology, University of Southern California, Distributed by Kinko's Academic Courseware Exchange.

Kunstadter, P., E.C. Chapman and S. Sabhasri (1978) *Farmers in the Forest*, Honolulu, East West Centre Publications.

Laderman, C. (1984) *Wives and Midwives: Childbirth and Nutrition in Rural Malaysia*, Berkeley, University of California Press.

Lakoff, G. (1987) The Instability of Graded Structure: Implications for the Nature of Concepts, in U. Neisser (ed) *Concepts and Conceptual Development: Ecological and Intellectual Factors in Categorisation* , Cambridge, Cambridge University Press.

Lal, R. (1974) 'Soil Erosion and Shifting Agriculture: Shifting Cultivation and Soil Conservation in Africa', *FAO Soils Bulletin* 24, Rome, FAO.

— (1987) *Tropical Ecology and Physical Edaphology*, New York, John Wiley and Sons.

Lambert, D.H. (1985) *Swamp Rice Farming: The Indigenous Pahang Malay Agricultural System*, Boulder, CO, Westview.

Lampert, R.J. (1967) Horticulture in the New Guinea Highlands – C14 Dating, *Antiquity* 41, pp. 307 *ff.*

Lansing, J.S. (1978) Economic Growth and the Traditional Society: A Cautionary Tale from Bali, *Human Organisation* 37 (4).

— (1983) *The Three Worlds of Bali* , New York, Praeger.

— (1986) Balinese Religion, Mircea Eliade, etc. *Encyclopaedia of Religion*. New York, Macmillan Press.

— (1987) Balinese Water Temples and the Management of Irrigation, *American Anthropologist* 89, pp. 326-341.

Law, D. (1973) *The Concise Herbal Encyclopaedia*, New York, Saint Martin's Press.

Law, R. (1980) *The Horse in the West African History: The role of the Horse in the Societies of Pre-Colonial Africa*, Oxford, Oxford University Press.

Lawrence, E.A (1982) 'Cultural Perspectives on Human-Horse Relationships: The Crow Indians of Montana', Paper presented at the Third International Symposium on Veterinary Epidemiology and Economics, Arlington, Virginia, USA, 6-10 September 1982.

— (1985) The Horse in the Crow Indian History and Culture, Paper presented at the Annual Meeting of the American History Society, Las Vegas, Nevada, USA, July 23, 1985.

— (1988) That by Means of which People Live: Indians and their Horses' Health, *Journal of the West*, 27 (1), pp. 7-15.

Leakey, L.S.B. (1977) *The Southern Kikuyu before 1903* , London, Academic Press.

Lebeau, F. (1986) *Technology Transfer Study: Operation Haute Vallee*, Washington, D.C., Checchi and Co.

Ledesma, A.J. (1982) *Landless Workers and Rice Farmers: Peasant Subclasses under Agrarian Reform in Two Philippine Villages*, Manila, International Rice Research Institute.

Lee, R.P.L. (1989) Perceptions and Uses of Chinese Medicine among the Chinese in Hong Kong, *Culture, Medicine and Psychiatry* 4, pp. 345-375.

Leff, E. (1985) Enthnobotanics and Anthropology as Tools or a Cultural Conservation Strategy, in J.A. McNeely and D. Pitt (ed.) *Culture and Conservation: The Human Dimension in Environmental Planning*, London, Crown Helm.

Lele, U. (1975) *The Design of Rural Development: Lessons from Africa*, Baltimore and London, Johns Hopkins University Press.

Lennon, T.J. (1982) *Raised Fields of Lake Titicaca, Peru: A Pre-Hispanic Water Management,* Ph.D. Dissertation, University of Colorado.

Lent, J.A. (1982) Grassroots Renaissance: Folk Media in the Third World, *Media Asia,* 9 (1), pp. 9-17.

Leparc, J.R.A.J. (1947) *La Medicine Vétérinaire Populaire au Bocage Normand*, Doctoral Thesis, Paris, France, Veterinary Medicine, Faculté de Médicine de Paris.

Leslie, Ch. (ed) (1977) *Asian Medical Systems; A Comparative Study*, Berkeley, University of California Press.

— (1978) 'Theoretical Foundations for the Comparative', Study of Medical Systems, Special Issue, *Social Science and Medicine* 12 (2B).

— (1980) 'Medical Pluralism', Special Issue, *Social Science and Medicine*, 14B (4).

Leslie, Ch. (1988) 'Foreword', in S. van der Geest and S. Reynolds White (ed.) *The Context of Medicines in Developing Countries; Studies in Pharmaceutical Anthropology*, i-xii, Dordrecht, Kluwer Academic Publishers.

Lestari (n.d.) 'Yayasan Pengelolaan Obat Tradisional Indonesia' (The Journal of the Association for the Promotion of Traditional Indonesian Medicine), Special Issue, *Original Jamu from Java*, Soeparto (ed.) Jakarta.

Lévi-Strauss, Cl. (1966) *The Savage Mind*, Chicago, IL, University of Chicago Press, (English translation).

Lewis, I.M. (1961) *A Pastoral Democracy: A Study of Pastoralism and Politics Among the Northern Somali of the Horn of Africa,* London, Oxford University Press.

Lewis, W.H. (ed) *(*1965) *French Speaking Africa*, New York, Walker and Company.

Lightfoot, C. (1987) 'Indigenous Research and On-Farm Trials', *Agricultural Administration and Extension*, 24, pp. 79-89.

Lightfoot, C., O. De Guia, A. Aliman and F. Ocado (1987) *Letting Farmers Decide in On-Farm Research*, Paper for the Workshop on Farmers and Agricultural Research: Complementary Methods held at the Institute of Development Studies, University of Sussex, July 26-31.

— (1988) 'A Participatory Method for Systems-Problem Research: Rehabilitating Marginal Uplands in The Philippines', *Experimental Agriculture*, 24, pp. 301-109.

Lin, W., G. Coffman and J.B. Penn (1980) *U.S. Farm Numbers, Sizes and Structural Dimensions: Projections to Year 2000,* Technical Bulletin 1625, National Economics Division, Economics, Statistics and Cooperatives Service, Washington, D.C., United States Department of Agriculture.

Lindo Revilla, J. (1982) 'Como Curar la Hinchazón', *Minka*, 8 (August), pp. 8.

Lingga, P. (1983) *Resep-Resep Obat Traditsonal*, Jakarta, Penebar Swadaya.

Lionberger, H.F. and P.H. Gwin (1982) *Communication Strategies: A Guide for Agricultural Change Agents*, Danville, IL, Interstate.

Lionberger, H.F., Chii-Jeng Yeh and G.D. Copus (1975) 'Social Change in Communication Structure: Comparative Study of Farmers in Two Communities', *Rural Sociological Society Monograph* 3, Morgantown, WV, West Virginia University for the Rural Sociological Society.

Lira, J.A. (1985) *Medicina Andina: Farmacopea y Ritual*, Cuzco, Peru, Centro de Estudios Rurales Andinos, Bartolomé de las Casas'.

Litsinger, J.A., A.T. Barrion and D. Soekarna (1987) *Upland Rice Insect Pests: Their Ecology, Importance and Control,* IRPS 123, Manila, International Rice Research Institute.

Little, P.D. and D. Brokensha (1987) 'Local Institutions, Tenure and Resource Management in East Africa', in D. Anderson and R. Grove (eds) *Conservation in Africa,* pp. 193-209, Cambridge, Cambridge University Press.

Litzenberger, S. and Ho Tong Lip (1968) 'Utilising *Eupatorium odoratum L.* to Improve Crop Yields in Cambodia', *Agronomy Journal*, 53, pp. 321-324.

Lozano Nathal, L.C. (1988) 'Las Tesis de Licenciatura sobre Plantas Medicinales en la Facultad de Medicina Veterinaria y Zootecnia, UNAM (1916-1987)', in L.L. Nathal and G.L. Buendía, (coords.), *Memorias, Primera Jornada sobre Herbolaria Medicinal en Veterinaria*, pp. 23-33, México DF, Universidad Nacional Autónoma de México, Facultad de Medicina Veterinaria y Zootecnia, Coordinación de Educación Continua.

Lozano Nathal, L.C. and G.L. Buendía (1988) 'Prólogo', in L.L. Nathal and G.L. Buendía, (*coordinators*), *Memorias, Primera Jornada sobre Herbolaria Medicinal en Veterinaria,*.pp. 1-3, México DF, Universidad Nacional Autónoma de México, Facultad de Medicina Veterinaria y Zootecnia, Coordinación de Educación Continua.

Lozano, J. C. and E.R. Terry (1976) 'Cassava Disease and their Control', *Proceedings of the 4th Symposium of the Society for Tropical Root Crops,* Ottawa, Canada, International Development Research Council.

López Buendía, G.L. (1988) 'Aproximación Histórica al Uso de las Plantas

Medicinales en Veterinaria a Través de la Tradición Oral', in L.L. Nathal and G.L. Buendía, (coord.), *Memorias, Primera Jornada sobre Herbolaria Medicinal en Veterinaria*, pp. 8-11, México DF, Universidad Nacional Autónoma de México, Facultad de Medicina Veterinaria y Zootecnia, Coordinación de Educación Continua.

López Buendía, G., L.C.L. Nathal and I.P. de la Aubert (1988) 'Proyecto HERVET, 10 Aspectos Teórico-Práctico para el Desarrollo de una Base de Datos Relacional sobre Plantas Medicinales para Uso en Medcina Veterinaria', in L.L. Nathal and G.L. Buendía, (*coordinators*), *Memorias, Primera Jornada sobre Herbolaria Medicinal en Veterinaria,* pp. 144-155, México DF, Universidad Nacional Autónoma de México, Facultad de Medicina Veterinaria y Zootecnia, Coordinación de Educación Continua.

Lubis, S. (1984) *Resep-Resep Obat Tradisional dalam Ramuan Jawa dan Cina*, Pekalongan, Bahagia.

Lugo, A.E., J.J. Ewel, S.B. Hecht, P.G. Murphy, C. Padoch, M.C. Schmink and D. Stone (eds) (1987) *People and the Tropical Forest,* A Research Report from the United States Man and the Biosphere Program, Washington, D.C., US Department of State.

Lumsden, R.D., R. Garcia-E., J.A. Lewis and G.A. Frias (1987) 'Suppression of Damping-off Caused by *Pythium* spp. in Soil from the Indigenous Mexican Chinampa Agricultural System' *Soil Biology and Biochemistry*, 19, pp. 501-508.

Lusigi, W.J.,(ed) (1984) *Integrated Resource Assessment and Management Plan for Western Marsabit District, Northern Kenya,* Integrated Project in Arid Lands (IPAL), Technical Report A-6, Nairobi, UNESCO.

Lusigi, W.J. (1984) 'The Integrated Project on Arid Lands (IPAL)', Kenya, in P.J. Joss, P.W. Lynch and O.B. Williams (eds) *Rangelands: A Resource Under Siege: Proceedings 2nd International Rangeland Congress,* pp. 338-349, Adelaide, Australia.

Machbub, B., H.F. Ludwig and G. Gunaratnam (1988) 'Environmental Impact from Agrochemicals in Bali (Indonesia)', *Environmental Monitoring and Assessment,* 11, pp. 1-23.

Macfarlane, A.D.J. (1976) *Resources and Population of the Gurungs of Nepal*, Cambridge, U.K., Cambridge University Press.

MacKill, D.J. (1987) *Trip Report: Kampuchea, November 26-December 3, 1987,* IRRI.

MacPherson, S. (1982) *Social Policy in the Third World*, Brighton, Wheatsleaf.

Macuch, P. (1976) Statement of the WHO, in H. Knotig (ed) *Proceedings of the International Meeting on Human Ecology*, Saphporin, Switzerland, Georgi Publishing Company.

Maddin, R., J.D. Muhly and T.S. Wheeler (1977) 'How the Iron Age Began', *Scientific American*, 237 (4), pp. 122-131.

Mahat, T.B.S., D.M. Griffin and K.R. Shepherd (1986-7a) Human Impact on Some Forests of the Middle Hills of Nepal, Forestry in the Context of the Traditional Resources of the State, *Mountain Research and Development,* 6 (3), pp. 223-232.

— (1986-7b) 'Some Major Human Impacts Before 1950 and the Forests of Sindhi Palchok and Kabhre Palanchok', *Mountain Research and Development,* 6 (4), pp. 225-234.

— (1986-7c) 'Forests in the Subsistence Economy of Sindhu Palchok and Kabhre Palanchock', *Mountain Research and Development,* 7 (1), pp. 53-70.

— (1986-7d) 'A Detailed Survey of Southeast Sindhu Palchok and North-east Kabhre Palanchok', *Mountain Research and Development,* 7 (2), pp. 111-134.

Makina, J.C. (1981) *Some Traditional Wildlife Conservation Practices and Their Role in the Planning of Conservation Education Programmes Using Mass Media with Special Emphasis on Radio and Television*, Harare, Zimbabwe, Department of Adult Education, University of Zimbabwe.

Maliki, A.B. (1981) *Ngaynaaka: Herding according to the WoDaaBe*, Rapport preliminaire—Discussion paper 2, Tahua, Niger, Ministry of Rural Development, Niger Range and Livestock Project.

Maliki, A.B. *et al.* (1984) 'The WoDaaBe', in J.J. Swift (ed.) *Pastoral Development in Central Niger: Report of the Niger Range and Livestock Project*, pp. 255-530, Niamey, USAID/Ministry of Rural Development.

Malla, Y.B. and R.J. Fisher (1987) 'Planting Trees on Private Farmland in Nepal: The Equity Aspect' Paper prepared for the Winrock International-F/FRED Workshop *Multipurpose Trees for Small Farm Use*, Pattaya, Thailand, November 1-5.

Malvestuto, S.P. and Earl K. Meredith (1986a) 'Assessment of the Niger River Fishery in Niger (1983-1985), With Implications for Management', Auburn University (unpublished report).

— (1986b) 'Rapport Final: Résultats de lé Valuation de la Pêcherie du Fleuve Niger au Niger', Enquête d'Evaluation des Captures (EEC), Auburn University (unpublished report).

Manandhar, P.K. (1982) 'Introduction to Policy, Legislation and Programmes of Community Forestry Development in Nepal', *CFDP Field Document* 19, Kathmandu, Community Forestry Development.

Manderson, L. (1981) 'Traditional Food Classifications and Humoral Medical Theory in Peninsular Malaysia', *Ecology of Food and Nutrition*, 11, pp. 81-93.

Marchand, A. (1984) 'Médecine Vétérinarie Populaire et Maladies Parasitaires', *Ethnozootechnie*, 34, pp. 19-23, Special issue entitled La Médecine Vétérinaire Populaire.

Mares, R.G. (1951) 'A Note on the Somali Method of Vaccination against Contagious Bovine Pleuropneumonia', *The Veterinary Record*, 63 (9), pp. 166.

— (1954a) 'Animal Husbandry, Animal Industry and Animal Disease in the Somaliland Protectorate', *The British Veterinary Journal*, 110 (10), pp. 411-423.

— (1954b) 'Animal Husbandry, Animal Industry and Animal Disease in the Somaliland Protectorate. Part II' *The British Veterinary Journal*, 110 (11), pp. 470-481.

Marinow, W. (1961) 'Die Schafzucht der Nomadisierenden Karaktschanen in Bulgarien, in L. Földe' (ed) *Viehzucht und Hirtenleben in Ostmitteleuropa: Ethnographische Studien*, pp. 147-196, Budapest, Akadémiai Kiadó, Verlag der Ungarischen Akademie der Wissenschaften, Budapest.

Marks, S.A. (1984) *The Imperial Lion: Human Dimensions in Wildlife Management in Central Africa,* Boulder,CO, Westview Press.

Marten, G.G. (ed) (1986) *Traditional Agriculture in Southeast Asia,* Boulder, CO, Westview Press.

Maro, P.S. (1988) 'Agricultural Land Management under Population Pressure: The Kilimanjaro Experience, Tanzania', *Mount. Res. Dev.,* 8, pp. 273-282.

Marten, G.G. and P. Vityakon (1986) 'Soil Management in Traditional Agriculture', in G.G. Marten (ed) *Traditional Agriculture in South-east Asia*, Boulder, CO, Westview Press.

Marten, G. G. (ed) (1986) *Traditional Agriculture in South-east Asia*, Boulder, CO, Westview Press.

Martin, P.S. (1984) 'Prehistoric Overkill: The Global Model', in P.S. Martin and R.G. Klein (eds) *Quaternary Extinctions: A Prehistoric Revolution*, pp. 354-403, University of Arizona Press.

Martin, R.B. (1986) *Communal Areas Management Programme for Indigenous Resources (CAMPFIRE),* Branch of Terrestrial Ecology, Working document 1/86, Department of National Parks and Wildlife Management.

Martínez A. and A. Miguel (1988) 'Investigaciones Multidisciplinarias en la

Sierra Norte de Puebla: Aspectos Metodológicos', in L.L. Nathal and G.L. Buendía, (coords.), *Memorias, Primera Jornada sobre Herbolaria Medicinal en Veterinaria,* pp. 156-163, México DF, Universidad Nacional Autónoma de México, Facultad de Medicina Veterinaria y Zootecnia, Coordinación de Educación Continua.

Marucchi, J. (1950) *Psychologie Paysanne: Empirisme et Médecine Vétérinaire,* Doctoral Thesis, Alfort, France, École Nationale Vétérinaire d'Alfort, France.

Marx, W. (1984) 'Traditionelle Tieraerztliche Heilmethoden unter besonderer Beruecksichtigung der Kauterization in Somalia', *Giessener Beitraege zur Entwicklungsforschung: Beitraege der Klinischen Veterinaermedizin zur Verbesserung der tierischen Erzeugung in den Tropen,* Reihe I, Band 10, pp. 111-116, Giessen, West Germany, Wissenschaftliches Zentrum Tropeninstitut, Justus Liebig Universitaet.

Marx, W. and D. Wiegand (1987) 'Limits of Traditional Veterinary Medicine in Somalia- The Example of Chlamydiosis and Q-Fever', *Animal Research and Development,* 26, pp. 29-34, Tuebingen, West Germany, Institute for Scientific Cooperation.

Matheron, M.E. and S.M. Mircetich (1985) 'Influence of Flooding Duration on Development of Phytophthora Root and Crown Rot of Juglans Jinsii and Paradox Walnut Rootstocks', *Phytopathology,* 75, pp. 973-976.

Mathewson, K. (1984) *Irrigation Horticulture in Highland Guatemala,* Boulder, CO, Westview Press.

Mathias-Mundy, E. (1989) 'Of Herbs and Healers: Traditional Veterinary Medicine and Sustainable Development', *ILEIA Newsletter,* 3 (October), pp. 20-22.

Mathias-Mundy, E. and C.M. McCorkle (1989) *Ethnoveterinary Medicine: An Annotated Bibliography,* Bibliographies in Technology and Social Change 6, Ames, IA, Iowa State University.

Maurya, D M. (1990) 'The Innovative Approach of Indian Farmers', in R. Chambers, A. Pacey and L. Thrupp (eds) *Farmers First: Farmer Innovation and Agricultural Research,* 9-13, London, Intermediate Technology Publication.

Maydell, H.J. von (1986) *Trees and Shrubs of the Sahel, Their Characteristics and Uses,* Rossdorf, Germany, Schriftenreihe der GTZ 196, TZ Verlagsgesellschaft.

Mayer, E. (1979) *Land-Use in the Andes: Ecology and Agriculture in the Mantaro Valley of Peru with Special References to Potatoes,* Lima, Peru, International Potato Centre, Social Science Unit.

— (1980) *Land Use in the Andes,* Lima, Peru, International Potato Centre.

Málaga, C.E. (1988) *Herbas Medicinales Peruanas: Plantas que Curan,* Lima, Peru, Editorial Litográfica La Confianza for Editorial Mercurio.

McCabe, J.T. (1983) 'Land Use Among the Pastoral Turkana', *Rural Africana,* 15-16, pp. 109-126.

McCall, M.K. (1987) 'Indigenous Knowledge Systems as the Basis for Participation: East African Potentials', *Working Paper 36,* Enschede, University of Twenty, Technology and Development Group.

— (1988) 'Indigenous Technical Knowledge in Farming Systems and Rural Technology. A Bibliography on Eastern Africa', *Working Paper 38,* Enschede, University of Twente, Technology and Development Group.

McCalla, T.M. and D.L. Plucknett (1981) 'Collecting, Transporting and Processing Organic Fertilisers', in D.L. Plucknett and H.L. Beemer, Jr. (eds) *Vegetable Farming Systems in China,* pp. 19-37, Boulder, CO, Westview Press.

McCamant, K.A. (1986) *The Organisation of Agricultural Production in Coporaque, Peru,* MA Thesis, Berkeley, University of California, Centre for Latin American Studies.

McConnell, D.J. and K.A.E. Dharmapala (1978) *The Forest Garden Farms of Kandy. In Farm Management Report 7, Economic Structure of Kandyan Forest Garden Farms*, Sri Lanka, FAO Agricultural Diversification Project, Peradeniya.

McCorkle, C.M. (1982) *Management of Animal Health and Disease in an Indigenous Andean Community*, Sociology Technical Report Series 4, Columbia, USA., University of Missouri-Columbia, Department of Rural Sociology, Small Ruminant Collaborative Research Support Program.

— (1983) *Meat and Potatoes: Animal Management and the Agropastoral Dialectic in an Indigenous Andean Community, with Implications for Development*, Ph.D. Dissertation, Stanford, CA, Stanford University, Department of Anthropology.

— (1986) 'An Introduction to Ethnoveterinary Research and Development', *Journal of Ethnobiology*, 6 (1), pp. 129-149.

— (1988) *Manejo de la Sanidad de Rumiantes Menores en una Comunidad Indígena Andina*, Lima, Peru, Editorial Hipatia for the Comisión de Coordinación de Tecnología Andina.

— (1989a) *Personal communication*, Columbia, MO, University of Missouri-Columbia, Department of Rural Sociology.

— (1989b) 'Veterinary Anthropology', *Human Organization*, 48 (2), pp. 156-162.

—(1989c) 'Veterinary Anthropology on the Small Ruminant CRSP/Peru', in C.M. McCorkle (ed) *The Social Sciences in International Agricultural Research: Lessons from the CRSPs*, Boulder, CO, Lynne Rienner Publishers.

— (1989d) 'Re-stating the Obvious: The Importance of Local Knowledge for Agricultural Research and Development, *Agriculture and Human Values*, 6 (3).

McCorkle, C.M., R.H. Brandstetter and G.D. McClure (1988) *A Case Study on Farmer Innovations and Communication in Niger*, Washington, D.C., Communication for Technology Transfer in Agriculture Project (AID/S&T 936-5826), Academy for Educational Development.

McDermott, J. and M.D. Ngor (1983) *Grazing Management Strategies Among the Tuic, Nyarraweng and Ghol Dinka of Kongor Rural Council: Prospects for Development*, Draft Report for Kongor Integrated Rural Development Project, Rome, FAO.

McDowell, R. (1986) *An Animal Science Perspective on Crop Breeding and Selection Programmes for Warm Climates*, Cornell, Ithaca, NY, Department of Animal Science.

McEwen, F.L. (1978) 'Food Production – The Challenge of Pesticides', *BioScience*, 28, pp. 773-777.

McGlinchey, C. (1986) *The Last of the Name*, Belfast, Northern Ireland, Blackstaff Press.

McKinion, J.M. and H.E. Lemmon (1985) 'Expert Systems for Agriculture', *Computers and Electronics in Agriculture*, 1, pp. 31-40.

McNeely, J.A. (1988) *Economics and Biological Diversity: Developing and Using Economic Incentives to Conserve Biological Diversity*, Gland, IUCN.

McNeely, J.A. and K.R. Millers (ed.) (1984) *National Parks, Conservation and Development: The Role of Protected Areas in Sustaining Society*, Washington D.C., Smithsonian Institution Press.

McNeely, J.A. and D. Pitt (ed.) (1984) *Culture and Conservation: The Human Division in Environmental Planning*, London, Croom Helm.

McNeely, J.A. and J.W. Thorsell (ed.) (1985) *People and Protected Areas in the Hindukush-Himalay*, Kathmandu, ICIMOD.

McNeely, J.A. and P.S. Wachtel (1988) *Soul of the Tiger*, New York, Doubleday.

Meehan, P. (1980) 'Science, Ethnoscience and Agricultural Knowledge-

Utilisation', in D. Brokensha, D.M. Warren and O. Werner (eds) *Indigenous Knowledge Systems and Development*, pp. 383-392, Lanham, MD, University Press of America.

Meillassoux, Cl. (1965) 'The Guro-Peripheral Markets Between the Forest and the Sudan', in P. Bohannan and G. Dalton (eds) *Markets in Africa: Eight Subsistence Economies in Transition,* pp. 67-92, Garden City, NY, Anchor Books.

Merker, M. (1910) *Die Maasai,* (second edition), Ethnographische Monographie eines Ostafrikanischen Semitenvolkes, Berlin.

Merwe, N.J. van der and D.H. Avery (1982) 'Pathways to Steel: Three Different Methods of Making Steel from Iron were Developed by Ancient Peoples of the Mediterranean, China and Africa', *American Scientist,* 70, pp. 146-155.

Messerschmidt, D.A. (1981) 'Hogar and Other Traditional Forms of Cooperation in Nepal: Significance for Development', *Human Organisation,* 40, pp. 40-47.

— (1981-4) 'RCUP Social Science Fieldtrip Report', Kathmandu, Resource Conservation and Utilisation Project (unpublished mimeo).

— (1986) 'People and Resource Management Systems of the Upper Kali Gandaki', *Common Proper Management,* pp. 455-480, Washington, D.C., National Academy Press.

— (1987) 'Conservation and Society in Nepal: Traditional Forest Management and Innovative Development', in P.D. Little and M.M. Horowitz, with A.E. Nyerges (eds) *Lands at Risk in the Third World: Local-Level Perspectives,* pp. 373-397, Boulder, CO, Westview Press.

— (1988) 'Success in Small Farmer Development; Paper making at Pang and Nanglibang, Nepal', *World Development,* 16 (6), pp. 733-750.

Metalié, G. (1984) 'Aperçu des Principes de la Médecine Vétérinaire Traditionnnelle en Chine', *Ethnozootechnie,* 34, pp. 43-50, Special issue entitled La Médecine Vétérinaire Populaire.

Michon, G. (1985) *De l'Homme de la Forêt au Paysan de l'Arbre – Agroforesterie Indonesienne,* Thèse, 273, Montpellier, U.S.T.L.

Middleton, J. and G. Kershaw (1972) *The Kikuyu and Kamba of Kenya,* London, International African Institute.

Millour, C. (1984) 'Les Saints Guérisseurs du Bétail en Bretagne', *Ethnozootechnie,* 34, pp. 53-58, Special issue entitled La Médecine Vétérinaire Populaire.

Ministry of Commerce, Industry and Transportation, Price Analysis and Marketing Division (n.d.) *Price List of Locally Produced Agricultural Commodities for Counties and Territories Excluding the Monrovia Area* (probably produced 1981), Gbarnga, Bond County, Liberia, Ministry of Commerce, Industry and Transportation.

Minja, M.M.J. (1984) 'Utilization of Medical Plants in Veterinary Practice', *Proceedings of the 2nd. Tanzania Veterinary Association Scientific Conference* II, pp. 257-263, Arusha, Tanzania, 4th-6th December, 1984, Medicine, Morogoro, Tanzania, Sokoine University, Faculty of Veterinary, Tanzania Veterinary Association.

Miracle, M.P. (1965) 'The Copperbelt: Trading and Marketing', in P. Bohannan and G. Dalton (ed.) *Markets in Africa: Eight Subsistence Economies in Transition,* pp. 285-341, Garden City, NY, Anchor Books.

— (1967) *Agriculture in the Congo Basin,* Madison, University of Wisconsin Press.

Mittleider, J.R. (1986) *Grow-bed Gardening,* Santa Barbara, CA, Woodbridge Press.

Moddie, A.D. (1981) 'Himalayan Environment', in J.S. Lall (ed.), *The Himalaya: Aspects of Change,* pp. 341-350, Bombay, Oxford University Press.

Mohammed, A.A. and M. Tiffen (1986) 'Water Management in the Gezira Scheme, Sudan: A Survey of Farmer's Attitudes on Two Minor Canals', *Report OD* 76, Wallingford, Hydraulics Research.

Moles, J.A. and H. Rukman Wagachchi (1989) *Sustainable Alternatives to Small Grain Carbohydrates and Sugar Cane: A Lesson in Agricultural Understanding*, Paper presented at the Annual Meeting of the Amerian Association for the Advancement of Science, San Francisco, CA, January 1989.

Mollison, B. (1988) *Permaculture: A Designers Manual,* Tyalgum, NSW, Australia, Tagari Publications

Molnar, A. (1981a) *The Kham Magar Women of Thabang. The Status of Women in Nepal* II (2), Kathmandu, Nepal, Tribhuvan University, Centre for Economic Development and Administration.

— (1981b) *The Dynamics of Traditional Systems of Forest Management in Nepal: Implications for the Community Forestry Development and Training Project*, Report to the World Bank/International Finance Corporation, Washington, D.C., The World Bank (unpublished report).

Monod, T. (1975) 'Introduction', in T. Monod (ed.) *Pastoralism in Tropical Africa*, pp. 8-98, London, Oxford University Press.

Moody, R. (ed) (1988) *The Indigenous Voices,* London, Zed Press.

Moon, T., P.B. Mann and J.H. Otto (1956) *Modern Biology*, New York, Henry Holt and Company.

Moore, G.T. and R.G. Golledge (eds) (1976) *Environmental Knowing: Theories, Research and Methods,* Stroudsburg, PA, Dowden, Hutchinson and Ross, Inc.

Morales, H.L. (1984) 'Chinampas and Integrated Farms: Learning from the Rural Traditional Experience', in F. di Castri, F.W.G. Baker, M. Hadley (ed.) *Ecology in Practice,* II, *The Social Response,* pp. 188-195, Paris, UNESCO/Dublin, Tycooly.

Moran, E.F. (1979) *Human Adaptability: An Introduction to Ecological Anthropology,* North Scituate, MA, Duxbury.

— (ed) (1984) *The Ecosystem Concept in Anthropology,* Epping, Bowker.

Morgenthau, R.S. (1979) 'Strangers, Nationals and Multinationals in Contemporary Africa', in W.A. Schack and E.P. Skinner (eds) *Strangers in African Societies,* pp. 105-120, Berkeley, University of California Press.

Moris, J.R. (1983)*What Do We Know about African Agricultural Development? The Role of Extension Performance Reanalysed,* Background Paper, Washington, D.C., USAID Bureau of Science and Technology.

— (1988) 'Options for Science based Interventions in African Agriculture', *Discussion Paper* 27, London, Agricultural Administration (Research and Extension) Network – AAU/ODI.

Morren Jr., G.E.B. (1986) *The Miyanmin: Human Ecology of a Papua New Guinea Society*, Ann Arbor, Michigan, UMI Research Press.

Morvan, H. and J. Vercruysse (1978) 'Vocabulaire des Maladies du Bétail en Langue Fulfuldé chez les Mbororo de l'Empire Centrafricain', *Journal d'Agriculture Tropicale et de Botanique Appliquée,* 25 (2), pp. 111-118.

Moscoso Castilla, M.(1953/1942) *Secretos Medicinales de la Flora Peruana y Guía de la Maternidad,* (second edition), Cuzco, Peru, Tipografía Americana.

Moseley, A. (1989) 'Rural Entrepreneurship: One Key to Rural Revitalisation', *American Journal of Agricultural Economics,* 71 (5), pp. 1305-1314.

Mosende, L.C. (1981) *Sociocultural Correlates of the Maternal Teaching Styles of Selected Filipino Women,* Ph.D. Dissertation. Ann Arbor, University of Michigan (unpublished).

Moser, C. (1989) 'Gender Planning in the Third World: Meeting Practical and Strategic Gender Ne(eds)", *World Development,* 17 (11).

Mowlana, H. (1975) 'Technology versus Tradition: Communication in the Iranian Revolution', *Journal of Communication*, 29 (3), pp. 107-112.

Mueller, S.C. and G.W. Fick (1987) 'Response of Susceptible and Resistant Alfalfa Cultivars to Phytophthora Root Rot in the Absence of Measurable Flooding Damage, *Agronomy Journal*, 79, pp. 210-204.

Muhly, J.D. (1982) 'How Iron Technology Changed the Ancient World', *Biblical Archaeology Review*, 8 (6), pp. 41-54 and replies to it in *Biblical Archaeology Review*, 9 (3), pp. 23-24.

Mulder, N. (1983) *Mysticism and Everyday Life in Contemporary Java: Cultural Persistence and Change*, Singapore, Singapore Univerity Press.

Müller, J. (1980a) *Liquidation or Consolidation of Indigenous Technology: A Study of the Changing Conditions of Production of Village Blacksmiths in Tanzania*, Development Research Series 1, Aalborg, Denmark, Aalborg University Press.

— (1980b) 'The Persistent Blacksmiths, Tanzania', [Summary of Müller (1980a)], in R.J. Mitchell (ed) *Experiences in Appropriate Technology*, pp. 11-20, Ottawa, Canada, The Canadian Hunger Foundation.

Mungai, D.N., C.L. Coulson and C.J. Stigter (1989) *An Integrated Quantification Approach of Agroforestry Interventions: A Kenyan Alley Cropping Case Study*, Paper presented at the 6th ISCO Conference, Addis Ababa, International Soil Conservation Organisation.

Muñoz, E. (1986) 'Producción de Maiz, Frijol, y Calabaza en un Sistema Hidráulico de Chinampa, [Maize, Bean and Squash Production in a Chinampa Irrigation System]', *Turrialba*, 36, pp. 369-373.

Murphy, J. (1983) 'Strengthening the Agricultural Research Capacity of the Underdeveloped Countries: Lessons from A.I.D. Experience', A.I.D. Program Evaluation Report 10, September 1983.

Nabhan, G.P., D. House, L. Hernandez, W. Hodgson and S.A. Humberto (1990) 'Conservation and Use of Rare Wild Plants by Traditional Cultures of the U.S./Mexico Border States', in M.O. Oldfield and J.B. Alcorn (ed.) *Biodiversity: Traditional Management and Development of Biological Resources*, Boulder, CO, Westview Press.

Nair, K. (1983) *Transforming Traditionally: Land and Labour Use in Agriculture in Asia and Africa, Perspectives on Asian and African Development*, New Delhi, India, Allied Publications Priv. Ltd.

Nanayakara, V.R. (1981) *Administration Report of the Conservator of Forests, Sri Lanka, 1980*, Colombo, Ministry of Lands and Land Development, Government of Sri Lanka.

Natawidjaja, P.S. (1982) *Apotek Hijau dan Kesehatan Kita*, Jakarta, Pustaka Dian.

National Academy of Science (NAS) (1986) *Common Property Resources Management*, Washington, D.C., National Academy Press.

National Census and Statistics Office (NCSO) (1980) *Census of Population: Preliminary Report*, Manila, National Census and Statistics Office.

National Research Council (1989) *Alternative Agriculture*, Washington, D.C., National Academy of Science.

Nations, J.D. and D.I. Kromer (1983) 'Central America's Tropical Rain Forests: Positive Steps for Survival', *Ambio*, 12 (5), pp. 232-238.

Nawari and I. Ardi (1979) 'Intensive Egg Production in Alabio, South Kalimantan', *Proceedings of the Second Poultry Science and Industry Seminar*, Bogor.

Nazhat, S.M and C.M. Coughenour (1987) *The Communication of Agricultural Information in Sudanese Villages*, Report 5, Lexington, KY, University of Kentucky, Department of Sociology, International Sorghum and Millet Collaborative Research Support Program.

NCDBA (1981) *National Commission for Development of Backward Areas*

Report on Development of Drought Prone Area, Planning commission, New Delhi.

Needham, J. and Lu Gwei-Djen (1969) 'Chinese Medicine', in F.N.L. Poynter (ed.) 'Proceedings of a Historical Symposium organised jointly by the Wellcome Institute of the History of Medicine, London, and the Wenner-Gren Foundation for Anthropological Research, New York', London, Wellcome Institute of the History of Medicine.

Nepal, H.M.C. of (1988) *Forestry Master Plan of 1988,* Kathmandu, Ministry of Forests and Soil Conservation.

Ngwa, A.T. and J. Hardouin (1989) 'Traditional Weaning Practices in the Semi-Arid zone of Mali', *African Small Ruminant Research and Development,* Proceedings of a Conference held at Bamenda, Cameroon, January 1989, Addis Ababa, Ethiopia, International Livestock Centre for Africa (ILCA).

Niamir, M. (1982) *Report on Animal Husbandry Among the Ngok Dinka of the Sudan: Integrated Rural Development Project, Abyei, South Kordofan, Sudan,* Cambridge, Harvard University, HIID Rural Development Studies.

— (1990) *Local Knowledge and Systems of Natural Resource Management in Arid and Semi-Arid Africa,* Rome, Italy, The Community Forestry Unit, FODP, FAO.

Niang, A. (1987) *Contribution a l'Étude de la Pharmacopée Traditionelle Mauritaniénne,* Thesis, Sidi Thabet, Tunisia, Ecole Nationale de Médecine Vétérinaire.

Nichols, S. (1982) *The Fragile Mountain,* (A film), Franklin Lakes, NJ, Nichols Productions Ltd.

Nield, R.S. (1985) *Fuelwood and Fooder – Problems and Policy,* A Working Paper, Kathmandu, Water and Energy Commissions Secretariat, His Majesty's Government of Nepal.

Niehof, A. (1985) 'Women and Fertility in Madura', Ph.D. Dissertation, Leiden, Leiden University.

Nilsson, N.J. (1980) *Principles of Artificial Intelligence,* Palo Alto, Tioga Publishing Company.

Nor, S. (1989) *The Potential of Minor Forest Products,* Kepong, Kuala Lumpur, Malaysia, Forest Research Institute.

Norem-Huisinga, R. (1983) *The Integration of a Family Systems' Perspective into Farming Systems Projects,* Proceedings of Family Systems and Farming Systems Conference, Blackburg, VA, Virginia Polytechnic Institute and State University.

Norgaard, R. (1980-81) *Post-harvest Technology. Aphids and Tuber Moth,* Thrust VIII Technical Report, Lima, Peru, International Potato Centre.

— (1984) 'Traditional Agricultural Knowledge: Past Performance, Future Prospects and Institutional Implications', *American Journal of Agricultural Economics,* 66, pp. 874-878.

Norman, D.W. (1980) 'Farming Systems Approach: Relevance for the Small Farmer', *MSU Rural Development Paper 5,* East Lansing, Michigan State University.

Noronha, R. and F.J. Lethem (1983) *Traditional Land Tenure and Land Use Systems in the Design of Agricultural Project,* Washington, D.C, World Bank Staff Working Paper 561 .

Norton, G.A. (1976) 'Analysis of Decision Making in Crop Protection', *Agroecosystems,* (1), pp. 27-44.

Novikoff, G. (1976) 'Traditional Grazing Practices and their Adaptation to Modern Conditions in Tunisia and the Sahelian Countries', *Ecol. Bull. (Stockholm),* 24, pp. 55-69.

Nuwanyakpa, M. (1989) Letter of 13 September to Evelyn Mathias-Mundy concerning Heifer Project International Activities in Cameroon (unpublished).

Nwude, N. and M.A. Ibrahim (1980) 'Plants used in Traditional Veterinary Medical Practice in Nigeria', *Journal of Veterinary Pharmacology and Therapeutics*, 3, pp. 261-273.

Nyoka, G.C. (1983) 'Potentials for No-Tillage Crop Production in Sierra Leone', in R. Lal, P.A. Sanchez and R.W. Cummings, Jr. (ed.) *Land Clearing and Development in the Tropics*, pp. 66-72, Rotterdam, Balkema.

Oasa, E.K. and B.H. Junnings (1983) 'Science and Authority in International Agricultural Research', *Bulletin of Concerned Asian Scholars*, pp. 30-41.

Oba, G. (1985) 'Local Participation in Guiding Extension Programs: A Practical Proposal', *Nomadic Peoples*, 18, pp. 27-45.

Ochse, J.J. (1961) *Tropical and Subtropical Agriculture*, New York, Macmillan Press.

Odell, M.J. (1982) 'Local Institutions and Management of Communal Resources: Lessons from Africa and Asia', *Pastoral Network Paper* 14e, London, ODI.

Odum, E.P. (1953) *Fundamentals of Ecology,* Philadelphia, WB, Saunders and Co.

Ohta, I. (1987) 'Livestock Individual Identification among the Turkana: The Animal Classification and Naming in the Pastoral Livestock Management', *African Study Monographs*, 8 (1), pp. 1-69.

— (1984) 'Symptoms are Classified into Diagnostic Categories: Turkana's View of Livestock Diseases', *African Study Monographs* , Supplementary Issue 3, pp. 71-93.

Okafor, J.C. and E.C.M. Fernández (1987) 'Compound Farms in South-eastern Nigeria: A Predominant Agroforestry Home Garden System with Crops and Small Livestock', *Agroforestry Systems*, 5, pp. 153-168.

Okigbo, B.N. and D.J. Greenland (1976) 'Intercropping Systems in Tropical Africa', in M. Stelly (ed.) *Multiple Cropping*, Special Publication 27, Madison, WI, American Society of Agronomy

O'Kting'ati, A. (1984) *An Analysis of the Economics of Agroforestry in Kilimanjaro*, Ph.D. Thesis, Morogoro, Tanzania, Sokoine University of Agriculture (unpublished).

Oldfield, M.L. and J.B. Alcorn (1987) 'Conservation of Traditional Agroecosystems', *BioScience*, 37, pp. 199-208.

Oldfield, M.L. (1989) *The Value of Conserving Genetic Resources*, New York, Sinauer.

Oliveros, B., J.C. Lozano and R.H. Booth (1974) 'A Phytophthora Root Rot of Cassava in Colombia', *Plant Disease Reporter*, 58, pp. 703-705.

Ollier, C.D., D.P. Drover and M. Godelier (1971) 'Soil Knowledge Amongst the Baruya of Wonerara, New Guinea', *Oceania*, 42 (1), pp. 33-41.

Olofson, H. (1983) Indigenous Agroforestry Systems, *Philippine Quarterly of Culture and Society* 11, pp. 149-174.

Orlove, B.S. (1980) 'Ecological Anthropology', *Annual Review of Anthropology*, 9, pp. 235-273.

Ortiz, S.D. (1979) 'The Effect of Risk Aversion Strategies on Subsistence and Cash Crop Decisions', in J. Roumasset (ed.) *Rice and Risk: Decision Making Among Low-Income Farmers*, Amsterdam/New York, Elsevier Publishing Company, Agricultural Development Council.

— (1980) 'Forecasts, Decisions and the Farmer's Response to Uncertain Environments', in P. Barlett (ed) *Agricultural Decision Making: Anthropological Contributions to Rural Development*, pp. 177-202, New York, Academic Press.

Ossenbruggen, F.D.E. van (1911) 'Eigenaardige Gebruiken bij Pokken Epidemieën in den Indischen Archipel', *Bijdragen tot Taal-, Land- en Volkenkunde*, 65, pp. 53-88.

OTA, Office of Technology Assessment (1984) 'Africa Tomorrow: Issues in

Technology, Agriculture and U.S. Foreign Aid: A Technical Memorandum', *OTA-TM-F-31*. Washington, D.C., U.S. Congress.

Padoch, C., J. Chota Inuma, W. de Jong and J. Unruh (1985) 'Amazonian Agroforestry: A Market-Oriented System in Peru', *Agroforestry Systems,* 3, pp. 47-58.

Pagezy, K. (1988) 'Coping with Uncertainty in Food Supply Among the Oto and the Twa Living in the Equatorial Forest Near Lake Tumba (Zaire)', in I. de Garine, I. and G.A. Harrison (eds) *Coping with Uncertainty in Food Supply,* pp. 175-209, Oxford, Oxford University Press.

Painter, T. (1986) 'In Search of the Peasant Connection: Spontaneous Cooperation Introduced Cooperatives and Agricultural Development in South-western Niger', in M. Horowitz and T. Painter (eds) *Anthropology and Rural Development in West Africa,* pp. 197-219, Denver, CO, Westview Press.

Palacios Ríos, F. (1985) 'Tecnología del Pastoreo', in H. Lechtman and A.M. Soldi (ed.) *La Tecnología en el Mundo Andino: Runakunap Kawsayninkupaq Rurasqankunaqa Tomo I: Subsistencia y Mensuración,* pp. 217-232, México DF, Imprenta Universitaria de la Universidad Nacional Autónoma de México.

— (1988) 'Tecnología del Manejo de Pastizales y Rebaños', in J.F. Ochoa (ed.) *Llamichos y Paqocheros: Pastores de llamas y Alpacas,* pp. 87-100, Cuzco, Peru, Editorial Universitaria UNSAAC for the Centro de Estudios Andinos Cuzco.

Pandey, Shanta (1983) *Social Science Fieldtrip Reports,* Kathmandu, Resource Conservation and Utilisation Project.

Parmar, S. (1975) *Traditional Folk Media in India,* New Delhi, Geka Books.

Parsons, J.J. and W.M.Denevan (1967) 'Pre-Colombian Ridged Fields', *Scientific American,* 217 (1), pp. 93-100.

Pearson, G. (1989) 'Respect for Nature Among Forest People', *BOS (Bosbouw Ontwikkelings Samenwerking),* 18 (1), pp. 11-27.

Pei, Sheng-ji (1985) 'Some Effects of the Dai People's Cultural Beliefs and Practices upon the Plant Environment of Xishuanganna, Yunnan Province, South-west China', in K.L. Hutterer, A.T. Rambo and G. Lovelance (eds) *Cultural Values and Human Ecology in South-east Asia,* pp. 321-339, Michigan Papers on South-east Asia 27, Ann Arbor, Michigan, University of Michigan, Centre for South and South-east Asian Studies.

Pelissier, P. and S. Diarra (1978) 'Traditional Strategies, Modern Decision-Making and Management of Natural Resources in Sudan, Africa', *Man and the Biosphere Technical Notes,* pp. 35-36.

Pelinck, E. and J.G. Campbell (1984) 'Management of Forest Resources in the Hills of Nepal', Paper for the *Franco-Nepalese Seminar on Ecology and Development,* Kathmandu, Community Forestry Development Project.

Pembinaan Kesejahteraan Keluarga (PKK) (1984) Departemen Dalam 1984 Negeri Republik Indonesia, Direktorat Jenderal Pembangunan Desa, Jakarta.

Peña Bellido, L.B. (1975) *La Agropecuaria Tradicional en la Provincia de Chumbivilcas – Cusco,* Thesis, Cusco, Peru, Universidad San Antonio Abad del Cusco, Department of Agronomy.

Peña Haaz, N., E.A.A. Angulo and H.S. López (1988) 'Evaluación Comparativa del Efecto Nematodicida del Ajo (*Allium sativa*), sus Extractos Liposoluble e Hidrosoluble y el Tartrato de Amonio y Potasio en Carpa (*Cyprinus carpio*)', in L.L. Nathal and G.L. Buendía (coords.) *Memorias: Primera Jornada sobre Herbolaria Medicinal en Veterinaria,* pp. 124-129, México DF, Universidad Nacional Autónoma de México, Facultad de Medicina Veterinaria y Zootecnia, Coordinación de Educación Continua.

Penkala, D. (1980) '"Hot" and "Cold" Classification in the Traditional Medicine of Afghanistan', *Ethnomedicine,* 6, pp. 201-228.

Perera, N.P. (1969) 'The Ecological Status of the Montane Grasslands (Patanas) of Ceylon', *Ceylon Forester,* 11 (1/2), pp. 27-51.

Perry, B.D., B. Mwanaumo, H.F. Schels, E. Eicher and M.R. Zaman (1984) 'A Study of Health and Productivity of Traditionally managed Cattle in Zambia', *Preventive Medicine,* 2, pp. 633-653.

Peters, C.M. and E. Pardo-Tejedo (1982) '*Brosimum alicastrum* (Moraceae): Uses and Potential in Mexico', *Economic Botany,* 36, pp. 166-175.

Peters, P. (1984) 'Struggles Over Water, Struggles Over Meaning: Cattle, Water and the State in Botswana', *Africa,* 54 (3), pp. 29-49.

Phillips, A.O. (1985) *Indigenous Agricultural Revolution: Ecology and Food Production in West Africa,* Boulder, CO, Westview Press.

— (1989) 'Indigenous Agriculture Knowledge Systems for Nigeria's Development: The Case of Grain Storage', in P. Richards, L.J. Slikkerveer and A.O. Phillips (eds) *Indigenous Knowledge Systems for Agricultural and Rural Development: The CIKARD Inaugural Lectures,* Studies in Technology and Social Change 13, Ames, IA, Iowa State University.

Pickett, S.T.A. and P.S. White (1985) *The Ecology of Natural Disturbance and Patch Dynamics,* Orlando, FL, Academic Press.

Pieczarka, K.J. and J.W. Lorbeer (1974) 'Control of Bottom Rot of Lettuce by Ridging and Fungicide Application', *Plant Disease Reporter,* 58, pp. 837-840.

Pielago, G., R. Distrajo, L. Gayon, D. Apura, O. de Guia, R. de Pedro and C. Lightfoot (1987) 'A Diagnostic Survey of the Problem Complex in Shifting Cultivation Systems of Upland Farmers in Basey, Samar', *FSDP-EV Working Paper* 11, Tacloban, The Philippines, Department of Agriculture.

Pijl, L. van der (1990) 'Djamoe-Djamoe', *Moesson,* 34 (18), pp. 4-5.

Pingali, P.L. (1988) *Kampuchean Rice Economy: An Overview of the Constraints to Output Growth,* IRRI-Economics (unpublished mimeo).

Plath, C.V. (1970) *Florida Shade Tobacco, Economics of Production, 1969,* Gainesville, Florida, University of Florida, Cooperative Extension Service.

Pompa, G. (1984) *Medicamentos Indígenas: Colección Extraída de los Reinos Vegetal Animal y Mineral – Ondice para sus Aplicaciones,* (51st edition), Caracas, Corporación Marca, Venezuela for Editorial América.

Posey, D.A. (1983) 'Indigenous Knowledge and Development: An Ideological Bridge to the Future', *Ciênca e Cultura,* 35 (7), pp. 877-894.

— (1985) 'Indigenous Management of Tropical Forest Ecosystems: The Case of the Kayapo Indians of the Brazilian Amazon', *Agroforestry Systems,* 3, pp. 139-158.

— (1987) 'Contact Before Contact: Typology of Post-Colombian Interaction with Northern Kayapó of the Amazon Basin', *Boletin de Museu Emílio Goéldi, Séne Antropologia Belém-Pará, Conselho Nacional de Desen Volvimento Científico e Tecnológico* (2), pp. 135-154.

PPEA-PRATEC (Proyecto Piloto de Ecosistemas Andinos y Proyecto Andino de Tecnologías Campesinas) (1989) *Manejo Campesino de Semillas en Los Andes,* Serie Eventos de Técnicos, Lima, Peru (no publisher given).

Pradhan, S., M.G. Jotwani and B.K. Rai (1962) The Neem Seed Deterrent to Locusts, *Indian Farming* 12, pp. 7, 11.

— (1963) The Repellent Properties of Aome Neem Products, *Bulletin Regional Research Laboratory, Jammu* 1, pp. 149-151.

Prain, G. (1987) *Personal Communication,* Lima, Peru.

PRATEC (Proyecto Andino de Tecnologías Andinas) (1988a) *Rondas Campesinas y Tecnología Andina: Taller Regional Nor-Andino de Tecnologías Campesinas,* Lima, Peru, Editorial Adolfo Arteta.

— (1988b) *Saber Campesino Andino: I Taller Regional Sur-Andino de Tecnologías Campesinas,* Lima, Peru, G. y G. Impresores.

— (1989) *Sorochuco: Chacra Campesina y Saber Andino* – II *Taller Regional Nor-Andino de Tecnologías Campesinas,* Lima, Peru (no publisher given).

Price, T.L. (1987) *Republic of Niger: A Report prepared for Socio-Economic Studies on Niger River*, FAO/Rome, FI, GCP/NER/027/USA (February 1987).

Primov, G. (1984) 'Goat Production within the Farming System of Smallholders of Northern Bahia, Brazil', *Technical Report Series* 35, Columbia, University of Missouri-Columbia, Department of Rural Sociology, Small Ruminant Collaborative Research Program.

Pringgohusodo (1986) *Jamu Jawa Gejala Penyakit dan Obatnya*, Yogyakarta, Nur Cahaya.

Prinz, D. and F. Rauch (1987) The Bamenda Model, Development of a Sustainable Land-Use System in the Highlands of Western Cameroon, *Agroforestry Systems*, 5, pp. 463-474.

Proyecto de Tecnologías Campesinas-CEPIA (`1988) *Tecnologías Campesinas de Los Andes*, Lima, Peru, Editorial Horizonte.

Puleston, D.E. (1978) 'Terracing, Raised Fields and Tree Cropping in the Maya Lowlands: A New Perspective in the Geography of Power', in P.D. Harrison and B.L. Turner II (eds)*Pre-Hispanic Maya Agriculture*, pp. 225-245, Albuquerque, University of New Mexico Press.

Putman, D.B (1984) 'Agro-Pastoral Production Strategies and Development in the Bay Region', in T. Labahn (ed) *Proceedings of the 2nd International Congress of Somali Studies*, 3, pp. 159-186, (1-6 August 1983), Hamburg, University of Hamburg 'Aspects of Development'.

Quijandria, B. (1989) 'Role of Animal Agriculture in Farm Enterprises/Household Production and Linkage to Regional and National Economies' *Summary Report of the Animal Agriculture Symposium: Development Priorities Toward the Year 2000,* (June 1-3, 1988), Washington, D.C., U.S. Agency for International Development.

Quinn, N. (1978) 'Do Mfantse Fish Sellers Estimate Probability in their Heads?' *American Ethnologist*, 5 (2), pp. 206-226.

Rabeh, O.O. (1984) 'The Somali Nomad', in T. Labahn (ed.) *Proceedings of the 2nd International Congress of Somali Studies* 3, pp. 57-69, (1-6 August 1983), Hamburg, University of Hamburg, 'Aspects of Development'.

Radcliffe, E.B., F.V. Dunkel, P.P. Strzok and S. Adam (1990) 'Antifeedant Effect of Neem, *Azadirachtin indica* A, Juss., Kernel Extracts on *Kraussaria angulifera* (Krauss) (Orthoptera: Acrididae) a Sahelian Grasshopper', (manuscript in review).

Radwanski, S.A. (1982) *Home Made Neem Insecticides for the Tropics* (unpublished manuscript).

Radwanski, S.A. and G.E. Wickens (1967) 'The Ecology of *Acacia albida* on Mantle Soils in Zalingei, Jebel Marra, Sudan', *Journal of Applied Ecology*, 4 (2), pp. 569-579.

Rahmato, D. (1987) *Famine and Survival Strategies: A Case Study from North-east Ethiopia.* Addis Ababa, Ethiopia, Institute of Development Research, Addis Ababa University.

Rajasekaran, B. (1987) *An Agricultural Extension Officer's Field Reports (1980-1987)*, Madras, India, Joint Directorate of Agriculture.

Rajasekaran, B. and D.M. Warren (1989) *The Relationship between Indigenous Rice Taxonomies and Farmers' Rice Production Decision-Making Systems in South India,* Paper presented at the Farming Systems Research and Extension Symposium, Fayetteville, AR, 9 October 1989.

Rambo, A.T. (1981) 'Orang Asli Adaptive Strategies: Implications for Malaysian Natural Resource Development Planning', East-West Environmental and Policy Institute Preprint, Honolulu, East-West Centre.

Rangagath, H.K. (1980) *Folk Media and Communication*, Chinthana Bangalore, Prakashana.

Rangel, R. and J.L.F. Ortiz (1985) *Medicina Tradicional para Animales en dos*

Comunidades de la Meseta P'urhépecha, Uruapan, México, URM/Dirección General de Culturas Populares/SEP (unpublished manuscript).

Rappaport, R.A. (1971) 'The Flow of Energy in an Agricultural Society', *Scientific American* 255 (3), pp. 116-132. (1984) *Pigs for the Ancestors: Ritual in the Ecology of a New Guinea People*, 2nd ed., New Haven and London, Yale University Press.

Ray, H.E., S.G. Saunders, D.R. Foote and J.I. Mata (1986) *CTTA Project Manual*, Washington, D.C., CTTA.

Recharte, J. (1981) *Los Limites Socio-Ecologicos del Crecimiento Agricola en la Ceja de Selva*, Tesis, Lic. Antropología, Lima, Pontificia Universidad La Catolica del Perú.

Redclift, M. (1984) *Development and the Environmental Crisis*, London, Methuen.

— (1987) 'Raised Bed Agriculture in Pre-Colombian Central and South America: A Traditional Solution to the Problem of Sustainable Farming Systems', *Biol. Agriculture and Horticulture*, 5, pp. 51-59.

Redfield, R. (1956) *Peasant Society and Culture: An Anthropological Approach to Civilization*, Chicago, The University of Chicago Press.

Reichel-Dolmatoff, G. (1965) *Colombia: Ancient People and Places*, London, Thames Hudson.

Reij, C. (1987) *The Agro-Forestry Project in Burkina Faso: An Analysis of Popular Participation in Soil and Water Conservation*, Paper presented at IIED Conference on Sustainable Development, London, 28-30 April 1987.

Reijntjes, C., B. Haverkort and A. Waters-Bayer (1992) *Farming for the Future: Introduction to Low-External-Input and Sustainable Agriculture*, Leusden, ILEIA.

Rembold, H. (1988) 'Isometric Azadirachtins and their Mode of Action', in M. Jacobson (ed.) *1988 Focus on Phytochemical Pesticides 1, The Neem Tree*, pp. 47-67, Boca Raton, FL, CRC Press.

Rembold, H., H. Forster, Ch. Czoppelt, P.J. Rao and K.P. Sieber (1983) 'The Azadirachtins: A Group of Insect Growth Regulators from the Neem Tree', in H. Schutterer and H. Rembold (ed.) *Natural Pesticides from the Neem Tree*, pp. 163-161, Proceedings, 2nd International Neem Conference, Rauisch-Holzenhause, 1983, Schriftenreihe der GTZ; Deutsche Gessellschaft für Technische Zusammenarbeit (GTZ) GmbH.

Repulda, R., F. Quero, R. Ayaso, O. de Guia and C. Lightfoot (1987) 'Doing Research with Resource Poor Farmers: FSDP-EV Perspectives and Programs', *International Workshop on Farmers and Agricultural Research*, Sussex, England, Sussex University, IDS.

Rhoades, R.E. (1978) 'Archaeological Use and Abuse of Ecological Concepts and Studies: The Ecotone Example', *American Antiquity*, 43 (4), pp. 608-614.

—_ (1984) *Breaking New Ground and Anthropologists in Agricultural Research*, Lima, Peru, International Potato Centre.

—_ (1986) *The Development and Transfer of Diffused Light Storage in Guatemala*, Manuscript.

—_ (1987) *Farmers and Experimentation*, Discussion Paper 21, Agricultural Administration (Research and Extension), London, Overseas Development Institute.

Rhoades, R.E. and A. Bebbington (1988) *Farmers Who Experiment: An Untapped Resource for Agricultural Research and Development*, Paper presented at the International Congress on Plant Physiology, New Delhi, India, 15-20 February 1988.

Rhoades, R.E. and R. Booth (1982) 'Farmer-back-to-Farmer: A Model for Generating Acceptable Agricultural Technology', *Agricultural Administration*, 11, pp. 127-137.

Rhoades, R.E. and J. Recharte (n.d.) *Farmers of the Chanchamayo,* Lima, Peru, International Potato Center (manuscript).

Rice, D. (1981) 'Upland Agricultural Development in The Philippines: An Analysis and a Report on Ikalahan Programs', in H. Olofson (ed.) *Adaptive Strategies and Change in Philippine Swidden-based Societies,* pp. 73-90, Los Baños, Laguna, University of The Philippines, Forest Research Institute.

Richards, A. (1939) *Land, Labour and Diet in Northern Rhodesia,* London, University of London Press.

Richards, P. (1980) 'Community-Environmental Knowledge in African Rural Development', in D. Brokensha, D.M. Warren and O. Werner (ed.) *Indigenous Knowledge Systems and Development,* pp. 181-194, Lanham, MD, University Press of America.

— (1983) 'Farming Systems and Agrarian Change in West Africa', *Progress in Human Geography,* 7, pp. 1-39.

— (1985) *Indigenous Agricultural Revolution: Ecology and Food Production in West Africa,* Boulder, CO/London, Westview Press, Hutchinson.

— (1986) *Coping with Hunger: Hazard and Experiment in an African Rice Farming System,* London, Allen and Unwin.

— (1987) 'Experimenting Farmers and Agricultural Research' (unpublished manuscript).

— (1989) 'Indigenous Agricultural Knowledge and International Agricultural Research', in P. Richards, L.J. Slikkerveer and A.O. Phillips (ed.) *Indigenous Knowledge Systems for Agriculture and Rural Development: The CIKARD Inaugural Lectures,* Studies in Technology and Social Change Series 13, pp. 4-18, Ames, IA, Iowa State University.

Richards, P., L.J. Slikkerveer and A.O. Phillips (eds) (1989) *Indigenous Knowledge Systems for Agricultural and Rural Development: The CIKARD Inaugral Lectures,* Studies in Technology and Social Change 13, Ames, IA, Iowa State University.

Rieger, H.Chr. (1978/79) 'Socio-Economic Aspects of Environmental Degradation in the Himalayas', *Journal of the Nepal Research Centre,* 2/3, pp. 177-184.

Riley, B.W. and D. Brokensha (1988) *The Mbeere in Kenya,* Lanham, University Press of America.

Risch, S.J., D. Andow and M.A. Altieri (1983) 'Agroecosystem Diversity and Pest Control: Data, Tentative Conclusions and New Research Directions', *Environmental Entomology,* 12, pp. 625-629.

Rivera, W. and S.G. Schram (ed.) (1987) *Agricultural Extension Worldwide,* London, Croom and Helm.

Robinson, D.W. (1977) *The Husbandry of Alabio Ducks in South Kalimantan Swamplands,* Report 3, Bogor, Centre for Animal Research and Development.

Roersch, C. and L. van der Hoogte (1988) *Plantas Medicinales del Surandino del Peru,* Cuzco, Peru, Visual Service S.R.L. for the Centro de Medicina Andina.

Rogers, E.M. (1962) *The Diffusion of Innovations,* New York, Free Press, (1983) *Diffusion of Innovations* (third edition), New York, Free Press.

— (1989) 'Evolution and Transfer of the U.S. Extension Model', in J.L. Compton (ed.) *The Transformation of International Agricultural Research and Development,* pp. 137-152, Boulder and London, Lynne Rienner.

Rogers, E.M. and R. Agarwala-Rogers (1976) *Communication in Organisations,* New York, Free Press.

Röling, N. and P. Engel (1989) 'Indigenous Knowledge Systems in Knowledge Management: Utilising Indigenous Knowledge in Institutional Knowledge Systems', in D.M. Warren, L.J. Slikkerveer and S.O. Titilola (eds) *Indigenous Knowledge Systems: Implications for Agriculture and*

International Development, pp. 121-137, Studies in Technology and Social Change 11, Ames, IA, Iowa State University.

Romero Ramírez, C., R.A.R. del Castillo R., A.C.M. Martínez and C.J.F. Calderón (1988) 'Estudios Preliminares de los Efectos Antibacterianos, Antiparasitarios y Toxicológicos de la Raíz del Chilcúan', in L.L. Nathal and G. López Buendía (coords.) *Memorias: Primera Jornada sobre Herbolaria Medicinal en Veterinaria,* pp. 134-143, México DF, Universidad Nacional Autónoma de México, Facultad de Medicina Veterinaria y Zootecnia, Coordinación de Educación Continua.

Rondinelli, D. (1983) *Development Projects as Policy Experiments,* London, Methuen.

Rouch, J. (1948) 'Banhgawi, Chasse á l'Hippopotame au Harpon par les Pêcheurs Sorko du Moyen-Niger', *Bulletin de Français d'Afrique Noire (IFAN),* X: Fascicule Unique, pp. 361-377.

— (1950) 'Les Sorkawas: Pêcheurs Itinerants du Moyen-Niger', *Africa: Journal of the International African Institute,* 20 (1), pp. 5-25.

Roumasset, J.A. (1976) *Rice and Risk: Decision Making Among Low-Income Farmers,* Amsterdam/New York, Elsevier Publishing Company.

Roy, S.K. (1987) 'Sustainable Development of Natural Resources in the Third World: The Human Equation', in D.D. Southgate and J.F. Disinger (eds) *Sustainable Resource Development in the Third World,* pp. 159-168, Boulder, CO, Westview Press.

Rubel, A.J., C.W. O'Neal and R. Collado-Ardon (1986) *Susto, A Folk Illness,* Berkeley, University of California Press.

Rumphius, D.A. (1741) *Het Amboinsche Kruydtboek,* Amsterdam.

Runge, C.F. (1986) 'Common Property and Collective Action in Economic Development', *World Development,* 14 (5), pp. 623-635.

Rupa, I.N. (1985) *Subak,* Jakarta, (in Indonesian), Baru.

Rusten, E. (1989) *An Investigation of Indigenous Management Practices of Tree Fodder Resources in the Middle Hills of Central Nepal,* Ph.D. Dissertation, Lansing, Michigan State University, Department of Forestry.

Ruthenberg, H. (1985) *Innovation Policy for Small Farmers in the Tropics: The Economics of Technical Innovation for Agricultural Development,* Oxford, Oxford University Press.

Sachs, I. (1984) *Development and Planning,* Cambridge, Cambridge University Press.

Salas, H. (1988) 'Ecological Reclamation of the Chinampa Area of Xochimilco, Mexico City', in P. Allen and D. van Dusen (eds) *Global Perspectives on Agroecology and Sustainable Agricultural Systems* II, pp. 469-473, Santa Cruz, University of California, Agroecology Program.

Sahly, S. (1983) *Pengobatan Dengan Resep-Resep Asli,* Solo, Aneka.

Salcedo, M.B. (1986) *Un Herbolario de Ch'ajaya Devela sus Secretos,* Edited by SOBOMETRA and the Department of SEMPAS, Artes Gráficas El Buitre for Ediciones SENPAS, La Paz, Bolivia.

Salisbury, R.F. (1962) *From Stone to Steel,* London, Cambridge University Press.

Sánchez V., C. (n.d.) 'Avances sobre el Proyecto Alpaca Convenio UNTA-NUFFIC Control de la Sarna de Alpacas con Alcaloides del Tarwi', *II Anales del Conversatorio Nacional Multisectorial sobre Desarrollo de Camélidos Sudamericanos* pp. 153-154.

Sandford, D. (1981) 'Pastoralists as Animal Health Workers: The Range Development Project in Ethiopia', *Pastoral Network Paper,* 12c, London, UK, Regent's College, Inner Circle, Agricultural Administration Unit, Overseas Development Institute (ODI).

Sandor, J. (1987) 'Initial Investigation of Soils in Agricultural Terraces in the Colca Valley, Peru', in W.M. Denevan, K. Mathewson and G. Knapp (eds)

Pre-Hispanic Agricultural Fields in the Andean Region, pp. 163-192, Oxford, British Archaeological Reports, International Series 359 (1).

— (1989) 'Investigation of Agricultural Soils at Lari, Colca Valley, Peru', in D. Guillet (ed.) *Cognitive, Behavioral and Agronomic Studies of Soil Management in the Colca Valley, Peru,* pp. 101-163, Technical Report to the National Science Foundation (Anthropology Program), Washington, D.C., Catholic University, Department of Anthropology.

Sanford, S. (1984) 'Traditional African Range Management Systems', in P.J. Joss, P.W. Lynch and O.B. Williams (eds) *Rangelands: a Resource Under Siege, Proceedings 2nd International Rangeland Congress,* pp. 475-478, Adelaide, Australia.

Sartono, R. (1986) *Perawatan Tubuh and Pengobatan Traditional,* Semarang, Dahara Prize.

Sastroamidjojo, S. (1965) *Obat Asli Indonesia,* Jakarta, PT Dian Rakyat.

Sattaur, O. (1988) The Lost Art of the Waru Waru, *New Scientist,* 118 (1612), pp. 50-51.

Sauer, C.O. (1969) *Seeds, Spades, Hearths and Herds. The Domestication of Animals and Foodstuffs,* Cambridge, MA, Massachusetts Institute of Technology Press.

Saussay, C. de (1987) 'Land Tenure Systems and Forestry Policy', *FAO Legislative Study 41,* pp. 48-52, Rome, Food and Agriculture Organization.

Sayahbuddin, A. (1984) *Berbagai Obat Sakit Demam,* Jakarta, Aqua Press.

Schank, R. and R. Abelson (1977) *Scripts, Plans, Goals and Understanding,* New York, John Wiley and Sons.

Schapera, I. (1940) 'The Political Organization of the Ngwato of Bechuanaland Protectorate', in M. Fortes and E. Evans-Pritchard (eds) *African Political Systems,* pp. 56-82, London, Oxford University Press.

Schefold, R. (1990) 'The Culinary Bode in the Puliaijat Ritual of the Mentawaians', *Bijdragen tot Taal-, Land- en Volkenkunde,* 138 (1), pp. 64-98.

Schillhorn van Veen, T.W. (1984) 'Observations on Animal Health, Especially Approaches to Identify and Overcome Constraints in the Subhumid Zone of West Africa', in J.R. Simpson and P. Evangelou (eds) *Livestock Development in sub-Saharan Africa: Constraints, Prospects, Policy,* pp. 303-317, Boulder, CO, Westview Press.

— (1986) 'Some Considerations in the Approach to Measure and Prevent Animal Health Problems in Traditionally raised Livestock', Adapted English version of a paper presented at Workshop Les Méthodes de la Recherche sur les Systèmes d'Elévage en Afrique Intertropicale, Dakar-Mbour, Sénégal, February 1986.

Schinkel, H.G. (1970) *Haltung, Zucht und Pflege des Viehs bei den Nomaden Ost- und Nordostafrikas: Ein Beitrag zur traditionellen Oekonomie der Wanderhirten in Semiariden Gebietem,* Berlin, GDR, Akademie-Verlag, Veroeffentlichungen des Museums für Völkerkunde zu Leipzig, Heft 21.

Schlippe, P. de (1956) *Shifting Cultivation in Africa: The Zante System of Agriculture,* London, Routledge and Kegan Paul.

Schmutterer, H. (1981a) 'Ten Years of Neem Research in the Federal Republic of Germany', in H. Schmutterer, K.R.S. Ascher and H. Rembold (eds) *Natural Pesticides from the Neem Tree,* 21-42, Proceedings, 1st International Neem Conference, Rottach-Edern, 1980, Schriftenreihe der GTZ; Deutsche Gessellschaft für Technische Zusammenarbeit (GTZ) GmbH.

— (1981b) 'Some Properties of Components of the Neem Tree' (*Azadirachta indica*) and their Use in Pest Control in Developing Countries, *Mededelingen van de Rijksfaculteit Landbouwwetenschappen,* 46, pp. 39-47, Gent.

— (1984) 'Neem Research in the Federal Republic of Germany since the First

International Neem Conference', in H. Schmutterer and H. Rembold (eds) *Natural Pesticides from the Neem Tree,* pp. 21-31, Proceedings, 2nd International Neem Conference, Rauisch-Holzenhausen, 1983, Schriftenreihe der GTZ; 161, Deutsche Gessellschaft für Technische Zusammenarbeit (GTZ) GmbH.

— (1985) 'Which Insect Pests can be Controlled by Application of Neem Seed Kernel Extracts under Field Conditions?', *Zeitschrift für Angewandte Entomologie* 10, pp. 468-475.

Schmutterer, H., K.R.S. Ascher and H. Rembold (eds) (1981) *Natural Pesticides from the Neem Tree,* Proceedings, 1st International Neem Conference, Rottach-Edern, 1980, Schriftenreihe der GTZ, Deutsche Gessellschaft für Technische Zusammenarbeit (GTZ) GmbH.

— Schmutterer, H. and K.R.S. Ascher (eds) (1987) *Natural Pesticides from the Neem Tree,* Proceedings 3rd International Neem Conference, Nairobi, Kenya, 1986, Schriftenreiche der GTZ, 206, Eschborn.

Schmutterer, H. and C. Hellpap (1988) 'Effects of Neem on Pests of Vegetable and Fruit Trees', in M. Jacobson (ed) *1988 Focus on Phytochemical Pesticides 1, The Neem Tree,* 87-96, Boca Raton, FL, CRC Press.

Schmutterer, H. and H. Rembold (eds) (1984) *Natural Pesticides from the Neem Tree,* Proceedings, 2nd International Neem Conference, Rauisch-Holzenhausen, 1983, Schriftenreihe der GTZ; 161, Deutsche Gessellschaft für Technische Zusammenarbeit (GTZ) GmbH.

Schmutterer, H. and H. Rembold (1980) 'Zur Wirkung einiger Reinfraktionen aus Samen von *Azadirachta indica* auf Fraßaktivotät und Metamorphose von *Epilachna varivestis* (Col. Coccinellidae)', *Zeitschrift für Angewandte Entomologie,* 2, pp. 179-188.

Schofen, J. (1989) 'Utilising Indigenous Agricultural Knowledge in the Planning of Agricultural Research Projects Designed to Aid Small-Scale Farmers', in D. Brokensha, D.M. Warren and O. Werner (eds) *Indigenous Knowledge Systems and Development,* Lanham, MD, University Press of America.

Schram, L.M.J. (1954) *The Monguors of the Kansu-Tibetan Frontier: their Origin, History and Social Organisation,* Philadelphia, American Philosophical Society.

Schroeder, R.F. (1985) 'Himalayan Subsistence Systems: Indigenous Agriculture in Rural Nepal', *Mountain Research and Development,* 5 (1), pp. 31-44

Schuh, G.E. (1984) *Policy Options for Improving the Trade Performance of U.S. Agriculture,* Washington, D.C., National Agricultural Forum.

Schultes, R.E. (1974) 'Palms and Religion in the Northwest Amazon', *Principles,* 18, pp. 2-21.

Schultz, T. (1964) *Transforming Traditional Agriculture,* New Haven, CT, Yale University Press.

Schulze, W. (1970-71) 'Early Iron Smelting Among the Northern Kpelle', *Liberian Studies Journal,* 3 (2), pp. 113-127.

— (1973) *A New Geography of Liberia,* London, Longman.

Schwab, G. (1947) *Tribes of the Liberian Hinterland,* XXXI, Papers of the Peabody Museum (ed.) with Additional Material by G.W. Harley, Report of the Peabody Museum Expedition to Liberia, Cambridge, MASS, Peabody Museum.

Schwabe, C.W. (1978) *Cattle, Priests and Progress in Medicine,* The Wesley W. Spink Lectures on Comparative Medicine IV , Minneapolis, University of Minnesota Press.

— (1984) 'A Unique Surgical Operation on the Horns of African Bulls in Ancient and Modern Times', *Agricultural History,* 58 (2), pp. 138-156.

— (1987) 'Traditional Veterinary Medicine of the Nilotic Dinka and Ancient Egyptians Compar(ed)' *Working Paper Series,* 40, Davis, CA, University of California, Agricultural History Centre.

Schwabe, C.W. and I.K. Kuojok (1981) 'Practices and Beliefs of the Traditional Dinka Healer in Relation to Provision of Modern Medical and Veterinary Services for the Southern Sudan', *Human Organization*, 40 (3), pp. 231-238.

Schwarz, R.A. (1983) *The Human Dimension of Integrated Pest Management*, Washington, D.C., USAID.

Scott, M. and B. Gormley (1980) 'The Animal of Friendship: An Indigenous Model of Sahelian Pastoral Development in Niger', in D. Brokensha, D.M. Warren and O. Werner (eds) *Indigenous Knowledge Systems and Development*, pp. 93-111, Lanham, MD, University Press of America.

Seaman, J. and J. Holt (1980) 'Markets and Famines in the Third World', *Disasters Journal*, 4, pp. 283-297.

Seidel, E. (ed.) (1988) *The Biosphere Reserve 'Vessertal' in the Thuringian Forest*, Berlin, GDR, MAB National Committee, Ministry of Environmental Protection and Water Management.

Senanayake, F. Ranil (1987) *Analog Forestry as a Conservation Tool*, Tigerpaper 14 (2), pp. 25-29.

Shanklin, E. (1985a) *Donegal's Changing Traditions: An Ethnographic Study*, New York, Gordon and Breach Science.

— (1985b) Sustenance and Symbol: Anthropological Studies of Domesticated Animals , *Annual Review Anthropology* 14, pp. 375-403.

Sharland, R.W. (1989) *Using Indigenous Knowledge in Relation to Subsistence Sector Extension: Interaction between the Agricultural and Wild Environments in Moru Agriculture in Southern Sudan*, Ph.D. Thesis AERDD, University of Reading (unpublished).

Sheng-Han, S.(1963) *Fan Sheng-Chich Shu*, An Agriculturist Book of China written by Fan Sheng-Chih in the First Century B.C., Peking, Science Press.

— (1982) *A Preliminary Survey of the Book, CH'I MIN YAO SHU, An Agricultural Encyclopaedia of the 6th Century* , Peking, Science Press.

Shigeura G.T., R.M. Bullock and J.A. Silva (1975) 'Defoliation and Fruit Set in Guave', *Hortic Sci*, 10, pp. 590.

Shinnie, P.L. (ed) (1971) *The African Iron Age* , Oxford, The Clarendon Press.

Shrestha, Vijaya, *et al.* (1982) 'Social Action/Adaptive Research Program', *Report to the Resource Conservation and Utilisation Project* , 3 vols, Kathmandu, New Era.

Siemens, A.H. (1980) 'Indicios de Aprovechamiento Agricola Prehispánico de Tierras Inundables en el Centro de Veracruz', *Biotica*, 5 (3), pp. 83-92.

Siemens, A.H. and D.E. Puleston (1972) 'Ridged Fields and Associated Features in Southern Campeche: New Perspectives on the Lowland Maya', *American Antiquity*, 37, pp. 228-239.

Sigaut, F. (ed) (1985) 'Une Discipline Scientifique à Développer: La Technologie de l'Agriculture', *Colloques et Séminaires,* A Travers Champs, Paris, ORSTOM.

Simmons, I.G. (1974) *The Ecology of Natural Resources*, London, Edward Arnold Ltd.

Simon, P. (1923) *Noticias Historiales de las Conquistas de Tierra Firme en las Indias Occidentales,* 1, Bogota, Biblioteca Banco Popular.

Simpson, P., S. McRae and S. Kays (eds) (1987) *Sound Science* , A Record and Commentary on a Hui at Waikawa Marae, Marlborough Sounds, New Zealand, 30 April-1 May 1986. New Zealand Man and the Biosphere Report 9, Wellington, National Commission for UNESCO.

Siregar, A.P. (1982) Sejarah Itik di Indonesia, *Poultry Indonesia* 11, pp. 35-36.

Slikkerveer, L.J. (1982) Rural Health Development in Ethiopia: Problems of Utilisation of Traditional Healers: *Social Science and Medicine* 16 (21), pp. 1859-1872.

— (1983) *Medisch Pluralisme in Noordoost-Afrika*, Ph.D. Dissertation, Leiden, Leiden University.

— (1987) *Apotik Hidup: Indigenous Indonesian Medicine for Self-Reliance*, Paper for the LIPI Workshop on Jamu and PHC Development, Jakarta, Indonesia, LIPI, pp.25.

— (1989) 'Changing Values of Social and Natural Scientists toward Indigenous Peoples and their Knowledge Systems', in D.M. Warren, L.J. Slikkerveer and S.O. Titilola (ed.) *Indigenous Knowledge Systems: Implications for Agriculture and International Development,* pp. 121-137, Studies in Technology and Social Change 11, Ames, IA, Iowa State University.

— (1990a) *Utilisation of Jamu in West Java: an Institution-Based Study on the Use of Traditional Herbal Pharmaceutical Medicines in Bandung, Indonesia,* Paper for the Third International Conference on Traditional Asian Medicine (IASTAM), Bombay, India, pp. 42.

— (1990b) *Plural Medical Systems in the Horn of Africa: The Legacy of 'Sheikh' Hippocrates,* Monograph from the African Studies Centre Leiden, London, Kegan Paul Int.

Smith, C.A. (1976) 'Regional Economic Systems: Linking Geographical Models and Socio-economic Problems', in C.A. Smith (ed.) *Regional Analysis: Economic Systems,* I, pp. 3-63, New York, Academic Press.

— (1978) 'Beyond Dependency Theory: National and Regional Patterns of Underdevelopment in Guatemala', *American Ethnologist,* 5 (3), pp. 574-617.

Soemarwoto, O. and I. Soemarwoto (1984) 'The Javanese Rural Ecosystem', in T. Rambo and P.E. Sajise (eds) *An Introduction to Human Ecology Research on Agricultural Systems in South East Asia,* pp. 254-287, Los Baños, University of The Philippines.

Soetjipto, N.W. and S.H.A. Lubis (1981) *Vegetables Projek Penelitian Potensi Sumber Daya Ekononmi ,* Jakarta, LIPI.

Sollod, A.E. (1981) *Patterns of Disease in Sylvopastoral Herds of Central Niger. An Epi-demiological Study of Herd Health in the Niger Range and Livestock Project Zone,* Niamey, Niger, The Niger Ministry of Rural Development and USAID.

—_ (1983) *The Influence of Trypanosomiasis on the Animal Disease Taxonomies of the Fulbe,* Paper presented at the 26th Annual ASS Meeting, Boston, December 7-10, 1983.

Sollod, A.E. and J.A. Knight (1983) *Veterinary Anthropology: A Herd Health Study in Central Niger,* pp. 482-486, Third International Symposium on Veterinary Epidemiology and Economics, Arlington, Virginia, 6-10 September 1982, Edwardsville, KAN, Veterinary Medicine Publishing Company.

Sollod, A.E., K. Wolfgang and J.A. Knight (1984) 'Veterinary Anthropology: Interdisciplinary Methods in Pastoral Systems Research', in J.R. Simpson and P. Evangelou (ed.) *Livestock Development in sub-Saharan Africa: Constraints, Prospects, Policy,* pp. 285-302, Boulder, CO., Westview Press.

Soukup, J. (n.d.) *Vocabulario de los Nombres Vulgares de la Flora Peruana y Catálogo de los Géneros,* Lima, Peru, Editorial Salesiana.

Southwold, M. (1964) 'Leadership, Authority and the Village Community', in L.A. Fallers and A.I. Richards (ed.) *The King's Men: Leadership and Status in Buganda on the Eve of Independence,* pp. 211-255, Oxford, Oxford University Press.

Spaandermann, A.L. (1985) *Recherche Agricole dans Trois Villages, République Togolaise,* Amsterdam, University of Amsterdam.

Spencer, P. (1965) *The Samburu: A Study of Gerontocracy in a Nomadic Tribe,* London, Routledge and Kegan Paul.

Spradley, J. (1979) *The Ethnographic Interview,* New York, Holt, Rinehart and Winston.

Spurr, S.H. (1969) The Natural Resource Ecosystem, in G.M. van Dyne (ed.) *The Ecosystem Concept in Natural Resource Management,* 3-7, New York, Academic Press.

Squire, E.G. (1958) *The States of Central America,* New York, Harper.

Steets, R. (1976) 'Zur Wirkung eines Gereinigten Extraktes aus Früchten von *Azadirachta indica* auf *Leptinotarsa decemlineata* Say (Coleoptera: Chrysomelidae)', *Zeitschrift für Angewandte Entomologie,* 82, pp. 169-176.

Steets, R. and H. Schmutterer (1976) 'Der Einfluß von Azadirachtin auf die Lebensdauer und das Reproduktionsvermogen von *Epilachna varivestis* Muls. (Coleoptera: Coccinellidae) (Influence of Azadirachtin on Longevity and Reproduction Capacity of *Epilachna varivestis* Muls. (Coleoptera, Coccinellidae)', *Zeitschrift für Pflanzenkrankheiten und Pflanzenschutz* 82, pp. 176-179.

Stenning, D.J. (1959) *Savannah Nomads: A Study of the WoDaaBe Pastoral Fulani of Western Bornu Province, Northern Region, Nigeria,* Oxford, Oxford University Press.

Stigter, C.J. (1984) Wind Protection in Traditional Microclimate Management and Manipulation: Examples from East Africa, in J. Grace (ed), *The Effects of Shelter on the Physiology of Plants and Animals. Progress in Biometeorology* 2, Lisse, Swetz and Zeitlinger.

— (1985a) 'Management and Manipulation of Microclimate in Tanzanian Traditional Farming', Final Contest Report, Dar es Salaam, University of Dar es Salaam, Agricultural Physics Section, Physics Department, Synopsis , *Neth. J. Agric. Sc.*, 33, pp. 303-305

— (1985b) *Microclimate Management and Manipulation in Traditional Farming Second Annual Report* (May 1984-May 1985) to the President, Commission for Agricultural Meteorology, World Meteorological Organisation.

— (1986) *Project – Traditional Techniques of Microclimate Improvement (TTMI), Fourth Progress Report.*

— (1987a) 'Tapping into Traditional Knowledge: African Revival Rediscovering their Own Resources (Centrepiece papers)', 20 (3), pp. 29-32.

— (1987b) Traditional Manipulation of Microclimatic Factors: Knowledge to be Us (ed) *ILEIA Newsletter,* 3 (3), pp. 5-6.

— (1988a) 'Microclimate Management and Manipulation in Traditional Farming', *CAgM Report 25, WMO/TD* 228, Geneva, World Meteorological Organisation.

— (1988b) 'Microclimate Management and Manipulation in Agroforestry', in K.F. Wiersum (ed) *Viewpoints on Agroforestry,* Wageningen, Agricultural University.

— (1989) 'The Project Traditional Techniques of Microclimate Improvement (TTMI-Project) and the Groningen Research Community to the Letter written by the Organising Committee of the Conference' Pre-Conference Paper for Conference on Development Related Research, The Role of the Netherlands, Groningen, University of Groningen.

Stigter, C.J., H.S. Adam and C.L. Coulson (1989) 'Meteorological Hazards and Research Education at National Institutes; An Interdisciplinary Approach Developed and Validated in East Africa, Proceedings of the International Symposium on Meteorological Hazards and Development', Lagos/Kano, Nigerian Meteorological Society/ICTP/WMO.

Stigter, C.J., C. Baldy, C.L. Coulson, C.D. Othieno, M.A. El-Tayeb, D.N. Mungai, R.M.R. Kainkwa and A.A. Ibrahim (1989) 'Meteorological Hazards and the Low External Input Farmer: Some Case Studies, Proceedings of the International Symposium on Meteorological Hazards and Development', Lagos/Kano, Nigerian Meteorological Society/ICTP/WMO.

Stigter, C.J., C.L. Coulson, A.M. El-Tayeb, D.N. Mungai and R.M.R. Kainkwa (1989a) 'Users' Needs for Quantification in Tropical Agrometeorology: Some Case Studies: Proceedings of the Fourth Technical Conference on Instruments and Methods of Observation,(TECIMO IV), Instruments and Observing Methods', *Report 35, WMO/TD* 303, 365-370, Geneva.

Stigter, C.J. and T. Darnhofer (1989) 'Quantification of Microclimate near the Soil Surface', Appendix F, in J.M. Anderson and J.S.I. Ingram (ed.) *Tropical Soil Biology and Fertility: A Handbook of Methods,* Wallingford, IUBS/ISSS/UNESCO and CAB International.

Stigter, C.J., C.O. Othieno, C.L. Coulson and the Kenyan TTMI-Team (1987) 'Mulching with Organic Materials: Knowledge is Power', *ILEIA Newsletter,* 3 (3), pp. 10-11.

Stigter, C.J. and the TTMI-Teams in Kenya, Sudan and Tanzania (1987) 'Traditional Techniques of Microclimate Improvement. The TTMI Project', *ILEIA Newsletter,* 3 (3), pp. 7-8.

— (1989) 'The Traditional Techniques of Microclimate Improvement (TTMI Project): An Approach Combining Local Interdisciplinary applied Research, Local Research Training and Development of Weather Advisories for Low-Resource Agriculture at National Research Institutes in Africa', Proceedings of the Second ICTP/SAPAM Workshop on the Applicability of Environmental Physics and Meteorology in Africa, Addis Ababa, ICTP/SAPAM.

Stigter, C.J. and M.T. Weber (1989) 'Food Security: Lessons from Practice for Research to Design and Validate Government Policies', Paper for the International Conference Development Related Research: The Role of The Netherlands, Groningen, University of Groningen.

Stigter, C.J. and A. Weiss (1986) 'In Quest of Tropical Micrometeorology for On-Farm Weather Advisories, A Guest Editorial', *Agric. For. Meteorol.* 36, pp. 289-296.

Stocking, G.W. (1981) The Ethnographer's Magic: Fieldwork in British Anthropology from Tylor to Malinowski, in G.W. Stocking (ed) *Observer's Observed,* 70-120, Madison, University of Wisconsin Press.

Storas, F. (1987) 'Intention or Implication – the Effects of Turkana Social Organisation on Ecological Balance', Paper for the Workshop *Changing Rights in Property and Problems of Pastoral Development in the Sahel,* Manchester University, April 1987.

Su, Kuang-chi (1979) Role of Tomato in Multiple Cropping, *Proceedings of the 1st International Symposium on Tropical Tomato,* Taiwan, Republic of China, Asian Vegetable Research and Development Centre.

Subedi, B.P., C.L. Das and D. Messerschmidt (1992) *Tenure on Trees and Land in East Nepal – A Case Study by Rapid Appraisal. Community Forestry Note,* Rome, FAO/UN.

Sumano López, H., A.A. Angulo and L.O. Camberos (1988) 'Comparación del Efecto Cicatrizante de Varios Preparados de la Medicina Tradicional y la Medicina de Patente', in L.L. Nathal and G. López Buendía, (coords.), *Memorias, Primera Jornada sobre Herbolaria Medicinal en Veterinaria,* pp. 80-84, México DF, Universidad Nacional Autónoma de México, Facultad de Medicina Veterinaria y Zootecnia, Coordinación de Educación Continua.

Sundström, L. (1972) Ecology and Symbiosis: Niger Water Folk, *Studia Ethnographica Upsaliensia,* XXXV.

Suparlan, P. (1991) *The Javanese Dukun,* Jakarta, Peka Publications.

Surjodiningrat, D.W. (1982) 'Shadow Puppets and Family Planning: The Indonesian Experience', *Folk Media and Mass Media in Population Communication*, Population Communication: Technical Documentation 8, pp. 12-14, Paris, United Nations Educational, Scientific and Cultural Organization.

Sutrisno, R.B. (1984) 'The Two-Way Approach in the Development of the Indonesian Traditional Drugs', in, *Proceedings of the Second International Congress on Traditional Asian Medicine (IASTAM),* Surabaya: Airlangga University.

Sutter, J.W. (1978) *Pastoral Herding in the Arrondissement of Tanout,* A Socio-

Economic Study for the Niger Range and Livestock Project, Zinder, Ministry of Rural Development.

Swantz, M-L. (1987) *Systems of Knowledge as Systems of Domination*, Helsinki, World Institute for Development Economic Research (WIDER), United Nations University.

Swift, J.J. (1975) 'Pastoral Nomadism as a Form of Land Use: the Twareg of the Adrar n Iforas (Mali)', in T. Monod (ed.) *Pastoralism in Tropical Africa*, pp. 443-454, London, Oxford University Press.

— (1977) 'Pastoral Development in Somalia: Herding Cooperatives as a Strategy Against Desertification and Famine', in M.H. Glantz (ed) *Desertification: Environmental Degradation in and Around Arid Lands,* pp. 275-305, Boulder, CO, Westview Press.

— (1979) 'Notes on Traditional Knowledge, Modern Knowledge and Rural Development', *IDS Bulletin*, 10 (2), pp. 41-43.

— (1988) *Mali Republic. Kidal Development Project Identification Report,* Rome, IFAD.

— (1989) 'Why are Rural People Vulnerable to Famine?' *IDS Bulletin*, 20 (2), pp. 8-15.

Taman Obat Keluarga (TOGA) (1983) Departemen Kesehatan Republik Indonesia, Jakarta.

Tansley, A.G. (1935) *Introduction to Plant Ecology*, London, George Allen and Unwin

Teit, J.A. (1930) 'Ethnobotany of the Thompson Indians of British Columbia', *Forty-fifth Annual Report of the Bureau of American Ethnology to the Secretary of the Smithsonian Institution 1927-1928*, Washington, D.C.,United States Government Printing Office.

Temple, P.H. (1972) 'Soil and Water Conservation Policies in the Ulguru Mountains, Tanzania', *Geografiska Annaler*, 54A (3-4), pp. 110-123.

Tennet, Sir James Emerson (1859) *Ceylon: An Account of the Island*, II, London, Longman, Green, Longman and Roberts.

Thomasson, G.C. (1987) *Indigenous Knowledge Systems, Sciences and Technologies: Ethnographic and Ethnohistorical Perspectives on the Educational Foundations for Development in Kpelle Culture*, Ph.D. Dissertation, New York, Cornell University.

Thompson, S. (1973) *Pioneer Colonisation: A Cross Cultural View*, Addison-Wesley Module in Anthropology, 33, Reading, MA, Addison-Wesley Publishing Company.

Thrupp, L.N. (1989) 'Legitimising Local Knowledge', 'Scientized Packages', or Empowerment for Third World People', in D.M. Warren, L.J. Slikkerveer and S.O. Titilola (eds) *Indigenous Knowledge Systems: Implications for International Development*, Ames, IA, Iowa State University, Technology and Social Change Studies 11.

Thurston, D.H. (1990) 'Plant Disease Management Practices of Traditional Farmers', *Plant Diseases*, 74 (2), pp. 96-101.

Thurston, H.D. and O. Schultz (1981) 'Late Blight', in W.J. Hooker (ed.) *Compendium of Potato Diseases*, pp. 40-42, St. Paul, MN, American Phytopathological Society.

Tillman, H.J. (1983) 'Planificar el Futuro de la Comunidad', *Minka*, 11 (June), pp. 21-25.

Timaffy, L. (1961) 'Das Hirtenwesen auf den Donauinseln (SzigetkÖz, Westungarn)', in L. Földe (ed) *Viehzucht und Hirtenleben in Ostmitteleuropa: Ethnographische Studien,* pp. 609-645, Budapest, Adadémiai Kiadó, Verlag der Ungarischen Akademie der Wissenschaften.

Torres, H. (1985) 'The Andean Native Peoples in the Conservation Planning Process, in J.A. McNeely and D. Pitt (eds) *Culture and Conservation: The Human Dimension in Environmental Planning*. London, Crown Helm.

Toulmin, C. (1983) 'Herders and Farmers or Farmer-herders and Herder-farmers?', *Pastoral Network Paper*, 15d, London, ODI.

Touré, A.H. (1987) *Etude de l'Organisation des Méthodes et Pratiques Traditionnelles des Pêcheurs dans une Région du Fleuve Niger: Possibilité d'Adaptation aux Aménagements Modernes.* Niger, République du Niger, Ministére de l'Agriculture, Institut Pratique de Développement Rural – Kolo, Forêts-Faune, Mémoire de Fin d'Etudes, Août 1987.

Trapnell, C.G. (1953) *The Soils, Vegetation and Agriculture of North-Eastern Rhodesia,* Lusaka, Zambia, Government Printer.

Tubiana, M.J. (1969) 'La Pratique Actuelle de la Cueillette Chez les Zaghawa du Tchad', *JATBA* XVI (2-5), pp. 4-83.

Tubiana, J. and J. Tubiana (1977) *The Zaghawa from an Ecological Perspective,* Rotterdam, Balkema.

Tucker, R.P. (1982) 'The Forests of the Western Himalayas: The Legacy of British Colonial Administration', *Journal of Forest History*, 26, pp. 112-123.

— (1984) 'The Historical Context of Social Forestry in the Kumaon Himalaya', *Journal of Developing Areas*, 18, pp. 341-356.

Turner, B.L., II (1974) 'Prehistoric Intensive Agriculture in the Mayan Lowlands', *Science* 185, pp. 118-124.

Turner, B.L., II and P.D. Harrison (1981) Prehistoric Raised-Field Agriculture in the Maya Lowlands, *Science*, 213, pp. 399-405.

Turton, D. (1985) 'Mursi Response to Drought: Some Lessons for Relief and Rehabilitation', *African Affairs*, 10, pp. 331-346.

Tversky, A. (1972) 'Elimination by Aspects: A Theory of Choice', *Psychological Review,* 79 (4), pp. 281-299.

Tweeten, L. (1983) *Impact of Federal Fiscal-Monetary Policy on the Farm Structure,* Paper presented at the Annual Meetings of the Southern Agricultural Economics Association, Atlanta, GA.

— (1984) *Causes and Consequences of Structural Change in the Farming Industry,* Washington, D.C., National Planning Association Food and Agriculture Committee.

Udupa, K.N. (1975) 'The Ayurvedic System of Medicine in India', in K.W. Newell (ed), *Health by the People*, Geneva, World Health Organization, pp. 53-69.

U.S. Agency for International Development (USAID) (1985) *A Soil and Water Conservation Project in Two Sites in Somalia: Seventeen Years Later*, A.I.D. Project Impact Evaluation Report 62, Washington, D.C., USAID.

U.S. Congress, Office of Technology Assessment (1984) *Africa Tomorrow: Issues in Technology Agriculture and U.S. Foreign Aid, A Technical Memorandum* Washington, D.C., OTA.

UNESCO (1978) *Tropical Forest Ecosystems,* A State-of-Knowledge Report prepared by UNESCO, UNEP and FAO, Natural Resources Research Series 14. Paris, UNESCO.

— (1979) *Man in the Humid Tropics,* MAB Audio-Visual Series 1, Paris, UNESCO. (1981) *Ecology in Action: An Exhibit*, Thumbnail Sketches of 36 Posters, Paris, UNESCO.

— (1983) *Swidden Cultivation in Asia,* Volume Two, Country Profiles: India, Indonesia, Malaysia, The Philippines, Thailand, Bangkok, UNESCO.

— (1987) *A Practical Guide to MAB,* Paris, UNESCO.

— (1988) *Man Belongs to the Earth. International Co-operation in Environmental Research,* UNESCO's Man and the Biosphere Programme, Paris, UNESCO.

— (1989) *Man and the Biosphere (MAB) Programme. Biennial Report 1987-1988,* Paris, UNESCO.

United Nations (1972) *Report of the United Nations Conference on the Human Environment.* U.N. General Assembly A/Conference, 48/14 3 July 1972, Conference held in Stockholm, 15-16 June 1972.

— (1980) *North-South: A Program for Survival*, Report of the Independent Commission on International Development Issues, Cambridge, MA, The MIT Press.

United States Congress, Office of Technology Assessment

— (1984) *Africa Tomorrow: Issues in Technology, Agriculture and U.S. Foreign Aid*. Washington, D.C., OTA.

United States Steel (anonymous committee authorship) (1957) *The Making, Shaping and Treating of Steel*, (seventh edition), Pittsburgh, Pa., United States Steel.

Uphoff, N. (1986) *Local Institutional Development. An Analytical Sourcebook with Cases*, West Harsford, CT, Kumarian Press.

USDA (Soil Conservation Service) (1981) *Soil Survey Manual*, Washington, DC, USDA-SCS.

USDA (United States Department of Agriculture) (1981) *A Time to Choose: Summary Report on the Structure of Agriculture*, Washington, DC, USDA.

— (1982) *Census of Agriculture*, Washington, DC, USDA.

— (1988) *Economic Indicators of the Farm Sector: Farm Sector Review, 1986*, Agriculture and Rural Economy Division. Economic Research Service, ECIFS 6-3.

Valbuena, V.T. (1986) *Philippine Folk Media in Development Communication*. Singapore, Asian Mass Communication Research and Information Centre.

Valdizán, H. and A. Maldonado (1985/1922) *La Medicine popular Perinea: Contribution al folklore Medico del Perú* I, II and III, Lima, Peru, Imprenta Torres Aguirre for the Consejo Indio de Sud-América.

Vanek, E. (1989) 'Enhancing Environmental Resource Management in Developing Nations through Improved Attitudes Toward Indigenous Knowledge Systems: The Case of the World Bank', in D.M. Warren, L.J. Slikkerveer and S.O. Titilola (ed.) *Indigenous Knowledge Systems: Implications for Agriculture and International Development*, pp. 121-137, Studies in Technology and Social Change 11, Ames, IA, Iowa State University.

Vavilov, N.I. (1949) *The Origin, Variation, Immunity and Breeding of Cultivated Plants*, Waltham, MA, Chronica Botanica Company.

Vásquez Manríquez, L., H. S. López and L.A. Calzada Nova (1988) 'Evaluación Comparativa de un Remedio de la Medicina Tradicional para el Tratamiento de la Traqueobronquitis en Caninos', in Luz Lozano Nathal and Gerardo López Buendía, (coords.), *Memorias, Primera Jornada sobre Herbolaria Medicinal en Veterinaria*, pp. 85-89, México DF, Universidad Nacional Autónoma de México, Facultad de Medicina Veterinaria y Zootecnia, Coordinación de Educación Continua.

Verma, M.R. and Y.P. Singh (1969) 'A Plea for Studies in Traditional Animal Husbandry', *The Allahabad Farmer*, XL III (2), pp. 93-98.

Villareal, R. (1980) *Tomatoes in the Tropics*, Boulder, CO, Westview Press.

Villemin, M. (1984) 'L'Empirisme, Une Necessité ou un Anachronisme?', *Ethnozootechnie* 34, pp. 25-39, Special issue entitled La Médecine Vétérinaire Populaire.

Vogeler, I. (1981) *The Myth of the Family Farm: Agribusiness Dominance of U.S. Agriculture*, Boulder, CO, Westview Press.

Vondal, P. (1984) *Entrepreneurship in an Indonesian Duck Egg Industry: A Case of Successful Rural Development*, Ph.D. Dissertation Brunswick, New Jersey, Rutgers University (unpublished).

— (1987) 'Intensification through Diversified Resource Use: The Human Ecology of a Successful Agricultural Industry in Indonesian Borneo', *Human Ecology*, 5 (1).

— (1989) 'The Ecology of Farm Management in a Swampland Region of Indonesia', in S. Smith and E. Reeves (eds) *Human Systems Ecology: Studies* in the Integration of Political Economy, Adaptation and Socionatural Regions, pp. 107-123, Boulder, CO, Westview Press.

Vorderman, A.G. (1894) 'De Transmigratie- en Signatuurleer in de Javaansche Geneeskunde', *Feestbundel voor Dr. P.J. Veth,* Leiden, Brill.

— (1900) 'Inlandsche Namen van eenige Madoereesche Planten en Simplicia', *Natuurkundig Tijdschrift voor Nederlandsch-Indie,* 59, pp. 140-198.

Waddell, E. (1972) *The Mound Builders: Agricultural Practices, Environment and Society in the Central Highlands of New Guinea,* Seattle, University of Washington Press.

Wagenaar, K.T., A. Diallo and A.R. Sayers (1986) *Productivity of Transhumant Fulani Cattle in the Inner Delta of Mal,* Research Report 13, Addis Ababa, ILCA.

Wagner, G. (1970) *The Bantu of Western Kenya with special reference to the Vugusu and Logoli. II: Economic life,* London, Oxford University Press.

Wagner, W. (1926) *Die Chinesische Landwirtschaft,* Berlin, Paul Parey.

Wahua, T.A.T. and U.I. Oji (1987) Survey of Browse Plants in Upland Areas of Rivers State, *Browse Use and Small Ruminant Production in Southeast Nigeria,* pp. 23-33 Proceedings of a Symposium held at the Federal University of Technology, Owerri, Imo State, 4 May 1987, Ibadan, Nigeria, International Livestock Centre for Africa (ILCA), Humid Zone Programme

Walker, A. (1983) *Indian Agriculture* I, Page 85 Quoted in P. Charam, *Indian Science and Technology in the Eighteenth Century,* 229-256, Hyderabad, Academy of Gandhian Studies.

Walker, A.R. (1986) *The Toda of South India: A New Look,* New Delhi, India, Hindustan Publishing Corporation.

Walker, P.J.C. (1988) *Food for Recovery: Food Monitoring and Targeting in the Red Sea Hills, Sudan,* Oxford, OXFAM Internal Report.

Wallace, M.B. (1987) 'Community Forestry in Nepal: Too Little, Too Late?', *Research Report Series,* 5 (June 1987), Kathmandu, HMG-USAID-GTZ-IDRC-Winrock Project Strengthening Institutional Capacity in the Food and Agricultural Sector in Nepal.

Wallerstein, I. (1976) 'The Three Stages of African Involvement in the World-Economy', in P.C.W. Gutkind and I. Wallerstein (ed.) *The Political Economy of Contemporary Africa,* 30-57, Sage Series on African Modernisation and Development I, Beverly Hills/London, Sage Publications.

Waminathan, M.S. (1973) 'Our Agricultural Balance Sheet: Assets and Liabilities. Sardar Patel Memorial Lecturers of the All India Radio', in S. Ramanujam, E.A. Siddq, V.L. Chopra and S.K. Sionha (eds) *Science and Agriculture,* New Delhi, Indian Society of Genetics and Plant Breeding IARI, 1980.

— (1976) 'Science and Integrated Rural Development: Presidential Address of Sixty-Third Session of the Indian Science Congress, Waltair, January 3-7', in S. Ramanujam, E.A. Siddq, V.L. Chopra and S.K. Sinha (eds) *Science and Agriculture,* New Delhi, Indian Society of Genetics and Plant Breeding IARI, 1980.

Wang, G. (1982) *Indigenous Communication Systems in Research and Development,* Paper presented at the conference on Knowledge Utilisation: Theory and Methodology, 25-30 April 1982, Honolulu, HI, East-West Centre.

Wang, G. and W. Dissanayake (1982) The Study of Indigenous Communication Systems in Development: Phased Out or Phasing In? *Media Asia,* 9 (1), pp. 3-8.

Wang, G. and W. Dissanayake (eds) (1984) *Continuity and Change in Communication Systems: An Asian Perspective,* Norwood, NJ, Ablex.

Ware, H. (1977) Desertification and Population: Sub-Saharan Africa, in M.H.

Glantz (ed) *Desertification: Environmental Degradation in and Around Arid Lands,* pp. 166-202, Boulder, CO, Westview Press.

Waring, E.J. (1868) *Pharmacopoeia India,* London, Allen.

Warren, C.P. (1964) *Progress Report* III: *Deliberate Instruction in Non-Literate Societies,* Chicago, IL, University of Chicago, Department of Anthropology, (ERIC document ED 040 121).

Warren, D.M. (1974) 'Disease, Medicine, and Religion Among the Techiman Bono of Ghana', Doctoral Dissertation, Indiana University.

— (1980) 'Ethnoscience in Rural Development', in D. Brokensha, D.M. Warren and O. Werner (eds) *Indigenous Knowledge Systems and Development,* pp. 363-376, Lanham, MD, University Press of America.

— (1982) 'The Techiman-Bono Ethnomedical System', in S.P. Yoder (ed.) *African Health and Healing Systems: Proceedings of a) Symposium,* pp. 85-107, University of California, Los Angeles, Crossroads Press.

— (1989a) 'Linking Scientific and Indigenous Agricultural Systems', in J.L. Compton (ed.) *The Transformation of International Agricultural Research and Development,* pp. 153-170, Boulder/London, Lynne Rienner.

— (1989b) 'Utilising Indigenous Healers in National Health Delivery Systems: The Ghanaian Experiment', in J. van Willigen, B. Ryiko-Bauer and A. McElroy (eds) *Making Our Research Useful: Case Studies in the Utilisation of Anthropological Knowledge,* pp. 159-178, Boulder, Westview Press.

— (1989c) *Language and Culture (Anthropology 500),* Class Notes, Ames, IA, Iowa State University.

— (1991) "Using Indigenous Knowledge in Agricultural Development. *Discussion Paper* 127, Washington D.C., World Bank.

Warren, D.M., S. Bova, M-A. Tregoning and M. Kliewer (1982) 'Ghanaian National Policy toward Indigenous Healers: The Case of the Primary Health Training for Indigenous Healers (PRHETIH) Program', *Social Science and Medicine,* 16, pp. 1873-1881.

Warren, D.M. and K. Cashman (1988a) *Indigenous Knowledge for Sustainable Agricultural Development,* Gatekeeper Series SA10, London, International Institute for Environment and Development.

— (1988b) *Indigenous Knowledge for Agriculture and Rural Development: Some Practical Applications,* Paper presented at the Conference on Indigenous Knowledge Systems, AED, Washington, D.C., December 1988.

Warren, D.M. and P.M. Meehan (1980) 'Applied Ethnoscience and Dialogical Communication in Rural Development', in D. Brokensha, D.M. Warren and O. Werner (eds) *Indigenous Knowledge Systems and Development.,* pp. 317-322, Lanham, MD, University Press of Warren, D.M., L.J. Slikkerveer, S.O. Titilola (eds) (1989) *Indigenous Knowledge Systems: Implications for Agriculture and International Development,* Studies in Technology and Social Change 11, Ames, IA, Iowa State University.

Waters-Bayer, A. (1988) *Dairying by settled Fulani Agropastoralists in Central Nigeria: The Role of Women and Implications for Dairy Development,* Farming Systems and Resource Economics in the Tropics 4, Vauk, Kiel, West Germany, Wissenschaftsverlag.

Watson, G. (1987) 'Make Me Reflexive – But Not Yet: Strategies for Maintaining Essential Reflexivity in Ethnographic Discourse', *Journal of Anthropological Research,* 43 (1), pp. 29-41.

Watt, A.S. (1947) 'Pattern and Process in the Plant Community', *Journal of Ecology,* 35, pp. 1-22.

WCED (1987) *Our Common Future,* World Commission on Environment and Development, Oxford, Oxford University Press.

Weatherwax, P. (1951) *Indian Corn in Old America,* New York, Macmillan Press.

Webster, C.C. and P.N. Wilson (1980) *Agriculture in the Tropics,* London, Longman.

Weck, W. (1937) *Heilkunde und Volkstum auf Bali,* Stuttgart.
— (1938) 'Taru Premana; Die Balische Pharmakopie', *Natuurkundig Tijdschrift voor Nederlandsch-Indie,* 98, pp. 250-282.
Weidman, H.H. (1979) 'On Mitchell's Changing Others', *Medical Anthropology Newsletter,* 8 (14), 25.
Weinstock, J.A. and N.T. Vergara (1987) 'Land or Plants: Agricultural Tenure in Agroforestry Systems', *Economic Botany,* 41 (2), pp. 312-322.
Wel, H.van der, L.A. Hladik, C.M. Hladik, G. Hellenkant and D. Glaser (1989) 'Isolation and Characterisation of Pentadin, The Sweet Principle of Pentadiplandra Brazzeana Baillon', *Chemical Senses,* 14, pp. 75-79.
Weninger, B. and L. Robineau (eds) (1987) *Recherches Scientifiques et Usage Populaire des Plantes Médicinales dans la Caraibe,* Séminaire Tramil 2, Santo Domingo, November 1986. Santo Domingo, ENDA.
Werner, O. and G.M. Schoepfle (1987) *Systematic Fieldwork,* Beverly Hills, CA, Sage Publications, Inc.
Werner, W. (1984) 'Die Hohen-und Nebelwalder auf der Insel Ceylon (Sri Lanka)', in R. Werner (ed) *Aus der Reihe: Tropische und Subtropische Pflanzenwelt 46,* Akademie der Wissenschaften und der Literatur, Mainz, Wiesbaden, Franz Steiner Verlag.
West, T.L (1981) *Alpaca Production in Puno, Peru,* Sociology Technical Report Series 3, Columbia, USA., University of Missouri-Columbia, Department of Rural Sociology, Small Ruminant Collaborative Research Support Program.
Westoby, J. (1987) *The Purpose of Forests: Follies of Development,* Oxford, Basil Blackwell.
Whiting, J. and B. Whiting (1970) 'Methods for Observing and Recording Behavior', in R. Narroll and R. Cohen (eds) *A Handbook of Method in Cultural Anthropology,* pp. 282-315, New York, Columbia University Press.
Whittaker, R.H. (1975) *Communities and Ecosystems,* New York, Macmillan Press.
WHO (1981) *Global Strategy for Health for All by the Year 2000,* Geneva, WHO.
Whyte, A.V.T. (1977) *Guidelines for Field Studies in Environmental Perception,* Man and the Biosphere Technical Notes, 5, Paris, UNESCO.
Whyte, W.F. and D. Boynton (eds) (1983) *Higher-Yielding Human Systems for Agriculture,* Ithaca, NY, Cornell University Press.
Wicks, T. and T.C. Lee (1985) 'Effects of Flooding, Rootstocks and Fungicides on Phytophthora Crown Rot of Almonds', *Australian Journal Experimental Agriculture,* 25, pp. 705-710.
Wilcox, W.F. and S.M. Mircetich (1985) 'Effects of Flooding Duration on the Development of Phytophthora Root and Crown Rots of Cherry', *Phytopathology,* 75, pp. 1451-1455.
Wilken, G.C. (1969) 'Drained-Field Agriculture: An Intensive Farming System in Tlaxcala, Mexico', *Geographical Review,* 59, pp. 215-241.
— (1971) 'Food Producing Systems Available to the Ancient Maya', *American Antiquity* 36, pp. 432-448.
— (1972) 'Microclimate Management by Traditional Farmers', *Geogr. Rev,* 62, pp. 544-566.
— (1977) 'Integrating Forest and Small Scale Farm Systems in Middle America', *Agro-Ecosystems,* 3 (4), pp. 291-302.
— (1987) *Good Farmers: Traditional Agricultural Resource Management in Mexico and Central America,* Berkeley, University of California.
Wilkes, G. (in press) '*In situ* Preservation of Agricultural Systems', in M.O. Oldfield and J.B. Alcorn (eds) *Biodiversity: Traditional Management and Development of Biological Resources,* Boulder, CO, Westview Press.
Williams, B.J. and C.O. Solorio (1981) 'Middle American Folk Soil Taxonomy', *Annals of the Association of American Geographers,* 71 (3), pp. 335-358.

Williams, P.H. (1981) 'Plant Protection', in D.L. Plucknett and H.L. Beemer (eds) *Vegetable Farming Systems in China*, pp. 129-162, Boulder, CO, Westview Press.

Wilson, M. (1979) 'Strangers in Africa: Reflections on Nyakyusa, Nguni and Sotho Evidence', in W.A. Schack and E.P. Skinner (ed.) *Strangers in African Societies*, pp. 51-66, Berkeley, University of California Press.

Wilson, R.T. (1986) *Livestock Production in Central Mali: Long Term Studies on Cattle and Small Ruminants in the Agropastoral System,* Addis Ababa, ILCA Research Report 14.

Wilson, R.T., K. Wagenaar and S. Louis (1984) 'Animal Production', in H.J.J. Swift (ed.) *Pastoral Development in Central Niger: Report of the Niger Range and Livestock Project*, pp. 69-144, Niamey, USAID, Ministry of Rural Development.

Wirth, C.L. (1980) *Parks, Politics and the People,* Norman, OKLA, University of Oklahoma Press.

Wittfogel, K.A. (1957) *Oriental Depotism: A Comparative Study of Total Power*, New Haven, Yale University Press.

— (1979) 'L'arbre et le Nomade', *JATBA*, 26 (2), pp. 103-128.

Wittwer, S., Y. Youtai, S. Han and W. Lianzheng (1987) *Feeding a Billion: Frontiers of Chinese Agriculture*, Lansing, Michigan State University Press.

Wolf, C.E. (1986) 'Beyond the Green Revolution: New Approaches for Third World Agriculture', *Worldwatch Paper,* 13, Washington, D.C., Worldwatch Institute.

Wolfgang, K. (1983) *An Ethno-Veterinary Study of Cattle Health Care by FulBe Herders of South Central Upper Volta*, Thesis, Amherst, MASS, Hampshire College (unpublished).

Wolfgang, K. and A. Sollod (1986) *Traditional Veterinary Medical Practice by Twareg Herders in Central Niger*, Integrated Livestock Project, Ministry of Animal Resources, BP 85, Tahoua, Niger and Tufts University, North Grafton, MASS, School of Veterinary Medicine,

Womack, M.K. (1976) *Gadsden: A Florida County in Word and Picture,* Montgomery, AL, Taylor Publishing Company.

Woodham-Smith, C. (1962) *The Great Hunger. Ireland 1945-9,* London, Hamish Hamilton.

World Bank (1979) 'Nepal Forestry Sector Review', *Report* 1952-NEP, Washington, DC, The World Bank, South Asia Projects Department.

— (1981) 'Accelerated Development in Sub-Saharan Africa: An Agenda for Action', Washington, D.C., The World Bank.

— (1981) *Economic Development and Tribal Peoples: Human Ecological Considerations,* Washington D.C., International Bank for Reconstruction and Development.

— (1985) *Agricultural Research and Extension: An Evaluation of the World Bank's Experience*, Washington, D.C., The World Bank.

— (1988) *World Bank Annual Report,* Washington, D.C., WBRD.

World Neighbors (n.d.) *Simple Soil and Water Conservation Methods for Upland Farms,* Cebu City, The Philippines.

Wormald, T.J. and T.D. Russell (1976) *An Account of the Salija*, Forest Inventory, Pokhara, Nepal, Lumle Agricultural Centre, Mimeograph.

Wormald, T.J. and D.A. Messerschmidt (1986) 'Management and Monitoring of Community Forestry Activities in Nepal', *Field Document* 12, Kathmandu, Community Forestry Development Project.

WRI (1986) *Tropical Forests: A Call for Action*, 3 vols, Washington, DC, World Resources Institute.

Yoder, Stanley P.(ed) (1982) *African Health and Healing Systems: Proceedings of a Symposium,* University of California, Los Angeles, Crossroads Press.

York, E.J. (Jr.) (1988) 'Improving Sustainability with Agricultural Research', *Environment*, 30 (9), pp. 18-24.

Young, A. (1982) The Amhara System, in S.P. Yoder (ed.) *African Health and Healing Systems: Proceedings of a Symposium,* 21-43, University of California, Los Angeles, Crossroads Press.

— (1986) *The Potential of Agroforestry for Soil Conservation, Erosion Control.,* Working Paper 42, Nairobi, ICRAF.

Young, J. C. (1981) *Medical Choice in a Mexican Village,* New Brunswick, NJ, Rutgers University Press.

Zabawa, R. (1984) 'The Transformation of Farming in Gadsden County, North Florida: A Micro-Level Example of a Macro-Level Phenomenon', Ph.D. Dissertation, Evanston, IL, Northwestern University, Department of Anthropology (unpublished).

— (1987) 'Macro-Micro Linkages and Structural Transformation: The Move from Full-Time to Part-Time Farming in a North Florida Agricultural Community', *American Anthropologist,* 89 (2), pp. 366-382

Zanno, P.R., J. Miura,. K. Nakanishi and D.L. Elder (1975) 'Structure of the Insect Phagorepellent Azadirachtin', Application of PRFT/CWD Carbon-13 Nuclear Magnetic Resonance, *Journal of American Chemical Society*, 97, pp. 1975-1977.

Zessin, K-H. and T.E. Carpenter (1985) 'Benefit-Cost Analysis of an Epidemiologic Approach to Provision of Veterinary Service in the Sudan', *Preventive Veterinary Medicine* 3, pp. 323-337.

Zuckerman, B.M., M.B. Dicklow, G.C. Coles, R. Garcia and N. Marban-Mendoz 'Suppression of Plant Parasitic Nematodes in the Chinampa Agricultural Soils', *Chemical Ecology.*

Zulauf, C. (1986) 'Changes in Selected Characteristics of U.S. Farms During the 1970s and Early 1980s: An Investigation Based on Current and Constant Dollar Sales Categories', *Southern Journal of Agricultural Economics,* 18 (2), pp. 113-122.

Index

579